GW00728786

ANNUAL REVIEW OF IRISH LAW 2004

UNITED KINGDOM
Sweet & Maxwell Ltd
London

AUSTRALIA
Law Book Co. Ltd
Sydney

CANADA AND THE USA
Carswell
Toronto

NEW ZEALAND
Brookers
Wellington

SINGAPORE AND MALAYSIA
Sweet and Maxwell
Singapore and Kuala Lumpur

Annual Review
of Irish Law 2004

Raymond Byrne
B.C.L., LL.M., Barrister-at-Law
Lecturer in Law, Dublin City University
Director of Research, Law Reform Commission

William Binchy
B.A., B.C.L., LL.M., F.T.C.D., Barrister-at-Law
Regius Professor of Laws, Trinity College, Dublin

Thomson Round Hall
2005

Published in 2005 by
Thomson Round Hall
43 Fitzwilliam Place,
Dublin 2, Ireland.

Typeset by
Gough Typesetting Services, Dublin.

Printed by
MPG Cornwall.

ISBN 1-85800-415-2

A catalogue record for this book
is available from the British Library.

All rights reserved. No part of this publication may
be reproduced or transmitted in any form or by any means,
including photocopying and recording,
without the written permission of the publisher.
Such written permission must also be obtained before any
part of this publication is stored in a retrieval system
of any nature.

© Thomson Round Hall 2005

Table of Contents

Preface

In this eighteenth volume in the Annual Review series, our purpose continues to be to provide a review of legal developments, judicial and statutory, that occurred in 2004. In terms of case law, this includes those judgments which were delivered in 2004, regardless of whether they have been (or will be) reported and which were circulated up to the date of this preface. In terms of legislation, we endeavour to discuss those Acts and statutory instruments enacted and made during the year. Once again it is a pleasure to thank those who made the task of completing this volume less onerous.

For this eighteenth volume of the Annual Review series, the authors are delighted to have had the benefit of specialist contributions on Asylum and Immigration Law, Company Law, Constitutional Law, Contract Law, Equity, Information Law, Land Law, Planning Law, Practice and Procedure, Social Welfare, Sports Law and also Succession Law included in this volume. The authors continue to take final responsibility for the overall text as in the past, but are especially grateful for the contributions of Nuala Egan and Patricia Brazil in Asylum and Immigration Law, Gráinne Callanan in Company Law, Oran Doyle and Estelle Feldman in Constitutional Law, Ruth Cannon in Contract Law and Land Law, Hilary Delany in Equity and Practice and Procedure, Estelle Feldman in Information Law, Garrett Simons in Planning Law, Gerry Whyte in Social Welfare, Albert Keating in Succession Law and Neville Cox in Sports Law.

Finally, we are very grateful to Thomson Round Hall, in particular Susan Rossney and Suzanna Henry, and to Gilbert Gough, whose professionalism ensures the continued production of this series.

Raymond Byrne and William Binchy,
Dublin

October 2005

Table of Cases

IRELAND

ENGLISH CASE LAW

EUROPEAN CASE LAW

INTERNATIONAL CASE LAW

Table of Legislation

CONSTITUTIONAL PROVISIONS

TABLE OF STATUTES

TABLE OF STATUTORY INSTRUMENTS

Rules of Court

EUROPEAN LEGISLATION

Directives

INTERNATIONAL TREATIES AND CONVENTIONS

Administrative Law

APPROPRIATION

The Appropriation Act 2004 provided as follows. For the year ended December 31, 2004, the amount of supply grants in accordance with the Central Fund (Permanent Provisions) Act 1965 was €33,074,174,280. Under the Public Accounts and Charges Act 1891, the sum for appropriations-in-aid was €2,899,679,383. The 2004 Act also provided, in accordance with s.91 of the Finance Act 2004, for carrying over into the year ending December 31, 2005, undischarged appropriations for capital supply services totalling €236,967,000. This, in effect, allowed this amount, which had not been spent on various large infrastructure projects in 2004, to be carried over into 2005. The 2004 Act also provided that the financial resolutions passed by Dáil Éireann on December 1, 2004 (after the 2004 Budget and which dealt with an increase in the farmers' flat rate and the livestock rate of Value-Added-Tax) would have legal effect provided that, in accordance with s.4 of the Provisional Collection of Taxes Act 1927, legislation was enacted in 2005 (in the Finance Act 2005) to give full effect to the resolutions. The 2004 Act came into effect on its signature by the President on December 17, 2004.

CIVIL REGISTRATION SERVICE

The Civil Registration Act 2004 provided for a major reorganisation, modernisation and renaming of the system for civil registration; supported and enabled the modernisation of the Civil Registration Service; and facilitated the decentralisation of the General Register Office. The main objectives of the 2004 Act are to rationalise the procedures for registering births, stillbirths and deaths; give An tÁrd-Chláraitheoir (the Chief Registrar) responsibility for overall policy for the Civil Registration Service, including maintaining standards of service; assign responsibility for the management, control and administration of the Civil Registration Service at local level to health boards; streamline the existing procedures governing the registration of adoptions; establish new registers of divorce and civil nullity; reform the procedures governing the registration and solemnisation of marriage and venues for marriage; and facilitate the future linking of what are described as "life events". The 2004 Act came into force generally on February 27, 2004.

Modernisation of civil registration During the passage of the 2004 Act, the Minister for Social and Community Affairs noted that, while there had been little change to the basic registration procedures since the introduction of the Registration of Births and Deaths (Ireland) Act 1863 and the Registration of Marriages (Ireland) Act 1863 (both of which were repealed by the 2004 Act, along with part or all of over 20 other Acts) there have been many changes in society as well as major developments in technology and increased expectations by citizens as to how public services should be delivered. In 2003, more than 110,000 life events were registered, approximately 500,000 certificates produced and some 1.2 million searches of registration records carried out. Recognising the importance of civil registration and acknowledging the changing needs of customers, the Minister stated that the Government approved a programme of work to modernise the Civil Registration Service. This involved the introduction of modern technology providing on-line registration, electronic certificate production and the capture of digitised signatures; the redesign of business processes and procedures; capturing and storing in electronic format all paper-based records from 1845 onwards; and the reform of legislation which gave rise to the 2004 Act. The benefits arising from the modernisation programme include improved service to customers, for example, extended opening times; greater efficiency in the use of resources; nationwide standards for registering life events; the registration of divorces and civil annulments on a central register; the electronic capture and transmission of all vital statistics on life events to the Central Statistics Office; the sharing of data with designated Departments and agencies; the facilitation of long-standing plans to decentralise the General Register Office; and reducing the demand for paper certificates for the purposes of Government services.

Relationship with e-government initiatives The 2004 Act may also be seen in the context of New Connections, the Government's information society action plan, which identifies e-government as a key infrastructural mechanism and the e-inclusion programme as a key supporting framework. In line with the commitment to improving the way services are organised, integrated and delivered to customers, a number of programmes were initiated, including the development of the REACH inter-agency messaging service; the automated establishment of public service identity in respect of children born in Ireland; and the service delivery modernisation project. To facilitate the sharing and e-enabling of life event data between Government agencies, REACH developed an inter-agency messaging service, IAMS, which will be used to transfer registration data between the Civil Registration System, the Department of Social and Community Affairs and the Central Statistics Office. By way of specific example, since 2003, all new birth registration data is transferred electronically to the Department of Social and Community Affairs from the civil registration computer system. This facilitates the allocation of a personal public service number (PPSN) to a child at registration which establishes a child's public service identity; the creation of family links on the national central database for all citizens, the client records system which is administered by the Department; and initiation of a child benefit claim for first-born children and automatic payment for second and subsequent children in a family.

Office of An tÁrd-Chláraitheoir (Chief Registrar) Part 2 of the 2004 Act provides for the administration of the civil registration service. Sections 7, 9 and 12 provide for the continuation of the existing offices of an tÁrd-Chláraitheoir, the assistant to an tÁrd-Chláraitheoir (an tÁrd-Chláraitheoir Cúnta and Oifig an Árd-Chláraitheora. Section 13 provides powers for an tÁrd-Chláraitheoir to establish and maintain registers of births, stillbirths, adoptions, deaths, marriages, divorce and civil nullity, the last two mentioned being new registers. In the future all life events will be stored in electronic registers.

Local registration offices Sections 14 and 15 provide for the establishment of local registration authorities, which are the health boards, who will appoint a superintendent registrar to administer the service at local level. Each registration authority is required to set out a formal scheme for the administration of the civil registration service in their area. Provision is also made to facilitate the delegation of certain functions, for example, late registration, from an tÁrd-Chláraitheoir to local registration authorities.

Registration of births and stillbirths Part 3 of the 2004 Act provides for the registration of births and stillbirths. The principal responsibility for registering a birth remains with the parents, who will be required to register the event within three months of the birth. To facilitate parents in fulfilling this obligation, the previous time limit of 42 days was extended to three months. Births may be registered with any registrar as opposed to the pre-2004 system where a birth could only be registered by the registrar of the district in which the birth occurred. Sections 23 and 24 of the 2004 Act allow a birth to be re-registered to include the father's details where they were not entered in the register at the time of registration. Sections 26 and 27 provide for the registration of certain births and stillbirths occurring outside the State. This includes the birth or stillbirth to an Irish citizen in jurisdictions where no registration system exists or the registration records are unavailable; on Irish-registered ships and aircraft; to an Irish citizen on foreign ships and aircraft; and to members of the Defence Forces and the Garda Síochána while serving abroad. The provision relating to births and stillbirths on aircraft was introduced for the first time. In addition, this provision addresses the current anomaly where the birth or stillbirth of a child on board an Irish-registered ship, in certain circumstances, cannot be registered. The Civil Registration Act 2004 (Section 27) (Commencement) Order 2004 (S.I. No.84 of 2004) brought s.27 into effect on March 2, 2004. Sections 28 and 29 provide for the registration of stillbirths, under which parents or a relative may register the stillbirth within 12 months. Prior to the 2004 Act, only the parents could register the stillbirth within 42 days. The new provisions were introduced to allow the family of the child more time to undertake the necessary registration procedures while coping with their loss. Section 30 requires institutions, including hospitals, to notify the local registration authority of the occurrence of each birth and stillbirth. This obligation also falls on doctors and midwives where such events occur outside these locations. This notification will be recorded electronically and is intended to assist parents in their registration obligations at the registrar's office of their choice.

Registration of adoptions Part 4 of the 2004 Act provides for the registration of adoptions. Under the Act, there will be one adoption register for the registration of all adoptions in the State. An authorised officer of the Adoption Board will act as registrar for the purposes of these registrations. Prior to the 2004 Act, adoptions were registered in either the adopted children's register for adoptions effected within the State, or the foreign adoption register for foreign adoptions. Section 35 reiterates the previous position to the effect that access to the register of adoptions or the index which makes traceable the connection between this register and the register of births will not be available except by order of the Adoption Board, or of a court which is satisfied that such access is in the best interests of the adopted person concerned. It was accepted that these provisions may be amended in light of the review of adoption legislation by the Department of Health and Children, which was ongoing at the time of the enactment of the 2004 Act.

Registration of deaths Part 5 of the 2004 Act concerns the registration of deaths. Section 37 provides that the primary responsibility for registering a death remains with the next of kin or persons who would have knowledge of the particulars of the death. This section also extends the list of persons who may provide details of a death to include specified staff of a hospital or institution where the death occurred, and undertakers. The period for registering a death was also extended from five days to three months from the date of death. Under the 2004 Act, a death may be registered at any registrar's office, which was intended to allow greater flexibility for the person responsible for registering a death. Sections 38 and 39 provide for the registration of deaths which occur on ships and aircraft or deaths of members of the Defence Forces or the Garda Síochána while serving abroad. These are similar to the provisions of ss.26 and 27, which provide for the registration of certain births and stillbirths occurring outside the State.

Reform of marriage registration Part 6 of the 2004 Act provides for significant reform of the law in respect of marriage and arises from recommendations of an inter-departmental committee on the reform of marriage law. Among the issues identified by the committee as requiring examination was the need for a universally applicable framework of clear and simple procedures to underpin the solemnity of the marriage contract. The requirement introduced in the Family Law Act 1995 that a couple notify the registrar of marriages of the district at least three months before the intended date of marriage was reiterated in s.46 of the 2004 Act. As under the 1995 Act, a couple may apply to a court for an exemption to the three months' notification rule because of extenuating circumstances. In specified circumstances a couple will be allowed to submit the three-month notification in writing, for example, where the couple are living outside the State. However, in all such cases, the couple will be required to attend at the registrar's office at least five days prior to the intended date of marriage to sign an undertaking that there is no lawful impediment to the marriage and to produce other necessary documentation. Section 48 of the 2004 Act introduces a new marriage registration form. This form will only be produced and given to a couple when they have completed all civil preliminaries for marriage. This must be signed immediately after the ceremony by all the parties to the marriage. Responsibility for returning the completed form to a registrar lies with the couple who must do so within one month of the date of the marriage. Section 49 provides for the registration of marriages, which is to be effected by either one of the married couple by giving the completed marriage registration form to the registrar within one month of the marriage taking place. Section 50 provides that if a marriage registration form is not returned within 56 days of the date of marriage, the registrar can pursue the matter by issuing a reminder to the couple requiring the return of the form within a further 14 days. This follow-up measure is intended to ensure that the marriage is registered as soon as possible after its solemnisation. Section 51 of the 2004 Act outlines the substantive requirements for the solemnisation of a valid marriage. It also provides for an interpretation service at the marriage ceremony, where necessary. Section 52 is concerned with the venues and times at which a marriage can take place. It allows a marriage to be solemnised at a place and time agreed by the couple and the solemniser. The section also provides for the payment of fees by the couple where a civil marriage is conducted by a registrar at a location other than the registrar's office. Section 53 provides for an tÁrd-Chláraitheoir to establish and maintain a new register of solemnisers, which will replace the previous register of churches and buildings. Only registered solemnisers and members of religious bodies temporarily authorised to do so may solemnise a marriage. Section 54 outlines the procedures to be followed by a religious body or local registration authority when applying to have one of its members entered in the register of solemnisers. Section 55 enables an tÁrd-Chláraitheoir to cancel an entry in the register of solemnisers and provides for the procedures involved in doing so. Section 56 introduces an appeals system which gives a person the right to appeal an tÁrd-Chláraitheoir's decision to refuse to register him or her in the register of solemnisers or to cancel his or her entry in that register. Section 57 allows an tÁrd-Chláraitheoir to grant a temporary authorisation to a member of a religious body to solemnise a specific marriage or to solemnise marriages within a specified time only. This is intended to facilitate, for example, a clergy person who wishes to visit the State specifically to solemnise the marriage of a relative. Section 58 provides for the lodging of an objection to an intended marriage to a registrar and for the processing of such an objection.

Registration of divorces and annulments   Part 7 of the 2004 Act provides for the registration of decrees of divorce and decrees of nullity by the Courts Service in new registers in accordance with s.13.

Miscellaneous   Part 8 of the 2004 Act contains a number of miscellaneous provisions relating to civil registration. Section 60 provides for the introduction of a formal appeals system for the first time. This will allow persons to appeal a decision of a registrar or an authorised officer to an appeals officer of the local registration authority. Section 61 provides for the conditions necessary for searches of registration records. Since civil registration records are a matter of public record, any person can carry out a search and obtain a certificate of any event, excluding stillbirths, by paying a specified fee. The introduction of electronic registers and the electronic capture of all paper-based records will provide easier and faster access to registration records. Section 61 allows any person to search the indexes to all the registers and to purchase copies of the records relating to the searches, with the exception of the index of stillbirths and an index which makes traceable the connection between an entry in the register of adoptions and the corresponding entry in the register of births. Section 66 allows an tÁrd-Chláraitheoir to share certain registration information for specified purposes with designated Departments and agencies. This provision will facilitate the sharing of information, reduce form filling and the need for certificates for the administration and control of schemes and services. Section 67 empowers the Minister for Health and Children to make Regulations for the charging of fees. For example, fees may be charged for issuing certificates or for undertaking the re-registration of an event, such as a marriage.

COMMISSIONS OF INVESTIGATION

Commissions of Investigation Act 2004   The background to the Commissions of Investigation Act 2004 is the intention to provide investigative mechanisms that might act as precursors to, or alternatives to, tribunals of inquiry conferred with the powers contained in the Tribunals of Inquiry (Evidence) Acts 1921 to 2004. The 2004 Act does not, therefore, replace or amend the tribunals of inquiry legislation. Nor does the 2004 Act establish a single or permanent investigations body, but rather enables the establishment of commissions when required. To that extent, the 2004 Act is consistent with the provisional recommendation in the Law Reform Commission's *Consultation Paper on Public Inquiries including Tribunals of Inquiry* (LRC CP 22–2003) to provide for a private low-key inquiry which would operate as a preliminary to, or in some cases an alternative to, a full-scale tribunal of inquiry. A key aspect of the 2004 Act is that a commission of investigation would operate primarily in private, whereas a tribunal of inquiry generally sits in public. Other significant aspects of the 2004 Act are that it focuses on the need to state with clarity the terms of reference of a commission of investigation and to encourage co-operation with its operation.

Establishment of commission Section 3 of the 2004 Act provides that a commission may be established on foot of a Government order approved by the Oireachtas, to investigate an issue giving rise to "significant public concern". As noted during the Oireachtas debate, such an issue must be one of more than mere passing interest to the public and must instead be an issue that has serious, including long-term, implications for public life. By way of general example, it was noted that those implications could include the welfare and safety of a sector in society or the effective and safe operation of a significant public service. It may also be noted that the "trigger" for the establishment of a commission of investigation may be contrasted with the phrase "definite matter of urgent public importance" in s.1 of the Tribunals of Inquiry (Evidence) Act 1921. The first Commission of Investigation was established in 2005, to investigate bombings in Dublin and Monaghan in 1974.

Terms of reference It was recognised during the passage of the 2004 Act that clear and well-defined terms of reference would be the key to a successful investigation. Section 4 provides that the establishment of a commission begins with the presentation to the Oireachtas of a reasoned statement of the need to establish a commission, along with the draft establishment order. Following the approval of the order by the Oireachtas, the terms of reference are to be set by the Government or the Minister having overall responsibility for the commission in question. Section 5 sets out very specific matters to be considered in setting the terms of reference and also requires that the terms of reference must be accompanied by statements setting out the likely duration and cost of an investigation. The terms of reference and the accompanying statements on costs and duration will be published. Section 6 provides for the amendment of terms of reference for specific purposes, namely to clarify, extend or limit the scope of an investigation. Amendments may be made only if the commission consents to them and it may withhold consent if it is satisfied that the amendment would prejudice the legal rights of any person who has co-operated with or provided information to the commission. The provisions and amending terms of reference reflect comparable provisions made in recent amendments to the tribunals of inquiry legislation, but it is worth noting that the provisions of the 2004 Act on setting terms of reference are not currently mirrored in the tribunals of inquiry legislation. In the *Annual Review of Irish Law 2005*, we will discuss the recommendations of the Law Reform Commission in this regard in its *Report on Public Inquiries including Tribunals of Inquiry* (LRC 73–2005).

Membership and independence Section 7 of the 2004 Act adopts a flexible approach to determining the membership of commissions. The experience and qualifications of the members can be supplemented by experts who can be recruited under s.8 to assist and advise the commission. Section 9 requires that a commission must be independent in the discharge of its functions.

Principle of co-operation and privacy Section 10 sets out the guiding principles by which commissions must operate, in particular that they are required to seek the voluntary co-operation of persons whose evidence is required. The 2004 Act places a responsibility on commissions to facilitate witnesses in that respect. Subject to certain safeguards, they may accept evidence in forms other than in person, for example, by live or pre-recorded video links or by affidavit. Section 11, which provides that, in general, evidence will be given to commissions in private, complements s.10. Section 11 provides that legal representatives of other parties will be present only if the commission is satisfied that their presence is necessary in the interests of the investigation and fair procedures. Similarly, cross-examination by or on behalf of other parties will take place only if the commission agrees. The commission may, however, question a witness on the evidence he or she has given.

It is important to ensure that private hearings are not abused in a way that would allow unfounded allegations and claims to be made or to go unchallenged. Section 12 addresses this concern by providing that a commission should inform any person who may be the subject of such claims or allegations of those claims or allegations. It provides that such persons should be given an opportunity to deal with them. While no obligation is being placed on a commission to reveal the source of any evidence given to it, such details should be disclosed on certain occasions.

Procedure and enforcement Section 15 requires a commission to establish or adopt rules and procedures pertaining to its operation. If a commission has several members, such rules may authorise the taking of evidence by one or more of them. Section 15 provides that evidence given in such circumstances will be regarded as having been given to the commission. While voluntary co-operation is central to the 2004 Act, it was also accepted during the Oireachtas debate on the legislation that commissions should be in a position to pursue investigations with vigour if co-operation is not forthcoming. Sections 16 and 28 of the 2004 Act provide powers to deal with a failure to co-operate. Section 16 specifies the powers that will be available to commissions in respect of witnesses, including the power to direct witnesses to attend, to answer questions and to produce and disclose documents. Section 28 provides for powers relating to entry into premises, inspecting and securing documents, taking copies of documents and requiring persons in charge of documents or related equipment to co-operate with the commission. All witnesses appearing before a commission will be made aware that, in the absence of co-operation, the commission may have recourse to the powers available to it under these sections. The 2004 Act also creates several offences, including failure to comply with directions, giving false statements and obstruction. The offences carry a maximum fine on summary conviction of €3,000, or a term of imprisonment of up to 12 months. On indictment, the offences are punishable by a maximum fine of €300,000 or five years' imprisonment. Standard provision is also made for the prosecution of corporate bodies and their senior officers and directors. As with the tribunals of inquiry legislation, the 2004 Act also provides that if a person does not comply with a direction to attend or produce documentation, a commission may apply to the High Court for an order seeking compliance. The failure to comply with such an order raises the issue of contempt of court.

Costs The issue of costs was discussed in detail during the passage of the 2004 Act, largely influenced by the increasing concerns as to the costs of tribunals of inquiries in recent years. As noted earlier, the terms of reference of a commission must be accompanied by a statement of the costs that are likely to be incurred by a commission. The statement is to be revised if the terms are altered. The costs covered by the statement will include the costs of staff appointed to advise and assist the commission, in accordance with s.8. Such staff may include barristers and solicitors. Section 8 provides that a competitive tendering process may be used for the recruitment of staff under the section, where it is appropriate to do so. Section 17 provides that if a witness is held to have failed to co-operate with, or obstructed, a commission, and the commission or other witnesses have incurred additional costs as a result, the party who causes the delay or obstruction may be held liable for the additional costs. Liability for the costs of a commission or other witnesses may be imposed on persons in addition to that person being proceeded against for the offence of obstruction. In other words, it should be understood that obstruction is likely to have serious consequences.

Section 23 provides for guidelines to be prepared by the relevant Minister with responsibility for a commission of investigation in respect of witnesses' legal costs. The guidelines will be drawn up in consultation with the Minister for Finance, in advance of the commission's hearings. The guidelines prepared under s.23 may restrict the types of legal services or fees to be recouped and may set limits on the level of legal costs to be paid. We note here that, in its *Report on Public Inquiries including Tribunals of Inquiry* (LRC 73–2005), the Law Reform Commission recommended that this provision be repealed, on the ground that it may conflict with the decision in *Re the Commission to Inquire into Child Abuse* [2002] 3 I.R. 459. We will return to this in the *Annual Review of Irish Law 2005*.

Section 24(5) makes a limited exception to the general regime on costs. This will occur where a witness incurs exceptional costs other than legal costs because of the volume or location of documents, for example, documents held outside the State. In those circumstances, the commission may direct that such exceptional costs be repaid to the witness and, as in the case of legal costs, the relevant Minister may request the commission to reconsider any direction about the repayment of such costs.

Reports and interim reports Section 32 provides not only that a commission must prepare a written report for the relevant Minister based on the evidence received by it, but also that it must identify the precise purpose of the report. It must set out the facts it has established in regard to the matter referred to it. Section 32(2) enables a commission to indicate its opinion as to the quality or weight of evidence relating to any area where the evidence is incomplete, insufficient, inconsistent or disputed. This permits a commission to point out that, for example, certain disputed facts are supported by corroboration from other sources or that a clear majority of witnesses affected by a particular event support one version as opposed to another. Statements of this kind merely summarise where the weight of the evidence lies and they are, to that extent, merely stating what is obvious to all. There is no general restriction in the 2004 Act on the identification of persons in reports of a commission. However, s.32(3) sets out considerations that may lead to the omission of certain details from a report identifying persons who gave evidence or any other person.

Sections 34, 35 and 36 contain provisions providing an opportunity to persons identified in or identifiable from a draft report to submit comments thereon to the commission on the grounds that there has been a failure to observe fair procedures or in order to protect commercially sensitive information. A commission is required to give due consideration to requests for alterations. It may either amend the report, apply to the High Court for directions, or submit the report to the relevant Minister without alteration. Alternatively, a person identified in or identifiable from a draft report may bring the matter before the High Court seeking an order from the court directing that the draft be amended before submission to the relevant Minister. The court may either order the commission to submit the report without alteration, or with such alterations as it may direct, or give a direction to the commission to provide an opportunity to the person to give evidence or make submissions to the commission before the report is finalised. The final decision on the publication of a report or interim report rests with the relevant Minister. He or she may seek directions from the High Court where there is a risk that anything in the report or interim report could prejudice any pending or ongoing criminal proceedings.

Section 42 confers absolute privilege on reports and interim reports as well as on other documentation of a commission, where published.

Connection with tribunals of inquiry It was accepted during the Oireachtas debate on the 2004 Act that in some instances a commission may be unable to establish or present the full facts in respect of some or all of the matters about which it has carried out an investigation. The 2004 Act therefore leaves open the possibility of a tribunal of inquiry being established under the Tribunals of Inquiry (Evidence) Acts 1921 to 2004 for the purposes of inquiring further into the matter. Section 45 provides that, in the event of a tribunal being established, all of the evidence collected by a commission of investigation may be made available to a tribunal. Section 46 provides that any affected person is to be informed of the effect of any such disclosure. As to the difference between a commission of investigation and a tribunal, it was pointed out during the Oireachtas debate that a tribunal hears arguments in public and, unlike what we generally expect to be the case with commissions, permits cross-examinations. A tribunal can therefore come to conclusions based on the balance of the evidence available to it. In other words, it is able to make judgments about the balance of evidence in a way that is not foreseen for commissions of investigation.

COMMISSION TO INQUIRE INTO CHILD ABUSE

In *Hillary v Minister for Education*, High Court, June 11, 2004, the applicant sought a declaration that the Commission to Inquire into Child Abuse Act 2000 (Additional Functions) Order 2001, empowering it to inquire into vaccine trials carried out in State institutions, was *ultra vires* the Commission to Inquire into Child Abuse Act 2000. The 2001 Order had been purportedly made under s.4(4) of the Act of 2000 following a report by the Chief Medical Officer into vaccine trials conducted in State institutions. Section 4(4) of the 2000 Act entitled the Government to confer on the Commission additional functions or powers connected with their functions and powers for the time being. The applicant contended that the investigation into vaccine trials was not connected with the functions and powers of the Commission then existing, which instead concerned inquiring into child abuse occurring in State institutions. Ó Caoimh J. agreed. He held that the conduct of the trials could not be said in any way to amount to "abuse" as defined in the 2000 Act. He also held that none of the issues raised in the report of the Chief Medical Officer even suggested the existence of abuse as defined by the 2000 Act in the conduct of the trials in question. He was of the view that there must be some real connection before an Additional Functions Order could be made. The report of the Chief Medical Officer did not suggest any connection, as required by the 2000 Act, such as to entitle the making of an Additional Functions Order in the circumstances. The essential issue raised was one of medical ethics and was not one suggestive of "abuse" as defined in the Act of 2000. The Additional Functions Order was, therefore, *ultra vires* the 2000 Act. Ó Caoimh J. also pointed out in conclusion that the approval of the 2001 Order by both Houses of the Oireachtas did not operate to validate the making of the Order, which could only be made within the limits of the 2000 Act itself.

COUNCIL OF EUROPE DEVELOPMENT BANK

The Council of Europe Development Bank Act 2004 provides for Ireland's membership of the Council of Europe Development Bank. The primary purpose of the bank is to help in solving the social problems with which European countries are or may be faced as a result of the presence of refugees, displaced persons or migrants consequent upon forced movements of populations as a result of natural or ecological disasters. However, in recent years the bank has expanded its operations to support projects relating to social housing, health, education, rural modernisation, support for SMEs and the improvement of the quality of life in disadvantaged urban areas and the protection and rehabilitation of historic heritage. The bank provides loans and guarantees, not subsidies, to its Member States, to local authorities and to financial institutions.

INTERNATIONAL DEVELOPMENT ASSOCIATION

The International Development Association (Amendment) Act 2004 provided for the State's contribution to the 13th round of funding for the International Development Association, the concessionary lending arm of the World Bank, which was agreed in 2003. The International Development Association provides grants or long-term loans at zero interest rates to the poorest developing countries. These are countries where *per capita* income is less than US$875. Ireland pledged a contribution of €50 million payable over the period to 2008, subject to the approval of the Oireachtas in the form of the enactment of the 2004 Act.

JUDICIAL REVIEW

Alternative remedies   In *Tomlinson v Criminal Injuries Compensation Tribunal*, High Court, March 3, 2004; [2005] 1 I.L.R.M. 394 (SC), the applicant sought judicial review to challenge part of an award made to her pursuant to the Criminal Injuries Compensation Scheme. A single member of the respondent Tribunal had ruled that the applicant fell within the scheme and made an award of compensation in her favour. The award included a sum in respect of loss of earnings. The figure awarded, however, contained a substantial deduction from the applicant's claimed figure. The legal basis for the deduction was not entirely clear but the parties assumed that it related to the payment of death service benefit to the applicant. Under the scheme, an award may be reduced where compensation is available from another source. The applicant claimed that the respondent was wrong in making those deductions and had acted *ultra vires*. Under the scheme a person who is unhappy with the decision of the single member has a full right of appeal to an appeal panel of three members. The applicant did not appeal but instead opted to pursue judicial review proceedings. The respondent contended that the applicant had failed to exhaust alternative remedies. Kelly J. agreed and refused the relief sought. He held that the court should be very slow indeed to intervene by way of judicial review except to correct a final decision made by the respondent. In this case, no such decision had been given. The entitlement of the court to intervene before the process contemplated by the scheme had been exhausted was very limited. He considered that there may well be cases where this would be justified if there was a failure to conform to the principles of natural and constitutional justice. However, that was not the case here. He also noted that there was no time limit provided for in the scheme for bringing an appeal so the applicant was not prejudiced in that regard. We note briefly here that the Supreme Court reversed this decision on appeal ([2005] 1 I.L.R.M. 394), to which we will return in the *Annual Review of Irish Law 2005*.

Delay: validity of statutory Orders In *Noonan Services Ltd v Labour Court and S.I.P.T.U.*, Supreme Court, May 14, 2004, the applicants challenged the validity of two Employment Regulation Orders (EROs) made by the respondent under the Industrial Relations Acts which provided statutory minimum rates of pay and conditions of employment for workers in the contract cleaning sector. The respondent made the order on July 28, 2003 to come into effect on January 1, 2004 to allow employers and workers rearrange their work systems to meet the EROs. The applicant made an *ex parte* application for leave to bring judicial review proceedings on December 15, 2003. The judge found that the issue of delay in bringing the application was fatal to the applicants' case. He held that since all sectors of industry were affected by the EROs a strict approach in granting judicial review must be taken, considering the practical difficulties that would arise should the court intervene in an industrial relations matter at that late stage. On appeal, the Supreme Court agreed. Speaking for the court, McGuinness J. referred to the court's decision in *Dekra Éireann Teo v Minister for the Environment and Local Government* [2003] 2 I.R. 270 (*Annual Review of Irish Law 2003*, p.40) and noted that that under Ord.84, r.21 of the Rules of the Superior Courts 1986, an application for leave to bring judicial review proceedings must be made promptly, particularly where it would affect others besides the parties. The court agreed with the view taken in the High Court that it would create considerable difficulty for the whole sector if the EROs were found *ultra vires*. McGuinness J. noted that they had been under negotiation for some time and it was likely that all parties were aware that the respondent intended to make such EROs as early as April 2003.

She concluded that there was no apparent reason why the applicants did not move the judicial review application at an earlier stage. The notice party, a trade union, had made a cross-appeal for an order for costs. The Supreme Court deemed them an appropriate party to be brought into the case because they represented a large number of workers affected by the Regulations. They were thus were entitled to their costs.

Procedure: law reform proposals   In 2004, the Law Reform Commission published its *Report on Judicial Review Procedure* (LRC 71–2004), which followed from its *Consultation Paper on Judicial Review Procedure* (LRC CP 20–2003). There has been an increased volume of judicial review applications coming before the courts in recent years: almost 1,300 judicial review applications were lodged in the High Court in 2002, of which over 500 were refugee/asylum/immigration cases. Three judges of the High Court are currently assigned to deal almost exclusively with judicial review cases, reflecting the complexity of these cases and the priority given by the High Court to them. The Report examined the long-established conventional judicial review procedure, contained in Ord.84 of the Rules of the Superior Courts 1986, as well as numerous special statutory regimes in such fields as planning and refugees. The recommendations are aimed at supporting the measures already taken in the courts to ensure that judicial review cases are dealt with in an efficient and timely manner consistent with the requirements of justice.

In conventional judicial review, the Report recommends retention of the *ex parte* leave stage and the "arguable case" test. It also recommends that, in exceptional cases, the leave stage be converted into a hearing involving both sides. It also recommends that, in relation to the availability of alternative remedies, a middle-ground approach be applied in which the potential availability of alternative remedies should not, in itself, prevent an application for judicial review. In the context of statutory schemes for judicial review, the Report recommended retention of the leave stage and of the higher standard of "substantial grounds", which it considers is justifiable. The Report recommends that the general time limit for applying for judicial review should be six months, subject to stricter time limits in some cases, such as planning and immigration cases. In that respect, the Report recommended that the fixed period within which applications for judicial review falling under the Illegal Immigrants (Trafficking) Act 2000 are to be made, should be changed from 14 to 28 days, subject to the same judicial discretion to extend as currently exists. The Report also recommended that there should be further development of active judicial case management by the courts, including judicially supervised timetables to ensure that judicial review cases are progressed as speedily as possible and greater flexibility use of case management. In the context of costs, the Report recommended that the courts may make greater use of the power to apportion the costs appropriately. The Report did not recommend the introduction of an "'Administrative Court" or of a "single order'" in judicial review cases.

Substantive law Other than the cases discussed above, much of the case law under Ord.84 of the Rules of the Superior Courts 1986 is discussed in the various chapters in this *Annual Review* where the substantive subjects arising are detailed, notably in the Planning Law chapter. Further reference may also be obtained through the Table of Statutory Instruments under the entry for the Rules of the Superior Courts 1986.

OFFICIAL LANGUAGES

Irish and English language An Tordú Acht Na Dteangacha Oifigiúla 2003 (Tosach Feidhme) 2004, the Official Languages Act 2003 (Commencement) Order 2004 (S.I. No.32 of 2004) brought the majority of the Official Languages Act 2003 (*Annual Review of Irish Law 2003*, p.7) into effect on January 19, 2004. The Order brought s.10 of the 2003 Act into effect from May 1, 2004 in the case of specified documents that relate to the year 2003 or any subsequent year. Particular provision is made for a county development plan that has been published prior to May 1, 2004 but not yet formally made on that date.

PRIVATE SECURITY AUTHORITY

Private Security Authority The Private Security Services Act 2004 provides for the establishment of the Private Security Authority. The Authority is, in effect, a regulatory body with the role of controlling and supervising individuals and companies providing private security services. The 2004 Act encompasses a broad range of security activities and services, including door supervisors ("bouncers"), private investigators, security guards and consultants, as well as suppliers and installers of security equipment. The 2004 Act gives general effect to the *Report of the Consultative Group on the Private Security Industry* (1997). The Authority also has an investigatory and adjudicative role concerning any complaints against such individuals or companies. In respect of its adjudicative role, the 2004 Act also provides for the establishment of the Private Security Appeal Board, which is empowered hear and determine appeals against decisions of the Authority.

Licensing As mentioned by the Minister for Justice, Equality and Law Reform during the passage of the 2004 Act, one of the Authority's immediate priorities will be to introduce and operate a licensing system and maintain an up-to-date and easily accessible register of all licensees. In the longer term, the aim will be to improve industry standards and delivery of the services concerned. It was envisaged that the licensing requirement would apply initially to door supervisors and security guards and be rolled out subsequently to other sectors. The 2004 Act defines "security service" as a service provided by a private security employer or any of the persons set out in the list which follows in the course of an employment or as an independent contractor. The effect of this is that both private security companies and the individual staff members who provide security services must be licensed. A number of exemptions to the licensing requirement are set out in s.3 of the 2004 Act; these include members of the Garda Síochána, the Defence Forces, authorised officers under the Air Navigation and Transport Acts or staff of a Department or State agency while undertaking official duties. Apprentices employed by a person providing a security service are also excluded. Additional exemptions may be made by means of Regulations under s.3(2).

Functions of Authority   The principal functions of the Authority are set out in s.8. In general, it is empowered to control and supervise persons providing security services with a view to maintaining and improving standards in the provision of those services. It will grant and renew licences to persons within the industry and, where appropriate, suspend or revoke licences. It may also specify standards to be observed in the provision of security services by licensees and qualifications or training requirements for the grant of licences. Standards and qualification requirements will be implemented by means of Regulations made by the Authority with the consent of the Minister under s.51. Section 13 empowers the Authority to investigate any security services being provided by any person. It may request information relevant to an investigation from any person and also request a person to appear before it with a view to furthering the investigation. If these requirements are not complied with, the authority may apply to the District Court for an order requiring compliance. The court may treat a failure to comply with such an order without reasonable excuse as a contempt of the court. Under s.14, the Authority may appoint members of its staff to be inspectors subject to terms and conditions determined by it. Each inspector shall, on appointment, be given a warrant which he or she shall produce when requested. Section 15 confers on inspectors powers of entry and inspection for the purpose of obtaining information on any matter under investigation by the Authority. Refusal to comply with any requirement of an inspector will be an offence. Section 48 deals with offences generally and empowers the authority to bring and prosecute summary proceedings for an offence under the Act.

Licensing arrangements   Section 21 sets out the conditions for obtaining a licence to provide security services. Application forms must be accompanied by references as to the applicant's character and competence, as well as the prescribed fee. The Authority may require an applicant to furnish such additional information as it may consider necessary, including certification by a senior member of the Garda Síochána, and may require verification of any information by affidavit. Investigations or examinations may also be undertaken regarding an applicant's character, financial position and competence. In the case of companies and partnerships, the information required will relate to directors and partners respectively, as well as any manager, secretary or other officer of the entity concerned. An individual who occupies any of these positions and is also directly involved in providing a private security service will require an individual licence. Section 22 provides that the Authority may grant or refuse to grant a licence. It shall refuse to issue a licence where the applicant is not a "fit and proper person" to provide a security service or does not comply with requirements under the legislation. In the case of companies and partnerships, the conditions apply to directors and partners, respectively, as well as to any manager, secretary or other similar officer of the entity concerned. It is also provided that a licence does not confer any right of property and that it may not, *inter alia,* be transferred or mortgaged. In so far as offences are concerned, s.36 requires an applicant for a licence or a licensee who has been convicted of an offence, or against whom proceedings are pending, to notify the Authority of the conviction or the proceedings in the prescribed manner and within the prescribed period. Section 39 provides that a person may make a complaint of misconduct against a licensee provided that it is made in good faith and not frivolous or vexatious. If, following investigation, the complaint is upheld, the Authority may take appropriate action, which range from revocation of the licence to the issuing of a caution or advice to the licensee concerned.

Appeals Section 40 provides for the establishment of the Private Security Appeal Board which will hear and determine appeals against decisions of the Authority. An applicant or licensee may appeal against any decision of the Authority to refuse to grant or renew a licence, suspend or revoke a licence or take action on foot of a complaint under s.39. Details of the composition and operation of the appeal board and the procedures for handling appeals are set out in Sched.2. Section 41 makes provision for an appeal to the High Court on any question of law arising from a determination by the Appeal Board.

Bodies licensed in other EU States Part 6 of the 2004 Act relates to the provision of security services in the State by persons who hold licences from comparable licensing authorities in other EU Member States. It was noted during the Oireachtas debate on the 2004 Act that many of the services in which the private security industry is involved, including transportation of works of art or high value goods, require the crossing of national frontiers. A transnational dimension can also arise where a company in one EU Member State wishes to tender for a private security contract in another or where an individual applies for a job in one Member State having acquired work experience or a qualification in another. Part 6 contains a set of procedures which will permit a person—referred to in the Act as a "relevant person"—who holds a licence from a comparable authority in another EU Member State —referred to as a "corresponding authority"—to provide a security service in the State. A number of safeguards are included in Part 6 to ensure persons who would not qualify for an Irish licence due to criminal convictions or inadequate qualifications cannot circumvent the standards in the 2004 Act by procuring, by whatever means, a licence to provide a security service from another Member State.

PUBLIC SERVICE RECRUITMENT AND APPOINTMENTS

Public Service Management (Recruitment and Appointments) Act 2004 The Public Service Management (Recruitment and Appointments) Act 2004 provides for fundamental change to the method of recruitment to the Civil Service, the Garda Síochána and to senior posts in local authorities. The general background to the 2004 Act is the modernisation of the civil service and public service derived from the Strategic Management Initiative (SMI), which began in the 1990s. More directly, a Human Resources Management Working Group, a cross-departmental body established under the SMI, recommended to the Government that the structures governing the recruitment of civil servants should be reformed. In particular, it was considered that there should be an option for public service bodies to recruit directly from the labour market. It was stated during the debate in the Oireachtas on the 2004 Act that it represented a significant element of the programme of public service modernisation which was agreed with the social partners in the public sector agreement *Sustaining Progress*. The 2004 Act provides for the creation of two new bodies, the Commission for Public Service Appointments and the Public Appointments Service. In effect, under the 2004 Act, the Commission for Public Service Appointments became the principal regulator for public service recruitment and thus replaced the Civil Service Commission and the Local Appointments Commission. The 2004 Act repealed the Civil Service Commissioners Act 1956 and amended substantially the principal legislation relating to the Local Appointments Commission, the Local Authorities (Officers and Employees) Act 1926.

Scope of 2004 Act Section 5 of the 2004 Act provides that it applies to: appointments to most positions in the Civil Service, including unestablished positions; appointments to the Garda Síochána; appointments to most managerial, professional and technical posts in local authorities and to vocational education committees. Section 6 authorises the Minister for Finance to provide by Orders for the extension of the 2004 Act beyond these appointments. Section 7 of the 2004 Act provides, however, that certain appointments are excluded from the scope of the 2004 Act: appointments to posts established under the Constitution; appointments made by the President or Government; or the appointment of special advisers within the meaning of the Ethics in Public Office Act 1995. The reference to special advisers was inserted during the debate on the 2004 Act to ensure that special advisers cannot be appointed by Ministers, or by Government, to established positions in the Civil Service and that, therefore, special advisers will continue to leave the Civil Service at the same time as their Ministers leave office. Subject to these exclusions, it was stated during the Oireachtas debate on the 2004 Act that it is the intention to ensure that in time the overwhelming majority of public service posts will be subject to the system of regulation established by the 2004 Act.

Commission for Public Service Appointments Under the 2004 Act, the Commission for Public Service Appointments will set standards for recruitment to the civil service and the public service and will monitor compliance with those standards. While initially the Commission will broadly oversee the same range of recruitment as the Civil Service Commission and the Local Appointments Commission, the 2004 Act also provides for the extension of its remit to cover the full range of public service recruitment in due course. As finally enacted, s.12 of the 2004 Act provides that the Commission comprises five *ex officio* members, namely the Ceann Comhairle of Dáil Éireann, the Secretary General to the Government, the Secretary General, Public Service Management and Development, in the Department of Finance, the Chairman of the Standards in Public Office Commission and the Ombudsman. As initiated, s.12 had provided for only three *ex officio* members of the Commission, and that up to six other commissioners could have been appointed by Government. To allay concerns that the power of appointment to the Commission might be open to question, s.12 was amended to add two more *ex officio* members and to delete the Government's power to appoint members to the Commission. Section 15 provides that persons who have knowledge of an attempt to influence a recruitment process may inform the Commission in order that it may take appropriate action. The Commission may investigate the exercise of recruitment functions by any licence holder or recruitment agency. Licence holders, recruitment agencies and any other person who may have information which is materially relevant to the exercise of functions under the Act must co-operate with an investigation and it is an offence to obstruct an investigation. A person found guilty of the offence will be liable on summary conviction to a fine not exceeding €3,000 or to imprisonment for a term not exceeding two years, or both.

Public Appointments Service Part 3 of the 2004 Act provides for the establishment of the Public Appointments Service (PAS), as the centralised recruitment body for the public service. The PAS will incorporate the staff of the Civil Service Commission and the Local Appointments Commission. The Public Appointment Service will be independent in the exercise of its functions, which will include acting as the centralised recruitment, assessment and selection body for the Civil Service and public service bodies where it is requested to do so; ensuring that the Commission's codes of practice are followed in the recruitment process, undertaking other selection competitions, including promotion competitions and competitions to posts in organisations outside the Civil Service where requested by the relevant Minister; and providing expert services on recruitment, assessment and selection matters. The board of the PAS comprises a chairperson, the chief executive of the PAS and seven ordinary members. Its functions include considering and approving plans and strategic objectives put forward by the chief executive, monitoring the PAS in the exercise of its functions and ensuring appropriate review procedures are put in place for recruitment and promotion procedures. The 2004 Act provides that the board members must not participate in political activity. This was considered essential to ensure there will be no suspicion of political interference in the work of the PAS.

Devolution of authority to recruit In a departure from the previous arrangements, Pt 4 of the 2004 Act provides that public service bodies regulated by the Commission for Public Service Appointments will be allowed to undertake their own recruitment under a licence to be issued by the Commission. If the Garda Commissioner or relevant Secretary General of each Department decides to apply for such a licence, they will be entitled to recruit directly from the labour market without the requirement to use the Public Appointments Service. Any licence will be subject to clear codes of practice, which will allow the Garda Commissioner or Department to recruit on its own behalf, or with the assistance of private sector recruitment agencies specifically approved by the Commission. Where licence holders delegate all or part of the task of recruitment to the PAS, the chief executive of the PAS, rather than the licence holder, will be responsible for adherence to the terms of the licence. Where a private sector recruitment agency is engaged, s.25(5)(b) of the 2004 Act provides that sole responsibility for the final selection of candidates for appointment or placement on a panel for appointment will rest with the public sector body rather than the recruitment agency. This provision was added during the Oireachtas debate and was intended to secure the probity of the recruitment process by placing responsibility for final selection of candidates unambiguously on the shoulders of the public body.

Recruitment and selection Part 5 of the 2004 Act sets out the obligations applying to candidates in respect of recruitment and selection procedures. Section 54 prohibits in any public service recruitment, selection or promotion competition the provision of false information, canvassing, bribery, personation and any interference with the competition. A person engaging in such activities is guilty of an offence. If a person who has been found guilty of such an offence was or is a candidate at a competition, he or she will be disqualified as a candidate. If he or she has been appointed, he or she will forfeit the appointment.

Selection for promotion Part 6 of the 2004 Act, which comprises s.57, deals with selection for promotion and provides that the Minister for Finance, following consultation with any relevant Minister, may ask the PAS to hold promotion competitions for civil servants or other public servants. Part 7, which comprises s.58, sets out the powers and responsibilities of the Minister for Finance and other Ministers in respect of recruitment and selection.

PUBLIC SERVICE SUPERANNUATION AND PENSION REFORM

The Public Service Superannuation (Miscellaneous Provisions) Act 2004 gave effect to the age related superannuation and pension reforms for the public service announced in the 2004 Budget, and based on the *Report of the Commission on Public Service Pensions*. The 2004 Act defines "superannuation benefit" as "a pension, gratuity or other allowance payable on resignation, retirement, discharge or death to or in respect of a member or former member of a public service pension scheme, in accordance with the terms of the scheme". The following age related reforms for most *new entrants* to the public service came into effect under the 2004 Act with effect from April 1, 2004: first, the minimum age for receiving a pension should generally be 65, and there should be no compulsion in the system for people to retire at a particular age, such as 65, if they are fit and willing to remain in employment. The 2004 Act implements these reforms by amending the relevant primary legislation which provides for a compulsory retirement age or a minimum pension age and by making the necessary overriding provisions in respect of other public service pension schemes. These include: the Superannuation Act 1859, the Superannuation Act 1887, the Superannuation Act 1909, the Superannuation Act 1914 and the Civil Service Regulation Act 1956. For the operational reasons identified in the Commission's Report, the 2004 Act provides for a minimum pension age of 55 for new entrant Garda Síochána, prison officers and specified fire officers, as defined in the 2004 Act, and new pension arrangements for new entrants to the Permanent Defence Forces. It was estimated in the 2004 Budget speech that the annual savings which will arise from the introduction of these changes will be of the order of €300 million in current terms in 30 to 40 years time, with some savings being realised earlier than that.

STATE AIRPORT AUTHORITIES

The State Airports Act 2004 gave legislative effect to the dissolution of the state-owned airports authority, Aer Rianta cpt, and the creation of three separate state-owned authorities to manage and control the three international airports in the State. The enactment of the 2004 Act came against the background of considerable public and political controversy about the decision to dissolve Aer Rianta. We do not propose to address that aspect of the legislation here, but will focus on its essential elements. The three new bodies are the Dublin Airport Authority plc, the Cork Airport Authority plc and the Shannon Airport Authority plc. The 2004 Act formally provided that Aer Rianta cpt was renamed the Dublin Airport Authority plc. The Dublin Airport Authority was thus conferred with the powers of Aer Rianta cpt. The intention expressed during the Oireachtas debate was that, after business plans were developed by the boards appointed to the Cork and Shannon airport authorities, responsibility for their management and control would be transferred from the Dublin Airport Authority.

In order to comply with the capital maintenance provisions of Pt 4 of the Companies (Amendment) Act 1983, the 2004 Act provides that Aer Rianta effectively transferred the assets relating to the airport businesses at Cork and Shannon to the new airport authorities established under the Act in return for the issue of shares by the new companies to the Minister for Finance. For the purposes of company law, the transfers are regarded as distributions made by Aer Rianta cpt to its shareholder, the Minister for Finance. Consequently, Aer Rianta cpt was only in a position to make the transfers when it had available distributable reserves equal to the net value of the assets transferred. As the distributable reserves available to Aer Rianta cpt at the time the 2004 Act was enacted were insufficient for this purpose, the 2004 Act provided for a phased approach, which allowed for Shannon Airport Authority to be vested in a relatively short term after enactment, while Cork Airport Authority would be vested once sufficient further distributable reserves have been built up within Aer Rianta cpt, as renamed the Dublin Airport Authority. The 2004 Act provided that a portion of the Cork Airport assets would remain in Aer Rianta cpt and be subject to a finance lease between Aer Rianta cpt and the Cork Airport Authority.

As a consequence of the restructuring, Pt 3 of the 2004 Act makes appropriate changes to the Aviation Regulation Act 2001. Thus, changes were made to the objectives of the Commission of Aviation Regulation in making a determination on maximum airport charges, the duration of such a determination and significantly the removal of Cork and Shannon from the scope of price cap regulation. It was stated during the Oireachtas debate that, as a result of the restructuring, it would no longer be appropriate to price regulate Cork and Shannon Airports because they would not have market dominance in the way that Dublin Airport had and would continue to have.

STATE BODIES

Aer Lingus The Aer Lingus Act 2004 gave effect to the Employee Share Ownership Plan (ESOP) agreed by Government and unions in the airline Aer

Lingus and to provide a legal framework to facilitate any private sector investment process in the event that the Government embarks on such a process. The 2004 Act thus provides for the repeal of provisions, in whole or in part and on different days, contained in the Air Companies Acts 1966 to 1993 as detailed in the Schedule to the Act. The 2004 Act also includes an enabling provision for the establishment of new pension schemes by Aer Lingus. Section 3 provides that the Minister for Finance may sell, exchange or dispose of his or her shares in Aer Lingus Group plc. The Minister for Finance is currently the major shareholder in the airline. Provision is also made that any funds received in respect of the sale or disposal of the State's shareholding in Aer Lingus will be paid into and disposed of for the benefit of the Exchequer. Section 4 makes provision for Aer Lingus Group plc to issue new shares and to create shares of different classes with different rights, subject to the Companies Acts 1963 to 2001. Section 5 provides enabling powers to facilitate a sale of all or part of the State's shareholding in Aer Lingus. Appropriate provisions are made to enable the Minister for Finance to enter one or more agreements in connection with the sale of the shares in the company including customary provisions contained in a shareholders' or underwriting agreement as the Minister may wish. Section 6, in order to facilitate ESOT Board representation, the terms of which have already been agreed between the parties and, where and when necessary, third party Board representation, provides for the full or partial disapplication from the Company of the Worker Participation Acts 1977 and 1993, for the retirement of directors upon such disapplication and for the Minister to appoint new directors to fill vacancies so created. Section 7 provides for employee shareholding schemes and their acquisition of shares in the company. Section 8 clarifies that s.60 of the Companies Act 1963, which prohibits a company from giving financial assistance for a purchase of shares in the company, does not apply to any warranties given, or financial obligations undertaken, by the company in connection with the disposal of shares and, in addition, does not apply to any financial arrangement in connection with the purchase of shares by an Employee Share Ownership Trust (ESOT). Section 9 provides that Aer Lingus may establish one or more superannuation scheme or schemes for their own employees. Under existing arrangements Aer Lingus shares a common pension scheme, the Irish Airlines (General Employees) Superannuation Scheme, with other employers. Section 10 provides that the money needed for the costs related to carrying out disposal of shares will be provided by the Oireachtas. Section 11 provides for the repayment by Aer Lingus Ltd to the Exchequer of €6,348,690 (£5,000,000) advanced to Aerlinte (now Santain Developments Ltd) under the Air Companies (Amendment) Act 1969, together with any outstanding interest. Section 12 provides for the non-application of certain legislation in the event of any future private sector investment process. This includes the Ethics in Public Office Acts 1995 and 2001, the Prompt Payment of Accounts Act 1997 and s.521 of the Taxes Consolidation Act 1997.

TRIBUNALS OF INQUIRY

Costs orders   The primary purpose of the Tribunals of Inquiry (Evidence) (Amendment) Act 2004, which contains one substantive provision, was to ensure that Judge Alan Mahon, chairperson of the Tribunal to Inquire into Certain Planning Matters and Payments (the Planning Tribunal), which had previously been chaired by Mr Justice Fergus Flood, was empowered to make orders for costs incurred during the tenure of the previous chairperson. The issue became apparent following the resignation in June 2003 of Mr Justice Flood as chairperson of the tribunal. Specifically, the issue arises in the determination of costs concerned with certain modules dealt with in the first two interim reports of the Planning Tribunal. These modules were dealt with at a time when Mr Justice Flood was the sole member of that tribunal and the reports were accordingly prepared by him. The determination of costs had not been made at the time of Mr Justice Flood's resignation.

Section 2 of the 2004 Act inserted a new s.6(1A) and s.6(1B) into s.6 of the Tribunals of Inquiry (Evidence) (Amendment) Act 1979, as amended by the Tribunals of Inquiry (Evidence) (Amendment) Act 1997. The effect of this is that the sole member of a tribunal, or the chairperson if there is more than one member, may make an order on any costs that were incurred before his or her appointment and that have not already been determined. In exercising this power, the sole member, or chairperson, must have regard to any report of the tribunal relating to its proceedings in the period before his or her appointment. The 2004 Act provides that the new provisions will apply to tribunals appointed and costs incurred before or after the passing of the legislation. During its passage in the Oireachtas, s.6(1B) was inserted to make clear that s.6(1A)(b) could not have the result of limiting the effect of the amended s.6(1) on matters which can be taken into account by the chairperson when making determinations on costs.

It is worth pointing out that the 2004 Act is the sixth Act passed since 1979 which has amended the original Tribunals of Inquiry (Evidence) 1921. The effect was a patchwork quilt of legislative provisions which did not even provide a comprehensive legislative code in this area. We note here that the Law Reform Commission, in its *Report on Public Inquiries Including Tribunals of Inquiry* (LRC 73–2005), recommended that the 1921 Act, as amended, be codified into a single Act. The 2005 Report includes the text of a draft codifying Tribunals of Inquiry Bill. We will return to the Commission's Report in the *Annual Review of Irish Law 2005*.

Planning tribunal: discontinuing inquiry into certain matters   The Tribunal of Inquiry into Certain Planning Matters and Payments Act 2004 was enacted to provide a statutory basis for the discretion granted in the amended terms of reference of the Planning Tribunal of Inquiry to decide which issues within its terms of reference to investigate. The Tribunal of Inquiry had been established in 1997 and, until 2002, its only member was Flood J. The Tribunals of Inquiry (Evidence) (Amendment) Act 2002 (*Annual Review of Irish Law 2002*, pp.6–9) provided for the appointment of more than one member to a tribunal of inquiry. Since 2002, the tribunal comprised three judicial members (since 2003, it has been chaired by Judge Alan Mahon). The 2002 Act was enacted to provide for a more speedy conclusion to the tribunal's functions. In the *Fourth Interim Report of the Planning Tribunal*, published in June 2004, the tribunal indicated that it still has a large volume of work on hand which, if investigated in full, could see the tribunal continuing until 2014 or 2015, that is, for 18 years since its establishment. The tribunal itself recognised that this situation could not and should not continue. As a result, the tribunal's fourth interim requested a change to its terms of reference to allow it more discretion in the issues that it investigates, with a view to shortening the anticipated duration of the tribunal's activities. The Minister for Local Government and the Environment stated during the Oireachtas debate on the 2004 Act that the tribunal had indicated that the amended terms of reference, together with additional resources which had been allocated to it, would allow the tribunal to complete its public hearings by March 2007, a substantially shorter time frame than that indicated in the tribunal's fourth interim report.

As provided for by the Tribunals of Inquiry (Evidence) (Amendment) Act 1998, the amended terms of reference had been approved by both Houses of the Oireachtas prior to the enactment of the 2004 Act. Under the amended terms of reference, the final date for receipt of any new complaint or request for investigation is fixed by the terms of reference as December 16, 2004.

The 2004 Act empowers the tribunal: to decide to carry out any preliminary investigations as it thinks fit, in private, using all the powers conferred on it under the Tribunals of Inquiry (Evidence) Acts 1921 to 2004, in order to determine whether sufficient evidence exists in relation to any matter before it to warrant proceeding to a public hearing if deemed necessary; to decide not to initiate a preliminary investigation or a public hearing of evidence in relation to the matter notwithstanding that the matter falls within the tribunal's terms of reference, or; in any case where it has initiated a preliminary investigation in private, whether concluded or not, but not yet initiated a public hearing of evidence in the matter, to decide to discontinue or otherwise terminate its investigation notwithstanding that the matter falls within the tribunal's terms of reference.

In exercising this discretion the tribunal must have regard to the following: the age or state of health of one or more persons who are likely to be in a position to provide useful information, including oral evidence to be given privately or publicly. This would include the age or likely state of health of any such person, at the possible date in the future when that person or persons might be expected to be called upon to give oral evidence, or otherwise to co-operate with the tribunal. In particular, the tribunal may consider whether or not their age or state of health would to be an impediment to such person being in a position to co-operate with the tribunal or to give evidence to the tribunal in private or in public; the likely duration of the preliminary investigation or public hearing into any matter; the likely cost, or other use of the resources of the tribunal, of such investigation or any stage of the investigation into any matter; whether or not the investigation into the matter is likely to provide evidence to the tribunal which would enable it to make findings of fact and conclusions or to make recommendations and; any other factors which in the opinion of the tribunal would, or would be likely to, render the continued investigation into any matter inappropriate, unnecessary, wasteful of resources, unduly costly, unduly prolonged or of limited or no probative value.

By May 1, 2005, the tribunal must decide what new matters on its books will proceed to a public hearing. To allow the tribunal to prepare its final report no new investigation can be referred to public hearing by the tribunal, other than matters that come to light during existing investigations. If the tribunal decides that the continued pursuit of its inquiries would be of limited or of no further value in discharging its mandate, it must report that to the Oireachtas and convey to the Oireachtas the wish of the tribunal that its investigations and inquiries should terminate on a date to be specified by the tribunal.

Asylum and Immigration Law

NUALA EGAN, Barrister-at-Law
and
**PATRICIA BRAZIL, Barrister-at-Law, Lecturer in Law,
Trinity College, Dublin**

INTRODUCTION

Over the past five years or so, a steadily increasing body of judicial review case law has begun to emerge in the area of refugee and immigration law, mirroring the considerable increase in numbers of persons arriving in the State from the mid-1990s onwards for the purpose of seeking recognition of their refugee status. Whilst initially such cases were dealt with in the general judicial review list of the High Court, by 1999 it was decided, in view of the number of cases instituted for the purpose of challenging decisions reached in the asylum and deportation processes, to create a separate court list dealing exclusively with such cases. A further reaction to the increasing numbers emerged the following year in the guise of the Illegal Immigrants (Trafficking) Act 2000 which raised the procedural bar for persons who sought to challenge such decisions. Thus, such an applicant is precluded from challenging same otherwise than by application for judicial review, which application must be made within fourteen days of receipt of the impugned decision, with an extension of the time period possible where the High Court considers that there is "good and sufficient" reason for doing so. The application for leave to apply by way of judicial review shall be on notice to the respondent parties and an applicant must, in order to obtain such leave, satisfy the court that his or her application discloses "substantial grounds". Finally, the determination of the High Court is final and no appeal lies therefrom to the Supreme Court unless the High Court grants leave to do so, being of the view that its decision involves a point of law of exceptional public importance and that it is desirable in the public interest that such an appeal should be taken.

The contentious sections of that Bill were referred by the President to the Supreme Court which upheld the constitutional validity thereof (*In the matter of Article 26 and in the matter of Sections 5 and 10 of the Illegal Immigrants (Trafficking) Bill 1999* [2000] 2 I.R. 360). While the court acknowledged that non-nationals are entitled to the same degree of natural justice and fairness of procedures as that to which a citizen is entitled, it concluded that the requirement to proceed by way of judicial review within a limited time period serves the legitimate public policy objective of seeking to bring about, at an early stage, legal certainty as regards administrative decisions and better facilitates the administration and functioning of the system for dealing with applicants for refugee status.

The regime set out in the 2000 Act has had a marked impact upon the jurisprudence of the courts in this area. Thus, although the High Court list remains full with new cases, there is, as yet, very little Supreme Court guidance on the impact of natural justice and fairness of procedure on the asylum application and deportation processes. As a result, different viewpoints persist in the High Court on such questions. Equally, the important question of whether the *O'Keeffe v An Bord Pleanála* test or a lower standard of review is to be employed by the courts where an applicant alleges that the impugned decision is irrational and/or unreasonable, though touched upon in brief, remains to be discussed and resolved by the Supreme Court (the Supreme Court specifically reserved consideration of this question in the case of *Z v Minister for Justice* [2002] 2 I.L.R.M. 215, while in *AL & DO v Minister for Justice* [2003] 1 I.R. 1 both McGuinness and Fennelly JJ. suggested that "where constitutional rights are at stake as in this case the standard of judicial scrutiny as set out in particular in *O'Keeffe v An Bord Pleanála* may fall short of what is likely to be required for their protection" (at pp.126 and 203)). Likewise, the requirement that an application for leave to apply by way of judicial review be conducted on notice has resulted in a situation in which cases are run and, by and large, determined, at that stage, with a resultant shortage of High Court jurisprudence at the final— substantive—judicial review stage. A further minor hindrance for practitioners arises from the prohibition upon the use of and reference to an applicant's full name in such proceedings; this arises as a result of s.19 of the Refugee Act 1996, subs.(2) of which provides:

> "no matter likely to lead members of the public to identify a person as an applicant under this Act shall be published in a written publication available to the public or be broadcast without the consent of that person and the consent of the Minister".

The penalties for breach of this provision are contained in s.19(3), which prescribes a maximum fine not exceeding £1,500 or imprisonment for a term not exceeding 12 months or both.

Nonetheless, there are now a large number of judgments addressing the standards to be employed by those persons who make the decisions in the asylum and deportation processes. The position regarding the reporting of judgments in this area is also improving. Whilst academic conferences on the topic often discuss solely the situation pertaining at European level and in other jurisdictions, it is to be hoped and expected that the importance of Irish jurisprudence will gain recognition and thus ensure a more widespread and thorough discussion of the issues arising.

LEGISLATION

The Immigration Act 2004   A detailed analysis of the judgments of the High and Supreme Courts in *Leontjava and Chang v DPP* [2004] 1 I.R. 591 is set out in the chapter on Constitutional Law in this issue of the *Annual Review of Irish Law*. It is therefore sufficient to say, for present purposes, that as a result of the High Court judgment in that case, delivered on January 22, 2004, no aspect of the Aliens Orders could be regarded as safe from challenge and that, as stated in the Explanatory Memorandum to the Immigration Bill 2004, introduced in the Seanad some seven days after the High Court delivered its judgment:

> "[t]here will be no reliable legislative basis for the operation of immigration controls on the entry or presence in the State of non-nationals. This Bill seeks to fill that legislative lacuna."

The Supreme Court judgment, delivered on June 23, 2004, reversed the High Court finding in relation to the constitutionality of s.5(1) of the Aliens Act 1935 and s.2(1) of the Immigration Act 1999. By that time, however, the Immigration Act was in operation, having acquired the force of law on February 13.

The Act seeks merely to give expression in primary legislation to matters such as the regulation of the entry into the State of non-nationals; the granting of permission to be in the State; the requirement upon non-nationals to register on a periodic basis with members of An Garda Síochána acting as registration officers; and the deportation of non-nationals from the State, all of which were, prior to the High Court judgment in *Leontjava and Chang v DPP*, regulated via the Aliens Orders of 1946 and 1975. The Act does replace the outdated term "alien", as found in the Orders, with the term "non-national" and interestingly, as its enactment pre-dated the passage of the 27th Referendum removing citizenship from certain persons born in the State, purports to exempt from certain forms of regulation "a non-national who was born in Ireland" (*per* s.9(6)(b) of the Act). It also makes clear that the terms of the Act regarding entry into and removal from the State shall not override the right conferred by s.9(1) of the Refugee Act 1996 to enter the State for the purpose of making and pursuing an application for refugee status.

The Irish Nationality and Citizenship Act 2004   This Act, which acquired the force of law on December 15, sets out the statutory framework by which effect is given to the principles embodied in the 27th Constitutional Amendment which, as discussed in detail later in the Constitutional Law chapter, inserted a new Art.9.2 into the Constitution removing the constitutional entitlement of all persons born in the State to citizenship. The new sub-Article provides:

"1. Notwithstanding any other provision of this Constitution, a person born in the island of Ireland, which includes its islands and its seas, who does not have, at the time of his or her birth, at least one parent who is an Irish citizen or entitled to be an Irish citizen is not entitled to Irish citizenship or nationality, unless otherwise provided for by law.

2. This section shall not apply to persons born before the date of the enactment of this section."

Section 4 of the Act, which inserts a new s.6A into the Irish Nationality and Citizenship Act 1956, contains the Act's central innovation. It adds to the list of citizens who are referred to expressly in Art.9.2 by providing that a person shall be entitled to citizenship if his or her parent has, during the period of four years immediately preceding the person's birth, been resident in the island of Ireland for a period of not less than three years in aggregate. The new s.6A(2)(e) of the Act of 1956 confirms that such a residence requirement shall not apply to a person born in the island of Ireland who has at the time of his or her birth one or more parents who is a British citizen or is otherwise entitled to reside in the State or in Northern Ireland without any restriction on his or her period of residence. This provision, affording automatic citizenship to such categories of person, had to be inserted in order to ensure compliance with the terms of the Good Friday Agreement. Although a person to whom refugee status has been conferred is lawfully in the State for the purposes of the assessment of the reckonable period of time described in s.6A, the Act makes clear that time spent by persons applying for refugee status and, indeed, persons in the State for the purpose of pursing a course of education, is not of relevance in that regard.

Finally, a separate concern is addressed in s.10 of the Act which provides that a person shall be of "Irish association" if he or she is related by blood, affinity or adoption to a person who is or was during his or her lifetime an Irish citizen or entitled to so be. Thus, this provision seeks to close off the "association" route formerly employed by persons making significant financial investment within the State and obtaining Irish citizenship on foot of such investments.

CASE LAW

Adverse findings as to credibility   There were a number of decisions of the High Court during 2004 which addressed the difficult issue of the circumstances in which adverse findings as to credibility may be made in respect of an applicant, and the obligations on the tribunal of fact when drawing such inferences. In *Z v Minister for Justice, Equality and Law Reform* High Court, November 26, 2004, Clarke J. considered this issue in some detail. The applicants applied for leave to judicially review decisions of the Refugee Appeals Tribunal to refuse their appeals from the recommendations of the Refugee Applications Commissioner not to grant declarations of refugee status. The applicants were a Russian couple from the Kaliningrad region; the second-named applicant, the husband, was Jewish. The applicants, and in particular the husband, alleged they had suffered discrimination and harassment for religious reasons.

The Tribunal member in his decision rejected the explanation given by the applicants for giving more detailed accounts on their appeals than had been given in their interviews or in their respective submissions. On that basis the Tribunal member went on to conclude that, in both cases, the evidence of the applicants generally was not credible and that on the basis that their credibility had been undermined, their evidence in relation to events of past persecution was not accepted.

It was submitted on behalf of the applicant that the Tribunal member was not entitled to dismiss the entirety of the applicants' evidence on the basis of an adverse finding as to credibility in respect of one aspect of their evidence. It was further submitted that the finding that their credibility had been undermined was based on errors of fact and law and was in breach of the principles of natural and constitutional justice. Finally, it was submitted that the Tribunal member's analysis of country of origin information was wholly inadequate and that conclusions drawn therefrom by the Tribunal member were not supported by the objective or subjective evidence provided.

Clarke J. noted that the claim advanced by the applicants was very similar in substance to the issues raised in *B v Minister for Justice, Equality and Law Reform* (High Court, Finlay Geoghegan J., May 7, 2003) regarding the obligations on the decision-maker, in accordance with fair procedures in assessing the credibility of the applicants, to consider and assess the explanation given for any alleged material inconsistency between the evidence given at oral hearing and at earlier stages in the application process.

Clarke J. also referred to the dicta of Peart J. in *DS v Refugee Appeals Tribunal* (High Court, July 9, 2004) where Peart J. stated that:

> "the assessment of credibility is one of the most difficult tasks facing the Commissioner and the Tribunal member. It is an unenviable task, and one that is fraught with possible danger. It is very easy, I suspect, to come to a conclusion in the light of the questionnaire answers and the interview and possibly the oral hearing on the appeal that the story as told is simply not believable. In everyday life one is so used to simply having a feeling that all we are told is not exactly as someone would have us believe. One's experience of life hones the instincts and there comes a point where we can feel that the truth can, if it exists, be smelt. But reliance on what one firmly believes is a correct instinct or gut feeling that the truth is not being told is an insufficient tool for use by

an administrative body such as the Refugee Appeals Tribunal. Conclusions must be based on correct findings of fact. A factual error of sufficient importance will often have capacity to at least cast some doubt upon the integrity of the decision-making process, and in those circumstances this court's function is to intervene and, if necessary, on a substantive hearing to provide redress".

Clarke J. noted that the decision in that case concerned clear errors of fact in the decision of the Refugee Appeals Tribunal. However, Clarke J. went on to widen the potential application of this approach by finding that it was at least arguable that:

"there is a wider principle, being the one identified by Peart J. when he says that the feeling cannot be based simply upon a gut feeling or a view based on experience or instinct that the truth is not being told. A finding of lack of credibility, it is at least arguable, must therefore be based on a rational analysis which explains why, in the view of the deciding officer, the truth has not been told".

In so holding, Clarke J. placed significant weight on the absence of analysis of why the Tribunal member felt it appropriate to disregard the explanations given by the applicants, by virtue of the fact that it was the sole reason that he was relying on for coming to his determinations. Clarke J. stated that while it is not necessary for a Tribunal member to give detailed reasons for each minor aspect of a determination, where the entire determination turns on one matter, then it is at least arguable that the Tribunal member must give a more detailed analysis justifying a conclusion on credibility.

Regarding the country of origin information, Clarke J. found that there were arguable grounds for suggesting that, based on the information before him, the Tribunal member could not have come to such a far-reaching conclusion, namely that he was not satisfied that there was non-state persecution of Jews in Russia. Clarke J. acknowledged that this issue raised the difficult question of the approach the courts should take in reviewing such decisions, and commented that: "[t]here may be arguments to the effect that the full effect of the test identified by the courts in *O'Keeffe v An Bord Pleanála* does not necessarily apply in human rights cases such as these" (at p.14). Clarke J. continued at p.16 as follows:

"... even accepting the principles in *O'Keeffe v An Bord Pleanála*, I am not sure that a selective quotation of one element, taken from a lengthy United Kingdom Home Office document ... is a justifiable exercise".

Another leave application addressing adverse findings as to credibility is that of *NK v Refugee Appeals Tribunal* [2004] 2 I.L.R.M. 550. The applicant sought leave to apply for judicial review seeking to quash the determination of the Refugee Appeals Tribunal that the applicant was not entitled to a declaration of refugee status. The applicant was an ethnic Russian who was a citizen of Uzbekistan. She claimed to have a well-founded fear of persecution in Uzbekistan by reason of her ethnicity and religion. The applicant claimed that the respondent had erred in law in relation to the three cumulative reasons set out by the member for his ultimate decision, namely (i) doubts as to the credibility of the applicant; (ii) that the failure of the applicant and her husband to seek protection from State authorities in Uzbekistan precluded them from asserting that their country of origin was unable or unwilling to provide them with protection from persecution; and (iii) the conclusions that the events complained of by the applicant did not constitute persecution within the meaning of s.2 of the Refugee Act 1996.

Finlay Geoghegan J. accepted that the assessment of the applicant's credibility in this application was relevant to both the subjective and objective elements of her claim to be a refugee. Finlay Geoghegan J. stated that:

> "there are substantial grounds for contending that the Tribunal or an adjudicator at first instance is obliged, where an issue is raised as to the credibility of the applicant, to assess the applicant's credibility either in general or in relation to particular factual issues and make a clear finding on that issue."

Finlay Geoghegan J. was satisfied that there were substantial grounds for contending that the Tribunal member had failed to reach such a clear determination in the decision in question.

The applicant also contended that where the Tribunal member makes a specific adverse finding as to the applicant's credibility, this must be based upon reasons which bear a legitimate nexus to the adverse finding, relying on the decision of the US Court of Appeals for the Ninth Circuit in *Aguilera-Cota v INS* (1990) 914 F. 2d 1375 in support of this proposition. Finlay Geoghegan J. concluded that there were substantial grounds for contending that the principle relied upon applies in this jurisdiction.

The applicant also submitted that the Tribunal member was obliged to assess the credibility of the applicant in the context of the available country of origin information. Noting that the Tribunal member at the conclusion of his decision stated that he had regard to country of origin information, Finlay Geoghegan J. stated that:

> "this bald statement is arguably different to the principle relied upon by the applicant as determined in *Milan Horvath v Secretary of State for the Home Department* [1999] INLR 7 and as explained with its appropriate subtleties by David Pannick QC (sitting as a Deputy Judge

of the High Court) in *R v Immigration Appeals Tribunal ex parte Sardar Ahmed* [1999] INLR 473."

In *Horvath*, Judge Pearl stated:

> "It is our view that credibility findings can only really be made on the basis of a complete understanding of the entire picture. It is our view that one cannot assess a claim without placing that claim into the context of the background information of the country of origin. In other words, the probative value of the evidence must be evaluated in the light of what is known about the conditions in the claimant's country of origin."

This statement of principle was expressly endorsed by David Pannick QC in *R. v IAT Ex p. Ahmed.* Finlay Geoghegan J. concluded that there were substantial grounds for asserting that the principles relied upon by the applicant as endorsed by David Pannick QC "properly form part of the correct legal approach to the assessment of the credibility of the applicant's claim to refugee status in this jurisdiction".

Regarding the Tribunal member's conclusion that the applicant could not assert a failure or lack of State protection in circumstances where she had failed to approach the State authorities, it was submitted by the applicant that the proper approach where an applicant has failed to seek state protection in her own country, was for the Tribunal to then consider whether it was objectively reasonable for the applicant to have failed to do so. In considering this submission, Finlay Geoghegan J. referred to the decision of the Supreme Court of Canada in *Canada (Attorney General) v Ward* [1993] 2 SCR 689. La Forest J., considering the test for determining fear of persecution, asked the question: "Does the plaintiff first have to seek the protection of the State, when he is claiming under the 'unwilling' branch in cases of State inability to protect?" and stated (at p.724):

> "... I prefer to formulate this aspect of the test for fear of persecution as follows: only in situations in which State protection 'might reasonably have been forthcoming' will the claimant's failure to approach the State for protection defeat his claim. Put another way, the applicant will not meet the definition of 'Convention refugee' where it is objectively unreasonable for the claimant not to have sought the protection of his home authorities; otherwise, the claimant need not literally approach the State".

Finlay Geoghegan J. concluded that there were substantial grounds for contending that the failure to approach the State will not necessarily defeat the applicant's claim and that the appropriate test to be applied was that stated by the Supreme Court of Canada. In so holding, Finlay Geoghegan J. approved the statement of La Forest J. in *Ward* at p.724:

"… it would seem to defeat the purpose of international protection if a claimant would be required to risk his or her life seeking ineffective protection of a State merely to demonstrate that ineffectiveness."

A substantive decision on the issue of adverse findings as to credibility is to be found in the judgment of Finlay Geoghegan J. in *AMT v Refugee Appeals Tribunal* [2004] 2 I.R. 607. The applicant was a national of Côte d'Ivoire who sought asylum based on a fear of persecution by reason of his Muslim faith and membership of a particular tribe. His application was refused at first instance by the Refugee Applications Commissioner and on appeal by the Refugee Appeals Tribunal. The applicant was granted leave to challenge the decision of the Refugee Appeals Tribunal on four of the five grounds sought, each of which attacked the manner in which the Tribunal member had assessed the applicant's credibility and the conclusions drawn therefrom. Finlay Geoghegan J. noted at the outset that:

"The assessment of the credibility of an applicant and/or his/her story is often crucial to the determination of his or her entitlement to a declaration of refugee status. As I observed recently in *K v Refugee Appeals Tribunal* [2004] 2 I.L.R.M. 550, credibility potentially comes into play in two aspects of the assessment of a claim. Firstly, in the assessment of the subjective element of the applicant's claim, that he/she has a fear of persecution for a Convention reason if returned to his/her own country and secondly, in assessing the objective facts relied upon by the applicant, to establish that the fear is well-founded."

Finlay Geoghegan J. quoted with approval from the judgment of Kelly J. in *SC v Minister for Justice* (High Court, Kelly J., July 26, 2000) and stated that:

"[t]he assessment by the decision-maker of the credibility of the applicant and his story forms part of the decision-making power conferred by the Refugee Act 1996. Hence, following *East Donegal Co-Operative Livestock Mart Ltd v Attorney General* [1970] I.R. 317, such assessment must also be carried out in accordance with the principles of constitutional justice."

The first ground relied upon by the applicant was an error made by the Tribunal member as to the applicant's evidence of his method of travel from Paris to Hamburg. In the applicant's grounding affidavit, he stated that he did not give evidence that he travelled by bus from France to Germany nor did any person make any suggestion to that effect in the course of the hearing before the Tribunal member. It was submitted that such error by the Tribunal member as to the evidence given was of sufficient importance to render the decision invalid. The respondents conceded that an error had been made but submitted that it was an error of fact and, as such, did not invalidate the decision. Finlay Geoghegan J. rejected this submission, and held:

> "Whether one considers the legal principles applicable to the assessment of credibility in claims for refugee status or the principles of constitutional justice, I have concluded that the obligation of the Tribunal member is to assess the credibility of the applicant in relation to the story as told or evidence given by him/her. This did not happen in this case. In assessing the credibility of the applicant, the Tribunal member has included as part of his story a fact for which she had no relevant material and, further, placed reliance upon such fact in a manner adverse to the applicant in reaching a conclusion against the credibility of his story. Such error renders the decision invalid.
>
> In reaching the above conclusion I do not wish to suggest that every error made by a tribunal member as to the evidence given will necessarily render the decision invalid. It will, obviously, depend on the materiality of the error to the decision reached. The error must be such that the decision-maker is in breach of the obligation to assess the story given by the applicant or the obligation to consider the evidence given in accordance with the principles of constitutional justice."

A further ground of challenge to the Tribunal member's decision was the manner in which the credibility of the applicant's story was assessed. It was submitted that the Tribunal member's conclusion was based on conjecture, being made in the absence of any evidence to support the basis on which she rejected the credibility of the applicant's story, and was therefore invalid. The fundamental issue was whether or not the Tribunal member was obliged to assess the story in the context of relevant country of origin information prior to coming to a conclusion such as that reached. Finlay Geoghegan J. noted that such an obligation appears to follow from the first issue identified by Professor Goodwin-Gill and approved by Kelly J. in *SC v Minister for Justice* (High Court, July 26, 2000). Finlay Geoghegan J. also referred to her decision in *NK v Refugee Appeals Tribunal* [2004] 2 I.L.R.M. 550 which had been given since the hearing in this case, noting her conclusion that there were substantial grounds for asserting that there is an obligation to assess the credibility of the applicant in the context of country of origin information. Accordingly, Finlay Geoghegan J. granted an order of certiorari quashing the decision of the Tribunal and remitting the matter to the Tribunal for hearing and decision by another Tribunal member.

Application for bail pending hearing of leave application   In *NA v Governor of Cloverhill Prison* (High Court, December 10, 2004) the applicant was granted leave on an ex parte basis to seek judicial review of his continued detention pursuant to s.9(8)(c) and (f) of the Refugee Act 1996 on a number of grounds. The principal grounds of challenge concerned the consistency of the applicant's detention with the Constitution and/or the European Convention on Human Rights. The applicant also contended that even if the impugned provisions were upheld, his detention based upon the determination of the District Court was flawed by reason of two grounds, namely

(a) the reinstatement on a subsequent hearing of a specific ground which had previously been ruled inapplicable at an earlier hearing; and

(b) that the applicant had done all that was required to establish his identity as required by the provisions of the 1996 Act.

The applicant also sought bail for the purpose of giving effect to his release pending the trial of the matter. Clarke J. held that it would be inappropriate to grant bail or otherwise release the applicant without giving the respondents an opportunity to be heard, and therefore directed that notice be served upon the respondents. The application for bail was therefore heard with the benefit of submissions and evidence from both sides.

Counsel for the applicant submitted that the grant or otherwise of bail in circumstances such as this differed in no material respect to the grant of bail pending a criminal trial so that the principles set out in *People (DPP) v O'Callaghan* [1966] I.R. 31 were applicable. On that basis it was submitted that the only real consideration for the court was whether the court was satisfied that the applicant would attend the hearing and be available to be recommitted to prison in the event that his case was unsuccessful.

Counsel for the respondents accepted that the question of the likelihood of the applicant attending was a material consideration but suggested that the range of matters which the court was entitled to take into account in a matter such as this were wider than those which the court would properly take into account in considering an application for bail pending a criminal charge. Clarke J. accepted this submission, having regard to the fact that the decision in *O'Callaghan* derived from the presumption of innocence which is accorded to a person prior to their conviction by a court of competent jurisdiction. Clarke J. contrasted the position of such a person with that of a person who has been convicted by a court of competent jurisdiction who was not, in the ordinary way, entitled to release pending an appeal. Clarke J. characterised the cases where such persons had been admitted to bail pending the appeal as the exception rather than the rule.

Clarke J. dismissed the applicant's claim that he had not been convicted of any criminal charge on the grounds that the applicant's detention stemmed from a finding by a court of competent jurisdiction that the circumstances set out in the sub-paragraphs of s.9(8) of the 1996 Act had been met so as to require his detention under the terms of the Act. Whilst Clarke J. accepted that the applicant had made an arguable case for a challenge to that detention, it did not follow that he was in the same position as a person accused of a criminal offence in respect of whom no court determination had been made and who enjoyed the presumption of innocence.

On the basis of evidence tendered by the respondents, Clarke J. was satisfied that it was probable in the event that the applicant secured his release that he would not attend at the trial of the substantive issue in this case. Clarke J. found as a matter of probability that the applicant had the means, ability and inclination to find ways to procure false documents and thereby put himself in a position to absent himself from the hearing. Therefore, even applying a traditional criminal bail test, Clarke J. held that it would not be appropriate to admit the applicant to bail.

Application for discovery in context of application for leave   The case of *GS v Minister for Justice, Equality and Law Reform* (High Court, March 19, 2004) concerned an application for discovery of certain documents which the applicant claimed were necessary for the purpose of his application for leave to apply by way of judicial review for an order of certiorari quashing the respondent's decision to revoke the applicant's declaration as a refugee. The ground upon which the revocation of refugee status was effected was a finding that the applicant was a person "whose presence in the State poses a threat to public policy" on the grounds that the applicant had been convicted in Belgium of the criminal offence of people trafficking.

The respondent furnished to the applicant's solicitor copies of some of the materials which had been considered by the Minister when making his decision, but stated that the material which was being furnished did not include "legal advice received and references to same as well as information received from the Belgian authorities which they wish to claim privilege on".

The applicant's solicitor sought discovery of those documents which the Minister had failed to furnish in his original disclosure of materials, on the basis that such documents were relevant and necessary for disposing of the cause, being the judicial review proceedings instituted by the applicant seeking to challenge the revocation of refugee status.

Considering the application for leave, Peart J. referred to the decision in *KA v Minister for Justice, Equality and Law Reform* [2003] 2 I.R. 93 where Finlay Geoghegan J. considered whether an applicant for leave was entitled to discovery of documents at the leave stage, in view of the normal rule that discovery ought not to be granted until pleadings were closed. Peart J. held that the applicant in the present case must be in a position to make his best possible case at the leave stage. The documents sought constituted part of the material which was before the Minister when he made the decision to revoke the applicant's refugee status, and Peart J. found that it was therefore arguable that the documents would be such as might have assisted the applicant in making submissions on the Minister's proposal to revoke the applicant's refugee status, and which the Minister would have been obliged to consider prior to making his final decision in the matter. It was held that to refuse the applicant's application for discovery of these documents at the pre-leave stage had the potential to place the applicant in a less advantageous position in making his application for leave, and that it therefore seemed unfair to require leave to be granted prior to discovery being ordered. Regarding the respondent's claim that the material in question was privileged, Peart J. was satisfied that this issue could be debated and dealt with once discovery had in principle been granted, if necessary by the court dealing with that aspect of the case looking at the documents and deciding the matter.

Application for habeas corpus In *VS & RT v Governor of Cloverhill Prison* (High Court, December 24, 2004) the applicants requested the court to inquire into the lawfulness of their detention pursuant to Art.40.4.2° of the Constitution. The applicants were both Romanian nationals who arrived in the State on false or forged passports.

The applicants' false or forged passports were impounded by the authorities on the day of arrival in the State. Whilst detained in Cloverhill Prison the applicants applied for asylum. The applicants were subsequently brought before the District Court which extended their detention pursuant to s.9(8) of the Refugee Act 1996 as amended, which provides:

> "where an immigration officer or a member of An Garda Síochána, with reasonable cause, suspects that an applicant—
>
> ...
> (f) without reasonable cause has destroyed his or her identity or travel documents or is in possession of forged identity documents,
> he or she may detain the person in a prescribed place ..."

The applicants' detention was extended by the District Court on a number of occasions thereafter, each time pursuant to s.9(8)(f) of the Refugee Act 1996. The only evidence before the District Court judge in relation to forged identity documents was that on a date prior to the application for asylum being made, the applicant had been in possession of a forged passport and that it had been impounded on that date. The applicant therefore submitted that on the date on which he applied for asylum, being two days after the passport was impounded, there could not have been a reasonable suspicion that the applicant was in possession of forged identity documents since the forged passport had been taken from him permanently immediately upon his arrival and on which date he did not claim asylum. It was therefore submitted that the District Court judge had no power to make an order of committal pursuant to s.9(8)(f) as at the time of the application for asylum the applicant was not in possession of a forged identity document.

Peart J. held that the provisions of the Refugee Act 1996, and in particular s.9(8), were not intended to cover a situation where, perhaps several weeks or months after an illegal entry into the State on forged documents, which were impounded, such a person then applied for asylum. It was held that there was a clear meaning capable of being gleaned from the plain and ordinary meaning of the words used in the section, which Peart J. held was designed to deal only with the situation where a person arrives in the State and immediately upon arrival seeks asylum by completing the ASY1 form on arrival and is thereafter processed. Peart J. concluded that to interpret the provisions of s.9(8) as applying to the applicants in the present case would be changing or amending the legislative provisions in order to fill a gap now perceived, and that to do so would go beyond what could be permissible by virtue of a purposive construction. In those circumstances, Peart J. found that the detention of the applicants was unlawful and ordered their release.

Applications for residency on basis of Irish children   Prior to February 2003, the Department of Justice, Equality and Law Reform operated a scheme which allowed non-nationals to make applications for residency on the basis of an Irish child. In *JE v Minister for Justice* (High Court, October 14, 2004) the applicant sought to challenge a decision by the Department of Justice that her application for residency pursuant to this scheme would not be considered, in circumstances where the application had been made two weeks before an announcement that the scheme was to be abolished.

The applicant arrived in the jurisdiction in late December 2002 and gave birth on January 9, 2003. Her application for residency was made in late January 2003 and was acknowledged on February 3, 2003. On February 19, 2003, the Minister announced that he was no longer accepting applications for residency based on the parentage of an Irish child. On July 18, 2003, he announced that the Government had decided it also would not consider (under the scheme which had existed before February 19, 2003) those applications for residency which were outstanding on that date. Also on July 18, 2003, a letter was written on behalf of the Minister to the applicant informing her that it was proposed to make a deportation order regarding her.

The applicant's solicitors wrote to the Department of Justice referring to the scheme for residency based on having an Irish child and asking for confirmation that moves would not be made to deport the applicant but rather that her application for residency would be processed. On August 22, the Department wrote to the applicant's solicitors stating that the residency scheme had been abolished and therefore she would not receive any reply to her application for residency. The letter also stated that where it was proposed to deport a person who was the parent of an Irish child, that person would be given an opportunity to make representations on the deportation. All relevant factors, including the family circumstances of the proposed deportee, would be taken into account. The letter noted that the Minister had a legal obligation to inform a person in writing of his proposal to deport them and to give that person the opportunity to make written representations. The Minister made a deportation order in respect of the applicant on March 11, 2004, which the applicant received on July 1. The applicant then applied for leave to seek judicial review of that decision.

In her judgment, Finlay Geoghegan J. stated that the issues in the case related to whether the actions of the Minister before making the deportation order breached the applicant's entitlement to fair procedures or compliance with the requirements of natural and constitutional justice. She held that the applicant had established substantial grounds to support her claim that she had a legitimate expectation to have her application for residency determined in accordance with the administrative scheme which was abolished on February 19, 2003.

A similar conclusion was reached in the decision of *SO v Minister for Justice, Equality and Law Reform* (High Court, November 4, 2004). The first-named applicant arrived in the State on October 26, 2002. His wife, the second-named applicant, arrived in the State on March 23, 2003. The third-named applicant was born in the National Maternity Hospital, Dublin on May 27, 2002. The second-named applicant applied for asylum subsequent to her arrival in the State. However, after the birth of the third-named applicant, the second-named applicant sought to apply for residency on the basis of her Irish child. This application was acknowledged by the Refugee Applications Commissioner, who informed her that there was a delay in processing such applications, but that her case would be dealt with in due course.

Some months thereafter, while awaiting a decision on the residency application, the second-named applicant was notified that the Minister proposed to make a deportation order in respect of her pursuant to s.3 of the 1999 Act. The reason for the Minister's proposal was that the applicant had withdrawn her application for asylum and that her entitlement to remain temporarily in the State had therefore ceased.

Finlay Geoghegan J. held that having regard to the uncontested facts in the application and the submissions of the parties, there were substantial grounds for contending that the proposal to deport was invalid. The first ground on which this could be argued was error on the face of the record, in relation to the reference in the proposal to deport that the applicant had remained in the State without the permission of the Minister. It was submitted that in accepting the applicant's application for residency, there existed an implicit consent to the applicant temporarily remaining in the State while the application for residency was processed and determined. Finlay Geoghegan J. also found that the applicant had made out substantial grounds for contending that the proposal to deport was invalid on the basis that the applicant had a legitimate expectation and/or procedural entitlement to have her application for residency determined in accordance with the administrative scheme under which she applied.

It should be noted that on January 14, 2005 the Department of Justice announced details of revised arrangements for the processing of claims for permission to remain from the non-national parents of Irish children who were born before January 1, 2005. Applicants for residency under this scheme were required to provide personal details, immigration history, other identities used in the State and details of their Irish children. The deadline for receipt of such applications was March 31, 2005. Applicants were also required to sign a statutory declaration to the effect that, if granted permission to remain, the applicant would not engage in criminal activity and would make every effort to become economically viable, and accept that there is no entitlement to family reunification. The effect of this statutory declaration, in particular in respect of family reunification, remains to be determined.

Deportation prior to hearing of judicial review proceedings   The decision of Peart J. in *BA v Commissioner of An Garda Síochána* (High Court, October 27, 2004) addressed the issue of the constitutional right of access to the court, and in particular the remedies which might be available where failed asylum-seekers have been deported from the State in circumstances where they have issued judicial review proceedings in respect of their proposed deportation, but where those proceedings have not yet been heard. The applicants in *BA* had lodged judicial review proceedings in February and March 2004 challenging the validity of deportation orders made in respect of them. These applications were returnable for various dates in April 2004. The solicitor acting for the applicants sent faxes to the Garda National Immigration Bureau (GNIB) on the evening of April 6, 2004 after he learned that his clients might be deported that night or the following morning, in which he drew attention to the existence of judicial review proceedings and the return dates in April 2004. He stated that he trusted in the circumstances that the applicants would not be deported, thereby depriving them of their constitutional right of access to the courts. Having received no reply to these faxes, the applicants' solicitor consulted counsel who advised that an application for habeas corpus should be made in respect of each of them. By 11.30 p.m. that night Gilligan J. granted orders of habeas corpus in each case and an injunction restraining the deportation of the applicants. Following the making of the orders, the applicants' solicitor attempted to notify the making of the orders to the GNIB by telephone but was unable to obtain any reply. The applicants' solicitor eventually made contact with "Command and Control" at Dublin Airport at 1.15 a.m. on April 7, 2004 at which time he was informed that the plane had taken off for Nigeria at 12.19 a.m. The solicitor thereupon sent a fax to GNIB insisting that the applicants be returned immediately and not placed on Nigerian territory, alleging that not to so return the applicants would be a contempt of court.

The applicants contended that there was a carefully premeditated plan by which the applicants were to be removed from the State on the date in question in such a way as would prevent any of them from consulting with their lawyers and making applications for restraining orders. Two of the applicants specifically complained that their mobile phones had been removed from them upon them being taken into custody, and that their requests to contact a solicitor had been refused. It was submitted that there was nothing to prevent the authorities from contacting the aircraft in order to have it return the applicants to this jurisdiction so as to be in compliance with the orders of the High Court. It was alleged that this had been a "sting operation" on the part of the authorities which had been planned and timed in order to make it as difficult as possible for the applicants to seek legal advice, and that the timing also resulted in difficulties in communicating the orders made to those to whom they were directed because it was well outside office hours. The respondents denied the allegations, and stated that any persons who sought access to legal representation were permitted to make contact with, and facilitated in making contact with, their solicitor prior to being placed on the aircraft. It was also stated that there was no policy in place to remove mobile phones or prevent access to lawyers.

The applicants sought to attach and commit to prison or otherwise penalise the Commissioner of An Garda Síochána for contempt of the orders made by Gilligan J. on April 6, 2004, and also applications for habeas corpus in respect of each applicant. In relation to the application for attachment and committal, Peart J. held that there was no evidence that the Garda Commissioner, his servants or agents, were aware of the orders made by Gilligan J. on April 6, 2004 injucting the removal of the applicants from the State prior to the departure of the flight. Peart J. was satisfied that the making of the orders became known only on the following morning after the aircraft had landed at Lagos, and the failure to immediately return the applicants could not in these circumstances amount to contempt warranting imprisonment of the Commissioner. Nevertheless, Peart J. acknowledged that the fact remained that in this case there were orders of a judge of the High Court which were still extant and had not been complied with. In the circumstances Peart J. was satisfied that it was appropriate to direct the Commissioner of An Garda Síochána to take "such steps as might be open to him to facilitate or enable in whatever manner is possible the return of these applicants to this State, so that the status quo ante can be resumed and the matters can then proceed in the same manner as if the orders had been communicated in sufficient time before the take-off of this aircraft".

Regarding the conflict of evidence as to the removal of two applicants' mobile phones, and the denial of their requests to consult a solicitor, Peart J. found that on the balance of probabilities he preferred the evidence of the applicants, and accepted that "any deliberate removal of the mobiles phones, when combined with a denial of a request to be permitted to communicate with a legal adviser, must amount to a denial of a constitutional right". On the balance of probabilities Peart J. was satisfied that the rights of the applicants had been so denied.

A further question which arose for consideration was whether the mere institution of judicial review proceedings in which interlocutory injunctive relief is being sought acts as a stay on the deportation order until such time as the injunction application has been heard and determined. It was submitted on behalf of the applicants that by not allowing the judicial process to determine an application for an injunction before giving effect to the deportation order which is the subject of the challenge in the proceedings, the executive arm of government was interfering in the functions of another arm of government, namely the judiciary, and as such was in breach of the separation of powers. It was submitted that in the provision within the 2000 Act of a 14-day time limit within which a deportation order can be challenged, it was implicit that no steps should be taken to give effect to such an order prior to the expiration of the limitation period.

The respondents submitted that the applications for habeas corpus by the applicants were now moot since the applicants all enjoyed freedom from their detention, whether lawful or unlawful, since arrival in Lagos, albeit a freedom not enjoyed in this State. The respondents further submitted that it is the fact of detention which gives rise to a remedy by way of habeas corpus, and that it is not a relief to be called in aid for the purposes of punishing a person after a possibly illegal detention has come to an end.

Peart J. accepted the respondents' submissions on this issue, and held that in circumstances where the applicants had their liberty, albeit not within this State, the question of whether their detention on April 6, 2004 was lawful or not was now moot. Peart J. further stated that because the facts surrounding their detention on that date were particular to that date, no finding as to legality or otherwise could serve any further purpose in relation to any detention of the same or other applicants on any future date on which the legality of a different arrest and detention might be the subject of a court's consideration. Peart J. also accepted that the fact that the applicants were outside the State was a bar to obtaining any relief by way of habeas corpus in the circumstances where the applicants could not be said to be within the custody or control of persons who were subject to the court's jurisdiction.

Extension of time pursuant to s.5(2)(a) of 2000 Act   The principles applicable to an application for an extension of time were considered by the Supreme Court in the case of *CS v Minister for Justice, Equality and Law Reform* [2005] 1 I.L.R.M. 81. The applicants were a mother and her two daughters of South African origin who arrived in the State in November 2001.

The applicants sought leave to bring judicial review proceedings seeking a number of reliefs pursuant both to Ord.84 of the Rules of the Superior Courts and to s.5 of the Illegal Immigrants (Trafficking) Act 2000. Since the application was made outside the 14-day period specified in s.5(2)(a) of the 2000 Act, among the reliefs sought by the applicants was an order extending the time for the bringing of the application. Leave was granted by the High Court

(O'Sullivan J.) including an order extending the applicants' time for making their application for leave to apply for judicial review. An application was subsequently made on behalf of the respondent pursuant to s.5(3)(a) of the 2000 Act for leave to appeal, which application was granted.

In the course of the hearing before the Supreme Court, it was accepted by the parties that the principal issue concerned the extension of time. The respondent submitted that there had been no satisfactory explanation provided for how the delay had arisen and that the trial judge had erred in attributing blame to the Refugee Legal Service. It was also submitted that the applicants had failed to establish an arguable case. The applicants laid emphasis on the admission by the applicants' solicitor that the major part of the delay was due to his fault and submitted that that fault should not be visited on the head of the applicants.

McGuinness J., giving the judgment of the court, referred to the judgment of Finnegan J. in *GK v Minister for Justice* [2002] 1 I.L.R.M. 81, which case concerned the extent to which an applicant should be held vicariously liable for the deficiency or inefficiency of his solicitor, wherein Finnegan J. drew a distinction between the situation where the deficiency is on the part of a legal aid solicitor or on the part of a private solicitor. McGuinness J. also considered the decision of the Supreme Court in *GK v Minister for Justice* [2002] 1 I.L.R.M. 401, where Hardiman J. held that when considering whether there was good and sufficient reason to extend time the court should consider the merits of the substantive case and not simply the merits of the application to extend time. Hardiman J. described the approach to applications for extension of time as follows (at p.406):

> "On the hearing of an application such as this it is of course impossible to address the merits in the detail of which they would be addressed at a full hearing, if that takes place. But it is not an excessive burden to require the demonstration of an arguable case. In addition, of course, the question of the extent of the delay beyond the fourteen-day period and the reasons if any for it must be addressed."

In considering whether the blame for the delay in the present case should be visited vicariously on the applicants so as to prevent their access to the court, McGuinness J. noted that the applicants had suffered many of the disadvantages described by the Supreme Court in the *Article 26 Reference*, including unfamiliarity with the Irish legal system, and the fact that the first-named applicant lived some considerable distance from her solicitor's place of business. McGuinness J. also noted that while the first-named applicant had been represented by the Refugee Legal Service up to the stage of her appeal, she was thereafter informed that the RLS could do nothing further for her, which would have caused her both confusion and distress.

McGuinness J. accepted that while the first-named applicant was responsible for her own actions in seeking further legal and other advice when the Refugee Legal Service withdrew its services from her, "it would be going too far to categorise her own actions as personally blameworthy". It was furthermore held that despite considerable reservations arising from the various deficiencies of her present solicitors, the first-named applicant should not be held vicariously liable for their actions. In so holding McGuinness J. referred to the observations of Finnegan J. (as he then was) in the *GK* case where he held (at p.87) that:

> "In determining the extent to which an applicant should be held vicariously liable for the default of his solicitor it is important to bear in mind the serious consequences which could result from an application failing because of the delay ... where however an applicant is deported the consequences for him may be very serious indeed in that he may be deported to a State in which his fundamental human rights would not be vindicated."

McGuinness J. stated a reluctance to accept the distinction made by Finnegan J. in *GK* between defaults attributed to the Refugee Legal Service and defaults attributed to a privately instructed solicitor, stating (at p.101):

> "Indeed it may well be that there has been an over-emphasis on the attribution of blameworthiness or fault, either direct or vicarious, in regard to the issue of extension of time. There is, it seems to me, a need to take all the relevant circumstances and factors into account. The statute itself does not mention fault; it simply requires 'good and sufficient reason'."

McGuinness J. also pointed out that in the context of the case before the court, it must be borne in mind that two of the applicants were infants, to whom blameworthy delay could not be imputed.

On the basis that the first-named applicant had demonstrated "reasonable diligence" in seeking access to the court, and having regard to the merits of her case, McGuinness J. therefore dismissed the respondent's appeal against the decision of the High Court to extend the time for the institution of judicial review proceedings.

This decision marks a significant shift in the focus of the courts on the issue of extensions of time. As McGuinness J. noted, previously the focus had rested to a large degree on the conduct and blameworthiness of legal advisers in failing to institute judicial review proceedings within the strict 14-day time limit prescribed by s.5(2)(a) of the 2000 Act. The Supreme Court in *CS* endorsed a move away from this focus, and the test advocated by McGuinness J. (namely the diligence of the applicant in seeking access to the court) is consistent with the approach of the courts to the issue of extensions of time more generally, and in particular in the leading case of *Éire Continental Trading Co. Ltd v Clonmel Foods Ltd* [1955] I.R. 170. In *Éire Continental* the Supreme Court held that one of the primary factors in considering an application for an extension of time for the taking of an appeal would be whether the applicant could demonstrate a bona fide intention to appeal, which intention must be formed within the permitted time.

Failure to seek assistance from non-governmental agencies This issue was considered in the context of an application for leave in *DM & VE v Nicholson sitting as the Refugee Appeals Tribunal* (Peart J.), July 14, 2004. The applicants were Moldovan nationals who applied for asylum in the State. The challenge to the respondent's decision was based solely on a finding contained in the decision that the applicants had failed to seek assistance from certain non-governmental agencies in Moldova. The applicants had maintained that the police were linked to the persons who had persecuted the applicants and that in the circumstances the police would not protect them. The applicants' challenge in particular objected to the finding by the respondent that the evidence given by the first-named applicant, that he did not know about non-governmental agencies operating in the capital of Moldova, was "not a valid reason for not making enquiries". The applicants contended that that respondent took into account an irrelevant matter and that the decision was unreasonable. It was contended that to decide that the first-named applicant ought to have sought assistance from organisations whose very existence was unknown to him was irrational and that accordingly the decision was flawed.

Peart J. held that the decision must be read as a whole, rather than examining one sentence in isolation, and in particular referred to findings of fact contained in the decision regarding the first-named applicant's claim, on which basis the respondent reached a conclusion that the events complained of did not amount to persecution. Peart J. concluded that the grounds contended for finding the decision of the respondent invalid were not arguable or weighty in the sense that the submission was based on a small part of the decision, and even if it was not reasonable to say or conclude that the first-named applicant ought to have made enquiries about non-governmental agencies whose existence he was not aware of, this did not go to the root of the decision. Peart J. found that this was only one of a number of things which the Tribunal considered that the applicants could have done, and that it was not unreasonable in the circumstances to decide that the applicants could have made enquires to ascertain the existence of any such organisations in the capital of their country. Leave to apply for judicial review was therefore refused.

Injunction to prevent hearing of refugee appeal pending judicial review of decision of Refugee Appeals Commissioner In *RDM v Refugee Appeals Tribunal* (High Court, May 27, 2004) the plaintiff sought an injunction pending the trial of the action restraining the respondent, its servants or agents, from hearing and determining the appeal of the applicant. The plaintiff had previously had a hearing before the Refugee Applications Commissioner which resulted in a negative decision. The plaintiff contended that there was a breach of fair procedures in respect of that hearing and sought an order of certiorari quashing the decision of the Refugee Applications Commissioner refusing to grant the plaintiff a declaration of refugee status in the State. As a result of certain applicable time limits the plaintiff was obliged to lodge a notice of appeal from the decision of the Refugee Applications Commissioner to the Refugee Appeals Tribunal which appeal was lodged notwithstanding the judicial review proceedings.

The plaintiff then proceeded by way of two separate applications to institute proceedings seeking an injunction restraining the holding of the appeal by the defendant, and also judicial review proceedings seeking various reliefs including an order of prohibition preventing the defendants from hearing the appeal pending the determination of the judicial review proceedings.

The respondents were anxious to proceed with the appeal, and submitted that the application was too late in the day and designed to disrupt the appeals procedures within the Tribunal. It was also contended that the relevant legislation permits both steps to be taken at the same time, and that there was an obligation on the Refugee Appeals Tribunal to move forward and that the appeal before the respondent constituted a full rehearing, but that in any event the plaintiff was entitled to maintain the judicial review proceedings.

Gilligan J. noted that following the Supreme Court decision in *Stefan* the existence of a pending appeal before the Refugee Appeals Tribunal was not a bar to the courts exercising their discretion, that an available appeal procedure may not be an appropriate or adequate alternative remedy so as to withhold certiorari in circumstances where an applicant has been denied a primary decision in accordance with fair procedures, and further that the availability of a fair appeal does not cure an unfair hearing.

Gilligan J. was satisfied that there was a serious issue to be tried which would be dealt with on the application for leave to apply by way of judicial review, and further held that the balance of convenience favoured the granting of the injunction to maintain the status quo pending the hearing of the application for leave.

Meaning of "refusal" under s.5 of the 2000 Act   This issue was considered by the Supreme Court in *S v Minister for Justice, Equality and Law Reform* Supreme Court, June 10, 2004. The applicant was a South African national who sought asylum in the State. Her application was refused by the Minister pursuant to s.17(1) of the Refugee Act 1996 having considered the recommendation of the statutory tribunal in that regard. The applicant subsequently sought to make a fresh application for a declaration that she was a refugee pursuant to s.17(7) of the 1996 Act, which provides:

"A person to whom the Minister has refused to give a declaration may not make a further application for a declaration under this section without the consent of the Minister".

The applicant sought the consent of the Minister for the making of such further application, which request was refused by the Minister by letter dated April 2, 2003. On May 27, 2000 counsel for the applicant applied ex parte for leave to seek judicial review in the form of declarations and injunctions attacking the Minister's refusal of his consent to the applicant's request. Amongst the reliefs sought by the applicant was:

"A declaration that the respondent has erred in law and acted ultra vires the Refugee Act 1996 in refusing consent to the applicant to make a further application for refugee status pursuant to section 17(7) of the Refugee Act 1996 as amended".

Further references were made in the statement of grounds to the purported "refusal" of the Minister pursuant to s.17(7) of the 1996 Act.

Section 5(1)(k) of the Illegal Immigrants (Trafficking) Act 2000 provides:

"A person shall not question the validity of—
    (k) a refusal under section 17 (as amended by s.11(1)(L) of the Immigration Act 1999) of the Refugee Act 1996
other than by way of an application for judicial review under Order 84 of the Rules of the Superior Courts".

Section 5(2) of the 2000 Act lays down a number of requirements in relation to an application for judicial review to which s.5(1) refers, including the requirement that an application must be made within 14 days commencing on the date on which the person was notified of the "decision, determination, recommendation, refusal or making of the order concerned" unless the court dispenses with this requirement. Section 5(2) also contains a restriction on the right of appeal of the losing party to the judicial review application to the Supreme Court, unless the High Court permits such appeal to be taken in the circumstances set out in the subsection.

The net point in this case was whether the Minister's decision, communicated to the applicant by letter of April 2, 2003, constituted a "refusal" within the meaning of s.5(1) of the 2000 Act, and in particular sub-paragraph (k) of that subsection.

The applicant argued that the reference to "a refusal under section 17 ... of the Refugee Act 1996" captured only a refusal to grant a declaration of refugee status pursuant to s.17(1), and did not extend to a refusal of consent to reapply pursuant to s.17(7). It was submitted on behalf of the applicant that whereas all refusals are decisions of a negative nature, not all decisions of a negative nature are refusals for the purposes of s.17 of the 1996 Act.

This argument was rejected by the Supreme Court on the basis that there was no ambiguity in the wording of s.5(1) of the 1996 Act, and that applying the ordinary and natural meaning of the word "refusal", it was clear that the section encompassed a refusal to grant consent pursuant to s.17(7) of the 1996 Act as amended.

Revocation of deportation order on basis of marriage to Irish national   An issue which has resulted in diverging views of the High Court is the effect upon the validity of a deportation order of marriage to an Irish national subsequent to the issuing of the deportation order. This matter was considered by Butler J. in *RP v Minister for Justice, Equality and Law Reform* (High Court, June 17, 2004). The first-named applicant arrived in the State from the Ukraine and applied for asylum. The first-named applicant's claim for asylum was rejected and a deportation order was made in April 2003. Some three weeks later the first-named applicant married an Irish national, the second-named applicant in the proceedings. The applicants informed the respondent of the marriage and sought revocation of the deportation order on that basis, and sought an undertaking that the first-named applicant would not be deported pending a determination of the application for residency. The respondent initially acknowledged the request for revocation of the deportation order, and indicated that "a more substantive response would issue at the earliest opportunity", but failed to provide the undertaking not to deport as requested. Leave to apply for judicial review was granted by Kearns J. on March 23, 2004, to seek an order of prohibition restraining the respondent from giving effect to the deportation order, a declaration that the respondent was not entitled to give effect to the deportation order without having regard to the material change in the first-named applicant's circumstances, and a declaration that the constitutional rights of the second-named applicant would be infringed if the respondent was to give effect to the deportation order without having regard to the material change in circumstances.

Butler J. accepted that it was either common case or not seriously in contention that the deportation order was validly made, that the applicants' marriage was bona fide and that they constituted a "family" within the meaning of Art.41 of the Constitution, and that in the light thereof the Minister was obliged to have regard to the application to revoke the deportation order having regard to the change of circumstances. Butler J. noted that it was not contended that either of the applicants had a right *per se* to have the deportation order revoked by reason of the marriage.

The only issue remaining to be decided was whether the court was entitled to grant a stay on the execution of the deportation order pending consideration of the change of circumstances by the respondent. Noting the constitutional rights which were at issue, Butler J. was satisfied that in the circumstances of the case, "the court not only has power to but must intervene", while also stressing that this decision could not be taken as affecting the right of the respondent to proceed with the implementation of the deportation order or to establish any sort of automatic stay on the operation of such order by reason of events, including marriage, after the making thereof.

Butler J. therefore granted the relief sought in the form of a declaration that the respondent was not entitled to affect the deportation order without first having regard to the material change in circumstances, but declined to grant the order of prohibition as also sought in the statement of grounds.

A related issue was considered by Quirke J. in *SC and RC v Minister for Justice* and *TC and AC v Minister for Justice* (High Court, December 21, 2004), where the applicants sought to challenge the refusal of the Minister to exercise his statutory power to revoke deportation orders made in respect of them in circumstances where the applicants had been residing as family units with their partners in Ireland prior to their deportation.

Section 3(11) of the Immigration Act 1999 (as amended) provides that:

"The Minister may by order, amend or revoke an order made under this section including an order under this subsection."

The applicants contended that the Minister had exercised the power conferred upon him by s.11(3) of the 1999 Act in an unlawful manner, namely that the respondent had fettered his discretion to make the appropriate decision by applying a seemingly inflexible policy consideration to the applications. Both applications for revocation of the deportation orders were refused on the grounds that the applicants were "not residing in a family unit..." and ... "not residing together as part of a subsisting family unit."

The applicants contended that the reasons advanced for these decisions gave rise to a clear inference that they were regulated by a strict and inflexible policy applied to applications of this kind by the respondent. The applicants also submitted that, on the evidence, it was not physically or practically possible for the applicants to reside together as family units throughout the periods in question having regard to the fact that both RC and AC had been deported to Albania and to Romania respectively while their spouses were required to remain within this jurisdiction caring for children. It was further submitted that a policy which required applicants to reside together for an "appreciable period" of time after their marriage was a policy which may not lawfully be applied by the respondent to applications to revoke deportation orders if it necessarily required that they live outside the jurisdiction before any consideration will be given to their applications. It was claimed on behalf of both applicants that their rights to reside in Ireland as a family unit were constitutionally protected pursuant to the provisions of Arts 40, 41 and 42 of the Constitution and Arts 8 and 14 of the European Convention on Human Rights, which had been incorporated into Irish law pursuant to the provisions of the European Convention on Human Rights Act 2003.

On behalf of the respondent it was submitted that the respondent was expressly empowered by s.3(11) of the 1999 Act (as amended) to make the decisions which had been made, and that valid and subsisting deportation orders remained in force in respect of each applicant, the validity of which had not been challenged. The respondent relied on the decision of *Laurentiu v Minister for Justice* [1999] 4 I.R. 26 in support of the proposition that the right to deport non-nationals is vested in the State "by virtue of its nature and not because it has been conferred on particular organs of the State by Statutes". Whilst the respondent acknowledged that family rights are protected under the Constitution, it was submitted that such rights were not absolute in nature and must be balanced with other potentially conflicting rights and obligations. The respondent further submitted that the State may enact laws for the common good which may impinge upon the rights of the family.

Quirke J. held that the respondent, in considering the applications of RC and AC, was required to consider each application on its individual merits but was entitled to take into account legitimate policy considerations relevant to the orderly administration of the immigration and asylum system within the State. Quirke J. accepted that in considering each applicant's application, the respondent (or his persona designata) was obliged to act judicially and within the bounds of constitutional justice. This included the requirement that each of the applications made had to be considered separately by the respondent on their individual merits. It was held that the evidence established that in both cases the Minister's persona designata had considered each application on its individual merits and had not applied a particular inflexible policy consideration. However, it was clear that in the case of RC the Minister had failed to have regard to the citizenship of the daughter of RC and his wife, and the constitutional rights of RC's daughter deriving from her citizenship were not taken into account by the respondent during the consideration of RC's application. In considering RC's application the respondent did not consider whether, notwithstanding those rights, there were, in the circumstances of the case, good and sufficient reasons associated with the common good for the deportation of RC with the inevitable consequences for CC and the consequences for the child resulting from the deportation of RC. Accordingly, Quirke J. granted an order of certiorari quashing the deportation order made against RC.

However, in the case of AC, Quirke J. was satisfied that it could not be said that his deportation was not lawful, nor was it contrary to the European Convention on Human Rights. In so holding Quirke J. referred to the decision of the Court of Appeal in England in *R. (Mahmood) v Secretary of State for the Home Department* [2001] 1 W.L.R. 840, and in particular the decision of Lord Phillips MR which made it clear that Art.8 does not impose upon any state a general obligation to respect the choice of residence of a married couple. Quirke J. held that the power exercised by the respondent pursuant to s.3(11) of the 1999 Act to refuse to revoke the deportation order in respect of AC was lawful and proportionate having regard to the rights of AC's wife and her daughter and the exigencies of the common good and did not in any respect offend the provisions of Art.8 of the European Convention on Human Rights or any other provision within that Convention. The reliefs sought by AC were consequently denied.

Standard of proof to be applied to applications for refugee status The question of the appropriate standard of proof in the determination of an application for refugee status was considered in *ARP v Minister for Justice, Equality and Law Reform* (Peart J.) November 2, 2004. The applicant sought leave to seek judicial review by way of certiorari to quash the decision of the Refugee Appeals Tribunal refusing his appeal against the finding that he was not entitled to a declaration of refugee status. The applicant had sought refugee status on the basis of persecution on account of his political opinions.

It was contended on behalf of the applicant that the respondent had applied the wrong standard of proof, by reason of the finding in the decision that the applicant had not convinced the respondent that he had suffered persecution for Convention reasons. The applicant also complained that it was never put to him during his appeal that he would have had the opportunity of taking a private suit against the alleged oppressors. However, Peart J. was not satisfied that this was a valid criticism, having regard to the fact that the applicant had previously accessed the police in respect of other matters and that it was therefore a reasonable assumption that he had access to the legal process in Romania. Peart J. therefore held that it was not necessary to put that to the applicant in order to refute it.

Peart J. thus concluded that even if a close parsing and analysis of the decision was undertaken and some minor flaws exposed, such as the use of the word "convinced" or the fact that the precise nature of the country of origin information was not set out, none of these matters constituted "substantial grounds" when the applicant's documentation and evidence was taken as a whole.

The standard of proof to be applied to refugee appeals was also considered by Herbert J. in *DH v Refugee Applications Commissioner* (High Court, May 27, 2004). The applicant sought leave to seek judicial review of the decision of the Refugee Appeals Tribunal confirming the recommendation of the Refugee Applications Commissioner that the applicant's request for refugee status be refused. The applicant contended that the Tribunal member had erred in law and failed to adopt fair procedures with reference to the conduct of the appeal, including the admission of material recorded at the interview of the applicant before the Refugee Applications Commissioner regarding the applicant's credibility and her mode of travel to the State. The applicant also complained in respect of the burden of proof adopted by the Tribunal member, the evaluation of country of origin information and alleged a failure to observe the principle of audi alteram partem by failing to put to the applicant findings made by him or inferences drawn from the evidence so as to afford the applicant and her legal representatives the opportunity to address those matters.

Herbert J. rejected the applicant's criticism of the conduct of the appeal, and reserved the question of the appropriate standard of proof to be applied to applications for refugee status for a case where the matter was fully argued, but held that the Refugee Appeals Tribunal member was entitled to apply the "reasonable likelihood" standard in reaching his decision. Herbert J. held that there was "some justification for the criticism" of the manner in which country of origin information was dealt with by the Tribunal member, stating:

> "I do not consider that placing total reliance on reports, and even more so, on extracts from reports, furnished to the governments or State Departments of the United States or America or Great Britain is always a sufficient compliance with the need to ascertain and evaluate relevant circumstances in the country of origin of a particular applicant. The reasons for and background to these reports could seriously limit their value as independent indicators of the circumstances in the country of origin of the particular applicant."

However, noting that the Tribunal member had reached his decision largely by accepting the applicant's own account of the prevailing circumstances in her country of origin, and applied the law to those facts, Herbert J. held that the Tribunal member could not be said to have failed to adopt fair procedures.

Standard of review where European Convention on Human Rights Act 2003 pleaded   The decision of Clarke J. in *AG v Minister for Justice, Equality and Law Reform* (High Court, December 3, 2004) is considered below in the context of whether a deportation order interferes in the exercise of family rights. However, Clarke J. in that decision also referred briefly to the issue of the appropriate standard of proof in cases where the European Convention on Human Rights was pleaded. Clarke J. referred to the dicta of the Supreme Court on the appropriate standard of review generally in *AO and DL v Minister for Justice* [2003]1 I.R. 1 to the effect that it was "at least arguable that where constitutional rights are at stake the standard of judicial scrutiny as set out in *O'Keeffe v An Bord Pleanála* [1993] 1 I.R. 39 may fall short of what is likely to be required for their protection." Clarke J. further commented that such an argument might perhaps be capable of being advanced with even greater strength in relation to decisions to which the provisions of the European Convention on Human Rights Act 2003 apply.

Whether applicant is an economic migrant or refugee   This issue was addressed in *GG v Minister for Justice, Equality and Law Reform* (High Court, November 4, 2004). This was an application for leave to issue judicial review proceedings seeking to quash the decision of the Refugee Appeals Tribunal in which it was determined that the applicant had failed to establish a well-founded fear of persecution for a Convention reason in accordance with s.2 of the Refugee Act 1996.

The conclusion of the Tribunal member was that the applicant had failed to demonstrate a well-founded fear of persecution for a Convention reason having regard to the definition of persecution, and further on the grounds that it could not be said that the applicant's life or fundamental rights were at risk. The Tribunal member also believed from the applicant's evidence that he was more an economic migrant than a refugee.

The key grounds advanced on behalf of the applicant were that the Tribunal member had erred in law in concluding that the applicant had not suffered from persecution, that this conclusion of the Tribunal member was irrational and unreasonable, and that the Tribunal member had erred in law in considering the relative balance between any economic motives of the applicant in seeking to come to this jurisdiction and his alleged fear of persecution.

Finlay Geoghegan J. referred to the decision of the Canadian Immigration Appeal Board in *Guillermo Lautaro Diaz Fuentes* [1974] 9 A.C. 323, where it was stated that:

> "A superficial examination of the appellant's testimony both at the special inquiry and at the appeal hearing might suggest that the appellant is seeking material security above all, and that he might be what is called ... an "economic migrant"... But we must not consider this testimony out of context; on the contrary, what we must find out is whether behind apparent personal and economic motives there exists a fear of persecution ... the distinction between an economic migrant and a refugee is not always easy to establish, but what is important to bear in mind is that if a person is a refugee, the fact that he also is or may be an economic migrant does not deprive him of his status as a refugee".

Finlay Geoghegan J. accepted that there were substantial grounds for asserting that this was the correct legal approach in this jurisdiction.

Whether deportation order interferes with constitutional right to family life of an Irish child At the core of the decision in *OEG v Minister for Justice* (High Court, May 27, 2004) was the validity of the process by which the Minister for Justice reached a decision to deport non-national parents of an Irish child subsequent to the decision of the Supreme Court in *AO and DL v Minister for Justice* [2003] 1 I.R. 1. The applicants sought leave to apply for judicial review for certain reliefs relating to deportation orders made by the respondent pursuant to s.3(1) of the Immigration Act 1999 deporting the first and second-named applicants. The primary reliefs sought were orders of certiorari quashing the decisions to make deportation orders and the concomitant decisions to refuse the applications of the first and second-named applicants, who were the parents of an Irish child, leave to remain in the State, on the basis that the decisions were ultra vires, void and of no force or effect.

The first and second-named applicants arrived in the State on November 7, 2002 and thereafter applied for asylum. At the time of their arrival the second-named applicant was in the eighth month of her pregnancy. The third-named applicant was the child of the first and second-named applicants who was born in the State on December 30, 2002, and was an Irish citizen. On April 23, 2003 the applicants withdrew their applications for asylum on the basis of their Irish child. By letters dated July 18, 2003, the first and second-named applicants were notified that the respondent proposed to make deportation orders in respect of both of them pursuant to s.3 of the Immigration Act 1999, and invited the applicants to make representations in writing to the Minister within 15 days of the sending of the notification. Representations were made on behalf of the applicants by the Refugee Legal Service. By letters dated October 16, 2003 the applicants were informed of the outcome of the representations. The letters stated that the respondent had decided to make deportation orders in respect of both applicants on the basis that they were persons whose refugee status had been refused, and went on to state that having had regard to the representations made by the applicants, the Minister was satisfied that the interests of public policy and the common good in maintaining the integrity of the asylum and immigration systems outweighed those features of the applicants' cases that might tend to support their being granted leave to remain.

Laffoy J. accepted that the characterisation of the applicants as persons whose refugee status had been refused was "patently incorrect", but nevertheless held that these errors and inconsistencies were not sufficient to invalidate the process or its outcome. The applicants' true legal status within the State was correctly set out in the letter of July 18, 2003 and was the basis of the respondent's consideration of their representations and his decision to make deportation orders.

In seeking leave to challenge the deportation orders by way of judicial review the applicants submitted that when reaching the impugned decisions, having regard to the "common good", the applicants should have been informed of which principles of the common good the respondent had in mind and what criteria he was applying. Further, the applicants should have been entitled to make representations in relation to those principles and criteria. The applicants submitted that the failure to afford them such opportunity constituted a breach of fair procedures. It was also contended that the applicants should have had an opportunity to address potential exclusionary considerations. Another aspect of the challenge to the respondent's decision related to the applicants' Irish child. It was submitted that the respondent failed to take into account all relevant considerations in relation to the Irish status of the child. This was canvassed in the context of the two choices available to her parents on deportation: either to take the child with them to Romania, or to leave the child in the State. In respect of the former option it was submitted that no consideration had been given to the conditions which the child would encounter or to the fact that the child might be discriminated against, while in respect of the latter it was submitted that the possibility that the child's parents might leave the child in the State had not been considered by the Minister, nor was the protection and welfare of the child in that eventuality considered. The contention of the applicants was not that too much weight was given to public policy in reaching the impugned decision, but that the applicants had not been informed which aspects of public policy outweighed the rights of the child and were not given an opportunity to make representations on the issue.

Finally, it was submitted that the rights of the child at issue in this application were constitutionally protected fundamental rights, and that in reviewing the impugned decision the court should adopt a standard of anxiously scrutinising the degree of interference with the rights of the child against the exigencies of the common good which the Minister relied upon to justify such interference, similar to the standard adopted by the Court of Appeal in *R. v Lord Saville, Ex p. A* [1999] 4 All E.R. 860.

It was held by Laffoy J. that the position in Irish law of the non-national parents of an Irish child and the right of an Irish child of non-national parents to reside in the State with his or her parents was definitively determined by the Supreme Court in the *AO and DL* case. Parentage of an Irish child gives non-national parents no rights of residence in the State. The constitutional right of an Irish child to the company, care and parentage of his or her parents within the State is not absolute and unqualified, and it can be displaced where there are grave and substantial reasons associated with the common good which require the deportation of the non-national parents. Laffoy J. referred in this regard to the decision of the Supreme Court in *AO and DL* that the integrity of the asylum and immigration systems was a factor to be weighed in the balance in determining whether to deport the non-national parents of an Irish child. Laffoy J. concluded that the first and second-named applicants had failed to establish an arguable ground for challenging the decision to deport notwithstanding that the consequence might be that the right of the child to reside in the State was effectively negated or that she was deprived of the company, care and parentage of her parents. Laffoy J. inferred from the decision of the Supreme Court in *AO and DL* that the proper exercise by the respondent of the State's power to control immigration did not require that persons who are the subject of such control be afforded an opportunity to make representations in relation to policy in this sphere.

Regarding the applicants' submissions as to the appropriate standard of review, Laffoy J. applied the normal *O'Keeffe* principles, which was the standard applied by the Supreme Court in *AO and DL*. Nevertheless, Laffoy J. stated that the applicants had established that there were substantial grounds for contending that "where constitutionally protected fundamental rights of a child are at issue, a more rigorous standard of review should be applied". In so holding, Laffoy J. referred to the dicta of Fennelly J. in *AO and DL*, and stated that "the application of the normal standard of review makes the decisions of the respondent virtually immune from review." However, Laffoy J. noted that the standard of review was already the subject of an appeal from the High Court to the Supreme Court in the matter of *Meadows v Minister for Justice* and in the circumstances held that it would not be appropriate to grant leave in this case on the basis of a "stand alone" ground as to the standard of review.

Reference should also be made under this heading to the decision of Clarke J. in *AG v Minister for Justice, Equality and Law Reform* (High Court, December 3, 2004). This decision also concerned the issue of whether a deportation order interfered with the constitutional, and Convention, rights of the family, and in particular whether the Minister in deciding to make the deportation order had had regard to all relevant considerations in carrying out the balancing exercise between the rights of the family and the interest of the common good. The second-named applicant was a Kosovan national who was deported on foot of a deportation order on May 16, 2003. The first-named applicant, an Irish citizen, was at this time pregnant. After the birth of the applicants' child, the first-named applicant travelled to Kosovo and married her husband there on September 2, 2003. The applicants thereafter applied to the respondent to revoke the deportation order but this application was refused on November 3, 2003. The applicants instituted proceedings seeking leave to bring judicial review with the aim of obtaining orders requiring the first-named respondent to act in various ways such that would permit the husband to return to the State, whether by revoking the deportation order, granting the visa application, or granting leave to reside in the State. The applicants also sought declaratory relief concerning the entitlements of the applicants including an entitlement under the Constitution and under the provisions of the European Convention on Human Rights Act 2003 to each of the applicants to reside together as a family unit in the State. The reasons advanced by the Minister for the making of the deportation order was that the husband and wife had not resided together for an appreciable period of time since their marriage.

Clarke J. held that the applicants had failed to advance substantial grounds in support of the orders sought which would allow the second-named applicant to return to the State, on the basis that the statutory regime made it clear that the relevant decision was ultimately one for the Minister. Clarke J. stated that it would only be in cases where the court was satisfied that there was only one decision that the Minister could properly take in the circumstances of such a case that it would be appropriate for the court to make any of the types of orders sought, and further stated that he was not satisfied that this was such a case. Leave to proceed on those grounds was therefore refused.

However, Clarke J. held that, as regards the issues concerning the issue of family rights as guaranteed by Art.41 of the Constitution and Art.8 of the European Convention on Human Rights, the applicants had raised substantial grounds for contending that the Minister had failed to consider all relevant matters when making the orders in question. In this respect, Clarke J. noted that wife and husband did live together within the State for a period of time before they were married, which period would be regarded as being an exercise of family life under the Convention but not, under the established jurisprudence of the courts, for the purposes of Art.41 of the Constitution. Clarke J. noted that the only basis given for the decision of the first-named respondent in this case was that the wife and husband had not resided together for an appreciable period of time since their marriage. He accepted that this was a legitimate factor to be taken into account by the Minister, but noted that the real thrust of the applicants' complaint was that none of the other factors which should properly be taken into account by the Minister had been weighed in the balance and in a proportionate manner against that fact. In particular, reliance was placed upon the grave difficulties which the first and third-named applicants would allegedly suffer in attempting to relocate to Kosovo. This, it was argued, amounted to a failure to accord any significant weight to their entitlements whether under Art.8 of the Convention or under Art.41 of the Constitution. Furthermore, it was suggested that no, or insufficient, weight had been placed on the interests of the child. Clarke J. granted leave to proceed on the basis that the determination of the Minister appeared to be based on one factor only, and it was thus at least arguable that he may be said to have failed to take into account appropriate factors which he was, arguably, required by law to put in the balance in a proportionate manner.

Whether deportation order in breach of Criminal Justice (UN Convention Against Torture) Act 2000 The UN Convention Against Torture was incorporated into Irish law by virtue of the provisions of the Criminal Justice (UN Convention Against Torture) Act 2000, which was signed into law on June 14, 2000. In *MJL v Minister for Justice, Equality and Law Reform* (High Court, November 30, 2004) the applicant was granted leave to challenge a deportation order made by the respondent under s.3 of the Immigration Act 1999 by O'Sullivan J. on November 12, 2003. The sole ground on which leave was granted was an allegation that the respondent's decision to deport was in breach of s.4 of the Criminal Justice (UN Convention Against Torture) Act 2000.

The decision to deport the applicant, as approved by the Minister, contained no reference to the question of whether the deportation of the applicant might amount to a breach of the 2000 Act. The question as to whether the Minister had wrongly failed to take account of the requirements of s.4 was wholly dependent on the true construction of the section.

Section 1(1) of the 2000 Act, the definition section, defines torture as follows:

"An act or omission by which severe pain or suffering, whether physical

or mental, is intentionally inflicted on a person—
    (a) for such purposes as—
            (i)   obtaining from that person, or from another person, in-
                  formation or a confession;
            (ii) punishing that person for an act which the person concerned
                  or a third person has committed or is suspected of having
                  committed; or
            (iii) intimidating or coercing that person or a third person; or
    (b) for any reason that is based on any form of discrimination,
    but does not include any such act that arises solely from, or is inherent
    in or incidental to, lawful sanctions."

Section 4(1) of the 2000 Act provides that a person shall not be expelled or
returned from the State to another State where the Minister is of the opinion
that there are substantial grounds for believing that the person would be in
danger of being subjected to torture. Subsection 2 provides that for the purposes
of determining whether there are such grounds, the Minister shall take into
account all relevant considerations including, where applicable, the existence
in the State concerned of a consistent pattern of gross, flagrant or mass violations
of human rights.

The respondent submitted that the definition of torture in Art.1 of the UN
Convention Against Torture refers to cases where the relevant pain or suffering
"is inflicted by or at the instigation of or with the consent or acquiescence of a
public official or other person acting in an official capacity". The respondent
therefore submitted that s.4 of the 2000 Act should be construed as confining
the risk of torture to circumstances where the pain or suffering concerned
might be apprehended as being likely to be inflicted by public officials or
those acting in consort or with the acquiescence of public officials. The
applicant submitted that on its plain meaning s.4 concerned an apprehension
of torture, as defined in s.1, which is not confined to cases involving directly
or indirectly public officials.

Clarke J. found that the literal meaning of s.4 of the 2000 Act, when
considered in conjunction with s.1, was such that it imposed a prohibition on
the Minister in expelling or returning from the State to another state a person
in circumstances where there are substantial grounds for believing that that
person would be in danger of being subjected to torture as defined in s.1 which
does not require that the fear or the infliction of pain and suffering must be a
fear that same will arise at the hands of public officials or their agents.

In the absence of submissions by the respondent as to whether there existed
special circumstances justifying deviation from the literal rule of interpretation,
and having regard to the significant consequences of the literal interpretation
on the State's immigration and refugee policy generally, Clarke J. held that it
was appropriate to require the parties to file further submissions on the correct
approach to the interpretation of s.4 of the 2000 Act. Clarke J. furthermore

suggested that the parties in their submissions address the possible significance of the provisions of the European Convention on Human Rights Act 2003 in this context, particularly s.2 of the 2003 Act which imposes an obligation on state bodies, including the courts, to interpret and apply legislative provisions having regard to, in so far as possible, the State's obligations under the Convention.

Whether standard of treatment available for AIDS capable of constituting persecution within meaning of s.2 of 1996 Act   In *EMS v Minister for Justice* (High Court, December 21, 2004) the applicant sought leave to challenge a decision by the Minister refusing consent under s.17(7) of the Refugee Act 1996 to allow the applicant to make a further application for a declaration of refugee status under that Act. The applicant contended that on a reading of the reasons given on behalf of the Minister for the refusal concerned, it was clear that the decision was made either on the basis of an erroneous view of the law which led to a failure to take into account appropriate matters, or that if all proper matters were taken into account the decision reached was irrational.

An initial issue which arose in the course of the hearing was as to the appropriate standard to be applied by the Minister in the case of an application for consent under s.17(7) of the Refugee Act 1996. Counsel for the applicant submitted that the appropriate test was that adopted by the courts in the United Kingdom, citing the decision of Bingham MR in *R. v Secretary of State for the Home Department Ex p. Onibiyo* [1996] 2 All E.R. 901 where he stated at p.497:

> "There is an overriding obligation to which states party to the convention commit themselves. The risk to an individual if a state acts in breach of this obligation is so obvious and so potentially serious that the courts have habitually treated asylum cases as calling for particular care at all stages of the administrative and appellate process."

Bingham MR described the "acid test" in such cases as follows:

> "The acid test must always be whether comparing the new claim with that earlier rejected, and excluding material on which the claimant could reasonably have been expected to rely in the earlier claim, the new claim is sufficiently different from the earlier claim to admit of a realistic prospect that a favourable view could be taken of the new claim despite the unfavourable conclusion reached on the earlier claim."

Clarke J. noted that s.17(7) of the 1996 Act did not specify any criteria by reference to which the Minister should exercise his discretion to grant consent to re-enter the process, and thus held that it was at least arguable that the test formulated by the courts in the United Kingdom (which in turn were based on ensuring compliance by the United Kingdom with its obligations under the Geneva Convention) would also be required in this jurisdiction having regard to the need to interpret s.17(7) in such a manner as to ensure, in so far as it is possible, compliance by Ireland with its obligations under the Geneva Convention.

On February 14, 2003 the applicant's solicitors forwarded to the Minister a detailed application seeking, amongst other things, the Minister's consent under s.17(7). The basis of the application made to the respondent Minister was stated to be the availability of new information, material facts and change of circumstances regarding the applicant's fear of persecution. This information was stated not to have been available to the office of Refugee Application Commissioner or the Refugee Appeal Tribunal and was stated not to have been available and/or presented when considering her application for a declaration of refugee status. The principal items were then set out in support of the application, including the applicant's recent confirmation of pregnancy, her significantly deteriorated medical condition, country information not previously available and/or presented, the applicant's psychological condition and the requirement to consider the applicant's fear of persecution and discrimination amounting to persecution by reason of her membership of the social group comprising persons from South Africa with HIV infection (and/ or women including pregnant women with HIV) and in respect of which group the State of South Africa fails to provide adequate protection against persecution.

The decision under s.17(7) was taken by a duly authorised deciding officer on behalf of the Minister and the results of same were set out in a letter of April 2, 2003, wherein the minister stated that the issue of the applicant's pregnancy and her present medical condition were not relevant to a s.17(7) application on the basis that they did not refer to persecution for a Convention reason, that the country of origin information had been considered and it was noted that inadequacy of medical treatment in the country of origin was not relevant and, with regard to the applicant's membership of a social group, the inadequacy of medical treatment in the country of origin was also stated not to be relevant.

Clarke J. noted that the first three grounds relied upon by the deciding officer related to the contention of the applicant that she was a member of a social group being persons suffering from HIV/AIDS in South Africa (and/or women including pregnant women with HIV) and the alleged legitimate fear of the applicant of persecution and discrimination amounting to persecution by reason of her membership of that group. In that context Clarke J. went on to consider the extent to which there may be an arguable case that persons may be entitled to refugee status for what might be termed health reasons. Clarke J. referred to the case of *Kuthyar v Minister for Immigration and Multicultural Affairs* (2000) FCA 110 which had been cited with approval by Peart J. in *AO v Minister for Justice* (High Court, May 26, 2004), and noted

Peart J.'s comment in that case that:

> "It is beyond any doubt that she has been diagnosed as HIV positive, and it therefore became a possibility once she articulated this in the limited way she could, that there might be discrimination against the group of HIV positive sufferers, and that the sharing of the burden of proof then kicked in, so to speak, in the sense that it then became necessary to pass on to a further stage of investigation of the application, perhaps by obtaining any available country of origin information about the condition or plight of HIV positive sufferers in Nigeria. It, at the least, merited investigation. She might as a result be part of a particular social group exposed to discrimination in Nigeria."

Having reviewed the material that was placed before the Minister, Clarke J. concluded that it was at least arguable that some of this material could give rise to a conclusion that by virtue of a view taken by the authorities within South Africa the level of treatment being given to persons suffering from AIDS within that jurisdiction fell below the level which could reasonably be expected having regard to the seriousness of the problem of AIDS within South Africa and the resources available within that country. Clarke J. was also satisfied that it had been established that there were, at least arguably, materials contained within the documentation supplied to the Minister that would place the Minister on inquiry as to whether there might not be other discrimination in the form of shunning or exclusion which the authorities were unable or unwilling to counteract.

Commercial Law

ARBITRATION

Foreign arbitral award In *Brostrom Tankers AB v Factorias Vulcano SA* [2004] 2 I.R. 191 the defendant was a Spanish company which entered into a shipbuilding contract with the plaintiff, a Swedish company. A dispute arose and was submitted to arbitration in Norway as required by the contract, which applied the New York Convention on the Recognition and Enforcement of Foreign Arbitral Awards. This resulted in an award in favour of the plaintiff. The plaintiff sought to enforce the award in Ireland pursuant to s.7 of the Arbitration Act 1980. The defendant opposed the making of the enforcement order by reference to s.9(3) of the Act of 1980 which provides that enforcement may be refused if it would be contrary to public policy. The defendant argued that the claim was captured by a Spanish court order which directed that it pay its creditors just 10 per cent of the debts due to them. It was contended that as a matter of public policy the High Court ought not to make an enforcement order as the 10 per cent limitation would not apply in this jurisdiction. Kelly J. held that the award should be enforced. He noted that there were strong public policy considerations in favour of enforcing New York Convention awards, though he accepted that this would not stand in the way of a refusal if it were required as a matter of public policy. The public policy referred to in s.9(3) of the 1980 Act was the public policy of this State, which was clear from Art.5(2)(b) of the New York Convention. There was no authority to support the contention that public policy required that enforcement be refused where it would confer a commercial advantage on the plaintiff which it might not get under Spanish law, or that the comity of courts would be imperilled by an enforcement order being made. Kelly J. applied the decision in *Parsons and Whittemore Overseas Co v Société Generale de l'Industrie du Papier* 508 F. 2d 969 in holding that the public policy defence to an enforcement application was of narrow scope and extended only to a breach of the most basic notions of morality and justice. Since the Convention's purpose was to permit parties to international transactions to promote neutral dispute resolution, he concluded that there was no illegality or even suggestion of illegality or any aspect of Irish public policy which could justify a refusal of an enforcement order.

Standard of review from decision of arbitrator In *Carrickdale Hotel Ltd v Controller of Patents, Designs and Trade Marks* [2004] 3 I.R. 410 Laffoy J. considered the standard of review to be applied by the High Court on the hearing of an appeal from an arbitrator appointed under the Copyright Act 1963 (since replaced by the Copyright and Related Rights Act 2000). The plaintiff appealed to the High Court against an award made by an arbitrator in pursuance of a reference made by the Controller under s.41 of the 1963 Act. The arbitrator had fixed amounts payable by the plaintiff to the second defendant, a music rights agency. The second defendant raised, as a preliminary issue, the standard of review to be applied. The second defendant contended that the standard was reasonableness *simpliciter*, namely, whether the decision in question was vitiated by a serious and significant error. The plaintiff contended that the court should treat the appeal in the same way that appeals to the Supreme Court from the High Court are dealt with. Laffoy J. preferred the test advocated by the second defendant. She held that the test to be applied on the appeal in determining whether the award should be varied is whether the plaintiff has established as a matter of probability that, taking the adjudicative process as a whole, the decision reached was vitiated by a serious and significant error or a series of such errors. In applying that test, regard must be had to the degree of expertise and special knowledge which the adjudicator has.

COMPETITION

EC Competition Rules   The European Communities (Implementation of the Rules on Competition Laid Down in Articles 81 And 82 of the Treaty) Regulations 2004 (S.I. No.195 of 2004) gave administrative effect in the State to EC Council Regulation No.1/2003, implementing Arts 81 and 82 of the EC Treaty. The 2003 Regulation introduces significant changes in the public and private enforcement of Community competition law and was directly applicable in all Member States from May 1, 2004. The 2004 Regulations designate the national authorities responsible for the implementation in the State of the public enforcement provisions of the EC Regulation. The courts are designated for the purpose of Article 5 of the Council Regulation (power to apply Art.81 and Art.82 in individual cases) and in accordance with their existing jurisdiction under the Competition Act 2002. Most of the other functions assigned to national competition authorities by the Council Regulation are allocated to the Competition Authority. Certain functions are allocated concurrently to the Authority, the Director of Public Prosecutions and the courts or are apportioned between the Authority and the courts. The 2004 Regulations also provide some clarification of the terms "national judicial authority" and "authority prosecuting the case".

Defence to Article 81 proceedings   The Competition Act 2002 (Commencement) Order 2004 (S.I. No.196 of 2004) brought s.6(4)(c) of the Competition Act 2002 into operation on May 1, 2004, under which it is a good defence in proceedings under Art.81(1) of the EC Treaty to prove that the agreement, decision or concerted practice fulfils the conditions of Art.81(3) of the EC Treaty. This change coincides with the coming into operation of EC Council Regulation No.1/2003 on the implementation of the rules on competition laid down in Arts 81 and 82 of the EC Treaty under which the provisions of Art.81(3) of the EC Treaty become directly applicable.

FINANCIAL SERVICES

Central Bank and Financial Services Authority of Ireland Act 2004   The Central Bank and Financial Services Authority of Ireland Act 2004 has its origins in three sources. First, it completes the legislative implementation of the recommendations of the 1999 *Report of the Implementation Advisory Group on the establishment of a Single Regulatory Authority for the Financial Services Sector* (the McDowell Report). A number of the recommendations in the McDowell Report had already been implemented by the Central Bank and Financial Services Authority of Ireland Act 2003 (see the *Annual Review of Irish Law 2003*, pp.31–32), which established the Irish Financial Services Regulatory Authority (IFSRA, but now increasingly referred to by itself as "the Financial Regulator") to oversee the activities of financial institutions, including their treatment of customers. Secondly, the provisions of the 2004 Act concerning reporting and auditing requirements for financial institutions are based on those recommendations in the 2000 *Report of the Review Group on Auditing* which relate specifically to financial institutions. As was noted during the Oireachtas debate, the Group's other recommendations were implemented in the Companies (Auditing and Accounting) Act 2003 (see the *Annual Review of Irish Law 2003*, pp.80–89). Thirdly, the provisions in the 2004 Act for money transmission and bureau de change businesses implement recommendations of the *Financial Action Task Force* (an OECD body) on the prevention of money laundering and the financing of terrorism.

Difficult layout of 2004 Act The arrangement of sections for the 2004 Act indicates that it comprises 35 sections only. But this figure disguises the reality that the 2004 Act, which comprises 208 printed pages, makes sweeping changes to the Central Bank Act 1942, a technique also used for the Central Bank and Financial Services Authority of Ireland Act 2003 (which itself runs to 228 printed pages). For example, s.10 of the 2004 Act, which comprises 16 pages of printed text, amends the Central Bank Act 1942 (previously amended by the 2003 Act) by the insertion of a new "Part IIIC: Enforcement of Designated Enactments and Designated Statutory Instruments" into the 1942 Act. This new Part IIIC comprises 19 new sections, s.33AN to s.33BF, of the 1942 Act. This form of amendment is unlikely to assist in the easy navigation of the legislative code on financial services, and there is a strong case at this stage for its consolidation. Indeed, given the enormous amendments effected by the 2003 and 2004 Acts to the Central Bank Act 1942, it is difficult to sustain the formal title of the 1942 Act as the "Principal Act".

Overview of 2004 Act Given the detailed nature of the 2004 Act, what follows comprises a brief overview. As noted in the Oireachtas debate, the 2004 Act provides for: the establishment of a Financial Services Ombudsman to deal with consumer complaints about financial institutions; the establishment of Consumer and Industry Consultative Panels to advise the IFSRA; new reporting and auditing obligations for financial institutions; the conferral of powers on the IFSRA to impose sanctions directly on financial institutions for failure to comply with regulatory requirements, subject to a right of appeal to the Irish Financial Services Appeals Tribunal (established by the 2003 Act); a right of appeal to the Appeals Tribunal in relation to certain supervisory decisions of IFSRA; new regulatory requirements for money transmission and bureau de change businesses; the amendment of the Consumer Credit Act 1995, including provisions to allow the Minister for Finance to extend some or all of the provisions of the 1995 Act to lending to persons other than consumers.

Enforcement powers for the IFSRA Sections 8, 9 and 15 of the 2004 Act provide that, where a financial service provider breaches a relevant statutory requirement or the provisions of an IFSRA Code of Conduct, the IFSRA may impose sanctions directly on that service provider as an alternative to court proceedings. From a procedural perspective, provision is made for a separation of investigation by the IFSRA, while the actual determination is conferred on a Panel appointed by the IFSRA. The decisions of the Panel must be confirmed by the Authority before they have effect. The 2004 Act provides for the following sanctions which may be imposed on a financial service provider: a caution or reprimand; an order to refund a charge; a fine of up to €5 million; and an order to pay the costs of the investigation. In addition, the following sanctions may be imposed on a director or manager of a financial service provider: a caution or reprimand; an order to refund a charge; a fine of up to €500,000; disqualification from being involved in the management of a financial service provider; and an order to pay the costs of the investigation. As already mentioned, a right of appeal to the Appeals Tribunal established under the Central Bank and Financial Services Authority of Ireland Act 2003, is also provided for. In addition, the 2004 Act makes a number of amendments to relevant legislation concerning other supervisory functions of the IFSRA, by substituting the Appeals Tribunal for the court in relation to appeals against supervisory decisions by the IFSRA. The 2004 Act also provides for a full right of appeal to the High Court from the decisions of the Appeals Tribunal.

Financial Services Ombudsman Sections 10 and 17 of the 2004 Act insert a new Pt VIIB into the Central Bank Act 1942 and provide for the establishment of an independent statutory Financial Services Ombudsman (FSO) scheme to deal with consumer complaints against financial service providers. These arrangements replace the non-statutory schemes, the Insurance Ombudsman and the Ombudsman for the Credit Institutions, which had been in operation for a number of years. Indeed, the 2004 Act provided that the existing non-statutory Ombudsmen, and their staffs, would be transferred into the statutory scheme, and that the existing Ombudsmen would be designated by the Minister for Finance as Deputy Ombudsmen-designate under the statutory scheme. A key feature of the 2004 Act is that the functions of the FSO apply to a comprehensive coverage of complaints from personal consumers against financial services providers, including banks, insurance companies, credit unions and intermediaries (brokers). In line with other elements of the 2004 Act, Pt 4 also provides for extension by way of ministerial Regulations of the FSO scheme to complaints from non-personal consumers. The 2004 Act provides for the appointment of a Bureau, overseen by a Council, which will be appointed by the Minister for Finance in consultation with the Minister for Enterprise, Trade and Employment. This will be composed of persons with relevant experience in consumer and financial services. The 2004 Act provides that the Council will appoint the Financial Services Ombudsman and Deputy Ombudsmen and will make detailed rules governing the scheme. The 2004 Act also provides that the Ombudsman will be fully independent in making decisions on individual complaints. The Act also provides that the determinations of the Ombudsman are binding on financial institutions, subject to a right of appeal to the High Court. The statutory scheme, which is independent of the IFSRA, is funded by levies and charges on financial service providers.

Consultative Panels Section 11 of the 2004 Act inserts a new Pt VIIC into the Central Bank Act 1942, and s.18 inserts a new Sch.8 into the 1942 Act and provides for the appointment by the Minister for Finance of separate Consumer and Industry Consultative Panels to advise the IFSRA. Thus, the IFSRA is obliged to consult both Panels before issuing general Regulations, directives or codes. In addition, the Minister is obliged to consult both Panels before approving the IFSRA's annual budget. The Authority is obliged to publish Panel reports and recommendations and, in addition, the Panels, separately or jointly, may appoint Advisory Groups to deal with specific issues. In line with recent legislation, each Panel must produce an annual report and the Chairperson of each Panel is obliged to appear, on request, before an Oireachtas Committee.

Governance oversight of financial service providers Part 3 of the 2004 Act amends the Central Bank Act 1997. Section 21 of the 2004 Act inserts a replacement Pt IV into the 1997 Act concerning corporate governance oversight and auditing of financial service providers. These complement the auditing oversight provisions in the Companies (Auditing and Accounting) Act 2003 (see the *Annual Review of Irish Law 2003*, pp.80–89).

Bureau de change and money transmission businesses Section 22 of the 2004 Act inserts a replacement Pt V into the 1997 Act to provide for revised arrangements for the supervision of bureau de change and money transmission businesses. This implemented recommendations of the *Financial Action Task Force* (an OECD body) on the prevention of money laundering and the financing of terrorism. It was pointed out during the Oireachtas debate that the revised provisions extend the system of authorisation that applied to bureaux de change to persons engaged in money transmission business. The main purpose of the authorisation system is to facilitate the effective implementation of the anti-money laundering and anti-terrorist funding provisions of the Criminal Justice Act 1994.

Consumer credit and moneylending It was noted in the Oireachtas debate on the 2004 Act that the McDowell Report had recommended that the Consumer Credit Act 1995 should extend to moneylending. The 2004 Act gives effect to this by amending the 1995 Act to enable the Minister to extend some or all of the provisions of the 1995 Act to lending to non-personal consumers.

Mortgage introducers and lenders It was also noted in the Oireachtas debate on the 2004 Act that the Director of Consumer Affairs had indicated that the practice of using mortgage "introducers" was on the increase and that the lack of regulation gave scope for abuse. "Introducers" are persons who, although not authorised as mortgage intermediaries in their own right, introduce clients to authorised intermediaries in return for a commission. The 2004 Act therefore amended the definition of "mortgage intermediary" in the Consumer Credit Act 1995 to include "introducers". The 2004 Act also amended the 1995 Act to provide that all institutions who lend on the security of a borrower's principal home are made subject to Pt 9 of the 1995 Act. This provides protection to a borrower by imposing various obligations on housing loan lenders (such as disclosure of charges, non-linkage of services, the "health warning" concerning the risk of loss of the person's home, and mortgage protection insurance). This amendment implemented another recommendation of the McDowell Report that all mortgage lenders should be subject to regulation.

Financial collateral arrangements The European Communities (Financial Collateral Arrangements) Regulations 2004 (S.I. No.1 of 2004) and the European Communities (Financial Collateral Arrangements) (Amendment) Regulations 2004 (S.I. No.89 of 2004) implemented Directive 2002/47/EC on financial collateral arrangements and the provision of financial collateral. As amended, the Regulations came into force on March 8, 2004.

INTELLECTUAL PROPERTY

Copyright and related rights The European Communities (Copyright and Related Rights) Regulations 2004 (S.I. No.16 of 2004) amended ss.2, 50, 87, 244 and 374 of the Copyright and Related Rights Act 2000 in order to complete the implementation into Irish law of Directive 2001/29/EC on the harmonisation of certain aspects of copyright and related rights in the information society. The explanatory note to the Regulations averred that while the State was already in substantial compliance with the 2001 Directive through the enactment of the 2000 Act, the Regulations made a small number of amendments to the 2000 Act to ensure it fully achieves the result intended by the Directive.

Public exhibition of copyright works The Copyright and Related Rights (Amendment) Act 2004 was enacted by the Oireachtas within a week of its presentation as a Bill. The single purpose of the 2004 Act was to amend s.40 of the Copyright and Related Rights Act 2000, which provides that the right of making available a work to the public includes, *inter alia*, performing, showing or playing a copy of the work in public. While the Minister of State introducing the 2004 Act to the Oireachtas asserted that the reference to "showing" in s.40 of the 2000 Act was intended to cover audio-visual works, for example, the showing of a film, he accepted that it had been suggested that the reference to "showing" effectively created a public exhibition right. This would mean that, for example, an artist could prevent the "showing" of his or her painting by a gallery. It could also be interpreted as allowing the copyright owners of a book or books to prevent the public exhibition of such books. This arose in 2004 in the context of a proposed public exhibition in the National Library of Ireland of an exhibition of the works of James Joyce to mark the centenary of Bloomsday, which of course is the day featured in Joyce's *Ulysses*. The material in question had been purchased by the State in 2001 for over €12 million in anticipation of the 2004 centenary, but it was also suggested that the copyright owners of the works in question might have been entitled to object to the exhibition under s.50 of the 2000 Act. While this was rejected by the Minister of State, the opposition parties, while not opposing the passage of the Act, considered that the 2004 Act was more than merely declaratory of existing law. The 2004 Act amended s.40 of the Copyright and Related Rights Act 2000 by inserting a new subs.(7A) after subs.(7), as follows:

> "(7A) For the avoidance of doubt, no infringement of any right created by this Part in relation to an artistic or literary work occurs by reason of the placing on display of the work, or a copy thereof, in a place or premises to which members of the public have access."

The 2004 Act also provided that this amendment would not affect any claim made before the passing of the Act. In the event, the exhibition in question proceeded.

Company Law

GRÁINNE CALLANAN, Waterford Institute of Technology

CORPORATE LITIGATION

Admission of additional evidence   *Ashclad Ltd (In Liquidation) and Barry Forrest v Eugene Harrington and Michael Culleton*, Supreme Court, *Extempore* Keane C.J., January 21, 2004.

The respondents appealed a decision of the High Court, which found that they had failed to keep proper books of accounts as required by s.202 of the Companies Act 1990. As a result of this failure the respondents were held personally liable for the debts of the company and were restricted under s.150 of the Companies Act 1990. The respondents appealed against the order of the High Court and sought to adduce new evidence of a cheque journal and bank statements in order to demonstrate that the findings of the High Court were not justified. The Supreme Court held that before it could admit additional evidence, it first had to be satisfied that the additional evidence had not been in existence at the time of the High Court hearing, and secondly that the evidence could not have been obtained by the person seeking to adduce the additional evidence. The respondents had only attempted to obtain the journal and bank statements after the High Court hearing, therefore they failed to meet the first requirement and the motion was dismissed.

Effect of failure to provide security for costs   *Superwood Holdings plc v Sun Alliance and London Insurance plc* [2004] Supreme Court, 2 I.L.R.M. 12.

The plaintiff's premises, which were insured by the defendants, had been damaged in a fire some years previously. The defendants repudiated liability for the consequential loss of IR£2 million on the grounds that the claim had been so grossly overstated as to be fraudulent. The defendants further refused the plaintiff's request to have their claim submitted to arbitration. The plaintiff's claim was dismissed by the High Court and the plaintiff appealed this decision to the Supreme Court. The defendants sought security for the costs of the appeal. In April 2002 the Supreme Court made an order for security for costs, pursuant to s.390 of the Companies Act 1963. The matter was remitted to the Master of the High Court to assess the amount of security. The amount fixed by the Master was upheld by the High Court. On appeal, not only did the

Supreme Court uphold the amount fixed but also fixed a period of three months within which the security must be provided. The plaintiff failed to provide the security and the defendants subsequently brought a motion seeking to dismiss or strike out the plaintiff's appeal. Counsel for the defendants relied on the decision of the High Court in *Lough Neagh Exploration Ltd v Morrice* [1999] 1 I.L.R.M. 62 (HC) to the effect that in circumstances in which there is no prospect of security for costs being provided, the court has an inherent jurisdiction to make an order dismissing the proceedings. Counsel for the plaintiff argued that s.390 of the Companies Act 1963 did not give the court the power to strike out proceedings and to construe the section on such a basis would be in conflict with Art.34.4.3 of the Irish Constitution, which provides that a right of appeal to the Supreme Court exists from all decisions of the High Court, subject only to exceptions prescribed by law. The court was urged to make it clear that the constitutional right of appeal conferred by the Article could be excluded only by the use of express and unambiguous language, which language was not evident in s.390 of the Companies Act 1963. Keane C.J. accepted the decision in *Lough Neagh Exploration Ltd v Morrice* that an order may be made by the court where there is no reasonable prospect that the security will be received. In the application before the court in the instant case, the order for security had been made two years previously and there had been no indication that there was a reasonable prospect of the plaintiff succeeding in raising the necessary sum. Accordingly, the court was satisfied that the order to strike out the plaintiff's appeal should be granted.

Pre-Incorporation Documents and Professional Privilege   *Ochre Ridge Ltd v Cork Bonded Warehouses Ltd and Port of Cork Company Ltd*, High Court, Lavan J., July 13, 2004.

The plaintiff company claimed legal professional privilege over 53 documents of which the defendant had sought discovery. The correspondence at issue concerned a range of documents, including a number of pre-incorporation documents. While the case primarily turned on the distinction between legal advice and legal assistance privilege (the court approved the decision of the Supreme Court in *Smurfit Paribas Bank Ltd v AAB Export Finance* [1990] 1 I.R. 469, which held that the law of professional privilege is limited to legal advice only), the defendants submitted that the plaintiff could not claim privilege over any documents that had come into existence before the company itself existed. Lavan J. held that it was irrelevant whether documents related to the pre-incorporation phase of the company provided that the communications formed part of the spectrum of legal advice between legal advisor and client. To decide otherwise would mean that a company could never claim privilege over documents relating to its pre-incorporation phase, which in turn would deny the benefit of privilege to a vast array of proceedings.

SHARE TRANSFER STOP NOTICE

Lee v Buckle, High Court, Laffoy J., July 30, 2004.

The applicant was President and Chief Investment Officer of a company that employed the respondent. The respondent's employment with the company ceased and a dispute arose as to the basis of this cessation, which was a matter of separate proceedings. At the date of cessation of his employment the respondent owned of a number of shares in the company. The respondent was party to a Shareholders Agreement that regulated the repercussions in the event of a shareholder ceasing to be employed by the company. The Shareholders Agreement provided for the valuation of the shareholding and the appropriate transfer procedure, depending on the scenario in which the employment had ceased. The applicant, contending that the shareholder had terminated his own employment, invoked this scenario, as provided under the Shareholders Agreement, and served notice in writing on the respondent of his wish to exercise his Call Right over the respondent's shares at par value. He enclosed with this notice a cheque for the par value of the shares and a stock transfer form for execution by the respondent. The respondent believed his employment has been terminated following constructive dismissal. Under the Shareholders Agreement this scenario would entitle him to a Put Right, which would oblige the applicant to purchase his shares at Fair Value. Not accepting the applicant's entitlement, the respondent refused to negotiate the cheque or to sign the stock transfer form under the applicant's terms. On foot of the Shareholders Agreement, an agent of the company executed a stock transfer form and the respondent's shares were transferred to the applicant. The respondent served notice on the company, in accordance with Ord.46, r.6 of the Rules of the Superior Courts 1986, that his shareholding was subject to the provisions of the Shareholders Agreement and "to stop the transfer" of his shares. In the proceedings before Laffoy J. the applicant sought an order ceasing the operation of "the Notice to Restrain Transfer of Stock".

It was accepted by the court that the real issue between the parties was not the transfer itself—which would ultimately occur—rather it was the amount of the purchase price. The applicant submitted that the stop order was akin to a *lis pendens* registered against land that is vacated when the person who has registered it no longer has a claim to the land. By analogy, the stop notice should be ceased as the respondent is obliged to sell the shares irrespective of the underlying dispute and has no rights in relation to the *res* that require to be protected by the stop notice. The applicant further submitted that to allow the stop order continue would have the consequence of permitting the respondent to have a quasi security for his monetary claim against the company prior to obtaining judgment, which the court should not allow. The purpose of a stop notice is to preserve the shares *in specie* while there is an unresolved dispute as to the entitlement of the shares *in specie*, so that they will be available to satisfy the claim, if successful. The rationale for continuing the stop order no longer existed when the claimant ceased to be entitled to the shares *in specie*. Laffoy J. accepted the analogy between the *lis pendens* and the stop notice. In ordering the cessation of the operation of the stop notice, Laffoy J. held that as it was established that the ultimate outcome of the respondent's claim, if successful, is a monetary award and not the retention of the shares, the respondent was not entitled to a continuation of the stop notice. Laffoy J. therefore ordered the cessation of the operation of the notice served by the respondent on the company.

RECEIVERS

Application for directions under s.316 of the Companies Act 1963 *Re Salthill Properties Ltd (In Receivership)*, High Court, Laffoy J., July 30, 2004.

The applicant, *i.e* the receiver of Salthill Properties (hereafter "the company"), applied for directions pursuant to s.316 of the Companies Act 1963. The notice party was the lessee named in three leases created by the company. The receiver sought directions as to a number of issues, namely: whether the leases contravened a negative pledge clause contained in certain mortgages between the company and First Active Bank Plc.; whether the leases were determined by reason of forfeiture notices served by the company on the lessees; whether the leases were surrendered by the lessee; and whether the lessee had any valid or enforceable leasehold or other interest in the lands thereby demised. The receiver also sought an order staying plenary proceedings taken by the lessees against the company. The lessees submitted that the issues between the company and the lessees should be dealt with in plenary proceedings and that an application under s.316 was inappropriate for the resolution of contested facts and further that a determination under such an application would be prejudicial to the lessees. It was also submitted by the lessees that the receiver was not entitled to any of the relief claimed, namely: that the negative pledge clause was contravened; or that the leases were determined by forfeiture; or that the leases were surrendered. Finally, the lessees submitted that the receiver had failed to demonstrate that the reversion on the leases was still vested in the company.

Laffoy J. held that the receiver was entitled to bring an application for directions under s.316. The objective of the legislative provision was that a receiver should not have to embark on a plenary action to resolve certain matters. It was accepted, however, that the provision was not without limitations, in that the directions sought must relate to the receiver's functions and the proceedings must be conducted in accordance with principles of constitutional justice. While the court is empowered to determine issues before it as to the rights of persons, such a determination must be just. Laffoy J. suggested that it would be difficult to envisage a situation in which it would be just to make an order declaring rights on the basis of affidavits where those affidavits clearly demonstrate that a dispute exists as to a material fact. In relation to the submission that the issues between the parties be resolved by plenary proceedings, Laffoy J. accepted that the courts would not readily permit actions that centre on the same issues and parties to be maintained separately. While acknowledging that there were similarities between the issues in plenary proceedings and those before the court, this was not a basis for the court to refuse to exercise its discretion under s.316. Laffoy J. further held that it was not established that the leases had been determined by forfeiture, or indeed surrender. It was held, however, that the lessees had contravened the negative pledge clauses contained in the mortgage debentures because the bank had not given consent to the leases, either prospectively or retrospectively. Nor had the lessee discharged the onus of establishing that it did not have notice of the actual negative pledge clause. No determination was made as to the validity or enforceability of the leasehold interests between the company and the lessee.

Whether claims for injuries sustained in the course of employment constituted an accident within the meaning of s.285(2)(g) of the Companies Act 1963 for the purposes of preferential status *Re Irish Ispat Ltd (In Voluntary Liquidation)*, High Court, Carroll J., February 4, 2004.

Section 285(2)(g) of the Companies Act 1963 provides, *inter alia*, that in a winding up there shall be paid, in priority to all other debts, all amounts due from the company to a person employed by it in respect of damages and costs payable in the course of his or her employment with the company. In this case a number of employees had sued in respect of hearing loss incurred during the course of employment. The employees claimed that their hearing loss was caused by an accident, or series of accidents, in the course of their employment. The liquidator brought an application under s.280 of the Companies Act 1963 for a determination of the status of the claims for the purposes of s.285(2)(g) of the Companies Act 1963, that is whether they ranked as preferential debts. The liquidator contended that the hearing loss was the result of ongoing exposure to high noise levels during the course of employment and therefore was caused by a process of work and not by an accident or series of accidents. Carroll J. referred to a number of Irish and English authorities which dealt with the term "accident" for the purposes of s.285(2)(g) and in respect of workers' compensation: *Irish Foundries limited (In liquidation) Burns v Paul Doyle and Others* (Unreported) [1977]; *Kelly v Cement Ltd* [1940] I.R. 84; *Roberts v Dorothea Slate Quarry Co. Ltd* [1948] 2 All E.R. 201; *Pyrah v Doncaster Company* [1949] 1 A.E.R. 883. On the basis of the authorities referred to, Carroll J. concluded that the repeated incidents of impulse noise which had caused the hearing loss were not unexpected or fortuitous and could not be said to have been caused by an "accident". Accordingly, the court held the employees' claims were not entitled to preferential status under s.285(2)(g) of the Companies Act 1963.

COMPANY INVESTIGATIONS

Re National Irish Bank Ltd, High Court, Kelly J., July 23, 2004.

In 1998 inspectors were appointed by the High Court under s.8 of the Companies Act 1990 to investigate the affairs of National Irish Bank (hereafter "the bank") and National Irish Bank Financial Services Limited (hereafter "the company"). The inspectors investigated the affairs over a six-year period and their final report was delivered to the court on July 12, 2004. The High Court made an order on that date, in accordance with s.11(3) of the Companies Act 1990, that a copy of the report be made available to the Director of Corporate Enforcement, upon an undertaking that no disclosure or publication of its contents would be made pending a further order of the court. On the same date an order was made that a hearing would take place on July 21, 2004 with a view to the court providing directions and making orders under ss.11, 12 and 13 of the Companies Act 1990 pursuant to the delivery of a final report.

Section 11(3) and (4) of the Companies Act 1990 relates to the court's statutory obligation to furnish a copy of every report to the Director of Corporate Enforcement and its discretionary power to forward, or furnish a copy of any report to various other parties, including those who are the subject of, or affected by the report. Furthermore, it provides the court with the discretionary power to cause any report to be printed and published. In the instant case the court held that the bank and the company under investigation should be furnished with a copy of the inspectors' report. The bank and the company requested that if the court should direct the printing and publication of the report, that they be furnished with the report in advance of such publication. This request was based largely on the bank's need to be prepared for customer queries, media queries, the protection of the bank's market position, the management of ongoing banking business and the need to proactively manage its response in the market place. In view of the fact that the bank had already been furnished with a draft of the inspector's report in 2003 and had not taken issue with any matter, including the adverse findings in the draft, when replying to the inspector, Kelly J. refused the application for a copy to be furnished to the bank in advance of any other entity of general publication. Kelly J. also made a number of orders to furnish other parties with a copy of the report. In relation to the printing and publication of the report, the court noted that the bank and the company sought publication, as did the inspectors, and no party was opposed to the publication. Despite these facts it was noted that the decision was solely a matter for the court. The one reservation on the question of publication related to the potential difficulties for the Director of Public Prosecutions in any subsequent prosecution. Nevertheless Kelly J. was satisfied that appropriate directions from a trial judge would negate any possible prejudice arising from the report's publication. Accordingly, he concluded that the public interest required that the report be published in full.

Section 12 of the Companies Act gives the court the power to make such orders, as it deems fit, in relation to matters arising from the report, including an order to wind up the company on its own motion, or on a petition from the Director of Corporate Enforcement. Furthermore, the court may make an order to remedy any disability suffered by a person whose interests were adversely affected by the conduct of the affairs of the company, provided that in making such an order the court has regard to the interests of any other person who may be affected by such order. The Director of Corporate Enforcement indicated that he did not intend petitioning the winding up of the company. The inspectors appointed to investigate the affairs did not consider it necessary that a winding up order be made, and the bank and the company also opposed the making of a winding up order. Nevertheless the decision, according to Kelly J., was one exclusively for the court. Given the uniqueness of the power to the company law of this jurisdiction, Kelly J. considered English authorities that deal with "public interest petitions" to be of relevance given that the power under s.12(1)(a) should be exercised if it is in the public interest to do so. Kelly J. cited, with approval, the judgment of Nicholls L.J. in *Re Walter L. Jacob & Co. Ltd* [1989] B.C.L.C. 345, where he stated that the court must carry out a "balancing exercise" and in so doing may take account of the submissions of interested parties and the regulator, but must also identify for itself the aspects of the public interest that would be promoted by issuing a winding up order. As part of the balancing exercise, Kelly J. summarised the improper practices carried out by the bank, the company, and by a number of senior bank personnel, practices which were widespread and carried out over a long period of time. On the other hand he considered the contrite attitude of the bank, its commitment to ensuring a high level of governance and the financial costs associated with addressing the issues identified in the investigation. Furthermore, such an order would likely delay the repayment programme already agreed and have consequences for the bank's customers and the banking system. Kelly J. therefore concluded that it would not be in the public interest to order the winding up of the company. Interestingly, Kelly J. did aver to the fact that the cessation of improper conduct was not in itself a ground for not winding up the company. Kelly J. did not consider it appropriate to make any order remedying any disability suffered by any person whose interests were affected by the conduct of the affairs of the company, but he suggested that any such person would have the report of the inspectors available to him and which would be admissible as evidence in any civil proceedings.

In relation to costs Kelly J. ordered that the bank and the company discharge the costs incurred by the inspectors, including their legal costs.

Re Ansbacher (Cayman) Ltd and Others, High Court, Finnegan P., May 25, 2004.

In 1999 the High Court appointed inspectors to investigate the affairs of Ansbacher (Cayman) Limited and report their findings to the court. The report was duly completed and presented to the High Court in June 2002. Access to the report, including the appendices, had been granted to the Revenue Commissioners. In this application the Revenue Commissioners sought an order, under s.12 of the Companies Act 1990, for access to documents obtained by the inspectors in the course of their investigation but not included in the report or the appendices. The Revenue Commissioners submitted that as the inspectors' report had concluded that there was a conspiracy to defraud the Revenue, the information sought would be of assistance to the Revenue in its investigation of the Ansbacher account-holders. The inspectors submitted that many of the parties who had furnished information and documentation had done so on the proviso that their affairs would be revealed by the inspectors only to the extent necessary for completing the report. In a number of cases the inspectors had expressly undertook not to disclose material, except insofar as it was necessary for the completion of the report. The inspectors expressed concern that further disclosure of information and documentation would have an adverse affect on future investigations, in that co-operation might be less likely.

Finnegan P. examined the scope and extent of s.12(1), which gives the court a wide discretion, including making an order as it sees fit. Section 12(1) provides as follows:

> "12(1) Having considered a report made under section 11, the court may make such order as it deems fit in relation to matters arising from that report including—
>
> (a) an order of its own motion for the winding up of a corporate body, or
>
> (b) an order for the purpose of remedying any disability whose interests were adversely affected by the conduct of the affairs of the company, provided that, in making any such order, the court shall have regard to the interests of any person who may be adversely affected by the order."

Finnegan P. stated that the discretion given to the court was not limited to that specified in s.12(1)(a) and s.12(1)(b) as these provisions were regulated by the word "including", indicating that the discretion of the court might be exercised in cases falling outside these provisions. In the circumstances of the present application he considered it appropriate to have regard to the contractual duty of confidentiality that exists between a bank and its customer, the constitutional right to privacy, and to balance these rights against the interests of the Revenue Commissioners. While these matters were relevant Finnegan P. did conclude that the public interest was paramount (*National Irish Bank Ltd & Another v Radio Telefís Éireann* [1998] 2 I.R. 465 applied). The court accepted that the Revenue Commissioners were adversely affected by the affairs of Ansbacher (Cayman) Limited and that information furnished to the inspectors involuntarily, or on foot of a undertaking of confidentiality, did not circumscribe the powers of the court to make an order. However, the court acknowledged that it could, as part of its discretionary powers, take into account other circumstances. One such circumstance was the effect such disclosure might have on the conduct of future enquiries. He cited the following passage from *Re Pergamon Press Ltd* [1971] Ch.388, where Denning M.R. stated:

> "This investigation is ordered in the public interest. It should not be impeded by measures of this kind. Witnesses should be encouraged to come forward and not hold back. Remember, this not being a judicial proceeding the witnesses are not protected by an absolute privilege, but only a qualified privilege: see O'Connor v Waldron [1935] A.C. 76. It is easy to imagine a situation in which, if the name of a witness was disclosed, he might have an action brought against him, and this might deter him from telling all he knew. No one likes to have an action brought against him, however unfounded. Every witness must therefore be protected. He must be encouraged to be frank. This is done by giving every witness an assurance that his evidence will be regarded as confidential and will not be used except for the purpose of the Report. This assurance must be honoured. It does not mean that his name and his evidence will never be disclosed to anyone. It will only have to be used for the purposes of the Report, not only in the Report itself, but also by putting it in general terms to other witnesses for their comments. But it does mean that the Inspectors will exercise a wide discretion in the use of it so as to safeguard the witness himself and any others affected by it."

On the basis of the matters to be taken into account, the court was not satisfied that documents and information obtained by the inspectors relating to persons not mentioned in the report could be said to be matters arising out of the report. However, the court was satisfied that in the assessment and collection of taxes the public interest outweighs the contractual right to confidentiality and the constitutional right to privacy of the individuals and companies mentioned in a report. In such circumstances any undertaking as to confidentiality, while a factor to which court ought to have regard, did not preclude the court from making an order. Accordingly, the court made the order sought by the Revenue, but only in relation to those Ansbacher clients and those persons and companies found to have failed to co-operate with the inspectors in the enquiries, which group included individual members of the board of Ansbacher.

LIQUIDATION

Main Insolvency Proceedings   Council Regulation (EC) 1346/2000 provides the rules governing the opening of insolvency proceedings in any Member

State. There are two categories of insolvency proceedings under the regulation, *viz.* main and secondary insolvency proceedings. The former can have extra-territorial effect, while the latter are confined to assets within the jurisdiction in which such proceedings are opened. The regulations provide that main proceedings may be opened in the Member State where the company has the centre of its main interests and where insolvency proceedings (as provided for in Annex 4 of the Regulation) are commenced in that Member State.

Re Eurofood IFSC Ltd, Supreme Court, July 27, 2004 [2005] 1 I.L.R.M. 161.

Eurofoods IFSC Ltd. (hereafter "the company") was an Irish-registered company that formed part of Parmalat, a group of Italian companies. In December 2003 Parmalat was placed in extraordinary administration to permit a financial restructuring of the group. In February 2004 the Italian court fixed February 17 as the date for the hearing of a petition concerning the insolvency of the company. It directed that notice of the proceedings be served on all interested parties.

On January 27, 2004 the main creditor of the company, Bank of America, petitioned the High Court to wind up the company. Bank of America expressed concern that an attempt would be made to move the centre of main interests of the company, for the purposes of Council Regulation (EC) 1346/2000, from Ireland to Italy. The High Court appointed a provisional liquidator, who notified the creditors and the extraordinary administrator of Parmalat in Italy. In March 2004 the High Court (Kelly J.) granted the order for the winding up of the company. It was held that the insolvency proceedings had commenced in Ireland, at the date of the presentation of the petition for the winding up, and that the centre of main interests was Ireland. It was therefore held that for the purposes of the Council Regulation the insolvency proceedings had opened in Ireland. The opening of main insolvency proceedings in Italy was contrary to the Regulation and could not alter the fact that proceedings were already in existence in Ireland. Finally, the failure of the Extraordinary Administrator in Italy to put the creditors on notice of the hearing, as directed by the Italian court, and the failure to furnish the Provisional Liquidator with the petition and other papers amounted to a lack of due process so as to warrant the Irish court refusing to give recognition to the Italian court under the Regulation.

The appellant—the Extraordinary Administrator in Italy—appealed against the decision of the High Court. The main issues that arose were where the insolvency proceedings first opened; where the company's centre of main interests was; whether it would be contrary to public policy to recognise the Italian court's decision. In relation to the first issue, Art.1(1) of the Regulation provides that it applies to "collective insolvency proceedings which entail the partial or total divestment of a debtor and the appointment of a liquidator". Under Annex A of the Regulation a "compulsory winding up by the court" is a proceeding within the meaning of Art.1(1). According to the Supreme Court the petition presented to the High Court on January 27, 2004 constituted such a proceeding. It further held that the appointment of a provisional liquidator involved at least a "partial divestment" of the debtor insofar as it deprived the directors of their powers and required the provisional liquidator to take possession of the company's property. Where a winding up order is later made—which in this case it was—then the effect of s.220(2) of the Companies Act 1963 is that the order is deemed to have been made on January 27, 2004. The Supreme Court then examined the effect of this provision. Article 16 of the Regulation provides that:

> "Any judgment opening proceedings handed down by a court of a Member State which has jurisdiction ... shall be recognised in all other Member States from the time that it becomes effective in the State of the opening of the proceedings."

The question then was whether the appointment of a provisional liquidator constituted the opening of insolvency proceedings. The Supreme Court examined Art.(2)(e) of the Regulation, which defines a "judgment" as including "the decision of any court empowered to open such proceedings or to appoint a liquidator". By virtue of Art.2(b) and Annex C of the regulation the word "liquidator" includes a provisional liquidator. However, as Art.2(e) does not refer to a judgment appointing a liquidator but rather to a judgment by a court "empowered" to make such an order, the question that had to be decided was whether an order appointing a provisional liquidator is to be considered as a judgment that opens insolvency proceedings and therefore entitled to recognition under Art.16.

While the Supreme Court acknowledged that it was not clear whether Art.2(e) intended to create a distinction between opening proceedings and the appointment of a liquidator for the purposes of Art.16, it stated that the definition of the appointment of a liquidator as a "judgment" does not appear to serve any purpose within the Regulation if it does not benefit from the recognition provided by Art.16. Furthermore, the appointment of a liquidator is an "essential component of the notion of collective insolvency proceedings" within Art.1(1) of the Regulation. Bank of America had relied on Art.2(f), which defines the "time of the opening of proceedings" as meaning "the time at which the judgment opening the proceedings becomes effective, whether it is a final judgment or not". The Supreme Court accepted that this argument was helpful, provided it could be shown that the "time of opening of proceedings", as defined, was relevant to determining the priorities between the opening of proceedings where conflicting orders are made in two Member States. Given these circumstances the Supreme Court decided to refer the question to the European Court of Justice for a decision as to whether the Irish Courts first opened insolvency proceedings.

In relation to the matter of the company's "centre of main interests", this was held to be a matter of fact. Recital 13 provides that the centre of main interests should correspond to the place where the debtor conducts the administration of its interests on a regular basis, which is ascertainable by third parties. Article 3(1) states that in the absence of proof to the company, the place of the registered office shall be presumed to be the centre of main interests. In relation to the first of these matters the company was registered in Ireland, conducted its business lawfully in Ireland and complied with all the legal and regulatory requirements imposed by Irish company, tax and financial services law. Furthermore, the appellant's only contention in this regard—in respect of holding board meetings—was not supported by the evidence. The court was satisfied that the company clearly conducted the administration of its business in Ireland. In relation to the second matter, namely that the centre of main interests must be ascertainable by third parties, it was clear from the evidence adduced that the creditors did not believe they were transacting business with a company whose centre of main interests was in Italy. The appellant argued that the company was a wholly owned subsidiary of Parmalat, whose sole object was to provide finance to the Parmalat group of companies and whose policy was determined at Parmalat headquarters. It further argued that the company had no employees in Ireland and that the company's liability to its note-holders was guaranteed by Parmalat. Thus, the appellant claimed, the company was a mere financial vehicle for Parmalat. The Supreme Court held that such submissions were far-reaching in relation to the fundamentals of company law. Of particular relevance to the Supreme Court was the compelling evidence of the creditors' reliance on legal and financial advice as to the legal and financial character of the company and the regulatory environment in which it operated. Accordingly, the court held that insofar as it could make judgment on the matter, the centre of main interests of the company was at all relevant times in Ireland. To decide otherwise would have serious implications for the future of international corporate structures, particularly if "financial control by a parent company" rather than the legal and corporate existence of a company were to be the determining factors. Nevertheless the Supreme Court addressed certain questions relating to this matter to the Court of Justice for determination.

The Supreme Court agreed with the High Court's decision that recognition should not be given to the judgment of the Italian court as there was no fair hearing in respect of the creditors of the company and of the provisional liquidator and that such was contrary to Irish public policy. It further stated that the principle of fair procedures in administrative proceedings is a principle of public importance and of cardinal importance, deriving from the rules of natural justice and constitutional rights. It referred the following question to the European Court of Justice: where it is manifestly contrary to the public policy of a Member State to permit a judicial or administrative decision to have legal effect in relation to persons whose rights to fair procedures and a fair hearing has not been respected, is that Member State bound to give recognition of such a decision?

The Supreme Court held that the appointment of both a liquidator in Ireland and an Extraordinary Administrator to the same company would render it impossible to administer the assets of the company, to the detriment of the creditors. The Supreme Court accordingly referred the questions, as to the matters described above, to the European Court of Justice for determination.

Presentation of a winding up petition is not a legitimate means of enforcing a debt that is bona fide disputed Section 213(e) of the Companies Act 1963 provides that a company may be wound up by the court if is unable to pay its debts. By virtue of s.214 of the Companies Act 1963 a company will be deemed to be unable to pay its debts where *inter alia* a creditor to whom the company is indebted in a sum exceeding €1,269 has served on the company a demand to pay the sum due and the company has failed to pay the sum for three weeks, or to secure or compound for it to the reasonable satisfaction of the creditor.

Coalport Building Company Ltd v Castle Contracts (Ireland) Ltd, High Court, Laffoy J., January 19, 2004.

The plaintiff company sought an injunction restraining the defendant from advertising or in any way publicising a petition seeking the winding up of the company, pursuant to s.214 of the Companies Act 1963, on the grounds that the company was unable to pay its debts. The plaintiff defended this claim on the grounds that it had been overcharged and the plaintiff's solicitor had given notice to the defendant of this defence. The plaintiff also suggested an alternative remedy to the bringing of a winding up petition whereby the defendant could have sued for the alleged debt. Laffoy J. followed the applicable principles as stated by Keane J. in *Truck and Machinery Sales Ltd v Marubeni Komatzo Ltd* [1996] 1 I.R. 12 at p.24 as follows:

> "It is clear that where a company in good faith and on substantial grounds, disputes any liability in respect of the alleged debt, the petition will be dismissed, or if the matter is brought before the court before the petition is issued, its presentation will in normal circumstances be restrained. This is on the grounds that a winding up petition is not a legitimate means of seeking to enforce payment of a debt which is bona fide disputed."

On the basis that the contractual relationship between the parties was characterised by a total lack of documentation and that liability had been disputed immediately upon receipt of the defendant's formal demand and that the plaintiff's solicitor had put on record the basis of the plaintiff's claim, the High Court was satisfied that the plaintiff company's defence to the debt claimed was bona fide and based on substantial grounds. The defendant had also argued that the plaintiff had not offered any security for the debt. The plaintiff informed the court that it had authorised its solicitors to lodge the amount claimed in security. The court agreed that the defendant had a suitable alternative remedy available to it, in that it could sue for the alleged debt. It was ordered that the defendant should not take any steps to advertise or otherwise publicise a petition for the purpose of seeking the winding up of the company on condition that the plaintiff lodged in court a sum of money as security for the alleged debt.

Re I.C.T. International Cotton and Textile Trading Company Ltd, High Court, Laffoy J., March 31, 2004.

A petition was presented to wind up the company, pursuant to s.214(a) of the Companies Act 1963, on the grounds that the company had not complied with a demand by the petitioner to pay sums owed by the company. The company contended that it was not indebted to the petitioner and that it was not insolvent. The parties both agreed that the test to be applied was that set out by Buckley L.J. in *Stonegate Ltd v Gregory* [1980] 1 All E.R. 241, which was approved by the Supreme Court in *Re Pageboy Couriers* [1983] I.L.R.M. 510 and subsequent cases. The test as stated by Buckley L.J. was that if the company, in good faith and on substantial grounds, disputes any liability in respect of the alleged debt, the petition would be dismissed because a winding up petition is not a legitimate means of enforcing payment of a debt that is bona fide disputed. Laffoy J. stated that in such circumstances the onus was on the company to demonstrate that it was acting bona fide in advancing the defence and that such a defence must be based on substantial grounds. The petitioner and the company presented conflicting accounts as to the nature of the debt and the actual debtor. It was submitted by the company that the dispute as to the liability of the company raised questions with regard to the credibility of witnesses and the inferences that should be drawn from the facts, and that these matters could not be resolved without a plenary hearing. Laffoy J. accepted that there were sufficient conflicting facts and these could only be resolved by a plenary hearing and therefore that there was insufficient evidence to establish that the company was unable to pay its debts so as to empower the court to grant the winding up order. Being satisfied that there were substantial grounds for disputing the debt, Laffoy J. turned to the question of whether the company was acting in good faith. While the evidence showed that there might be a concern as to the bona fides of the company's dealings with the petitioner, this was not, in fact, relevant. Rather it was the company's bona fides in defending the claim for indebtedness that was relevant. As there was no evidence that the company was not lacking good faith in this regard and as the company had consistently denied any indebtedness to the petitioner, Laffoy J. held that it was not appropriate to make the order.

CONVERSION FROM A VOLUNTARY WINDING UP TO A COMPULSORY WINDING UP

Re Hayes Homes Ltd, High Court, O'Neill J., July 8, 2004.

The company was in voluntary liquidation. Over 90 per cent of its debt was owed to the Revenue Commissioners. A creditors' meeting was held following the appointment of the liquidator and the Revenue Commissioners sought to avail of s.267(3) of the Companies Act 1963, which provides as follows:

> "(3) if at a meeting of creditor mentioned in s.266(1) a resolution as to the creditors nominee or liquidator is proposed, it shall be deemed to be passed when a majority, in value only, of the creditor's present personally or by proxy and voting on the resolution have voted in favour of the resolution."

At the meeting the Revenue was represented by proxy, and an issue arose as to whether or not the form of proxy had been properly executed or transmitted to the registered office of the company. Following an adjournment of the meeting the Chairman refused to allow the Revenue Commissioners' proxy to vote to appoint its nominee as liquidator. The Chairman asserted that the Revenue had not notified the instrument of proxy to the company prior to the meeting in accordance with Ord.74, r.82(1) of the Rules of the Superior Court. The Revenue Commissioners petitioned the court to have this order reversed, or, in the alternative, to have the court convert the liquidation into a compulsory one. The petitioner undertook to discharge the costs of the voluntary liquidation to date and all future expenses if the court were disposed towards granting the order of conversion. O'Neill J. held that the Chairman of the creditors meeting was correct in not allowing the Revenue to vote because the instrument of proxy was not duly notified to the company within the time specified by Ord.74, r.82(1) of the Rules of the Superior Court. With regard to the matter of replacing the voluntary winding up with a compulsory winding up, O'Neill J. examined the differing approaches taken in Irish and English cases (*Re Palmer Marine Services Ltd* [1986] B.C.L.C. 106, *Re Falcon RJ Developments* [1987] B.C.L.C. 437, *Re Eurochick (Ireland) Ltd*, unreported, McCracken J., High Court March 23, 1998 and *Re Naiad Ltd*, unreported, McCracken J., High Court February 13, 1995) and concluded that there was no significant divergence in principle in the approach adopted when the question at issue was that of converting from a voluntary liquidation to a compulsory liquidation. It was suggested that any divergence could be explained by the justifiability of the creditors' grievances in each case. On the basis of the facts presented, in particular the entitlement and intent of the petitioner, the fact that the petitioner was the only substantial creditor, the fact that the company's only potentially realisable asset had been transferred to an associate company without proper consideration, and the fact that the petitioner had undertaken to discharge the costs and expenses of the voluntary liquidation, O'Neill J. exercised the court's discretion and granted the order to convert the liquidation from a voluntary to a compulsory one.

FOSS v HARBOTTLE

Re Heaphy v Heaphy, High Court, Peart J., January 15, 2004.

The plaintiff and defendant were brothers. The plaintiff sued the defendant for damages for fraud, breach of contract, misrepresentation and breach of fiduciary duty. The defendant brought an application for an order dismissing the plaintiff's claim on the ground *inter alia* that the claim asserted rights on behalf of a company and not on behalf of the plaintiff. In 1974 the plaintiff had incorporated and was the principal shareholder in a company known as Springmound Holdings Ltd. The company purchased two hotels. In 1986 the plaintiff moved abroad and he alleged that he left his brother in charge of a number of matters relating to the running of the hotels and the discharge of the company's loan. The plaintiff claimed that when he returned to Ireland the defendant had caused Springmound Holdings Ltd to sell the two hotels, without his knowledge or consent. He claimed that as a result, the sale was a fraud on the plaintiff, the defendant was in breach of contract and in breach of his fiduciary duty to the plaintiff. The defendant argued that even if the claim were valid—which he in fact disputed—it could only be brought by the company, which was in liquidation, because the alleged damage was suffered by the company, namely the sale of two company assets at an undervalue. Accordingly, any such claim to damages by the company could not give rise to a claim by a shareholder arising from any diminution in the value of his shares. The court was referred to the principle in *Foss v Harbottle* [1843] 2 Hare 461, which provides that where a wrong is done to the company, only the company can bring proceedings. The court was also referred to the case of *O'Neill v Ryan and Others* [1990] I.L.R.M. 140, where the Supreme Court accepted the principle that a shareholder's investment follows the fortunes of a company and he may exercise his influence over the fortunes of the company only by the exercise of his voting rights at a general meeting. It was submitted by the defendant that any alleged loss is a loss to the company and that it is open to the company's liquidator to investigate such loss and to take an action, should he so choose. Peart J. concluded that the plaintiff operated his business by means of a limited liability company and that in doing so he ceased to have the control over the affairs he would have had if he had dealt personally with the matters. It was further held that the plaintiff's allegations were, in substance, an allegation of fraud against the company and on this basis that while the loss may have felt personal, it was in fact a company loss. As the law was clear that any such claim, if substantiated, is a matter for the company and not for the plaintiff, the plaintiff's claim against the defendant was dismissed.

EFFECT OF RESTORATION TO REGISTER OF COMPANIES ON LIABILITY OF DIRECTORS

Richmond Building Products Ltd v Soundgables Ltd, James Butler, John O'Keefe and Gerry Spillane, High Court, Finnegan P., November 4, 2004; [2005] 1 I.L.R.M. 497.

The plaintiff had obtained judgment against the first- and third-named defendant for goods delivered to the company during the period when it had been struck off the register. The plaintiff sought further relief against the second- and fourth-named defendants, who were directors of the company. The company had since been restored to the register and the defendants claimed that the effect of such restoration was to release the directors from personal liability. The plaintiff contended that the liability survived, irrespective of the restoration order. While there was some doubt as to the specific statutory provision under which the application to restore the company was made, Finnegan P. stated that it was irrelevant because in either case the company is nonetheless deemed to have continued in existence as if its name had not been struck off. He further stated that s.12(3) of the Companies (Amendment) Act 1982, which provides that the liability of every director of a company that has been struck off the register shall continue as if that company had not been so struck off, was not helpful to the applicant's case as that provision was relevant only where the company had not been restored and, in any event, affects only a director *qua* director and does not relate to liability incurred by any person purporting to act in the name of the company while the company is dissolved. With regard to the effect of a restoration order, Finnegan P. referred to the decision of O'Neill J. in *Re Amantiss Enterprises Ltd* [2000] 2 I.L.R.M. 177, where it was accepted that the effect of the restoration provision was to validate all acts carried out by the company in the interim between its dissolution and its restoration. This "as you were" approach had also found favour in most of the English cases referred to (*Tymans Ltd v Craven* [1952] 2 QB 100, *Re Huntington Poultry Ltd* [1969] 1 All E.R. 328, *Re Lindsay Bowman Ltd* [1969] 3 All E.R. 601 and *Re Priceland Ltd* [1997] 1 B.C.L.C. 467). On the basis of the authorities, Finnegan P. was satisfied that the order restoring the company had the effect of releasing the directors from the personal liability they had incurred while the company was struck off, and the plaintiff's claim failed.

LATE FILING FEES AND PROSECUTION FOR LATE FILING OF ANNUAL RETURNS—DOUBLE JEOPARDY?

The Registrar of Companies v Judge David Anderson and System Partners Ltd, Supreme Court, December 16, 2004.

The Registrar of Companies appealed a High Court decision that refused to grant his application for an order of certiorari by way of judicial review of a decision of the first-named respondent, who struck out two summonses that had been issued by the appellant against the second-named respondent company for breach of s.125 of the Companies Act 1963, by failing to file annual returns. There was no dispute that the company had failed to file the returns for the years 2000 and 2001. Subsequent to the summonses, but before the matter came for hearing before the District Court, the company had filed its annual return in respect of the years in question and had paid to the Registrar of Companies the late filing fees. Subsequently, the prosecution of the company for failing to make its returns came before the District Court. The District Judge raised the question as to whether—in circumstances where the company had already received a penalty for filing its returns late in the form of late filing fees—the subsequent prosecution under s.125 of the Companies Act 1963 amounted to, or exposed the second-named respondent to the risk of double jeopardy. In concluding that there might be a risk of double jeopardy, the District Judge struck out the two summonses. The High Court had questioned whether there was a difference between a criminal sanction and an administrative sanction and had concluded that in the instant case the offence gave rise to a criminal sanction when there was already a sanction in place (*McLoughlin v Tuite, The Revenue Commissioners* [1989] I.R. 82 distinguished). Accordingly, the High Court held that the District Judge was correct and refused the relief sought. On appeal, the Registrar of Companies submitted that the late filing fee did not constitute, either in form or in substance, a criminal penalty, but rather was in the nature of a civil, or administrative sanction. Such a sanction was applied solely to encourage timely filing and as its purpose was administrative it was further submitted that the payment of the late filing fee did not preclude prosecution under s.125. It was further submitted by the Registrar that the late filing fee had no relationship with the prosecution and is relevant only to issues of mitigation in respect of any fine to be imposed for the actual offence. The issue of double jeopardy did not apply where there was an overlap between the criminal law, on the one hand, and the civil law, on the other. The Supreme Court accepted the Registrar's submission and held that the District Judge was wrong in law in striking out the summonses. The appeal was allowed.

SECTION 204 OF THE COMPANIES ACT 1963

Patrick Walls v Walls Holdings Ltd, High Court, Smyth J., November 5, 2004.

The applicant sought to prevent the respondent from acquiring his shares in Walls Properties Limited (hereafter "Properties") and Thornhill Properties Limited (hereafter "Thornhill") pursuant to the provisions of s.204(1) of the Companies Act 1963. The companies, including the respondent, had common shareholders who were all members of the Walls family. The applicant held shares in each of Properties and Thornhill and in the respondent holding company. The applicant submitted that the respondent was not an independent bidder in that its controlling shareholders and directors were the sole directors and, together with their children, the majority shareholders of Properties and Thornhill. The applicant further submitted that the respondent's offer was extortionate for the following reasons:

(1) the offer was at a substantial undervalue;

(2) the proposal to pay the purchase price by instalments would leave the transferor shareholder not only unsecured during the period of the instalments but also liable to capital gains taxation on transfer;

(3) the offer process was fundamentally and materially unfair in terms of the information that was not given to shareholders, the short time period imposed for acceptance and the advice that was provided by the solicitors in relation to these; and

(4) the attempt to "expropriate" the applicant's shares was made in contravention of the pre-emption provisions in Properties' articles of association.

In relation to the independence of the offeror, the court was satisfied that the majority shareholders had not exercised unjust influence or coercion and that s.204 did not require that the holders of the four-fifths majority be independent or disinterested in the transferee company. The court stated that the test as to whether "the court thinks fit to order otherwise" is a discretion that is generally dependent on whether or not the offer is unfair and that the onus is on the applicant to prove unfairness. While circumstances may justify reversing the onus (*Re Bugle Press Ltd* [1961] 1 C.H. 270), there were no such circumstances in the present case. In regard to the sale at an undervalue, the court was satisfied that the proper test to be applied was that of Vaisey J. in *Re Sussex Brick Co.* [1961] Ch. 289 at p.291, where he stated:

> "A scheme must be obviously unfair patently unfair, unfair to the meanest intelligence. It cannot be said that no scheme can be effective to bind a dissenting shareholder unless it complies to the extent of 100 per cent, with the highest possible standard of fairness, equity and reason."

On the basis of the evidence before the court, in particular the views of the majority and the fact that the outcome of the offer was not a foregone conclusion and the fact that the applicant's shareholding in the respondent company would be increased, the court could not accept that the applicant had shown convincingly that the offer was unfair.

In regard to the matter of the unsecured instalments, the court accepted the business reasons for such a scheme and was satisfied that the acceptors of the scheme were not unaware of the capital gains taxation issue or the element of risk in accepting deferred payments without security. As regards the failure to provide information, the court was satisfied that while not all information was forthcoming in the manner required by the applicant, this did not justify rejecting the entire scheme (*Re Evertite Locknuts* [1945] 2 CH 220 applied). In the matter of the inadequate time period allowed for acceptance and the inadequacy of advice given, the court was satisfied that these submissions were unsustainable. The final matter related to the breach of the pre-emption scheme provided in Properties' articles of association. The court accepted the respondent's contention that where there is a conflict between the articles of association and the provisions of the Act, the Act prevails. Furthermore, the discretion to deny the right to acquire under s.204 was vested in the court and not in a dissenting shareholder through reliance on the articles. Accordingly, the standard pre-emption rights did not intrude into the process to which s.204 applies. On this basis the court concluded that the offer was not unfair and refused to order the relief sought by the applicant.

RESTRICTION OF DIRECTORS

Transactions between the Company and Directors   *Stafford v Higgins and Others, Re Xnet Information Systems Ltd (In Voluntary Liquidation)*, High Court, Finlay Geoghegan J., May 6, 2004.

The liquidator applied to have the four respondent directors restricted under s.150 of the Companies Act 1990. The first and second respondents were the initial shareholders and directors of the company. The third- and fourth-named respondents became directors at a later time because of their relevant expertise. In May 2001 the first- and second-named respondents purchased premises, which were leased to the company. While the third- and fourth-named respondents appeared to have knowledge of the purchase and the rent to be paid by the company, the lease did not appear to have been approved by the board. The company moved to the new premises in June 2001, at a time when it was facing significant business problems. At a board meeting in July 2001 the manner in which the first- and second-named respondents had financed the purchase of the premises came to light: they had obtained, on behalf of the company, a business development loan. The company then loaned this amount to the first- and second-named respondents, who used it to provide the balance of the purchase price for the premises. The first- and second-named respondents, having become aware of these transactions, raised an objection at the board meeting. The first- and second-named respondents indicated the loans were temporary and would be repaid within six months, following refinancing. In August 2001 the first- and second-named respondents—without seeking the approval of the board of directors—procured an increase of the rent payable to them by the company, which was still in difficult financial circumstances. In autumn 2001 the refinancing had not been obtained and the loan was not repaid to the company. In January 2002, following legal advice that the loans to the first- and second-named respondent were illegal, the company called in the loans. The first- and second-named respondents were unable to pay them. Shortly thereafter the company was wound up. The liquidator and the third- and fourth-named respondents took the view that the loans given by the company to the first- and second-named respondent contributed to the demise of the company.

With regard to the first- and second-named respondents, despite their intentions and previous record with the company, the court was satisfied that in entering into significant financial transactions between the company and themselves without obtaining approval from the board they did not act responsibly. They had failed to distinguish between the company and themselves, had failed to appreciate their obligations to the company, the other shareholders and creditors and had failed to comply with their statutory obligations, in particular the disclosure requirements of s.194 of the Companies Act 1963 and the prohibition of loans to directors under s.31 of the Companies Act 1990. Accordingly, a restriction order was granted against the first- and second-named respondents. The court was satisfied that the third- and fourth-named respondents had discharged the onus of satisfying the court that they had acted honestly and responsibly as directors of the company. In particular, when the matters came to light they took such steps as was necessary to procure the repayments of the loans and to ameliorate the perceived damage to the company. The application for a restriction order against the third- and fourth-named respondent was not granted.

De facto directors and undercapitalised companies   *Gray v McLoughlin, Re First Class Toy Traders Ltd*, High Court, Finlay Geoghegan J., July 9, 2004.

The official liquidator made an application for an order of restriction under s.150 of the Companies Act 1990 against the three respondents. The first two respondents were appointed and acted as directors of the company up until the date of commencement of the winding up. The third respondent, Mr Tuohy, was not formally appointed as director, but the liquidator submitted that he was a person who was a *de facto* director of the company within the 12 months prior to the commencement of the winding up. Section 2(1) of the Companies Act 1963 provides that a director includes any person occupying the position of director, by whatever name called. This definition therefore includes not only *de jure* directors but also *de facto* directors. All directors, whether *de facto* or *de jure,* are amenable to restriction under s.150. It was accepted by the liquidator that the onus was on him to establish that Mr Tuohy was a *de facto* director and further accepted that the court must decide the issue on the balance of probabilities. The court was referred to a number of authorities in Ireland and in England and Wales in relation to establishing whether or not a person is a *de facto* director. In *Re Lynrowan Enterprises* (Unreported, High Court, July 31, 2002) O'Neill J. followed the approach of Timothy Lloyd Q.C., sitting as deputy High Court judge, in *Re Richborough Furniture* [1996] 1 B.C.L.C. 507 and in so doing identified three circumstances in which a person may be considered a *de facto* director of a company:

(1) Where there is clear evidence that the person has been the sole person directing the affairs of the company; or

(2) that the person is directing the affairs of the company equally with others who also lack valid appointment; or

(3) that the person was acting on an equal or more influential basis with other validly appointed directors in directing the affairs of the company.

O'Neill J. also followed Timothy Lloyd Q.C.'s limitations on those three circumstances by stating that in the absence of clear evidence of any of the foregoing circumstances, and where there is evidence that the role of the person can be explained by the exercise of a role other than a director, then the person should not be amenable to a s.150 restriction order. Finlay Geoghegan J. noted that the test formulated by Timothy Lloyd Q.C. had since been subjected to further consideration, and some criticism, and next considered the approach taken by Jacob J. in *Secretary of State for Industry v Tjolle and others* [1998] B.C.C. 282, as expanded by Robert Walker L.J. in *Re Kaytech International plc, Potier v Secretary of State for Industry* [1999] B.C.C. 390 which he found to be more helpful. Essentially, in these decisions the crucial test was whether the individual had assumed the status and functions of a company director so as to make himself responsible as if he were a *de jure* director. Adopting this approach, Finlay Geoghegan J. considered that in deciding whether a person has assumed the functions of a director it was of assistance to recall what those duties were at common law. She endorsed the formulation of the duties of directors adopted by Jonathan Parker J. in *Re Barings plc (No.5) Secretary of State for Trade and Industry v Baker* [1991] B.C.L.C. 433 as follows:

> "Each individual director owes duties to the company to inform himself about its affairs and to join with his co-directors in supervising and controlling them."

On the basis of this formulation Finlay Geoghegan J. concluded that Mr Tuohy was, as a matter of probability, a *de facto* director for the following reasons: (1) The *de jure* directors considered him to have acted as a director; (2) Mr Tuohy accepted that he had agreed to the description of finance director for his position; (3) Mr Tuohy met regularly with the other directors at what have been categorised as board meetings; (4) Mr Tuohy was an authorised signatory for the purposes of company cheques; (5) Mr Tuohy appears to have had full information about the affairs of the company and he controlled the availability of financial information; (6) Mr Tuohy accepted that he had responsibility for the financial function of the company; and (7) Mr Tuohy's involvement in the control and supervision of the affairs of the company went beyond the financial function and he appears to have had a role in the negotiation of property matters and in dealings with the principal supplier. The court therefore concluded that Mr Tuohy had assumed the status and function of director and was a director of the company within the meaning of s.2(1) of the Companies Act 1963.

Having reached this conclusion the matter to be considered was whether the three respondents had satisfied the court as to their honesty and responsibility. There was no issue raised in relation to the directors' honesty. In relation to the responsibility of the directors, however, the liquidator did raise the matter as to whether the directors ought to have traded and incurred liabilities on behalf of the company, which was undercapitalised from the outset. Finlay Geoghegan J. referred to leading Irish cases dealing with the issue of irresponsibility. In *Re Squash Ireland Ltd* [2001] 2 I.R. 35 the Supreme Court held that the question to be decided as to the responsibility of a director must be judged by an objective standard and that commercial errors and misjudgments did not necessarily amount to irresponsible conduct. In *La Moselle Clothing Ltd v Soualhi* [1998] 2 I.L.R.M. 345 Shanley J. raised the "lack of commercial probity or want of proper standards" as one element of any test for establishing whether a director's conduct could be said to be irresponsible. Finlay Geoghegan J. concluded that trading with an undercapitalised company and incurring significant debts could raise questions about a lack of commercial probity, or want of proper standards. On the evidence submitted, however, Finlay Geoghegan J. was not satisfied that this was such a case. Accordingly, the application for restriction against all three directors was dismissed.

Executive and non-executive directors *Re Colm O'Neill Engineering Services Ltd (In Voluntary Liquidation)* Finlay Geoghegan J., February 13, 2004.

The liquidator applied under s.150 of the Companies Act 1990 for a declaration of restriction against the four respondents who were directors of the company in the 12 months prior to the commencement of the winding up. Mr Colm O'Neill was the founder and Managing Director of the company. He was diagnosed with cancer in 2000 and was undergoing treatment for the disease up until the case came for hearing. His son, Mr Ruairi O'Neill, had joined the board in 1999. Initially he was an executive director, but for some time prior to the commencement of the winding up he had been a non-executive director. There was a suggestion, however, that prior to the liquidation he had attempted to take over some of the burden from his father. Mr Oliver Reddy had joined the company in 1990 as a non-executive director. Dr Patrick Galvin had joined the company as a non-executive director in 1999 when an associated company, referred to as "Complete", was being established.

The liquidator raised a number of matters in relation to the responsibility of the directors. The first related to the possibility that the board had failed to obtain sufficient financial information from the executives of the company and as a result of this incompetency had in turn failed to recognise in due time the deterioration of the financial condition of the company. The second matter related to the establishment of an associated company, "Complete", by the directors in 1999 and the investment of monies by this company in "Complete" and the adequacy of the recording of financial transactions between this company and "Complete". Finally, for the purposes of the court considering whether there was any other just and equitable reason that the directors should be restricted, the liquidator alleged that there was non-effective co-operation in the course of the liquidation on the part of some of the directors. Finlay Geoghegan J. described the purpose of s.150 of the Companies Act 1990 as a provision designed to "protect the public against the future supervision and management of companies by persons whose past record as directors of insolvent companies have shown them to be a danger to creditors and others." She referred to leading Irish authorities (*La Moselle Clothing Ltd v Soualhi* [1998] 2 I.L.R.M. 345 and *Re Squash Ireland Ltd* [2001] 3 I.R. 35), which held that the responsibility that must be established by directors goes beyond simple compliance with the principal features of the Companies Acts. Directors who display a lack of commercial probity or want of proper standards may not be considered to have acted responsibly. However, the court did observe that bad commercial judgment does not in itself amount to a lack of responsibility and that the courts must be careful not to permit the conducting of "witch hunts" against directors and should not view matters with the "inevitable benefit of hindsight which arises in the course of the liquidation". It was suggested that the courts should instead look at the actions of the directors on the basis of a company being a going concern.

In relation to the first matter raised by the liquidator, the court was satisfied that the company had complied with its statutory obligation and that its books and records were reasonable. In regard to the lack of financial information and the incompetent manner in which the board dealt with financial information, the court accepted that no executive director was the financial controller of the company. In the final stages of the company's life the board had taken steps to strengthen the financial reporting by appointing an individual and, when dissatisfied with that individual, by appointing a Mr Scott as financial controller. On foot of this the court was satisfied that there was no incompetence and certainly no irresponsibility in respect of this matter.

In regard to the second matter, relating to the establishment of the associated company "Complete" and the irresponsible actions of the directors in diverting monies from the company to "Complete", the court was satisfied that the company's net investment in "Complete" was more than compensated for by loans given to and pension contributions left by some of the directors in the company. Any alleged inadequacy in respect of recording transactions between the company and "Complete" appeared to relate to back-up documentation and clarity of entries. As such matters rested with the financial controller of the company, who was not a director, the court concluded that it could not be said that the directors had been irresponsible in relation to that matter. Accordingly, Finlay Geoghegan J. was satisfied that the directors had discharged the onus placed on them of establishing that they had acted responsibly.

Finally, in regard to the matter raised by the liquidator as to the alleged lack of co-operation, the court held that each director had done what he could when asked, and that the board had even, at the expense of "Complete", retained the financial controller of the company to assist the liquidator. The court acknowledged that there was some fault on both the liquidator and one of the directors in relation to the provision of timely information, but it was not such that the blame could rest on the director. On this basis Finlay Geoghegan J. held that there was no additional matter that would, on a "just and equitable" basis, justify restriction. The application against all four directors was dismissed.

Duties of non-executive directors *Kavanagh v Delaney and Others, Re Tralee Beef and Lamb Ltd (In Liquidation)*, High Court, Finlay Geoghegan J., July 20, 2004; [2005] 1 I.L.R.M. 34.

The Official Liquidator brought an application for restriction against the four respondents, who were each directors of a cattle- and lamb-slaughtering company at the date of the commencement of the winding up. The first-named respondent, Mr John Delaney, was the sole executive director. The second-named respondent was Mr Delaney's wife, who only became a director at her husband's request. The third-named respondent, Mr Terry Dunne, was a non-executive director and Managing Director of the holding company of the Garvey group of companies. He took up the unremunerated position as non-executive director following the purchase by the company of a business previously owned by Garvey. As part of the purchase deal it was agreed that Mr Dunne would have no day-to-day dealings with the company, his role being instead to foster and maintain the business relationship of the company with the Garvey group and the Musgrave group. While he did fulfil this role for two years, he did not resign as director when the business relationship between the company, Garvey and Musgrave came to an end. The fourth-named respondent, Mr Simon Coyle, was a chartered accountant and insolvency practitioner. He was nominated to join the board as a non-executive director by a fund-manager for the Business Enterprise Scheme (BES), which had invested certain sums in the company.

Mr Coyle submitted that his remit was to receive and review financial information from the company executives and to attend certain board meetings, but he was not to have any active part in the control of the company.

Each of the non-executive directors stated that he or she relied on Mr Delaney to provide them with financial information in relation to the company. The evidence suggested that there were no board meetings, formal or informal, during the final two years of the company's trading. In 2000 the BSE crisis led to a number of difficulties for the company. In March 2001 Mr Delaney realised that the company was facing significant financial difficulties, and he attempted to find outside investors to save the company. In October the company's auditors informed him that the position was much worse than originally thought. Thereafter, and without consulting the third- or fourth-named respondent, Mr Delaney took steps to have a receiver appointed by Anglo Irish Bank in October 2001. Mr Coyle asserted that throughout 2000 and 2001 he had unsuccessfully attempted to seek financial information from Mr Delaney. He was informed by Mr Delaney in September 2001 that the company had traded at a loss of £200,000, where in fact the draft accounts showed a loss of over £1 million. Subsequent to the appointment of the receiver, Mr Coyle appears to have arranged that his nominee company would petition for the winding up of the company.

Finlay Geoghegan J. examined the purpose and scope of s.150, under which the liquidator has a statutory obligation to put before the court those matters he considers the court should take into account in determining whether the directors acted honestly and responsibly. The liquidator is also obliged to raise any other matters that might be relevant to a determination as to whether there is any other reason why it would be just and equitable for the court to grant a restriction order. While directors are obliged primarily to satisfy the court in relation to the matters raised by the liquidator, that in itself does not relieve them of the general onus established by s.150. Directors must also deal with any other matters raised in the course of the application, including, as in the present case, matters raised by their fellow directors.

Finlay Geoghegan J. cited, with approval, the matters set out by Shanley J. in *La Moselle Clothing Ltd v Soualhi* [1998] 2 I.L.R.M. 345 when the court is determining a s.150 application (as approved by the Supreme Court in *Re Squash (Ireland) Ltd* [2001] 3 I.R. 35). In regard to the first of these matters, namely the extent to which the director has complied with the Companies Acts, Finlay Geoghegan J. suggested that this matter required some amplification in relation to the present application. Reference was made to the common law duties owed by directors, which are based on fiduciary duties and the duty of skill and care. There was nothing in the previous decisions of the courts to suggest that these should be ignored in a s.150 application. The general formulation of the duty of a director set out by Jonathan Parker J. in *Re Barings plc. (No.5) Secretary of State for Trade and Industry v Baker* [1999] 1 B.C.L.C. 433 was cited with approval, namely that "Each individual director owes duties to the company to inform himself about its affairs and to join with his co-directors in supervising and controlling them." Reference was also made to the three propositions derived from earlier authorities by Jonathan Parker J. as follows:

"(i)   Directors had, both collectively and individually, a continuing duty to acquire and maintain a sufficient knowledge and understanding of the company's business to enable them properly to discharge their duties as directors.

(ii)   Whilst directors were entitled (subject to the articles of association of the company) to delegate particular functions to those below them in the management chain, and to trust their competence and integrity to a reasonable extent, the exercise of the power of delegation did not absolve a director from the duty to supervise the discharge of the delegated functions.

(iii) No rule of universal application can be formulated as to the duty referred to in (ii) above. The extent of the duty, and the question whether it has been discharged, depended on the facts of each particular case, including the director's role in the management of the company."

Finlay Geoghegan J. found these propositions helpful, but noted that they did not specifically address the potentially differing responsibilities of executive and non-executive directors. Finlay Geoghegan J. observed that it was a fact of commercial life that persons are appointed as non-executive directors to act alongside executive directors. It was further obeserved that common sense dictated that the duties and responsibilities of executive and non-executive directors may differ. A non-executive director may be invited to join the board to bring a range of skills and it is appropriate to consider the discharge of their duties in relation to their particular skills and their agreed role on the board. Nevertheless, she endorsed the formulation that all directors must take reasonable steps to place themselves in a position to guide and monitor the management of the company (*Re Barings plc* [1999] 1 B.C.L.C. 433 and *Daniels v Anderson* [1995] 16 A.C.S.R. 607). Applying this formulation to an objective standard, it was suggested that it would be difficult to establish that directors acted responsibly, within the meaning of s.150, if during a significant period they failed to inform themselves about the company's affairs, or failed to take steps to join with their co-directors in supervising and controlling the company's affairs.

The court was satisfied that there was no issue as to the honesty of directors, but the question remained as to the responsibility of the directors. In relation to Mr Delaney, as the sole executive director it was his responsibility to produce the relevant financial information and distribute it at board meetings. The financial information so produced was inadequate, and indeed Mr Delaney, while aware of the financial difficulties, was not made aware of the extent of same. Mr Delaney failed to inform his fellow directors of this situation, as he was obliged to do under his duty to exercise skill and diligence. Nor did he arrange to hold board meetings in order to allow the directors to seek collectively to discharge their duty of supervising and controlling the affairs of the company during this crucial period. Furthermore, Mr Delaney requested the appointment of a receiver by the lending bank without informing his fellow directors. On this basis Mr Delaney could not have been said to have acted responsibly in relation to the conduct of the affairs of the company.

In relation to Mrs Delaney it was clear that she brought no particular skills to bear to the company. Apart from signing off the accounts and attending the AGM there was little to suggest that she took any active role in the company. Despite this, she was aware of the financial difficulties and although she did advise her husband to seek outside assistance, she failed to inform her fellow directors of the situation, leaving it in the hands of her husband. Finlay Geoghegan J. made it clear that by agreeing to become a director of the company she undertook a separate and distinct role that imposed on her certain obligations, which she did not discharge in a responsible manner.

With regard to Mr Dunne, despite his non-executive role and his specific function in fostering a commercial relationship between the company and other specific businesses, when that role ended he remained a director. He was therefore under a duty to discharge the minimum obligation of informing himself about the company's affairs and joining with his co-directors in supervising and controlling such affairs. This duty was not adequately discharged, particularly during the period of financial difficulty. Even taking into account his earlier tenure with the company, the court was not satisfied, when looking at his entire tenure, that he had acted responsibly.

In relation to Mr Coyle, the liquidator was satisfied that he had acted honestly and responsibly. However, the Director of Corporate Enforcement did not relieve him of his obligation to bring the application, so presumably he did not agree with the liquidator. Accordingly, the onus remained on Mr Coyle to satisfy the court as to his honesty and responsibility, regardless of whether the liquidator did not raise any matters in relation to him. While the evidence showed that Mr Coyle had made some attempt to obtain information from Mr Delaney, there appeared to be no attempt at direct communication between Mr Coyle and Mr Delaney, or any other directors, during the period between January 2000 and September 2001 which was in fact a crucial time for the company. Despite his role as a "watching brief" for BES investors, Mr Coyle remained obliged to discharge the minimum duty of a non-executive director, namely to inform himself about the company's affairs and to join with his co-directors in supervising and controlling those affairs. Finlay Geoghegan J. held that this onus had not been discharged. Furthermore, his entire tenure, described as one of "total inactivity", was not a mitigating factor.

On the basis of the above Finlay Geoghegan J. made a restriction order against all four directors, noting that the court was confined to looking at the conduct of the directors in respect of the company in liquidation and could not take into account the conduct of the directors in relation to any other companies.

See also *Kavanagh v Riedler and Others, Re RMF (Ireland) Ltd,* High Court, Finlay Geoghegan J., May 27, 2004.

Abdication by directors of their duties to other group companies *O'Ferral v Coughlan and Others, Re 360atlantic (Ireland) Ltd (In receivership and in Liquidation),* High Court, Finlay Geoghegan J., December 21, 2004.

The liquidator applied for an order of restriction under s.150 of the Companies Act 1990 against the four respondent directors of the company. The company was part of a worldwide group that was in the business of designing and constructing fibre-optic cable networks. A global downturn in the telecommunications industry had ultimately led to the collapse of the group. The Irish company was then placed in receivership and also in liquidation. Only one of the directors was resident in Ireland. Finlay Geoghegan referred to *Re Euroking Miracle (Ireland) Ltd,* unreported), High Court, June 5, 2003, where it was held that s.150 applies to persons resident outside the jurisdiction. While it was incumbent that such persons, insofar as practicable, be given notice of an application in respect of them, the court was satisfied that as a matter of probability each of the directors had been given notice of the application. Finlay Geoghegan J. reviewed s.150 and the applicable authorities (*La Moselle Clothing Ltd v Soualhi* [1998] 2 I.L.R.M. 345, *Re Squash (Ireland) Ltd* [2001] 3 I.R. 35 and *Re Tralee Beef and Lamb Ltd,* unreported), High Court, Finlay Geoghegan J., July 20, 2004). Reference was then made to the issue raised by the liquidator as to whether the directors had satisfied the courts that they had discharged the minimum duties as directors of the company and, in particular, whether they had informed themselves about the financial affairs of the company and whether they had joined with their co-directors in supervising and controlling the affairs of the company. In respect of these matters the court made the following factual conclusions:

(1) the operations of the company were financed as part of worldwide operations;

(2) the company was formed only by reason of professional advice relating to the worldwide operations of the overall group;

(3) the company was part of a closely intertwined group of companies and not in a position to operate independently;

(4) the financing of the Irish company was determined in Barbados as part of group operations, and while the Irish resident director was given financial information it was in a consolidated form and did not identify the financial position of the company;

(5)   the minutes of the board meetings indicated that they related to regulatory matters and there was no substantive matters (other than approval of the annual accounts) dealt with at these board meetings;

(6)   the accounts presented for approval in June 2001 appear to have been inaccurate; and

(7)   one of the non-resident directors acknowledged that he did not give the requisite attention to reviewing and appreciating the affairs of the company.

On the basis of the above conclusions an issue was raised as to whether and to what extent the court should have regard to the fact that the company was a wholly owned subsidiary when considering whether the respondents had acted responsibly. In this regard the court held that being a wholly owned subsidiary does not alter the applicable legal principles. The company had a separate corporate and legal identity, with separate employees and separate creditors. Each respondent agreed to act as a director of that corporate entity. Despite their obligation to follow the policies of the entire group, the directors cannot abdicate all their responsibilities. They must be considered to remain under a duty to inform themselves about the affairs of the company, as distinct from any other part of the group, and to join with each other in supervising and controlling the affairs of the company. If this were not the case, their position would be meaningless. While the court acknowledged that their margin of discretion may have been small in terms of business decisions, this did not absolve them from their obligation to take decisions. On this basis, and given the fact that a complete abrogation of responsibility for the financial affairs of the company took place and the fact that proper books of accounts were not maintained, the court concluded that an order of restriction be made against all four respondents.

See also *O'Ferral v Coughlan, Re 360Networks (Ireland) Ltd (In Receivership and in Liquidation)*, High Court, Finlay Geoghegan J., December 21, 2004.

LEGISLATION

The Companies (Amendment) Act 1982 (s.13(2)) Order 2004 (S.I. No.506 of 2004) allows limited partnerships registered under the Limited Partnerships Act 1907 to have up to 50 partners where the partnership is formed for the purpose of, and whose main business consists of, the provision of investment and loan finance and ancillary services to persons engaged in industrial or commercial activities.

The Companies (Forms) Order 2004 (S.I. No.133 of 2004) introduces a new Form B1 that must be completed when furnishing a company's annual return to the Registrar of Companies.

The Companies (Auditing and Accounting) Act 2003 (Commencement) Order 2004 (S.I. No.132 of 2004) sets out the commencement dates for some of the provisions of the Act. April 6 is appointed as the day on which the following provisions of the Act come into operation: (a) Pt 1; (b) ss.52, 53(a), (c), (d) and (e), 54, 55, 56 and 57; (c) Sch.2 (other than the amendments at item 1 to ss.115(6) and 128(4) of the Companies Act 1963 and the amendments at item 9 of the Companies Act 1990). July 1 is appointed as the day on which s.53(b) of the Act comes into operation in relation to a company as respects any financial year of the company beginning on or after that day. May 17 is appointed as the day on which the following provisions of the Act come into operation: (a) s.46; (b) s.47 in so far as it substitutes for s.128(6) of the Companies Act 1963—(i) subss.(6) and (6A), (ii) subs.(613) other than para.(b) of that subsection, and (iii) subs.(6)(C).

European Communities (Companies) Regulations 2004 (S.I. No.839 of 2004), replaces the requirement to have certain particulars published in *Iris Oifigiúil* in relation to companies with the requirement to publish in the Companies Registration Office Gazette, which is to be kept solely in electronic form.

Conflicts of Law

ARBITRATION

Public Policy   In *Brostrom Tankers AB v Factorias Vulcano SA*, unreported, High Court, May 19, 2004, Kelly J. had to determine the scope of the public policy basis for non-enforcement of an arbitral award under s.9 of the Arbitration Act 1980. Section 9 is contained in Pt 3 of the Act, which deals with New York Convention awards. Section 9(1) makes it clear that enforcement of an award is not to be refused otherwise than pursuant to subs.(2) (which had no relevance to the instant case) or subs.(3), which provides that enforcement may be refused when, *inter alia*, it would be contrary to public policy to enforce the awards.

The case concerned a contract governed by Norwegian law, containing an arbitration clause whereby all disputes were to be resolved by arbitration in Oslo in accordance with Norwegian law. The plaintiff was a Swedish ship-owner; the defendant a Spanish ship manufacturer. The contract was for the construction and supply of a chemical tanker. A dispute arose which culminated in an award, the enforcement of which was sought in Ireland under s.7 of the 1980 Act. (Ireland was relevant because it appeared that there might be an intercompany debt owed to the defendant by an Irish company which could be garnished.)

The defendant invoked s.8, arguing that it had obtained a form of court protection in Spain under which it was liable to pay its creditors only 10 per cent of the debts due to them and that the Irish court as a matter of public policy ought not to enable the plaintiff to get around the Spanish court's radical reduction of its liability. The plaintiff contested the defendant's claim that the Spanish order affected the defendants' contractual liability to the plaintiff. Kelly J. resolved the matter of the public policy defence without deciding these "vexed questions", since, even on the assumption that the Spanish order captured the defendant's contractual liability to the plaintiff, it did not in his view constitute a reason for the Irish court's refusing to enforce the arbitral award under s.9(3).

Kelly J. was satisfied that the public policy referred to in s.9(3) was "[that] of this State". This was clear from the wording of Art.5(2)(b) of the New York Convention which provides that recognition and enforcement of an arbitral award may be refused if the competent authority in the country where recognition and enforcement is sought finds that recognition or enforcement of the award "would be contrary to the public policy of *that country*" (emphasis added).

Kelly J. stated:

> "Counsel for the defendant was unable to produce a single authority from here or anywhere else in the common law world supportive of her contention that public policy requires that I refuse enforcement in this country because to order enforcement would confer a commercial advantage on the plaintiff which it might not get under Spanish law, or that the comity of courts would be imperilled by an enforcement order being made.
>
> I am quite satisfied that a refusal of an enforcement order on grounds of public policy would not be justified in this case. To do so would extend to a very considerable extent the notion of public policy as it has come to be recognised in the context of the enforcement of an arbitral award. The case law and the textbook writers make it clear that the public policy defence to an enforcement application is one which is of a narrow scope. It extends only to a breach of the most basic notions of morality and justice...
>
> I am satisfied that a broad interpretation such as is contended for by the defendant would defeat the Convention's purpose of permitting parties to international transactions to promote neutral dispute resolution.
> ..."

Kelly J. was of the opinion that he would be justified in refusing enforcement only if there was (as is stated in Cheshire and North's *Private International Law* (13th ed.)):

> "[s]ome element of illegality, or ... the enforcement of the award would be clearly injurious to the public good, or possibly [if] enforcement would be wholly offensive to the ordinary responsible and fully informed member of the public."

The instant case came "nowhere near that position". There was no illegality or even suggestion of illegality, nor had any of the other elements been even remotely demonstrated.

Kelly J.'s approach is in line with that adopted in other countries: see Peter Turner & Jan Paulsson, "Grounds for Refusal of Recognition and Enforcement under the New York Convention: A Comparative Approach" (OECD Experts Group Meeting on Dispute Resolution and Corporate Governance, UNCITRAL Secretariat, Vienna, June 25, 2003).

COMPANY

Insolvency In *Re Eurofood IFSC Ltd*, unreported, High Court, March 23, 2004, Kelly J. had to determine a series of crucial issues relating to the Insolvency Regulation (Council Regulation (EC) 1346/2000). His resolution of these issues was not the last word: the case was appealed to the Supreme Court which, on July 27, 2004 referred a series of questions to the Court of Justice. The opinion of Advocate General Jacobs, delivered on September 27, 2005, was largely in harmony with Kelly J.'s approach. We await the judgment of the Court of Justice and will analyse it in detail when it is handed down. Here we examine Kelly J.'s judgment.

Eurofood IFSC Ltd was an Irish company. It was a wholly owned subsidiary of Parmalat SpA, a major global food company incorporated in Italy. Eurofood's principal business activity was that of providing financial facilities for companies in the Parmalat Group.

Eurofood operated pursuant to a certificate issued by the Irish Minister for Finance pursuant to s.39(b)(2) of the Finance Act 1980, granted subject to a number of conditions relating to transparency. Its day-to-day administration was conducted on its behalf by the Bank of America in accordance with the terms of an administration agreement which was governed by Irish law and which contained an Irish jurisdiction clause.

Eurofood's annual accounts were prepared and audited in accordance with Irish law and accounting principles. Its books of account were maintained in Dublin. Its auditors and solicitors were Irish. It paid corporation tax in Ireland on its trading operations.

Until November 2003 it had four directors, two of whom were Irish and two Italian. In November 2003 one of the Italian directors resigned. The second resigned in January 2004. Fourteen of the 15 board meetings were held in Dublin. At all board meetings two Irish directors or their nominees were present at all times. Virtually all of Eurofood's assets were represented by debts due by Parmalat companies or were guaranteed by the ultimate Parmalat parent. Parmalat SpA was part of a group of companies which had operations in over 30 countries throughout the world with in excess of 30,000 employees. The group had a turnover in excess of €7.5 billion for the year ending December 2002. The group went into a deep financial crisis which led to the insolvency of many of its key companies, the making of allegations of fraud on a large scale and the arrest in Italy of a number of persons associated with it. On December 23, 2003 the Italian parliament passed into law Decree No.347 which permits extraordinary administration of companies. On Christmas Eve 2003, Parmalat SpA was admitted to extraordinary administration proceedings. One Signor Enrico Bondi was appointed the extraordinary administrator.

Bank of America NA presented a petition to the Irish High Court for the winding up of Eurofood on January 27, 2004 alleging a debt due to it in excess of US$3.5 million. A provisional legislator was appointed that day.

Following his appointment the provisional liquidator took steps to preserve the assets of the company insofar as that was possible. He met with representatives of Bank of America in its capacity as administrator of the company. He notified the creditors of his appointment. On January 30, 2004 he notified Signor Bondi of the fact that he had been appointed provisional liquidator of Eurofood.

On February 9, 2004 Signor Bondi was appointed extraordinary administrator of Eurofood by the Italian Ministry for Productive Activities. This appointment was made notwithstanding knowledge on the part of Signor Bondi that the Irish court had appointed a provisional liquidator to Eurofood almost two weeks beforehand.

On February 10, 2004 the provisional liquidator received a fax from Signor Bondi giving notice that he was appointing three Italians as directors of Eurofood with immediate effect and was also removing an Irish director from her directorship. No consent was sought or obtained from the Irish Department of Finance in respect of this purported change of directors.

Late on the afternoon of Friday, February 13, 2004, the provisional liquidator was personally served by the Irish solicitors acting for Signor Bondi with a short form notice of a hearing which was to take place before the Parma court the following Tuesday. The notice made it clear that the Parma court was going to hear an application concerning Eurofood with a view to declaring the insolvency of that company.

Despite the direction of the Parma court neither the Bank of America nor the note holders were given notice of the Parma court hearing of February 17, 2004.

Although the provisional liquidator had only received a bare notice of the proposed hearing in Parma and did not have sight of the petition which had been presented to that court, he thought it likely that the application to be heard there was with the view to admitting the company into insolvency proceedings before the Parma court. He took the view that the Irish court had already opened main insolvency proceedings and it was only open to the Parma court to open secondary proceedings. However, the notice which he had received suggested to him that the Parma court might not appear to regard itself as so restricted. He therefore made an application to the Irish court on February 16, 2004 and was given leave by Lavan J. to appear at and participate in the hearing before the Parma court for the purpose of putting before that court such arguments and evidence in relation to the affairs of the company, the issue of jurisdiction and in particular the location of Eurofood's centre of main interests, as the provisional liquidator might consider appropriate.

As of February 17, 2004 Signor Bondi had not furnished a copy of the petition which grounded his application before the Parma court to the provisional liquidator. This was so despite repeated written and verbal requests from the provisional liquidator's Italian lawyers. The provisional liquidator appeared, together with his Italian lawyer, at the hearing in Parma on February

17, 2004. Three Italian judges conducted an oral hearing which lasted for about an hour.

In addition to seeking to defend the substance of the case, which sought to have Eurofood brought into extraordinary administration and a determination that the company's centre of main interests was in Italy, the provisional liquidator's Italian lawyer sought an adjournment of the hearing on the basis that Signor Bondi's petition had not yet been received. The Parma court refused an adjournment but granted both parties permission to file further briefs by February 19, 2004. This second defence brief did, however, have to be furnished to Signor Bondi's lawyers by February 18, 2004. This was done and a counter-brief was filed by Signor Bondi's lawyers on February 19, 2004.

The Parma court reached its decision on February 20, 2004. It declared the company to be insolvent and found that the centre of its main interests was in Italy.

Neither the petitioning creditor nor the note holders had been given notice of the hearing despite the order of the Parma court.

The petitioning creditor and note holders sought to challenge the validity of the orders of the Italian court. They argued that the centre of main interests of Eurofood had always been in Ireland and that the appointment of the provisional liquidator on January 27 had constituted the opening of main insolvency proceedings. If that was not so, they contended that, by virtue of the relation back concept contained in s.220(2) of the Companies Act 1963, the making of the winding up order of Eurofood would have effect retrospectively to the date of the presentation of the petition and that accordingly the Irish winding up order would antedate the Italian insolvency proceedings. They argued that, by virtue of Art.16(1) of the Insolvency Regulation, recognition should not be afforded to the orders of the Italian court and that the breach of the principles of natural justice which excluded the creditors involved from being heard meant that these orders should not be recognised on public policy grounds.

Kelly J. first had to determine whether main insolvency proceedings had been opened in Ireland. He concluded that they had. The definition of "judgment" in Art.2 of the Regulation, in relation to the opening of insolvency proceedings or the appointment of a liquidator, included the decision of any court empowered to open such proceedings or to appoint a liquidator. The definition of "liquidator" in Art.2(6) and Annex C with reference to Ireland included a provisional liquidator. Thus, it was "beyond argument" that a decision of the Irish High Court appointing a provisional liquidator was a judgment in relation to the opening of insolvency proceedings within the meaning of Art.3(1).

Furthermore, "the time of the opening of proceedings" was expressly defined in Art.2(f) as "the time at which the judgment opening proceedings becomes effective, whether it is a final judgment or not". The order appointing the provisional liquidator became effective on the day upon which it was made.

That date therefore was the time of the opening of insolvency proceedings within the meaning of the Regulation. Clearly an order appointing a provisional liquidator was not a final judgment, but that did not matter having regard to the definition contained in Art.2(f) of the Regulation.

Kelly J. went on to observe:

> "The argument which is advanced on behalf of Signor Bondi to the effect that the definition of the 'time of opening of proceedings' in Article 2 is when the final winding up order is actually made is completely inconsistent with the definition in Article 2 (f). Indeed, even if there had never been a provisional liquidator appointed it is clear that under Irish insolvency law and in particular s. 220 (2) of the Companies Act 1963, an order appointing an official liquidator becomes effective as of the date of presentation of the petition which in this case was the 27th January, 2004 even though an order directing the winding up of the company post dates the date of presentation of the petition. This provision of Irish insolvency law mirrors a similar provision in the law of England and Wales. Such a provision may appear peculiar in other jurisdictions but it has long been a part of the law of this State and its nearest neighbour and was known to the drafters of the Regulation."

Kelly J. went on to consider whether the centre of the main interests of Eurofood was situated in Ireland so as to confer jurisdiction on the Irish court to open main insolvency proceedings.

The starting point was the presumption that the centre of main interests was the place of the registered office of the company in the absence of proof to the contrary. The registered office of Eurofood was Ireland. Recital 13 to the Directive provided that the centre of main interests should correspond to the place where the debtor conducted the administration of its interests on a regular basis and was therefore ascertainable by third parties. Moss, Fletcher and Issacs in *EC Regulation on Insolvency Proceedings* (2002) had commented that this recital indicated that the centre of main interests was:

> "intended to provide a test in which the attributes of transparency and objective ascertainability are dominant factors. This should enable parties who have dealings with the debtor to found their expectations on the reasonable conclusions to be drawn from systematic conduct and arrangements for which the debtor is responsible. In principle therefore it ought not to be possible for a debtor to gain advantages, at creditors' expense, from having resorted to evasive or confusing techniques of organising its business or personal affairs, in a way calculated to conceal the true location from which interests are systematically administered."

The clear perception of the Eurofood creditors had been that they were dealing with investments issued by a company that was located in Ireland and was subject to Irish fiscal and regulatory provisions. There was "no evidence whatsoever" that they had considered the company was run out of Italy. The whole basis for the making of the order of January 27, 2004 was that the court was satisfied that the centre of main interests was in Ireland. The whole thrust of the application and the object of it was to prevent a perceived attempt on the part of Signor Bondi to take steps to remove the centre of main interests from Ireland.

Since the appointment of the provisional liquidator constituted the opening of the main proceedings, the jurisdiction for that judgment was founded on Art.3 of the Regulation; the judgment had to be recognised in all the other Member States from the time that it became effective, on January 27, 2004.

That position was further underscored by the provisions of recital 22 of the Regulation to the effect that the decision of the first court to open proceedings should be recognised in the other Member States without those Member States having the power to scrutinise the court's decision. The fact that the Italian court had purported to do so contrary to recital 22 and Art.16 could not alter the fact that main insolvency proceedings were already extant.

It followed that Kelly J. did not have to consider the merits of the Italian court's decision since it lacked jurisdiction under the Regulation to do what it had purported to do.

Kelly J. gave a very clear analysis of the Irish court's obligations relative to the Regulation and to the Italian court's judgment regarding the Regulation:

> "Signor Bondi's argument boils down to a contention that because the Parma court has purported to determine the issue its order is binding on this court. But that cannot be so in circumstances where there is a presumption under the Regulation that the centre of the main interests lay in Ireland, that the objective evidence establishes that fact, that the Irish court in appointing the provisional liquidator must have so concluded having regard to the evidence placed before it and its order antedated that of the Parma court. The Parma court was obliged pursuant to Article 16 to recognise that. The Regulation does not require an express determination by a court that the centre of main interests lies in the jurisdiction of that court. Article 3 (1) merely lays down the rule of jurisdiction. If the centre of main interests lies as a fact in a given jurisdiction then insolvency proceedings opened in that jurisdiction are the main insolvency proceedings if they otherwise comply with the terms of the Regulation. Such being the case it is not open to this court to cede jurisdiction to the Parma court."

Kelly J. also considered that the Italian decision should not be recognised by virtue of Art.26 of the Regulation, which permits any Member State to refuse to recognise insolvency proceedings opened in another state or to enforce a judgment handed down in the context of such proceedings where the effects of such recognition or enforcement would be manifestly contrary to the state's public policy and in particular its fundamental principles or the constitutional rights and liberties of the individual.

General principles of European Union law, whose observance was ensured by the European Court of Justice (ECJ), included respect for fundamental rights. In this regard the European Convention on Human Rights had particular significance. These general principles included the right to a fair hearing. This had been elaborated on by the ECJ in *Transocean Marine Paint Association v Commission* [1974] E.C.R. 1063.

In the instant case it was clear that the creditors of the company had not been heard on the application despite the fact that the Italian court apparently had directed that all interested parties ought to be. Nor had the note holders been given the opportunity to put evidence to the Parma court.

Moreover, the provisional liquidator, although notified of the Italian proceedings, had received notification after close of business on a Friday that the proceedings would take place at midday the following Tuesday; he had not been furnished with the petition or the other papers grounding the application until after the hearing before the Italian court had actually concluded. This lack of due process appeared to Kelly J., quite apart from the other considerations, to warrant the court's refusing to give recognition to the decision of the Italian court.

Kelly J. was satisfied that on the evidence before him Eurofood was grossly insolvent and that creditors were entitled to have it wound up in accordance with the legislation in force in Ireland. They were not required to participate in a procedure under Italian law which manifestly was not a winding up but a form of re-organisation. Accordingly Kelly J. made an order for the winding up of the company which, pursuant to s.220(2) of the Companies Act 1963, related back to the date of presentation of the petition: January 27, 2004.

On appeal by Signor Bondi to the Supreme Court, the Supreme Court in two separate judgments, delivered on July 27, 2004, affirmed Kelly J.'s holding that recognition should be denied to the Italian orders as offending Irish public policy under Art.26 of the Regulation and referred the following questions to the Court of Justice for its preliminary rulings ([2005] 1 I.L.R.M. 161):

> "1. Where a petition is presented to a court of competent jurisdiction in Ireland for the winding up of an insolvent company and that court makes an order, pending the making of an order for winding up, appointing a provisional liquidator with powers to take possession of the assets of the company, manage its affairs, open a bank account and appoint a solicitor all with the effect in law of depriving the directors of the company of power to act, does that order combined with the presentation of the petition constitute a

judgment opening of insolvency proceedings for the purposes of Article 16, interpreted in the light of Articles 1 and 2, of Council Regulation (EC) No 1346 of 2000?

2. If the answer to Question 1 is in the negative, does the presentation, in Ireland, of a petition to the High Court for the compulsory winding up of a company by the court constitute the opening of insolvency proceedings for the purposes of that Regulation by virtue of the Irish legal provision (section 220(2) of the Companies Act, 1963) deeming the winding up of the company to commence at the date of the presentation of the petition?

3. Does Article 3 of the said Regulation, in combination with Article 16, have the effect that a court in a Member State other than that in which the registered office of the company is situated and other than where the company conducts the administration of its interests on a regular basis in a manner ascertainable by third parties, but where insolvency proceedings are first opened, have jurisdiction to open main insolvency proceedings?

4. Where,
   (a) the registered offices of a parent company and its subsidiary are in two different Member States,
   (b) the subsidiary conducts the administration of its interests on a regular basis in a manner ascertainable by third parties and in complete and regular respect for its own corporate identity in the member state where its registered office is situated and
   (c) the parent company is in a position, by virtue of its shareholding and power to appoint directors, to control and does in fact control the policy of the subsidiary,
   in determining the 'centre of main interests', are the governing factors those referred to at (b) above or on the other hand those referred to at (c) above?

5. Where it is manifestly contrary to the public policy of a Member State to permit a judicial or administrative decision to have legal effect in relation to persons or bodies whose right to fair procedures and a fair hearing has not been respected in reaching such a decision, is that Member State bound, by virtue of Article 17 of the said Regulation, to give recognition to a decision of the courts of another Member State purporting to open insolvency proceedings in respect of a company, in a situation where the court of the first Member State is satisfied that the decision in question has been made in disregard of those principles and, in particular, where the applicant in the second Member State has refused, in spite of requests and contrary to the order of the court of the second Member State, to

> provide the provisional liquidator of the company, duly appointed
> in accordance with the law of the first Member State, with any
> copy of the essential papers grounding the application?"

On September 27, 2005, the Advocate General Jacobs produced his opinion,
which was largely an endorsement of the approach taken by Kelly J. He
answered the first question in the affirmative. Such an answer seemed to him
consistent with both the aim and language of the Regulation. In the light of the
affirmative answer to the first question, it was not necessary to answer the
second; nevertheless Advocate General Jacobs considered that it could be dealt
with briefly, again with an affirmative answer. He stated:

> "Article 16(1) of the Regulation, which concerns the recognition of
> judgments opening insolvency proceedings, requires recognition from
> the time a judgment 'becomes effective in the State of the opening of
> proceedings'. Thus it is national law which determines when the
> judgment becomes effective. That is consistent with Article 4 which
> provides that in general the law of the State where the proceedings are
> opened is the law 'applicable to insolvency proceedings and their effects'
> including the opening, conduct and closure of those proceedings. Recital
> 23 makes it clear that that law includes procedural as well as substantive
> rules. I accordingly cannot accept Dr Bondi's assertion that the
> Regulation in some way 'overrides' domestic law provisions. It must
> also be borne in mind that the Regulation was not intended to be a
> harmonisation measure.
>
> Section 220(2) of the Irish Companies Act, 1963, provides that in
> the case of a compulsory winding up by the court (such as the
> proceedings at issue in the present case), the winding up 'shall be
> deemed to commence at the time of the presentation of the petition for
> the winding up'.
>
> The terms of that provision, applicable by virtue of the Regulation,
> seem to me conclusively to resolve the national court's second question.
>
> It might be added that, as the Certificate/Note Holders point out,
> the Virgós-Schmit Report explicitly recognises the existence of national
> 'relation back' doctrines, stating that the law of the State of opening of
> insolvency proceedings 'determines the conditions to be met, the manner
> in which the nullity and voidability function (automatically, by allocating
> retrospective effects to the proceedings or pursuant to an action taken
> by the liquidator, etc) and the legal consequences of nullity and
> voidability'."

We may here interpose a cautionary observation. The strategy of "relation
back" involves a reconstruction of factual reality in that what happens in the
future can retrospectively affect the present. The Insolvency Regulation,

however, is concerned with actual reality, not deemed reality. There is much to be said for the application of a stern scrutiny on any national law which results in queue-jumping by courts.

Advocate General Jacobs interpreted the third question as being "essentially" whether, in a situation where the courts of two Member States assert jurisdiction over the insolvency of a company, the court in one of those Member States may review the jurisdiction of the court in the other Member State.

The petitioning creditor, note holders and the Irish government had taken the position that foreign insolvency proceedings had to be recognised only if the foreign court objectively had jurisdiction. They submitted that the obligation on the courts of other Member States to recognise a judgment opening insolvency proceedings in a given Member State pursuant to Art.16(1) applied only if the Member State in which the insolvency proceedings were opened "ha[d] jurisdiction pursuant to Article 3", and therefore only if the centre of the debtor's main interests was situated in that Member State. The courts of only one Member State had jurisdiction to open main insolvency proceedings and those were the courts of the Member State within whose territory the centre of a debtor's main interests was situated; it was quite clear from the Regulation that a company could have only one centre of main interests. The test as to where the centre of a debtor's main interests is situated was an objective one. A court of a Member State might not open main insolvency proceedings in respect of a corporate debtor where neither its registered office nor the place where it conducted the administration of its assets on a regular basis in a manner ascertainable by third parties was in that Member State. Thus, any court faced with the possibility that insolvency proceedings had been opened in another jurisdiction had to ascertain whether the other court actually had jurisdiction pursuant to Art.3 and more particularly whether (a) the court claiming to have determined the locus of the centre of main interests applied the correct legal criteria and (b) the factual evidence was capable of supporting such a conclusion. Although recital 22 in the preamble to the Regulation required that "the decision of the first court to open proceedings should be recognised", it was notable that that requirement was not reflected in the main text of the Regulation.

Advocate General Jacobs did not agree. He referred to the principle of mutual trust which underlay the Regulation, made explicit in recital 22 of the preamble. That recital stated:

> "Recognition of judgments delivered by the courts of the Member States should be based on the principle of mutual trust. To that end, grounds for non-recognition should be reduced to the minimum necessary. This is also the basis on which any dispute should be resolved where the courts of two Member States both claim competence to open the main insolvency proceedings. The decision of the first court to open

proceedings should be recognised in the other Member States without those Member States having the power to scrutinise the court's decision."

Advocate General Jacobs acknowledged that the text of the Regulation did not include a provision to the same effect as recital 22. The importance of the principle articulated in that recital was, however, confirmed by the Virgós-Schmit Report, which stated that the "courts of the requested State may not review the jurisdiction of the court of the State of origin, but only verify that the judgment emanates from a court of a Contracting State which claims jurisdiction under Article 3." Numerous commentators had accepted this. The proper remedy for any party to insolvency proceedings who was concerned that the court opening the main proceedings had wrongly assumed jurisdiction under Art.3 should be sought in the domestic legal order of the Member State where that court was situated, with the possibility of a reference to the Court of Justice if appropriate.

Advocate General Jacobs accordingly concluded in purported answer to the third question that, where insolvency proceedings are first opened by a court in the Member State in which a company's registered office is situated and in which the company conducts the administration of its interests on a regular basis in a manner ascertainable by third parties, the courts of the other Member States do not have jurisdiction to open main insolvency proceedings. With respect, this is an answer to a question quite different from that asked by the Irish Supreme Court. The actual question addressed the situation of a court in a Member State *other than* that in which the registered office of the company is situated and *other than* where it conducts the administration of its interests on a regular basis in a manner ascertainable by third parties. Moreover, it addressed the situation in respect of those courts where insolvency proceedings are first opened. The question related to jurisdictional competence assessed objectively; it did not address the matter of the entitlement of courts other than those professedly opening the main proceedings to assess whether jurisdiction under the Regulation existed for their opening.

Turning to the fourth question, Advocate General Jacobs considered that the fact of the parent company's control was not sufficient to rebut the presumption in Art.3(1) of the Regulation that the centre of main interests of a subsidiary company was situated in the Member State where its registered office is to be found. That conclusion seemed to him to follow from the scheme and wording of the Regulation.

The Advocate General was of the view that, where the registered offices of a parent company and its subsidiary were in two different Member States, the fact that the subsidiary conducted the administration of its interests on a regular basis in a manner ascertainable by third parties and in complete and regular respect for its own corporate identity in the Member State where its registered office was situated would "normally be decisive" in determining the centre of its main interests:

> "It is clear that nothing can necessarily be inferred from the fact that a debtor company is a subsidiary of another company. The Regulation applies to individual companies and not to groups of companies; in particular it does not regulate the relationship of parent and subsidiary. Under the scheme of the Regulation, jurisdiction exists for each debtor with a separate legal entity. Both subsidiary and parent company have separate legal identities. It follows therefore that each subsidiary within a group must be considered individually."

The Advocate General went on to counsel that it was not the case that the purely formal criterion of the locus of a subsidiary company's registered office would necessarily determine the Member State whose courts had jurisdiction over any insolvency. An inherent aspect of the "centre of main interests" concept was to ensure that functional realities were capable of displacing purely formal criteria. Any party seeking to rebut the presumption that insolvency jurisdiction followed the registered office had, however, to demonstrate that the elements relied on satisfied the requirements of transparency and ascertainability.

Advocate General Jacobs accordingly concluded that, where the debtor is a subsidiary company and where its registered office and that of its parent company are in two different Member States and the subsidiary conducts the administration of its interests on a regular basis in a manner ascertainable by third parties and in complete and regular respect for its own corporate identity in the Member State in which its registered office is situated, the presumption that the centre of the subsidiary's main interests is in the Member State of its registered office is not rebutted merely because the parent company is in a position, by virtue of its shareholding and power, to appoint directors, to control, and does in fact control, the policy of the subsidiary.

In view of his answer to the first question referred by the Supreme Court, the Advocate General did not have to answer the fifth question. He made it clear, however, that he considered that the judgment of the Court of Justice in *Krombach v Bamberski* Case C–7/98 [2000] E.C.R. I–1935, while acknowledging the need to review the limits within which the courts of a Contracting State might have recourse to the concept of public policy, nonetheless had given weight to the general principle of community law that everyone was entitled to fair legal process, inspired by the fundamental rights which formed an integral part of the general principles of law whose observance the court ensured and which were enshrined in the European Convention on Human Rights.

Jurisdiction An interesting question of characterisation arose in *Volker Spielberg v Rowley*, unreported, High Court, November 26, 2004. Proceedings had been initiated in England by a company—Charley Acquisitions Limited—

which had originally been domiciled in Ireland but which had purportedly been changed to that of the Island of Nevis in the Caribbean. Volker Spielberg took proceedings in Ireland against a number of defendants; the third defendant, resident in England, contested the asserted jurisdictional base for the proceedings against him, which was Art.22(2) of Council Regulation (EC) 44/2001 of December 22, 2000 on jurisdiction and the recognition and enforcement of judgments in civil and commercial matters (Brussels I). Article 22(2) confers exclusive jurisdiction, regardless of domicile,

> "in proceedings which have as their object the validity of the constitution, the nullity or the dissolution of companies or other legal persons or associations of natural or legal persons, or of the validity of the decisions of their organs, [on] the courts of the Member State in which the company, legal person or association has its seat. In order to determine that seat, the court shall apply its rules private international law."

The essential question at issue was the scope of Art.22(2). In order for proceedings to "have as their object" the matters specified in Art.22(2), must these matters be their principal subject matter (as stated by Layton and Mercer, *European Civil Practice* (2nd ed., 2004), p.625) or can they be less central, if not collateral? Finlay Geoghegan J. favoured the former interpretation. In order to determine what was the principal subject matter of the proceedings, she considered that the court should primarily look at the statement of claim and other pleadings, but that it might also have regard to the facts set out in the affidavits sworn in the application.

Applying these principles, Finlay Geoghegan J. concluded that the plaintiff had failed to discharge the onus of unequivocally establishing that the object in the sense of the principal subject matter of these proceedings was the validity of a decision of an organ of Charly Acquisitions in either its Irish or Island of Nevis manifestations.

Counsel for the plaintiff had identified the subject matter of the proceedings as a challenge to the validity of a decision of the board of directors of the Irish manifestation of the company to apply to the regulatory authorities of the Island of Nevis to transfer the domicile and place of incorporation of the company to the Island of Nevis. The contention was that it was null and void by reason of a lack of a capacity of an Irish company to seek to transfer its domicile and place of incorporation to another jurisdiction.

Finlay Geoghegan J. did not agree. It appeared to her that the principal subject matter of the proceeding was the question as to whether Charly Acquisitions Limited had been validly incorporated and registered on the Island of Nevis and continued to have a corporate existence notwithstanding the dissolution of its Irish manifestation. It was possible that the principal subject matter might also extend to the issue of whether that company was the owner of the copyright in musical recordings previously owned by its Irish manifestation, but nothing turned on this.

Finlay Geoghegan J. went on to observe:

> "The determination of the relevant issues as to the principal subject matter of the proceedings undoubtedly includes the validity of the transactions which took place on the Island of Nevis in December, 1999. I accept that it is envisageable that a consideration of such issues may include a consideration as to whether [the Irish manifestation of the company] had the capacity to make an application to the Registrar of Companies on the Island of Nevis to change its domicile. However, even if the resolution of that issue were to be considered to include a determination as to the validity of a decision of an organ of [the Irish manifestation] within the meaning of Article 22(2) (without necessarily deciding that it does so), it does not appear to me that the determination of such issue could be considered to constitute the principal subject matter of the proceedings. It is simply one of a number of issues which may have to be determined by a court in reaching conclusions in relation to the principal subject matter of the proceedings."

Accordingly, Finlay Geoghegan J. concluded that the court did not have jurisdiction to hear and determine the plaintiff's claim against the third named defendant under Art.22(2).

EUROTORT

In *Short v Ireland, Attorney General and British Nuclear Fuels Plc*, unreported, High Court, April 2, 2004, the plaintiffs, residents of County Louth, sought a number of declaratory and injunctive reliefs against British Nuclear Fuels Plc (BNFL), which included declarations that the nuclear fuel reprocessing activities which it was carrying out at Sellafield in its THORP project were being conducted in contravention of Council Directive 85/337 of June 27, 1985 in not having had an environmental impact assessment as to their effects carried out, and of Council Directive 80/836 Euratom, in lacking "justification" before the purported authorisation of liquid air or other discharges from the THORP project was given, as well as breaches of the precautionary principle contrary to Art.130R of the Treaty of European Union and customary international law. The plaintiffs also claimed damages against BNFL under a range of headings, including assault, nuisance, trespass and negligence.

Peart J. had to determine a limited number of issues: whether the court had jurisdiction to make such declarations or to grant a mandatory injunction against BNFL, what was the applicable law for determining the plaintiffs' claim and whether the court should decline jurisdiction or stay the proceedings on the ground of *forum conveniens.*

Peart J. held, first, that the court did not have jurisdiction to make the declarations. He did not find it necessary to address arguments based on the "act of state" doctrine or on sovereign immunity because he was satisfied on the basis of general principles that the courts had no jurisdiction to make any finding of invalidity in respect of a foreign administrative decision. In *Adams v DPP* [2001] 2 I.L.R.M. 401, the applicant had unsuccessfully sought an order of certiorari quashing a certificate of the British Home Secretary waiving the rule of speciality in respect of charges other than those for which he had been extradited to Britain. McGuinness J. had thought it:

> "surely necessary to consider the possible practical effect of the order sought by the applicant. Even if the High Court (or this court on appeal) had theoretical jurisdiction to grant an order of certiorari directing that the certificate of the third respondent be brought up to be quashed, how would such an order be enforced? One has only to pose the question to recognise that the applicant's position is unsustainable."

As rgards the relationship between public law and private law remedies, it is worth bearing in mind that the victim of a default in public law obligations may in some circumstances have a remedy in tort, for misfeasance in public office or negligence, for example. It is true that in *Kennedy v Law Society*, Supreme Court, April 21, 2005, Geoghegan J. sought to restrict the entitlement to sue for negligence in cases where one has initiated a claim for misfeasance in public office, but in *Beatty v Rent Tribunal*, October 21, 2005, Fennelly J. appears to have rejected an *a priori* resolution of this question.

Counsel for the plaintiffs in the instant case argued that the breach of an EC Directive was a tort, and had been so characterised by courts in Ireland and England. He referred to *Tate v Minister for Social Welfare* [1985] 1 I.R. 418 where Carroll J. had held that a breach of obligation to observe community law was a tort within the meaning of s.11(2) of the Statute of Limitations 1957.

Peart J.'s analysis deserves extended quotation:

> "[T]he of action in *Tate* arose out of this State's failure to implement Council Directive 7/79/EEC relating to the equal treatment of men and women in matters of social security payments. Carroll J. found that the case amounted to a claim not for a simple debt in respect of the amount which the plaintiff ought to have received under the Directive, but was a claim for general damages for breach of the Directive in accordance with the damages principles enunciated in *Frankovich v The Italian Republic* (Cases C-6/90 and C-9/90) [1991] 1 E.C.R. 5357. While in the present case there is a claim for damages included, it is not the primary claim, and certainly the Replies to Particulars furnished have

not particularised this aspect of the claim in any substantial way, and this is in contrast to the Particulars provided in respect of the regulatory claims. These proceedings could not realistically be classified as a claim primarily for damages.

In any event it certainly is not a claim for damages of the kind brought in *Tate*, namely against the State for its failure to implement a Directive. Simply because there has been a breach of a Directive does not mean that there is an entitlement to damages, just as a breach of statutory duty does not automatically give rise to a claim for damages for breach of that statutory duty. There must be a causal link established. In this case it can certainly be submitted, as it has been by BNFL, that even supposing that there has been a breach of the requirements under the Directives, this has not given rise to any compensatable damage to the plaintiffs, just as in the converse, if damage was negligently caused to the plaintiffs, BNFL could not simply rely by way of defence on the fact that they had complied with the terms of the Directives.

In my view it is clear therefore that, while the learned Carroll J. found that such a failure to implement the Directive gave rise to a claim in tort, it was nevertheless a tort committed in this jurisdiction, and therefore one over which an Irish Court has jurisdiction. It may be that a breach of a Community law by the UK authorities, namely, as in this case, a failure to adopt procedures mandated by certain Directives incorporated into UK domestic law by legislation, comes within a broad definition of a tort, but, in the present case, it must be regarded as a tort committed in the UK, and therefore justiciable only before the Courts in that jurisdiction, just as a person who suffers personal injuries in a road traffic accident in England, must bring his action in tort thereby arising before a court in that jurisdiction.

It should also be noted that, in *Tate*, the classification as a tort of the breach of an obligation to observe Community law was in the context of whether the claim was a tort within the meaning of s.11, subs.2 of the Statute of Limitations, 1957, and on that basis it was held that the doctrine of laches which had been pleaded did not arise. That decision must be confined to that context, and cannot be extended to the question of this court's jurisdiction to deal with a breach of another State's obligation to observe Community law ...

The logic following from [the] submission [of counsel for the plaintiffs], it seems to me, would be that if the plaintiff in *Tate*, and all the other associated plaintiffs, were by now dispersed among several EU Member States, there could be possible a multiplicity of different actions, taking place in perhaps all such Member States in which such plaintiffs now resided, and at different times, in all of which the same issue would arise for determination, namely whether the Irish Government, being in breach of its obligation to implement the

Directive, was liable to the plaintiff in question. That would be an absurdity, and a result which could never have been intended by a decision such as that in *Tate*, where the definition of a tort was stated to include a breach of a European law obligation by the State. It could not be the case that any such breach could be litigated in any Member State."

Let us consider the several points made in this passage. The first is that the *Frankovich* principle has no application because the instant proceedings could not realistically be classified as a claim primarily for damages. One wonders whether this is a crucial factor. The breach by a Member State of its obligation to comply with EC law by properly implementing a Directive generates liability to those who suffer, or who may suffer, as a result. This is why the *Frankovich* decision is often described as involving recognition of the phenomenon of a "Eurotort". Whether the remedy sought is for damages or an injunction does not seem crucial.

The next point is that, whereas in *Tate* there had been a failure by the State to implement a Directive, the instant case involved the breach of a Directive that the Member State had in fact implemented. This in itself is not relevant to *Frankovich*, which does not restrict Member State liability to cases of non-implementation as opposed to breach. But Peart J. immediately goes on to point out that the breach of a statutory duty is not actionable for damages unless a causal link between breach and injury is established. In the instant case Peart J. ventured to observe that "it certainly can be submitted, as it has been by BNFL, that even supposing that there has been a breach of the requirements under the Directives, this has not given rise to any compensatable damage to the plaintiffs …". Peart J. did not hold that no such damage would be sustained in the future. One is entitled to an injunction against a threatened tort, provided one can reach the threshold required in *quia timet* proceedings. It seems, therefore, that the nature of the plaintiffs' claims—whatever their strength might be—was not such as to warrant the denial of jurisdiction on the basis that damages were not at their core or that a causal link might be hard to sustain.

The next point relates to whether it is necessary for a plaintiff under the *Frankovich* principle to establish that the Eurotort was committed within the jurisdiction of the State. Peart J. considered that a failure by the British authorities to adopt procedures mandated by EC Directives incorporated into British domestic law by legislation "must be regarded as a tort committed in the UK, and therefore justiciable only before the courts in that jurisdiction, just as a person who suffers personal injuries in a road accident must bring his action in tort thereby arising before a court in that jurisdiction."

It is true that in cases where the wrongful conduct and the damage both occur in a single state, jurisdiction will be found in that state under Art.5(3) of the Brussels Convention and its replacement Regulation (*Brussels I*); but in cases where the conduct occurred in one state and the damage occurred (or may occur) in another state, the plaintiff may choose to sue in either state. This was established in *Bier v Mines de Potasse d'Alsace* [1976] E.C.R. 1735, a judgment of the Court of Justice to which Peart J. referred later in his judgment when he sought to distinguish it from the instant case as follows:

> "In the *Bier* case it is important to bear in mind that it is a river water pollution case, and this has the potential to give rise to claims by citizens and bodies in a multiplicity of Member States since the river flows through a number of states. It is also a claim in which actual damage occurred, the success of which was not dependent upon a finding of illegality or invalidity of any administrative decision. In other words it was not a 'euro-tort' claim ...
>
> [T]here is nothing in the wording of Article 5(3) of the Convention, or in the judgment in *Bier*, which suggests that it was contemplated that a challenge to the validity of an administrative act, or a 'euro-tort' dependent upon such a challenge, could be mounted other than in the jurisdiction in which the administrative decision was made. In other words, the question of jurisdiction would come within the terms of Article 2, the general provision, and not under any of the special cases referred to in Article 5 of the Convention. Article 2 provides a general rule, subject to Article 5, that the courts of the state in which the defendant is domiciled shall have jurisdiction. Given the fact that a decision in favour of the plaintiffs would of necessity entail the court making a finding of invalidity in respect of the authorizations based on a failure to adhere to procedures laid down by the Directives, and also bearing in mind the fact that the Queen's Bench Division in England has already decided that the Directives are inapplicable to the operation of the THORP plant, it seems inconceivable that, even if the plaintiffs' claim is accepted as coming within the concept of a 'euro-tort', it could possibly have been contemplated that it would constitute a claim under Article 5(3) of the Convention, but would rather be a claim to which Article 2 would more naturally apply. Hence, I would not consider that the decision in Bier as broadly stated in the headnote which I have quoted in full, would automatically apply in the present case so as to entitle the plaintiffs to elect whether to bring the proceedings in this jurisdiction rather than in England."

While of course *Bier* was not a direct authority on the issue that arose in the instant case about the entitlement of the plaintiffs to challenge the validity of an administrative act, it surely was a direct authority on the specific question as to a plaintiff's entitlement to sue in tort in either the place of wrongful conduct or the place where the damage is suffered. It contradicts the proposition that the allegedly inadequate incorporation of certain Directives into British domestic law by legislation "must be regarded as a tort committed in the UK, and therefore justiciable only before the courts in that jurisdiction …". If injury is caused to a person in another state, it should be his or her choice as to whether to sue in Britain or in that other state.

It is worth noting that Art.5(3) of the Brussels Convention was drafted in such a way as to presuppose that the tort has already been committed at the time the plaintiff takes proceedings in that it referred to the place "where the harmful event *occurred*" (emphasis added). Cheshire & North, *Private International Law* (13th ed., 1999), p.215, observed that this was "a serious omission" since, with certain torts, it was common to seek an injunction in the Contracting State in which the threat existed. (They noted, however, that it was possible to obtain an injunction in such cases by using Art.24, which related to provisional, including protective, measures.) The *Brussels I* Regulation has cured this defect in that Art.5(3) has been redrafted to confer jurisdiction in matters relating to tort on "the courts for the place, where the harmful event occurred *or may occur*" (emphasis added).

As to the final concern that there might be a multiplicity of actions by plaintiffs dispersed among several EU Member States, which would be "an absurdity", one can agree that it would be unfortunate but this in itself is not a reason for declining jurisdiction on the basis that England (or Britain) is the *forum conveniens*. Such a principle has no place under the Brussels Convention or the *Brussels I* Regulation.

Peart J. went on to note the argument of counsel for the plaintiffs that, under EU law, national rules must not stand in the way of a litigant who has a good cause of action under European law: the plaintiffs in the instant case were such litigants. Peart J. responded to this argument as follows:

> "That is undoubtedly so as a general proposition—see, for example, the case of *Van Schijndel and Van Veen v Stichling Pensioenfonds voor Fysiotherapeuten*, Cases C–430, 431/93, [1995] ECR I–4705, and also cases such as *R v. Secretary of State for Transport, ex parte Factortame (No.2)* Case C–213/89, [1990] ECR I–2433; [1990] 3 WLR 818. But the present case is not really a case under European Law in the sense of the plaintiffs seeking relief against the State, because for example the State has failed to implement a directive. The plaintiffs are seeking an ordinary common law remedy which has been characterised at times as a tort or *quia timet* action, and also as a judicial review type action in which certain declaratory reliefs and injunctions are sought, the basis for which is an alleged failure on the part of BNFL to adhere to procedures mandated by certain EU Directives. In such cases the ordinary rules as to jurisdiction apply. The plaintiffs have their right to litigate and a remedy is available. It is simply a question of which court is the appropriate court to hear and determine the issues. There is no suggestion that some absence of national rules is standing in the way of

an effective remedy for these plaintiffs in this jurisdiction. If that were so, then the effect would be to overwrite and eliminate the existing principles by which matters of jurisdiction are determined, and would mean that by virtue of such decisions litigants could choose at will the forum in which they wish to bring their claim."

Peart J. was surely correct in saying that litigants should not be free to choose at will the forum in which they bring their claim but it can be argued that the plaintiffs were not seeking to make such a choice. They were claiming to have been injured (or at the risk of future injury) in Ireland as the result of a Eurotort where the defendant had engaged in tortuous conduct in England. They were claiming further that under the national law, which includes Irish private international law, they were entitled to sue in Ireland under Art.5(3) of the Brussels Convention. The decisions cited by Peart J. do not assert that the requirements of EU law are discharged by the availability of an entitlement to claim only in the state where the wrongful conduct of the defendant allegedly occurred or is likely to occur.

Peart J. went on to answer in the negative the second issue falling for consideration. If the court had no jurisdiction to make the declarations specified in the first question, it followed that it could not have jurisdiction to grant any injunction the basis of which would be those declarations. He went on to observe:

> "Such a finding is independent of any general principle which I would have thought existed that this Court has jurisdiction only within the territory of the State. The question posed by McGuinness J. in *Adams* as to how, supposing the Court had jurisdiction to quash by *certiorari* an order of the British Home Secretary, such an order would be enforced, has resonance in the circumstances of the present case, if one was to presume that this court had jurisdiction to grant an injunction, the effect of which would be to close down the THORP operation at Sellafield. This Court has no capacity to enforce its own orders outside the State, and since the Court ought not to act in vain, it follows that it would not make an order which it has no capacity to enforce."

In the light of his answers to the first two questions, Peart J. did not consider it necessary to answer the third and fourth questions.

CHILDREN

1. Hague Convention on Child Abduction

Custody Rights In *Re the Minor, AO; AO v MO*, unreported, High Court, December 15, 2004, the crucial issue was whether the plaintiff, the father of a child taken by the respondent from Ireland to Germany without his consent, was married to the defendant at the time of the removal. The plaintiff did not contest that, if he was not in fact married to the defendant, he could not assert that any custody rights in relation to his child.

The plaintiff was Nigerian; the defendant was originally from Mauritius. They arrived in Ireland in June 2001 and both then made a claim for refugee status. The child was born in September 2001. They lived together until September 2002. The defendant took the child with her to Germany a couple of months later. When the plaintiff requested the return of the child, the defendant denied that they had ever in fact married each other. This denial was communicated in correspondence between the Irish and German Central Authorities.

The plaintiff, in affidavit evidence, asserted that he had married the defendant in the civil registry office in Abbia in Nigeria but that, despite his best efforts, he had been unable to procure a copy of the marriage certificate. He exhibited documentation, backed by evidence of an official of the hospital in Ireland where the child had been born, in which the defendant had represented that she was married to him. An official of the Department of Justice, Equality and Law Reform also produced files relating to their applications for refugee status. The answers to 83 questions appeared to have been completed on each form in similar handwriting. The answers to the 84th question—the final question on the form—which related to the reasons for which they were seeking asylum, were in very similar terms.

Counsel for the plaintiff sought to rely on the defendant's communication with the Irish state authorities as admissible declarations by analogy with the law relating to declarations in applications for declarations of legitimacy. Counsel also relied on a presumption of marriage that might arise from cohabitation.

Finlay Geoghegan J. referred to *Pazpena de Vire v Pazpena de Vire* [2000] 1 F.L.R. 460 where Michael Harrison QC, sitting as a Deputy Judge of the English High Court, had discussed a number of judicial authorities between the end of the 18th century and 2001. He had concluded:

> "The cases show that the presumption relates to two distinct aspects of marriage: first the fact of a marriage ceremony, then the secondary issue of compliance with formalities. In Rayden and Jackson's *Law and Practice in Divorce and Family Matter* (Butterworths, 17th edn, 1997), it is put as follows, (the same appears in Halsbury's Laws):

4.11 Presumption from cohabitation and reputation. Where a man and woman have cohabited for such a length of time, and in such circumstances, as to have acquired the reputation of being man and wife, a lawful marriage between them will be presumed, though there may be no positive evidence of any marriage having taken place, particularly where the relevant facts have occurred outside the jurisdiction; and this presumption can be rebutted only by strong and weighty evidence to the contrary ...

(12) There is no doubt from the cases that there is a strong presumption in favour of a valid marriage where parties have long cohabited as man and wife ..."

Finlay Geoghegan J. rejected the plaintiff's claim. The first reason for doing so was that the plaintiff had not satisfied the court of his inability to obtain a marriage certificate from Nigeria. He had not set out any steps taken to try and obtain the certificate or why it could not be obtained through friends who presumably remained in Nigeria.

Secondly the court could not be satisfied that as a matter of probability the marriage had taken place by reason of the declarations made by the defendant in Ireland:

"The Court has been made aware that there is now a dispute between the parties as to the fact of the marriage. In such circumstances it appears that the Court should require stricter proof of marriage as has been required *inter alia* for bigamy and divorce ... Further if the Court were to conclude on the basis of the declarations made by the defendant in this Country that the plaintiff and defendant are married it would effectively be holding that the defendant is by reason of those declarations estopped from now denying that she was ever married to the plaintiff which would be contrary to the decision of the Supreme Court in *K. v K.* [2004] 1 I.R. 224 [analysed below, p.307].

Accordingly the Court must consider whether in accordance with the principle referred to above the cohabitation, its length of time and circumstances are such that the plaintiff and the defendant should be considered to have acquired the reputation 'of being man and wife' such that a lawful marriage between them will be presumed."

Turning to consider the presumption of marriage based on long cohabitation, Finlay Geoghegan J. noted that it derived from cases decided at a time when it was less common for unmarried persons to live together as "man and wife" than it was in the 21st century. The principle, she thought, "must now be applied with considerable caution".

In relation to the length of time, there had no evidence as to how long before they arrived in Ireland the plaintiff and the defendant might have cohabited. Finlay Geoghegan J. went on to observe:

> "The circumstances of the cohabitation in Ireland appear to be that they arrived together [and] made a claim for refugee status when the defendant was already approximately six months pregnant. They appear to have continued to cohabit together for approximately one year after the birth of the child. In the intervening period it appears from an exhibit to the plaintiffs affidavit that on or about the 5th October, 2001 they lodged with the office of the Refugee Applications Commissioner a withdrawal of their application for asylum by reason of a stated intention to apply to the Minister for Justice, Equality and Law Reform for residency based upon an Irish born child. It is a well established fact that in October, 2001 there existed an administrative scheme under which parents of Irish born children applied for residency by reason of the birth of an Irish child and that a significant number of such applications were granted.
>
> I have concluded that having regard to the period of cohabitation of which there exists evidence in Ireland of approximately 15 months and the specific circumstances relating to the applications for declarations of refugee status, the withdrawal of same and the applications for residency based on the birth of an Irish born child that the facts are not such as to give rise to a presumption that the plaintiff and the defendant acquired a reputation 'of being man and wife' such that a lawful marriage between them should be presumed."

Accordingly, Finlay Geoghegan J. concluded that the plaintiff had failed to discharge the onus of satisfying the court that he was married to the defendant at the date of the alleged abduction. It followed that the application must fail.

Risk of Harm or Intolerable situation If a parent who has removed or retained a child argues that returning the child will involve a grave risk of exposing the child to harm or otherwise placing the child in an intolerable situation, must the risk in some way be connected with circumstances that provoked the removal or retention in the first place or is it sufficient to establish a risk arising from other circumstances? In *Re TM and DM Minors; Minister for Justice Equality and Law Reform Ex p. EM v JM* [2003] 3 I.R. 178 at 187, Denham J. sought to answer this question as follows:

> "*Prima facie* the basis of the defence that there was great risk that the child's return would expose the child to physical or psychological harm, or otherwise place the child in an intolerable situation, must spring from the circumstances which prompted the wrongful removal and/or retention. Events subsequent to the removal and/or retention would be

material only insofar as they tended either to aggravate any original intolerable situation, or to create one, and also would normally relate to matters which had occurred in the requesting state."

It has to be said that the justification for this approach is less than obvious. While Denham J. lays down no absolute rule, why should there even be a prima facie preference for its adoption? Of course, as a matter of empirical experience, the vast majority of cases where Art.13(b) is invoked will invoke an account of previous problems which precipitated the removal or retention; but neither the language of Art.13(b) nor the simple policy which it seeks to effectuate would support the notion that, in the face of an admittedly grave risk of harm, the court should nonetheless order the return of the child simply because that harm is not attributable to the circumstances provoking the removal or retention. Article 13(b) does not seek to punish applicants for having been bad to their children: its focus is on protecting children from the risk of future harm, regardless of its provenance or the time when that risk began.

In *CN v PK-D*, unreported, High Court, December 16, 2004 (*ex tempore*), Finlay Geoghegan J. addressed this issue. The facts were tragic. The child was in the final stages of a terminal illness from a brain tumour; the process of returning him to Illinois would expose him to the risk of serious physical and psychological harm.

Finlay Geoghegan J. quoted the passage from Denham J.'s judgment and commented:

> "I have concluded that that passage does not preclude this court from considering the very serious medical condition of the child as potentially a matter which constitutes grave risk on the facts of this case. Denham J, undoubtedly, is stating a general principle as is clear from the use of the term 'prima facie' and also it appears to me expressly recognises in the second sentence of the quotation that events subsequent to the removal may be material where they create an intolerable situation.
>
> It also appears to me that there is considerable common sense to the approach of Justice La Forest in the Canadian Supreme Court in *Thompson v Thompson* [1994] 3 SCR 551 where … in considering the question of the allowable source of harm, it is stated…
>> 'As this court stated in *Young v Young* [1993] 4 SCR 3 from a child-centred perspective harm is harm. If the harm were severe enough to meet the stringent test of the Convention it would be irrelevant from whence it came.'"

Turning to the facts of the case, Finlay Geoghegan J. noted that they involved a highly unusual set of circumstances. There was a grave risk that the mere return process would expose the child to physical harm. The court did not have to look beyond that to address what his circumstances would be if returned to Illinois. If, however, that question were to be addressed, there was a grave risk that the child would also suffer psychological harm. He was in a condition in which, effectively, he was unable to do anything for himself and extremely dependant on the mother and her husband. She was in the late stages of pregnancy. It was impossible for her to travel at the time of the judgment and, therefore, any order for return would be separating the child from his mother, on whom in the final stages of his life and illness he appeared to be entirely dependant.

Accordingly, Finlay Geoghegan J. declined to order the return of the child to Illinois.

In *Re HH, a Child; EH v SH*, unreported, High Court, April 27, 2004, an important issue of principle was addressed, and seemingly resolved, by Finlay Geoghegan J. If a child is to be returned to a state whose laws are fully protective of children from the risk of harm, but the abducting parent will not be able in fact to protect the child from harm on account of being under the domination of the applicant, should the court order the child's return? In this case, the applicant father had been violent to the respondent mother, but not the child. The mother had "failed to pursue any complaints of violence to the point of proceedings"; Finlay Geoghegan J. concluded, as a matter of probability, that this had been "primarily caused by either fear of or dominance by the applicant." The mother had taken the child from England to Ireland. At the time of the hearing of the husband's application for the return of the child, it was clear that the spouses would not resume cohabitation. Finlay Geoghegan J. also concluded that the pattern of violence from the applicant had "had a significantly adverse effect on the respondent" and that he had actually threatened her verbally outside the Four Courts.

Finlay Geoghegan J. observed that it was "well settled" by the cases in Ireland that the exception provided for in Art.13 "must be strictly construed". Laws L.J. had "clearly and succinctly summarised" the court's jurisdiction in this regard in *TB v JB* (*Abduction: Grave Risk of Harm*) [2001] 2 F.L.R. 515 at 547, where he had stated:

> "In summary, then, these following features of this jurisdiction are in my judgment interdependent functions of each other:
> (1) The Convention's policy is that substantive questions of a child's welfare should be decided by the courts of the state of the child's habitual residence.
> (2) A child unlawfully removed from the state of habitual residence will therefore be promptly returned unless it is shown, exceptionally, that an order of return would create grave risk of intolerable harm to the child.
> (3) The decision whether such grave risk is made out has to be assessed summarily, else (a) the policy stated at (1) might be

undermined, and (b) otherwise the parent left behind in the home jurisdiction is potentially put to unjust disadvantage in seeking to make a case for the child's return.

(4) The considerations set out at (3), the words of Art.13(b), and the exceptional nature of what has to be demonstrated, show that 'clear and compelling evidence' (*per* Ward LJ, *Re C (Abduction: Grave Risk of Psychological Harm)* [1999] 1 FLR 1145, 1154) is required if the obligation to return is in any particular case to give way in light of Art. 13(b)."

The respondent in her affidavit acknowledged that there were remedies available under English law to persons who had suffered domestic violence but expressed the view that these remedies were insufficient to protect her and the child in the particular circumstances of her situation. She also stated that she believed that, if she lived in proximity to the applicant, by reason of his dominance she would be unable to seek effective protection for herself and the child. A psychiatrist who gave affidavit evidence on her behalf concluded that "she would lose whatever confidence she has gained in the few months here and not be in a position to protect either herself or her daughter, if forced to return to England."

Counsel on behalf of the respondent sought to pursue the defence under Art.13(b) on the basis that the psychiatrist's affidavit and report were evidence that, as a matter of probability, the respondent would be unable to apply for effective protection if an order for her return was made. In response to this, counsel for the applicant sought to rely upon the majority decision of the English Court of Appeal in *TB v JB* [2001] 2 F.L.R. 515 and, in particular, the judgment of Arden L.J. In that case, there was evidence that the mother had previously been unwilling to avail herself of the protection of the courts of New Zealand. In the High Court Singer J. had proceeded on the basis that the mother was likely to make the same choice in the future. In the Court of Appeal, Arden L.J. stated:

"The policy of the Convention as set out above seems to me to require that the evaluation of risk is carried out on the basis that the abducting parent will take all reasonable steps to protect herself and her children and that she cannot rely on her unwillingness to do so as a factor relevant to the risk. The onus would thus be on the mother in this case to show that, even if she took all reasonable steps, she would not be adequately protected from Mr. H. in New Zealand."

Finlay Geoghegan J. stated:

"I agree with the above as a general statement of the approach which this court must take to the assessment of grave risk. The facts of this case are different to *TB v JB* insofar as it is not an unwillingness to seek protection which is alleged but rather an inability to do so by reason of psychological frailty resulting from the alleged violence and dominance of the applicant. However, even in such differing circumstances it appears to me that the principle as stated by Arden L.J. must be considered, at minimum, to be the starting point of any consideration by this court. A respondent who attempts to persuade this court of an inability to seek protection from the courts of the habitual residence of the child by reason of the respondent's own psychological frailty would have to establish by clear and compelling evidence that on the particular facts pertaining to her (including her psychological frailty) it would be reasonable for her not to seek the protection from the courts of the habitual residence of the child. I am not satisfied that the respondent has so established on the facts of this case.

The evidence in this case establishes that even while the applicant and respondent were residing together the respondent did on occasion seek assistance from the police in England and also advice from Bexley's Women's Aid. … I accept that she did not pursue matters at the relevant time. However, the situation is now quite different as she has separated from the applicant and it appears to be accepted by both parties that their marriage is at an end. The respondent has sought and obtained legal assistance and fully defended these proceedings. In the changed circumstances, where it is accepted that if she returns to England and Wales the respondent will not be living with the applicant, I am not satisfied that the respondent, as a matter of probability, will be unable to seek protection from the courts of England and Wales or that it would be reasonable for her not to seek such protection."

Finlay Geoghegan J. referred to the psychiatrist's conclusion that, if the respondent were forced to return to England "she would lose whatever confidence she has gained in the few months here and not be in a position to protect either herself or her daughter". It appeared to Finlay Geoghegan J. that the latter part of this conclusion was of a very general nature and not specifically addressed to seeking assistance, if necessary, from the courts of England and Wales. In general, it appeared to Finlay Geoghegan J. that the psychiatrist's report was directed to welfare issues which the Irish court was not competent to consider in relation to an Art.13 defence. Finlay Geoghegan J. observed:

"Welfare issues concerning the child must … be dealt with by the courts of habitual residence of the child. It would be a matter for the courts of England and Wales, if proceedings are brought before them, as to whether or not the welfare of the child would be best served by permitting the mother and the child to live in Ireland. [The psychiatrist]'s report is clearly relevant to any such consideration. It is well established that the courts of England and Wales consider that they have jurisdiction and will in appropriate cases permit a parent to remove a child to live in another jurisdiction."

As the respondent had not made out a defence under Art.13(b) of the Hague Convention Finlay Geoghegan J. considered herself bound under Art.12 to make an order for the return of the child.

Finlay Geoghegan J.'s conclusion that the dominance exercised by the husband would not be likely in the future to prevent the mother from protecting her child may perhaps be considered to be supported by the new fact that the spouses were separated, although the psychiatrist's conclusion, on its face, may suggest a different assessment. What is more significant is the general principle. The test adopted by Finlay Geoghegan J. is that the abducting parent should have to establish by clear and compelling evidence that on the particular facts pertaining to her (including her psychological frailty) "it would be reasonable for her not to seek the protection from the courts of the habitual residence of the child." The reference to reasonableness needs to be probed. This involves engagement with the murky area where objective value judgments encounter subjective factors. In one sense, a person who is under another's domination is not "reasonable" in failing to act to protect his or her daughter from harm. The failure is excusable, and no blame attaches to one for being the victim of domination, but the failure cannot easily be described as an exercise of rationality or a matter capable of being characterised as reasonable. (One is reminded here of the Supreme Court decision in *Fletcher v Commissioners of Public Works* [2003] 1 I.R. 465 where the reasonableness of the plaintiff's fear of mesothelioma was his undoing even though the fear was associated with a mental illness foreseeably caused by the defendant's negligence.)

The larger question of how best to deal with domestic violence in an international context is increasingly engaging courts and commentators: see Klein, Orloff & Sarangapani, "Border Crossings: Understanding the Civil, Criminal and Immigration Implications for Battered Women Fleeing Across State Lines with Their Children", 39 Family L.Q. 109 (2005), Lewis, "The Hague Convention on the Civil Aspects of International Child Abduction: When Domestic Violence and Child Abuse Impact on the Goal of Comity", 13 Transnat'l L. 391 (2000), Kayl, "The Hague Convention and the Flight from Domestic Violence: How Women and Children Are being Returned by Coach and Four", 13 Int'l J. of L., Policy & the Family 191 (1999).

Information relating to a child's social background The final paragraph of Art.13 of the Hague Convention provides that:

"in considering the circumstances referred to in this Article, the judicial and administrative authorities shall take into account the information relating to the social background of the child provided by the Central Authority or other competent authority of the child's habitual residence."

In *Re HH, a Child; EH v SH*, unreported, High Court, April 27, 2004, Finlay Geoghegan J. admitted into evidence under this provision a letter from a person working with the Community Safety Unit of the Metropolitan Police at Woolwich police station, as the Metropolitan Police Service appeared to her to be a "competent authority of the United Kingdom" for the purposes of Art.13.

Habitual Residence The failure of the Hague Convention on International Child Abduction of 1980 to include a definition of habitual residence has recently, and with good reason, been criticised as being "probably one of the greatest deficiencies in [its] drafting": Linda Silberman, "Interpreting the Hague Convention: In Search of a Global Jurisprudence", New York University Law School Institute for International Law and Justice W.P. No.2005/5, May 2005, p.15. In *Re CAS, a Minor; PAS v AFS*, unreported, Supreme Court, November 24, 2004, important guidance was given on the question of how to determine the habitual residence of a minor where the parents are in conflict.

Habitual residence is an excellent and simple connecting factor—far less complicated than domicile—in cases where adults are concerned. Once the focus shifts to the habitual residence of a minor, problems emerge, for three reasons in particular.

First, and most obviously, where the minor is very young, his or her presence in any particular country will be the result, not of the minor's decision, but of the decision by people in whose custody or under whose control the minor happens to be. Usually parents are exercising such custody or control, but not always. Domicile is at least frank on this issue and specifically acknowledges that the minor is not in charge and has no real control over his or her place of residence. This explains, though perhaps does not justify, the doctrine of a minor's domicile of dependency. The rhetoric in favour of habitual residence emphasises that it is a question of fact rather than of law; the truth is that every finding of such "fact" has to be based on an acknowledged legal framework. If the minor is too young to make an effective choice on where he or she is to live, how is the court to regard decisions on the matter made by parents? It is very hard for courts to avoid slipping into a mindset which involves, in practice, a legal concept of "habitual residence of dependency". Any judicial statement which asserts that parents determine the habitual residence of their children adds to this danger. Several courts have made this mistake, which would have been avoided if they had treated the phenomena of the constriction on free choice of the minor and actual choices by the parent or parents, not as determinative *in themselves* of the minor's habitual residence, but rather as important elements of the compendium facts from which a finding of habitual residence would have to be made.

The second danger is that courts will confuse legal custody entitlements as determinative of the factual question of habitual residence. If they do this, there is a real danger that they will regard the violation of a custody right as presumptively inconsistent with an ascription of the child's habitual residence which, in its result, would aid the custody violator. In the context of the Hague Child Abduction Convention, this danger is particularly prevalent. Inevitably, courts form some view of the merits of the case and there has to be some natural human resistance to the prospect of being obliged to deny a deserving applicant a remedy under the Convention because he or she has not established the jurisdictional basis for the application's success, based on the child's habitual residence at the time of the wrongful removal or retention.

A third problem with habitual residence is that it simply provides no convincing answer in cases where a child is born or spends a period of time in a state entirely unconnected with the centre of gravity of the parents' interests. In such a case, a question arises as to whether it is theoretically defensible to ascribe to the child an habitual residence in a state where the child has never in fact resided at all.

In the instant case two of these three issues arose for consideration and Fennelly J. gave guidance on the third. The respondent, an Irish woman, had gone to Canada in 1999. She had married the applicant, a Canadian man, in 2001. In February 2003 the respondent became pregnant. In May 2003 she travelled to Ireland to visit her parents for a family event. A couple of days after arriving in Ireland, she suffered epileptic seizures and was hospitalised. The applicant came to Ireland to be with her. It turned out that she had a brain tumour. The applicant paid brief return visits to Canada but for most of the time he was with his wife in Ireland. Their child was born in December. The respondent had surgery in London for the brain tumour in January 2004. Arrangements were made for the return of the parents and their child to Canada in February 2004. They stayed with the applicant's mother. In April 2004 the respondent, without the consent of the applicant, took the child back with her to Ireland.

Murphy J. in the High Court concluded that the child's habitual residence at the time of his removal was in Canada. He stated:

> "It does not appear to me that habitual residence can be lost where the parties left Canada where there was no settled intention by the parties to remain in Ireland. Moreover a short period of residence may suffice where somebody is resuming residence in a country where they were form[er]ly habitually resident as in the case of the parties returning in February of this year even if the respondent had no intention of remaining. What is relevant is the habitual residence of the child at the date of the alleged abduction. She had been registered for medical purposes, had lived for seven weeks in Canada but, most importantly her parents had been habitually resident in that jurisdiction.
> It is clear from the case law that one or two parents with joint parental

responsibility cannot change the habitual residence of their child unilaterally."

The Supreme Court reversed. Fennelly J. delivered a judgment with which McGuinness J. and McCracken JJ. concurred.

Fennelly J. stressed that by "universal accord, the issue of habitual residence is essentially one of fact." He quoted from McGuinness J.'s judgment in *Re CM (a minor)*; *CM and OM v Delegacion Provincial de Málaga Consejería de Trabajo y Asuntos Sociales Junta de Andalucía* [1999] 2 I.R. 363 at 381:

> "Having considered the various authorities opened to me by counsel, it seems to me to be settled law in both England and Ireland that 'habitual residence' is not a term of art, but a matter of fact, to be decided on the evidence in this particular case. It is generally accepted that, where a child is residing in the lawful custody of its parent (in the instant case the mother), its habitual residence will be that of the parent. However, the habitual residence of the child is not governed by the same rigid rules of dependency as apply under the law of domicile and the actual facts of the case must always be taken into account. Finally, a person, whether a child or an adult, must, for at least some reasonable period of time, be actually present in a country before he or she can be held to be habitually resident there."

Fennelly J considered that this passage, subject to one *caveat*, stated correctly the approach that a court should adopt to assessing the issue of habitual residence. The last sentence seemed, however, to state too broad a proposition. (Fennelly J. returned to this matter later in his judgment.)

Fennelly J. went on to observe:

> "The Convention deliberately left the notion of habitual residence undefined. The courts of the Contracting States have to be free to apply it to the facts, having considered all the circumstances of the case. Human situations are infinitely variable. Habitual residence will be perfectly obvious in the great majority of cases. It is an obvious fact that a new-born child is incapable of making its own choices as to residence or anything else. What the courts have to look at is the situation of the parents and their choices. Where the child has, for a substantial period, been resident in one country with both its parents, while they are in a stable relationship particularly if they are of the same nationality, the answer will usually be fairly obvious."

Fennelly J. noted that this normal state of affairs had been described by Waite J. in *Re B* [1993] 1 F.L.R. 993 at 995 in the following terms:

"1. The habitual residence of young children of parents who are living together is the same as the habitual residence of the parents themselves and neither parent can change it without the express or tacit consent of the other or an order of the court.

2. Habitual residence is a term referring, when it is applied in the context of married parents living together, to their abode in a particular place or country which they have adopted voluntarily and for settled purposes as part of the regular order of their life for the time being whether it is of short or of long duration.

3. All that the law requires for a 'settled purpose' is that the parents' shared intentions in living where they do should have a sufficient degree of continuity about them to be properly described as settled.

4. Although habitual residence can be lost in a single day, for example upon departure from the initial abode with no intention of returning, the assumption of habitual residence requires an appreciable period of time and a settled intention. ... Logic would suggest that provided the purpose is settled the period of habitation need not be long."

Fennelly J. next turned to the question whether a child could, for the purposes of the Convention, be habitually resident in a country where he or she had never physically been present. In *CM*, McGuinness J. had cited respectable authority for a negative answer. In *Re M. (Abduction: Habitual Residence)* [1996] 1 F.L.R. 887, Sir John Balcombe had stated: "Before a person, whether a child or an adult, can be said to be habitually resident in a country, it is clear that he must be resident in that country. Of course, residence does not necessarily require physical presence at all times."

In *Re A (Abduction: Habitual Residence)* [1998] 1 F.L.R. 497, Stuart-White J. had cited that passage and gone on to say, "Not only would it offend against common sense to hold that a child of 6 months of age, who had never actually resided in Greece was habitually resident there, it would also be inconsistent with authority."

There was, however, some English authority to the contrary. In *B v H (Habitual Residence)* [2002] 1 F.L.R. 388, Charles J. had postulated the possible example of "the unexpectedly early birth to a married couple who are habitually resident in England during a weekend break in France." He asked rhetorically why the baby should "not be habitually resident in England at birth rather than at the moment ... he or she is brought back to England." He had continued in a passage with which Fennelly J. agreed:

"Given that habitual residence is not defined and is an issue of fact to be determined in all the circumstances of the case by reference to the intentions and actions of the parents to my mind the answer to that question is that there is no compelling reason why the baby should not be habitually resident in England at birth."

Charles J. had applied this reasoning to a case where a family of Bangladeshi origin, but habitually resident in England, travelled for a holiday to Bangladesh with their three children but between the conception and birth of a fourth who was born in Bangladesh. The court had held that the baby was habitually resident in England. This case was followed by Hedley J. in *W & B v H* (Family Division, February 18, 2002).

In an important passage, Fennelly J. observed:

> "I do not say that the place of birth of a child is an irrelevant fact. Clearly, it will be of prime importance in many cases. The facts of many cases will not be as benign as that of the premature birth during a weekend break in France. I do say, however, that to exclude, in every case, the possibility of a child being habitually resident in a country where it has never physically been is to introduce an unjustified restriction into the open and flexible notion adopted by the Convention.
>
> It is also clear that, in cases of conflict, some or all of the propositions of Waite J regarding 'settled purpose' and 'shared intentions' simply may possibly not apply at all. It would be undesirable to lay down rigid criteria for the assessment of situations which are as variable as human nature. However, where the parties have, for some time, had a settled relationship and shared intentions before a child is born, both parents will normally have equal custody rights, which cannot be ruptured unilaterally. However, in situations of deep conflict, particular weight must necessarily attach to the relationship of a mother with a new-born child. To quote Butler-Sloss LJ in *Re F (A Minor)* [1992] FLR 548 at 556, 'When the parents separate, the child's habitual residence may change and will, in due course, follow that of the principal carer with whom he resides.'"

This downplaying by Fennelly J. of technical legal rules relating to habitual residence is to be welcomed. It seeks to ensure that a finding of habitual residence remains what it was originally intended to be: essentially one of fact. It makes it less likely that courts will favour an elaborate network of legal concepts, comparable to the domicile of dependency of minors. One could do well to heed the observations of Pippa Rogerson in "Habitual Residence: The New Domicile?", 49 Int'l & Comp L.Q. 86 at 100 (2000) that:

> "it is in the very nature of the common law to have to decide cases which are at the borderlines even with a rule that is generally very clear. It is then impossible for legal principles not to evolve from this inevitable accretion of decisions in these marginal cases and some

contradictory or artificial consequences result. If habitual residence is
to retain its appeal as a concept with a factual, objectively ascertainable
basis then the courts will have to bear this in mind."

Turning to the facts of the case, Fennelly J. thought it reasonable to start by
enquiring whether the parties had lived together in Canada in a stable marital
relationship, with a "settled intention" and "shared purpose" prior to May 1,
2003, of bringing up their child in Canada. Fennelly J. was of the view that
Murphy J. should have fully considered the events in Ireland from May 2003
to February 2004 in seeking to discern what this earlier intention and purpose
had been. Murphy J. had failed to "grasp the nettle" in that the respondent's
stay in Ireland was no longer going to be temporary once she was diagnosed
as suffering from a brain tumour. She was going to remain in Ireland until the
baby was born and until after she had had her operation. Furthermore, she had
claimed that she told the applicant long before the birth that she intended to
bring the baby up in Ireland. This matter required a clear finding of fact. If the
respondent had expressed her intention of remaining in Ireland and bringing
up her child here, this would have inevitably undermined the idea that the
parties had, at that time, a shared intention and settled purpose of living in
Canada.

In Fennelly J.'s view Murphy J. had not made the necessary findings of
primary fact to justify his conclusion on habitual residence. The birth of the
child in Ireland in this case had not been the sort of fortuitous event recognised
in some of the cases as not being inconsistent with habitual residence in another
country. Accordingly the Supreme Court allowed the appeal and remitted the
matter to the High Court for re-hearing.

In *CN v PK-D*, unreported, High Court, December 16, 2004 (*ex tempore*),
Finlay Geoghegan J. gave short shrift to the argument that, because the courts
of Illinois had "retained" proceedings relating to a child after his mother had
moved from there to Arizona, where she acquired a new habitual residence,
the habitual residence of the child remained in Illinois. The mother and father
of the child were not married.

Finlay Geoghegan J. concentrated on the habitual residence issue rather
than whether the Illinois courts had acquired or retained rights of custody in
relation to the child by reason of the proceedings in Illinois (in respect of
which the judgment does not elaborate). She quoted the passage from
McGuinness J.'s judgment in *Re CM (a minor)*; *CM and OM v Delegacion
Provincial de Málaga Consejería de Trabajo y Asuntos Sociales Junta de
Andalucía* [1999] 2 I.R. 363 which Fennelly J. also quoted in *Re CAS, a Minor;
PAS v AFS*, unreported, Supreme Court, November 24, 2004, see above, p.134.

Finlay Geoghegan J. noted that in *C v S (A Minor) (Abduction)* [1990] 2
All E.R. 961 Lord Brandon had said that the question whether a person is
habitually resident in a specified country was "one of fact to be decided by
reference to all the circumstances of any particular case."

Emphasising that the habitual residence of the minor was a matter of fact, Finlay Geoghegan J. went on to observe that:

> "[f]urther, on the facts of this case at the time of the move to Arizona, the minor was in the lawful custody of his mother and the applicant father did not have at that time any rights of custody. The onus is on the applicant to establish that [at the relevant date] the habitual residence of the minor remained in Illinois."

More than two years had passed subsequent to the mother's going to Arizona, where she married another man, before she took the child to Ireland.

2. Luxembourg Convention   In *RW v CC*, unreported, High Court, March 26, 2004, Finlay Geoghegan J. gave a comprehensive analysis of the circumstances in which, under the Luxembourg Convention, a decision relating to custody (which term includes access orders) should not be recognised or enforced in another Contracting State. Article 10 of the Convention provides in part as follows:

> "1. In cases other than those covered by articles 8 and 9, recognition and enforcement may be refused not only on the grounds provided for in article 9 but also on any of the following grounds:
> a. if it is found that the effects of the decision are manifestly incompatible with the fundamental principles of the law relating to the family and children in the State addressed;
> b. if it is found that by reason of a change in the circumstances including the passage of time but not including a mere change in the residence of the child after an improper removal, the effects of the original decision are manifestly no longer in accordance with the welfare of the child;
> ...
> d. if the decision is incompatible with a decision given in the State addressed or enforceable in that State, after being given in a third State, pursuant to proceedings begun before the submission of the request for recognition or enforcement, and if the refusal is in accordance with the welfare of the child."

The Child Abduction and Enforcement of Custody Orders Act 1991 implemented the Luxembourg Convention in Ireland. Section 28 provides as follows:

> "(1) The Court shall refuse an application made under this Part for recognition or enforcement in the State of a decision relating to custody where—
> (a) in relation to a decision to which article 8 of the Luxembourg

Convention applies, the Court is of opinion on any of the grounds specified in article 10.1 a, b, c or d of that Convention that the decision should not be recognised or enforced in the State;

(b) in relation to a decision to which article 9 or 10 of that Convention applies, the Court is of opinion on any of the grounds specified in the said articles that the decision should not be recognised or enforced in the State;

(c) the Court is of opinion that the decision is not enforceable in the Contracting State where it was made and is not a decision to which article 12 of the Convention applies."

The instant case involved a long history of litigation. Two girls, aged nine and 14, had been taken from England to Ireland in 2002 to live with their maternal aunt when their mother had been diagnosed with cancer. The mother came to Ireland shortly afterwards and died a month later. The mother appointed her sister and her sister's husband as testamentary guardians. The girls continued to live with them in Ireland, having settled down well and integrated successfully into the Irish educational system.

The children's father, who had been married to their late mother and who had been living apart from her for some time before her death, had had a contact order (equivalent to an order for access in Irish law) made in his favour by the English High Court before the girls had been taken to Ireland. This litigation continued after the mother's death. The maternal aunt successfully applied to be joined as respondent in place of her late sister. In the meantime the father unsuccessfully invoked the Hague Convention before the High Court where Murphy J. on October 8, 2002 refused the father's application for the return of the children to England.

In November 2002 O'Neill J. made an interim order granting the maternal aunt and her husband custody of the girls pending further order and restraining their father from removing them from the jurisdiction until after the hearing of the aunt and husband's summons seeking sole custody of the girls. In October 2003 a date was fixed for the hearing of those proceedings in February 2004. In the meantime, in January 2003 in the English High Court, the maternal aunt complied with the request to give an undertaking that she would withdraw the proceedings then before the Irish High Court and would not institute any other proceedings during the currency of the English proceedings.

The English High Court made an order to the effect that the girls should continue to live with their testamentary guardians, with their father being entitled to have contact with them in London on specified days. In regard to this contact, the order provided that the younger daughter was to stay overnight with her father unless she did not wish to do so and that the elder daughter was to stay overnight with him if she wished to do so.

In February 2003 the father insisted that, if the girls came to London, they would have to stay with him or his adult daughter. The girls were unwilling to travel on these terms. Their maternal aunt did not in fact discontinue the Irish proceedings as she had undertaken. She wrote to the English High Court informing it that, by reason of the unsuccessful proceedings which the father had taken under the Hague Convention in Ireland, she considered it more appropriate that the matters be dealt with in the Irish High Court. She also apprised the English High Court of the father's stance regarding contact which, she said, had led to the failure of the access in February 2003. The proceedings continued in England, culminating in the making of an order in July 2003 granting the father contact with his daughters. It was this order which the father sought to enforce under Art.7 of the Luxembourg Convention. Being an order for access, it fell within the definition of an "order for custody", within the meaning of Art.1 of that Convention.

Finlay Geoghegan J. approached the matter as follows. The onus of establishing the facts that would justify the refusal to enforce the order rested on the respondent: the Supreme Court decision in *RJ v MR* [1994] 1 I.R. 271 (noted in *Annual Review of Irish Law 1993*, pp.131–135) had clearly so held. Article 10 gave "an authorisation to the Contracting States to permit refusal" on the grounds stated in that Article. The Oireachtas had "taken up such permission by specifically enacting s. 28 (1) of the Act of 1991." Article 10 provides that "recognition and enforcement may be refused" in specified circumstances. Section 28(1) provides that the court "shall refuse" recognition or enforcement where "the Court is of opinion on any of the grounds specified" in, *inter alia*, Art.10 that the decision should not be recognised or enforced in the State.

Counsel for the children's maternal aunt argued that there were only three matters to which the court should have regard when considering the defence raised under Art.10(1)(d): whether there was a relevant decision of the Irish courts given in proceedings commenced before the submission of the request for recognition and enforcement of the English order of July 2003, whether that English order was incompatible with the order of O'Neill J. in November 2002 and, if so, whether the refusal to recognise or enforce the English order was in accordance with the welfare of the girls. If the court considered that the order should not be recognised or enforced on the basis of these three factors, it had no residual discretion to recognise or enforce it nonetheless. Counsel for the father, however, submitted that the court did in fact retain such a discretion and was entitled to consider additional matters relevant to achieving the objectives of the Luxembourg Convention. In particular, the court should have regard to the fact that the maternal aunt had made, and broken, undertakings to the English High Court; if she had acted in accordance with her undertakings, there would not have been any order by O'Neill J. in existence as a potential barrier to the enforcement of the English order.

Finlay Geoghegan J. rejected the argument put forward on behalf of the father. She stated:

"Considering s.28(1) and Article 10 in accordance with the above principles I have concluded that the Oireachtas, by the express wording of s. 28(1)(b), intends a court in forming a view as to whether a decision should or should not be recognised or enforced in the State, to be limited to the specific matters set out in each of the sub-paragraphs of Article 10. I derive that intention particularly from the wording of s.28(1)(b) '... the court if of opinion on any of the grounds specified in the said articles ...'. Further that the court having formed the view on grounds specified in one of the sub-paragraphs of article 10(1) is then obliged by reason of the opening words of s. 28(1) to refuse the application."

Finlay Geoghegan J. went on to observe:

"The construction which I am placing on Article 10 as implemented by s.28(1), appears to me to accord with the express objectives of the Convention. Undoubtedly the express objectives of the Convention are that orders made in one Contracting State and enforceable there should be recognised and enforced in another Contracting State unless the facts are such that the respondent establishes one of the very limited exceptions set out *inter alia* in Article 10. It is absolutely clear that the court in considering an objection to recognition or enforcement may not take into account matters which go outside the specific grounds referred to in Article 10 (or Article 9 as appropriate). The grounds specified in Article 10 appear intended to reflect an objective of tempering the rigid rule of recognition and enforcement with limited exceptions directed to circumstances where courts on the specified grounds would consider the recognition or enforcement of the order not appropriate by differences in fundamental principles of the law relating to the family or a need to refuse in the interest of the welfare of the child in certain very limited circumstance. It appears to me to be consistent with the objectives of the Convention that the Oireachtas would, in accordance with our constitutional principles relating to the protection of the personal rights and the statutory principles relating to the welfare of the child being paramount, decide that it would take up the option given to it under Article 10 of the Convention, by requiring a court to refuse to recognise or enforce a foreign order where the court has formed the view on one of the grounds specified in Article 10 that the order should not be recognised or enforced in the State.

Accordingly, it appears to me that [the] exercise which the court must undertake where a defence raised is under Article 10 is to consider on the specific grounds under the relevant sub-article whether the respondent has discharged an onus of establishing facts such that the court should refuse recognition or enforcement in accordance with the relevant sub-article and if so then the Court is obliged under s. 28(1)(d) to refuse the application for recognition and enforcement."

The children's maternal aunt also put forward the argument that the failure of the English High Court to have bound her husband, one of the two joining guardians of the children, meant that its order should not be enforced. Finlay Geoghegan J. had little doubt that this failure to have involved the husband was undesirable since it could have opened the possibility of a dispute between the guardians in addition to their combined dispute with the father. Nonetheless she did not consider that the order had met the threshold of being "manifestly incompatible" with the fundamental principles of the law of the State relating to family and children. She was guided by two earlier decisions. The first was that of the Supreme Court in *RJ v MR* [1994] 1 I.R. 271, which she had already quoted in her judgment on the question of the onus of proof. In *RJ v MR,* Finlay C.J. had stated that it was necessary that the court, in construing the provisions of Art.10, paras (1)(a)(b):

> "should give to the word 'manifestly' a definite and commonsense meaning. The insertion of the word 'manifestly' must indicate that the standard of proof which is necessary for a person objecting to the making of an order for the return of a child is a standard which is something more than the probability appropriate for ordinary proof in civil actions.
>
> I am satisfied that there are no grounds for suggesting that it could be as much as an onus of proving the matter as a certainty or beyond a reasonable doubt.
>
> I am satisfied that to give effect to the word 'manifestly' it must be interpreted as placing upon the party objecting to the making of the order an onus to prove the incompatibility as a matter of high probability."

The second decision was that of Charles J. of the English High Court in *T v R (Abduction: Forum conveniens)* [2002] 2 F.L.R. 544. That case had concerned the recognition and enforcement of a Swedish order granting custody to a father of a child residing with his mother following the removal of the child from Sweden and the failure by the mother to participate in proceedings in Sweden. The test applied by Charles J. in considering a defence under Art.10(1)(a) had been whether or not the Swedish order "is within the range of orders that would have been open to an English court in the difficult circumstances that face the Swedish courts following the mother's removal of the child from Sweden and her failure to take a full part in the preparation of the care report and thus the Swedish proceedings."

Finlay Geoghegan J. observed:

> "Whilst the court is directed by article 10(1)(a) to look at the effects of the order there is an attractive simplicity in the approach of Charles J.

> Applying his test to the facts of this case, where following the death of the mother only CC had applied to be joined as a respondent to the English proceedings and notwithstanding that it appears to have been disclosed to the English court that both FC and CC were appointed testamentary guardians and the fact that FC and CC are married to each other I am not satisfied that (despite as I have indicated the potential undesirability of such an order) it can be concluded that it would not be competent for an Irish court to make an access order in such circumstances in favour of the father by requiring one guardian namely CC who has, at her request was joined in the proceedings to make the girls available for access. Accordingly I find that the defence raised under article 10(1)(a) fails."

Finlay Geoghegan J.'s rejection of the application of the public policy bar to the recognition of the English order seems eminently sensible. It may, however, be suggested that neither of the two decisions to which she referred offered the strongest of analysis. Finlay C.J.'s approach was to treat the word "manifestly" as one relating to the strength of the evidence whereas it can better be understood as relating to the extent to which the impugned order was at variance with Irish public policy. Charles J.'s approach seems dangerously provincial. The mere fact that the impugned order was not within the range of orders that would have been open to the court of the state addressed to make is not a reason to invoke public policy. Something more than this is essential.

Turning to the question of the change of circumstances, to which Art.10(1)(b) refers, Finlay Geoghegan J. was satisfied that this change must relate to the period after the making of the foreign order sought to be enforced. She was assisted in coming to this conclusion not only by the wording of Art.10(1)(b) itself, but also by Art.9(3) which provides that in no circumstances may the foreign decision be reviewed as to its substance:

> "In considering what were the circumstances at the time of the order of 29th July, 2003, this court must start from a presumption, as I am sure it was the case, that the order of 29th July, 2003, was an order made by the English High Court in what it perceived in the circumstances then prevailing and made known to it to be the appropriate provisions for contact between the girls and the father in accordance with the English principles of paramount welfare of the girls. The purpose of Article 10(1)(a) is only to permit this court to take into account a change in circumstances after the date of the making of the English order and article 9(3) precludes this court from revisiting the decision of the English Court."

There was a further complication. Counsel for the maternal aunt submitted that it was clear that the substance of the contact provisions had been considered in January and that the two further orders had been made following the perceived default by the maternal aunt to comply with the terms of the January order. Accordingly, the court should consider the July order as part of a series of orders made from January to July whose substance was considered in January and therefore should consider a change in circumstances after January rather than July.

It was not, in the circumstances of her holdings on other issues, necessary for Finlay Geoghegan J. to resolve this issue on the facts of this case. She did, however, express the view that:

> "[w]hilst undoubtedly ... the general principle appears to be that the court must only look at a change in circumstances after the date of the order being sought to be enforced it may be that, in circumstances where it is clear that the order sought to be enforced is an order made without substantive consideration of facts and for the purposes of continuing an earlier order, ... it would be consistent with the terms of Article 10(1)(b) to consider a change in circumstances from the date of the earlier order."

Finlay Geoghegan J. noted that, in August 2003, as in January earlier in the year, the father had again indicated that, if the girls came to London, they would have to stay with him or his adult daughter. This represented one change in circumstances subsequent to the English High Court order in July. The second change in circumstances concerned the serious deterioration in the elder daughter's relationship with her father, triggered by his insistence about where she or her sister should stay when in London. A similar deterioration had occurred in the younger daughter's relationship with her father, caused in part by this insistence and in part by his failure to respond to a Christmas card she had sent him in December 2003. There had been no contact between the father and his daughters since 2003. Finlay Geoghegan J. further concluded by reason of these changes in the circumstances that it was manifestly no longer in accordance with the welfare of either of the girls that the July order be recognised and enforced.

Finally, Finlay Geoghegan J. held, under Art.10(1)(d), that the July order was incompatible with the order of O'Neill J. in November 2002 insofar as it required the children to be taken out of the jurisdiction of the Irish High Court. Counsel for the father had argued, in the light of the Supreme Court decision in *DK v Crowley* [2002] 2 I.R. 744 (analysed in *Annual Review of Irish Law 2002*, pp.255–262), that O'Neill J.'s order, being an interim one made on an ex parte basis but expressed to last until the hearing of the summons was an order which it was not competent for the High Court to make.

Finlay Geoghegan J. rejected this submission for two reasons. First O'Neill J.'s order had been made in proceedings intended to be issued and to be served on the applicant and actually so issued and served. The applicant had not sought to have that order set aside by applying to the High Court, as he would be entitled to do, but on the contrary had filed a replying affidavit and proceeded to the hearing of the summons. A date had been fixed for the hearing prior to the issue of the instant proceedings. The only reason for which those proceedings had not been heard was the automatic stay provided for in s.27 of the Act of 1991 following the institution of the instant proceedings.

Secondly, Finlay Geoghegan J. did not accept that it followed from the decision of the Supreme Court in *DK v Crowley* that there were no circumstances in which a judge might make an order restraining the removal of children from the jurisdiction of the court pending the hearing of the relevant proceedings even on an ex parte basis. There were significant differences between such an injunction and the barring order at issue in *DK v Crowley*. The interim barring order was mandatory in nature, requiring the respondent to leave the family home whereas an order of the type made by O'Neill J. was prohibitive in nature and for the purpose simply of preserving the status quo pending the hearing of the proceedings. Moreover, the failure to comply with the interim barring order automatically entailed the commission of a criminal offence, unlike the position of a person who failed to comply with an injunction.

3. Jurisdiction in guardianship proceedings   In *Re EO, a Minor and MO, a Minor; FN and ED v CO, HO and EK*, unreported, High Court, March 26, 2004, Finlay Geoghegan J. held that the habitual residence of two Belgian children, aged 13 and 14, in Ireland afforded a sound basis of jurisdiction in guardianship, custody and access proceedings, even though all the parties were Belgian nationals. She referred to *LR v DR* [1994] 1 I.R. 239, analysed in *Annual Review of Irish Law 1992*, pp.112–115, where Costello J. had held that the mere presence of the child within the State gave the Irish courts jurisdiction. Moreover, it appeared to Finlay Geoghegan J. to be desirable, in the absence of compelling reasons to the contrary, that the courts in the jurisdiction where a child was habitually resident should be the forum for determining disputes relating to guardianship, custody or access. Resolving such disputes normally needed an enquiry into issues surrounding the child's welfare. This was most easily done in the jurisdiction where the child was habitually resident. In the instant case, there were no active proceedings pending in Belgium relating to the children at the time the Irish proceedings were heard. This was a further reason for the Irish court to accept jurisdiction.

DIVORCE

Estoppel   The decision of *CK v JK*, unreported, Supreme Court, March 31, 2004 raises substantial questions about the values underlying family law in the present constitutional dispensation. At one level the court's holding can be described simply: the doctrine of estoppel has no place in determining whether a foreign divorce should be recognised under Irish private international law. At a deeper level, more troubling issues arise relating to the notion of marriage as involving a status and the extent to which marriage is to be regarded as accommodating personal or social goals.

In *CK v JK* the respondent had married in 1968. There was one child of the marriage. In 1972 the spouses separated. The respondent's wife, who was a school teacher, did not look to him for maintenance for herself or her child. In 1979 the respondent met the applicant and, according to the Circuit Court judge, Judge McCartan, "they started to date". The respondent moved to work in the same company as the applicant shortly afterwards. His work involved going to Ohio on training courses lasting three to four weeks. He went on two of these trips in 1981. On one of them he initiated divorce proceedings against his wife based on a false assertion of residence in Ohio. He returned to Ohio in March 1982 for the final hearing and the grant of the decree.

The respondent's wife had received notification of the divorce petition but (according to Judge McCartan's findings) "decided to ignore it as affairs with the respondent had long been settled." When she received notice of the actual decree, she "was amused by the reference to child support which she confidently and correctly anticipated would amount to nothing in reality."

The applicant had not been "involved directly in the attempts by the respondent to clear the way for their marriage. [She] had sought the divorce document and on its reading it seemed to her that a judge of capable authority, who had the attendance of the respondent in court and was satisfied of all legal requirements, had granted the divorce sought."

In early 1983, the respondent applied to the General Register Office in England for recognition of the Ohio divorce but this was refused. In March of that year the parties married at the Registry Office in Dublin. The application to the Registrar was on the basis that the respondent was a bachelor. The Circuit Court recorded that the respondent, "realising that he was not properly divorced, actively concealed that fact from the Registrar and [the applicant]."

Here we may pause briefly in the narration of the facts to make a possibly impertinent observation. The judgments in the Supreme Court proceeded on the basis that the applicant was a victim of the respondent's fraudulent behaviour and that she was completely unaware of the position. Yet the Circuit Court judge's findings on this matter were more carefully crafted, so far as it is possible to glean from the Supreme Court judgments. He did not hold that the applicant was unaware of the description of her prospective husband as a bachelor or of his earlier attempt to obtain recognition in England for the divorce. It appears that she was fully aware of his earlier marriage and the continuing existence of his wife and teenage child. As regards the Ohio divorce proceedings, she knew that a man all of whose long-term connections were with Ireland, at a time when divorce was constitutionally prohibited, had obtained a divorce having visited Ohio for two brief periods of three to four weeks. It is surely ascribing a degree of naivety to the applicant beyond what is credible to conclude that she could have accepted without qualms the legal effectiveness of the Ohio divorce.

Reverting to the narrative, the parties after their 1983 marriage ceremony stayed together for almost 17 years. They had two children. The applicant took proceedings for judicial separation against the respondent, seeking ancillary reliefs. The respondent filed a defence and counterclaim in which he sought a declaration of nullity of marriage on the basis of a prior subsisting marriage.

Judge McCartan considered that justice could be achieved only by the use of estoppel whereby the respondent would not be allowed to challenge the validity of the Ohio divorce. His factual findings included the following:

> "The respondent's original spouse ... was aware of the making of the application and did not object [and] was not adversely affected by the making of the order of divorce....
>
> The child of the respondent's marriage [in 1968] is not adversely affected by the continued existence of the divorce....
>
> The applicant and her two children would suffer significant diminution of status and reduction of financial rights should the validity of her marriage be undermined....
>
> No collusion or complicity can be laid at the feet of the applicant in the application for a licence to marry the respondent."

Judge McCartan stated a case to the Supreme Court on the application of the applicant.

The Supreme Court unanimously held that estoppel had no application. The earlier decision of the Supreme Court in *Gaffney v Gaffney* [1975] I.R. 133 had rejected the idea that estoppel should have such a role. In that case a couple domiciled in Ireland had obtained a divorce in England on the basis of a false assertion of a jurisdictional entitlement there. The husband remarried. The first wife was held entitled to a legal right under the Succession Act 1965.

Walsh J. had stated:

> "The paramount issue in the present case is the status of the plaintiff and her husband at the date of his death. The plaintiff was either his wife or she was not. Apart from other legal incidents in this country, certain constitutional rights may accrue to a woman by virtue of being a wife which would not be available to her if she were not. The matter cannot, therefore, by any rules of evidence be left in a position of doubt nor could the Courts countenance a doctrine of estoppel, if such existed, which had the effect that a person would be estopped from saying that he or she is the husband or wife, as the case may be, of another party when in law the person making the claim has that status. In law it would have been quite open to the husband to have denied at any time after

his marriage to the defendant that he was in law her husband. If during the currency of that marriage the plaintiff had claimed that she was his wife, she might have been met with the answer which is being offered on behalf of the defendant in this case—that the plaintiff was estopped from doing so because she had submitted to a jurisdiction which purported to change that status. Consent cannot confer jurisdiction to dissolve a marriage where that jurisdiction does not already exist. The evidence which the plaintiff sought to offer in the present case was directed towards showing that the court in question did not have jurisdiction. In my view, the learned trial judge was quite correct in admitting that evidence."

Henchy J. said that he failed:

"to see why, although the decree seems good on its face, evidence should not be received to show that its façade conceals a lack of jurisdiction no less detrimental to its validity than if it had been written into the order. To hold otherwise would be to close one's eyes to the available truth and to give effect instead to a spurious divorce which the English court was deluded by sworn misrepresentations into making.

The position is not affected by the fact that it is a foreign decree. The comity of courts under private international law does not require or permit recognition of decisions given, intentionally or unintentionally, in disregard of jurisdictional competence. Counsel for the defendant is unable to point to any authority showing that a party to a foreign divorce which was given without jurisdiction was debarred from giving evidence pointing out the want of jurisdiction. On the contrary, a number of authorities cited in the High Court (or cases referred to in those authorities) exemplify or support the reception of such evidence: see, for example, *Bonaparte v. Bonaparte* [1892] P. 402, *Shaw v. Gould* (1868) L.R. 3 H.L. 55, *Middleton v. Middleton* [1996] 2 W.L.R. 512. I am satisfied that there can be no estoppel by record when the record arose in proceedings, domestic or foreign, upon which the court in question had no jurisdiction to adjudicate."

The issue of estoppel has come before the courts in the intervening three decades.

In *RB v AS (Nullity: domicile)* [2002] 2 I.R. 428, which we analyse in *Annual Review of Irish Law 2001*, pp.57–60, Keane C.J. stated:

"While it was suggested ... that the petitioner, by his conduct at the time in encouraging and facilitating the divorce, was estopped from contesting the validity of his marriage, I do not think that that argument was seriously pressed during the oral submissions and, in my view, correctly, so. It is clear from the judgment of Walsh J. in this court in *Gaffney v. Gaffney* [1975] I.R. 133 that the doctrine of estoppel cannot operate so as to change a person's status where that status, as a matter of law, has not been changed."

In *PK (otherwise C) v TK* [2002] 2 I.R. 186 Fennelly J. noted that the dictum of Walsh J. in *Gaffney* had not been challenged in that case. He went on, however, to make the following observations:

> "The evidence to which objection was taken in that case was evidence which the plaintiff had given to show that she had been coerced by threats into presenting a divorce petition in England, a petition which on its face asserted that the plaintiff was domiciled in England. It would have been egregious to exclude it. The dictum of Walsh J. was recently approved in the judgment of Keane C.J. in *R.B. v. A.S. (Nullity: Domicile)* [2002] 2 IR 428. The matter was not, it appears, fully argued in that case. Nonetheless, the principle appears to have been broadly accepted in many jurisdictions though with occasional dissent ... For my own part, I would not wish categorically to exclude the possibility that a person who had acted so in relation to a decree of divorce granted by a foreign jurisdiction might be precluded from questioning its validity. However, the issue has not been argued on this appeal ... ."

In the instant case, four judgments were delivered: by Denham, Murray, McGuinness and Fennelly JJ., McCracken J. concurring with his four judicial colleagues. There was a complete agreement on the central issue: estoppel had no application. There were nuanced differences of emphasis on related aspects of the subject.

Denham J. had an objection in principle of the use of estoppel in this context. She was:

> "satisfied that in relation to such an important area as status and the constitutional family it is inappropriate to consider using a rule which, by analogy, creates or uses a legal fiction. This is an inappropriate device to be used in a modern constitution. The rule of law is not supported by such a subterfuge ...
>
> To preclude the respondent from relying on the facts of the case, to apply estoppel, would mean that for the purpose of this case the applicant would enjoy a status to which she is not entitled in law. While it is clear that there have been enormous legal changes since 1975, the core principle in Gaffney remains the same. Indeed, if as a consequence of the enormous legal changes, there are many anomalous and difficult cases where litigants might seek to gain an unfair advantage, there is no merit in making the situation more complex and potentially more

problematical by using estoppel in some circumstance and not others. It would have the effect of introducing an element of legal fiction into this already complex field."

Denham J. also considered that the status of marriage was incompatible with a doctrine of estoppel:

> "At the core of this case is the issue of status. The status of the parties gives rise to constitutional, as well as legal, rights. The status of a person is important for the individual, for the families involved and the community. A person and their status is a building block in the fundamental unit group of our society, under the Constitution, the family.
>
> All the reliefs sought by the applicant are predicated on the fact that she is a spouse. Yet under the law and the Constitution she is not. I am satisfied the applicant cannot evade the reality of the situation by her legal argument such as submitting that the decision is inter partes only, that it is in personam, or that the respondent be estopped from proving all the circumstances of the case. The law is as stated in *Gaffney* and precludes the operation of the doctrine of estoppel in relation to marital status. The doctrine of estoppel cannot operate to change a person's status in law."

McGuinness J. acknowledged that the approach favoured by McCartan J. had "many attractions" but she was ultimately swayed by the difficulties it would create. Decrees affecting marital status were not purely private law matters. The estoppel doctrine might, moreover, work injustice on the first spouse while endeavouring to do justice to the second partner. She noted that, in the decision of the Supreme Court of Canada in *Downton v Royal Trust Company* (1972) 34 D.L.R. (3d) 403, Laskin J. had expressed support for the application of a doctrine of estoppel (or "preclusion") where one spouse, having obtained a decree of divorce or nullity from a foreign court incompetent to give it, later seeks to assert that incompetence in order to gain a pecuniary advantage against the other spouse (or the estate of that other spouse). Laskin J. had, however, indicated that "[a]ny ethical factors underlying the preclusion doctrine are submerged in overriding considerations when an invalid foreign decree is pressed in a strictly matrimonial cause in which divorce or nullity is sought. Marital status *per se* cannot be altered or perpetuated by a preclusion doctrine …".

In McGuinness J.'s view, there was considerable difficulty in the distinction made in *Downton* between "strictly matrimonial causes" and other cases in which the preclusion doctrine applied:

> "In the present case, for example, the applicant argues that the preclusion doctrine should apply in her judicial separation proceedings. Yet the

respondent in the same proceedings by way of counterclaim seeks a decree of nullity which is, presumably, a 'strictly matrimonial cause'. Are the present proceedings as a whole, therefore, a 'strictly matrimonial cause' or not?

The notice party, whatever be the outcome of the applicant's proceedings, clearly cannot rely as she has hitherto done on the validity of the Ohio divorce. As can be seen from her letter she wishes to obtain a divorce in this jurisdiction from the respondent (for which she appears to have the clearest grounds). Her divorce proceedings would also be a 'strictly matrimonial cause'.

Thus within one set of circumstances two forms of relief could be sought which are essentially based on the invalidity of the foreign divorce, while in the applicant's proceedings no reliance could be placed on the invalidity of the same foreign divorce if a doctrine of estoppel or preclusion is accepted. The application of this principle would, it seems to me, be likely to cause confusion and inconsistency in future cases where the factual circumstances might not be so clear as in the present case."

McGuinness J. was clearly unimpressed by the argument against estoppel based on the importance of certainty in regard to marital status.
    She observed:

"This argument would, in my view, carry more weight if there was in reality any great degree of clarity and certainty in the current law in this field. As it is, the marital status of certain persons is governed by the Domicile and Recognition of Foreign Divorces Act 1986; that of others by the decision of this Court in *W v W* [1993] 2 IR 476. Our own legislation bases jurisdiction in judicial separation, divorce and nullity on 'ordinary residence' for a period of one year in addition to jurisdiction based on domicile. (See Judicial Separation and Family Law Reform Act 1989 section 31(4), Family Law (Divorce) Act 1996 section 39, Family Law Act 1995 section 39.) The marital status of some may, or perhaps may not, be affected by the judgments of the High Court in *G.McG v D.W.* [2000] 1 IR 96 and *D.T. v E.L.* [2002] 2 ILRM 152. Those who have obtained divorces which were initiated in Member States of the European Union since 1st March 2001 are governed by an entirely different regime, that of Council Regulation (EC 1347/2000) of 29th May 2000 on Jurisdiction and the Recognition and Enforcement of Judgments in Matrimonial Matters and in Matters of Parental Responsibility for Children of Both Spouses, generally known as Brussels II. This regime of recognition bases jurisdiction in the main on habitual residence, although a subsidiary alternative role is played by domicile and/or nationality. Presumably this recognition regime will later this year be extended to the ten new Member States. Brussels II does not, however, apply to Denmark. In certain cases the Regulation may apply to divorces obtained after 1st March 2001 where proceedings were instituted before that date, but this is quite uncertain.

To all this must be added the inherent complexity of the law of domicile, which over the years has led to much litigation. Still further uncertainty may be added by the provisions of section 29 of the Family Law Act 1995 which appears to mean that a declaration of marital status made by the Court will affect the parties in all cases but will not affect the State unless the Attorney General has been a party to the action. Bearing all this in mind it is not really surprising that at a recent conference a lecture by Mr Alan Shatter, author of 'Family Law in the Republic of Ireland', on the recognition of foreign divorces was entitled 'The Application of Chaos Theory'.

In these circumstances I would find it difficult to be swayed by any argument in the present proceedings based on the desirability of certainty regarding matrimonial status. Certainty may well be desirable, but it does not at present exist."

Perhaps this critique of the existing position is a little severe. The application of any legal connecting factor for recognition of foreign divorces to the facts of particular cases will always have some element of uncertainty. Domicile admittedly has its distinctive complexities but even habitual residence is not immune from uncertainty in its application, less so in cases of divorce, where the parties are adults, than in cases relating to the Hague Convention on child abduction: see above, p.125. The complexities created by Council Regulation (EC) 1347/2000 of May 29, 2000 apply to all Member States (save Denmark) and are unlikely to involve many individual instances of uncertainty in deciding whether the Regulation rules for recognition apply.

McGuinness J. went on to make the following interesting observation:

"[A] considerable number of persons in this country are involved in situations where a second marriage has followed on a prior foreign divorce which is possibly invalid. Such persons may well find themselves in a position comparable to that of the applicant. It is not satisfactory for the Court to deal with these complex and anomalous situations on a case by case basis, whether through the principles of estoppel or otherwise. It would be preferable that legislation be enacted both to create a clear and consistent code of recognition and to provide a remedy for persons who through no fault of their own have become parties to a marriage which later proves to be invalid."

Such a law would be formidably difficult to draft. Earlier in her judgment McGuinness J. had observed that, "due to the unavailability of divorce in this jurisdiction until recent times, a considerable number of persons are involved in situations where a second purported marriage has followed on an invalid prior foreign divorce." The applicant was "by no means alone in her unenviable position". This observation, in conjunction with McGuinness J.'s expression of preference for legislation, may suggest a willingness to countenance recognition to a range of second marriages following a divorce that was not capable of recognition. Whether this would involve statutory recognition of that divorce is not clear. It is noteworthy that s.2 of the Marriages Act 1972 conferred retrospective validation on marriages celebrated at Lourdes in breach of the formal requirements of the *lex loci celebrationis*. It did not address the position of people who, having celebrated such a void marriage, might have entered a second marriage which was (naturally) valid at the time of celebration. The Minister for Health, Mr Childers, was content to let the courts sort out the potential mess that the Oireachtas had—at least in theory—created.

The numbers involved in the Lourdes marriages problem were quite modest—considerably fewer than the numbers involved in unrecognisable divorces and void remarriages. Moreover, the possibility that parties to the Lourdes marriages had actually remarried other spouses was infinitesimally small.

If one moves away from cases of fraudulent inducement of a person to marry, such as the Supreme Court interpreted the facts in the instant case, McGuinness J.'s preference for legislation creating a new code for recognition of foreign divorces raises issues of justice and of public policy. As to justice, why should spouses who were in unsatisfactory marriages and who chose to obtain a foreign divorce which they knew to be incapable of recognition under Irish private international law now be rewarded when other spouses with equally unsatisfactorily marriages complied with the law and did not go through this process?

Perhaps the answer is that spouses who sought foreign divorces which they knew could not be recognised under the then-prevailing constitutional dispensation were exercising an autonomous choice (albeit often involving breaches of the law of the state where they obtained the divorce), marking a protest against the restraints which the absence of a domestic divorce regime imposed. Whether this is a fully satisfactory answer may be debated.

As to public policy, let us assume for the purposes of argument that the contemporary public policy is to be indifferent about whether people obtain foreign divorces incapable of recognition in Ireland and furthermore that this indifference extends to whether people have actually told lies in order to assert a jurisdictional basis to which they were not entitled. This assumption is not particularly controversial, since the effect of Art.17 of Council Regulation (EC) 1347/2000 of May 29, 2000 (Brussels II) (replicated in Art.26 of Council Regulation (EC) No.2201/2003) (Brussels II *bis)* is that Irish courts have to recognise decrees obtained in such circumstances. One may ask whether it is good public policy to beam the value of indifference back into a time when

Irish society largely embraced the opposing value of concern that the constitutional prohibition on divorce should not be sidestepped by falsehoods in foreign courts.

The Supreme Court judgment in *W v W* [1993] 2 I.R. 477 is interesting in this context because it was decided in 1992, six years after the constitutional prohibition on divorce had been strongly reaffirmed in a referendum. The Supreme Court there adopted a rule for recognising foreign divorces obtained in the years before the enactment of the Domicile and Recognition of Foreign Divorces Act 1986. This new rule required that courts have regard to contemporary policy. In the *Annual Review of Irish Law 1992*, pp.115–126, we criticised this approach on the basis of the inappropriateness of applying public policy values in a time warp. Spouses many years ago made decisions in the context of the social values that then applied. It can yield quite inappropriate solutions to apply contemporary values to those decisions, which were the product of the culture of that time.

In the instant case, a number of the judges addressed a series of related questions, of marriage as a status, whether a divorce or a judicial decree was a judgment *in rem* and how precisely a declaration made under s.29 of the Family Law Act 1995 affected the marital status of the parties. Their analysis ranged from the formal, in which an *in rem* characterisation was considered to represent, of itself, a refutation of the argument in favour of applying the estoppel doctrine, to a more substantive concentration on underlying social policies. Fennelly J. favoured the latter approach. He stated:

> "There was much discussion at the hearing about the distinction between actions *in rem* and *in personam*. It was generally agreed that judicial decisions concerning marital status have traditionally been regarded as judgments *in rem*. They affect the entire world. Decrees in matrimonial suits have long been considered to be judgments *in rem*. (See *Bater v Bater* [1906] P. 209])… It is perhaps unattractive to describe a marriage, even indirectly, as a thing. The essential point is that, whatever language is used, marriage involves status and has public-interest implications."

Counsel for the applicant had argued that matrimonial proceedings heard *in camera* could not bind the whole world, since the public did not know about them. The court did not accept this contention. Fennelly J. was:

> "satisfied that the purpose of the *in camera* rule applied to family law proceedings in this jurisdiction is to protect private and family life from potentially distressing public and media intrusion and that it does not diminish the character of the decisions made by those courts. They remain decisions as to status."

McGuinness J. referred in this context to the imminent legislative changes about to be effected by the Civil Registration Act 2004, Pt 7 of which provided for a full system of registration of decrees of divorce and decrees of nullity of marriage: see further below. It must be said that the privacy attaching to divorce decrees was hard to understand. One of the central arguments in favour of introducing divorce was that if a marriage was dead the court should be empowered to grant a death certificate. Divorce was seen as a public social endorsement of that fact and the conferral of "the right to remarry". It necessarily involved a public dimension: what is the point of obtaining a divorce if no one else is aware of it? A possible answer might be that one's personal relationships are such an intimate aspect of one's life that one should be free to choose whether to disclose the fact that one has been divorced, but this is hard to reconcile with the socio-legal phenomenon of the marriage ceremony which (like divorce) involves a change of status.

On the question whether a decree for judicial separation was *in rem* rather than *in personam*, Fennelly J. observed that such a decree:

> "does not change status, because it merely affects t[he] parties['] mutual obligations to cohabit. On the other hand, the entire jurisdiction is predicated on the existence of a marriage. Mr Durcan accepted that, in England, it has, for that reason, been held to be an action *in rem*. The fact of the grant of a decree of judicial separation has a number of legal consequences either flowing from the mere fact of the decree itself or from ancillary orders. The respondent would be entitled to tax relief on maintenance payments. Assets transferred pursuant to property orders are exempt from capital gains taxation. None of these matters are, of course, undesirable in themselves. They merely demonstrate that the decree has certain objective legal effects amounting to recognition in law of the marital status, though separated, of the parties ...
>
> I am convinced ... that judicial separation proceedings relate to the marital status of the parties to the action, even if they do not change that status. Such proceedings depend on the parties being lawfully married to each other. The problem is not merely that anomalies would flow from estopping the Respondent from impugning the validity of the Ohio divorce. The law is capable of accommodating anomalies. The objection is more fundamental. It is that the effects of a decree of judicial separation would not be limited to the private and personal rights and interests of the parties. The public interest is involved. The court itself is very directly involved. The jurisdiction of the court presumes that the parties are married. Once they are not, the court can not entertain the application. It would be closing its eyes to blatant evidence that it lacked jurisdiction."

The question of how the court should regard proceedings for judicial separation was important for the following reasons. Some courts in the United States of

America and, as we have seen, Laskin J. in the Canadian decision of *Downton v Royal Trust Company* (1972) 34 D.L.R. (3d) 403, have taken the view that, outside the context of decrees affecting status, it should be possible for the estoppel principle to apply so as to preclude a party from claiming some financial advantage by an inequitable invocation of the validity or incapacity for recognition of a foreign divorce or other decree-affecting status. This argument received the support of William Duncan in "Foreign Divorces Obtained on the Basis of Residence, and the Doctrine of Estoppel" 9 Irish Jurist (NS) 59 (1974).

Fennelly J. had this to say:

> "I am prepared to accept, as a hypothesis, the argument propounded by Mr Duncan in his Irish Jurist article. A person who has behaved as the respondent in this case has done should, as a matter of general principle, be precluded by the doctrine of estoppel from proving the invalidity of the divorce obtained by him from a foreign court on concocted and fraudulent evidence, where his object is to obtain an unfair advantage over another or where he seeks a specific remedy. The real question is to identify the sort of advantage or remedy which he should be precluded from getting. If, for example, he were to seek recovery of sums paid on foot of the divorce decree, or otherwise to readjust property ownership with his lawful wife, the plea might have merit. Such a spouse might, depending on the circumstances, find it difficult to maintain a claim to share in the estate of his deceased lawful wife. It will be recalled that Walsh J was of the opinion that, if it had not been for the duress, the plaintiff in *Gaffney v Gaffney* would have been bound to apply to the English court to set aside the divorce decree. None of those situations, however, so directly affect marital status as does this one."

McGuinness J. observed that:

> "The applicant in reality seeks through the means of estoppel to obtain certain orders in regard to maintenance and, more importantly, to property. These orders, however, can only be obtained as a result of, and ancillary to, a decree of judicial separation. In order to grant such a decree the Court must itself hold (a) that the parties were legally married and (b) that the marriage has broken down on the grounds set out in section 2 of the Judicial Separation and Family Law Reform Act 1989."

The idea here appears to be that the ancillary claims for maintenance were so integrally connected with a claim based on marital status that they stood or fell by reference to the status issue. One is reminded here of the time when Irish courts were nervously venturing towards recognising awards for maintenance made in foreign divorce proceedings. In *Sachs v Standard Chartered Bank*

(Ireland) Ltd [1987] I.L.R.M. 297, Barrington J. observed that "[a] woman's right to have such a financial provision made for her arises not because she was divorced but because she was married and the marriage has broken down."

Is it possible to make a distinction in principle between the following two cases? In the first, a man has divorced his first wife abroad in circumstances known by both him and his first wife to render the divorce incapable of recognition. The man and the wife both enter second marriages to partners who reasonably believe that the divorce was capable of recognition. The man in due course dies and the first wife re-appears to assert her "legal right" under the Succession Act 1965. Fennelly J. appears to countenance the application of the estoppel doctrine in such an instance. The result will be that the second "wife" can claim a legal right under the 1965 Act.

The second case—involving facts similar to those in the instant case—involves a woman who seeks a judicial separation and ancillary orders only to discover that her "husband" is still legally married to his first wife because his foreign divorce is not capable of recognition. McGuinness J. expressly, and the other judges in the instant case implicitly, held that she cannot invoke the estoppel doctrine against her "husband" because her claim is founded integrally on her having the status of lawful wife. How is it that one innocent wife can succeed and another not?

We suggest that there is in fact no difference in principle between these cases. Form is obscuring a clear vision of what is just. What is needed is for the courts to recognise that family law should be seeking to have a series of principles which are just and humane and protect dependant members of the family. Of course these principles have to be articulated in a formal structure, but that formal dimension should not be permitted to defeat the efficacy of the operation of these principles. It may well be that the language of estoppel is unfortunate in that it forces the court to resolve just claims through the use of formal characterisations that are simply not true. That explains Denham J.'s rejection of "legal fictions" as being inappropriate for use in a modern constitution.

This brings us to Murray J.'s reflections on the subject. He constructed a constitutional edifice for ensuring that justice would be done to people in the position of the applicant. He stated:

> "In a society based on the rule of law it would certainly be a major gap in its fabric if persons who have been wronged in the manner in which the applicant has been in this case were to be left without remedy. In such a society the system of law is intended to be complete, that is to say that within its framework it provides, in principle, a remedy for any denial of rights conferred by law or its constitution (the extent of the remedy may be constrained by public policy considerations in the interests of the common good or, where the right is conferred by law by the limited nature of the right, but none of these extra considerations

seem to me to arise in this context). Either the applicant has some remedy against the applicant or she has not ... .

The applicant has sought to rely on the doctrine of estoppel as a means of defending the consequences of being stripped ignominiously of the legal and constitutional status of a duly married wife. *Gaffney v Gaffney* says that estoppel cannot apply in these circumstances as a remedy for the applicant. If, as has been suggested, estoppel was the only remedy available to the applicant and in the absence of which she had no remedy at all, I would be bound to entertain grave doubts as to whether that case was indeed a complete statement of the law on this matter. Therefore, I feel it necessary to consider whether, as argued by the Attorney General in defence of the law as laid down in *Gaffney v Gaffney*, whether there are indeed any alternative remedies available to a plaintiff in a similar fact situation as the learned Circuit Court Judge found the applicant in this case to be.

Thus, this is a question of law arising in this Case Stated which for me is directly relevant to the question whether the law as reflected in *Gaffney v Gaffney* is indeed the law as it applies to these circumstances having regard to the protection which the Constitution gives to the institution of marriage, and married persons."

Murray J. interpreted Art.41.3 of the Constitution as being intended not only to protect the institution of marriage as such against attack but as also "clearly envisag[ing] that the rights of individuals, as married persons, should be protected". He referred to his own judgment in *DT v CT* [2002] 3 I.R. 355 (analysed in *Annual Review of Irish Law 2002*, pp.263–282 where he had emphasised the fact that marriage was a solemn contract of partnership with a special constitutional status, under which the law held the parties to certain obligations. He went on to make the following important statement:

"That status, with its concurrent obligations and liabilities, is protected by the Constitution. When a person in good faith enters into a marriage contract, solemnised in accordance with law, he or she is entitled to expect to enjoy their constitutional status and the protections which the law affords, even in the event of its breakdown or ultimate dissolution.

If the law permitted a person to induce, by deceit or fraudulent mis-representation, another to enter into an otherwise lawful marriage and after many years of ostensible marriage to cut himself adrift without any obligation to the other person it would in my view undermine the status of the marriage contract itself and the constitutional rights which that person was entitled to have protected by virtue of that status. A prosecution for bigamy where a person enters into a second marriage in the full knowledge that a first marriage is valid and subsisting may be a means of protecting the public interest but it is not a remedy which vindicates or protects the rights of the injured party. A declaration as to status can afford protection to the legitimate spouse of the first marriage. In my view it is a direct attack on the constitutional rights of a person for another to induce them or cause them to enter into a duly solemnised marriage contract by deceit when the latter knows that he lacks the capacity to enter into a valid marriage by reason of a pre-existing and subsisting marriage.

In *bona fide* participating in a marriage ceremony before a person duly authorised in the eyes of the State to perform it she was entitled to the constitutional status of a married person; 'certain constitutional rights may accrue to a woman by virtue of being a wife' (*Gaffney v Gaffney*, [1975] IR, at 152). That was a right she was entitled to enjoy at least throughout the seventeen years when they lived together as husband and wife with the consequential protections which the law provides should the marriage irretrievably break down. She was denied those rights by the deceit and fraudulent misrepresentations of the respondent.

If a conspiracy to dismiss or a dismissal of an employee because of his refusal to undertake to join a trade union as a condition of his employment is an actionable infringement of his constitutional right to associate or dissociate (*Meskell v C.I.E.* [1973] I.R. 121). I can see no reason why it is not an actionable infringement of, in this case, a woman's right to marital status if, having been ostensibly lawfully married, she is denied it by reason of the deceit and/or fraudulent misrepresentations of her partner."

The *Meskell* principle, in Murray J.'s view, ensured that the applicant was entitled to the protection of the courts for the infringement of her constitutional rights. The question, therefore, was whether the existing framework of torts afforded her a remedy: if it did, there would be no need for the court to grant her a remedy outside what Walsh J. in *Meskell* had described as "ordinary forms of action".

Murray J. was "quite satisfied", for the purposes of the Case Stated, on the basis of the facts as found, that the applicant would have a remedy in law for actionable deceit grounded on the fraudulent misrepresentations of the respondent. In such an action for deceit, a court would be entitled, when awarding damages, to take into account the statutory and other entitlements of a plaintiff who was separated from her ostensible husband if the marriage had in fact been valid. The Statute of Limitations 1957 should not represent a bar in the light of the continuing fraud or concealment on the part of a defendant as to his or her true capacity to marry.

Constitutional Law

ORAN DOYLE, Lecturer in Law, Trinity College, Dublin
and
ESTELLE FELDMAN, Research Associate, Trinity College, Dublin

CONSTITUTIONAL AMENDMENT

On June 10, 2004, the people voted to insert a new Art.9.2 into the Constitution:

> "1° Notwithstanding any other provision of this Constitution, a person born in the island of Ireland, which includes its islands and its seas, who does not have, at the time of his or her birth, at least one parent who is an Irish citizen or entitled to be an Irish citizen is not entitled to Irish citizenship or nationality, unless otherwise provided for by law.
>
> 2° This section shall not apply to persons born before the date of the enactment of this section".

The previous Art.9.2, which states that fidelity to the nation and loyalty to the State are fundamental political duties of all citizens, was renumbered as Art.9.3.

This amendment essentially changes the constitutional basis for Irish citizenship previously set out in Art.2. In *Lobe and Ossayande v Minister for Justice* [2003] 1 I.R. 1, a number of members of the Supreme Court commented that the effect of Art.2 of the Constitution was to entitle all persons born on the island of Ireland to Irish citizenship. This has been changed by Art.9.2.1°. Pursuant to Art.9.2.1°, one is now *constitutionally* entitled to citizenship only if (a) one is born on the island of Ireland, and (b) at the time of one's birth one has at least one parent who is an Irish citizen or entitled to be an Irish citizen. Alternatively, but of increasingly less relevance, one is constitutionally an Irish citizen if one was a citizen of Saorstát Éireann at the time the Constitution came into force. In all other circumstances, one's entitlement to citizenship is determined by non-constitutional law.

The inconsistency between Art.2 and Art.9.2.1° is resolved in favour of Art.9.2.1° by its opening phrase "notwithstanding any other provision of this Constitution". This phrase effectively elevates Art.9.2.1° over Art.2 and immunises the legislative regime envisaged by Art.9.2.1° from constitutional challenge by reference to Art.2. However, it also immunises that legislative regime from constitutional challenge by reference to any other provision of the Constitution. Thus it is no longer open to a person, as it was in *Somjee v Minister for Justice* [1981] I.L.R.M. 324, to challenge citizenship laws by reference to other provisions of the Constitution, such as Art.40.1. Assuming that "provision" does not mean "Article", it also appears that citizenship laws can no longer be invalidated by reference to Art.9.1.3°, which provides that no person may be excluded from Irish nationality and citizenship by reason of the sex of such person. In short, citizenship legislation cannot be constitutionally challenged, save by reference to Art.9.2.1°.

As a number of constitutional rights depend on one's status as a citizen, this amendment to constitutional citizenship laws has a number of significant effects. Most obviously, one's right to reside in the State and one's right to vote in national elections depend on whether one is a citizen. With respect to other constitutional rights, the situation is less clear. The general tendency has not been to see non-citizenship as a bar to the invocation of constitutional rights (see *Re Article 26 and the Illegal Immigrants (Trafficking) Bill 1999* [2000] 2 I.R. 360 at 384). However, given the wording of a number of constitutional rights provisions which limit protection to "citizens" in apparent contradistinction to human persons in general, it remains possible that Art.9.2.1° lessens the constitutional protection of some persons in respects other than residence and voting. (See generally William Binchy, "Citizenship and the International Remit of Constitutional Protection" in Binchy ed., *The Citizenship Referendum: Implications for the Constitution and Human Rights* (Trinity College Law School, 2004)).

At a more general level, Art.9.2.1° introduces a pedigree distinction into the core of constitutional law. One's constitutional entitlement to Irish citizenship now turns primarily on who one's parents are. This alters the basis for the Supreme Court's judgment in *An Blascaod Mór Teoranta v Commissioners of Public Works* [2000] 1 I.R. 6 at 19; [2000] 1 I.L.R.M. 401 at 409:

> "In the present case the classification appears to be at once too narrow and too wide. It is hard to see what legitimate legislative purpose it fulfils. It is based on a principle – that of pedigree – which appears to have no place (outside the law of succession) in a democratic society committed to the principle of equality. This fact alone makes the classification suspect. The Court agrees with the learned trial judge that a Constitution should be pedigree blind just as it should be colour blind or gender blind except when those issues are relevant to a legitimate legislative purpose. This Court can see no such legitimate legislative purpose in the present case and has no doubt but that the plaintiffs are being treated unfairly as compared with persons who owned or occupied and resided on lands on the island prior to November 1953 and their descendants".

Article 9.2.1° provides clear constitutional authorisation for pedigree distinctions in public law. For this reason, the courts' evolving case law on Art.40.1 might need to be reconsidered in light of Art.9.2.1°. On the other hand, it might be argued that the opening phrase of Art.9.2.1°, "notwithstanding any other provision of the Constitution", immunises the other provisions of the Constitution from Art.9.2.1° in the same way that it immunises Art.9.2.1° from other provisions of the Constitution. If the courts were to adopt that interpretation of Art.9.2.1°, its effect on constitutional doctrine would not be as significant. (For further discussion, see Oran Doyle, *Constitutional Equality Law* (Thomson Round Hall, 2004) at pp.142–143.)

CONSTITUTIONAL CHALLENGE TO INFRASTRUCTURAL PROJECTS

Carrickmines Castle challenges *Dunne v Minister for Environment, Heritage and Local Government* [2004] I.E.H.C. 304 (September 7, 2004) was the third in the series of High Court challenges in connection with the construction of the South Eastern Route, M50 motorway, and the archaeological site colloquially known as Carrickmines Castle. In the first action, *Dunne v Dun Laoghaire-Rathdown County Council* [2003] 1 I.R. 567, (*Dunne No.1*), whilst the Supreme Court held that there was a fair and bona fide question to be determined in relation to the absence of a consent by the Minister under s.14 of the National Monument Act 1930 as amended by s.15 of the National Monuments Act 1994 for works on the Carrickmines Castle site, the case never went to plenary hearing. The county council and the State put a consent in place, and the injunction preventing any works was discharged. This provoked the second proceedings, *Mulcreevy v Minister for Environment, Heritage and Local Government and Dun Laoghaire-Rathdown County Council* [2004] 1 I.L.R.M. 419. The Supreme Court gave leave to apply by way of judicial review for an order of certiorari, and in the High Court Kearns J. quashed the Minister's approval order to proceed with the works (this case is discussed below under "Legislative Power"). Subsequently, the Oireachtas enacted the National Monuments (Amendment) Act 2004 which amended the 1930 Act and introduced a special provision in relation to the South Eastern Route. In the instant case, the plaintiff, a co-plaintiff in *Dunne No.1*, was questioning the permissibility of s.8 of the 2004 Act having regard to the Constitution and to European Union law (some aspects of this case are also discussed below under "Legislative Power").

Imperative to complete M50 Laffoy J. expressed no doubt whatsoever as to the meaning and effect of the impugned provision.

"On its face, when considered in the context of the entire National

Monuments Acts code and, in particular the provisions of the Act of 2004, in my view, the meaning and effect of s.8 is absolutely clear. The history of the South Eastern Route [the M50 motorway], which is partially recounted earlier, leaves one in no doubt as to the policy by which the enactment of s.8 was driven. It was to ensure the completion of the South Eastern Route without any input in relation to national monument protection implications from any party external to the Minister and his advisors and the Council and its advisors. *Prima facie*, the Oireachtas has given statutory force to that policy in s.8". *Dunne v Minister for Environment, Heritage and Local Government* [2004] I.E.H.C. 304.

Nebulous constitutional challenge   In addition to challenging the statutory provision by reference to Art.15.2, a challenge was taken under Arts 5, 10 and 40. In relation to this aspect of the plaintiff's case, Laffoy J. commented:

"Counsel for the Minister submitted, not unfairly in my view, that the plaintiff's claim based on Articles 5, 10 and 40 is nebulous and hard to pin down. The plaintiff's own counsel acknowledged, realistically in my view, that it is an ambitious claim and that it sails into uncharted waters" [2004] I.E.H.C. 304.

The claim did, indeed, fail on all three counts, but not before an in-depth excursion in the judgment citing such authorities as, *inter alia*, *Tuohy v Courtney* [1994] 3 I.R. 1 at 47 regarding the court's role in a challenge to the constitutional validity of a statute; *Heaney v Ireland* [1994] 3 I.R. 593 at 607 regarding proportionality; *Webb v Ireland* [1988] I.R. 353 regarding the State's entitlement to possession and ownership of antiquities and protection of archaeological heritage; and several authorities on *locus standi* including *J.M. Kelly: The Irish Constitution* (4th ed., LexisNexis Butterworths, Dublin, 2003) at p.807.

Of particular relevance to the Carrickmines Castle saga and the issue of *locus standi*, Laffoy J. cited extensively from the judgment of Keane C.J. in *Mulcreevy* [2004] 1 I.L.R.M. 419 at 426:

"It has been made clear in decisions of the High Court and this court in recent times that it is not in the public interest that decisions by statutory bodies which are of at least questionable validly [*sic*] should wholly escape scrutiny because a person who seeks to invoke the jurisdiction of the court by way of judicial review cannot show that he is personally affected, in some sense peculiar to him, by the decision. ... It is at the same time essential to bear in mind that, while it is undesirable that invalid legislation or unlawful practices should escape scrutiny because of the absence of an indisputably qualified objector, it is also important

to ensure that unfounded and vexatious challenges are not entertained"
[2004] I.E.H.C. 304.

Laffoy J. dismissed the Minister's challenge to the plaintiff's *locus standi*
relying on the aforementioned authorities:

> "The essence of this aspect of the plaintiff's claim, as I understand it, is
> that, in enacting s.8, the Oireachtas has put in place arrangements which
> are inimical to, and fail to safeguard and protect, a monument which is
> part of the natural heritage in contravention of the States obligation
> derived primarily from Article 5 of the Constitution. I am of the view
> that there is authority for the proposition that he has *locus standi* to
> maintain this challenge". [2004] I.E.H.C. 304.

Safeguarding national assets not a personal right   Noting beyond doubt
that it is a constitutional imperative that the State safeguard national assets,
including monuments of cultural and historical significance, Laffoy J. could
not see how this duty could translate into a personal right of the type which,
although unspecified, is protected by Art.40.3.

> "It is not inconceivable that in a hypothetical case, a person in the
> position of the plaintiff, a concerned private citizen, could successfully
> challenge a statutory measure on the basis that it purported to permit a
> clear-cut breach of the State's duty to protect the national heritage.
> This is not such a case. In inviting the court to review s.8 in the light of
> the State's duty to safeguard the national heritage and the other
> requirements of the common good, the plaintiff is asking the court, to
> use the metaphor used by Keane C.J. in *TD v Minister for Education*
> [2001] 4 I.R. 259 at 288, to cross a Rubicon and to undertake a role
> which is conferred by statute on the Oireachtas under the Constitution.
> The court cannot do that".   [2004] I.E.H.C. 304.

Safeguarding heritage, a warning knell   While motorists caught in the traffic
congestion exacerbated by the legal challenges to the construction of the M50
have cause to celebrate the judgment in the second *Dunne* case, one needs to
consider the implications of legislation driven by the impatience of seemingly
endless delays. Laffoy J., in considering s.8, stated:

> "Although the Minister must issue valid directions if such are necessary
> for the completion of the South Eastern Route, which clearly is the
> case, his consideration as to the content of the directions is untrammelled
> by archaeological considerations even to the extent that he may direct
> the destruction in whole or in part of the national monument at
> Carrickmines Castle, taking account of the public interest". *Dunne v*

Minister for Environment, Heritage and Local Government [2004] I.E.H.C. 304.

The question the courts may well have to reconsider is whether an "untrammelled" discretion to a Minister, albeit lawfully passed by the Oireachtas, is constitutionally sound. Assuming such delegated legislation passes the *Cityview* and *East Donegal* tests, the former discussed elsewhere in this chapter, is it really in accord with Art.5 and modern understanding of the needs of a democratic state that concerned citizens will be reduced to reliance on trying to inject substance into nebulous challenges? Indeed, this was an element of the arguments presented by counsel for the plaintiff in the Supreme Court appeal which will be considered in greater detail in the *Annual Review of Irish Law 2005*.

ELECTORAL ISSUES

The electoral system and the right to stand for election were considered in three cases in 2004. In the one substantial case, *Ring v Attorney General* [2004] I.E.H.C. 88, [2004] 1 I.R. 185, local government and the rights of members of Dáil Éireann to stand for county council election was at issue; the High Court took the opportunity to analyse Art.28A which enshrines local government in the Constitution. *Redmond v Minister for Environment, Heritage and Local Government* [2004] I.E.H.C. 24 (February 13, 2004) was a consideration of the damages to which the plaintiff was entitled following a judgment in his favour in the earlier case of *Redmond v Minister for the Environment* [2001] 4 I.R. 64 that requiring a deposit from an electoral candidate was unconstitutional. Finally, the President of the High Court refused the reliefs sought in *Riordan v Minister for the Environment, Heritage and Local Government* [2004] I.E.H.C. 89 (May 26, 2004), *inter alia*, to order the insertion of the plaintiff's name on the ballot paper for the European Parliament Elections due to take place on June 11, 2004.

Local government and the dual mandate   In *Ring*, the plaintiff, a member of Dáil Éireann and also a member of Mayo County Council, sought a declaration that s.13A of the Local Government Act 2001 (as inserted by s.2 of the Local Government (No.2) Act 2003), was contrary to the Constitution, in particular, Arts 5, 6, 16, 28A, 40.1 and 40.3. Section 13A(1) provides that a person who is a member of either House of the Oireachtas is disqualified from being elected or co-opted to, or from being a member of, a local authority. Subsection (2) provided that the section would come into operation and be applied with respect to the local elections to be held in the year 2004 and thereafter. Local elections were due to be held in June 2004. In colloquial terms, s.13A abolished the dual mandate and added a further category of persons who are disqualified from membership of a local authority to the categories already provided for in s.13(1) of the Act of 2001; it also introduced a further category of disqualification from holding public office for members of the Dáil and Seanad.

The plaintiff broadly based his contention as to the invalidity of s.13A on four grounds:

> "(1) the right of citizens to stand for election to local authorities is constitutionally guaranteed: s.13A unlawfully interferes with that right;
>
> (2) the right of citizens to stand for election to Dáil Éireann is constitutionally guaranteed: s.13A unlawfully interferes with that right;
>
> (3) the Constitution guarantees that all citizens shall, as human persons, be held equal before the law. As regards eligibility for membership of a local authority, s.13A invidiously discriminates between citizens who are eligible to become members of local authorities, on the one hand, and citizens who would be so eligible but for membership of Dáil Éireann on the other hand. As regards eligibility for election to Dáil Éireann, s.13A invidiously discriminates between citizens eligible to be elected to Dáil Éireann, on the one hand and citizens who would be so eligible but for membership of a local authority on the other. Thus s.13A infringes the constitutional guarantee of equality;
>
> (4) section 13A interferes with the constitutionally protected rights identified in a manner which cannot be objectively justified and which does not comply with the principle of proportionality". [2004] I.E.H.C. 88 at para.15.

In response, the defendant contended that there is no constitutional entitlement to stand for local government election: the entitlement is statutory and subject to regulation by the Oireachtas. Section 13A neither prevents a person standing for election to a local authority nor does not it impose any constraint on the entitlement of a person to stand for election to Dáil Éireann. It is a matter of choice, the provision of which is not unconstitutional. Any interference there might be with a constitutionally guaranteed right by s.13A is fair, reasonable, and proportionate, having regard to the interests of the State in the efficient, orderly and effective conduct of the business of the Oireachtas and of local government, having regard to their separate evolving roles.

It was noted in evidence that, should his legal challenge be unsuccessful, the plaintiff, a member of Fine Gael, would be constrained to choose between membership of the Dáil and membership of Mayo County Council. He would choose the former, but in so doing he feared that he would lose a major part of his political base and would lose touch with a major part of his constituency.

He "candidly acknowledged" that he was concerned about his prospects of re-election to the Dáil if he were no longer a member of the local authority. He anticipated that he would be "watching over his shoulder to see who is in the constituency and what they were at". He anticipated that he would have to spend more time in the constituency, thus defeating the purpose of the abolition of the dual mandate. Other serving politicians and political theorists gave conflicting evidence for both parties.

Article 28A construed   Laffoy J. summarised the plaintiff's case as having a constitutional right to stand for election to Mayo County Council. Accordingly, she deemed that the core issue for determination in the proceedings was whether the right of a citizen to stand for election to a local authority is a constitutionally guaranteed right. She opined that whether there is a constitutionally protected right of election to membership of a local authority turns on the proper construction of Art.28A, in the context of all of the provisions of the Constitution:

> "An analysis of Article 28A indicates limited constitutional protection for local government and local representative assemblies. The role of local government is recognised, rather than guaranteed. Significantly, insofar as the role of local government is recognised in exercising and performing at local level powers and functions, s.1 stipulates that such powers and functions are 'conferred by law'. While the constitutional protection is limited, nonetheless, Article 28A contains the following mandatory provisions which are fundamental in ensuring that the democratic representation of local communities is safeguarded:
>   (a) that local authorities exist
>   (b) that they shall be directly elected;
>   (c) that elections shall be held at five-yearly intervals; and
>   (d) that, as regards a core element of the electorate, eligibility to vote at such elections shall correspond with eligibility to vote at elections for the Dáil". [2004] I.E.H.C. 88 at para.38.

Having noted the mandatory constitutional provisions enshrined in Art.28A, Laffoy J. continued by noting the areas which were constitutionally left to the Oireachtas to regulate:

> "That the function of defining the parameters of the role of local government and how it operates in certain respects is left to the Oireachtas is clear on the face of Article 28A. As I have already mentioned, the powers and functions of local authorities are to be determined by the Oireachtas (Article 28A.1). Even in relation to the mandatory provisions a vast area of regulation is left to the Oireachtas. The number, the territorial extent and the demographic features of the

local authority areas are matters for the Oireachtas, as are their powers
and functions (Article 28A.2). The elections which are to be held at
five-yearly intervals are to be regulated by law. The right to vote, even
in relation to the core element of the electorate, is to be regulated by
law (Article 28A.4). Other matters which Article 28A expressly leaves
for regulation by the Oireachtas are the expansion of the core element
of the electorate (Article 28A.4) and the filling of casual vacancies in
membership of local authorities (Article 28A.5)". [2004] I.E.H.C. 88
at para.39.

Difference between constitutional electoral provisions Comparing and
contrasting Art.28A with Art.16, Laffoy J. cited O'Higgins C.J. in *Re The
Electoral (Amendment) Bill, 1983* [1984] I.R. 268, in which he described Art.16
as "'a constitutional code for the holding of an election to Dáil Éireann, subject
only to the statutory regulation of such election'." However, Laffoy J. stated:

"In contradistinction to Article 16, Article 28A only provides for two
of the foregoing 'essential features of elections' (*per* O'Higgins C.J.):
entitlement to vote, which is partially provided for; and the maximum
term of a local authority". [2004] I.E.H.C. 88 at para.41.

The comparison of Art.28A and Art.16 indicated that, in the area of local
authority elections, there is a considerable range of matters, both in relation to
matters which O'Higgins C.J. described as "essential" in the context of elections
to the Dáil and other matters not so described, which are not referred to in
Art.28A in respect of which regulation would be required to be put in place.
Laffoy J. concluded that it must be assumed that where Art.28A is silent as to
the regulation of local government and local authority elections, including the
criteria for eligibility for membership of a local authority, such regulation has
been left to, and is within the competence of, the Oireachtas:

"It is neither necessary nor logical that there should be implied in Article
28A a provision which corresponds to Article 16.1.1°. The whole thrust
of Article 28A is that constitutional regulation of local government is
minimal and that regulation is to be by statute". [2004] I.E.H.C. 88 at
para.44.

Laffoy J. could not discern any imperative anywhere in the Constitution which
necessitates that regulation of eligibility to stand for election to a local authority
should not be regulated by statute. Nor could she discern any basis in logic for
the proposition that the framers of Art.28A, and the people enacting it, intended
that eligibility to stand for a local election should be regulated in precisely the
same manner as eligibility for membership of the Dáil. As constitutionally
established, the two representative assemblies are not the same. Laffoy J. noted

that s.12 of the 2001 Act regulated eligibility to stand for a local authority election on a basis which differs from Art.16.1.1° in that it fixed the age threshold for eligibility at 18 years and did not limit it to citizens:

> "Although not determinative, it seems to me that the express linkage in Article 28A.4 of the right to vote at local elections to Article 16.1.2°, coupled with the absence of any reference in Article 28A to entitlement to stand for election to a local authority and, in particular, the omission to provide for entitlement similar to the entitlement to stand for an election to Dáil Éireann provided in Article 16.1.1°, must carry an implication of some weight that it was not intended that such an entitlement should be provided for constitutionally in Article 28A". [2004] I.E.H.C. 88 at para.45.

***Expressio unius exclusio alterius* not applicable**   Counsel for the plaintiff had submitted that applying the *expressio unius exclusio alterius* principle of construction, the Constitution necessarily excludes by implication a prohibition on the dual mandate. Laffoy J. found untenable an argument, by reference to the presence of Art.15.14, Art.33.3, Art.35.3, and Art.12.6.3°, in the Constitution, that it must have been the intention of the framers of the Constitution in 1937, or the framers of Art.28A in 1999, that entitlement to dual membership of the Oireachtas and a local authority would be immured against abolition other than by constitutional amendment, on the ground that it was not expressly proscribed.

> "The rationale which underlies the prohibition on simultaneous membership of both Houses of the Oireachtas and the rationale which underlies the prohibition on membership of either House and the holding of any other office in the case of constitutional office holders, being concerned, as they are, with concepts of separation of powers, independence, avoidance of conflicts and such like, are fundamentally different from the rationale underlying s.13A. Moreover, in the case of the constitutional office holders, the effect of the constitutional prohibition is fundamentally different from the effect of s.13A: the former are precluded from holding any other office or position". [2004] I.E.H.C. 88 at para.46.

She concluded that Art.28A of the Constitution is not open to the construction that there is implicit therein a right to stand for election to a local authority on terms similar to Art.16.1.1°. Moreover, she concluded that the right of a citizen to stand for election to a local authority is not constitutionally guaranteed.

Does s.13A interfere with constitutional right to stand for election to the Dáil?   Following from this decision, a remaining issue was whether s.13A interfered with the constitutionally protected right of a citizen to stand for election to the Dáil. Laffoy J. noted that there is an assumption that s.13A was crafted and structured in such a way as to avoid interfering with the constitutionally protected rights of the citizen. She found that as there is no constitutionally protected right to stand for election to a local authority, s.13A imposed no constraint on the plaintiff's eligibility for membership of the Dáil. Thus, she held that his argument based on Art.16.1 failed *in limine*.

Does s.13A infringe the equality guarantee? In respect of Art.40.1, Laffoy J. accepted as a correct statement of law the following passage from the judgment of McKechnie J. in *Kelly v Minister for the Environment* [2002] 4 I.R. 191 at 218:

> "[it] ... now seems clear that the State must in its electoral laws have regard to the concept of equality and must ensure that with any provisions passed into law the guarantee of equality as contained in Article 40.1 of the Constitution will be respected. It cannot, therefore, by any provision of a statute, or by any manner and way in which it might implement such a provision, cause unjustified advantage to accrue to one person, class or classes of the community as against or over and above another person or class of that same community. Equals must be treated equally." [2004] I.E.H.C. 88 quoted at para.58.

Accepting that there must be equality in the democratic process, the question to be considered was whether s.13A has caused unjustified advantage to accrue to a third party, or a class of persons, to the disadvantage of the plaintiff. Laffoy J. held that the arguments put forward by the plaintiff were unsustainable. He was in a similar position to every member of the Oireachtas who would wish to stand for membership of a local authority, but because of s.13A, must exercise a choice between membership of the Dáil and membership of a local authority. She noted that understandably the plaintiff may feel aggrieved that he is disadvantaged by comparison with the situation which prevailed a year ago, before the enactment of s.13A, but that was not relevant.

Laffoy J. stated that should she be incorrect in relation to the application of Art.40.1, any interference by s.13A with the guarantee of equality is reasonable and proportionate, *Heaney v Ireland* [1994] 3 I.R. 593. She concluded that on the evidence:

> "the objective of the Oireachtas in abolishing the dual mandate was to strengthen governance at both national and local level in Ireland, in the manner represented by the defendant in defending these proceedings. If the plaintiff's constitutional right under Article 40.1 has been interfered with, I am satisfied that the stated objective is sufficiently important to justify such interference. Further, I am satisfied that the

objective, relating as it does to enhancing the democratic process, is of pressing and substantial importance in a free and democratic society. As to the means chosen to achieve the objective, the enactment of s.13A is one of a number of measures introduced to fulfil that objective: other means include the insertion of Article 28A in the Constitution and the enactment of the Act of 2001. I am satisfied:

(a) that the provisions of s.13A are rationally connected to the objective, ... and

(b) that s.13A impairs the plaintiff's right to equality as little as possible, although, in truth, in terms of the value at issue here, I cannot see that there is any impairment of the plaintiff's right consequential on the enactment of s.13A". [2004] I.E.H.C. 88 at para.67.

Costs preclude Supreme Court appeal   As this was the first occasion where a substantive issue allowed the High Court to give a determination on Art.28A, it is regrettable that the plaintiff found himself unable to take an appeal to the Supreme Court solely arising from cost factors. See contemporaneous media reports.

Damages for breach of constitutional right   *Redmond v Minister for Environment, Heritage and Local Government* [2004] I.E.H.C. 24 (February 13, 2004) was a hearing for an award of damages in relation to Herbert J.'s earlier judgment in *Redmond v Minister for the Environment* [2001] 4 I.R. 64, in which he found unconstitutional the requirement for a deposit when standing for election (*Annual Review of Irish Law 2001*, pp.103–107). In the instant case he dismissed the submission on behalf of the respondent:

"that this Court should either always decline or should at least be very slow and then only in the most extreme circumstances, to make an award of damages against the legislative arm of the State for the infringement in an Act of the Oireachtas of a right guaranteed by the Constitution".

Relying on Supreme Court decisions in *State (Quinn) v Ryan* [1965] I.R. 70; *Byrne v Ireland and the Attorney General* [1972] I.R. 241; and *Murphy v The Attorney General* [1982] I.R. 241, he declared himself satisfied that the court had full power to award damages:

"ordinary compensatory damages or aggravated or increased compensatory damages and even punitive or exemplary damages (see *Conway v Irish National Teachers' Organisation & Ors.* [1991] 2 I.R. 305)— against the legislative arm of the State for breach of a constitutional right by an Act of the Oireachtas or by a provision of such an Act."

> However, I do not think that it is reasonably possible or even desirable
> to attempt to formulate any principles of general application as to the
> circumstances in which the Court might so award damages or as to the
> type or amount of those damages."

In this respect, the court adopted the judgment of Henchy J. in *Murphy v
Attorney General* [1982] I.R. 241 at 315, where he stated, when speaking of
such redress and of the sometimes "transcendent considerations" which may
render any or some particular forms of redress unavailable, *i.e.* damages or
restitution:

> "in any event, I think experience has shown that such constitutional
> problems are best brought to solution, step by step, precedent after
> precedent, and when set against the concrete facts of a specific case."

Injury without loss   Herbert J. held that the injury in this case was one without
loss, although nonetheless actionable without proof of actual loss. He was
satisfied that there was no wilful nor conscious wrongdoing by the legislative
arm of the State in knowing disregard of the constitutional rights of the plaintiff:

> "While the enactment into Law of the impugned statutory provisions
> was deliberate and in that sense intentional, I am satisfied that the
> resulting breach of the plaintiff's constitutional right was not intended
> but was a wholly undesired and altogether inadvertent consequence of
> the legislation."

He was quite satisfied that the sole intention of the Oireachtas in maintaining
the deposit requirement for Dáil Éireann and European Parliament Elections
was to protect the electoral system from abuse.

Nominal but not derisory damages   On the balance of probabilities Herbert
J. was satisfied that Mr Redmond had not made any real plans or given any
real consideration to putting his political proposals and ideas before the
electorate. The plaintiff was awarded nominal damages in the sum of €130
with the stricture that the damages are not and should not be considered to be
in any sense derisory or contemptuous.

Challenge to elections   In *Riordan v Minister for the Environment, Heritage
and Local Government* [2004] I.E.H.C. 89 (May 26, 2004), the plaintiff applied
for injunctive relief to require the insertion of his name on the ballot paper for
the European Parliament Elections due to take place on June 11, 2004, and for
an order restraining the Minister for the Environment, Heritage and Local
Government from holding elections for membership of local authorities until
such time as legislation has been enacted by the Oireachtas to require the

conduct of the elections as required by Art.28A.3 of the Constitution. In addition, the plaintiff sought a declaration that s.12(1A) of the European Parliament Elections Act 1997 as inserted by s.2 of the Electoral (Amendment) Act 2002 is repugnant to the Constitution.

As described elsewhere in this chapter, Finnegan P. held that there was a fair issue to be tried in relation to the delegation of legislative power. However, in deciding whether or not to grant the reliefs sought he considered the balance of convenience, the factor of delay, and the inadequacy of any undertaking as to damages. With regard to the balance of convenience, Finnegan P. took account of the very considerable inconvenience and disturbance to both the election process and to the declared candidates in the European Parliament Election and the Local Elections. With regard to delay, it is instructive to quote the President of the High Court in full:

> "Had the proceedings been instituted promptly and an application been made to me at any time thereafter I would have ensured that any interlocutory application would be dealt with promptly and that the matter received an appropriately early trial date. Immediately preceding the most recent Dáil Elections proceedings were instituted by a number of persons and in each case hearing dates were allocated within a matter of days and in advance of polling day and the same facility having regard to the importance of the electoral process would have been afforded to the parties here. No such application was made. Had such application been made the balance of convenience might well have been found to lie elsewhere. As matters stand the balance of convenience lies heavily in favour of refusing the application".

Finally, the plaintiff admitted that an undertaking as to damages would be worthless in that he had not the means to satisfy the same if called upon to do so.

> "While not determinative of the application it is a factor which I must take into account. I take into account the expense which has been incurred by the Defendants and I also take into account the expense which has been incurred by other candidates and indeed their efforts in their election campaigns. They will not be recompensed for these should the Plaintiff ultimately fail in these proceedings".

It seems clear from the judgment of the President of the High Court in *Riordan* that in electoral cases where there is a fair issue to be tried, if proceedings are instituted in good time, relief may well be granted notwithstanding the inability of the plaintiff to pay costs.

EQUALITY

In *Criminal Assets Bureau v S.*, High Court, October 19, 2004, Finnegan P. considered a challenge to s.10(7) of the Criminal Assets Bureau Act 1996, which allows a judge to grant anonymity to a member of staff of the bureau who is giving evidence. The defendant argued that Art.40.1 was infringed by this provision. Finnegan P. referred to the phrase "as human persons" in that provision, coming to the conclusion that the applicant had not been treated differently in relation to his dignity as a human person. This appears to endorse the "basis of discrimination" understanding of the human personality phrase. (See Oran Doyle, *Constitutional Equality Law* (Thomson Round Hall, 2004) at pp.125–132.) Finnegan P. also rejected a challenge on the basis of Art.40.3, observing that the section itself was not unconstitutional and that any unconstitutional operation of the section could be challenged as being *ultra vires*.

EXCLUDING RIGHT OF APPEAL TO SUPREME COURT

In *Holland v Information Commissioner* Supreme Court, December 15, 2004, the High Court's decision (Ó Caoimh J.) to refuse leave to cross-examine on an affidavit was confirmed. A question was raised on behalf of the Information Commissioner as to whether a statutory prohibition on an appeal to the Supreme Court such as that in s.42 of the Freedom of Information Act 1997, prior to its repeal by the 2003 Amending Act, *Annual Review of Irish Law 2003*, p.391, could be circumvented by appealing on an interlocutory ruling of this nature. *Per curiam*, Keane C.J. (Murray and Geoghegan JJ.) noted that the query raised implications for other cases in which the Oireachtas has excluded a right of appeal to the Supreme Court.

> "[A] question remains or may remain as to the jurisdiction of this court to entertain appeals in interlocutory matters. Having regard to the fact that this is a constitutional issue, the right of appeal to this court can only be excluded where that has been clearly and unequivocally done by the Oireachtas, and this court has repeatedly emphasised that this is not a matter for implication or uncertainty of any sort, that it is only where this court's appellate jurisdiction is conclusively and unequivocally removed by an Act of the Oireachtas, that a person's constitutional right of appeal from a decision of the High Court to the final court of appeal is removed".

See chapter on Information Law and the Ombudsman.

FAIR PROCEDURES

The plaintiff in *Joyce v Minister for Health and Children* [2004] I.E.H.C. 158 (July 30, 2004) was a consultant surgeon employed at Cavan General Hospital who had been suspended under s.22 of the Health Act 1970. The second-named and subsequent defendants were members of a committee established under s.24 of the Health Act 1970 to inquire into a proposal to remove the plaintiff from office and to make recommendations to the Chief Executive of the North Eastern Health Board. The second-named defendant was chairman of the committee. Among other points, the plaintiff complained to the effect that from an early stage of the hearings, and on many occasions throughout the hearings, the plaintiff got a strong smell of alcohol from the chairman. Further, the chairman, without any notification, failed to appear to conduct scheduled hearings of the committee, without any explanation for his non-attendance. It was submitted for the plaintiff that the cumulative effect of this has left him with a complete loss of confidence in the capacity of the second-named defendant to discharge his statutory function as chairman and, as a result, he has been, is being, and will continue to be denied a fair hearing into issues which are of the gravest importance to him, having regard to his livelihood and his personal and professional reputation. Consequently, there has been a breach of his constitutional right to fair procedures.

O'Neill J. found that although neither the chairman nor the committee in general had fallen into demonstrable error, the plaintiff had had to endure a hearing before a committee, the chairman of which had lacked the capacity to discharge his function. In his view, the plaintiff's constitutional right to fair procedures had been breached, and if this committee were to be permitted to continue its hearings there would be an ongoing breach of his constitutional right to fair procedures. O'Neill J. accepted that to invoke the principle that not only must justice be done but it must be seen to be done requires a very high threshold of proof. This is in order to protect the proceedings of the many and varied tribunals that sit on a daily basis in this jurisdiction from unmeritorious allegations designed to frustrate their proceedings. However, in the instant case, the subject matter of the plaintiff's complaints were of such a serious nature as to cross that threshold and justify the granting of a relief on that ground alone. On the balance of convenience, O'Neill J. deemed the appropriate relief would be better served by granting an injunction restraining the entire committee from resuming its hearings as scheduled. Finally, he observed that it was:

> "perhaps no more than a statement of the obvious, that this suspension has now been in existence for almost one year during which the plaintiff has been kept out of his office without pay and that this must be having a grossly detrimental effect on his livelihood and on his professional and personal reputation and must be a source of the utmost hardship to

him and his family. I do not think that it was ever conceived that suspensions for the purpose for which this one was imposed would continue for that kind of length".

The issue of fair procedures in relation to the deceased and to living members of the congregation of Christian Brothers was raised in *Murray v Commission to Inquire into Child Abuse* [2004] I.E.H.C. 225; [2004] 2 I.R. 222. Abbott J. made a declaration as to the importance of the right to cross-examine in this regard. The substantive constitutional issues are dealt with elsewhere in this chapter.

FAMILY RIGHTS

In 2004, the implications of the Supreme Court's decision in *A.O. and D.L. v Minister for Justice* [2003] 1 I.R. 1 continued to be worked out by the courts. In *F. v Minister for Justice* [2004] I.E.H.C. 8, the second applicant challenged her deportation on the grounds that she had been married to her husband, the first applicant, after the deportation order was made, but before the deportation order was executed. A similar circumstance had arisen in *Malsheva v Minister for Justice,* High Court, July 25, 2003, in which Finlay Geoghegan J. had granted leave to seek judicial review on the basis that there was an arguable case that the Minister should reconsider the deportation of the applicant in the light of her marriage to an Irish citizen. However, in *F.*, Murphy J. refused to apply *Malsheva* on the basis that in *Malsheva* the applicant had had a valid visa at the time of deportation. Nevertheless, Murphy J. appeared to approve the decision of Finlay Geoghegan J. in *Malsheva*.

P. v Minister for Justice [2004] I.E.H.C. 223 demonstrates general acceptance of the *Malsheva* principle, in that Butler J. granted a declaration that the Minister was not entitled to give effect to the deportation order without first having regard to the material change in the first applicant's circumstances since the date of the making of that deportation order, in particular his marriage to the second applicant. However, Butler J. emphasised that this gave the first applicant no substantive right to remain in the State. Similarly, in *C. v Minister for Justice*, High Court, December 24, 2004, Quirke J. declared a deportation order invalid where the Minister had failed to consider the constitutional rights of the proposed deportee's citizen spouse. A similar approach was adopted by Clarke J. in *Gashi v Minister for Justice* High Court, December 3, 2004.

In *Margine v Minister for Justice* [2004] I.E.H.C. 127, the applicant sought to rely on his status as the father of an Irish citizen child to resist his deportation. Relying on *A.O. and D.L.*, Peart J. observed that the State was entitled to control and regulate its borders and that the Minister was entitled to take reasonable and proportionate steps to maintain the integrity of the asylum system. This objective was sufficient to outweigh the family rights that were asserted in this case.

LEGISLATIVE POWER

In *Leontjava v DPP* and *Chang v DPP* [2004] 1 I.R. 591, the applicants were before the District Court on charges pursuant to arts 5(6) and 15 of the Aliens Order 1946 as amended. Article 5(1) of the 1946 Order provides that an immigrant must, on arrival in the State, present herself to an immigration officer for leave to land. Article 5(6) provides that an immigration officer may attach conditions as to the duration of stay and the business in which such an immigrant may engage. Article 15 of the 1946 Order provides that every immigrant shall produce on demand her registration certificate (if registered) or a valid passport or other such document, unless she can give a satisfactory explanation of the circumstances which prevent her from doing so. The applicants were prosecuted for offences in connection with these provisions.

The applicants then sought, by way of judicial review, to prohibit their trials on the grounds (a) that arts 5(6) and 15 were *ultra vires* the powers of the Minister for Justice under s.5(1) of the Aliens Act 1935, (b) (if necessary) that s.5(1) of that Act was inconsistent with Art.15.2 of the Constitution and (c) (if necessary) that s.2(1) of the Immigration Act 1999 was unconstitutional. These grounds raised issues both about the limits on delegated legislation and the correct process for adopting primary legislation.

Section 5(1) of the Aliens Act 1935, as amended, provides, *inter alia*:

> "The Minister may, if and whenever he thinks proper, do by order (in this Act referred to as an aliens order) all or any of the following things in respect either of all aliens or of aliens of a particular nationality or otherwise of a particular class, or of particular aliens, that is to say:
>> (b) impose on such aliens restriction and conditions in respect of landing in or entering into Saorstát Éireann, including limiting such landing or entering to particular places or prohibiting such landing or entering at particular places;
>> (e) make provision for the exclusion or the deportation and exclusion of such aliens from Saorstát Éireann and provide for and authorise the making by the Minister of orders for that purpose;
>> (h) require such aliens to comply, while in Saorstát Éireann, with particular provisions as to registration, change of abode, travelling, employment, occupation, and other like matters".

Section 5(1)(e) had been struck down by the Supreme Court in *Laurentiu v Minister for Justice, Equality and Law Reform* [1999] 4 I.R. 26; [2000] 1 I.L.R.M. 1 on the basis that it effectively delegated the policy-making function of the State in that regard to the Minister for Justice, thereby breaching the principles and policies test laid down in *Cityview Press Ltd v An Comhairle Oiliúna* [1980] I.R. 381. Under the *Cityview* test, primary legislation must deal with all matters of principle and policy; secondary legislation can constitutionally be authorised only to give effect to those principles and policies:

> "In the view of this Court, the test is whether that which is challenged as an unauthorised delegation of parliamentary power is more than a mere giving effect to principles and policies which are contained in the statute itself. If it be, then it is not authorised; for such would constitute a purported exercise of legislative power by an authority which is not permitted to do so under the Constitution. On the other hand, if it be within the permitted limits – if the law is laid down in statute and details only are filled in or completed by the designated Minister or subordinate body—there is no unauthorised delegation of legislative power". [1980] I.R. 381, 399.

Sections 5(1)(b) and (h) of the 1935 Act were constitutionally challenged in *Chang and Leontjava*.

Was the secondary legislation *ultra vires*?   In the High Court, Finlay Geoghegan J. concluded that art.5(6) of the 1946 Order was *ultra vires* the legislative powers granted by s.5(1) of the 1935 Act. She reasoned that the conditions envisaged by s.5(1)(b) related to the actual landing or entering of immigrants into the State. Further, nothing in s.5(1)(b) delegated to the Minister a legislative power to authorise an immigration official to determine the length of time for which an immigrant might be permitted to remain in the State. Finlay Geoghegan J. concluded that art.15(1) of the 1946 Order, in contrast, was *intra vires* the legislative power delegated by s.5(1)(h) of the 1935 Act:

> "[A] provision which authorises the Minister to require aliens to comply with provisions to be specified by the Minister relating to 'registration, change of abode, travelling, employment, occupation and other like matters' purports to give the Minister a very broad authorisation as to the provisions which he may specify with which an alien may be required to comply". [2004] 1 I.R. 591 at para.30.

The Supreme Court, *per* Keane C.J., agreed with Finlay Geoghegan J.'s conclusions on these two points. However, Fennelly and Murray JJ. dissented slightly from Keane C.J.'s reasoning in commenting that art.5(6) was *ultra vires* only because it ascribed the power to an immigration official rather than the Minister. The sorts of conditions envisaged by art.5(6) were not themselves *ultra vires*. Fennelly J. reasoned:

> "[I]t is inherent in the very notion of authorising an alien to land in the State that provision be made for the duration of his permitted stay. It is something that arises so naturally from the very fact of entering a foreign country that it did not need to be spelled out. The first type of condition

that would spring to mind, where an alien is given permission to enter the State, is one relating to the duration of his or her permitted stay" [2004] 1 I.R. 591 at para.625.

Was the delegation of legislative power constitutional?   As art.5(6) of the 1946 Order had been held *ultra vires*, there was no need for either Court to consider the constitutionality of s.5(1)(b) of the 1935 Act. However, given that art.15(1) of the 1946 Order had been held *intra vires* s.5(1)(h), the constitutionality of that subsection remained an issue in the proceedings. In the High Court, Finlay Geoghegan J. held that s.5(1)(h) fell foul of the *Cityview* test for the same reasons as given by the Supreme Court in *Laurentiu*:

> "[T]he Act of 1935 does not set out any policies and principles according to which the power given to the Minister under s.5(1)(h) to require aliens to comply whilst in the State in relation to the matters set out therein with 'particular provisions' should be exercised .... Further, there is no indication, even in relation to the specific matters referred to in para. (h), as to the policies according to which the Minister should determine either those aliens to which any requirements should apply or the 'particular provisions' with which such aliens should be required to comply in any order made under s.5(1)(h). The broad nature of the 'particular provisions' purported to be authorised (as already concluded) intrinsically requires a policy decision for their determination. Hence, as was concluded by the Supreme Court in *Laurentiu v Minister for Justice* [1999] 4 I.R. 26 in relation to s.5(1)(e), s.5(1)(h) simply gives to the Minister the power to determine such policies and principles" [2004] 1 I.R. 591 at para.38.

The Supreme Court, however, overturned this conclusion on appeal. Keane C.J., with whom the other members of the court agreed on this point, reasoned that the policy enunciated in s.5(1)(h) was plain:

> "the desirability of regulating the registration, change of abode, travelling, employment and occupation of aliens while in the State and the further desirability of regulating 'other like matters'" [2004] 1 I.R. 581 at para.34.

Keane C.J. did not consider problematic the use of phrases such as "particular provisions" or "other like matters", reasoning that they were wholly consistent with a legislative scheme whereby primary legislation dealt with matters of broad scope and secondary legislation filled in the details.

The decision of the Supreme Court appears consistent with previous case law. Doyle and Whyte have argued that the case law on this point does not, however, reflect the test actually stated in *Cityview Press*:

"The most plausible interpretation of the case law on this point is that the test stated by the Supreme Court in *Cityview* does not accurately represent the courts' position. The real test is not whether the Oireachtas has dealt with all matters of policy and principle, but rather whether the Oireachtas has dealt with no matters of principle or policy. Only in *Laurentiu v Minister for Justice* did the courts strike down primary legislation as being in breach of Article 15.2.1. In *Laurentiu*, the legislation contained no principles or policies, leaving everything to the Minister by delegating to the Minister the power to make provision for the deportation or exclusion of aliens'. In other cases, such as *Lovett v Minister for Education* [1997] 1 I.L.R.M. 88, the courts have employed the double construction rule to preclude delegates of legislative power from implementing principles and policies that were not envisioned by the primary legislation. However, in cases such as *Cityview* and the *Health Bill Reference case*, where the grant of legislative power on its face *requires* the delegate to make decisions of principle or policy, the courts seem prepared to uphold the validity of the legislation, provided that the primary legislation deals with *some* matters of principle and policy". (Doyle and Whyte, "The Separation of Powers and Constitutional Egalitarianism after the Health (Amendment) (No.2) Bill Reference" in O'Dell (ed.), *Older People in Modern Ireland: Essays on Law and Policy* (Firstlaw, Dublin, 2005).

Put another way, the courts have tended to draw from the fact that the primary legislation deals with some matters of principle and policy the false inference that the primary legislation deals with all matters of principle and policy, thus satisfying the *Cityview* test. This is what the Supreme Court did in *Leontjava and Chang*. The Court noted the legislative policy that it was desirable to regulate certain aspects of an immigrant's life in the State and concluded that the legislative power had not been constitutionally delegated. However, the Court did not advert to the absence of any principles and policies capable of informing the way in which those aspects of an immigrant's life should be regulated. If the Supreme Court, as it indicated, was applying the *Cityview* test, it made the false inference of concluding that the primary legislation dealt with all matters of principle and policy, simply because that legislation dealt with some matters of principle and policy. Finlay Geoghegan J., on the other hand, applied the *Cityview* test correctly, holding that the primary legislation did not deal with all matters of principle or policy.

It may be that the *Cityview* test is too restrictive. To preclude secondary legislation from dealing with any matters of principle or policy may be to reduce it to the level of administrative action, thereby depriving it of any legislative character. Against this, however, the trenchant statement in Art.15.2 that the Oireachtas is the sole legislative authority in the State perhaps supports such a limited role for secondary legislation. In any event, given that the courts, with the exception of Finlay Geoghegan J. in *Leontjava and Chang*, have consistently applied the *Cityview* test in this emasculated way, a judicial restatement of that test to reflect the real position would be welcome.

Was s.2 of the 1999 Act unconstitutional?   Following the Supreme Court's decision in *Laurentiu*, the Oireachtas had enacted the Immigration Act 1999. Section 2 provides:

> "(1) Every order made before the passing of this Act under section 5 of the Act of 1935 other than the orders or provisions of orders specified in the Schedule to this Act shall have statutory effect as if it were an Act of the Oireachtas.
>
> (2) If subsection (1) would, but for this subsection, conflict with a constitutional right of any person, the operation of that subsection shall be subject to such limitation as is necessary to secure that it does not so conflict but shall be otherwise of full force and effect".

The intention of the Oireachtas in enacting this provision seems to have been to ensure that the provisions of the Aliens Order 1946 (other than those provisions directly invalidated as a result of *Laurentiu*) had legal force and effect, independent of the validity or otherwise of the original enabling provision under which it was made. Applied to the facts of this case, s.2 of the 1999 Act would have rendered art.15 valid, even if the Supreme Court had agreed with Finlay Geoghegan J. in holding that its parent provision (s.5(1)(h) of the 1935 Act) was unconstitutional. A second and less obvious effect, however, was that a provision of the 1946 Order would have been rendered valid, notwithstanding that it was *ultra vires* its enabling statute. If s.2 was constitutionally valid, therefore, art.5(6) would have been valid, notwithstanding that it was *ultra vires* s.5 of the 1935 Act, and art.15 would have been valid, notwithstanding whether the delegation of legislative power in s.5(1)(b) was itself constitutional. For these reasons, it was necessary for both Finlay Geoghegan J. and the Supreme Court to examine the constitutionality of s.2 of the 1999 Act.

The constitutionality of s.2 turns on whether the Oireachtas is procedurally constrained by the Constitution from enacting primary legislation that either purports to confer the status of primary legislation on some other provision not enacted pursuant to the procedures established by the Constitution for primary legislation, or purports to incorporate such a provision by reference. In the High Court, the State argued that the 1946 Order remained a statutory rule and, as such, did not become an Act of the Oireachtas. Finlay Geoghegan J. accepted this contention. However, the State also argued that the 1946 Order, although secondary legislation, had as part of its legal status characteristics of an Act of the Oireachtas: these special characteristics were, as noted above, that the 1946 Order did not depend on the 1935 Act for its validity or effect.

Finlay Geoghegan J. summarised the effect of s.2 in the following way:

"The clear and unambiguous meaning of s.2(1), insofar as is relevant to these proceedings, is that the substantive provisions of the Aliens Order 1946 ... are to have statutory effect as if they are an Act of the Oireachtas but whilst not being contained in an Act of the Oireachtas". [2004] 1 I.R. 591 at para.52.

Finlay Geoghegan J. then referred to a number of provisions of the Constitution that led her to conclude that there was a procedural constraint on the law-making powers of the Oireachtas. In particular, she concluded that Art.25.4.3° and Art.25.4.5° required that the text of any provision which is to be treated as a "law" or as an "Act of the Oireachtas" must be contained in the Bill signed by the President and must be enrolled in the office of the registrar of the Supreme Court. This was further confirmed, in her view, by Art.26.1.1°:

"This [Article] appears to require that every provision which may subsequently have the status of a "law" made by the Oireachtas pursuant to Article 15.2 of the Constitution be capable of being referred to the Supreme Court as a Bill or as a specified provision of a Bill for a decision on its constitutionality prior to its signature by the President. Neither arts. 5(6) or 15 of the Aliens Order 1946, at issue in these proceedings nor any other provision of any Aliens Order referred to in s.2(1) of the Act of 1999 could have been referred by the President to the Supreme Court pursuant to Article 26". [2004] 1 I.R. 581 at para.77.

From her consideration of these constitutional provisions, she reasoned that a "law" in Art.25 was exclusively an Act of the Oireachtas and that, therefore, "law" in Art.15.2 referred solely to an Act of the Oireachtas. Accordingly, she ruled that s.2 of the 1999 Act was unconstitutional, as it purported to deem something a statutory law which could not be such a law.

The Supreme Court allowed the State's appeal. Keane C.J. noted that the Constitution was silent as to the form of legislation. He further noted a widespread practice of incorporation by reference, whereby primary legislative status had been conferred on such diverse sources of law as international conventions and secondary legislation. He concluded:

"[T]he Constitution affords a strikingly wide latitude to the Oireachtas in adopting whatever form of legislation it considers appropriate in particular cases. Under Article 15 it enjoys the sole and exclusive power of making laws for the State and where, as here, it has expressed its clear and unequivocal intention that particular instruments should have the force of law in the State, it is difficult to see on what basis it can be asserted that it has exceeded or abused its exclusive legislative role. In the view of the court, the choice by the Oireachtas to incorporate the instruments in question by reference rather by setting out their text *verbatim* in the body of the Act was one which they were entitled to make, unless it can be clearly established that the result was in conflict with specific provisions of the Constitution". [2004] 1 I.R. 591 at para.82.

It is clear from this passage that the State's argument in the Supreme Court was somewhat different to that advanced in the High Court. In the High Court, the State had argued that it was constitutionally permissible for s.2 to deem the 1946 Order a statutory law, notwithstanding that it had not been enacted according to the constitutional procedures. In the Supreme Court, the State argued that the 1946 Order was actually incorporated into the 1999 Act and was therefore part of a statute.

Addressing the more particular constitutional provisions mentioned by Finlay Geoghegan J., the Supreme Court held that the purpose of Art.25 was to ensure that an official and authoritative text of every Act passed by the Oireachtas and signed by the President was available in the office of the Supreme Court: those requirements had been met in this case. The Court also rejected the contention that the requirements of the Art.26 reference procedure mitigated against the constitutional validity of this type of legislation:

"If the President, after consultation with the Council of State, was of the view that a reference was desirable because one or more of the provisions contained in the orders being of statutory effect were of questionable constitutional validity, there was nothing to prevent her from referring s.2 of the Bill to this court for a decision as to its constitutionality. That would be the reference of a 'specified' provision within the meaning of Article 26.1.1° and the fact that only part of the specified provision was, in the view of the President, of questionable validity would not in the slightest degree affect her power to make such a reference. Holders of the Office of President have, in the past, referred an entire Bill to this court for a decision as to its constitutionality, although it was inconceivable that every single provision in the Bill was regarded as of questionable validity: see, for example, *The Employment Equality Bill 1996* [1997] 2 I.R. 321; [2004] 1 I.R. 581 at para.88.

The court concluded that the applicant had not successfully rebutted the presumption of constitutionality.

Although the Supreme Court's interpretation of Art.25 was at least as convincing as that of Finlay Geoghegan J., its interpretation of Art.26 was not so convincing. Keane C.J. implied that the Supreme Court, if s.2 of the 1999 Act had been referred pursuant to Art.26 reference, could consider the constitutional validity of the provisions of the Aliens Order 1946. In this way, he reasoned, Art.26.1.1° was satisfied. However, Keane C.J.'s acceptance that s.2 alone could have been referred by the President implied two further points. First, the President would not have been able to refer the provisions of the 1946 Order independently of s.2 of the 1999 Act. Secondly, the President would, if she wanted to refer any provision of the 1946 Order, have to refer all the provisions of that Order, under the guise of referring s.2 of the 1946 Act. This appears inconsistent with Art.26 of the Constitution, which clearly envisages that the President be able to specify the provisions of a Bill which she wants the Supreme Court to assess the constitutionality of:

> "The President may, after consultation with the Council of State, refer any Bill to which this Article applies to the Supreme Court for a decision on the question as to whether such Bill or any specified provision or provisions of such Bill is or are repugnant to this Constitution or to any provision thereof."

In *Re Article 26 and the Employment Equality Bill 1996*, the Supreme Court interpreted Art.26.1.1° in the following way:

> "It would have been possible for the President to specify some specific provision or provisions of the Bill on which she needed the Court's decision but she was not obliged to do that". [1997] 2 I.R. 321 at 331.

Keane C.J.'s observation—that Presidents in the past had referred a whole Bill even though it was inconceivable that all provisions of the Bill were considered to be of questionable validity—failed to address the issue of whether it was legitimate for the Oireachtas to deprive the President of the facility to refer specific provisions of a Bill.

Thus the Supreme Court's decision in *Leontjava and Chang*, to the effect that the 1946 Order was validly incorporated into the 1999 Act, deprived (albeit retrospectively and hypothetically) the President of certain of her powers under Art.26, principally her power to specify certain provisions of that Order to be referred to the Supreme Court. This deprivation, although retrospective and hypothetical in *Leontjava and Chang*, operates prospectively and really for future legislation that adopts the technique of incorporation by reference. If it is a constitutionally necessary feature of a Bill that the President be able to refer specified provisions of that Bill to the Supreme Court, it was unconstitutional for s.2 of the 1999 Act to deprive the President of this power. If that is the case, it follows that the attempt of s.2 to make those provisions part of the 1999 Act should have been held constitutionally invalid.

On the other hand, the State's argument in the High Court (to the effect that the provisions of the Order were not part of the Act but were nevertheless accorded the status of primary legislation) would also have been inconsistent with Art.26. For on this argument, none of the provisions of the Order could have been referred, even indirectly and en masse, to the Supreme Court. Therefore, those provisions would have the status of primary legislation without having been subject to all the procedural requirements for the enactment of primary legislation.

Even if the Supreme Court was correct in its interpretation of Art.26, its general reasoning raises concerns for future cases. The court, in upholding the capacity of the Oireachtas to adopt this type of legislation, emphasised both the procedural freedom accorded to the Oireachtas as to the form of legislation, and the prevalence of the legislative technique of incorporation by reference. The question is whether each of these rationales stands on its own. It seems clear that procedural freedom cannot, of itself, justify the court's decision. For there are legislative exercises of procedural freedom that the court would presumably not countenance. Most obviously, the court would presumably, if pushed, require that the incorporation by reference device be confined to existing legal provisions that could meaningfully be "ratified" by the Oireachtas. If the Oireachtas were allowed to incorporate into primary legislation all future Orders issued pursuant to the 1935 Act, that would set at nought Art.15.2.1°, as interpreted by the courts in assessing delegation of legislative power.

For this reason, procedural freedom could not, of itself, have been a sufficient basis for the court's decision. Yet the court's views on the legislative technique of incorporation by reference were not wholly convincing either:

> "This court cannot accept the proposition that the framers of the Constitution in 1937, while conferring on the Oireachtas the exclusive role of making laws for the State, intended to limit their powers to legislate by prohibiting them from incorporating other instruments, such as secondary legislation and treaties, in an Act and giving them the force of law without setting out their provisions *in extenso*. As the decision of the House of Lords in *Institute of Patent Agents v Lockwood* [1894] A.C. 347 demonstrates, that precise form of statutory incorporation by reference was already established towards the end of the nineteenth century and there is nothing in the Constitution to indicate that the choice of the Oireachtas to legislate in that rather than another form was in any way inhibited". [2004] 1 I.R. 591 at para.87.

As is generally the case, the court's views on the intentions of framers were apparently reached without any study of documentary sources that might have enabled the Court to identify the intentions of framers. Moreover, constitutional law is replete with examples of cases which the courts have decided in a manner scarcely envisaged by the framers of the Constitution. In the absence of guidance as to when the intentions of the framers are relevant, there remains considerable uncertainty as to the sort of freedom that the Oireachtas can legitimately exercise in enacting legislation.

In *Mulcreevey v Minister for Environment* [2004] 1 I.R. 72; [2004] 1

I.L.R.M. 419, the applicant sought leave to challenge the validity of the Minister's decision to approve the joint consent given earlier by the Minister and Dun Laoghaire-Rathdown County Council (the second respondent in these proceedings) for the removal of part of a national monument (Carrickmines Castle) to facilitate the construction of a motorway. The High Court had refused leave on the grounds that the applicant had not acted promptly, as required by Ord.84 of the Rules of the Superior Courts. The Supreme Court, however, granted leave.

Of relevance to the issue of legislative power, the court held that the applicant had established an arguable ground of challenge to the approval order on the basis that the Heritage (Transfer of Functions of Commissioners of Public Works) Order 1996 had sought to amend by statutory instrument the provisions of an Act of the Oireachtas. The somewhat complicated legislative background is as follows. Section 14 of the National Monuments Act 1930 provided that a person must obtain the consent of the Commissioners of Public Works and the relevant local authority in order, *inter alia*, to remove a protected structure. Section 15 of the National Monuments (Amendment) Act 1994 amended the consent scheme to provide that, where the removal was not in the interests of archaeology, the additional consent of the Minister for Arts, Culture and the Gaeltacht would be required. The 1996 Order purported to transfer the Commissioners' responsibilities in this regard to the Minister for Arts, Culture and the Gaeltacht with the result that the second consent now had to be obtained from one of the legal persons that had given the first consent. The responsibilities of the Minister for Arts, Culture and the Gaeltacht in this regard were transferred to the Minister for the Environment (the first respondent in these proceedings) by the Heritage (Transfer of Departmental Administration and Ministerial Functions) Order 2002 (S.I. No.356 of 2002).

In *Cooke v Walsh* [1984] I.R. 710, it had been established that it would be an unconstitutional delegation of power for primary legislation to empower a person to amend primary legislation by way of secondary legislation. Given the rule of double construction, the courts must read primary legislation, if at all possible, in a manner that does not grant such an amending power to secondary legislation. If the primary legislation is open to that narrower interpretation, it follows that the secondary legislation that purports to amend primary legislation is *ultra vires* its parent statute.

In *Mulcreevey*, Keane C.J., with whom Hardiman and McCracken JJ. agreed, concluded that the 1996 Order purported to amend s.15 of the 1994 Act. As the parent provision—s.9(2)(a) of the Ministers and Secretaries Act 1924—could easily be read in a way that did not authorise the secondary legislation to amend primary legislation, the applicant had (at the very least) established an arguable case that the 1996 Order was *ultra vires* its parent statute and therefore invalid. The applicant was granted leave to seek judicial review on this ground. Two days later, Kearns J. granted the relief sought, setting aside the approval order granted by the Minister for the Environment.

Subsequent to this decision, the Oireachtas enacted the National Monuments Act 2004. In *Dunne v Minister for Environment* [2004] I.E.H.C. 304, a case again concerning the proposed motorway at Carrickmines Castle, the plaintiff challenged, *inter alia*, the constitutionality of s.8 of the 2004 Act on the grounds that it unconstitutionally delegated legislative power to the Minister. Section 8(1) of that Act provides that the various consents normally required for works affecting national monuments will not be required for any works affecting any national monument in connection with the completion of the South Eastern Route of the M50 motorway. Instead, such works shall be carried out in accordance with the directions of the Minister. Section 8(2) provides guidance to the Minister on the issuing of directions:

"In considering to issue directions under subsection (1) of this section—
(a) the Minister is not restricted to archaeological considerations but is entitled to consider the public interest notwithstanding that such exercise may involve—
   (i) injury to or interference with a national monument, or
   (ii) the destruction in whole or in part of a national monument,
(b) the Minister may have regard to the following to the extent that they appear to the Minister to be relevant in exercising discretion to issue directions in respect of a national monument:
   (i) the preservation, protection or maintenance of the archaeological, architectural, historical or other cultural heritage or amenities of, or associated with the national monument,
   (ii) the nature and extent of any injury or interference with the national monument,
   (iii) any social or economic benefit that would accrue to the State or region or immediate area in which the national monument is situated as a result of the carrying out of the road development,
   (iv) any matter of policy of the Government, of the Minister or of any other Minister of the Government,
   (v) the need to collect or disseminate information on national monuments or in respect of heritage generally,
   (vi) the cost implications (if any) that would, in the Minister's opinion, occur from the issuing of a direction, or not issuing a direction, under subsection (1) of this section."

Laffoy J. rejected the plaintiff's challenge on the basis that s.8 gave the Minister an administrative power, not a legislative power. Accordingly, s.8 could not infringe Art.15.2.1° of the Constitution. In any event, she held that the principles and policies guiding the exercise of such power were clearly stated in s.8.

The Supreme Court had earlier in the year come to the same conclusion about s.12 of the National Monuments Act 1930 in *Casey v Minister for Arts* [2004] 1 I.R. 402 (see also "Right to Earn a Livelihood"). Section 12, as amended, provides the Minister with certain powers and obligations in relation to the management and maintenance of national monuments. The applicant argued that this breached Art.15.2.1° of the Constitution. Murray J., with whom McGuinness and McCracken JJ. agreed, gave short shrift to this argument, holding that the power accorded to the Minister here was administrative, not regulatory in character. Although there might be similarities between the test for the validity of administrative action and the test for the validity of (secondary) legislative action, the case raised no issue as to the constitutionality of the assignment of power to the Minister.

Finally, in *Riordan v Minister for Environment* [2004] I.E.H.C. 89, the plaintiff sought an injunction restraining the holding of local elections. As discussed elsewhere in this chapter, the applicant was refused an injunction on the basis of the balance of convenience. However, Finnegan P. did hold that there was a fair issue to be tried in relation to the delegation of legislative power effected by s.27 of the Local Government Act 2001, the relevant provisions of which state:

> "27(1)(a) Local Elections shall be held in accordance with Regulations made by the Minister under this section.
> (2) Without prejudice to the generality of sub-section (1) regulations under this section may in particular include provision for all or any of the following matters in relation to local elections:
> (a) Nominations".

Finnegan P. considered that there was a fair issue to be tried as to whether the Regulations made pursuant to that section were more "than simply implementing the policy and provisions of the Act in question". It is unclear from the judgment whether the plaintiff's focus was on the *vires* of the Regulations or the delegation of legislative power in s.27 itself.

MANDATORY ORDERS

In *Cronin v Minister for Education* [2004] 3 I.R. 205, the plaintiff, a four-year-old boy suffering from attention deficit hyperactivity, autistic features and/or hearing deficit, and speech delay, sought various declaratory reliefs in relation to his constitutional, statutory and other legal entitlements to be provided with appropriate free primary education and also appropriate free therapies and care. In addition, he sought a mandatory order, pursuant to the Education Act 1998, directing the Minister to provide forthwith free primary education, including support services, appropriate to his needs. More specifically, he sought a mandatory injunction that the Minister provide for the cost of 29 hours per week one-to-one ABA tuition from appropriately qualified staff throughout the calendar year in his home during the plaintiff's pre-school phase, and also the cost of supervision of the plaintiff's educational programme, measured at €300 per month, during the pre-school phase. The plaintiff's mother had put these arrangements in place and the Minister was, in effect, simply being asked to pay for the arrangements. At this stage of the proceedings, the plaintiff was seeking such an order on an interlocutory basis.

In *T.D. v Minister for Education* [2001] 4 I.R. 259, the Supreme Court held that constitutional rights could only be enforced through mandatory orders in the most limited of circumstances. Murray J. put the matter in the following way:

> "[A] mandatory order directing the executive to fulfil a legal obligation (without specifying the means or policy to be used in fulfilling the obligation) *in lieu* of a declaratory order as to the nature of its obligations could only be granted, if at all, in exceptional circumstances where an organ or agency of the State had disregarded its constitutional obligations in an exemplary fashion. In my view the phrase 'clear disregard' can only be understood to mean a conscious and deliberate decision by the organ of state to act in breach of its constitutional obligation to other parties, accompanied by bad faith or recklessness. A court would also have to be satisfied that the absence of good faith or the reckless disregard of rights would impinge on the observance by the State party concerned of any declaratory order made by the court". [2001] 4 I.R. 259 at 337.

Cronin differed from *T.D.*, however, in at least two ways: first, *Cronin* was concerned with interlocutory rather than permanent injunctions; secondly, the orders sought in *Cronin* were grounded on statutory rights, not constitutional rights.

Laffoy J. held that the matter should be addressed on the basis of the principles laid down in *Campus Oil Ltd v Minister for Industry and Energy* [1983] I.R. 88. Applying these principles, Laffoy J. held that there was a fair issue to be tried as to the appropriate provision of pre-school education for the plaintiff. She further held that the balance of convenience lay in favour of granting the injunction, and that damages would not be an adequate remedy. Finally, Laffoy J. held that the plaintiff's mother's undertaking in damages was adequate, and would sufficiently compensate the Minister if the plaintiff were unsuccessful at trial.

Of more interest, perhaps, are Laffoy J.'s views on the consistency of this decision with that of Keane C.J. in *T.D.* In particular, she referred to Keane C.J.'s observations to the following effect:

> "The difficulty created by the order of the High Court in this case is not

simply that it offends in principle against the doctrine of the separation of powers, though I have no doubt that it does. It also involves the High Court in effectively determining the policy which the Executive are to follow in dealing with a particular social problem. This difficulty is not met by the contention advanced on behalf of the applicants that the Ministers are being asked to do no more than carry into effect a programme prepared by them and which they assert it is their intention to implement. The evidence in this case establishes clearly that, in what is unarguably an extremely difficult area, approaches which at one time seemed appropriate may have to be reconsidered: in particular, officials are naturally concerned with how equivalent problems are being dealt with in other countries. There is no reason in principle why the Executive should not adopt a flexible and open minded approach to the problems of children with special needs, while at the same time ensuring that their constitutional right to have those needs met is respected. The making of the High Court order in this form, as the judgment of the trial judge emphasises, will make it necessary for the Minister to return to the High Court to obtain its sanction to any change in policy which necessitates a departure from the precise terms of the order. It cannot be right that the executive power of the Government can only be exercised in a particular manner, even though so to do would not contravene any person's constitutional rights, without the sanction of the High Court". [2001] 4 I.R. 259 at 287.

Laffoy J. briefly concluded that granting a mandatory injunction in *Cronin* did not fall foul of the Supreme Court's decision in *T.D.*, observing that the relief granted was limited to the particular needs of the plaintiff and was merely extending a programme that the Minister had already sanctioned. Laffoy J. thus appears to have distinguished *Cronin* from *T.D.* on the grounds that the relief sought in *Cronin* was limited to a particular plaintiff whereas the relief sought in *T.D.* was for a class of plaintiffs. If this distinction accurately represents the law, it follows that a mandatory order can be granted to remedy an individual interference with constitutional rights, but not a systemic interference with constitutional rights. Although a plausible interpretation of Keane C.J.'s specific comments in *T.D.*, this would appear to be inconsistent with the tenor of the Supreme Court majority's judgments, *i.e.* that mandatory orders should be reserved for the most egregious breaches of constitutional rights.

Laffoy J. did not address the separation of powers arguments as to the permissibility of mandatory orders in enforcing statutory, as opposed to constitutional, rights. In this regard, Hardiman J. had commented in *Sinnott*:

"It is hardly necessary to point out that a case based on a duty to provide services imposed by statute would avoid the difficulties of principle described in *O'Reilly v Limerick Corporation* and elsewhere. It is clearly not possible to say, in the abstract, whether other difficulties might await a specific case, but the enforcement of duties imposed by the legislature is obviously an exercise of a different kind to the devising or inferring of such duties without legislative intervention". [2001] 2 I.R. 545 at 711–712.

This observation of Hardiman J. has been taken by some to signify that mandatory orders might be granted in the case of legislative, as opposed to constitutional, duties. However, it is worth noting that the two parts of Hardiman J.'s distinction addressed different issues. In the first half of the last clause of the last sentence quoted above, Hardiman J. addressed the issue of the *enforcement* of duties. In the second half of that clause, he addressed the issue of the *devising* or *inferring* of duties. On the one hand, it could be argued that Hardiman J. was simply addressing the issue of duty recognition, rather than duty enforcement. On the other hand, at this point in his judgment, Hardiman J. was addressing enforcement issues, and he specifically referred to enforcement in the second half of the clause. As such, the precise import of Hardiman J.'s comments is unclear. On the basis of first principles, it is difficult to see why a clearly stated constitutional right should be less enforceable than a clearly stated legislative right. However, as Laffoy J. did not directly address this issue in *Cronin*, we must await a later judgment to interpret the remarks of Hardiman J. in *Sinnott*.

Finally, one must consider the appropriateness of Laffoy J.'s application of the *Campus Oil* test. In the context of a plenary hearing, there are clear principles that govern whether an injunction or award of damages is the appropriate remedy. These principles are adequately reflected by the *Campus Oil* test for interlocutory hearings. If *Cronin* had gone to a full hearing, however, there would have been a substantial issue as to whether a mandatory order or a declaration was the appropriate remedy. That issue is not addressed at all by the *Campus Oil* principles. Accordingly, one can argue that the *Campus Oil* test was not wholly appropriate to this type of case, as there is at least a suspicion that it would allow a plaintiff to obtain on an interlocutory basis an onerous order that could never be obtained at full hearing. The courts may need to reconsider this point in future, and in particular whether the appropriateness of a mandatory injunction can adequately be dealt with under the "fair issue to be tried" limb of the *Campus Oil* test.

The case was appealed to the Supreme Court and came before the court in November 2004. In light of changed circumstances, the court, on consent, discharged the injunction granted by Laffoy J. without deciding on the merits of the appeal one way or the other. The issues raised by *Cronin* will probably fall to be decided in another case.

RIGHT OF ACCESS TO THE COURTS

In *White v Dublin City Council* [2004] 1 I.R. 545, the applicants challenged a decision of the first respondent to grant planning permission to the applicants' neighbours and sought a declaration that s.82(3B)(a)(i) of the Local Government (Planning and Development) Act 1963 as amended, was unconstitutional. This provision required that applications for judicial review of decisions on planning applications be made within two months of the date of the decision.

The applicants' neighbours had applied for planning permission and had advertised their applications as required by the planning code. Having inspected the planning applications, the applicants were satisfied that their property would not be overlooked. However, the Council allowed the neighbours to alter the planning application so as to facilitate a grant of planning permission but did not exercise its discretion under reg.17 of the Local Government (Planning and Development) Regulations 1994 to require the neighbours to advertise the modified plans. Planning permission was granted, on the basis of the revised plans, which involved the proposed development overlooking the applicants' property. The applicants sought judicial review on the basis that the Council should have required the neighbours to advertise the revised plans. However, the application for judicial review of the Council's decision was made outside the two-month period imposed by s.82(3B)(a)(i) of the 1963 Act, as the applicants were unaware of the facts giving rise to their claim until after that time period had elapsed.

Fennelly J., with whom the other members of the court agreed, first held that the court was required to consider the planning challenge, even though it remained (in a sense) hypothetical pending the court's decision on whether the limitation period in s.82(3B)(a)(i) was unconstitutional. This ordering of the issues correctly follows from *Brady v Donegal County Council* [1989] I.L.R.M. 282, in which an equivalent provision had been constitutionally challenged. In that case, Finlay C.J. held that the court must establish first whether the applicant had a good factual basis for his planning law challenge (*i.e.* whether the newspaper in which the planning application was advertised was actually circulating in the local area), before considering the constitutional validity of the limitation period.

Addressing the planning law issue, Fennelly J. held that the decision not to require notification of the modified plans was irrational, not in the sense of *O'Keeffe v An Bord Pleanála*, but in the sense that it did not give proper consideration to the radical effect of the required modifications. This was particularly the case given the planning history of the site in which the possibilities of overlooking had played a prominent role.

Having decided the planning issue hypothetically in favour of the applicants, the court's decision on the constitutionality of s.82(3B)(a)(i) was delivered by Denham J. At issue was not so much the shortness of the two-month time limit, but rather the fact that this time limit was absolute. She accepted that the applicants had a personal right to litigate, protected by Art.40.3.1° of the Constitution. It was, she reasoned, unnecessary to decide whether the applicants' right was also a property right which benefited from the protection of Art.43.

Denham J. followed *Tuohy v Courtney* [1994] 3 I.R. 1 in accepting that the weighing of all relevant considerations and striking a balance in the form of a limitation period was "quintessentially a matter for the judgment of the legislator" [2004] 1 I.R. 545 at para.80. In *Tuohy*, the court upheld a six-year limitation period while acknowledging that a person might, through no fault or neglect of her own, not become aware of her loss within that limitation period. Denham J. also referred to *Re Article 26 and the Illegal Immigrants (Trafficking) Bill 1999* [2000] 2 I.R. 360, in which the court upheld the validity of a two-week limitation period which was extendable by the court.

From *Tuohy* and the *Illegal Immigrants Bill* case, Denham J. derived a number of principles. First, that lengthy limitation periods were usually laid down in civil actions between private persons or bodies. Their length was a relevant factor in deciding whether they were just, but the omission of a stipulation for extension where the wrong was not reasonably discoverable did not render them unconstitutional. Secondly, that it was inherent in the principle of respect for the rule of law that citizens should have an opportunity to challenge the legality of decisions of public law bodies. Judicial review was the appropriate procedure for such challenges, but there was a strong public interest in the certainty and finality of administrative decisions. Accordingly, any attack on their validity should be made at the earliest reasonable date.

Denham J. then noted that the factors that influenced the Supreme Court in *Tuohy*, such as the need to protect defendants from stale claims and the need for the courts to have oral evidence before it, based on the accuracy of recent recollection, did not count so strongly against an extension stipulation where the limitation period itself was only two months. The imperative of certainty in administrative decisions (planning decisions in particular) had to be weighed against:

> "the equally important principle laid down ... that, in a state based on the rule of law, any person affected by an administrative decision has a constitutionally protected right of access to courts to contest its legality". [2004] 1 I.R. 545 at para.98.

Denham J. concluded that s.82(3B)(a)(i) was unconstitutional in that it undermined or compromised a substantive right of access to the courts. The effect of this judgment would presumably have been to strike down the two-month limitation period as it would not have been open to the court to write into the statute an extension stipulation. However, given that s.50 of the Planning and Development Act 2000, which provides an eight-week limitation period but with an extension stipulation where an applicant can satisfy the court that there is good and sufficient reason for doing so, had been commenced by the time of the Supreme Court's decision in *White*, the practical effect of the court's decision for other litigants was minimal.

In *O'Donoghue v Legal Aid Board*, High Court, December 21, 2004, Kelly J. held that the plaintiff's constitutional right to legal aid had been infringed in circumstances where the plaintiff was statutorily entitled to legal aid but had experienced a 25-month delay in receiving that legal aid. Kelly J. reasoned as follows:

> "The Act of 1995 gives substance, in many ways, to the constitutional entitlement to legal aid for appropriate persons. The legislature is entitled to define reasonable limits to that right. But the right cannot be effectively set at nought for years in the manner that it was here."

Kelly J. awarded damages to the plaintiff. He did not accept that he was precluded, by the Supreme Court decision in *T.D.*, from intervening in this way, on the basis that there was no question of a mandatory order being granted.

RIGHT TO COMMUNICATE

The applicant in *Holland v Governor Portlaoise Prison* [2004] I.E.H.C. 208, [2004] 2 I.R. 573 is serving a sentence in Portlaoise Prison on drug charges. He sought access to the media, by way of visits and letters, for the purpose of attempting to secure their support, by public media presentation, in order to highlight what he says has been a miscarriage of justice in his criminal case. His application was strictly confined to this purpose and he expressed no objection to the respondent putting in place all reasonable means to ensure this. At the outset, McKechnie J. noted that no suggestion had been made on behalf of the respondent that the activity of the applicant lacked bona fides, or was designed for some criminal or illegal purpose, or was driven by a desire to create unrest, or whether the prisoner otherwise had some ulterior motive.

The reliefs sought by the applicant were first, an order of certiorari quashing specified decisions of the respondent, secondly a declaration that the respondent's refusal pursuant to rule 59 of the 1947 Prison Rules to allow him visits by a journalist and members of the media was unlawful and *ultra vires*, as the refusal was discriminatory, arbitrary, unfair, and unreasonable, and, thirdly, a declaration that the application of Prison Rules 59 and 63, as they relate to the applicant's access to journalists and the media was so unreasonable as to be *ultra vires* and void. The respondent submitted that he was operating a long-standing policy of the Irish Prison Service based on the interests of security and good order within the prison, and on the desire to prevent any further trauma to victims and their families. In addition, he said that there could not be any scope for individualisation because of the absolute requirement of consistency of treatment as between all prisoners.

May courts review prison policy or rules?   This application presented a challenge to prison policy rather than to the Prison Rules *per se*, and as such was a cause of concern to the authorities. Referring to the decision of Murphy J. in *Duff v Minister for Agriculture (No.2)* [1997] 2 I.R. 22 at 43–44, McKechnie J. opined:

> "Whilst one would have to await a case in which the point became pivotal, nevertheless, I would be greatly surprised if this judicial organ of government, which by Article 34 of the Constitution is enjoined to administer justice, was not available to a citizen who alleges that his Article 40 personal rights have been infringed by the exercise of such a policy. If it were otherwise, such a person would have no forum in which to make a case and the constitutionally established courts of this country would be debarred from performing one of the most fundamental duties and obligations entrusted to them, namely the vindication of such rights". [2004] I.E.H.C. 208 at para.15.

Furthermore, the applicant was seeking to impugn as unconstitutional the manner in which the respondent has interpreted and applied Prison Rules 59 and 63 rather than the rules themselves. It was claimed that as a consequence his constitutionally protected rights under Arts 40.3.1°, 40.3.2°, and 40.6.1° had been violated. This "perfectly permissible" approach was based on reliance on the presumption of behaviour "in accordance with the principles of constitutional justice", *East Donegal v Attorney General* [1970] I.R. 317 at 341.

Stardust **and** *O'Keeffe* **inappropriate tests**   McKechnie J. expressed doubts as to the relevance of the principles enunciated in *State (Keegan) v Stardust Compensation Tribunal* [1986] I.R. 642, and *O'Keeffe v An Bord Pleanála* [1993] 1 I.R. 39 in the instant action. He commented that the factual context of these cases, in particular the latter, were totally distinguishable:

> "If *O'Keeffe v An Bord Pleanála* was to apply, it would mean that this court should ask itself whether or not the respondent had before him any relevant material which would support its decision. I do not believe that when the exercise of a fundamental right such as the right to communicate is at the core of an application that this test is either proper or appropriate. Accordingly, I do not propose to decide this case on the basis either of *State (Keegan) v Stardust Compensation Tribunal* or *O'Keeffe v An Bord Pleanála*". [2004] I.E.H.C. 208 at para.18.

Is right to communicate based in Article 40.3 or Article 40.6.1°? In acknowledging the acceptance within our system of law that there is a right to communicate, McKechnie J. called in aid Costello J.'s judgment in *Attorney General v Paperlink Ltd* [1984] I.L.R.M. 373, and in the later case of *Kearney v Minister for Justice* [1986] I.R. 116, concluding that:

> "… whatever its true basis may be, the right to communicate is not an absolute right and by law its exercise can be subject to lawful conditions, restrictions or limitations." [2004] I.E.H.C. 208 at para.23.

With regard to the interaction between Art.40.3 and Art.40.6.1° of the Constitution in the context of this right to communicate, having considered the judgments in *Paperlink* and in *Murphy v IRTC* [1999] 1 I.R. 12, McKechnie J. held as follows:

> "It, therefore, seems quite clear that depending on the circumstances of any particular case, a claimant or plaintiff may be able to rely, not only on Article 40.3 of the Constitution but also on Article 40.6.1°. In the instant proceedings, it appears to me that, in all probability, the applicant can rely upon both sub-articles in furtherance of his claim. His attempts to communicate with R.T.É. involved apparently a mixture of fact, information, convictions and opinions and with the result that, by seeking to influence the media to bring to the attention of the public what he describes as a miscarriage of justice, he was undoubtedly, in a most direct way attempting to influence public opinion. Consequently, I believe that both sources of protection are available in principle to him …. If, however, I should be incorrect in this view it seems to me that for practical purposes, in the particular circumstances of this case, there is no valid distinction in the consequences which would follow from confining reliance to one or other but not both of these sub-articles. No issue on the facts of this case arises which could be said to involve 'public order or morality or the authority of the State' as that phrase is contained in Article 40.6.1°. Therefore, in my opinion it is not necessary to conclusively decide on the preferment of one sub-article to the exclusion of the other". [2004] I.E.H.C. 208 at paras 24–25.

"Necessary" abrogation of constitutional rights Citing as authority *State (McDonagh) v Frawley* [1978] I.R. 131, *State (Fagan) v Governor of Mountjoy Prison,* unreported, High Court, March 6, 1978, and *State (Richardson) v Governor of Mountjoy Prison* [1980] I.L.R.M. 82, McKechnie J. accepted that a prisoner lawfully detained is a person whose normal constitutional rights are abrogated or suspended in so far as is necessary. He went on to say:

> "[I]t appears to me that the rights, the exercise of which can be suspended

or abrogated or otherwise interfered with, are those which 'necessarily' follow from the prisoner having to serve a term of imprisonment and from the requirements of the prison service to sustain security and good order therein as between all inmates. Disregarding for a moment the scope or extent of the interference which could thus be justified, it seems to me that apart from the rights which are identifiable in this way, all other rights survive a prisoner's incarceration. If that is so, such surviving rights must be capable of exercise by him". [2004] I.E.H.C. 208 at para.28.

Continuing by citing *Murray v Ireland* [1985] I.R. 532 and two American authorities, *Wolff v McDonnell* 418 US 539 (1973) and *Procunier v Martinez* 416 US 296 (1973), McKechnie J. referred again to Costello J.'s judgments in both *Murray v Ireland* [1985] I.R. 532 and *Kearney v Minister for Justice* [1986] I.R. 116 in which the applicant had challenged the constitutionality of rule 63 of the Prison Rules. McKechnie J. was concerned with the *Kearney* judgment and its:

> "clear and definite enjoinder that any infringement or restriction on the exercise of a constitutional right of a prisoner must be no more than what is 'necessary or essential' for the protection of the interest or objective which grounds the justification for such interference or restriction in the first place. In *Procunier v Martinez* it was said to be security, order and rehabilitation". [2004] I.E.H.C. 208 at para.30.

Restriction must be proportionate, onus on respondent   Since the right in issue in the case was constitutionally based, McKechnie J. held it un-questionable that he must consider whether the policy of the prison service and the operation of rules 59 and 63, as these had been applied to the applicant, were proportionate to the objectives of the respondent, namely the maintenance of security and good order. Furthermore, any permissible abolition, even for a limited period or any interference, restriction, or modification on that right should be strictly construed with the onus of proof on the respondent. Referring first to the test in *Heaney v Ireland* [1994] 3 I.R. 593, he noted that it was important to mention that the case law in this jurisdiction as set forth is very similar to that emerging from the European Court of Human Rights, although for instant purposes the Convention was not yet part of our domestic law.

No legal basis for respondent's decision   The power of a prison governor in dealing with prisoners derives from the Prison Rules. Consequently, McKechnie J. was somewhat uncertain as to how it could have been asserted that he could make a decision on the applicant's request on the basis of what has been described as a longstanding policy of the Irish Prison Service. He knew of no authority, and none had been advanced, for the proposition that this body had any legal entitlement to establish a practice, or policy, which, on its own, could be used to determine the position of a prisoner. The legal foundation commences with the power vested in the Minister for Justice pursuant to the Acts or regulations mentioned in the preamble of the Prison Rules 1947, and having exercised this power, the immediate basis of authority is in fact the rules themselves. In respect of all requests made in relation to both communications and letters, the respondent must operate rules 59 and 63 and in so doing is given, what appears on the face of the rules, to be a very considerable discretion. McKechnie J. could find no specific exclusion in either rule dealing with the media, either by way of personal visits or by way of correspondence. Moreover, he could not find within the rules:

"… any provision which would entitle the respondent to adopt either the position of the Irish Prison Service [noted above] or indeed any independent policy of his own would have the effect of enabling him, when dealing with the media, to refuse every prisoner, in all circumstances, every request, no matter what the purpose of the intended communication was. On that general basis alone it is very difficult to see how the stated position of the respondent could be upheld" [2004] I.E.H.C. 36.

Respondent *must* exercise discretion *Mishra v Minister for Justice* [1996] 1 I.R. 189 was cited for the settled proposition that "'the use of a policy or set of fixed rules must not fetter the discretion which is conferred by the Act'", [1996] 1 I.R. 189 at 205 quoted at [2004] I.E.H.C. 208 at para.37. In holding that the impugned decisions taken by the respondent were invalid, McKechnie J. concluded as follows:

"I have come to the clear conclusion that even if in principle the respondent was entitled to take into account a policy emanating from the Irish Prison Service, or to have his own, this particular policy, by reason of its very scope is fundamentally at variance with the correct operation of rr. 59 and 63 and is also fundamentally contrary to a prisoner's entitlement to have a request made by him properly considered and evaluated by the said respondent. This policy, which is automatically triggered not by the nature of the request itself, had, by the identity of the addressee the effect of preventing and restraining the respondent from exercising any discretion under rr.59 and 63, which discretion undoubtedly he has. Therefore, as the facts of this case amply demonstrate, the respondent does not concern himself with the purpose of such request, or with the underlying intention behind its making, or with its content or with what effect it might have on any of the matters said by him to justify this outright restriction. Therefore, his approach in my opinion, violates both of the rules in" [2004] I.E.H.C. 38.

McKechnie J. completed his judgment finding that the respondent is not entitled to apply the policy as described, and is not entitled to utilise it in the way in which he has.

> "He must, in my opinion, give individual consideration to each request made by a prisoner to either write to or receive letters from members of the media and must likewise evaluate any application for a prison visit by members of the said media. Only then can it be said that the Rules have been operated in the manner envisaged by their provisions" [2004] I.E.H.C. 208 at para.40.

Blanket ban unjustified   The judgment was concluded by some general comments, at the request of the parties, on the more fundamental point where it was assumed that the prisoner's requests were properly considered by the respondent but that his response was similarly, that on grounds of security and prison discipline he was justified in coming to the conclusion that every request by every prisoner for communication, either by visit or letter, to the media should be refused. In acknowledging that it is not the function of the court to make the decision for him, nor to substitute its own views for those of the respondent, McKechnie J. opined that the imposition of a blanket ban on such communications is entirely disproportionate to the penal objective to maintain discipline and good order.

> "This objective is one which I think is properly legitimate but, it is the means adopted to achieve its results which, in my view, are unlawful. Therefore, I remain of the opinion that this ban cannot be justified". [2004] I.E.H.C. 208 at para.44.

Investigative journalism and miscarriages of justice   Finally, McKechnie J. considered the relationship between investigative journalism and miscarriages of justice. Noting that it would be an exercise in self-deception to believe that our criminal institutions are immune from such miscarriages, he did not doubt the involvement of the media and its capacity in this regard. In this context he compared *Kearney* and the instant case:

> "It can, therefore, I think be immediately seen that as between *Kearney v Minister for Justice* [1986] I.R. 116 and the instant proceedings, the former was in reality concerned with a potential restriction or interference with the exercise of the right in question whereas in this case one is confronted with its total and absolute abolition. What might be a perfectly acceptable justification to confer the status of legality on a limitation may be entirely ineffectual to sustain an abolition, in particular one which permits of no exception, ever, irrespective of the circumstances". [2004] I.E.H.C. 208 at para.47.

McKechnie J.'s final comments were an endorsement of the judgment of Lord Steyn in *R v Secretary of State for the Home Department*, ex parte *Simms* [2000] 2 A.C. 115, which he found wholly persuasive. In particular, he endorsed the views on freedom of expression of which the following is an extract:

> "'The value of free speech in a particular case must be measured in specifics. Not all types of speech have an equal value ... the prisoner's right to free speech is outweighed by deprivation of liberty by the sentence of a court, and the need for discipline and control in prisons. But the free speech at stake in the present case is qualitatively of a very different order. The prisoners are in prison because they are presumed to have been properly convicted. They wish to challenge the safety of their convictions. In principle it is not easy to conceive of a more fundamental function which free speech might fulfil' ... whilst the evidence in the present case is significantly less detailed than that which presented itself before their Lordships, nevertheless I believe that this court is entitled to take the view that such an agency as investigative journalism is and can be a productive and probative vehicle in the overall administration of justice" [2000] 2 A.C. 115 at 408 quoted at [2004] I.E.H.C. 208 at paras 50–51.

RIGHTS OF DECEASED PERSONS

Primarily dealing with evidentiary matters, constitutional issues were also raised in *Murray v Commission to Inquire into Child Abuse* [2004] I.E.H.C. 225, [2004] 2 I.R. 222. Simply put, the issue in the proceedings was whether the investigation committee of the Commission was empowered to make a finding of serious sexual abuse by one person in a particular institution of another, also within that institution, within a period many years ago in circumstances where that first person is either dead, under a disability, unplaced, or disadvantaged in the inquiry by reason of being hampered or hindered from rebutting the allegations, due to prejudice caused by the lapse of time since the alleged incidents took place. The plaintiffs were members of the congregation of the Christian Brothers, and were representing the congregation's interests. The Commission, colloquially known as the Laffoy Commission, had been established by the Commission to Inquire Into Child Abuse Act 2000. In its final ruling, the subject of the challenge by the plaintiffs, the investigation committee of the Commission set out extensive procedural arrangements and clarified in detail how the rights of parties are to be determined, and the standard of proof, together with procedures for determining whether the inquiry mandated by the Commission and its committee ought to be halted in respect of a particular complaint and other important issues.

Do common law rights of deceased exist?   Abbott J. found no case law to justify the existence of a constitutional right of the deceased to their good name or reputation. Referring to *Hilliard v Penfield Enterprises* [1990] 1 I.R. 138 and *Kelly v United Kingdom* [2001] E.C.H.R. at paras 91–92 cited by the plaintiffs, he held that these and other cases mentioned, related primarily to the right to life, rather than to any rights being asserted on behalf of the deceased. He found it clear from the judgment of Keane C.J. in *McDonnell v Brady* [2001] 3 I.R. 588, that no final decision was being made at the interlocutory stage of the hearing in relation to the right of the plaintiff to defend her late husband's reputation against unjust attack.

> "Apart from the cases mentioned I can find no authority in the history of the common law asserting a right of the deceased to a good name or to any property rights. Indeed in the area of property rights, the common law from ancient times is noteworthy for the extremes to which the courts went to free up land from the rule of the grave as in the cases of the evolution of the fiction laden fines and recoveries procedures which evolved for the purpose of barring the entail, and the development of the rule against perpetuities. A similar approach was adopted with the onset of legislative intervention as shown by the Mortmain Acts and indeed the Fines and Recoveries Act, 1883" [2004] I.E.H.C. 225 at para.126.

Do constitutional rights of deceased exist?   Adopting a literal interpretation of the Constitution, Abbott J. found that:

> "when such interpretation is tested schematically by testing it against other rights in the Constitution such as the right to equality before the law, the right to bodily integrity, the right to inviolability of the dwelling and other rights of the living, I find that there is no place in the Constitution from where the rights of the deceased may be rationally inferred" [2004] I.E.H.C. 225 at para.127.

Notwithstanding that the plaintiffs did not directly represent the deceased, he considered it necessary for the purpose of disposal of the issues in the instant case to decide on the issue. He did not accept the validity of the claims of the plaintiffs as to the existence of the rights.

Does a congregation have a right to good name?   Acknowledging the right of the committee to give any person, alive or deceased, the facility of representation for the purpose of assisting the committee and eliciting the true facts, Abbott J. considered whether in the particular circumstances of an adverse finding being possible against the members of the congregation, either past or present, the congregation as representing its existing members has a right in law and under the Constitution to such representation, and the right to protection against a finding adverse to them, and a right to their good name. He looked first at the law on group defamation and specifically at the Law Reform Commission consultation paper on the Civil Law of Defamation published in March 1991. He found it by no means certain that an allegation of abuse which, if made against one or a group of members or deceased members of the congregation, could be held to be defamatory of the group and thus, he found it unlikely that the constitutional rights of the other members of the group to their good names would be violated. However, in the circumstances of the instant case this conclusion had to be examined in the light of the mandate of the committee to investigate the management responsibility of the institutions involved. Abbott J. found that not only had the congregation a management responsibility at the time involving complaints back to 1940, but that they were now effectively the only available representatives of management. He continued:

> "Added to this consideration is the fact that the evidence indicated that the members of the congregation, through their association with its founder and his examples and ideals and their antecedents within the congregation, held themselves out as leading selfless and exemplary lives. These factors lead me to the conclusion that the application of the scheme of the Act of 2002 to the facts of the association of the members of the congregation with the persons and members of management against whom complaints are made, have a right under the Constitution to protect their good name, which arises by reason of their positive association with these people in the context of setting out the aims and ideals of the congregation and to the constitutional right of protection, by way of representation, against an adverse finding" [2004] I.E.H.C. 225 at para.136.

He concluded this point by stating that this right of representation and constitutional rights will be general and certainly not greater than the rights of living present or past members.

Constitutional justice on behalf of deceased and incapacitated   Abbott J. noted the importance of cross-examination for the purpose of ensuring fair procedures and constitutional justice as set out in *Maguire v Ardagh* [2002] I.E.S.C. 21, [2002] 1 I.R. 385. He held that the right of the representative of the deceased and incapacitated to cross-examine (notwithstanding difficulties in obtaining the fullest instructions for such cross-examination) is vitally important for ensuring the operation of fair procedures and constitutional justice in the context of inquiries by the committee, and made a declaration in this regard. In his consideration of the issue of the plaintiffs' *locus standi* to challenge the constitutionality of the 2000 Act, which he denied, Abbott J.

expanded on this point:

> "I find that, while the deceased and the persons suffering from an incapacity may not cross-examine as successfully as a person of full capacity, the right to cross-examine is no more denied to them than to similar persons in ordinary litigation. Moreover, the disadvantage suffered by such persons is considerably balanced by the introduction of a statutory mandate for the committee to seek corroboration as appropriate. Even if there were some attenuation or diminution of the constitutional rights of such persons by reason of a less advantageous position to cross-examine this is more than balanced by the statutory mandate and requirement to seek corroboration, as appropriate" [2004] I.E.H.C. 225 at para.187.

Article 40.3 guarantees not breached With regard to the alleged disadvantage of the plaintiffs in the attempted investigation of "the deceased, the disabled, the unlocated and the disadvantaged, or the alleged right of cross-examination being further circumscribed, apart altogether from the impossibility of taking instructions," Abbott J. found no breach of Arts 40.3.1° and 2° nor of the right to fair procedures. He held that fairness of basic procedures is guaranteed by:

> "(a) the statutory requirement of corroboration as appropriate, (b) the commitment of the committee to test the evidence as appropriate, (c) the acknowledged right and inability of the committee to stop the inquiry, either exceptionally, at the outset, or at a concluding stage of the inquiries, by reason of prejudice arising from delay, death or disability using the standards of jurisprudence evolved by the Courts in civil and criminal litigation" [2004] I.E.H.C. 225 at para.191.

Is 2000 Act constitutional? For the substantive purposes of the case, Abbott J. had not found it necessary to rule on the constitutionality of the 2000 Act. However, he did so for two reasons. In the first place, he found that for the committee to proceed with a complaint against the deceased brothers was *intra vires* the Act: this was fundamentally contrary to the case argued on behalf of the plaintiffs. Secondly, both parties had requested him from the outset to refrain from acting with judicial restraint in relation to the issue by reason of the public importance and urgency of having the inquiry of the committee and the work of the Commission continue without protracted delays by a re-submission of the constitutional issues to the Court. As noted, he denied the plaintiffs *locus standi* to challenge the constitutionality of the Act. Nevertheless, the final words of his judgment were as follows:

"In conclusion, if compelled to do so, I find no reason advanced by the plaintiffs to displace the presumption of constitutionality of the Act and would find the Act to be consistent and in accordance with the Constitution" [2004] I.E.H.C. 225 at para.191.

RIGHT TO EARN A LIVELIHOOD

In *Casey v Minister for Arts* [2004] 1 I.R. 402, the applicant, a boat operator, challenged the decision of the respondent to implement a new scheme of landing permits for Sceilig Mhícil and not to issue a permit to the applicant. As well as arguing that s.12 of the National Monuments Act 1936 (as amended) was an unconstitutional delegation of legislative power, the applicant argued that his right to earn a livelihood had been infringed. Murray J., with whom McGuinness and McCracken JJ. concurred, confirmed that the right to earn a livelihood included the right to earn a living from any lawful vocation, trade, business, or profession and was one of the unspecified rights protected by Art.40.3.1°. Murray J. first considered whether the refusal of a landing permit constituted an attack on the applicant's right to earn a livelihood. He noted that the applicant could use his boat for commercial purposes other than landing on Sceilig Mhícil, such as sight-seeing, bird-watching and sea angling. The applicant's complaint, in Murray J.'s view, was essentially based on the assertion that he had a constitutional right to land on Sceilig Mhícil. Murray J. rejected this contention:

> "[T]he applicant has misconceived the nature and ambit of the right to earn a livelihood. To engage in such a lawful business activity for the purpose of earning a livelihood is something which a citizen is entitled to do as of right. It is self-evident that the right to carry on such a business does not entitle the citizen to have access, as of right, to the property of third parties and use it for business purposes. It does not matter whether the property, in this case a national monument, is privately owned or owned by the State" [2004] 1 I.R. 402 at para.52.

Essentially, the court held that the right to earn a livelihood does not extend to a right to use other people's property in support of one's own livelihood. Interestingly, Murray J. concluded by describing the right to earn a livelihood as a liberty. This implicitly confirmed that the right to earn a livelihood is seen by the courts as a negative right that imposes no positive obligation on the State to assist people in earning a livelihood. The legislative power aspects of the court's decision are considered above. The applicant also made various administrative law arguments challenging the Minister's exercise of her powers. These arguments were rejected.

In *Kenny v The Dental Council and Minister for Health* [2004] I.E.H.C. 29 (February 27, 2004), Gilligan J. held that the right to earn a livelihood was not a right to earn a livelihood in whatever manner a person chooses. The plaintiff described himself as a denturist, an occupation which involves the design, construction and fitting of removable dentures including their repair and alteration. The effect of the Dentists Act 1928 made it illegal for a person who was not a dentist to perform any operation or give any treatment, advice or attendance on or to any person preparatory to or for the purpose of, or in connection with the fitting, insertion, or fixing of artificial teeth. Following publication of the Restrictive Practices Commission Report in 1982, the Dentists Act 1928 and the Dentists (Amendment) Act 1983 were repealed, and a Dental Council was established, pursuant to the provisions of the Dentists Act 1985. Section 6 of that Act provides that the general concern of the Council is to promote high standards of professional education and professional conduct among dentists and that the Council shall in particular fulfil the functions assigned to it by the Dentists Act 1985. Section 51 maintained the prohibition on the practice of dentistry other than by registered dentists and provided for fines, and, at the discretion of the court, a term of imprisonment. Section 53, dealing with auxiliary dental workers, states as follows:

> "(1) The Council may, with the consent of the Minister, make a scheme for establishing classes of auxiliary dental workers who may undertake such class or classes of dental work as shall be specified by the Council notwithstanding that the doing of such work would constitute the practice of dentistry within the meaning of this Act."

There is no scheme in place to regulate the practice of denturism, and accordingly the plaintiff carried on his work as a denturist contrary to law although he has never been prosecuted. *Inter alia*, the plaintiff sought a declaration that the defendants had failed to vindicate his constitutional rights to work and earn a livelihood guaranteed by Art.40.3 and an order directing the defendants to take such steps as would be necessary to vindicate the plaintiff's constitutional rights.

The plaintiff argued that s.53 of the 1985 Act gives the defendants a discretionary power, and both defendants have to exercise their discretion reasonably and fairly. Having found that the Dental Council and the Minister did exercise their respective discretion fairly and reasonably, Gilligan J. considered the constitutional issue in light of those findings. The constitutional right to earn a livelihood is not an absolute right, *Attorney General v Paperlink Ltd* [1984] I.L.R.M. 373. Gilligan J. stated that the plaintiff knew when he started to hold himself out as a denturist that he was acting in breach of the law, and he was satisfied on the evidence that the plaintiff was not qualified to practise as a denturist. He was further satisfied that:

> "there is justifiable legitimate legal restraint in the public interest in respect of persons holding themselves out to practise as denturists for the obvious public health issues that arise. This is not a case dealing with bus drivers or persons wishing to act as couriers or a person who

is improperly restrained from taking up employment which they are entitled to carry on as of right or in respect of which they meet the required standards and qualifications legitimately required to enable them to perform the duties required of such employment."

Gilligan J. was satisfied that the legislation does not mandate the introduction of a scheme, and it does not require that the legal prohibition on persons other than dentists practising denturism be removed.

It is noteworthy that the plaintiff had not challenged the constitutionality of the Dentists Act 1985. As such, the court, having regard also to the fact that it was not in a position to direct the defendants to bring in a scheme, could not override the provisions of the 1985 Act. Accordingly, Gilligan J. rejected the contention that because there is no scheme in place that enables the plaintiff to lawfully practise denturism that the plaintiff's constitutional right to earn his livelihood pursuant to Art.40.3 had been infringed.

RIGHT TO LIFE

In *Cosma v Minister for Justice*, High Court, November 5, 2004, Peart J. accepted that the applicant had demonstrated substantial grounds that her deportation order should be quashed. There was medical and personal evidence, from after the deportation order was made, indicating that the applicant might commit suicide if she were forced to return to her home country. As this was only a leave application, and as there was some confusion as to whether "arguable case" was the appropriate standard by which leave should be granted, one must wait until the full hearing for a complete consideration of this interesting argument.

RIGHT TO PRIVACY SUBORDINATE TO PUBLIC INQUIRY

Immense burden to challenge public document   At first glance there is nothing of deep constitutional significance decided in *Desmond v Moriarty* [2004] I.E.S.C. 3, [2004] 1 I.R. 334, a challenge against decisions taken in its proceedings by a Tribunal of Inquiry. The Tribunal in question is the Tribunal of Inquiry into Payments to Messrs Charles Haughey and Michael Lowry, Sole Member, Moriarty J. In the instant case, the Tribunal was engaged in investigating whether the award of the second mobile telecommunications licence to the ESAT Digifone consortium was compromised or influenced in any improper manner by Michael Lowry, in return for any payment received by him. At issue in the case were the decisions and the ruling by the Tribunal in relation to the court-appointed Inspector's report, *Final Report on Chestvale*

Properties Ltd and Hoddle Investments Ltd—the Glackin Report. The applicant's complaint was that as a consequence of the manner in which the respondent had caused or permitted witnesses appearing before the Tribunal to be questioned in detail and repeatedly upon the contents of the Glackin report, he has been compromised in his capacity to vindicate his good name. The High Court dismissed the complaints, [2004] 1 I.R. 334, *Annual Review of Irish Law 2003*, pp.12–13. This refusal of reliefs was affirmed by the Supreme Court. Noting a certain air of shadow boxing in the case, Denham J. (McGuinness and McCracken JJ. *nem. diss.*) found that the information in issue was already in a public document, the Glackin Report, which has been the subject of considerable media coverage over recent years. Thus, the information was already in the public domain.

> "To challenge references to a public document by the Tribunal was to assume an immense burden. For a court to exclude references to a public document by the Tribunal and its counsel in questions or submissions would be an extraordinary intrusion on the working of the Tribunal which I would envisage arising only in wholly extraordinary circumstances" [2004] I.E.S.C. 3 at para.57.

The court did not consider that such circumstances existed in the current case.

Free speech of Tribunal of most importance   What is of significance in the case is the decision on the relationship between the applicant's constitutional right to privacy and the right of free speech in the context of a tribunal of inquiry and the *obiter* which concludes this passage:

> "The Tribunal is an arena where free speech is of significant importance. The Tribunal was set up by the representatives of the people to inquire into matters of public importance. The inquiry is to find out relevant facts and determine whether there is reason for the disquiet or not. It is thus an arena where freedom of expression is an important tool in the public interest in our democracy. The Tribunal was the mode chosen by the public representatives to inquire into the stated matters, to track down wrongdoing if it exists, and to allay concerns if it does not. Thus, in this inquiry, freedom of speech has an important function as part of an open democracy" [2004] I.E.S.C. 3 at paras 47–48.

Denham J., commenting once again that the information was already in the public domain, held that there was no interference with the constitutional right to privacy of the applicant. Accordingly, the issue of weighing that right against the exigencies of the common good does not arise for consideration. She continued:

"However, if it did, the rights of the applicant are not such as to curb the public inquiry established by the representatives of the people from their use of the Glackin Report. To allow the applicant's right to his good name to prevail over freedom of speech in such a situation in the Tribunal on this issue would be wholly disproportionate" [2004] I.E.S.C. 3 at para.53.

Public interest versus personal rights   Denying leave to seek judicial review against the Moriarty Tribunal, Herbert J. in an exhaustive judgment in *O'Brien v Moriarty* [2004] I.E.H.C. 362 (November 26, 2004) stated: "A Tribunal of an Inquiry must always maintain a proper sense of proportion between the public interest and the rights of individual citizens". On various grounds, Mr Denis O'Brien sought to challenge the decision of the Sole Member of the Tribunal of Inquiry into payments to Mr Charles Haughey and Mr Michael Lowry, to proceed to, or to continue with, public hearings by the Tribunal of evidence relating to the Doncaster Rovers Football Club Limited (D.R.F.C.L.) Transaction. *Inter alia*, relief was sought in the form of a declaration that the procedures adopted by the respondent and the delay by the Tribunal in concluding its inquiry had infringed the applicant's rights to fair procedures, to natural and constitutional justice, and his rights under the European Convention on Human Rights as incorporated into Irish law. In addition, the applicant sought relief by way of an order of *mandamus* directing the respondent to report back forthwith to the Clerk of Dáil Éireann claiming that the failure of the respondent to so report for a period of seven years is in breach of the terms of reference establishing the Tribunal, and a breach of the applicant's rights to fair procedures, to natural and constitutional justice, and to his rights under the European Convention on Human Rights as incorporated into Irish law.

In considering all the grounds of claim, Herbert J. relied on the Supreme Court decision in *G. v Director of Public Prosecutions and Judge Kirby* [1994] 1 I.R. 374:

"that the facts averred in the [verifying] Affidavit would be sufficient, if proved, to support a stateable ground for the relief sought by way of Judicial Review [and] that on those facts an arguable case in law can be made that the Applicant is entitled to the relief which he seeks."

However, in applying this test in the context of the instant application, he was also cognisant of the Supreme Court decision in *Goodman International v Hamilton* [1992] 2 I.R. 543 at 592, *per* Finlay C.J. that it would require "a very clear breach of an unambiguous constitutional provision for the courts to consider impeding such an inquiry, which is of such manifest public importance".

Must demonstrate actual damage to constitutional rights   Herbert J. opined that even without any delay, if a complainant could demonstrate some actual and material prejudice to his personal or property rights, there would be an arguable case that the court must provide an appropriate remedy which might well extend to forbidding any further investigation by the Tribunal of the complainant's affairs whether in preliminary investigative mode or in public or private sittings of the Tribunal.

> "In reaching its decision the court will consider all of the relevant factors including:
>
> > The nature and seriousness of the matters under investigation and the degree of public disquiet occasioned by these matters.
> > The degree of connection of the complainant with these matters.
> > The evidence and nature of the actual damage to the personal and additionally or alternatively property rights of the complainant.
> > The degree of responsibility of the complainant for the length of the inquiry into his or her business or private affairs.
> > The proportion between the amount of further investigation deemed reasonably and actually necessary in relation to the complainant and the degree of benefit likely to accrue in the context of the nature and seriousness of the public disquiet sought to be allayed."

He concluded that, of course, this was not intended to be an exhaustive list of the matters to be considered in any individual case. In the instant case, no attempt had been made on the part of the applicant to quantify any actual loss or damage to his business or property interests because of the alleged delay on the part of the Tribunal. Nor had any evidence been offered of any actual damage to the applicant's personal or business reputation. It had to be accepted as an unavoidable consequence of the establishment of this Tribunal of Inquiry that some of the applicant's business and private affairs have become public as a result of the Tribunal's investigations. Herbert J. thus held that no arguable case could be made, and certainly no arguable case with a reasonable chance of success, that as a consequence of the manner in which the Tribunal had conducted its investigations into the D.R.F.C.L. transaction to date that actual damage to the personal, and additionally or alternatively property rights of the applicant had been caused. Herbert J. denied all other reliefs requested on procedural grounds. The Supreme Court decision in *O'Brien v Moriarty* [2005] 2 I.L.R.M. 321 will be discussed in the *Annual Review of Irish Law 2005*.

Contract Law

**RUTH CANNON, Barrister-at-Law, Lecturer in Law,
Trinity College, Dublin**

AGREEMENT

The key question at issue in *McGill Construction v McKeon,* unreported, High Court, Finnegan J., May 15, 2004, was whether or not there had been a concluded oral agreement between the plaintiff company and the defendants for the sale of the entire issued share capital in the fourth-named defendant, Whitefield Construction Limited. The first-named defendant, a director of the fourth-named defendant, met with his bank manager to express interest in selling on behalf of the fourth-named defendant's lands at Eaglewood which had been developed by it. The bank manager subsequently informed Mr Hugh McGill, a director of the plaintiff company, whose agents met with the first and second-named defendants and made clear to them that any such transaction could only proceed by way of a sale of the issued share capital in Whitefield Construction Limited rather than by way of the transfer of the Eaglewood lands originally proposed by the first-named defendant. The plaintiff alleged that following earlier abortive discussions as to price, Mr Hugh McGill had phoned the first-named defendant on the July 2, 2002 and offered him the sum of €3.62 million for the issued share capital of Whitefield Construction Limited, which sum was then accepted by the first-named defendant on behalf of the other defendants. This allegation of fact was disputed by the defendants.

Finnegan J., rejecting the plaintiff's claim, stated that it was unnecessary to decide whether such actual acceptance by the defendant took place. Even if an agreement on price had been reached in the telephone conversation of July 2, 2002, same was not sufficient to give rise to a concluded agreement for the sale of the issued share capital in Whitefield Limited. A number of issues, such as the deposit to be paid in respect of the said transfer, had not been decided.

In *JC v WC* [2004] 2 I.R. 312 the plaintiff initiated proceedings to exclude the defendant, his son, from his lands. The defendant counterclaimed, *inter alia*, that he and his father had entered into an agreement whereby his father would transfer the lands to him. The plaintiff succeeded in the Circuit Court and the defendant's counterclaim was dismissed. The defendant's appeal to the High Court was rejected by Murphy J. who held that there had been no definite terms of offer and acceptance sufficient to constitute an agreement between the parties regarding the transfer of the land. Nor had any consideration been requested from the defendant by the plaintiff. Since there was no contract, the question of part-performance did not arise. However Murphy J. indicated that, even if there had been a contract to transfer the land to the defendant, the defendant's work on the land could not be said to constitute part-performance of same since he had been paid for this work and had also been provided with a house and other land by the plaintiff. In the circumstances, the alleged acts of part-performance were not unequivocally referable to the type of contract alleged.

COMPLETION NOTICES

In *Birmingham v Coughlan*, unreported, High Court, June 9, 2004, Smyth J. held a completion notice in relation to a contract for the sale of land was invalid on the ground that the plaintiff vendors were not in fact ready, willing and able to complete at the time when it was served by them. The issue of wayleaves held by Westmeath County Council over the property, the subject of the sale, remained unresolved at the date of service of the notice. Citing the decision of the Supreme Court in *Tyndarius v O'Mahony*, unreported, March 3, 2003, Smyth J. referred to the penal and draconian nature of a completion notice and stated that it was vital that the party serving same be ready, willing and able to complete. In this case,

> "The problem of the Purchasers was that they purchased a parcel of land and when documentation was received the conditions on site varied from those shown on such map or maps as were furnished to them. They could not be expected to buy into a law suit or close a sale when the Vendors were not in a position to give good marketable title and clearly explain whatever discrepancies had been highlighted in the correspondence. Appreciating the argument that was made in the course of the hearing that any developer would be anxious to have as clean a site as possible so as to maximise such development as might be possible on the site, I am nonetheless satisfied that notwithstanding that the number of linear metres by which the pipeline might be said to be out of 'alignment' per the maps furnished with the way leave, does not mean that the Purchasers were obliged to conclude a sale which had certainly, to adopt the Plaintiffs/Vendors' euphemism, 'paper difficulties'. In my judgment, this was not a case of mere paper difficulties—the difficulties were real and not imaginary."

At the date of service of the completion notice, "[T]he Plaintiffs/Vendors, through their solicitors, had been advised by their own engineers that certain steps still required to be taken to resolve the mapping, measurement and boundaries of the way leaves".

In the circumstances the plaintiffs could not be said to have been ready, willing and able to complete at the time of service of the completion notice, which was consequently invalid. The plaintiffs' claim was dismissed pursuant to the inherent jurisdiction of the court to stay frivolous and vexatious proceedings.

CONDITIONAL CONTRACTS

The appellant vendor in *O'Connor v Coady* [2004] 3 I.R. 271 had entered into a contract of sale with the respondent purchaser in respect of lands at Ashbourne County Meath. The contract was expressly described as subject to the respondent obtaining planning permission within four months of the date of conclusion of same. The respondent failed to obtain a grant of planning permission within the period specified whereupon the appellant purported to terminate the contract. The respondent argued that this termination was invalid since no completion notice had issued, and commenced proceedings for specific performance. Carroll J., in the High Court, found in favour of the respondent, holding that, *per* Costello J. in *Sepia Limited v O'Hanlon* [1979] I.L.R.M. 11, time was not of the essence in conditions precedent. The service of a completion notice and the expiry of the notice period specified therein was therefore necessary before the contract could be terminated. This had not happened, consequently the contract was still in existence, and the appellant was bound to complete same.

The Supreme Court, taking a different interpretation of *Sepia v O'Hanlon*, allowed the appellant's appeal. There were some differences in the approaches of Geoghegan and McCracken J. *Per* Geoghegan J., non compliance with a time clause in a condition renders a contract voidable. McCracken J., on the other hand, felt that non-compliance might automatically make the contract void, removing the need for a letter of rescission. Both judges recognised that their statements in this regard were *obiter*, since counsel for the appellant had argued the case before the Supreme Court on the basis that the contract had been avoided. The remaining judge, McGuinness J., agreed with both judges. It should be added that the court deliberately failed to categorise the condition in question as a condition precedent or a condition subsequent, expressing doubts as to the usefulness of this distinction. The principles as set out by the court, therefore, apply to both types of conditions.

See also *Hand v Greaney*, unreported, High Court, Clarke J., December 15, 2004, which also involved the non-fulfilment of time clauses in conditional contracts. It was sought to distinguish this case from *O'Connor v Coady* (see immediately above) on the grounds that the defendant purchaser in this case had opted to waive the condition in question, which had been inserted for his benefit. Clarke J. rejected this argument, holding that a waiver by a purchaser of a special condition relating to planning permission could only take place within the time limits specified in this condition. Once fulfilment of a condition in a conditional contract was no longer possible according to its terms, the plaintiff was no longer entitled to waive it. In this case, compliance with the special condition became impossible when An Bord Pleanála allowed the appeal against the decision to grant permission; any waiver by the defendant had occurred after this point and was consequently, ineffective.

CONSIDERATION

See *JC v WC* [2004] 2 I.R. 312 above, Agreement. See also Proprietary Estoppel.

EXPRESS TERMS

In *Horan v O'Reilly*, unreported, High Court, Clarke J., December 3, 2004, the plaintiff had been a member of a syndicate which had won the Lotto. However, at the time the winning ticket was bought, the plaintiff had fallen behind with his dues. Relations between members of the syndicate were not governed by any written contract. Looking at the previous conduct of the syndicate in order to determine the terms of the contract between the members, Clarke J. held that the fact that the plaintiff had been in arrears at the time the winning ticket was bought should not deny him the right to share in the winnings. The practice of the syndicate in this case was to carry members, even if they did not pay for the particular ticket which won. On at least one occasion other members of the syndicate had paid on Mr Horan's behalf with the intention of recouping it from him at a later date. Payment to catch up was accepted at a later date. *Per* Clarke J.:

> "Mr Horan is entitled to succeed, on the basis that the contract between the parties permitted arrears and the arrears at the relevant time were within permitted and established bounds ... The syndicate operated in a way which vested in Mr O'Brien the authority to carry out all practical matters. Mr O'Brien permitted the system to operate whereby Mr Horan would be in arrears, as he was trustworthy ... At the time the winning ticket was drawn [Mr Horan] was not in any greater arrears than in the past ... therefore I am driven to the conclusion that he remained in the syndicate up to the date when the winning ticket was drawn. Therefore he is entitled to share in the proceeds of the winning ticket."

In *McCrory Scaffolding v McInerney Construction Ltd*, unreported, High Court, Peart J., November 5, 2004, an application for stay of summary proceedings between the parties pending the referral of the dispute to arbitration involved the interpretation of an agreement between plaintiff and defendants. A letter of intent dated April 3, 2001 and forwarded by the defendants to the plaintiffs in response to a tender submitted by it stated that the contract between them was to be in accordance with, *inter alia*, "the Conditions of Contract of GLDA 82".

On facts of the case Peart J. held that the letter of intent dated April 3, 2001, contained the terms of the contract which was subject to the said conditions, and granted the stay sought. In coming to this conclusion, he followed the approach of Morris J. in *Lynch Roofing Systems v Bennett & Son (Construction) Limited* [1999] 2 I.R. 45 which also treated a letter of intent following on a tender as embodying binding contract terms. He rejected the decision in *Smith v Gordon & John Lewis Building Limited* 44 Con L.R. 11, which had held that a subsequent written contract was needed to bring the terms specified in a letter of intent into force, on the basis that same failed to refer to the earlier judgment of Lord Denning in *British Crane Hire v Ipswich* [1975] 1 Q.B. 303, to which it ran contrary.

IMPLIED TERMS

Dakota Packaging v AHP Manufacturing, unreported, Supreme Court, December 15, 2004 involved an appeal from the High Court judgment of Peart J. dated October 10, 2003. The issue before the High Court had been whether or not the appellants, who had been major purchasers of packaging from the respondents, were contractually bound to give reasonable notice to the appellants of the termination of this trading relationship. Peart J. had held that the appellants were so bound on the basis of an implied term. The appellants appealed, claiming that the High Court judge had been wrong in law in implying such a term given that he had also held that there was no long-term purchase agreement between the parties in existence. The respondents, on the other hand, while accepting that no term could be implied in the absence of a valid contract between the parties, argued that Peart J. had in effect held such valid contract to be in existence.

The Supreme Court, in a judgment delivered by Fennelly J. (Murray C.J. and Hardiman J. concurring) allowed the appeal and found in favour of the appellants. Fennelly J. held that "unless there was some long-term agreement between the parties for the sale and purchase of packaging, there was no contract into which Peart J was entitled to imply a term that reasonable notice had to be given of its termination".

Fennelly J. stated that it was clear from the judgment of Peart J. and from the evidence of the parties as given in the High Court proceedings that there was no such long-term agreement in existence between the parties, each order by the respondents representing a separate contract for the supply of the goods so ordered. He rejected the argument of counsel for the appellant that Peart J., in stating that there was no long-term business agreement between the parties, was merely referring to the absence of a written agreement. *Per* Fennelly J.:

> "[T]he learned trial judge was not entitled to imply a term into the 'arrangements' or 'the relationship' between the parties ... there must be a contract before a term can be implied. Peart J., having determined that there was no contract of the relevant type, was not entitled to infer or imply any term."

Fennelly J. also went on to state, *obiter*, that even if such a long-term contract had in fact existed, Peart J. would not have been correct in implying the term in question. He emphasised that:

> "[T]he courts do not have 'a broad discretion' to imply terms. It is not enough that a term to be implied is 'fair and reasonable' ... the courts will not lightly infer terms".

In addition, for a term to be implied, it must be capable of being formulated with reasonable precision, and this was not the case here.

Mullarkey v Irish National Stud Company Limited, unreported, High Court, Kelly J., June 30, 2005 raised the issue of whether a court should imply a term in the plaintiff's contract of employment with the defendant, a semi-state body, entitling him to payment of salary while sick for a period in excess of 13 weeks. Kelly J. held that the High Court, in *Charlton v His Highness The Aga Khan's Stud*, unreported, Laffoy J., December 22, 1998, and *Rooney v Kilkenny* (2001) E.L.R. 120, had already recognised an implied term in the contract of employment to the effect that sick pay should continue for a reasonable time. Given the fact that the defendant was in the semi-state sector, a reasonable time in this case would be equivalent to that provided for sick pay in the public sector: full pay for 26 weeks with a reduction in pay to half pay for the 26 weeks thereafter.

In *McGrath v Trintech*, unreported, High Court, Laffoy J., October 29, 2004, the plaintiff, a senior project manager employed by the first-named defendant, which was a subsidiary of the second-named defendant, argued that his removal on the grounds of redundancy breached an implied term in his employment contract that he would not be so dismissed if, as in this case, he was on sick leave and reliant on prospects of permanent health insurance cover.

Laffoy J. refused to imply a term to this effect, stating that same

> "would be inconsistent with the express terms of the contract of employment, in that it was expressly provided that the plaintiff's

employment could be terminated on one month's notice and that, even where payment had commenced under the PHI scheme, it would cease on the termination of the employment".

However she ultimately found for the plaintiff on the basis that specific representations which had been made to him, to the effect that he would have 12 months' job security, had been breached by the defendants. *Per* Laffoy J., these representations were actionable in contract even though the plaintiff had not provided any consideration for same, stating that:

"[R]epresentations which were intended to vary or add to the terms and conditions of representations which were acted on by the Plaintiff … give rise to contractual liability".

In *Orr v Zomax Limited*, unreported, High Court, Carroll J., March 25, 2004, the plaintiff engineer was appointed client services manager of Microsoft Business, by the defendant in May 2000. In 2003 he was informed that a new role of business relationship manager was to be created, amalgamating his role as client services manager and the position of contract centre manager. His application for this new job was unsuccessful whereupon he was made redundant from his original position. He sought a declaration that this purported termination of his tenure by means of redundancy was invalid and in breach of contract. His argument, at the interlocutory relief stage, that a term should be implied in his contract of employment to the effect that his employer had a duty to act reasonably and fairly in the case of his dismissal, whether for redundancy or misconduct, was rejected by Carroll J., who held that he had not shown a fair case to answer that such a term existed. In any case, damages were an adequate remedy in the circumstances.

In *Barry v Medical Defence Union*, unreported, High Court, Carroll J., March 31, 2004, the plaintiff, who had taken out professional indemnity insurance from the defendant, sued it for breach of contract, claiming that it had breached an implied contractual term to act in accordance with the rules of natural and constitutional justice when considering his claim. Carroll J. held that the contract between the parties was to be found in the memorandum and articles of the defendant. Since the plaintiff did not give evidence, the issue of an additional preliminary or collateral contract between them did not arise. Carroll J. refused to imply the term put forward by the plaintiff, following the approach of McCracken J. in *Carna Foods Ltd v Eagle Star Insurance Company Ireland Limited* [1995] 1 I.R. 526 (affirmed on appeal to Supreme Court [1997] 2 I.R. 193) who had rejected the application of the principles of natural and constitutional justice to a decision of an insurance company to give reasons for its decision to cancel a policy of insurance, expressly stating that to decide otherwise would be a serious interference in the contractual position of parties in a commercial contract with very wide-ranging consequences. Carroll J. agreed with this stating that "In my opinion there is no justification for extending what is essentially public law to the area of private contract."

Although she held that the defendant was under a related implied obligation to act fairly in its dealings with the plaintiff "on the basis that it may not act unreasonably in carrying out its obligations under the contract with the plaintiff rather than that it was constrained by the Constitution to apply fair procedures", Carroll J. ultimately found that the defendant had not breached this implied term.

PART PERFORMANCE

See *JC v WC* [2004] 2 I.R. 312 above, Agreement.

Owens v Duggan, unreported, High Court, Hardiman J., April 2, 2004 (detailed later in the Land Law Chapter of this *Annual Review* under Proprietary Estoppel, p.350) is a case involving an oral agreement for the sale of land in which part-performance was pleaded, but not discussed in the judgment which found for the plaintiff on the alternative ground of proprietary estoppel.

PROMISSORY ESTOPPEL

For 2004 case law on the related doctrine of proprietary estoppel regarding promises of interests in land, see *JC v WC* [2004] 2 I.R. 312 and *Owens v Duggan*, unreported, High Court, Hardiman J., April 2, 2004, in the Land Law Chapter of this *Annual Review* under Proprietary Estoppel, p.350.

REMEDIES

Specific performance In *Keane v Irish Amateur Swimming Association Limited t/a Swim Ireland* [2004] 15 E.L.R. 6, following the plaintiff's appointment as Chief Executive Officer of the defendant company, the defendant tried to avoid appointing her to this position. The plaintiff sought an interlocutory injunction restraining the defendant from appointing any other person to the said position and directing the defendant to pay her salary and all benefits due. Gilligan J. held that the plaintiff had an arguable case and granted the prohibitory injunctions sought together with a mandatory injunction to pay the plaintiff's salary (but not other benefits received).

Criminal Law

COURT POOR BOX

In 2004 the Law Reform Commission published its *Consultation Paper on the Court Poor Box* (LRC CP 31–2004). This Paper deals with the procedure which has been adopted over many years by the courts, particularly the District Court, where the judge may take the view that, although the prosecution has proved its case, it is not appropriate to enter a conviction, but that a contribution is made to the Court Poor Box, the content of which is then given to relevant charities. Typical cases where the Court Poor Box is used include being drunk or disorderly in a public place, careless driving, petty larceny, minor assaults or cruelty to animals. The payments are generally less than €1,000 in each case, but there is a great deal of variation and the amount paid to the Court Poor Box has grown steadily in recent years. In both 2002 and 2003, €1 million was donated to the Court Poor Box.

The Commission acknowledged in the Consultation Paper that one of the most important positive features of the Court Poor Box is that it reflects principles of restorative justice, in which the offender and the community can be reconciled. But the Commission also concluded that there were a number of disadvantages with the current system. For example, the Court Poor Box is not used by all judges of the District Court and so it is not universally available to first-time offenders. It has also been suggested that it allows the rich to buy their way out of a conviction and/or term of imprisonment. The Commission did not accept that this is the case, but nevertheless believes that such negative public perception is damaging to the administration of justice. While the Court Poor Box is usually used in minor cases where a conviction would not be appropriate (and is therefore often used in conjunction with the Probation of Offenders Act 1907 to avoid a criminal record), the Commission pointed out that it has sometimes been used where a conviction is recorded.

The Commission provisionally recommended that the essential elements of the existing arrangement be put on a statutory basis, while omitting its adverse features. The proposed new statutory procedure would include the criteria to be used in its application, using an expanded version of the factors in the Probation of Offenders Act 1907, and also incorporating a revised version of the compensation order regime in the Criminal Justice Act 1993. The new disposition would be available only in respect of summary offences subject to a prescribed list of factors which the judge may take into account, including the trivial nature of the offence, the personal circumstances of the offender including character, family circumstances, age or health, and the need to avoid an injustice in a particular case. The Commission recommended that if the court records a conviction, the proposed statutory disposition should not be available.

DEFENCES

Provocation: evidential threshold   In *People (DPP) v Kelly*, Court of Criminal Appeal, February 6, 2004, the applicant sought leave to appeal against his conviction by a majority verdict for the murder of a New Age traveller at a campsite on December 28, 1999 at Curreeny, County Tipperary. The sole ground of appeal was that the trial judge erred in law in finding that the issue of provocation should not be left to the jury. On the morning of December 28, 1999 the applicant and the deceased were driving on a narrow road from the New Age encampment to a nearby village. An incident arose in which the deceased deliberately drove his car into the open door of the applicant's car and did considerable damage to it. When the applicant returned to the camp he entered a nearby caravan and emerged with a stick and a kitchen knife. Insults and obscenities were exchanged between the applicant and the deceased. In the course of a struggle between the two men the applicant inflicted four stab wounds on the deceased with the kitchen knife, as a result of which he died. Following legal argument at the conclusion of the evidence, the trial judge (O'Higgins J.) held that as far as he was concerned there was not sufficient evidence before the court to permit the issue of provocation to go to the jury. The Court of Criminal Appeal, whose judgment was delivered by McGuinness J., disagreed and ordered a retrial. Applying the decision in *People (DPP) v Kelly* [2000] 2 I.R. 1, the court held that a successful defence of provocation presupposes, at the critical time, the existence, not of a calculating mind, but of a mind subject to a sudden and temporary loss of control, rendering the accused so subject to passion as to make him or her for the moment not master of his or her own mind. The court considered that, in this respect, there is a low threshold for allowing provocation to go to the jury. On the accumulation of the various pieces of evidence put forward for the applicant, there was sufficient evidence, albeit not of a particularly strong variety, to allow provocation to go to the jury. The court noted, of course, that it would be for the jury to decide the weight and credibility of the evidence that was included in the trial.

DELAY

Appeal and re-trial   In *Sweetman v Director of Public Prosecutions*, High Court, April 1, 2004, the applicant sought an order restraining the respondent from prosecuting him for, *inter alia,* murder, firearms offences and false imprisonment. The applicant and a co-accused were convicted of the offences 15 months after the incident. On appeal, the Court of Criminal Appeal quashed the conviction and ordered a retrial. The applicant claimed that this retrial should be prohibited because of the delay by the prosecuting authorities. There had been a total delay of six years and one month between the date of original conviction and the prospective retrial date. Murphy J. refused the application. He considered that the delays since the quashing of the conviction were contributed to mainly by the applicant and his legal representatives; that the applicant was entitled to change his legal representation, expert witnesses and to adduce fresh evidence, but that this could not be classed as prosecutorial delay. It was reasonable for the prosecution to await both the decisions in the separate appeal of a former co-accused and the amended appeal of the applicant. He also held that it had been reasonable for the Court of Criminal Appeal to refuse to proceed until all grounds of appeal were before it. Further delay was caused by the non-availability of a judge on the day listed for trial, and the non-availability of the applicant's expert witness at the date to which the trial was adjourned. The applicant was on bail, and therefore might not have got the priority that an applicant in custody might have got. Murphy J. recognised that delay may have added to the anxiety of the applicant and caused some general prejudice to someone who was entitled to the presumption of innocence, but that in the present case this did not justify the prohibition of the applicant's retrial.

Rape and incest In *J.H. v Director of Public Prosecutions*, High Court, April 2, 2004, the applicant sought judicial review restraining his further prosecution on charges of, *inter alia*, rape and incest. The applicant had been tried and convicted of the rape of his daughter but that conviction was quashed by the Court of Criminal Appeal and a retrial ordered. The charge related to events allegedly occurring between 1985 and 1987, but although a complaint was made to the Gardaí in 1990, criminal proceedings were not instituted until 1998. No adequate explanation was available in respect of the delay. Murphy J. granted the relief sought. He accepted that if there was evidence of inordinate, even if excusable, delay between charge and prosecution, the applicant would be entitled to an injunction. He held that the court must look not to the date of the original trial but also to the date of his pending retrial, which would probably take place five years after his original trial. He also noted that the applicant had not only suffered anxiety but had also served part of a prison sentence. Balancing all the factors, he concluded that the applicant was entitled to the relief sought.

Sexual assault In *H.M. v Director of Public Prosecutions*, High Court, January 26, 2004, the applicant applied for an injunction restraining the respondent from further prosecuting him in relation to a number of charges of indecent assault. The charges related to incidents allegedly occurring in the mid-1980s, although the applicant was not charged until 2000. While the applicant admitted two of the charges, he denied the remainder. He argued that the delay in making the complaints had unfairly prejudiced his defence. He also argued that the non-availability of three witnesses who could have given evidence on his behalf, but who had died during the lapse of time between the alleged offences and the complaint, had prejudiced his defence. Murphy J. refused the relief sought. He considered that it did not appear that the applicant would suffer prejudice at his trial. He noted that the applicant had not stated what evidence these witnesses could have given and in any event the alleged incidents had occurred in private. Significantly, he held that the community had a right to have the offences prosecuted and that since many of the issues related to the credibility of the parties, they were best dealt with by a jury.

EUROPEAN ARREST WARRANT

European Arrest Warrant Act 2003   The European Arrest Warrant Act 2003, which came into effect on January 1, 2004, provides, in effect, for a court-based mutual recognition of warrants procedure to replace the extradition procedure under the Extradition Act 1965, at least in respect of those European Union Member States which have implemented the relevant Council Framework Decision of June 13, 2002 on the European arrest warrant and the surrender procedures between Member States. The Council Framework Decision is a clear manifestation of the increasing role of the European Union in the area of Justice and Home Affairs, arising from the inclusion of that as a competence of the EU in the amendments effected to the EU Treaties by the Treaty of Amsterdam (1997). It also represents a practical implementation of the principle of mutual recognition in civil and criminal matters in the 1999 Tampere Declaration of the Council of Ministers of the EU. We note briefly here that the 2003 Act was amended by the Proceeds of Crime (Amendment) Act 2005, to which we will return in the *Annual Review of Irish Law 2005*.

Court-based mutual recognition   In introducing what became the 2003 Act to the Seanad, the then Minister of State in the Department of Justice, Equality and Law Reform noted that, historically, extradition had been regarded as an aspect of a State's sovereignty and, as a result, extradition arrangements involved a significant role for the executive arm of government. It was thus noted that the 2002 Framework Decision replaced, in large measure, the inter-state aspects of extradition with a system of surrender based on the recognition by the judicial authorities of one Member State of orders issued by the judicial authorities in another Member State for the arrest and surrender of wanted persons. In the wake of the enactment of the 2003 Act, the role of the executive agencies of the State would be to provide administrative and technical support for this inter-court system. This will be done through the central authority in the State which, in Ireland, is the Minister for Justice, Equality and Law Reform and his or her Department. Therefore, the new system can, to a significant extent, be described as an inter-court system.

Designated Member States   Section 3 of the 2003 Act, which was inserted during the Oireachtas debate, provides for the designation of Member States for the purposes of the European arrest warrant by the Minister for Foreign Affairs, thus ensuring that Ireland can operate the new system on a reciprocal basis with those other Member States that have enacted the necessary legislation. The European Arrest Warrant Act 2003 (Designated Member States) Order 2004 (S.I. No.4 of 2004) designates, for the purposes of the 2003 Act, those EU Member States that have, under their respective national laws, given effect to the 2002 Council Framework Decision. The Order came into effect on January 1, 2004.

Timeframes for dealing with applications   The Minister of State noted that the extradition arrangements in place prior to the 2003 Act had regularly been criticised for being slow, often taking several years to complete. The 2002 Framework Decision addresses these concerns by the introduction of timeframes for the taking of decisions on European arrest warrants. Thus, a decision on whether to surrender the person should normally be taken within 60 days of the person's arrest or within a further 30 days where the initial period cannot be met. These timeframes are included in the 2003 Act, but as the Minister of State noted, they are not time limits; they are indicative rather than prescriptive because it would be inappropriate for the Executive or the Oireachtas to seek to limit the exercise of judicial discretion through the imposition of strict time limits when dealing with cases before the courts.

Absence of exceptions   Traditionally, many States refused to extradite their nationals and considered certain offences as being non-extraditable. The 2002 Framework Decision, and the 2003 Act implementing it, do not provide for exceptions or exclusions based on, for example, categories of offences or offenders. There are, therefore, no provisions permitting refusal to surrender on the grounds that the person being sought is a national of the executing Member State or that the offence falls into a particular category of offences such as revenue or political offences. Existing Irish law had, in any event, greatly curtailed the political offence exception and extradition for revenue offences has been in place since 2001, under the Extradition (European Union Conventions) Act 2001 (see the *Annual Review of Irish Law 2001*, pp.194–196).

"Positive list" offences: dual criminality not generally applicable   Another significant aspect of the 2002 Framework Decision and, therefore, of the 2003

Act is a curtailment of the dual criminality requirement, namely, the requirement that a person may be extradited to face prosecution or service of a sentence in another State only where the offences concerned are offences under the laws of the issuing and executing States. The 2002 Framework Decision introduced a significant curtailment of this requirement. Under the arrangements now in place under the 2003 Act, surrender may be sought for offences, carrying a penalty of 12 months' imprisonment or more under the law of the issuing Member State, provided also that the alleged offence corresponds to an offence under the law of the executing Member State. In that general sense, the dual criminality requirement still applies. But the 2003 Act also provides that where the alleged offence comes within any of the 32 categories of major offences listed in Art.2.2 of the Framework Decision—generally referred to as the "positive list" offences—and it is an offence that carries a penalty of three years' imprisonment or more under the law of the issuing Member State, the position under the law of the executing Member State does not arise for consideration by the executing court, so that the dual criminality requirement does not apply in those cases.

It was acknowledged by the Minister of State that this element of the 2002 Framework Decision presented some difficulty for several Member States, including Ireland, because it represented a significant departure from pre-2003 law and practice. However, on examination of the "positive list" offences in Art.2.2, the Government concluded that, leaving aside their description, all of the offences in question are already regarded as serious offences under Irish law. In that respect, the removal of the dual criminality requirement was not regarded as being as significant as had appeared at first glance.

Human rights safeguards In light of the significant changes effected by the 2002 Framework Decision and the 2003 Act, it is not surprising that a considerable number of safeguards by reference to human rights and constitutional protections have been included in the legislation. The 2002 Framework Decision sets out general principles on which the safeguard provisions are based. In addition, it contains specific provisions that list mandatory and discretionary grounds upon which requests for surrender can be refused. It also lists guarantees that may be sought before a person is handed over. On the general principles, Recital 12 of the Framework Decision affirms that it respects the fundamental rights and observes the principles recognised by Art.6 of the Treaty on European Union. Article 6 states, *inter alia*, that: "the Union shall respect fundamental rights, as guaranteed by the European Convention for the Protection of Human Rights and Fundamental Freedoms". Recital 12 goes on to state that:

> "nothing in this framework decision may be interpreted as prohibiting refusal to surrender a person for whom a European arrest warrant has been issued when there are reasons to believe, on the basis of objective

elements, that the said arrest warrant has been issued for the purpose of prosecuting or punishing a person on the grounds of his or her sex, race, religion, ethnic origin, nationality, language, political opinions or sexual orientation, or that that person's position may be prejudiced for any of those reasons."

Recital 12 adds that the Framework Decision "does not prevent a Member State from applying its constitutional rules relating to due process, freedom of association, freedom of the press and freedom of expression in other media." Recital 13 provides that "no person shall be removed, expelled or extradited to a State where there is a serious risk that he or she would be subjected to the death penalty, torture or other inhuman or degrading treatment or punishment". Part 3 of the 2003 Act reflects the provisions in Recitals 12 and 13 and the corresponding provisions of Art.1.3 of the Framework Decision.

Mandatory non-execution In specific terms, Art.3 of the 2002 Framework Decision lists mandatory grounds for the non-execution of European arrest warrants. First, a person may not be surrendered if he or she has been the subject of an amnesty in respect of the offence in question. Secondly, a person who has been finally judged and has completed any sentence imposed in a Member State or is no longer required to serve it in respect of the offences in question may not be surrendered. Thirdly, a person who cannot be held criminally responsible for the offence in question, by virtue of his or her age, may not be surrendered. Sections 39, 41(1) and 43 of the 2003 Act reflect these provisions.

Discretionary non-execution Article 4 of the Framework Decision lists grounds upon which Member States may rely for non-execution of European arrest warrants. In this respect, s.38 of the 2003 Act implements Art.4.1 and requires that, with the exception of the offences on the positive list, the offences specified in the warrant must correspond to offences under Irish law with a necessary qualification to allow for variations in the designation of certain revenue offences. Section 38, therefore, implements the dual criminality requirement for offences other than those covered by the "positive list".

Proceedings halted and delay Section 42 implements Arts 4.2 and 4.3 and provides that a person may not be surrendered where he or she is being proceeded against in the State for the same offence or where it has been decided not to proceed or to halt proceedings against the person in the State in respect of the offence on which the warrant is based. Section 40 implements Art.4.4 in prohibiting surrender where a prosecution for the same offence would not be permitted in the State by virtue of lapse of time.

Sentence completed and territoriality Section 41(2) implements Art.4.5 by prohibiting surrender where the person had been finally judged in a non-EU State and had served the sentence imposed, or was no longer required to serve it. Section 44 implements Art.4.7 and prohibits surrender where the offence occurred on the territory of the executing State or outside the territory of the issuing and executing States and the offence is one over which the executing State does not have jurisdiction.

Trial in absentia Section 45 provides that where the person had been tried *in absentia*, surrender may be made subject to guarantees from the issuing State that he or she will have the opportunity of a new trial and of being present at that trial.

Legal representation and interpretation A person arrested under either s.13 or s.14 of the 2003 Act must be informed of their rights to legal representation and interpretation services entitlements, in accordance with Art.11 of the Framework Decision.

Bail Sections 13(5) and 14(7) of the 2003 Act, reflecting Art.12 of the Framework Decision, provide that a person may be remanded on bail pending a decision on his or her surrender.

Consent to surrender Section 15 of the 2003 Act, implementing Art.13, provides that a person who consents to surrender may withdraw that consent. In such cases the person is then entitled to a full hearing of the surrender application. Before accepting that the person has consented to his or her surrender, the court must be satisfied that the consent was voluntary and informed.

Right to hearing Article 14 provides a guarantee that an arrested person has a right to a hearing before being surrendered. This is given effect by ss.15 and 16 of the 2003 Act.

Sentence served to be taken into account Section 36 gives effect to Art.26. It ensures that, in the case of persons returned to Ireland, any time served in custody in the executing State pending a decision on the request will be taken into account in any sentence to be served here.

Non-surrender to third States Sections 23 and 24 provide that a person surrendered by Ireland to another Member State on foot of a European arrest warrant may not be surrendered or extradited by that Member State to either a third Member State or a non-EU State without the consent of the Minister for Justice, Equality and Law Reform.

Surrender only for trial purpose In addition to these provisions, the Minister of State drew attention to the statement Ireland made when the Framework Decision was being adopted, namely that "Ireland shall, in the implementation in domestic legislation of this Framework Decision provide that the European arrest warrant shall only be executed for the purposes of bringing that person to trial or for the purpose of executing a custodial sentence or detention order". Thus, where the person has not yet been convicted, the emphasis is on ensuring that he or she is being sought to face trial. This is designed to ensure that persons are not surrendered for investigative purposes, with the possibility of prolonged detention before a decision is taken on whether to charge him or her. Section 11(3) of the 2003 Act gives effect to this statement: it requires that the issuing judicial authority must provide written undertakings that the warrant is for the purpose of the person being charged with and tried for the offence specified. In addition, it requires that there must be written confirmation that the person has been charged and that a decision to bring him or her to trial has been made or, alternatively, that a decision has been taken in the issuing Member State to proceed to charge and try the person once he or she has been returned to that Member State.

Application in new EU States As to the application of the 2003 Act to the 10 new EU Accession States (as to which, see the *Annual Review of Irish Law 2003*, p.262), it was noted they were expected to implement the Framework Decision as part of the *acquis communautaire* as and from May 2004. However, given the importance and sensitivity of the justice and home affairs issues, a special safeguard clause has been inserted into each of the accession treaties. The clause provides that the Commission should monitor implementation of framework decisions by the new Member States. It also provides for remedial actions, including the suspension of the operation of framework decisions by those new Member States in certain cases. This measure was intended to allay any concerns about the implementation of measures such as the European arrest warrant in the early years of EU membership by the new Accession States.

Central authority The 2003 Act is, as indicated, designed to be in large measure an inter-court system. Nevertheless, the Framework Decision permits each Member State to nominate a central authority. Its role is to provide administrative and technical assistance. It will also liaise with relevant authorities in other Member States in connection with arrangements for the handing over of wanted persons and property. The 2003 Act provides that in Ireland the Minister for Justice, Equality and Law Reform and his or her Department will perform this function. An amendment introduced into the 2003 Act at Committee Stage in the Dáil provides that the Minister for Justice, Equality and Law Reform must make a report to each House of the Oireachtas on the operation in the preceding year of Pt 2 of the 2003 Act.

Applications to High Court   The High Court is the judicial authority designated under the 2003 Act with responsibility for the execution of European arrest warrants received by Ireland. This is in line with the recent designation of the High Court for other extradition arrangements under the Extradition (European Union Conventions) Act 2001 (see the *Annual Review of Irish Law 2001*, pp.194–196). Any Irish courts having jurisdiction in criminal matters may issue a European arrest warrant, on application from or on behalf of the Director of Public Prosecutions, where a person now in another Member State is facing charges or is required to serve a sentence in Ireland. In all cases the warrants will be transmitted, inwards and outwards, by the central authority. European arrest warrants may be in their original form or sent by fax or electronically. Electronic transmission may in due course be via the Schengen information system, SIS. The Minister of State indicated that Ireland has opted to participate in elements of this Convention and arrangements are being made to establish the necessary systems and procedures. Under s.12, there is provision allowing for the possibility of receiving European arrest warrants in a language other than Irish or English. Section 13 provides that following receipt of a European arrest warrant, it will be brought to the High Court for its endorsement. Endorsement of the warrant by the High Court will have the effect of authorising the arrest of the named person.

Arrest powers   The powers of the Garda Síochána to make an arrest in these circumstances are contained in s.25. They include the power to enter premises to effect the arrest and seize goods and property considered to be connected with or the proceeds of the offence specified in the European arrest warrant. The possibility of an arrest where a Garda is satisfied, based on information available on the SIS (when the system is operational), that a European arrest warrant exists but has not yet been received is provided for in s.14. The information on the SIS must indicate that, where the person has not yet been convicted, he or she is to face trial, rather than being sought for investigative purposes. An arrest under s.14 must be based on a reasonable belief that the person will leave the State prior to the European arrest warrant being received here. Where there are no grounds for such a belief, the question of an arrest must await the arrival of the European arrest warrant. In those circumstances the procedures I have outlined for s.13 apply. In cases of arrests under s.14 the European arrest warrant must be produced within seven days of the arrest, otherwise the person must be released. A person who has been arrested, whether under s.13 or s.14, must be brought before the High Court as soon as possible after his or her arrest. The court may remand the person in custody or on bail and will also fix a date for the full hearing of the application. However, a person has a right to consent to surrender at this or any later stage. In these cases, s.15 provides that a full hearing will not be required if the court is satisfied that the person has given his or her consent voluntarily and in full knowledge of the consequences. As already indicated, a person who has consented may withdraw that consent. Withdrawal of consent will give rise to the need for a full hearing.

Order for surrender   Section 16 of the 2003 Act provides that the High Court may, after satisfying itself that the person before it is the person named in the European arrest warrant and after hearing the application, make an order for the person's surrender. However, it may do so only where it is satisfied that all the provisions in the 2003 Act are complied with. There is a stay of 15 days before the order takes effect and the person will normally be surrendered within a further 10-day period. Upon making the order, the court must remand the person in custody and inform him or her of the provisions of Art.40.4.2° of the Constitution which allow for *habeas corpus* applications. Section 16(12) also provides for appeals on points of law to the Supreme Court against the High Court's order. Sections 17, 18 and 19, which were inserted during the Oireachtas debate, deal, respectively, with European arrest warrants that relate to more than one offence, postponement of surrender and conditional surrender. Section 20, which deals with procedural and evidential matters, contains procedures for dealing with affidavit evidence.

Rule of specialty   Section 22 of the 2003 Act deals with the rule of specialty, which provides that a person who has been extradited or surrendered to another state may be proceeded against in that other state in respect only of the offence or offences for which he or she was extradited or surrendered unless the consent of the extraditing country has been previously obtained. This remains the basic position in the 2003 Act, subject to certain limitations. The 2002 Framework Decision and the 2003 Act provide that a person may be proceeded against for offences other than those for which he or she was surrendered where such offences attract financial penalties only or where a sentence of imprisonment will not arise. Neither will the rule apply where the person in question consents, either before or after his or her surrender, to being proceeded against for other offences. In both cases the court must satisfy itself that any consent given has been or will be given freely and in awareness of the consequences. As is the case under pre-2003 extradition legislation, the rule of specialty will not be applied in cases where the issuing judicial authority requests the central authority in this State to waive the rule and the Minister agrees to do so.

Third State surrender   Sections 23 and 24 provide that a person who has been surrendered on foot of a European arrest warrant may not be surrendered to a third Member State or third country, a non-EU state, unless the person gives voluntary and informed consent or unless the Minister in this State agrees to the onward surrender, having regard to the safeguard provisions in Pt 3 of the 2003 Act and the 2002 Framework Decision. In cases where the request is for the extradition of the person from the Member State to which he or she has been surrendered to a non-EU state, the High Court will also be required to give its consent. It may do so only where it is satisfied that the requirements of the Extraction Act 1965 are met.

Applications from different Member States Sections 29 and 30 set out the procedures and criteria to be applied when there are several European arrest warrants for the same person but from different Member States or where there are European arrest warrants from one or more Member States and extradition requests from one or more non-EU states.

Applications from Ireland Sections 31 to 36 deal with the arrangements for the issuing of European arrest warrants in this State. Section 32 is designed to assist Irish courts that are issuing European arrest warrants by enabling offences under Irish law to which Art.2.2 of the Framework Decision applies—the "positive list" offences—to be identified in regulations to be made by the Minister for Justice, Equality and Law Reform. Section 33 provides that applications may be made by or on behalf of the Director of Public Prosecutions to any court having jurisdiction in criminal matters, namely, the District Court, the Circuit Criminal Court, the Central Criminal Court and the Special Criminal Court. A European arrest warrant may be applied for where a warrant for the arrest of the person has already issued in the State and the person is not in the State. The warrant must be in respect of an offence having a penalty of 12 months' imprisonment or more or, where the person has already been convicted, a sentence of four months or more has to be served. The court that issues the European arrest warrant will be required to indicate whether the warrant is in respect of an offence that comes within the "positive list", namely, an offence listed in Art.2.2 of the Framework Decision that carries a penalty of three years' imprisonment or more under Irish law. The executing judicial authority in the other Member State will be obliged to accept that certification and the question of the dual criminality of the offence shall not be considered further. As already indicated, the reverse applies in the case of European arrest warrants that are to be executed in this State.

Isle of Man and the Channel Islands Part 4 of the 2003 Act contains miscellaneous amendments to the Extradition Act 1965. First, provision is made to ensure that extradition arrangements with the Isle of Man and the Channel Islands can continue to operate. Those territories will not be operating the Framework Decision on the European arrest warrant and it has been agreed with the UK authorities that extradition arrangements with those territories should, instead, operate on the basis of the European Convention on Extradition 1957.

United Kingdom: abolition of "backing of warrants" procedure Part 4 of the 2003 Act also amended the Extradition Act 1965 to replace the "backing of warrants" arrangements between the State and the United Kingdom with the European arrest warrant procedure. Article 31.2 of the 2002 Framework Decision deals with circumstances where there are bilateral arrangements in force, such as the "backing of warrants" arrangement which had been in place between the State and the United Kingdom under the 1965 Act. Article 31.2 provides:

> "Member States may continue to apply bilateral or multilateral agreements or arrangements in force when this Framework Decision is adopted in so far as such agreements or arrangements allow the objectives of the Framework Decision to be extended or enlarged and help to simplify or facilitate further the procedures for surrender of persons who are the subject of European arrest warrants".

The Minister of State explained during the passage of the 2003 Act in the Oireachtas that it had been agreed with the United Kingdom Government that the existing "backing of warrants" arrangement did not satisfy the legal test in Art.31.2 and would therefore be replaced with the European arrest warrant. The 2003 Act therefore provides for the repeal of Pt III of the Extradition Act 1965, which provided the legal basis for the "backing of warrants" arrangement. The equivalent United Kingdom legislation on the implementation of the Framework Decision has also provided for the repeal of its legislation on the "backing of warrants" arrangement, namely, the Backing of Warrants (Republic of Ireland) Act 1965.

Orders under the 2003 Act Section 50 of the 2003 Act amended the procedural requirements in s.10 of the Extradition (European Convention on the Suppression of Terrorism) Act 1987 for the laying of orders before each House of the Oireachtas. It provides that orders shall take effect 21 days after their being laid before the Houses unless they are annulled. The orders under s.10 of the 1987 Act are for the purpose of extending the provisions of that Act to apply between Ireland and countries that are not parties to the European Convention on the Suppression of Terrorism. The amendments bring the procedures under s.10 into line with the amendments to s.4 of the 1965 Act, introduced by s.21 of the Extradition (European Conventions) Act 2001.

EXTRADITION AND EUROPEAN ARREST WARRANT

Corresponding offence In *Attorney General v Tothova*, High Court, February 24, 2004, the Attorney General applied under the Extradition Act 1965 for an extradition order returning the respondent to the Czech Republic pursuant to a request by the Czech Minister of Justice. The request was supported by a warrant for the arrest of the respondent. The respondent had gone into a shop in the Czech Republic, taken two leather jackets and concealed them in a bag beneath her clothing. The respondent was convicted by a Czech District Court and sentenced to eight months' imprisonment on foot of a larceny charge. Regard was had to the respondent's previous conviction for a similar offence within the preceding three years. The central issue was whether the offence with which the respondent had been convicted corresponded to an offence in this jurisdiction. Peart J. held it did. For correspondence to be established, he considered it must be shown that the criminal act complained of in the requesting state would, if done here, constitute a crime and enable the respondent to be convicted of an offence. He concluded that the offence corresponded with the offence of theft under the Criminal Justice (Theft and Fraud Offences Act 2001 (*Annual Review of Irish Law 2001*, pp.219–227).

In *Attorney General v Heywood*, High Court, February 24, 2004, the issue of correspondence was considered in the context of the evidential proofs required. The applicant sought an order under s.47 of the Extradition Act 1965, as amended, for return of the respondent to the United Kingdom on foot of three warrants. Warrant A related to conspiracy to supply a controlled drug, namely heroin. The equivalent offence in this jurisdiction was the offence of possession of controlled drugs for the purpose of supply in s.15(1) of the Misuse of Drugs Act 1977. Warrants B and C related to charges of unlawfully causing grievous bodily harm. The equivalent offence in this jurisdiction was the offence of causing serious harm in s.4 of the Non-Fatal Offences Against the Person Act 1997. Peart J. refused to order the respondent's extradition and ordered his release. Peart J. accepted that diamorphine (heroin) was a controlled drug for the purposes of the Misuse of Drugs Act 1977, but he held that it could not be assumed that the offence of supplying, which was the substantive offence in respect of which the conspiracy charge in warrant A was laid, was the same as the offence of possession for the purpose of supplying. In order for the offence of supplying as stated in warrant A to correspond with an offence in this jurisdiction, it was necessary for the applicant to show that on the day on which the warrant was produced to the Assistant Commissioner for endorsement, there were regulations in place for the purpose of making it an offence here for a person to supply a controlled drug and no attempt had been made to do this. As to warrants B and C, the court had to be satisfied that the act which constituted the offence in the United Kingdom would, if done here, be an offence here. The act referred to in the warrants was simply a general one, namely of causing grievous bodily harm with intent, but there was no detail given as to what act was done or performed by the respondent. Peart J. thus concluded that warrants B and C were deficient in that they contained no factual detail upon which the court could decide that the act complained of would constitute an offence in this country. We can note here that Peart J. had taken a similar view in *Attorney General v Parke*, High Court, February 24,

2004, which also concerned the issue of drugs offences where there had also been an absence of evidence concerning the relevant Regulations under the 1977 Act.

European arrest warrant and surrender procedure   The terms of the European Arrest Warrant Act 2003, which came into effect on January 1, 2004, are discussed separately, above.

FIREARMS AND OFFENSIVE WEAPONS

Northern Ireland   The Independent Monitoring Commission Act 2003 provided for the establishment of an independent Commission to monitor the activities of paramilitary organisations in Northern Ireland, particularly in connection with their continued use of firearms and offensive weapons, including their use in criminal acts. The establishment of the Commission came in the context of negotiations between the various political parties in Northern Ireland and the Governments of the United Kingdom and of Ireland on the implementation of the 1998 Good Friday Agreements (see the *Annual Review of Irish Law 1998*, pp.118–127). The Independent Monitoring Commission Act 2003 (Commencement) Order 2004 (S.I. No.5 of 2004) brought the 2003 Act into operation on January 7, 2004.

INTERNATIONAL MARITIME SECURITY

The Maritime Security Act 2004 implemented the 1988 United Nations Convention for the Suppression of Unlawful Acts against the Safety of Maritime Navigation. It also gave effect to the 1988 Protocol to that Convention for the Suppression of Unlawful Acts against the Safety of Fixed Platforms on the Continental Shelf. The texts of the Convention and Protocol are contained in Sch.1 and 2 to the 2004 Act. The enactment of the 2004 Act became a priority after the attacks in New York on the World Trade Centre on September 11, 2001. The UN Security Council passed Resolution 1373 on September 28, 2001 to urge all UN Member States which had not yet done so to become party to the 1988 Convention and Protocol and 10 other international instruments in order to strengthen international co-operation against terrorism. Of those 12 international instruments, six relate to aviation security and transport of nuclear material and had already been implemented by Ireland. The Criminal Justice (Terrorist Offences) Act 2005 (to which we will return in the *Annual Review of Irish Law 2005*), implemented four others, so the Maritime Security Act 2004 completed the legislative enactment of the relevant instruments.

The need to proceed with the Maritime Security Act 2004 had also been reinforced by the train bombings in Madrid in 2004. Thus, a key aspect of the EU European Council Declaration of March 25, 2004 on combating terrorism was a commitment by all EU Member States to improve implementation of commitments already undertaken following the events of September 11, 2001.

As required by the Convention and Protocol, s.2 of the Maritime Security Act 2004 creates certain offences against the safety of Irish ships and other ships which are in Irish territorial waters, and against any fixed platforms on Ireland's continental shelf, while s.3 is a standard-type extension of Ireland's jurisdiction to allow prosecution in the State for breaches of the Convention or Protocol committed outside the State. In either case, the penalty is life imprisonment on conviction on indictment. The specific offences listed in s.2 of the 2004 Act mirror those set out in Art.3 of the Convention and Art.2 of the Protocol.

Sections 4 to 8 of the 2004 Act supplement those principal provisions by providing powers for search on a ship or fixed platform on which an offence was believed to have been committed or where an alleged offender is on board, and for the apprehension, detention and prosecution of alleged offenders or handing them over for prosecution to the appropriate authorities of another state which is party to the Convention and Protocol. Sections 9 to 12, while ensuring the avoidance of double jeopardy in any case arising under the 2004 Act, also ensure that, because of the gravity of the offences referred to, the most stringent requirements of the Bail Act 1997 and other relevant Acts will apply. Thus, bail may be refused to a person charged with a serious offence under the 2004 Act if the court considers it necessary to refuse bail in order to prevent the commission of a further serious offence. Moreover, offences under the 2004 Act cannot be regarded as political offences so as to prevent the extradition of the alleged offender from the State to the requested state.

INTERNATIONAL POLICE INVESTIGATION TEAMS

EU Framework Decision on Joint Investigation Teams   The Criminal Justice (Joint Investigation Teams) Act 2004 owes its origins, like the European Arrest Warrant Act 2003 (see p.224 *et seq.*), to the conclusions of the EU European Council meeting in Tampere in 1999, which established a "mutual recognition" principle in connection with Justice and Home Affairs. The Tampere European Council called for joint investigation teams (as foreseen in the Amsterdam Treaty) to be set up without delay as a first step to combat trafficking in drugs and human beings as well as terrorism. Article 13 of the 2000 Convention on Mutual Assistance in Criminal Matters between Member States of the European Union provided for the establishment of such teams. Following the attack on the World Trade Centre in New York of September 11, 2001, the Council of the European Union decided that a specific instrument providing for such teams should be adopted as soon as possible. As a result, Art.13 of the 2000 Mutual Assistance Convention, together with Arts 15 and 16 which make provision for criminal and civil liability, became the basis for a 2002 European Union Council Framework Decision on Joint Investigation Teams, which is scheduled to the 2004 Act. Although the Framework Decision is targeted in particular at setting up joint investigations to combat trafficking in drugs and human beings as well as terrorism, the 2004 Act is not confined to these offences.

Northern Ireland It was also noted during the Oireachtas debate that the 2004 Act involved implementation of a number of the recommendations of the 1999 Patten Report on Policing in Northern Ireland, such as the recommendations that the Police Service of Northern Ireland and the Garda Síochána should have written protocols covering key aspects of co-operation; there should be a programme of long-term personnel exchanges between them in specialist areas; and consideration should be given to providing for an immediate exchange of officers and pooling of investigative teams after major incidents with a substantial cross-border dimension. In this respect, Art.9 of the 2002 Agreement between Ireland and the United Kingdom on police co-operation provides that the Police Service of Northern Ireland and the Garda Síochána shall, as appropriate, make full use of existing arrangements for facilitating joint investigations and additional arrangements that are put in place in the context of European Union initiatives.

Competent authorities Section 2 of the 2004 Act provides that the Commissioner of the Garda Síochána is the competent authority for the State for the purposes of the 2002 Framework Decision except where other Member States require a judicial authority for the making or receiving of a request. In that case the Minister for Justice, Equality and Law Reform is the competent authority. The purpose of nominating the Minister as a competent authority is to allow Ireland to make and receive requests from other Member States, which in accordance with either their legislative or constitutional arrangements require and have named judicial authorities, rather than chiefs of police, as their national competent authorities for the purpose of giving effect to the Framework Decision.

Establishment of Joint Investigation Teams Section 3 deals with the establishment of joint investigation teams in the State. Where the Irish competent authority is satisfied that either an offence has been committed in the State or there are reasonable grounds for suspecting that an offence has been committed in the State and the investigation of the offence or suspected offence has links with one or more Member States or that conduct which would constitute an offence or a reasonable suspicion thereof has occurred partly in the State and partly in another Member State, it may request the relevant competent authority in the other Member State or States to establish a joint investigation team. Section 4 provides for the establishment of joint investigation teams on receipt of requests from other Member States and contains provisions which are similar in nature to those contained in s.3.

Section 5 elaborates on the provisions relating to the establishment and termination of joint investigation teams and provides for the agreement governing the establishment of such teams. A joint investigation team can be established for a specific purpose and for a limited period which can be extended for such periods as are agreed by the competent authorities concerned. A team can operate for as long as is necessary for the purpose of conducting the investigation concerned and parts of the team can operate in more than one Member State at the same time. Provision is also made for Member States to join a team which has already been established. Section 5(4) of the 2004 Act was amended during its passage in the Oireachtas in order to include the criteria which must be considered by the Irish competent authority when deciding whether to join an investigation team which has already been established by other Member States. These criteria are similar to those contained in s.4(3) of the 2004 Act. Section 5(5) provides that a Member State may join a team already established by more than one Member State including the State on such terms and conditions as may be agreed. The agreement to establish the team can be amended to reflect changing needs on any of these matters. Section 5(6) allows a joint investigation team to be terminated when the purposes for which it was established have been achieved or when there is no further benefit to be gained from its continued operation.

Membership and operation of Joint Investigation Teams   Section 6 deals with membership of a joint investigation team and the terms and conditions of such membership, including remuneration and allowances. National membership can be drawn from the Garda Síochána, Customs and Excise, the Revenue Commissioners, other Departments and persons who, in the opinion of the Minister, have experience or expertise relevant to the investigation concerned. Members of the Garda Síochána and civil servants will continue to be subject to the same terms and conditions of employment as they were subject to immediately before they became members of the team. Provision is made for the removal of members from the team by the Commissioner in the case of members of the Garda Síochána, or by the Minister, at the Commissioner's request, in the case of other team members. Members of the Garda Síochána and officers of Customs and Excise will continue to be vested with and can exercise their Garda or Customs and Excise powers while operating as members of a team.

Section 7 provides for the operation of a joint investigation team. A team will perform its functions in accordance with the law of the state of operation. In Ireland, a team will operate under the control and general supervision of the Garda Commissioner who will make the necessary organisational arrangements, including the appointment of a team leader. Team members, including seconded members, will perform their functions under the direction and control of the team leader.

While Art.1.6 of the 2002 Framework Decision provides for discretion as to whether seconded members of a joint investigation team are to be entrusted with the task of taking certain investigative measures in the host state, it was noted during the Oireachtas debate that s.7(4) of the 2004 Act prohibits this. It was explained that this was in line with the practice being adopted in other Member States on the role of seconded members in a joint investigation team. Seconded members may, however, be present when investigative measures are being undertaken, unless otherwise decided by the team leader. Evidence obtained during the course of an investigation will remain in the possession of the Garda Síochána or, if not already in their possession, will be taken into their possession.

Section 7 also provides for one of the more innovative aspects of the 2004 Act, namely, that where investigative measures are required by a joint investigation team in one of the Member States involved in the team, seconded members can request their own national authorities to take such measures. This means that it will not be necessary for the Member State of operation to submit a formal request for mutual assistance to another Member State. The relevant measures sought will be considered in the Member State in question, in accordance with the conditions which would apply had the measures been sought in a national investigation. In order to give effect to this, s.7(7) provides that evidence which is obtained directly by a seconded member operating in the State from his or her competent authority of appointment will be considered as if it had been obtained on foot of a mutual assistance request made under s.52 of the Criminal Justice Act 1994. Section 7(8) and 7(9) also provide for a member of the Garda Síochána who is operating as a seconded member in another Member State to make a request, on behalf of the team, for mutual assistance under s.51 of the Criminal Justice Act 1994, or for a search warrant authorising entry, search and seizure under s.55(4) of the Criminal Justice Act 1994. Another innovative measure is s.7(11) which allows a member of a joint investigation team operating as a seconded member in another Member State to provide to that team information which is available in the State and which is relevant to the investigation being conducted by the team.

Section 8 deals with the written agreement for the establishment of a joint investigation team and lists the provisions which must be included in any agreement: the parties to the agreement; the purpose for which the team is established; the identity of the person or persons to be investigated, if known, and details of membership of the team. Financial arrangements must also be agreed and included in any agreement drawn up between Member States involved in the establishment of a team. Provision is also made for the agreement to be amended in order to allow for issues such as the extension of the period of operation, changes of membership and other incidental matters.

Section 9 provides for additional assistance and expertise to be provided to a joint investigation team by appropriate persons, described as "participants", from EU bodies or authorities of countries other than Member States. Participants can be drawn from Europol, bodies established under Title VI of the Treaty on the European Union, such as Eurojust, the European Commission or other institutions of the European Communities, and authorities of countries other than Member States which have been designated by the Minister. The role of participants is similar to that of seconded members and, similarly, they will not be permitted to take investigative measures.

Section 10 amends the Garda Síochána Act 1989, as amended by s.5 of the Europol Act 1997, to allow the Garda Commissioner to assign a member of the Garda Síochána as a member of a joint investigation team abroad and to provide for the making of regulations to allow for the registration of his or her death or the birth or death of a member of his or her family while serving in that capacity outside the State. While it is not envisaged that the length of time served by a member seconded to a joint investigation team will necessitate his or her family joining him or her abroad, the length of time for which a member is seconded to a team will depend to a great degree on the nature of the investigation in question.

Information obtained by Joint Investigation Teams Section 11 is concerned with the use of information lawfully obtained by a member of a joint investigation team which is not otherwise available to the competent authorities of the Member States that established the team. Such information can only be used for the purposes for which the team was established. It may be used in other circumstances but only where the prior consent of the Member State in which such information became available has been obtained or where the Member State has been informed. Consent to the use of the information for the detection, investigation and prosecution of criminal offences other than those in respect of which the team was established may be withheld where it would be likely to prejudice criminal investigations being conducted in the State or where a request for mutual assistance or co-operation could be refused under the international co-operation provisions of the Criminal Justice Act 1994.

Criminal and civil liability Section 12 provides for criminal liability in respect of offences committed by or against seconded members while they are operating in the State as part of a joint investigation team. Specific provision is made for seconded members who are also members of a foreign police force, in that they will be deemed to be members of the Garda Síochána for the purpose of criminal liability.

Section 13 provides for the satisfaction of civil claims which may arise from operations carried out by members from another Member State operating in the State as part of a joint investigation team and also by Irish members operating abroad. The State will reimburse another Member State in full for any amount paid in respect of injury, loss or damage caused by our national members in the performance of their duties as seconded members. The State will also pay compensation or damages or provide another appropriate remedy for any injury, loss or damage caused by seconded members in the State in the same way as would apply to injury, loss or damage caused by national members. The State may seek reimbursement of compensation or damages it has paid or other loss incurred from the Member State which appointed the seconded members or from third parties who may be liable for injury, loss or damage caused.

LEGAL AID

Refusal: gravity of offence and means of applicant Section 2 of the Criminal Justice (Legal Aid) Act 1962 empowers a judge to grant a certificate of legal aid where he is satisfied that the applicant is of insufficient means and where the gravity of the charge or some other exceptional circumstances indicate that she should be afforded legal aid. In *Costigan v Brennan*, High Court, February 6, 2004, the respondent judge of the District Court refused to grant legal aid in circumstances where he had concluded it was unlikely that the applicant would receive a prison sentence if convicted of the charge preferred against her. It was acknowledged by all parties that the applicant did not have sufficient assets to enable her to obtain professional legal representation from her own resources. The applicant sought to quash the respondent's refusal, but Quirke J. refused the relief sought. He held that the respondent was acting within his jurisdiction under the 1962 Act in refusing to grant a certificate of legal aid to the applicant. The respondent fulfilled all the necessary legal requirements in his consideration of the application in that he conducted an inquiry into the applicant's means, the gravity of the charge preferred and whether any exceptional circumstances existed.

MISUSE OF DRUGS

Exemptions for medicinal products The Misuse of Drugs (Scheduled Substances) (Exemption) (Amendment) Order 2004 (S.I. No.91 of 2004) exempted from s.3 of the Misuse of Drugs Act 1977 (which makes unauthorised possession an offence) the substances, medicinal products, other preparations and other products specified in the Schedule to the Order. The Order came into force on March 1, 2004. The Misuse of Drugs (Scheduled Substances) (Amendment) Regulations 2004 (S.I. No.92 of 2004) implemented Directive 2003/101/EC relating to the manufacture and placing on the market of certain substances used in the illicit manufacture of narcotic drugs and psychotropic substances. The Regulations came into force on March 1, 2004.

PROCEDURE

Burden of proof: direction to jury In *People (DPP) v Reid* [2004] 1 I.R. 392 the Court of Criminal Appeal (Hardiman, Lavan and deValera JJ.) discussed an aspect of the burden of proof. The defendants had been convicted for affray contrary to s.16 of the Criminal Justice (Public Order) Act 1994. Section 16 provides, *inter alia,* that where two or more persons at any place unlawfully use or threaten to use violence towards each other they shall be guilty of an offence. The first applicant appealed on the ground that the trial judge was wrong to refuse his application for a direction of no case to answer and should have withdrawn the matter from the jury. The first applicant contended that there was no evidence that he had used or threatened to use violence towards the other persons gathered there. The second applicant contended that the trial judge had misdirected the jury in relation to giving him the benefit of the doubt. The trial judge had directed the jury that if two views were equally open they must take the one most favourable to the accused, unless it had been excluded beyond all reasonable doubt. The Court of Criminal Appeal allowed both appeals. As to the first applicant, the court noted that the actual or threatened use of violence required by s.16 of the 1994 Act must be violence towards each other. In the present case, there was no evidence of the first applicant using violence towards any person except the two prosecuting Gardaí concerned. That being so, there was no prima facie case against the first applicant and the charge should have been withdrawn from the jury. In relation to the second applicant, the court held that the trial court had misdirected the jury. The Court of Criminal Appeal noted that it is not necessary that two views be equally open to the jury. Two views might be reasonably open to the jury, even if one was less probable than the other. All that was required was that two views be possible on some part of the evidence, so that the jury was then required to adopt the view most favourable to the accused, unless the prosecution had established the other beyond all reasonable doubt.

Jury directions: remarks "giving seal of approval" to prosecution witness In *People (DPP) v Hourigan*, Court of Criminal Appeal, March 19, 2004, the applicants sought leave to appeal against their conviction for murder. The main grounds of appeal related to the remarks of the judge at the conclusion of the closing speech of counsel for the second-named applicant and immediately prior to his charge to the jury, in which he described the deceased's mother, whose evidence was crucial to the conviction of both applicants, as a "victim". The applicants also claimed the judge's charge to the jury regarding their options as to the verdict was inadequate; and that a photograph printed in a newspaper during the trial of the second-named applicant in the company of a uniformed person who appeared to be a prison guard was prejudicial. The Court of Criminal Appeal, whose judgment was delivered by McGuinness J., allowed the appeal and ordered a new trial. The court held that the trial judge's remarks concerning the deceased's mother gave her evidence a "seal of approval" and rendered the trial unfair and unsatisfactory, as he did not go on to state that her circumstances bore no relation to the veracity of her evidence. The court found that use of the term "walking free" in the judge's charge explaining the consequences of a verdict of "not guilty" was unfortunate, but was not in itself sufficient to quash the verdict of the jury. As to the publication of the photograph, the court noted that it might amount to contempt of court but that while it was open to criticism, it had been sufficiently dealt with in the trial judge's charge to the jury.

PROCEEDS OF CRIME

Assets freezing order In *Murphy v M.C.*, Supreme Court, March 8, 2004, the applicant appealed to the Supreme Court against a decision of the High Court refusing to discharge a previous order made by the High Court against the applicant pursuant to s.3 of the Proceeds of Crime Act 1996. The order in question froze any dealings in relation to a particular property on the grounds that it represented the proceeds of crime. The applicant argued that the earlier High Court proceedings had proceeded on the basis that the order was interlocutory but that a subsequent decision of the Supreme Court had made it clear that, though described as an interlocutory order, it was in effect a final order. The applicant claimed that this resulted in a situation where he had been deprived of the trial to which he was entitled because he would never have a final trial of the matter as was originally anticipated in the High Court. The Supreme Court (Keane C.J., Murray, Hardiman, Geoghegan and Fennelly JJ.) refused the relief sought. The court held that the applicant had not been put at any serious disadvantage. He had elected not to give oral evidence as to whether the property in question constituted the proceeds of crime. It was difficult to see, the court concluded, that the applicant had in fact suffered any tactical disadvantage in the proceedings other than disadvantages that were of his own choice because of the manner in which he had chosen to meet the case. The court therefore refused to discharge the previous order and dismissed the appeal.

PROSECUTION APPEALS FROM THE DISTRICT COURT

In 2004, in response to a request from the Attorney General made in 2003, the Law Reform Commission published a *Consultation Paper on Appeals against Unduly Lenient Sentences in the District Court* (LRC CP 33–2004). The Paper provisionally recommended that the Director of Public Prosecutions be empowered to appeal against unduly lenient sentences in the District Court. In coming to this conclusion, the Commission considered that the most persuasive argument is that it is in the public interest that offenders should be sentenced appropriately in relation to the crime that they have committed, and that a procedure should be in place for rectifying any undue leniency in the sentencing outcome. The Commission was also of the view that it is in the public interest that any real or perceived inconsistency (failure to apply appropriate sentencing principles), rather than disparity (appropriate different sentencing outcomes, taking account of different circumstances), in sentencing practices in the District Court be remedied by way of appeal.

The Commission accepted that there are arguments to be made against the introduction of such an appeal procedure, but concluded that such arguments are outweighed by introducing safeguards, notably a requirement to seek the consent of the Director of Public Prosecutions, into the procedure. This "filter system" would mean that, without affecting any existing right of appeal of any prosecuting authority (such as in health and safety at work cases), where a prosecutor is of the opinion that a District Court sentence is unduly lenient, the prosecutor should refer the case to the Director of Public Prosecutions to seek approval for an appeal within a defined time limit. The Commission recommended that the appeal system envisaged would be from any sentence imposed in the District Court on conviction including fines, imprisonment, community service orders, as well as conditional acquittals including orders made under the Probation of Offenders Act 1907 or any other order made on a finding of guilt without entry of a conviction. The Commission recommended that the appeal should be brought to the Circuit Court and that such an appeal provision should reflect the terms of s.2 of the Criminal Justice Act 1993, allowing for the variation of the sentence as appropriate. The Commission concluded that, in considering appeals, the Circuit Court should use the test applied by the Court of Criminal Appeal when considering appeals taken from sentences on indictment under s.2 of the 1993 Act, that is, that there must be a substantial departure from the appropriate sentence amounting to an error of principle. The Commission also recommended that in respect of acquittals on the merits, the form of appeal should be the existing method in the Summary Jurisdiction Act 1857, namely an appeal on a point of law by way of case stated to the High Court.

In the Paper, the Commission also considered other possible methods of dealing with any perception or reality of inconsistent sentencing in the District Court. It addressed the question of introducing sentencing guidelines, and reiterated its recommendation in its *Report on Sentencing* (LRC 53–1996) that presumptive sentencing guidelines should not be introduced in this jurisdiction as they would be inconsistent with the discretionary nature of Irish sentencing policy. However, the Commission supported the views in the *Report of the Committee on Judicial Conduct and Ethics* (2000) that sentencing bench books might be prepared by the proposed Judicial Studies Committee (part of the proposed Judicial Council), an approach which is consistent with the views expressed by the Commission in its *Report on Sentencing*. The Commission also addressed the issue of the present and future scope of prosecuting counsel's role in the sentencing process, including counsel's role in expressing a view as to the merits or otherwise of a particular sentencing disposition.

PUBLIC ORDER

Threatening, etc. behaviour: failure to include "in a public place" in summons or conviction In *Murphy v Director of Public Prosecutions* [2004] 1 I.R. 65, the applicant had been charged and convicted in the District Court with the offence of engaging in threatening, abusive or insulting behaviour with intent to provoke a breach of the peace, contrary to s.6 of the Criminal Justice (Public Order) Act 1994. On judicial review, the applicant argued that the absence of the words "in a public place" in the summons that brought him before the District Court, and in the order recording his conviction, rendered his conviction unsafe. The High Court accepted this argument and quashed the conviction. On appeal by the respondent, the Supreme Court noted that it had to determine whether the requirements in relation to the form of the conviction had been met. Delivering the court's decision in an *ex tempore* judgment, Keane C.J., speaking for the court, held that, in order to be safe, a conviction order must identify with precision the actual offence of which the applicant has been convicted. In this case, as the summons and conviction order indicated that the offence occurred at a licensed premises, a public house, the court concluded there could be no uncertainty in the mind of any person reading the order convicting the applicant as to the precise offence of which he was convicted and that that offence occurred in a public place.

ROAD TRAFFIC

Intoximeter: application for inspection In *Whelan v Kirby* [2004] 2 I.L.R.M. 1, the appellant had sought to challenge by way of judicial review a decision of the first respondent judge of the District Court convicting him of the drink driving offence under s.49 of the Road Traffic Act 1961, as amended. Prior to his trial the appellant had sought inspection of the intoximeter apparatus which had been used to take his breath specimen. The prosecuting gardaí in the case had no objection to such an inspection; however, the Medical Bureau of Road Safety, whose property the intoximeter was, indicated that it would only agree to an inspection if there was a court order authorising this. The first respondent refused the appellant's application for inspection and proceeded to convict the appellant. The appellant sought an order of certiorari quashing the conviction on the grounds that the first respondent had acted in breach of natural and constitutional justice in failing to properly entertain the application for inspection and/or failing to accede to same. Relief was also sought on the basis that the relevant District Court order, when taken up by the appellant's solicitor, purported to impose a penalty but did not formally contain an order recording conviction. The prosecution subsequently bespoke a certified copy of the order that contained a corrective statement recording conviction that had been inserted into the order. No explanation was provided by the second respondent for the discrepancy between the two orders. The High Court refused the relief sought but, on appeal, the Supreme Court (Keane C.J., Denham, Hardiman, Geoghegan, and Fennelly JJ.) allowed the appeal. The court held that the first respondent had refused to entertain the appellant's application regarding inspection of the intoximeter. The appellant, the court concluded, had an arguable case that an inspection was reasonable given the novelty of the apparatus and the fact that he stood to be convicted based on the result of a printout from that apparatus. It was not necessary for the appellant to adduce evidence of what such an inspection might have helpfully revealed, so the court should have entertained the application in the interests of ensuring that the appellant was not unfairly handicapped in the conduct of his defence. The court pointed out that since the intoximeter printout gives rise only to a rebuttable presumption of guilt, by refusing to entertain the application the first respondent was cutting the appellant off from any opportunity of rebutting the statutory presumption. It was also relevant that the Medical Bureau of Road Safety did not object to the inspection provided that the court authorised it by way of an order. There is jurisdiction in the District Court to make any order necessary for the fulfillment of the constitutional right to a fair trial and fair procedures. As to the question of the form of the two orders in this case, the court pointed out that s.14 of the Courts Act 1971 requires the District Court to have regard to the record. By bespeaking and exhibiting in court a certified copy of the order that recorded no conviction against him, the Supreme Court stated that appellant had satisfied the prima facie burden of showing that there was an error on the face of the record. By producing a second certified copy of the order without providing any explanation for the difference between it and the original order, the court concluded that the second-named respondent had failed to produce any evidence to displace the record.

It is worth noting that, following this judgment, the second respondent applied to the court for an order remitting the cases for rehearing to the District Court. In *Whelan v Kirby (No.2)*, Supreme Court, March 1, 2004, the court (Keane C.J., Denham, Hardiman, Geoghegan, and Fennelly JJ.) declined to do so. The court held that the error of the first respondent was not an error made within jurisdiction and therefore the applicants were not entitled to raise a defence of *autrefois acquit*. He was deprived of jurisdiction to make the order he did. The applicants were not in peril and accordingly the court was entitled in principle to exercise a power of remittal. In this respect, it held that its discretion was to be exercised taking all the circumstances into account. In these cases, a lengthy period of time had elapsed from the date of the alleged offences and difficulties might arise due to the lapse of time. The court also noted that the proceedings were summary and it was in the interests of the public and the persons accused that they should be disposed of within a reasonable time from when they were allegedly committed. The delay in the present cases had occurred due to no fault of the applicants. The court, therefore, in the exercise of its discretion refused to remit the cases to the District Court.

General   For general changes to road traffic legislation, see the Road Traffic Act 2004, discussed in the Transport Chapter below, p.567.

SENTENCING

Attempted robbery   In *People (DPP) v Doyle*, Court of Criminal Appeal, February 19, 2004, the respondent had been sentenced to one year's imprisonment on a count of attempted robbery. The Director of Public Prosecutions sought review on the grounds of undue leniency. No issue was taken by the Director with sentences on three subsequent counts. The respondent committed these later offences whilst on bail for the attempted robbery, and under s.11(1) of the Criminal Justice Act 1984 a trial judge is obliged to impose consecutive sentences to date from the expiration of any term of imprisonment for the first offence. The trial court imposed the one-year sentence for the attempted robbery but commented that, in the absence of the requirement to impose consecutive sentences, three years was an appropriate sentence. The Court of Criminal Appeal granted the application for review. The court accepted that the trial judge committed an error of principle in that he had sought to ensure that the consequences of s.11(1) of the Criminal Justice Act 1984 were avoided. The court substituted a sentence of three years' imprisonment.

Co-accused   In *People (DPP) v Tighe*, Court of Criminal Appeal, February 19, 2004, the applicant sought leave to appeal against severity of sentence in relation to a three-year sentence imposed on him for robbery. The sentencing judge had been informed that the defendant's two co-accused had also been sentenced, but that an application for leave to appeal on the grounds of undue leniency had been brought by the Director of Public Prosecutions. The trial judge proceeded to impose sentence on the defendant without reference to the sentences imposed on his co-accused. The Court of Criminal Appeal (Keane C.J., O'Neill and deValera JJ.) upheld the sentence. The court held that the trial judge had adopted the correct course in sentencing the defendant without regard to the sentences imposed on the other persons concerned. Had he taken them into account then, depending on the outcome of the Director's application to the Court of Criminal Appeal, an unjustifiable discrepancy might have resulted. Having regard to the serious nature of the offence, the significant role of the defendant and his previous record, the court could not detect any error of principle by the trial judge and it accordingly refused leave to appeal.

Drugs offences: statutory guidelines and mitigation   In *People (DPP) v Botha* [2004] 2 I.R. 375, the applicant had been convicted of possession with intent to supply drugs with a value in excess of €12,780 (£10,000). Section 15(A) of the Misuse of Drugs Act 1977, as inserted by s.4 of the Criminal Justice Act 1999, provides that where the value is in excess of this amount, the sentence to be imposed is a minimum of 10 years, unless there are "exceptional and specific" circumstances which would make it unjust to impose the 10-year sentence. The applicant had been sentenced to five years' imprisonment and sought to appeal against severity of sentence. He appealed on grounds of his South African nationality, his age, his unfortunate financial background, his good behaviour in prison, his plea of guilty, and a statement that he had made. It was submitted that the "exceptional and specific circumstances" referred to in s.15(A) of the 1977 Act, as amended, were not limited to the circumstances set out in it, and that "exceptional" and "specific" are alternate, and not cumulative, considerations. It was emphasised that the controlled drug in question was cannabis. The Court of Criminal Appeal dismissed the appeal, concluding that there had been no error in principle in the approach of the trial judge in sentencing the applicant.

The court noted that every mitigating factor had been taken into account and each had been given due weight. The trial judge had been correct in regarding that these mitigating factors rendered the minimum sentence unjust in the circumstances of the case. The court noted that s.15(A) of the 1977 Act, as amended, does not distinguish between the type of drug involved, rather it provides for the minimum sentence on the basis of value, rather than nature, of the substance. The court also held that it was clear from the conjunctive form of the wording of s.15(A) of the 1977 Act, as amended, that the unenumerated circumstances relied upon as putting the case into a category where it would be unjust to impose the minimum sentence, must be both exceptional and specific. At sentencing, the applicant's previous convictions had been disregarded due to remoteness in time.

The court referred to a number of other decisions on the interpretation of s.15(A) of the 1977 Act, as amended, but also noted that no reference to another case is useful unless the facts and circumstances of the offence and offender in that case are put before the court in written form. In this respect, the court considered that it would be appropriate that more assistance by prosecuting counsel should be provided to a sentencing judge. The court acknowledged that this might require alteration to the long-standing convention (incorporated into the Code of Conduct of the Bar Council of Ireland) that prosecuting counsel should not engage in any form of direct advocacy as to the sentence to be imposed.

Manslaughter In *People (DPP) v Aherne,* Court of Criminal Appeal, July 5, 2004, the applicant sought leave to appeal against the imposition of a 14-year sentence for manslaughter. He had been charged, together with two others, with the murder of one Brian Mulvanney in the Templeogue area of Dublin in 2000. The applicant had also been charged on one count of assault and one count of assault with intent to rob respectively, which had occurred on the same date as the murder. The applicant pleaded guilty to the latter two counts and was sentenced to three years' detention on each of them, to run concurrently with each other. The applicant was 15 years old at the time the crime was committed and had consumed about 10 pints of lager on the night in question. A co-accused of the applicant had lured the deceased from a party in a house in Templeogue on a pretext, but actually with the intention of assaulting him. The applicant had been asked by the co-accused to join him in attacking the deceased. The applicant had struck the deceased with a stick or plank on a number of occasions. When imposing the 10-year sentence, the trial judge White J. had taken into account the following factors: the previous good character and age of the applicant, the contents of the various reports submitted at the trial, the applicant's learning difficulties, his co-operation with the Gardaí and that he had not been the ring leader or prime mover on the night in question. The Court of Criminal Appeal allowed the application and imposed a 10-year sentence in its place. The court had regard to the evidence of the victim's father in relation to the impact of the crime on the deceased's family and found that the grief of the deceased's family had been aggravated by the severity of the deceased's bodily injuries and the fact that he was left to die when his assailants ran away without notifying the emergency services or anyone else of his whereabouts. The court found that there were a number of aggravating aspects to the crime. Thus, the applicant joined in the crime willingly and without being in any way overborne. The applicant did not suffer from a psychiatric illness and any learning difficulties he had provided no sort of excuse. In all the circumstances, the offence disclosed would have to be regarded as being in the most serious category of manslaughter. There were only three mitigating factors in the case, namely, the age of the applicant, that he had no previous convictions and that he offered a guilty plea to manslaughter. These were very weighty factors. The court imposed a sentence of 14 years' imprisonment but reduced that to 10 years in light of the powerful mitigating factors.

In *People (DPP) v Cooney,* Court of Criminal Appeal, July 27, 2004, the applicant sought leave to appeal against the severity of his sentence of 14 years' imprisonment for manslaughter. The principal ground of appeal was that the trial judge did not provide full or specific reasons for the sentence imposed. The applicant submitted that a sentence must be proportionate to the circumstances of the case having regard to the nature of the offence, its effect on the victim and the circumstances of the convicted person. A necessary factor to be considered was the prospect of successfully rehabilitating the convicted person. The applicant argued that neither the possibility of rehabilitation nor the applicant's early admission of guilt had been taken into account by the sentencing judge. It was also argued that it was an error in principle to treat manslaughter with a knife as being in a different category from other forms of manslaughter, as had occurred in this case. The court of Criminal Appeal accepted these arguments. Allowing the appeal and reducing the sentence from 14 years to eight years' imprisonment, the court accepted that the trial judge did not properly consider the established relevant factors which should be taken into account in imposing sentence but was overly influenced by the presence in court of the victim's family. The court also acknowledged that, as the law currently stood, a sentencing judge is not under an obligation to give reasons for the particular sentence which he imposes but it is, however, a desirable practice. In the present case, the judge had erred in treating the matter as an action between the appellant and the victims rather than as an action between the State and the appellant. The trial judge also erred in regarding manslaughter by stabbing as being in a different and more serious category than other types of manslaughter.

Suspended sentence: activation for breach of terms of suspension   In *People (DPP) v Stewart*, Court of Criminal Appeal, January 12, 2004, the applicant had been convicted on drugs charges. He had been sentenced to a total of 10 years' imprisonment, but the sentences had been suspended in the hope that the applicant would be cured of his drug addiction and on terms that he attend Coolmine Centre, a drug addition and counselling centre. The applicant had repeatedly breached these terms and the Circuit Court judge had, as a result, activated the suspended sentences in full. The applicant sought leave to appeal against the activation order. The Court of Criminal Appeal declined to interfere with the order. Delivering the court's *ex tempore* decision, Hardiman J. noted that the Circuit Court judge had jurisdiction to reactivate the sentences and in the circumstances it was difficult to see how she could have done otherwise. It was accepted that the sentencing court has power to reactivate sentences but that this is not mandatory. In exercising discretion the sentencing court will have regard to the nature of the breach of the terms on which the sentence was suspended. In this case, the Court of Criminal Appeal concluded that the breach of the terms by the applicant could not be described as a minor breach; thus, the Circuit Court judge, having exercised her discretion to activate the sentences, was constrained to reactivate the sentences in whole and it was not open to her to reactivate them in part.

Education

RECOGNITION OF PROFESSIONAL QUALIFICATIONS

The European Communities (General System for the Recognition of Higher Education Diplomas and Professional Education and Training and Second General System for the Recognition of Professional Education and Training) (Amendment) Regulations 2004 (S.I. No.36 of 2004) must be worth noting, not least because there are 30 words in their title. The 2004 Regulations give effect to Directive 2001/19/EC insofar as it relates to the amendment of Directive 89/48/EEC and Directive 92/51/EEC on the general system for the recognition of professional qualifications. The 2004 Regulations also amended the European Communities (General System for the Recognition of Higher Education Diplomas) Regulations 1991. The 1991 and 2004 Regulations deal with recognition of qualifications of nurse responsible for general care, dental practitioner, veterinary surgeon, midwife, architect, pharmacist and doctor.

SPECIAL EDUCATIONAL NEEDS

The Education for Persons with Special Educational Needs Act 2004 establishes a system to address the right to an education of persons with special educational needs comparable to those who do not have such needs. The background to the 2004 Act can be traced to a number of constitutional challenges in the High Court to the existing arrangements for such children, beginning with *O'Donoghue v Minister for Health* [1996] 2 I.R. 20. During the course of the Oireachtas debate, the Minister for Education and Science stated that the intention of the 2004 Act was to establish an educational context that would reflect the approach of O'Hanlon J. in *O'Donoghue*. In that case O'Hanlon J. had adapted comments of Ó Dálaigh C.J. in *Ryan v Attorney General* [1965] I.R. 294 on the meaning of "education" in Art.42 of the Constitution, and had concluded that the provision of education for a child with special educational needs must be such as to enable him or her "'to make the best possible use of his [or her] inherent and potential capabilities, physical, mental and moral,' however limited these capacities might be" [1996] 2 I.R. 20, at 62. The main effect of the 2004 Act is that children with special educational needs arising from an educational disability will have a right to an assessment, a right to an individual education plan and a right to have that plan implemented with all the requisite services. Parents will have a right to be involved and consulted at every stage of their child's development.

A key principle of the 2004 Act is that every child with special needs will be educated in an integrated and inclusive setting, unless this would not be in the best interests of the child or the effective provision of education for other children. It is also worth noting that the title of the 2004 Act was changed during the Oireachtas debate by the insertion of "special educational needs" in place of "disabilities". This was done with a view to ensuring that the 2004 Act included children with conditions such as dyslexia and Attention Deficit Disorder (ADD), and to encourage the inclusive and empowering nature of the approach adopted in the legislation.

The right of the child and his/her parents to services is also protected by a right of appeal to the Special Education Appeals Board (established by the 2004 Act) against any incorrect or inadequate statement or description contained in his or her individual education plan and against any failure by a school or a health board to implement any part of the plan. For the first time the 2004 Act also provides that the Minister for Education and Science and the Minister for Finance will have statutory duties to consider the requirements for funding, education and support services for children with special educational needs, and to make available adequate resources to discharge the State's duties to these children. Section 13 of the 2004 Act acknowledges the constitutional duty of the State to ensure the equal and fair treatment of all children so that children with special educational needs have the same opportunities as children without disabilities. It was also stated during the Oireachtas debate that the 2004 Act represented the first instance of primary legislation directly dictating how resources are to be allocated to a specific need. The 2004 Act stipulates that all its provisions must be fully implemented within five years of its enactment.

Under the 2004 Act schools also have a range of new duties in respect of children with special educational needs. They must respect the principle of inclusive education; ensure that parents are consulted regarding their child's needs; co-operate with the National Council for Special Education; ensure that teachers are aware of the special educational needs of the students and the importance of identifying children with those needs; and inculcate in students an awareness of the needs of people with disabilities.

The 2004 Act requires that individual education plans be devised to meet the educational needs of children with special educational needs. Where a school principal believes that a child is not benefiting from the regular education programme, he or she must take measures to meet the child's needs. If these measures do not succeed, the principal must consult the parents and arrange for an assessment of the child. School-based assessments must be completed no later than three months from the time the principal formed his or her opinion about the child. Where an assessment establishes that a child has special needs, the principal must ensure that an individual education plan is prepared within one month and that, in preparing the plan, the parents, special educational needs organiser and any other relevant person is consulted. Where the child's needs are relatively uncomplicated, it is intended that a school will draw up the plan. However, the principal and his or her staff will be able to avail of the assistance of a special educational needs organiser, where necessary. For those children whose needs are more complex, a formal planning process will be undertaken by the National Council for Special Education. In the case of a plan prepared by the Council, a special educational needs organiser will convene a team of people that must include the child's parents and may also involve the child, school principal and a psychologist.

Reflecting the large amount of litigation that preceded the 2004 Act, s.38 (which was inserted during the Dáil Report Stage debate on the 2004 Act) introduces a form of mediation to special education litigation. If either side refuses to take part, or does so in an obstructive manner, s.38 provides that the courts will be entitled to take that into account in dealing with later issues as to costs, although not with regard to the substantive issues in the case.

Electricity and Energy

ESB borrowing limit   The Electricity (Supply) (Amendment) Act 2004 raised the statutory borrowing limit of the Electricity Supply Board (ESB) to €6 billion to facilitate the ESB's major infrastructure investment programme. Prior to the 2004 Act, the ESB's borrowing limit stood at €2.03 billion, which had remained unchanged since 1982. Section 1 of the 2004 Act, the only substantive provision, gives effect to the change of limit to €6 billion by amending s.4(4) of the Electricity (Supply) (Amendment) Act 1954, as amended by the Electricity (Supply) (Amendment) Act 1982. Given the nature of the amendment and the size of the provision, the Office of the Parliamentary Counsel advised it was appropriate to re-state the subsection in its entirety with the new higher amount included, rather than merely providing for the insertion of the new amount. This was regarded as being consistent with the Government's 2004 White Paper *Regulating Better.*

Public service obligation levy   The Electricity Regulation Act 1999 (Public Service Obligations) (Amendment) Order 2004 (S.I. No. 174 of 2004) amended the Electricity Regulation Act 1999 (Public Service Obligations) Order 2002, which provided for the imposition on ESB of public service obligation requiring ESB to purchase, up until December 31, 2019, the output of certain peat and renewable, sustainable or alternative electricity generating stations, in the interests of security of supply and environmental protection respectively. It also provided for the introduction of a PSO (public service obligation) levy mechanism from January 1, 2003 to compensate the ESB for the additional costs incurred. This new order imposes a PSO on the ESB requiring it to purchase the output of additional renewable sustainable or alternative electricity generating stations in the interest of environmental protection and to provide for compensating it for the additional costs incurred. This Order also amended the 2002 Order to extend the closure date of the Shannonbridge U1 station to 2004.

Equality

EQUALITY ACT 2004

The Equality Act 2004 amended the Employment Equality Act 1998 (the 1998 Act) and the Equal Status Act 2000 (the 2000 Act) in order to implement the three recent EU equality Directives, Directive 2000/43/EC (the race and ethnic origin Directive), Directive 2000/78/EC (the framework employment Directive) and Directive 2002/73/EC (the gender equal treatment in employment Directive). The Directives deal with equal treatment on the grounds of gender, racial or ethnic origin, religion or belief, disability, age and sexual orientation. The race Directive, 2000/43/EC, provides a flexible general framework for combating discrimination on the grounds of racial or ethnic origin in both the employment and non-employment areas. The framework employment Directive, 2000/78/EC, provides a general framework for the prohibition of discrimination in regard to employment and occupation on the grounds of religion or belief, disability, age or sexual orientation. The gender equal treatment in employment Directive, 2002/73/EC, updates and improves the 1975 equal pay and 1976 equal treatment Directives. The 2004 Act also implemented Directive 97/80/EC, which shifts the burden of proof in gender discrimination cases, and which had already been implemented by the European Communities (Burden of Proof in Gender Discrimination Cases) Regulations 2001 (S.I. No.337 of 2001). The provisions of the Directives dealing with occupational pensions were implemented in the Social Welfare (Miscellaneous Provisions) Act 2004 (discussed in the Social Welfare chapter, p.449, below). For an excellent overview, see Kerr, Annotations, Irish Current Law Statutes Annotated. For a critical analysis, see Irish Human Rights Commission, Observations on the Equality Bill 2004 available at www.ihrc.ie/documents.

Alignment of 1998 and 2000 Acts The 2004 Act aligns, as far as possible, the provisions of the 1998 Act and the 2000 Act, for example, by the extension of the definition of discrimination under the 1998 Act to include discrimination by association or imputation, as was the case under the 2000 Act, and extension of sexual harassment under the 1998 Act to encompass same-sex sexual harassment, as under the 2000 Act. The 1998 Act was also amended to incorporate the provisions of the gender Directive, which reflect the case law of the European Court of Justice on discrimination on the grounds of pregnancy or maternity leave, within the meaning of the Maternity Protection Acts 1994 and 2004. On the burden of proof in discrimination cases, it was noted that the

1997 Directive applies to gender discrimination only, but the race and framework employment Directives extend this rule to the circumstances covered by them. The 2004 Act shifts the burden in cases involving all nine grounds, including the original ground of gender.

SCOPE OF CHANGES TO EMPLOYMENT EQUALITY ACT 1998

Part 2 of the 2004 Act, ss.3 to 46, amended the Employment Equality Act 1998. Section 3 of the 2004 Act makes a significant extension to the scope of the 1998 Act by amending the definition of "contract of employment" in s.2 of the 1998 Act, to include contracts to personally execute work or services and to deem references under the 1998 Act to employees or employers to include the parties to such contracts. As a result, persons who are or were employed under a contract personally to execute any work or labour, as well as partners and former partners in firms, are protected from discrimination. Section 7 of the 2004 Act inserts a new s.13A into the 1998 Act to include the self-employed and partnerships in its scope. Section 13A includes a specific provision in respect of partners within partnerships, including general partners within limited partnerships. Section 13A deems references to employees to include reference to partners and references to employers to include reference to partnerships. Similarly, the 2004 Act removed broad exclusions concerning private households by amending the definition of "employee" in s.2 of the 1998 Act to include, where the context admits, members or former members of a regulatory body and to exclude, only in so far as access to employment is concerned, persons employed in the provision of personal home services affecting the private or family life of those concerned. Thus, ss.26 and 37 of the 1998 Act and s.6 of the 2000 Act were amended and replaced with provisions which relate specifically to access to employment involving the provision of personal services and the provision of accommodation in a person's home, where the private or family life of those concerned is affected. This was intended to provide for balance between the protection of privacy and equal treatment. It should be noted that the failure to include all aspects of employment in a domestic context, particularly employment by close relatives, was criticised by the Irish Human Rights Commission, particularly as this failure may breach obligations under, for example, the 1996 Revised European Social Charter. The 2004 Act also provides for revision of some of the categories of exclusion which were originally allowed under the 1998 Act, so that there are no longer blanket-type exclusions in the case of employment in the Garda Síochána and Prison Service, such as age or height restrictions.

Less favourable treatment by imputation or association   Section 4 amended s.6 of the 1998 Act to include less favourable treatment by imputation or association with another person. This ensures comparability with the 2000 Act.

Pregnancy or maternity leave   Section 4 also inserted a new s.6(2A) into the 1998 Act to provide that less favourable treatment on a ground related to pregnancy or maternity leave comes within discrimination on the gender ground.

Age ground   Section 4 also inserted a new s.6(3) into the 1998 Act to amend significantly the existing exclusion from discrimination on the age ground in respect of persons less than 18 years, or 65 years or over. In the case of persons under 18, a provision based on the statutory age for school leavers is included in the 2004 Act, but employers may continue to set minimum recruitment ages where these do not exceed 18 years. In respect of persons over 65, no upper age threshold is provided for but compulsory retirement ages may continue to be set. A consequential amendment to s.2(1)(*b*) of the Unfair Dismissals Act 1977 was also made.

Harassment and sexual harassment   Section 8 of the 2004 Act inserts a new s.14A into the 1998 Act to deal with harassment and sexual harassment. Under the equality and race Directives, a common approach is taken to the treatment of harassment and sexual harassment on any of the discriminatory grounds. This is reflected in the new s.14A, which inserts a single provision on harassment and sexual harassment and removes the present separate provisions in s.23 (gender-related sexual harassment) and s.32 (non-gender related harassment) of the 1998 Act. As a consequence, ss.14 and 21 of the 2004 Act repealed ss.23 and 32 of the 1998 Act.

Accommodation of person with disabilities   Section 9 of the 2004 Act replaces s.16(3) of the 1998 Act dealing with the duty of employers and persons engaged in vocational training to accommodate the needs of persons with disabilities enabling those persons to access and participate in employment or training. Section 16(3) of the 1998 Act had limited the duty on employers to make "reasonable accommodation" or take "appropriate measures" where this gave rise to no more than "a nominal cost". This phrase was used by way of response to the decision of the Supreme Court in *Re the Employment Equality Bill 1996* [1997] 2 I.R. 321, which had found unconstitutional the provisions on this issue in the Employment Equality Bill 1996, which the court interpreted as imposing virtually all costs associated with this matter on employers (rather than the State, which the court felt was more appropriate, as this was a societal issue). Since s.9 of the 2004 Act implemented Art.5 of the framework employment Directive, this would appear to provide sufficient protection against any challenge. As amended, s.16 of the 1998 Act now requires the employer to take "appropriate measures" (which are not specified) "unless the measures would impose a disproportionate burden on the employer." As enacted, the amended s.16(3)(c) of the 1998 Act provides for three factors to be taken into account in determining what constitutes a "disproportionate burden" on the employer: "(i) the financial and other costs entailed, (ii) the scale and financial resources of the employer's business, and (iii) the possibility of obtaining public funding or other assistance". These factors are precisely those listed in Art.5 of the framework employment Directive. A similar amendment in respect of the provision for reasonable accommodation in the Equal Status Act 2000 is not contained in the 2004 Act. This is because since there is, as yet, no similar EU provision in the area of goods and services, the views of the Supreme Court in *Re the Equal Status Bill 1997* [1997] 2 I.R. 387 (the companion case to *Re the Employment Equality Bill 1996* [1997] 2 I.R. 321) remain a constitutional barrier to any such extension.

Compliance with statutory requirements   Section 10 amended s.17(2) and (4) of the Act of 1998, under which compliance with specified statutory provisions is excluded from discriminatory action on the grounds of race and age. Section 10 amended s.17(2) of the 1998 Act to give effect to Art.3.2 of the framework employment Directive, which excludes from its scope differences of treatment based on nationality, with particular reference to the provisions and conditions relating to the entry into and residence of third-country nationals and stateless persons in the Member States and to any treatment arising from their legal status. The exclusion will apply only to actions taken in accordance with the Employment Permits Act 2003. Section 10 also takes account of the differences of treatment on the ground of age which are permitted in accordance with Art.6 of the framework employment Directive, and allows for exclusion for compliance with the Protection of Young Persons (Employment) Act 1996, the National Minimum Wage Act 2000 or s.3 of the Redundancy Payments Act 1971, as amended.

Comparators for pregnancy or maternity   Section 11 amended s.18 of the 1998 Act, arising from the amendment made to s.6 of the 1998 Act by s.4 of the 2004 Act, allowing a comparator in the case of less favourable treatment on a ground related to pregnancy or maternity to be either male or female.

Indirect discrimination on gender: Equal remuneration   Section 12 amended s.19 of the 1998 Act on entitlement to equal remuneration. It amended the definition of indirect discrimination on the gender ground in relation to equal remuneration in s.19(4) of the Act to take account of the definition of indirect discrimination in the gender Directive. It applies to provisions which are apparently neutral and may be claimed only where the person considers that he or she has experienced discrimination. An employee or trainee will not be required to evidence his or her claim by reference to the proportion of other employees of the same gender who are similarly affected. However, either party may use statistical evidence in relation to a claim. This provision is paralleled, in the non-gender area, in s.19 of the 2004 Act, amending s.29 of the 1998 Act.

Indirect discrimination on gender generally   Section 13 amended s.22 of the 1998 Act, dealing with indirect discrimination on the gender ground other than in relation to remuneration. This parallels the amendment made by s.12 to s.19 of the 1998 Act. The separate reference to the grounds of marital and family status in s.22(4) of the 1998 Act is no longer required as a result of this amendment and was deleted.

Positive action on equal opportunities   Section 15 of the 2004 Act aligns s.24(1) of the Act of 1998, which concerns positive action on equal opportunities, more closely in line with Art.2.8 of the gender Directive.

Exclusion for genuine and determining occupational requirements Section 16 of the 2004 Act completely replaces s.25 of the Act of 1998, which permitted discrimination on the gender ground where a person's gender is "an occupational qualification". In line with Art.4 of the framework employment Directive, the new s.25 contains a more limited provision which only allows account to be taken of a characteristic which is "a genuine and determining occupational requirement for the post" and where "the objective is legitimate and the requirement proportionate". This provides a higher level of protection from discrimination on the gender ground than had previously been the case by imposing strict tests on employers in each case where it is proposed to restrict recruitment to one or other gender. As a result of this, s.18 of the 2004 Act made a further amendment to s.27 of the 1998 Act (which deals with the Garda Síochána and Prison Service) to provide that s.27 is "without prejudice to section 25" of the 1998 Act. In parallel to this amendment, s.25 of the 2004 Act amended the corresponding non-gender provision in s.37(2) of the Act of 1998, subject to certain operational requirements applicable to the Garda Síochána and the prison and emergency services. Section 37(5) of the 1998 Act continues to provide for the exemption for the Defence Forces in respect of the age and disability grounds.

Equality Tribunal   Section 30 of the 2004 Act made a number of changes to s.75 of the 1998 Act arising from the renaming of the Office of the Director of Equality Investigations as the Equality Tribunal. It also amended s.75(3) and (4) of the 1998 Act to remove references to equality officers of the Labour Relations Commission and empowers the Director of Equality Investigations to issue guidelines or guidance notes, appoint persons as equality mediation officers and delegate functions. The power to appoint mediation officers facilitates the Director in preventing any backlog building up in the Tribunal of cases which may be suitable for fast resolution by means of mediation by the appointment of additional mediation officers on a short-term contract basis from a panel of qualified and experienced non-civil servant mediators.

Redress process   Section 31 amended s.76(2)(*c*) of the 1998 Act to allow an employee claiming discrimination to seek information about the scale or resources of the employer's business, other than confidential information. Section 32 includes a number of amendments to s.77 of the 1998 Act on the operation of the redress procedures under the 1998 Act. For example, it extended the grounds on which a member of the Defence Forces may seek redress to include all the discriminatory grounds other than the grounds of age and disability. It also adds new provisions to s.77 permitting parties to any proceedings under the 1998 Act to be represented and deals with appeals in respect of decisions to accept or refuse late claims. Section 33 inserts a new s.77A into the 1998 Act dealing with dismissal of claims, allowing the Director or the Labour Court to dismiss claims considered to have been made in bad faith or to be frivolous, vexatious, misconceived or trivial. Section 35 amended s.79 of the 1998 Act so that where a set of circumstances gives rise to more than one claim of discrimination or to one or more claims of discrimination and a claim of victimisation, they can be investigated as a single case. Similarly, s.36 amends s.82 of the 1998 Act, which allows compensation to be awarded on the basis of a single case.

SCOPE OF CHANGES TO EQUAL STATUS ACT 2000

Part 3 of the 2004 Act, ss.47 to 65, amended the Equal Status Act 2000. Section 47 widens the scope of the definition of "proceedings" in s.2 of the 2000 Act to include any proceedings, including subsequent proceedings, before a person, body or court dealing with a request or referral under the 2000 Act. It also provides for the definition of a new term, "provision", meaning a term in a contract or a requirement, criterion, practice, regime, policy or condition affecting a person. It also helps to clarify the relevant date to be applied in relation to a claim of prohibited conduct.

Indirect discrimination   Section 48 amended s.3(1) of the 2000 Act by inserting a new definition of indirect discrimination to reflect the more advanced definition in the race Directive. The original s.1(3) provided generally that treating a person who has not attained the age of 18 years less favourably or more favourably than another, whatever that person's age, would not be regarded as discrimination on the age ground. It is compulsory for licensed drivers under the age of 18 to have motor insurance and it is reasonable, therefore, that such drivers be protected from unreasonable differences in treatment. In this regard, s.3(b) of the 2000 Act was amended to enable licensed drivers under the age of 18 to have recourse to the 2000 Act in cases of unreasonable treatment.

Statistical data   In addition, s.48 of the 2004 Act amended s.3 of the 2000 Act by providing that statistics are admissible for the purpose of determining whether indirect discrimination has occurred. This implemented recital 15 to the race Directive, which provides that, in accordance with the rules of national law or practice, such rules may provide, in particular, for indirect discrimination to be established by any means, including on the basis of statistical evidence.

Educational grants   Section 50 amended s.7 of the 2000 Act to provide that the Minister for Education and Science does not discriminate where, in exercising his or her powers, he or she prescribes requirements for the making of grants for the purpose of assisting persons to attend, or continue to attend, an educational establishment providing higher or further education which confine the making of such grants to persons who are nationals of a Member State of the European Union or allow for difference of treatment between those who are nationals of Member States and those who are not.

Harassment   Section 51 redefines harassment as any form of unwanted conduct related to any of the discriminatory grounds, and defines sexual harassment as any form of unwanted verbal, non-verbal or physical conduct of a sexual nature. It also provides that a person's rejection of, or submission to, sexual or other harassment may not be used by any other person as a basis for a decision affecting that person. These changes reflect the newer definitions set out in the relevant Directive.

Immigration and residency   Section 52 amended s.14 of the 2000 Act to provide for an exclusion from the provisions of the 2000 Act of actions taken by public authorities relating to specified persons and governing or arising from their entry into and residence in the State, as permitted under Art.3 of the race Directive. This is confined to cases of asylum and immigration and differences of treatment in the provision of public services to asylum seekers and those not lawfully resident in the State. Otherwise, the 2000 Act will apply to differences of treatment based on nationality.

Redress procedure   Section 53 extended the definition of complainant in s.20 of the 2000 act to allow a parent or guardian of a complainant with an intellectual or psychological disability to act in place of the person concerned. Section 54 amended s.21 of the 2000 Act concerning the operation of the redress procedures under the 2000 Act. Section 55 inserted a new s.21A into the 2000 Act to provide clarification that the date on which a claim or appeal is lodged is the date it is received by the Director or Circuit Court. Section 56 provides for an amendment to s.22 of the 2000 Act to enable the Director to dismiss a claim because it has been made in bad faith or is frivolous, vexatious or misconceived or relates to a trivial matter. Comparable changes to those made to the 1998 Act concerning the consolidation of claims into a single set of proceedings are also provided for. Section 60 inserts a new s.38A into the 2000 Act to take account of Art.8 of the race Directive. It provides that the burden of proof is placed on the respondent where a prima facie case of discrimination under any of the nine discriminatory grounds has been established by the complainant.

Equity

HILARY DELANY, Law School, Trinity College, Dublin

INTERLOCUTORY INJUNCTIONS

The well-established principles governing the grant of interlocutory injunctions have once again been applied in a number of cases this year, although the courts continue to recognise the fact that there are certain defined situations in which their application is not appropriate.

In *Mullarkey v Irish National Stud Company Ltd*, High Court, Kelly J., June 30, 2004, the plaintiff sought interlocutory injunctions requiring that his salary be paid to him, pending trial, whilst on sick-leave for a period in excess of that for which the defendant was prepared to allow. Kelly J. stated that he had to consider whether a fair case could be made, based on the wording of the contractual arrangements between the plaintiff and the defendant for the existence of an implied term entitling the plaintiff to payment of his salary when incapacitated by illness for a term in excess of the 13-week period conceded by the defendant. He further stated that the court could only conclude that the plaintiff had made out a fair case if it were of the view that there was a reasonable prospect that at trial the trial judge, having regard to all of the circumstances, might imply such a term into the contract of employment. Kelly J. concluded that, on balance, it appeared to him that a fair case had been made out by the plaintiff to support the claim that, in the context of a manager employed by the defendant, a reasonable time could be interpreted as a period of full pay whilst on sick-leave for a period in excess of 13 weeks, particularly as that the defendant operated in the public sector. Given this conclusion, Kelly J. stated that he must next ask whether damages would be an adequate remedy for the plaintiff. He concluded that damages would not constitute an adequate remedy because the plaintiff had ongoing financial obligations which would fail to be met and therefore could not await an award of damages which might ultimately be obtained at trial. In these circumstances, Kelly J. held that the balance of convenience was in favour of the grant, rather than the refusal, of the injunction. From the defendant's point of view the only inconvenience arising from the granting of the injunction was the payment of a definite sum of money for a defined period of time, whilst the inconvenience to the plaintiff if the injunction were refused was far greater. Therefore, Kelly J. held that the injunction should be granted.

A less positive outcome, from the plaintiff's point of view, was reached in

Orr v Zomax Ltd (High Court, Carroll J., March 25, 2004), in which the plaintiff sought a declaration that the purported termination of his position as client services manager with the defendant company for reasons of redundancy was invalid. He also sought, *inter alia*, an injunction restraining the purported termination of his employment and an injunction restraining the performance of his functions and duties by any person other than him. In addition, he sought an order that the defendant continue to pay his salary until the trial of the action. The circumstances of the purported termination were as follows. The defendant had announced a reorganisation of company structures, which involved the creation of a new position—business relationship manager—which amalgamated the position of client services manager (held by the plaintiff) and the position of contract centre manager. The plaintiff applied for this new position, but was unsuccessful. On foot of this he was informed that he was being made redundant, whereupon he instituted proceedings seeking declaratory and injunctive relief. The plaintiff claimed that the issue to be tried was that he had been unfairly dismissed on the grounds that there was no valid redundancy and that he had really been dismissed as a result of criticisms previously levelled against him.

Carroll J. stated that in deciding whether to grant interlocutory injunctive relief the guiding principles are those set out in *Campus Oil v Minister for Industry and Energy (No.2)* [1983] I.R. 88, namely that there must be a fair issue to be tried, that damages must not be an adequate remedy and that the balance of convenience must favour the granting of the injunction. In the instant case it was submitted on behalf of the defendant that there was not a fair issue to be tried as unfair dismissal is governed by the Unfair Dismissals Acts, which provide a statutory remedy that is mutually exclusive to the common law remedy for damages. Having referred to the decision of the Supreme Court in *Parsons v Iarnród Éireann* [1997] E.L.R. 203 and of the House of Lords in *Johnson v Unisys Ltd* [2001] 2 All E.R. 801, Carroll J. stated that these decisions illustrated that the common law claim for damages for wrongful dismissal and the statutory claim for unfair dismissal were mutually exclusive, therefore she concluded that it was not open to the plaintiff to argue that the principles applicable under the statutory scheme should be imported into the common law. She continued by saying that in the event that she was wrong to hold that there was not a fair issue to be tried, she would go on to consider whether damages would be an adequate remedy. Carroll J. stated that, in her opinion, they would be adequate. In her view the plaintiff could not seriously hope that he would be re-instated in employment in circumstances where the defendants were unwilling to take him back and had no position for him. Accordingly, his remedy, if he were successful, would be in damages.

Carroll J. then stated—again on the assumption that she might be wrong in her earlier finding—that she would consider whether a mandatory injunction should be made requiring the defendant to pay the plaintiff's salary over and above the period of notice. She noted that the plaintiff had been given one month's extra notice and pay over and above the two months provided for in his contract and moreover that if the plaintiff did not succeed, there would be a real injustice to the defendant if it was obliged to pay him his salary until the date of the trial. Having referred to the relevant authorities, Carroll J. suggested that the position *vis-à-vis* such payment had apparently moved from being appropriate in either special or exceptional circumstances to being a "well established practice". However, she stated that in her view cases where there was no suggestion of a breakdown of trust or confidence had no relevance to this case, nor had those cases where there was alleged breach of a fixed-term contract. She pointed to the fact that in his grounding affidavit the plaintiff had sought reinstatement only and had not alleged irreparable loss and damage if deprived of his salary. Carroll J. held that in her view the plaintiff had not made out a case on the balance of convenience that he should be paid his salary after the period of notice had expired, and that it would constitute a serious injustice for the defendant if it was obliged to pay his salary until the trial of the action. It followed that there was no justification for permitting the performance of functions and duties by the plaintiff, or for restraining the performance of those functions and duties by any person other than the plaintiff. Carroll J. concluded that the most appropriate course of action in the circumstances was to have an early trial and suggested that, provided the pleadings were complete and the case was ready for trial, it could be given priority in the list to fix dates at the end of the following term.

It is clear from the decision of Laffoy J. in *Miss World Ltd v Miss Ireland Beauty Pageant Ltd*, High Court, Laffoy J., February 10, 2004, that she approved of the idea that in considering where the balance of convenience lies, the adequacy of damages is a very important element and indeed may frequently be the decisive element. In this case the plaintiffs sought an interlocutory injunction restraining the defendants from passing off any of their events as or for, or as being associated with the plaintiffs' Miss Ireland Pageant, and certain ancillary interlocutory orders. Laffoy J. stated that it was the function of the court to first ascertain whether the plaintiffs had raised a fair and bona fide question to be tried. If they had, the court must then determine whether, in the event of being refused an injunction and succeeding in the action, the plaintiffs would be adequately compensated by damages. If they would not be so compensated, the court must then determine whether, in the event of the injunction being granted and the plaintiffs failing to succeed in the action, the defendants would be adequately compensated by damages. Finally, the court must consider whether the balance of convenience lay in favour of granting or refusing the injunction.

Laffoy J. stated that the wrong the plaintiffs contended the court ought to intervene to remedy is passing off, and she referred to the three-part test formulated by Lord Oliver in *Reckitt & Colman Products Ltd v Borden Inc.* [1990] 1 All E.R. 873, 880. First, in relation to the goods or services that he supplies, the plaintiff must establish a goodwill or reputation in the mind of the purchasing public by association with the identifying "get-up". Secondly, he must demonstrate a misrepresentation by the defendant, which would lead, or be likely to lead, the public to believe that goods or services offered by the defendant were the goods or services of the plaintiff. Thirdly, he must demonstrate that he has suffered or, in a *quia timet* action, that he is likely to suffer damage by reason of the erroneous belief engendered by the defendant's misrepresentation that the source of the defendant's goods or services is the same as the source of those offered by the plaintiff.

On the first point, Laffoy J. concluded that there was a fair and bona fide issue to be tried on whether there was goodwill attached to the plaintiffs' Miss Ireland Pageant in the mind of the public by association with the name "Miss Ireland", which is recognised by the public as attaching specifically to the plaintiffs' national pageant in Ireland. In addition, she said that it seemed to her that the plaintiffs had established that there was a fair and bona fide question to be tried concerning the potential for the public to confuse the defendants' business with the plaintiffs' business. Finally, she stated that it appeared that the plaintiffs had established that there was a fair and bona fide question to be tried that their goodwill was likely to be affected adversely if the defendants ran a pageant that, of itself, would give rise to an assumption of resulting damage. Laffoy J. then quoted from the judgment of McCracken J. in *B & S Ltd v Irish Autotrader Ltd* [1995] 2 I.R.142 as follows:

> "While Lord Diplock only used the phrase, 'balance of convenience' when considering the position if damages were not an adequate remedy for either party, I would be more inclined to the view that the entire test rests on a balance of convenience, but that the adequacy of damages is a very important element, and may frequently be the decisive element in considering where the balance of convenience lies."

Laffoy J. added that she respectfully agreed with this statement. In considering whether the plaintiffs could be adequately compensated by an award of damages, Laffoy J. concluded that it seemed to her that it would be impossible, not merely difficult, to quantify in damages a loss of the nature which the plaintiffs might suffer if the defendants were permitted to run a rival Miss Ireland Pageant. However, she also concluded that the loss the defendants would suffer if prevented from using the name "Miss Ireland" in connection with their pageant, and it transpired that they should not have been so prevented, would also be impossible to quantify. Therefore, she stated that the granting or refusal of an interlocutory injunction would have to be decided on the basis of the balance of convenience. In this instance, Laffoy J. held that the balance of convenience lay in favour of the plaintiffs because the first-named plaintiff had been in the market place in its own right, either directly or through franchisees, for over 50 years and had run a Miss Ireland Pageant each year during that period. The second-named defendant had not been in the market place other than as a franchisee of the first-named plaintiff: the defendants had never run a Miss Ireland Pageant in their own right. Laffoy J. therefore granted interlocutory relief to the plaintiffs.

Well-established principles were again applied in *Cavankee Fishing Co. Ltd v Minister for Communication, Marine and Natural Resources*, High Court, Kelly J., March 4, 2004, in which the defendant minister had given a written policy directive to the second-named defendant in accordance with s.3 of the Fisheries (Amendment) Act 2003. Reasons given for this new policy included the Government Programme, the provisions of Council Regulation (EC) 2371/2002 and a comprehensive review of the situation of the Irish fishing fleet and related capacity. The plaintiff owners of fishing vessels questioned the legality of para.H of the ministerial policy directive, the essence of their complaint being that while replacement capacity had been a feature of the Common Fisheries Policy of the European Community for some years, the new requirement that they decommission dormant, off-register capacity at the prescribed ratio in an entirely different segment of the Irish fleet was unacceptable. Accordingly, they sought an injunction restraining the defendants from applying para.H of the policy directive to their vessels until the outcome of the proceedings. The plaintiffs contended that they had shown a serious issue to be tried, that damages would not constitute an adequate remedy and that the balance of convenience lay in favour of the grant, rather than the refusal, of the injunction sought.

Kelly J. stated that the defendants had made strong arguments to the effect that the plaintiffs did not have any serious issue for trial, adding that if the defendants were correct in that contention, then no question of an injunction could arise. He decided not to express any view on this question and held that for the purposes of the judgment he was prepared to assume, without deciding the matter, that the plaintiffs did have a serious issue for trial in relation to at least some of the arguments they had made in relation to para.H. Kelly J. then considered whether damages would constitute an adequate remedy for the plaintiffs if no interlocutory injunction were granted but they subsequently succeeded at trial. He stated that he was quite satisfied that the damage suffered by the plaintiffs could be quantified as the loss they had allegedly suffered was clearly a commercial loss. Kelly J. added that there was no doubt about the capacity of the defendants to pay any damages awarded against them. That being the case, he was satisfied that damages would be an adequate remedy. He maintained that it would not be difficult to assess such damages in the instant case, but even if it were, he would have to take into account the assertion of Finlay C.J. in *Curust Financial Services v Loewe-Lack-Werk* [1994] 1 I.R. 450, to the effect that difficulty, as distinct from complete impossibility in the assessment of damages, should not be a ground for characterising the awarding of damages an inadequate remedy.

Kelly J. then stated that if he were wrong in reaching this conclusion, he would consider the question of the balance of convenience. He noted that the plaintiffs sought only to suspend para.H of the policy for the purposes of an application for vessel registration and pointed out that even if the relevant paragraph were suspended, the remainder of the policy would remain in place. In these circumstances Kelly J. held that he could not see how the plaintiffs would benefit from the order they were seeking. He said that he would also bear in mind that what was being sought was to suspend a provision of a policy that had been specifically provided for by the 2003 Act, which had been formulated by the Minister and laid before both Houses of the National Parliament. Kelly J. stressed that he was not suggesting that the court would be powerless to intervene to prevent the implementation of such a policy in a suitable case, but he expressed the view that the jurisdiction was one that had to be exercised sparingly and only in a very clear case. In this case it would have the effect of requiring the second-named defendant to effectively ignore such a policy in circumstances where it had not been condemned, and Kelly J. referred to the following comments made by Murphy J. in *Riordan v Ireland (No.6)* [2002] 4 I.R. 404:

> "This court would find it difficult to imagine any circumstances in which a public official would be directed by means of interlocutory mandatory order to carry out an act which would be in direct breach of the express terms of legislative provisions unless and until those provisions have been condemned by a court of competent jurisdiction."

While Kelly J. acknowledged that the injunction sought in the case before him was not mandatory, the effect of it would be to require the second-named defendant to consider an application for registration without the provisions of para.H, before the court had had an opportunity of deciding whether that paragraph should be condemned or not. He concluded that, given these considerations and the fact that the grant of the injunction sought would have the effect of placing the State in breach of its EU legal obligations, he was quite satisfied that despite the losses allegedly being suffered by the plaintiffs the balance of convenience lay against, rather than in favour of, an injunction being granted and he refused the relief sought.

Traditional principles were also followed in *Dublin City Council v McGrath* (High Court, Carroll J., March 12, 2004), although Carroll J. made it clear that preserving the status quo is not always desirable where an interlocutory injunction is sought. In this case the plaintiff sought a mandatory order that the defendant deliver up vacant possession of her flat in a Ballymun tower block, which was due to be demolished as part of the Ballymun Regeneration Programme. After failing in attempts to reach an agreement with the defendant by offering her alternative accommodation, in November 2003 the council gave notice to quit and the defendant was classified as a trespasser by the time the proceedings were brought. At the outset, Carroll J. stated that she would prefer to treat the application as one seeking an injunction to restrain trespass because the plenary summons claimed damages on this basis. She stated that an application for an interlocutory injunction must be considered in the light of the principles laid down in *Campus Oil v Minister for Industry and Energy (No. 2)* [1983] I.R. 88, *i.e.* that to succeed in obtaining an injunction there must be a fair question to be tried, damages must not be an adequate remedy and the balance of convenience must be in favour of granting the injunction.

The defendant submitted that the status quo must be preserved, citing the passage in *Campus Oil* at p.106, where O'Higgins C.J. stated that, "interlocutory relief is intended to keep matters *in status quo* until the trial and to do no more". Carroll J. said that while the court will generally preserve the status quo, in her opinion the court was not constrained *ab initio* from considering whether an injunction should be granted. She accepted that there were a number of issues to be tried at the hearing of the action, including whether the council had failed to deal properly with the question of whether the defendant should have been moved to the top of the medical priority list for rehousing due to her son's ill-health, and whether the State had failed to respect the private and family life and home of the defendant under Art.5 of the European Convention on Human Rights. Having considered the issue of damages, Carroll J. concluded that she was satisfied that damages would not be an adequate remedy for the council.

In relation to the balance of convenience, Carroll J. stated there were many weighty reasons why the council required possession of the tower block. The balance of convenience for the defendant, on the other hand, was that she wanted to be rehoused in an area of her choice; she was not defending a home in which she wished to stay. In the view of Carroll J., the conditions in which the defendant was currently living in the tower block threatened the health and safety of her and her son and she pointed to the fact that the defendant had been offered reasonable alternative accommodation elsewhere. She concluded that the balance of convenience was very much in favour of the council and therefore granted an injunction to restrain trespass by the defendant in the tower block, subject to the defendant being given a temporary tenancy in the area in premises made available by the council.

It has been confirmed by Laffoy J. in *Coalport Building Co. Ltd v Castle Contracts (Ireland) Ltd* (High Court, Laffoy J., January 19, 2004) that where an interlocutory injunction is sought to restrain the presentation of a petition for the winding up of a company, different principles of those laid down in the *Campus Oil* case apply. Laffoy J. stated that where it is sought to restrain the presentation of a winding up petition the principles applicable are well settled and were set out by Keane J., as he then was, in *Truck and Machinery Sales Ltd v Marubeni Komatzo Ltd* [1996] 1 I.R. 12. She quoted the following fundamental principle, stated by Keane J. at p.24 in the following terms:

> "It is clear that where a company in good faith and on substantial grounds, disputes *any* liability in respect of the alleged debt, the petition

will be dismissed, or if the matter is brought before the court before the petition is issued, its presentation will in normal circumstances be restrained. This is on the ground that a winding up petition is not a legitimate means of seeking to enforce payment of a debt which is *bona fide* disputed."

As Laffoy J. pointed out, that was the factual position in the case before the Court in *Coalport Building*, and the plaintiff disputed any liability in respect of the sum claimed by the defendant. The issue that therefore arose was whether the plaintiff was acting in good faith in and had substantial grounds for disputing the alleged debt. She referred further to the dicta of Keane J., to the effect that the power to restrain proceedings should be exercised only where the plaintiff company has established at least a prima facie case that its presentation would constitute an abuse of process. Keane J. had added that in many cases a prima facie case would be established where the plaintiff adduced evidence that satisfied the court that the petition was bound to fail, or at least that a suitable alternative remedy was available.

It was submitted on behalf of the defendant that there was not a genuine, bona fide dispute in relation to the alleged debt. However, Laffoy J. made reference to the fact that liability for the debt had been immediately disputed when the formal demand was issued, and that before the petition had been issued the plaintiff's solicitors had put on the record the basis of the plaintiff's defence to the claim. In addition, the plaintiff had suggested an alternative remedy to the bringing of a petition to wind up the company, *i.e.* that the defendant could sue for the alleged debt. Laffoy J. stated that the plaintiff's solicitors had authority to accept service of proceedings for recovery of the alleged debt and that it had also being indicated to the court that they had authority to lodge the amount of the alleged debt in court as security, pending the resolution of the proceedings. In these circumstances she said that it seemed to her that there was a suitable alternative remedy available to the defendant, and it was therefore unnecessary to put the existence of a substantial building company and employer at risk.

Laffoy J. concluded that an order would be issued restraining the defendant from taking any steps to advertise or otherwise publicise a petition for the purpose of seeking the winding up of the plaintiff company, until further order from the court, on condition that the plaintiff lodged a sum of money in court as security for the alleged debt.

European Union Law

EUROPEAN PARLIAMENT ELECTIONS

The European Parliament Elections (Amendment) Act 2004 amended the European Parliament Elections Act 1997 primarily to amend the boundaries of the constituencies for which candidates are elected from the State to the Parliament of the European Communities. The 2004 Act, which implemented recommendations of the Boundary Commission in this respect, also provided for amendments to the number of members to be elected for these Euro constituencies. The 2004 act also gave effect to Council Decision 2002/772 amending the Act concerning the election of the representatives of the European Parliament by direct universal suffrage. The 2004 Act came into effect on February 27, 2004 and the constituency changes it effected applied to the elections to the European Parliament held in 2004.

Family Law

CHILDREN

In the chapter on Information Law and the Ombudsman, below, p.321, Estelle Feldman analyses *N. McK. v Information Commissioner*, High Court, January 14, 2004, in which Quirke J. interpreted s.28(b) of the Freedom of Information Act 1997 as involving a rebuttable presumption that the best interests of children would be served by giving their parents access to records containing personal information. We limit ourselves here to a few observations.

First, the Supreme Court decision of *North Western Health Board v HW* [2001] 3 I.R. 622 (analysed in the *Annual Review of Irish Law 2001*, pp.316–338), on which Quirke J. placed strong reliance, was concerned with parental decision-making, not with the disclosure of confidential information by third parties to parents. It is one thing to presume that decisions made by parents about their children are in their best interests; it is another to presume that the desire of a parent to acquire knowledge of confidential information regarding their children is necessarily in the best interests of the children. Of course parents can make the argument, as the plaintiff did in the instant case, that access to this information may assist them in their decision-making about their children's health and general welfare, but there is a gap between situations where this may be helpful and the *a priori* proposition that parents are simply entitled to breach confidentiality in every case by invoking the theoretical possibility that disclosure may assist them in their decision-making relating to their children's welfare. This is the distinction which the Information Commissioner was seeking to draw in her decision. Quirke J.'s holding makes no attempt to find a base on any specific need or benefit associated with disclosure. Rather, he adopts the presumption *a priori*, while accepting the possibility of its rebuttal in specific cases.

There was a difficult element in the instant case. In 1993, during family law proceedings between himself and his wife "an allegation was made" that the applicant had abused his daughter in 1991 when she was three years old. The applicant vigorously denied this allegation at all stages and a Garda investigation concluded that there was no evidence to warrant a prosecution. The applicant was seeking access to "joint personal information" which was confined solely to material relating to his daughter and himself. Quirke J. considered that, although the complaint against the applicant had been made, it remained unsubstantiated and the applicant came before the court "enjoying the presumption of innocence which is enjoyed by every citizen of the State".

Let us imagine a more troublesome situation, where a parent has been prosecuted for incest and has been acquitted because of some procedural technicality. The presumption of innocence applies to that parent, as it does to the applicant in the instant case, but should hospital authorities be obliged to hand over joint personal information to that parent simply on the basis of that presumption? Surely, at some point, suspicious circumstances have to count in determining what is in the best interests of a child?

Finally, we may note the lack of extended discussion in Quirke J.'s judgment of the rights (as opposed simply to the best interests) of the child. A child has a range of rights in the zone of the child's dignity and privacy. Parents are not automatically entitled to violate the privacy and confidentiality of their children by the simple invocation of the mantra of the children's best interests. This general theme is well discussed by Finlay Geoghegan J. in *Re EO, a Minor and MO, a Minor; FN and EB v CO, HO and EK*, High Court, March 26, 2004, analysed immediately below.

One should not minimise in any way the serious responsibilities falling on parents as guardians of their children to exercise that role conscientiously and the corresponding entitlements that this involves. Nor is there any easy solution for courts in seeking to balance these parental functions with the emergence into full autonomy of their children. It is, nonetheless, respectfully suggested that the *a priori,* albeit rebuttable, presumption of parental entitlement to access to joint personal information in relation to children tilts the preference for parental rights too far.

None of these observations is intended to cast doubt on the holding in the instant case, which seems well justified on the evidence.

In *Re EO, a Minor and MO, a Minor; FN and EB v CO, HO and EK*, High Court, March 26, 2004, Finlay Geoghegan J. adopted a novel approach to the question of the entitlement to a child to have his or her views heard and heeded in guardianship proceedings affecting the child's welfare. Section 25 of the Guardianship of Infants Act 1964 requires the court, "as it thinks appropriate and practicable having regard to the age and understanding of the child, [to] take into account the child's wishes on the matter". This is a relatively mild obligation, since it leaves a very considerable discretion to the court, not merely to make empirical assessments about the particular child's "understanding", but also to make value judgments on the crucial questions of how age and maturity should affect the child's entitlement to be heard and (a separate question) to be heeded by the court.

In the instant case Finlay Geoghegan J. injected a new element into the court's responsibility under s.25. Acknowledging that any decision taken by the court would have to be "in accordance with the principles of constitutional justice", as first mentioned by Walsh J. in *East Donegal Co-operative Ltd v Attorney General* [1970] I.R. 317 at 341, Finlay Geoghegan J. went on to observe that it was:

"also well established that an individual in respect of whom a decision of importance is being taken, such as those taken by the courts to which s.3 of the Act of 1964 applies has a personal right within the meaning of Article 40.3 of the Constitution to have such decision taken in accordance with the principles of constitutional justice. Such principles of constitutional justice appear to me to include the right of a child, whose age and understanding is such that the court considers it appropriate to take into account his/her wishes, to have such wishes taken into account by a court in taking a decision to which s.3 of the Act of 1964 applies. Hence s.25 should be construed as enacted for the purpose of *inter alia* giving effect to the procedural right guaranteed by Article 40.3 to children of a certain age and understanding to have their wishes taken into account by a court in making a decision under the Act of 1964, relating to the guardianship, custody or upbringing of the child."

This passage merits close scrutiny, both for what it says and for what it does not say. First, it identifies in a child, about whom "a decision of importance" is being taken, the right to invoke the principles of constitutional justice in respect of the decision-making process. Note that this recognises children as rights-holders, on an equal basis with adults when it comes to the application of the principles of constitutional justice to them; it does not necessarily mean that compliance with these principles entails ignoring differences of physical or moral capacity related to age and maturity. Note also that Finlay Geoghegan J. does not commit herself to the proposition that constitutional justice involves the right of all children to be heard, even though one of the central principles of constitutional justice is that of *audi alteram partem*.

In *Re EOA, a Minor and MOA, a Minor; FN v CO*, High Court, March 26, 2004, Finlay Geoghegan J. addressed, but was not ultimately required to resolve, the question whether the strong and controversial interpretation of s.3 of the Guardianship of Infants Act 1964 in *Re J.H., an Infant* [1985] I.R. 375 as involving a constitutional presumption that the welfare of the child was to be found within the family save for compelling reasons or in exceptional cases had been modified by *Re Article 26 and the Adoption (No. 2) Bill 1987* [1989] I.R. 656. In the instant case, the maternal grandparents of children whose mother had died were appointed guardians under s.8(2) of the 1964 Act. In a dispute as to custody with the children's father, Finlay Geoghegan J. found that there were compelling reasons why the welfare of the children could not be achieved by living with their father. She therefore awarded custody to the grandparents. The question as to whether the principle stated in *Re J.H., an Infant* still retained its full force and did not need to be resolved but Finlay Geoghegan J. called attention to the fact that the principle had been expressly stated to apply "in this case" and that reference had been made to the very young age of the child involved in the proceedings, who was just over two years old. In telegraphed language, Finlay Geoghegan J. thus succeeded in modifying the worst excesses of the principle.

NULLITY OF MARRIAGE

Informed consent If the law on nullity of marriage is to retain any credibility it simply cannot expand so as to enable, or require, the court to grant a decree in an uncontested case where the petitioner proves in evidence some aspect of the respondent's character or personal biography which came as an unpleasant surprise. Yet in *M. O'M. v B. O'C.* [1996] 1 I.R. 208, the Supreme Court ventured close enough to that position. The husband in this case had failed to tell his wife before they were married that he had attended a psychiatrist on several occasions over a period of six years. Blayney J. (Hamilton C.J. and O'Flaherty J. concurring) stated:

> "So the issue comes down to this: Was this a relevant circumstance such that the failure to disclose it meant that the wife did not have adequate knowledge so that her consent lacked the quality of an informed consent? It seems to me that the answer must be that it was a relevant circumstance.
>
> The test is subjective. Because of this, great weight must be attached to the wife's evidence that had she known that the husband had attended [the psychiatrist] for approximately six years she would not have married him. It is possible that another person would not have reacted in the same way, but this was the wife's evidence of how she would have reacted if she had known and this was accepted by the learned trial judge. For her, accordingly, the fact that the husband had attended [the psychiatrist] was a circumstance which would have influenced her in making up her mind. And it could not be said that it was not a circumstance of substance. Apart altogether from any question of psychiatric illness - and there was no evidence that the husband had ever suffered from such an illness - a person's mental health or mental stability is obviously a matter of great importance and anything which might throw doubt upon it calls for serious consideration.
>
> Because of this, the husband ought to have told the wife that he had attended [the psychiatrist]. His failure to do so deprived her of knowledge of a circumstance which was clearly relevant to the decision she was making.
>
> For these reasons I would allow the wife's appeal and declare that her marriage was null and void by reason of the fact that her consent to it was not an informed consent."

Two aspects of this approach are a source of concern. The first is the court's willingness to grant an annulment on the basis of lack of informed consent on "a matter of great importance" or "a circumstance which was clearly relevant to the decision" to marry the other party. The generality of the type of circumstance that might be sufficiently relevant to constitute a test of the validity of the marriage is striking. The second is the adoption of the subjective test. This means that a petitioner could claim that, *for him or her*, the particular circumstance was more important than for most other people. The effect is to dilute still further the stringency of the test.

In *P.F. v G.O'N (otherwise G.F.)*, Supreme Court, November 28, 2004, a differently constituted Supreme Court sought to distance itself from *M. O'M. v B. O'C.* The case concerned a wife who had engaged in sexual relations with another man before and after the marriage. O'Higgins J. declined to grant a decree of nullity on the basis of the husband's lack of informed consent and the Supreme Court affirmed his decision. In an elaborate and strongly reasoned judgment, with which Murray and Geoghegan JJ. concurred, McGuinness J. reviewed the authorities in detail. She stated:

> "The formulation of the need for an informed consent by Blayney J. in *M.O'M. v B.O'C.* as contended for by the petitioner would appear to be so wide as to cover almost any situation where a petitioner has at the time of the marriage lacked relevant information on a matter of substance concerning the conduct, character or circumstances of the respondent, and that this will ground a decree of nullity. This, it appears, would apply regardless of whether or not the information had been deliberately concealed by the respondent. The test is subjective. Presumably all that would be required would be for the petitioner to give evidence that he or she would not have married the respondent had this information been available before the marriage. One has only to formulate the test in this way to realise that it could readily give rise to an undue widening of the grounds for nullity which would lead to precisely the type of difficulty so well set out by Sir. F.H. Jeune P. in *Moss v Moss*:
>
> > '… To assent to the proposition for which the petitioner contends would be to introduce into a law which now is, and beyond question should be, and believed to be certain, a new principle not resting on any sound basis, and, develop as it must in several directions, sure to give rise to many doubts and much confusion.'
>
> This cannot have been the intention of Blayney J. in *M.O'M. v. B. O'C.* I must conclude that the case of *M.O'M v B. O'C.* should be distinguished from the present case on the facts and on the particular nature of the information involved which gave rise to considerations of inherent disposition and mental stability. I respectfully agree with O'Higgins J. that it cannot be extended to cover concealed misconduct and other forms of misrepresentation."

McGuinness J. went on to place the issue in a constitutional context:

> "The courts have always stressed the necessity for certainty in marriage,
> as did the learned judge in *Moss v. Moss*. This is reinforced ... by Article
> 41.3.1 of Bunreacht na hEireann:
>> 'The State pledges itself to guard with special care the institution
>> of marriage, on which the family is founded, and to protect it against
>> attack.'
> The introduction of a ground for nullity which, taken to its logical
> conclusion, could bring uncertainty into a wide variety of marriages is
> not only undesirable as a matter of public policy but is contrary to the
> clear intention of Article 41.1.3."

It is worth noting here another decision of the Supreme Court, also in 2004,
seemingly in an entirely different context. In *CK v JK,* Supreme Court, March
31, 2004, which we analyse in detail above, p.147, Murray J. invoked Art.41.3
of the Constitution in support of the argument that a person who is deceived
into believing himself or herself to be lawfully married to another should be
entitled to obtain monetary compensation from the deceiving party in the form
of a tort action for fraudulent misrepresentation. Would it be stretching Murray
C.J.'s analysis too far to ask whether the action for deceit should logically be
extended to the benefit of those who enter not merely bigamously void
marriages, as a result of misrepresentation, but also marriages that are not
capable of being annulled (by virtue of the principles laid down in *P.F. v G.O'N
(otherwise G.F.)*) but which nonetheless were entered into as a result of a
serious misrepresentation?

In *L.B. v T. MacC.*, High Court, December 20, 2004, the petitioner sought
an annulment on the basis of the fraud and lack of capacity of the respondent
to maintain a normal marital relationship with her. The respondent did not
defend the proceedings; O'Higgins J. was satisfied that no question of collusion
arose. The petitioner was a successful professional. The respondent was a less
successful partner in a firm of chartered surveyors in Scotland. The marriage
took place in 1993. The respondent's professional and business life after the
marriage was unsuccessful. He left his practice in 1994 and became a
considerable financial drain on his wife's resources. He became involved in a
series of unsuccessful business enterprises. The wife's refusal to go guarantor
for security of £150,000 for a fast food franchise in which he wished to invest
was in her view "what eventually brought an end to the marriage" in 1997.

O'Higgins J. considered it:

> "difficult to avoid the conclusion that the constant financial demands
> of the respondent were a real factor in the failure of the marriage and
> although the respondent was unsuccessful in his business endeavours
> during the marriage I am satisfied that his financial dependency on the

petitioner was not deliberate. The evidence does not disclose that the respondent was incapable of earning a living or keeping a job by virtue of his personality. Had circumstances been different he may well have been successful in business. The financial dependency issue in this case is not in my view of assistance, in assessing the respondent's ability to contract to a valid marriage."

A psychiatrist was appointed to carry out a psychiatric examination of the petitioner and of the respondent and to report to the court. He interviewed the petitioner for a total of four hours and interviewed the respondent for a total of four hours. He gave the court his opinion that at the time of his marriage the respondent had a personality disorder to such an extent as to make it impossible for him to consent to and sustain a marriage with the respondent. In his view, the respondent had a fundamental difficulty with trust and allowing himself to be trusted.

The psychiatrist, according to O'Higgins J., quoted from the International Classification of Diseases, which set the meaning of a personality disorder as follows:

"it is a condition which comprises deeply ingrained and enduring behaviour patterns manifesting themselves as inflexible responses to a broad range of personal and social situations, they represent either extreme or significant deviations from the way that the average individual in a given culture perceives, thinks, feels thinks [*sic*] and particularly relates to others. Such behaviour patterns tend to be stable and to encompass multiple domains of behaviour and psychological functioning. They are frequently, but not always, associated with various degrees of subjective distresses and problems and social functioning and performance. They emerge early in the course of the person's development, usually present by early adulthood and generally persist throughout life."

(This coincides with the World Health Organisation definition.)

The psychiatrist went on to say that the particular personality disorder the petitioner had was:

"what is called a narcissistic personality disorder and that has a triad for diagnosis and the triad is self-importance or grandiosity, the need for admiration and the inability to empathise with others. They are usually people who have a very strong negative reaction to criticism; they show manipulative behaviour and an exaggerated sense of achievement and special abilities, a strong sense of entitlement and a requirement for constant attention while being indifferent to the feeling of others."

The psychiatrist said that he formed his opinion based on a number of factors in the history given to him by the petitioner and the respondent and on the documents furnished by him and referred to in his report.

The matters he relied on included the following:

(1) a letter seeking the franchise in which the respondent said he had been head-hunted by a particular company to be a director;

(2) a letter found addressed to a celebrated Q.C. in England;

(3) his asking for delivery of paintings from persons to whom he was in debt;

(4) his descriptions of himself in his C.V.

As regards the first letter, O'Higgins J. noted that the respondent had not been head-hunted by the company since the company had in fact been founded at his behest. In O'Higgins J.'s view, the psychiatrist was not correct in attributing any significance to this document in assessing that the respondent was grandiose or self-important. It was "nothing but a minor puff to cover up a gap in his curriculum vitae and to account for a period of unsuccessful business activity".

O'Higgins J. disposed of the significance of the second letter as follows:

> "[The psychiatrist] also places reliance on a draft letter from the respondent to a celebrated Q.C. as being evidence of pomposity and self-importance. In my view, any such reliance is totally misplaced. [The psychiatrist] is not in a position to tell the court whether or not the respondent knew the person in question and consequently could not be justified in placing any reliance on the fact of correspondence itself. It appeared moreover from the letter itself that it is not the first letter in correspondence and appears to be in response to 'papers you forwarded'. However, [the psychiatrist] attaches significance not to the letter itself but to the following sentence, 'Finally on a more personal note we are hoping to see you in [B] … on the 29th.' It would appear that the petitioner knew nothing of this invitation. In my view, it would be wrong to draw any inference however slight from that sentence. It may be a casual invitation or a meaningless polite phrase. It might have been something already discussed between the parties. There are no grounds in my view for forming an opinion that that sentence is evidence of grandiosity or pomposity without further information about the dealings between the respondent and the Q.C."

As regards the third matter, the correspondence with the firm of art dealers, the respondent wrote concerning the removal of three pictures from Dublin to Glasgow and referred to three unwrapped pictures which were to be taken from Dublin to Glasgow. The psychiatrist found it "rather unusual that he would be writing to these people to whom he owed money and expecting them to move the pictures for him and also they would be wrapping them and they would send him a bill for this as well". He found an element of grandiosity in an expectation that they would take care of the matter even though the applicant owed them money. O'Higgins J. did not agree. He stated:

> "I do not consider it in any way unusual for a person to deal with a company to whom that person owes money. In particular, I find nothing strange about the request in the letter especially when the same letter contains a cheque towards his account which he trusts 'will bring me close to balance'. (It appears from the previous correspondence which refers to balance payable of UK£252.88 on the 13th August, 1997 that the contention that the sum of UK£240.00 will bring me close to balance may well be correct). ..."

The final matter related to the respondent's C.V. in which the respondent described himself as "one of the most high profile chartered quantity surveyors in Scotland" and "one of Glasgow's best public speakers". O'Higgins J. commented:

> "Again, in my view it is not reasonable to use that, even as part of a jigsaw of findings and observations, on which to base the opinion that he formed. The assertions in the C.V. might be considered brash or excessive but the prevalent standards in self-promotion in the business world by way of a C.V. could well be at variance with those in the professional world. I do not think that [the psychiatrist] was justified in attaching any significance to that document in arriving at this diagnosis. With regard to his assertions about his prowess as a public speaker, it appears there was some basis for this view of himself."

O'Higgins J. was conscious of the fact that the psychiatrist had told the court:

> "One of the difficulties in making a diagnosis with a personality disorder is that if one picks any one particular feature then it does not necessarily have to be outside the norm, it is a feature that one might see in other people. In making the diagnosis of a personality disorder you look at the general pattern of behaviour across many domains of the person's functioning. I would refer to a number of features of Mr. MacC, the most obvious one is his *curriculum vitae* and the manner in which it is written."

It was clear from this that the proper approach was to look at the overall pattern rather than to place too much emphasis on any one specific factor. Nevertheless, it appeared from the evidence that the psychiatrist considered the matters referred to above as being factors, all of which were to be taken into account in coming to his diagnosis, and a very considerable amount of his evidence had been devoted to commenting on these matters.

There had been other matters involved in the diagnosis. The psychiatrist had referred to a letter in which the respondent wrote to the person from whom he had hoped to obtain the fast food franchise. In the letter, he referred to the very serious illness of his wife and, as the psychiatrist put it, went on to embellish matters by using the phrase "it's funny how life turns". In fact, his wife was not seriously ill following the birth of the child; in this regard the psychiatrist said: "He cannot simply state what the truth is and then deal with the consequences of it, he will make a statement which is untrue and then will go on to embellish it".

The respondent had written a letter to the petitioner expressing love and admiration on the same day that he sold items belonging to the petitioner. The psychiatrist had concluded that this indicated an absence of empathy on the respondent's part.

The respondent had told the psychiatrist that he had just ended a seven-year relationship with another person. This matter had not been probed at all by the psychiatrist because he did not think that the respondent was a very credible person to interview. Nonetheless O'Higgins J. considered it unfortunate not to have had any information on this topic. Furthermore, the psychiatrist had made no reference in evidence to the respondent's relationship with his parents.

The psychiatrist had also commented on the fact that the agreement reached between the parties three years after separating was that the petitioner should have full responsibility for the rearing of the children and that the respondent was not seeking access. He also told the court of a time when the child was ill and the respondent appeared to be indifferent and mentioned that in the interview the respondent denied authorship of a document which, the psychiatrist thought, was clearly in his handwriting.

O'Higgins J. observed that the psychiatrist:

> "conducted quite extensive interviews with the petitioner and respondent and had access to the documentation provided by the petitioner and referred to in his report. He had the benefit of information from the petitioner but not from other informants and referred in his evidence to the difficulties in not being able to use informants in these types of procedures.
>
> The court is aware of the experience and expertise of [the psychiatrist] but it would be wrong of the court to accept unquestioningly the evidence of an expert and to substitute expert opinion for the independent judgment of the court. Some of the matters which, cumulatively, are part of the basis of his opinion, and which formed a major part of his evidence, have not been accepted by the court as valid material on which reliance should be placed.

I am aware that the matters in question are only part of the full picture, and that the opinion was not based solely on the matters referred to but also on the interviews with both the petitioner and the respondent. I am not satisfied, however, that the totality of the evidence discloses that the personality traits of the respondent were so outside the norm as to constitute a personality disorder such as would preclude him from contracting to a valid marriage. Nor am I convinced that his personality was such as to preclude him from sustaining a relationship with the petitioner. Furthermore, it has not been shown to the satisfaction of the court that the respondent 'constructed a persona entirely at variance with reality'."

O'Higgins J. relied strongly on McGuinness J.'s judgment in *P.F. v G. O'M (Otherwise G.F.)*. In his view, the lack of full disclosure by the respondent about his financial affairs, family and social circumstances were not grounds on which one could base a claim for nullity:

"Neither the failure of the respondent to be the breadwinner for the family nor the failure of his business endeavours constitutes grounds on which to grant a declaration of nullity."

During the marriage, the respondent had provided little emotional support and did not appear to have been good at parenting the child born prior to the break-up of the relationship. He was inconsiderate to the applicant and sometimes deceitful. O'Higgins J. thought that one could be justified in concluding from the evidence that the respondent was very selfish, egotistical, deceitful and dishonest and that he had behaved badly. Nonetheless, the evidence did not convince O'Higgins J. that the personality traits which he had displayed were of "such a nature or quality as to bring him outside the norm". Since the respondent was not suffering from such personality disorder as would have prevented him from contracting a valid marriage, O'Higgins J. refused to grant a decree of nullity of marriage.

This decision can be greeted with relief. The careful and detailed manner in which O'Higgins J. expressed his disagreement with aspects of the psychiatric evidence is an impressive reminder of the responsibility resting on courts in undefended nullity proceedings.

DISCOVERY

In *F.D. v P.J.D.*, High Court, July 28, 2004, Master Honohan gave guidance as to the circumstances in which general discovery should operate in matrimonial cases.

Master Honohan observed:

"Inevitably ... a certain lack of rigour has crept into general (means/ financial) discovery in matrimonial cases at this point. More often than not the 'further and better' discovery sought is not on the basis of any analysis of evidential difficulties, or issues, or 'necessity', but simply on the strength of whatever the party's accountant/expert (sometimes referred to as a forensic accountant) has found to be missing in the documentation already furnished/discovered."

In Master Honohan's view, the stated requirements of the accountant were not the determining factor. The lawyers, and ultimately the court, had to weigh the significance of the missing jigsaw pieces in the overall picture before ordering their discovery. The mere fact of omission was insufficient to persuade the court of the need for discovery. There had to be "fairly clear evidence" that a party might have concealed a materially significant portion of income or wealth for the court to be persuaded to grant a further and better discovery order. That evidence might be inferential.

Master Honohan was inclined to adopt an English rule which exhorted solicitors not to seek a further affidavit unless it dealt with a serious allegation made by the other party or set out a change of circumstance.

In the instant case, the wife's solicitor had complained about tardy delivery of an affidavit of means and had gone to request voluntary discovery (under S.I. No.233 of 1999) of documentation in relation to tax relief, bank statements, financial records and accounts of companies in which the husband had an interest, and other categories of documentation.

In affidavits supporting the application for discovery, the applicant made the case that she was a beneficial shareholder in the companies listed in the respondent's affidavit of means—a case not made in her own affidavit of means—and pressed for access to up-to-date documentation relative to that case.

Master Honohan commented:

"[I]t is not the stuff of a serious allegation of concealment of assets or understatement of income. The wife's concerns are not about the company's balance sheet, or indeed the value of the shares, but rather about share ownership—an entirely separate line of inquiry. And there may be something in what she asserts, though from his description (which is hardly disputed) of the business and trade of the companies, the underlying net asset values may be small. There is the usual assertion that the husband's company credit cards mask personal income and expenditure and there is an allegation to the effect that the husband has in recent years funded an extravagant lifestyle by, in effect, asset stripping his companies by re-mortgaging property a matter relevant only to an interlocutory application—but apart from these, the application for further and better discovery of documentation pertinent to the means of the husband reduces to requests for updating of previously furnished accounts. There is no suggestion that such updating will transform the financial picture. The request for discovery is prompted out of a desire for completeness rather than to uncover any deliberate falsehoods or disingenuousness on the husband's part. It is a general discovery type demand rather than one which is focussed on any particular 'issue'."

Dismissing the application, Master Honohan observed that the parties should each consider whether corrective affidavits of means were called for. If the wife's financial advisors eventually "ma[d]e sense" of the husband's financial position, and could point to evidence in support of a "serious allegation", an application for further and better discovery might be renewed.

CONSTITUTION

In *SC and RC and CC (A Minor) v Minister for Justice, Equality and Law Reform,* High Court, December 21, 2004, the impact of the Supreme Court decision in *O and L v Minister for Justice, Equality and Law Reform* [2003] 1 I.R. 1 (analysed in the *Annual Review of Irish Law 2003*, pp.147–158) was measurable. The case involved two separate claims for judicial review by people who had been validly deported and whose application for revocation of the deportation order had been refused. In the first of these, the applicant, after having been deported, married the mother of his Irish-born child. A report and recommendation by an employee of the Immigration Division against granting a revocation made no reference to the child. It was acknowledged during the proceedings that the rights and interests of the child were not factors which had been taken into account.

Quirke J. made an order of certiorari quashing the decision to refuse revocation. He quoted from the judgments in *O & L* and in *Fajujonu v Minister for Justice* [1990] 2 I.R. 151, including the following passage from Murray J.'s judgment in *O & L*:

"[U]nlike a family of non-nationals who can be deported simply because they are non-nationals, having no personal right whatever to be within the State (where rights arising under the immigration and asylum systems have been excluded) the Minister must take into account in a case such as the present one, the prima facie constitutional rights deriving from the citizenship of the infants and consider whether, notwithstanding those rights, there are, in the circumstances of the case, good and sufficient reasons associated with the common good for the deportation of their parents with the inevitable consequences for their child."

Quirke J. observed that:

> "Accepting, as I of course do without hesitation, that ... paragraph as
> a clear statement of the law and of the respondent's obligation when
> considering the potential deportation of non-nationals and adopting the
> principle identified as being applicable equally to applications made to
> the respondent pursuant to s.3(11) of the [Immigration] Act ... 1999 it
> follows that the decision of the respondent to refuse to revoke the
> deportation order in respect of the [first applicant] was and remains
> invalid.
>
> This is so because of the candid acknowledgment on behalf of the
> respondent that the prima facie constitutional rights of [the child]
> deriving from her citizenship were not taken into account by the
> respondent during the consideration of the [first applicant's] application.
> In considering the [first applicant's] application the respondent did not
> consider whether, notwithstanding those rights, there were, in the
> circumstances of the case, good and sufficient reasons associated with
> the common good for the deportation of [the first applicant] with the
> inevitable consequences for [his daughter]."

In the second case, there was no Irish-born child, but the applicant had married
his Irish wife in Romania after he had been deported from Ireland. Quirke J.,
relying on Murray J.'s judgment in *O & L*, considered that it was "clear from
the decision of the Supreme Court" in that case that the protection afforded by
the Constitution to the family was "not dependent entirely upon whether it
counts amongst its members an Irish citizen". Whether all judges in *O & L*
took this view is, however, debatable. At all events, such protection as the
applicant was able to assert as attaching to his family did not avail him since
Quirke J. was satisfied that the decision made by the Minister to refuse to
revoke his deportation had been lawfully and proportionately made having
regard to the exigencies of the common good, having given due and proper
consideration to all relevant material before him.

The decision of the English Court of Appeal in *R. (Mahmood) v Secretary
of State for the Home Department* [2001] 1 W.L.R. 840 did not avail the
applicant in asserting a claim based on Art.8 of the European Convention on
Human Rights. In *R. (Mahmood)* Lord Phillips M.R.'s judgment made it clear
that Art.8 did not impose on any State a general obligation. In particular the
court had held that:

> "(5) Knowledge on the part of one spouse at the time of marriage that
>   rights of residence of the other were precarious militates against
>   a finding that an order excluding the latter spouse violates article
>   8.
> (6) Whether interference with family rights is justified in the interests

of controlling immigration will depend on:
(i) the facts of the particular case and
(ii) the circumstances prevailing in the State whose action is impugned."

In *RP and O'S v Minister for Justice, Equality and Law Reform*, High Court, June 17, 2004, Butler J. made a declaration that the respondent was not entitled to give an order of deportation to the first-named applicant, a Ukrainian whose application for asylum had failed, without first having regard to the material change in his circumstances since the making of the deportation order, in particular, his marriage to the second-named applicant who was an Irish citizen. Butler J. declined, however, to grant an order of prohibition as he considered that a declaration was "sufficient to meet the application".

No paternal preference A claim doomed to fail was put forward in ex parte habeas corpus proceedings taken in the instant proceedings by the applicant in *R. v R. and The State*, Supreme Court, April 2, 2004 (*ex tempore*). The applicant was a married man living apart from his wife who was the first respondent. The Circuit Court had awarded custody of their two children to the wife and the High Court had upheld this order. The applicant sought to impugn the order on the basis that, under the common law, the Constitution and s.18(2) of the Guardianship of Infants Act 1964, a father had a right superior to that of his wife to the custody of the children and that, since he had not committed any crime, he could not be divested of the custody of his children. Dismissing the application, Murray J. (Hardiman and McCracken JJ. concurring) stated:

"Now it is quite understandable that in circumstances of this nature when parents are separated and a court has to take a decision as to whether those children should be placed, with one parent or the other, that the parent who does not have the custody may feel seriously aggrieved and upset by it but I am satisfied that neither the common law in so far as it is applicable at all, nor, in particular, s.18(2) of the Guardianship of Infants Act makes any provision for giving a superior status or rights to the father over the mother nor indeed do the provisions of the Constitution which clearly recognise the role of both parents in the welfare of the children. It expressly recognises the need to make special provision for the children outside the custody of their parents in particular circumstances. The relevant legislation and in particular the Guardianship of Infants Act makes provision for the custody of infants to be awarded to one parent or another in certain circumstances, not on the basis that one or the other is necessarily unfit in themselves to have custody, but in all the circumstances on the basis of what is in the best interests of the child. That was the jurisdiction which was accorded to the Circuit Court and the High Court on appeal and which was exercised in this case. There is nothing in the submissions that have been put before this court which in my view could be a basis for impugning any order which was made by those courts either from the point of view of the Constitution or statutory law. It was the clear intention of parliament that the courts should have a discretion to award custody to either separated parent according to what was in the best interests of the children in the circumstances."

PRIVACY OF PROCEEDINGS

The subject of privacy of proceedings in family litigation involves a delicate balance between protecting people from having intimate aspects of their lives exposed to public scrutiny and ensuring that the broader public interest is served by some system of scrutiny of decision-making to protect both parties from the risk of arbitrary or biased adjudication. Until the passage of the Civil Liability and Courts Act 2004, a policy of intense privacy was in place. This had the beneficial effect of protecting the parties and their children from publicity in the media and otherwise, but at a serious price. The degree of access to family litigation was so limited as to make it impossible to know how the system was operating in practice, whether judges were adopting consistent standards and whether, as men's groups strongly asserted, there was gender bias in the adjudication.

Section 40 of the 2004 Act deals with the matter as follows. In regard to legal proceedings under a range of enactments (defined in s.39), including those relating to divorce and judicial separation but not guardianship of infants or domestic violence, s.39(3) facilitates the publication by a barrister, solicitor or other class of persons to be designated by the Minister for Justice, Equality and Law Reform of a report of the proceeding or the publication of the decision, without information enabling the parties or their children to be identified. It goes on to state that "accordingly, unless in the special circumstances of the matter the court, for reasons which shall be specified in the direction, otherwise directs, [the barrister, solicitor or other designated] person ... may, for the purposes of preparing such a report, attend the proceedings subject to any directions the court may give in that behalf."

In the Civil Liability and Courts Act 2004 (Section 40(3)) Regulations 2005 (S.I. No.337 of 2005), the Minister specified the following clauses to persons who are entitled to make reports under s.40(3):

"(a) family mediators who are—
    (i)   accredited to the Mediators Institute Ireland,
    (ii) nominated by the Family Support Agency, and
    (iii) approved by the Minister.
 (b) persons engaged in family law research who are—

(i) nominated by a body specified in the Schedule to these Regulations, and

(ii) approved by the Minister.

(c) persons engaged by the Court Service to prepare court reports of proceedings under relevant enactments."

The Schedule lists the following bodies:

"A college within the meaning of the Universities Act 1997 (No.24 of 1997)
University of Dublin, Trinity College Dublin
Dublin City University
University of Limerick
Dublin Institute of Technology
A college within the meaning of the Regional Technical Colleges Act 1992 (No. 16 of 1992)
Institute of Technology, Blanchardstown
Economic and Social Research Institute
Law Reform Commission."

Section 40(5) removes any prohibition contained in the relevant enactments on a party to the proceedings being accompanied in court by another person subject to the approval of the court and any directions it might give.

Section 40(6) applies, not just to the proceedings in the specific family law enactments listed as "relevant enactments" in s.40(1), but to any enactment that prohibits its proceedings from being heard in public. It provides that this type of prohibition is not to operate to prohibit the production of a document prepared for the purposes of or in contemplation of the proceedings or given in evidence in these proceedings to:

(a) a body or other person when it, or he or she, is performing functions under any enactment consisting of the conducting of a hearing, inquiry or investigation in relation to, or adjudicating on, any matter, or

(b) such body or other person as may be prescribed by order made by the Minister, when the body or person concerned is performing functions consisting of the conducting of a hearing, inquiry or investigation in relation to, or adjudicating on, any matter as may be so prescribed.

Section 40(7) contains a similar provision in relation to the giving of evidence. Nothing contained in an enactment prohibiting proceedings to which it relates from being heard in public is to operate to prohibit the giving of information or evidence given in such proceedings to a body or person in one of the categories described in s.40(6).

The Civil Liability and Courts Act 2004 (Matters prescribed under section

40) Order 2005 (S.I. No.339 of 2005) prescribes two matters to which s.40(6)(b) and s.40(7)(6) are to apply. These are the hearing of a complaint of misconduct against a barrister and an appeal against such a complaint.

The Civil Liability and Courts Act 2004 (Bodies Prescribed under section 40) Order 2005 (S.I. No.170 of 2005) prescribes under s.40(6)(b) and s.40(7)(b) the following bodies which may be given documents, information or evidence when conducting a hearing, enquiry or investigation or adjudication on a matter to which the *in camera* rule applies:

> "The Barristers' Professional Conduct Tribunal of the Bar Council;
> The Benchers of the Honourable Society of the King's Inns;
> The Professional Conduct Appeals Board of the Bar Council;
> The Professional Practices Committee of the Bar Council;
> The Professional Practices Committee of the Council of King's Inns."

Section 40(4) removes the prohibition on a party to proceedings to which a relevant enactment relates from supplying copies of (or extracts from) orders made in these proceedings to anyone else. It gives the Minister power to prescribe persons to whom the orders may be shown.

The Civil Liability and Courts Act 2004 (Section 40(4)) Order 2005 (S.I. No.338 of 2005) deals with the matter. It lists 26 categories of prescribed persons who may be given such copies where this is necessary to enable them to perform their functions; they must not show or supply the copies to anyone else except those to whom it is necessary for them to be shown or supplied to enable the prescribed person to perform his or her duties. The categories are as follows:

1. a recognised school within the meaning of the Education Act 1998;

2. a vocational education committee established under s.7 of the Vocational Education Act 1930;

3. a certified reformatory or industrial school under Pt IV of the Children Act 1908;

4. a children's detention school under the Children Act 2001;

5. the Minister for Foreign Affairs when performing functions relating to the granting of passports under s.1 of the Ministers and Secretaries Act 1924;

6. the Minister for Justice, Equality and Law Reform when performing functions under the Aliens Act 1935, the Refugee Act 1996 (No.17 of 1996), the Immigration Act 1999 or the Irish Nationality and Citizenship Acts 1956 to 2004;

7. a consular officer under the Diplomatic Relations and Immunities Act 1967 (No.8 of 1967) when performing the function of issuing passports

or other similar travel documentation to nationals of a state (other than the State), or visas or other similar travel documentation to persons wishing to travel to that state;

8. An Garda Síochána;

9. a designated credit institution under the Asset Covered Securities Act 2001 (No.47 of 2001);

10. a bank holding a licence under s.9 of the Central Bank Act 1971;

11. a solicitor;

12. a barrister-at-law;

13. the Land Registry;

14. a local authority within the meaning of the Local Government Act 2001;

15. the Health Service Executive;

16. the Minister for Social and Family Affairs when performing functions under the Social Welfare Acts;

17. An Bord Uchtála;

18. a guardian under the Guardianship of Infants Act 1964 (No.7 of 1964);

19. a guardian *ad litem* appointed under Pt IV (inserted by s.11 of the Children Act 1997 (No.40 of 1997)) of the Guardianship of Infants Act 1964 or s.26 of the Child Care Act 1991;

20. the Central Authority in the State under Pt II or Pt III of the Child Abduction and Enforcement of Custody Orders Act 1991;

21. the Central Authority under the Maintenance Act 1994;

22. the Central Authority for the State under the European Communities (Judgments in Matrimonial Matters and Matters of Parental Responsibility) Regulations 2005;

23. an t-Árd Chláraitheoir;

24. the governor of a prison within the meaning of s.7 of the National Treasury Management Agency (Amendment) Act 2000;

25. officers of the Minister for Justice, Equality and Law Reform assigned for the time being to the Probation and Welfare Service of the Department of State of which that Minister has charge;

26. the Revenue Commissioners.

Section 40(9) provides that a hearing, inquiry or investigation referred to in s.40(6) or (7), in so far as it relates to a document referred to in s.40(6) or information or evidence referred to in s.40(7), is to be conducted otherwise than in public and that no such document, information or evidence is to be published. One wonders how precisely the reports of adjudications resulting from these hearings, enquiries or investigations can meaningfully justify their conclusions without in some cases having to refer to the document, information or evidence.

Section 40(8) gives discretion to a court hearing proceedings under a relevant enactment, either on its own motion or on the application of one of the parties, to order disclosure of documents, information or evidence connected with or arising in the course of the proceedings to third parties if such disclosure is required "to protect the legitimate interests of a party or other person affected by the proceedings".

FINANCIAL PROVISION

In the *Annual Review of Irish Law 2003*, pp.346–349, we analysed the decision of *B.D. v J.D.,* High Court, December 11, 2003, an "ample resources" case in which McKechnie J. ordered the husband to pay his wife a total sum of €4 million between 2004 and 2006, as well as a €100,000 contribution to the wife's costs. The husband had control of companies worth €10 million. As regards the realisation costs and taxation issues, McKechnie J. stated:

> "As a result of the orders which I have made in this case, it is evident that Mr. D. will have a period of over two years to discharge his full liability to Mrs. D. and that for the entire duration of this time he will be solely in charge of this group of companies. With such position, he will have maximum flexibility to structure his resources in the most advantageous way possible from a taxation point of view. During the hearing of this case evidence was given, largely by Mr. Grant, as to how any lump sum payment could be extracted from the company. Such evidence touched upon a number of possibilities including the obtaining of money by way of dividend, by way of director's salary and by way of sale share to a third party. This evidence was, as it had to be, vague, uncertain and unclear in that there were no concrete circumstances surrounding the issue. Given the manner in which I have approached the granting of relief to Mrs. D., which as a result confers fully ownership on and gives total flexibility to Mr. D., I do not believe that it would be correct or appropriate for this Court to stand in the shoes of a taxation adviser to the respondent in the post litigation situation. It becomes entirely a matter for him as to how he discharges these financial obligations, which obligations have been deliberately staggered and which, of course, subsume all monies and other benefits which the applicant previously has been in receipt of from this group of companies."

The husband successfully appealed to the Supreme Court, which handed down its judgment on December 8, 2004. The essence of the husband's argument was that McKechnie J. had erred in failing to make any finding as to the financial incidents of the extraction of sufficient monies from the company to discharge the lump sums ordered to be paid to the wife. Counsel for the wife defended McKechnie J.'s approach on the basis that he had been entitled to leave it up to the husband to perform the extraction of the sums in the most fiscally and commercially effective fashion. It would be asking too much of trial judges in effect to take commercial decisions on a highly complicated issue relating to the taxation and commercial consequences of particular options.

In upholding the husband's arguments, Hardiman J. (Denham and Kearns JJ. concurring) stated:

> "I note that a considerable amount of evidence was heard on this topic. From this it emerged that the likely tax payable on the payment of the lump sums could vary between 20% and 42%, i.e. a sum of between €800,000 and €1,680,000. These are clearly very substantial sums in the context of the total worth of the parties. Moreover, they make no account of the commercial costs of realising them, on top of the basic sum of €4 million on which they are computed.
>
> In my view, these sums are simply too significant to be dealt with simply by according the husband total flexibility in raising them. This indeed might be more aptly described as simply imposing no additional constraint on him in doing so.
>
> If one envisages that, instead of a possible tax liability of up to €1,680,000 there were some other liability in that maximum amount, it would plainly be unjust for the Court not to take it into account. If either the husband or the company had personal or commercial debt which might amount to that sum there is no conceivable basis on which it could be excluded from consideration having regard, for example, to the terms of s.16(i) which requires the Court to consider, *inter alia*:
>> '(a) The income, earning capacity, property and other financial resources which each of the spouses concerned has or is likely to have in the foreseeable future,
>> (b) The financial needs, obligations and responsibilities which each of the spouses has or is likely to have in the foreseeable future (whether in the case of remarriage of the spouse or otherwise) ...'."

Hardiman J. noted that, in *T. v T.* [2002] 3 I.R. 334 at 415, Fennelly J. had said:

> "... The parties accept also that, in order to make provision in the form of a lump sum for the wife in accordance with the law, assets will have to be realised. This, in turn, necessarily entails the incurring of realisation costs and expenses in the form of legal and other professional expenses

and tax liability, in particular capital taxes. On this last basis, it is accepted that the relevant value of the assets is reduced..."

It appeared to Hardiman J. that both statute and case law positively required realisation costs (in this case, tax liability), to be taken into account, in a specific way.

Hardiman J. went on to observe that the valuation and the lump sum award, together with the cost of buying the wife out of the family home, transaction costs and tax liability, were such that the costs to the husband of making the provision ordered substantially exceeded one half of the value of the company. Whether this was appropriate in the circumstances, and if not what sum would be appropriate, could only be addressed after a view had been taken as to the mechanism to be used for the extraction of funds from the company and the tax effects of that extraction.

One can appreciate the concern for fairness underlying the Supreme Court's approach. There is, however, another view of McKechnie J.'s resolution of the issue, which was that he was seeking to maximise the husband's freedom of commercial decision-making, provided he ensured the payment of the particular sum that McKechnie J. judged to represent proper provision for the wife. In giving the husband that freedom, McKechnie J. must have been perfectly aware of the large range of choices that he was giving the husband and their differing financial impacts.

On a question of costs, since the wife had been unsuccessful in her primary claim that she was entitled to a 50 per cent equity in the companies, Hardiman J. saw no cogent reason why either party should contribute to the other's costs. Accordingly, the order for the payment by the husband of €100,000 as a contribution to the wife's costs was set aside.

Hardiman J. made an interesting observation as to costs in family litigation, unconnected to the circumstances of the instant case:

> "We make no comment as to the amounts of the costs in this particular case, which was one of some, but not extreme, complexity. But we would observe that the cost figures mentioned or deposed to affidavits of means in family law actions are sometimes very high, out of proportion it would appear to what is involved even in an ample resources case. They can be very burdensome, especially but not exclusively in less prosperous circumstances. Those charging instruction fees or brief fees must bear in mind that they are to be related to the work done and not directly to the asset value in a case. Obviously the latter will affect the complexity and the level of responsibility involved in the case but these are not the sole determining factors. One bears in mind, of course, that the solicitor's fee in particular will reflect outlay and that the costs of professional witnesses may be a very substantial factor in this. These costs, too, require to be kept within bounds. The

assets in family law cases often extend to valuable house property, commercial property and other items whose value may have increased very rapidly in recent times. It is not to be assumed that this rate of price inflation is to be applied automatically to legal costs inflation. These observations are not made with particular regard to the present case."

WARDSHIP

In *Dolan v Registrar of Wards*, High Court, March 19, 2004 (*ex tempore*), noted by Anne-Marie O'Neill, *Wards of Court in Ireland* (2004), paras 5.3.42 and 7.6, a young man who had cerebral palsy and physical and mental disability successfully settled an action for negligence against medical personnel involved at the time of his birth. The amount of the settlement was £3 million. Johnson J. approved the settlement and ordered that the bulk of the money be placed on deposit with the Accountant General of the High Court pending "application to the President" (implicitly an application for wardship). The young man's family did not, however, wish to take this step as they were concerned that his constitutional rights might be interfered with. The President of the High Court, over a year later, made an order directing that a medical visitor visit the young man for the purpose of enquiring into his capacity to manage his person and property. Several months later, the transaction not yet having taken place, the President directed that a letter be sent to his father making it clear that the assistance of the Gardaí would be involved if he did not allow the examination to take place. When the father's solicitors replied indicating that proceedings would be instituted, the President made the order invoking the help of the Gardaí. The medical visitor began, but felt he could not complete, his visitation. The family applied for injunctions restraining the Registrar of Wards of Court and any medical visitor, as well as members of the Gardaí, from entering their home. They claimed that the procedure that was already in operation offended their constitutional rights as a family and their son's constitutional rights as an individual and was offensive to the notion of constitutional justice.

Kelly J. dealt with the application for interlocutory injunctions. He considered that, if the order made by the President was in the nature of a judicial, as distinct from administrative, function being exercised by him, he "could not possibly intervene". One High Court judge could not enjoin the carrying out of the order of another judge. The only remedy in such circumstances would be to seek to have the original order set aside, preferably by the judge who made it, or to appeal to the Supreme Court.

The plaintiffs argued that the order made by the President, both as to the carrying out of the medical visitation and the subsequent order calling in aid the Gardaí, was administrative in character. Kelly J. did not agree. He acknowledged that there were many aspects of the wardship jurisdiction which did not involve the administration of justice or the exercise of judicial functions.

In *Re Wards of Court: Eastern Health Board v MK* [1999] 2 I.R. 99, Barrington J. had observed, however, that, although the wardship jurisdiction of the President of the High Court was a venerable and useful jurisdiction directed to protecting wards of court which was largely administrative in character, decisions which affected constitutional rights, such as the issue of whether to accept a person into wardship, could not be regarded as purely administrative.

Lynch J. had observed that there was "nothing merely administrative as regards the issues to be determined on its application to take children into wardship". Administrative issues would arise in the course of conducting and administering the wardship of children after they had been made wards of court and not when determining whether or not they should be taken into wardship.

Kelly J. did not think that the order directing the medical visitor to carry out his examination, as a necessary condition precedent to the possibility of wardship orders being made, could be characterised as administrative:

> "It is judicial. It can only be made by a judge. It can be enforced as any other order of court. Indeed the police can be and were in this case called upon to enforce it. It is part and parcel of a judicial process. It is a necessary condition precedent to the hearing of an application for admission to wardship. The order made affects constitutional rights."

On the basis that it was not possible to restrain the execution of a judicial order of a High Court colleague, Kelly J. concluded that he should refuse the injunction. He stressed that the making of a wardship order was a judicial function which had to be exercised in accordance with the Constitution and with constitutional propriety.

Kelly J. noted that in *Re Wards of Court: Eastern Health Board v MK* [1999] 2 I.R. 99, Denham J. had stated:

> "Wardship proceedings must be fair and in accordance with constitutional justice. The constitutional rights of all parties the children and the patients must be protected. Where rights are in conflict they must be balanced appropriately. Due process must be observed by the Court while exercising this unique jurisdiction. Consequently if a legal right or a constitutional right is to be limited or taken away by a court, this must be done with fair procedures. Fundamental principles such as those enunciated in *In re Haughey* [1971] IR 217 apply. There must be fair procedures…"

It followed that, in exercising his wardship jurisdiction in the instant case, the President had had to comply with those constitutionally mandated norms in deciding on whether or not to take the young man into wardship.

In an important passage Kelly J. expressed the view that the plaintiffs had:

> "misconstrued what wardship involves. It is a beneficent jurisdiction to assist a person such as Francis Junior who labours under a legal disability by reason of his health. It attempts to remedy that so as to enable his property to be administered. Given his impeccable family and the support which it has given to him, I cannot conceive of any order being made which would interfere with the family as a unit or have the sundering effects contended for. An order which might be made, if such be the case, would deal only with Francis Junior's assets. Whilst of course the plaintiffs are correct in saying that a wardship order may deal with the person of the ward, on the present evidence there would be no basis for any order with the far-reaching consequences for the family which the plaintiffs apprehend. Regrettably I have to hold that their apprehensions in that regard are simply not reasonable. There is on the evidence no basis for anticipating that any order would be made which would remove Francis Junior from his family or would otherwise interfere with the family unit, still less break it up."

Kelly J. accordingly concluded that the plaintiffs had not demonstrated a serious issue for trial in so far as permitting the medical examination to proceed was concerned. Even if he was wrong on that matter, Kelly J. considered that the injunction should also be refused on the grounds of adequacy of damages and balance of convenience.

Kelly J.'s holding seems eminently defensible on the facts. Nonetheless, it is worth reflecting on the wider problems concerning the constitutionality of the wardship jurisdiction. We have mentioned them in previous Annual Reviews: see, for example the *Annual Review of Irish Law 1995*, in our analysis of the decision of the Supreme Court in *Re a Ward of Court (Withholding Medical Treatment) (No.2)* [1996] 2 I.R. 79. See also Anne-Marie O'Neill, *Wards of Court in Ireland* (FirstLaw, Dublin, 2004), paras 1.9–1.14. If we assume for the purposes of this discussion that the *parens patriae* jurisdiction can be rehabilitated in constitutional clothing, no longer being entitled to find a foundation on a British royal prerogative, the question arises as to how the welfare of a ward should be permitted to override the constitutional right of the ward and his or her family. The most obvious rights at risk here are the ward's own right to autonomy, recognised in *Re Ward of Court (Withholding Medical Treatment (No.2)* and the ward's parents' autonomy as members of a constitutionally protected family under Arts 41 and 42. This latter right was clearly acknowledged in *North Western Health Board v HW* [2001] 3 I.R. 622.

It is not at all fanciful to envisage cases where the placing of a young person into wardship could indeed have radical implications for the exercise by parents of their guardianship functions and their autonomous decision-making in respect of their child. Let us modify the facts in the *Ward of Court* case to imagine a case where a young woman is in a persistent vegetative state with less cognitive capacity than in the *Ward of Court* case; the doctors in the hospital wish to withdraw a feeding tube because they, like O'Flaherty J. in the *Ward of Court* case, regard her life as one "without purpose, meaning or dignity."

The parents object. The hospital institutes wardship proceedings. If the court makes the young woman a ward of court, although it will heed the parents' objections, it will not be bound by them. It may order the withdrawal of the feeding tube, resulting in the death of the parents' daughter. Whatever faith we may have in the welfare test and its philosophical cosmology, we can scarcely deny that a judicial initiative of this kind can have radical incursions into the rights of the parents.

One can raise the question, therefore, whether these parental rights are deserving of full respect during the application stage for an order making the person a ward of court or whether, on the contrary, they are secondary to other questions relating to the welfare of the person in respect of whom the wardship application has been initiated. The cumbersome statutory framework is less than clear on this question but one can say with some degree of assurance that to date the courts have laid little emphasis on parental rights during the application process. The constitutional problem therefore remains as to how the happenstance of an application for wardship can have such radical effects on the exercise of otherwise constitutionally protected rights of the person who may be made a ward and his or her parents.

ADOPTION

O'Higgins J.'s decision in *Re L.R. an Infant; W.H.B. v An Bord Uchtála*, High Court, May 27, 2004, involved a discussion of such troublesome questions as what constitutes failure of parental duty and abandonment of parental rights for the purposes of the Adoption Act 1988 and the potential conflict between giving priority to the welfare of the child whose prospective adoption is in issue and protecting the welfare of that child's siblings.

The facts of the case were disturbing. The parents of the child whose prospective adoption was in issue had married in 1980. They had five children. One daughter, born in 1983, had died in 1985, having swallowed an open safety pin. Her sister, born in 1984, had died later in 1985, apparently in a cot death. In 1986, the mother disclosed that she had smothered her daughter. She was tried for murder, convicted of manslaughter and sentenced to seven years' imprisonment suspended on certain conditions. The eldest child of the family, a boy born in 1980, made complaints of chronic physical and emotional abuse, including an attempt by his mother to smother him. Concerns were also expressed that the child's mother might have sexually interfered with him. He was received into voluntary care in December 1985 and a fit person order was made in respect of him four months later.

L., the child who was the subject of the instant proceedings, was born in 1987. A place of safety order was obtained within a fortnight of her birth. She was then placed with the applicants, with whom she continued to live without interruption. The natural parents applied unsuccessfully for the discharge of the fit person order. In 1996, L. was made aware of her mother's admissions concerning the death of her sister. Around this time, L. discovered that it was possible for children to be adopted even where their parents were married. She expressed the wish to be adopted by her foster parents.

The health board conducted inquiries and was satisfied that it would be in her best interest to be adopted. Her mother strongly opposed this. Proceedings for an order under s.3(1) of the Adoption Act 1988 wended their way very slowly through the courts. (O'Higgins J. addressed the question of whether the delay was such as to warrant his refusing the order sought, under the European Convention on Human Rights; he concluded on the evidence that it was not.)

It will be recalled that the crucial provision in s.3(1) is the requirement that the court be satisfied that:

"(A) for a continuous period of not less than 12 months immediately preceding the time of the making of the application, the parents of the child to whom the declaration under section 2(1) relates, for physical or moral reasons, have failed in their duty towards the child, (B) it is likely that such failure will continue without interruption until the child attains the age of 18 years, (C) such failure constitutes an abandonment on the part of the parents of all parental rights, whether under the Constitution or otherwise, with respect to the child, and (D) by reason of such failure, the State, as guardian of the common good, should supply the place of the parents."

The first question in the instant case was whether the parents had failed in their duty towards L. and whether the failure would continue until she was 18 years old. O'Higgins J. rejected the argument made by counsel for the guardian *ad litem* of Lor, the younger sister of L., born in 1992, that the matters that had caused a fit person order to be made in respect of L. shortly after her birth were not properly matters capable of supplying the proof required under s.3(1)(I)(A) on the basis that they had arisen many years previously and not in the 12-month period immediately preceding the time of the making of the application. In O'Higgins J.'s view, although the failure had to relate to that period, it was not essential that the physical or moral reasons for the failure had to be evidenced by conduct which had taken place within that period. He considered that the court was:

"entitled and obliged to have regard to the reasons for the failure to fulfil the parental duties; not only would it be unrealistic to disregard the reasons for such failure merely on the basis that those reasons were attributable to events more than twelve months prior to the bringing of the application, but there is nothing in the Act requiring such an interpretation."

O'Higgins J. went on to express the view that:

"if the failure were due to a combination of physical or moral reasons the requirements of the legislation would be met because, notwithstanding the word 'or' in the legislation, it seems unlikely that the legislators intended to strictly compartmentalise the physical and the moral reasons. I am satisfied that the words 'physical reasons' should be interpreted so as to encompass mental illness. I accepted in the case of *Southern Health Board and M.D. and J.D. v. An Bórd Uchtála* (unreported, O'Higgins J., High Court, 20th December, 2001) that it would be an anomaly if mental incapacity, no matter how severe, accounting for the failure of the parent in his or her duty towards the child, would preclude the making of an adoption order (other than on grounds of moral failure). The unfortunate actions of the mother in respect of the brother who suffered physical abuse on an ongoing basis, (as well as emotional and sexual abuse) and her sister who was smothered were the prime reasons why L. was taken into care and were properly and understandably the cause of great concern. The death of S., another sister of L. gave rise for concern and was part of the circumstances in which L. was taken into care. I wish to make it clear, however, that the decision in this case is made on the basis that the mother is entitled to be presumed innocent of her death. The fact that L. has lost contact with her mother for many years following the disclosure of the mother's actions cannot be attributed to any unreasonable behaviour of L. or her foster parents but must be held to be a consequence of the actions of the mother, especially the actions giving rise to the manslaughter conviction. The combination of those actions and the illness of the mother satisfy the court that, in her case, the failure of duty was due to physical or moral reasons, as provided for by the Act. It is clear and is not in dispute that the mother has suffered from psychiatric illness for many years (at least from 1985) and she continues to be troubled with mental ill health. It is regrettable that psychiatric evidence was not furnished to the court in this case. The father must be considered to have acquiesced in this behaviour of the mother in that he was living at home and failed to take any action to prevent ongoing abuse notwithstanding that such would have been readily apparent to him if he exercised appropriate parental care. He

> has not seen L. for many years and has not attempted or even aspired to
> have any involvement parenting her."

O'Higgins J.'s analysis on the question of parental failure of duty merits a few observations. First, he is surely unquestionably correct in holding that mental illness falls within the scope of the words "physical reasons". Mental illness is not a moral failing. It would be a serious lacuna (as well as involving unconstitutional discrimination) if a distinction were to be drawn in this context between physical and mental disability. Secondly, O'Higgins J. was also surely right not to exclude the evidence regarding what the mother had done to one of her daughters simply because it had not occurred in the 12-month period immediately before the application. If it was relevant to the question of proof of failure of parental duty as required by s.3(1), then it clearly should not have been excluded. There is, however, a danger of eliding two separate questions. If a parent has unquestionably failed in his or her duty towards one child, (A), that is not a reason in itself, under s.3(1), why that parent should be held to have failed in his or her duty towards another child, (B), born after the earlier failure of duty by the parents towards (A), for the period of a year immediately before the application. O'Higgins J.'s analysis appears to address this requirement when he notes that the mother's smothering of L.'s sister and her ongoing abuse of her brother "were the prime reasons why L. was taken into care". Certainly the mother's ongoing abuse of L.'s brother was a failure of duty towards him and could credibly be regarded as a failure of duty, albeit indirectly, to L. also as the taking of L. into care was an entirely foreseeable consequence. Can it be so easily said, however, that the earlier failure of duty to L.'s late sister, however egregious its character, constituted failure of duty by the mother to L. 18 months later? Undoubtedly, the *effects* of that earlier failure continued to resonate, with damage to L., but is there not a difference between an occurrence and its effects? In the instant case it was perfectly sensible to infer from the dreadful act that had occurred that the mother might harm L., but the legislation does not in express terms permit the making of an order under s.3(1) on the basis simply of proof of risk of future failure of duty, however grave that risk or likely its occurrence may be.

O'Higgins J. next turned to consider the requirement that the failure of parental duty should constitute an abandonment on the part of the parents of all parental rights with respect to the child. The courts have had difficulty with giving conceptual substance to this requirement, as we have noted in earlier Annual Reviews, most recently, the *Annual Review of Irish Law 2002*, pp.247–255; in the instant case, O'Higgins J. was guided by Denham J.'s observations in *Southern Health Board v An Bord Uchtála* [2000] 1 I.R. 165 to the effect that s.3 did not require that there be an intention to abandon parental rights and that "abandonment" in s.3 did not have its ordinary meaning in common parlance but:

"should be deemed to be an abandonment within the legal term. The evidence must be such that it established the parents by acts or omissions so failed in their duty to the child that the circumstances are such that they may be deemed to have abandoned the child."

Undoubtedly this is true so far as it goes. The problem is that it still leaves undeveloped the conceptual substance to the notion of abandonment of parental rights. Is it concerned with the moral quality of the failure of duty? If intention is not a necessary element, has it nonetheless relevance?

In the instant case, O'Higgins J. did not engage in an analysis of the concept. He addressed aspects of the evidence which counsel for the mother and for the guardian *ad litem* for Lor had suggested constituted indications that the parents had not abandoned their parental rights.

Neither the mother's application for access between L. and Lor and improved access for herself nor the fact that the mother had taken opportunities to involve herself in issues concerning her son and L. was relevant to this question, in O'Higgins J.'s view. The mother's response to the possibility of L.'s adoption expressed in a letter to the Adoption Board in reply to a query could "not be said to be of any significance", in his opinion, though he acknowledged that the contents of such a letter could in some circumstances be of very considerable importance in deciding whether there had been abandonment. A "clear, informed and calm consent to adoption" might, in certain cases, be regarded as evidence bearing on the question of failure or abandonment.

O'Higgins J. concluded that the various elements mentioned by counsel were not of sufficient cogency to negate the rest of the evidence, which compelled the court to find a total failure of parental duty. He considered that there were "striking similarities" between the instant case and *Northern Area Health Board v An Bord Uchtála* [2002] 4 I.R. 252.

There McGuinness J. had observed that:

"the notice party has agreed to the continuing care of J. by the second and third named applicants over virtually J.'s entire life to date."

In the instant case, since 1991, and the failure to discharge the fit person order, no steps had been taken by either birth parent to attempt to exercise parental duties and they had to be taken to have acquiesced in, if not agreed to, the continuation of the order since they had failed to seek any review of the order over the following 13 years.

In the *Northern Area Health Board* case, McGuinness J. had stated:

"She is in addition happy that this situation could continue. She has allowed and willingly continues to allow J. to become in a practical sense a member of the second and third applicants' family. She has, in

> my view, abandoned the custody and care of her daughter to the second
> and third applicants."

It seemed clear to O'Higgins J. that some of McGuinness J.'s remarks had
application in the instant case:

> "There are no expressions of interest, intention or even aspiration to,
> on behalf of either parent to supply a parenting role in respect of L. I
> cannot conclude that the mother is 'happy' that the situation pertaining
> since 1991 should continue. However, she has acquiesced in the present
> arrangements. She has allowed—and continues to allow—and has not
> expressed unwillingness to allow—L. to become, in a practical sense,
> a member of the applicants' family."

Another important question that arose in the case concerned the possible impact
of making an order under s.3(1) on the best interests of Lor. On the evidence,
O'Higgins J. had little hesitation in concluding that the impact was not
detrimental since it would not discourage access between the sisters and in
any event their relationship was likely to improve as Lor became a teenager.
On the legal aspects of this question, O'Higgins J. rejected the argument that
the welfare of Lor should be regarded as "the first and paramount consideration"
in the proceedings under s.3(1) and thus of equal status to the position of L.
Section 2 of the Adoption Act 1974 required the court to have regard to the
welfare of the child involved in proceedings for the making of an adoption
order as the first and paramount consideration; this was L., not Lor. Section 3
of the Guardianship of Infants Act 1964 did not apply. It provides as follows:

> "Where in any proceeding before any court the custody or guardianship
> or upbringing of an infant, or the administration of any property
> belonging to or held in trust for an infant, or the application of the
> income thereof, is in question, the court, in deciding that question shall
> regard the welfare of the infant as the first and paramount consideration."

O'Higgins J. observed:

> "Although the question of access to Lor is extremely important and a
> consideration to be given due weight and attention I do not think the
> 'upbringing' of Lor is really in question in these proceedings. Nor does
> this case concern her guardianship or custody. In my view, the court
> has to take the interests of L. as being the first and paramount
> consideration. However, it is clearly obliged to take other considerations
> into account as well including the issues in relation to Lor about which
> evidence has been given."

The final argument advanced on behalf of Lor against adoption was that, because she was part of a family unit with the rights guaranteed under Art.41 of the Constitution, there was no power in the court (absent some wrong by Lor) to make the order sought because to do so would "deconstitute" the family unit so that it would cease to contain L. O'Higgins J. did not agree. In *The Adoption (No.2) Bill 1987* [1989] I.R. 656 the Supreme Court had rejected the contention that the nature of the rights of a family unit under Art.41 of the Constitution made it impermissible for the court to make an order of adoption in an appropriate case if such order was necessary to restore the constitutional rights of which a child had been deprived. It had specifically contemplated such an order being made in a situation which "disturbs or alters the constitution of the family".

FINANCIAL PROVISION

Separation agreement If spouses who separated many years ago have made a separation agreement which sought to wind up finally their respective rights and obligations relative to each other, how should the court in divorce proceedings today respond to an application by one of the spouses for extensive ancillary orders? The legislation gives an answer, albeit in general terms. Under s.5 of the Family Law (Divorce) Act 1996, the court, before granting a divorce, must be satisfied that "such provision as the court considers proper having regard to the circumstances exists or will be made for the spouses and any dependent members of the family". Section 20 reiterates this obligation and sets out a list of 12 matters to which the court must "in particular have regard". Section 20(3) provides that: "[i]n deciding whether to make an order under a provision referred to in subsection (1) and in determining the provisions of such order, the court shall have regard to the terms of any separation agreement which has been entered into by the spouses and is still in force." Section 20(5) provides that: "[t]he court shall not make an order under a provision referred to in subsection (1) unless it would be in the interests of justice to do so." Thus the court is placed under a double restraint: it *must* "have regard" to the terms of the separation agreement and *must not* make an order under subs.(1) *unless* it would be in the interests of justice to do so.

In *W.A. v M.A.*, High Court on Circuit, December 9, 2004, both spouses applied for a divorce, the wife seeking extensive ancillary orders. The spouses, who came from "comfortable agricultural backgrounds", had married in 1978. The matrimonial relationship had "collapsed by 1988 and probably sometime earlier". In 1993 they entered into a deed of separation and a side agreement, each having received full legal and accountancy advice. They divided their assets more or less evenly and undertook not to maintain proceedings against each other for a decree of judicial separation or any ancillary relief in the future. The side agreement contained the following term:

"... Neither of us will obstruct the other in seeking and/or obtaining a divorce a vinculo in the event of such other being entitled to seek and obtain a divorce a vinculo without infringing the constitutional rights of the party not so seeking such divorce and provided further that such of the financial and property terms contained in the [separation agreement] as remained to be performed at the date of application for such divorce a vinculo shall be incorporated on the application and by the consent of the moving party in such application into any decree which may be granted on foot of such application and provided further that any of the said financial terms or property terms that shall have been performed as of the date of such application for divorce a vinculo shall be excluded from the consideration of the court by and on the consent of the moving party in such application.

It is further agreed ... that this letter is not intended by the parties and shall not in fact approbate their alleged marriage and is intended solely to facilitate the parties in regulating their financial and property affairs and their marriage status insofar as such status be deemed invalid."

In the years after 1993, the husband prospered; with the assistance of his elderly mother, "a shrewd and formidable business woman", he invested wisely, using substantial borrowings. By 2004 his net worth was in the region of €7 million. In sad contrast the wife made bad economic decisions over the years. She engaged a supplier of labour services to work the farm. Hardiman J., on the evidence, regarded this as a highly inefficient solution. She sold off portions of the estate over the years and built a house which her accountant considered was too big for her needs. The wife said in evidence that she had been suffering from a form of emotional incapacity and a sense of being ostracised but Hardiman J. considered that this was "an afterthought" since she had not made this claim in the Circuit Court. Her asset value in 2004 was around €1.25 million.

Hardiman J. referred approvingly to the judgment of O'Neill J. in *K v K* [2000] 2 I.R. 416. Hardiman J. observed that O'Neill J. had analysed the relevant statutory and constitutional provisions "in a thorough and persuasive fashion". Hardiman J. went on to state:

"O'Neill J. distinguishes between a separation agreement which is relatively recent and one which is of more distant origin. The agreement in that case had been entered into in 1982. In my view, the significance of the date of the separation agreement depends entirely on the general circumstances of the case, at least in the case of an agreement made after the enactment of the Judicial Separation and Family Law Reform Act, 1989.

There are, of course, obvious differences between the circumstances in *K*, and those in this case. Firstly, there are no children in the present case: there were six in *K*. The wife in *K* had been for many years a full time homemaker: the wife here was at all material times engaged in an agricultural enterprise, firstly on her own account, then jointly with the husband and latterly on her own account again. In *K*, the learned judge held that the wife's work in the home 'was an integral part of the process which initially built [the husband's] career and ultimately led to his great success'. In this case, the husband's great financial success, so sharply distinguished from the wife's position, did not begin to take shape until after the collapse of the marital relationship. On the facts of this case it cannot be said that the wife made any direct or indirect contribution to the great commercial success which the husband has enjoyed in recent times. The contrary was not contended.

I have already made relevant findings in relation to the separation agreement of 1993. I am also conscious of the fact that s.20(1) of the Act obliges the Court to consider whether such provision as it considers proper 'exists' or will be made for the spouses. This phrase appears to direct the attention of the Court to the time at which the decree of divorce is granted. Into this exercise there must be factored firstly the twelve matters set out in the following subsection as well as other matters which the Court considers relevant and the terms of the separation agreement. While the events of the period since the separation agreement was entered into require to be considered so too must be what O'Neill J. called 'the length of disconnection [of the spouses] from one another'. In my view they have been 'disconnected' for about 17 years and formally separated for 11 and a half years. A marital relationship existed for something short of a decade at the most."

Hardiman J. went on to consider the question of finality or the "clean break". After quoting passages from the judgments in *DT v CT (Divorce: ample resources)* [2002] 3 I.R. 334, he observed:

"It appears, therefore, that the *desideratum* of certainty and finality, where that is attainable, has been fully recognised by the Courts. It is, perhaps, particularly obtainable in cases where the parties' resources are relatively substantial. The fact that this is so under the current statutory regime must colour the manner in which the Court 'has regard to' the terms of a separation agreement which, in the context of certain financial and property provisions, sought finality."

Turning to consider the matter specified in s.20(2) of the Act of 1996, Hardiman J. stated:

"The standard of living enjoyed by the parties before separation seems to me to have been one of comfortable but unostentatious sufficiency on a farm of approximately 350 acres. The parties, as found above, are 54 and 50 years old respectively. I find that they lived together in the matrimonial sense of the term for something under ten years. Neither has any physical or mental disability. I am satisfied that, subsequent to the separation agreement, neither party made any contribution to the welfare of the other in any shape or form. Prior to the separation, too, I believe on the evidence that neither party made any contribution over and above the other to the joint enterprise and that the division of assets between them in 1993 reflected the contributions each had made. I do not believe that the earning capacity of either party was impaired or foregone by virtue of any marital responsibility. Neither party, on the evidence, is entitled to any income or benefit under statute. The accommodation needs of each of the parties is amply met. I have no evidence that either party will forfeit any benefit or potential benefit by reason of the granting of a decree of divorce. Finally, I do not believe that the rights of any person other than the spouses will be at all affected by the making of a decree of divorce or of any imaginable ancillary order...

In relation to the separation agreement, I have already set out my findings on that topic. I believe it was a fair and approximately equal one."

Although most of the applications for provision under matrimonial statutes were by wives, some were by husbands. *Beech v Beech* [1995] 2 F.L.R. 160 was such a case, and the principal family asset was a dairy farm. However, it was heavily encumbered, an attempt to settle the parties' differences by agreement had been unsuccessful and the argument concerned provision for the parties out of the balance, over and above the encumbrances, received on a forced sale. In those circumstances the High Court in England had considered the husband's contribution to the financial embarrassment to be a consideration relevant to the determination of what payment should be made to him. First, the court posed the question:

"So the crux of the case is really the responsibility for the present near destitution of the husband. How has this come about? Who is responsible for this state of affairs? Is it the product of the husband's misconduct?"

The court found that the husband:

"... has proved over the course of the last twenty years to be a bad, even a disastrous, businessman. He had considerable talent as a stock man but could not harness that talent to financial controls... he obstinately, unrealistically and selfishly trailed on to eventual disaster, dissipating in the process not only his money but his family's money, his friends' money, the money of commercial creditors unsecured and eventually his wife's money, insofar as the disaster that eventually developed did not even pay for her specified agreed sum. The responsibility is, in my judgment, not shared, not hers, but his."

Hardiman J. therefore concluded that the position in England was that an agreement not to seek further provision was not binding on a court but should be given great weight when it was entered into in a considered manner and with advice. Furthermore, the conduct of a party in himself (or herself) bringing about the circumstances giving rise to the alleged need for (further) provision was itself of relevance to considering whether such provision should be made, and in what amount.

Hardiman J. then considered the impact of s.20(5). He concluded that it would not be in the interests of justice to make an ancillary order against the husband. He stated:

"I must in justice record my view that any difficulties which the wife now experiences are wholly of her own making and that the husband has contributed to them in no way whatever. Equally, the wife contributed to the husband's present state of prosperity in no way whatever.

Particularly having regard to the terms of s.20(3) of the Act of 1996, I cannot approach the question of what is 'proper' in the circumstances of this case without giving very significant weight to the terms of the separation agreement. I must also construe the word 'proper' having regard to its context as part of a statutory provision.

In all the circumstances, I do not consider it proper, that is 'fit, apt or suitable', much less 'correct or in conformity with rule', to make any ancillary order against the husband in the circumstances of this case. Still more fundamentally, I do not consider it just to do so and therefore I am precluded from doing so by the terms of s.20(5). I will accordingly grant a decree of divorce and make no further or ancillary order under s.12, 13, 14, 15, 16, 17 or 22 of the Act of 1996."

Garda Síochána

INTERNATIONAL POLICE INVESTIGATION TEAMS

EU Framework Decision on Joint Investigation Teams The Criminal Justice (Joint Investigation Teams) Act 2004 is discussed in the Criminal Law Chapter, p.236, above.

Health Services

The European Communities (Clinical Trials on Medicinal Products for Human Use) Regulations 2004 (S.I. No.190 of 2004) implemented Directive 2001/20/EC on the implementation of good clinical practice in the conduct of clinical trials on medicinal products for human use. They came into effect on May 1, 2004. It is worth noting that these very detailed Regulations do not completely supercede the Control of Clinical Trials Acts 1987 and 1990, though where they apply they are more detailed than the terms of the 1987 and 1990 Acts.

HEALTH SERVICE EXECUTIVE

Health Act 2004   The Health Act 2004 provided for the establishment of the Health Service Executive (HSE) with effect from January 1, 2005. The HSE took over responsibility for the management of the health services from the various health boards, which had been established under the Health Act 1970, and 27 other agencies which are listed in Sch.3 to the 2004 Act. These other agencies include the General Medical Services (Payments) Board, the Health Service Employers Agency and Comhairle na nOspidéal. The essential elements of the 2004 Act were based on the Government's 2003 Health Service Reform Programme, which in turn emanated from the *Report of the Commission on Financial Management and Control Systems in the Health Service* (the Brennan Report) and the *Report of the Audit of Structures and Functions in the Health System* (the Prospectus Report). The 2004 Act provides for the establishment of the HSE, to take over responsibility for the management and delivery of health services from the Eastern Regional Health Authority, the health boards and a number of other specified agencies. It also provides for the establishment of a national health consultative forum, regional health forums, advisory panels and a statutory complaints framework.

Health Service Executive   Section 6 of the 2004 Act provides for the establishment of the HSE. The Health Act 2004 (Establishment Day) Order 2004 (S.I. No.885 of 2004) established the HSE with effect from January 1, 2005. The Interim Health Service Executive (Establishment) Order 2004 (S.I. No.90 of 2004) had established an interim HSE, pending the enactment of the 2004 Act. Section 7 of the 2004 Act sets out the object and functions of the

HSE, notably, to use the resources available to it in the most beneficial, effective and efficient manner to improve, promote and protect the health and welfare of the public. The HSE is required to perform the functions under the enactments listed in Sch.3 which, prior to its establishment, were performed by the health boards and the other bodies dissolved on January 1, 2005. The HSE is also required to facilitate the education and training of students in health professions and its employees and the employees of service providers to the extent practicable and necessary to enable it to carry on its functions. The HSE is also required to have regard to the services similar or ancillary to its own provided by the voluntary and community sector, and to co-operate with other statutory authorities when performing its functions. As the activities of other public authorities can also impact on the health of the public, the HSE is required to co-ordinate its activities and co-operate with those other authorities. It must also have regard to the policies and objectives of the Government or of any Minister to the extent that those policies may impact on the functions of the HSE. Section 10 provides that the Minister for Health and Children may issue general directions in writing to the HSE for any purpose in the 2004 Act or any other enactment. The Minister is also empowered to issue directions regarding the provision by the executive of information and statistics which relate to its performance. The HSE is required to comply with any directions issued by the Minister under this section. The Minister is obliged to lay copies of any such directions before the Houses of the Oireachtas.

Board of HSE and Chief Executive Officer   Part 3 of the 2004 Act deals with the board of the HSE, which comprises a chairperson and 11 members appointed by the Minister, along with the chief executive officer, who is an *ex officio* member. Section 12 provides that the board is to be the governing body of the HSE. The chief executive officer has operational responsibility for the day-to-day running of the HSE. He or she will be responsible to the board for the performance of his or her functions and for the implementation of the board's policies. The board is empowered to appoint a deputy chief executive officer in the absence of a chief executive officer or if the position is vacant for any reason.

Section 20 provides that the chief executive officer is the Accounting Officer of the executive within the meaning of the Comptroller and Auditor General Acts 1866 to 1998. The chief executive officer will therefore be responsible for the preparation of the appropriation accounts and the Oireachtas appropriations vote of the HSE in the same way as a Secretary General of a Department. The chief executive officer is required to appear before the Oireachtas Committee of Public Accounts in his or her role as Accounting Officer, and s.21 also requires him or her to appear before Oireachtas committees when requested by those committees to account for the performance of the HSE.

The 2004 Act provides for the appointment of the first chief executive officer by the Minister on the recommendation of the board of the HSE. The first chief executive officer, Professor Brendan Drumm, was appointed in 2005. Any subsequent chief executive officer will be appointed by the appointed members of the HSE board following a recruitment process carried out in accordance with the Public Service Management (Recruitment and Appointments) Act 2004.

The Minister must appoint persons to the board whom he or she considers have sufficient experience and expertise on matters connected with the HSE's functions so as to enable them to make a substantial contribution to the work of the HSE. Members of the Houses of the Oireachtas, the European Parliament or a local authority will not be eligible for appointment to the board. This marks a significant departure from the arrangements for appointment to the now-disbanded health boards, whose membership included a significant number of local authority public representatives. The Brennan Report recommended that this should not feature in the HSE. Nonetheless, it was recognised that there should be some involvement of public representatives in the HSE. The 2004 Act therefore provides for the establishment of four Regional Health Forums which will comprise members of city and county councils within the functional area of the forum. This will give local public representatives an opportunity to make representations to the HSE on the delivery and operation of health and personal social services within their area. Schedule 2 of the 2004 Act contains the detailed provisions relating to the operation of the HSE board. Section 14 provides that the Minister may remove all of the board members in the event of the board failing to meet any one of a number of specified obligations including failure to comply with a direction of the Minister or any other requirement under the 2004 Act. The Minister may also appoint an independent person to review any matters related to the board's performance of its functions, if he or she is of the opinion that they are not being performed effectively. In the event of this independent review being undertaken, the HSE is required to co-operate with the person undertaking the review and provide him or her with all reasonable assistance.

Section 15 empowers the HSE to establish committees to provide it with assistance and advice. The persons appointed to these committees need not be members of the board, but may be persons who have the experience and knowledge required to advise the board.

Section 18 provides for the delegation by the HSE of some or all of its functions to the chief executive officer. Section 19 provides for the delegation by the chief executive officer of some or all of his or her functions to other employees within the organisation and their subsequent sub-delegation by those employees. This system of delegation is intended to provide employees of the HSE with clarity regarding their roles and responsibilities within the organisation.

Section 22 provides that the HSE is empowered to recruit its employees subject to the terms of the Public Service Management (Recruitment and

Appointments) Act 2004. The overall numbers, grades and terms and conditions will be determined by the HSE with the approval of the Minister for Health and Children and with the consent of the Minister for Finance. In relation to any proposed dismissal of HSE staff, the 2004 Act provides that the Unfair Dismissals Acts 1977 to 2001 will apply. The Health Act 1970 had provided a health board employee with access to appeal to the Minister in the event of a proposal to dismiss him or her. It was considered more appropriate that the employees of the HSE have the protection of general employment legislation, and it was pointed out that similar arrangements for local authority employees were made in the Local Government Act 2001.

The 2004 Act provides that the members of the HSE board and senior management will be subject to a code of conduct under s.10 of the Standards in Public Office Act 2001. The HSE must prepare a code of conduct which it must make available to all its employees and advisers and which must indicate the standards of integrity and conduct to be maintained by these persons in the performance of their functions and will form part of the terms and conditions under which a person is employed by the executive or engaged as an adviser.

Service plan and corporate plan   Section 31 provides that the HSE must prepare and submit a service plan to the Minister for his or her approval. The service plan must indicate the period to which the plan relates, the type and volume of health and personal social services it intends to provide, and estimate the number of employees for the period in question. It must comply with any directions issued by the Minister and accord with the policies and objectives of the Minister and the Government. It is also required to submit an estimate of its income and expenditure relating to the plan. Section 33 requires the HSE to manage the delivery of the services indicated in an approved service plan to ensure they are delivered in accordance with the plan. Section 35 of the 2004 Act requires the HSE to prepare a corporate plan which will set out its key objectives for the three-year period concerned, the manner in which it proposes to measure its achievement of these objectives and how it intends to use its resources. This must include a code of governance, including procedures relating to internal audits, risk management, public procurement and financial reporting. The corporate plan must be laid before both Houses of the Oireachtas once it is approved by the Minister and will be published on the Internet or in accordance with any other arrangement specified by the Minister.

Funding of voluntary groups   Section 65 of the Health Act 1953, which was repealed by the 2004 Act, was the basis on which many voluntary groups were funded for services which are similar or ancillary to the services (such as home helps and meals-on-wheels services) provided by health boards: these were commonly known as "section 65 grants". The 2004 Act retains this function within the HSE.

Complaints mechanism   Part 9 of the 2004 Act provides for the establishment of a statutory complaints framework which initially seeks to resolve the complaint at local level but with access to independent review if the complainant is dissatisfied with the outcome of the complaint. It also provides for access to the Office of the Ombudsman or the Office of the Ombudsman for Children if the complainant is still dissatisfied following the outcome of a review. This statutory framework will also apply to all service providers providing services on behalf of the HSE. If a person is unable to make a complaint because of illness or age or disability, a complaint may be made on his or her behalf by certain specified persons. Complaints must be made within 12 months of the actions giving rise to the complaint. Complaints cannot be made about certain issues which include matters which are or have been the subject of legal proceedings, matters relating to clinical judgment and matters relating to the recruitment and appointment of employees.

MEDICINAL PRODUCTS

Public supply   The Medicinal Products (Prescription and Control of Supply) Regulations 2003 (S.I. No.540 of 2003), made under the Irish Medicines Board Act 1995, consolidated and updated the controls applicable to the prescription and supply of medicinal products to the public in line with Directive 2001/83/ EC in so far as that Directive relates to the classification for the supply of medicinal products for human use. They also set out the classification for supply of medicinal products to the public as required by the 2001 Directive. The Regulations, which came into force on November 11, 2003, revoked a number of previous Regulations in this area, namely, the Medicinal Products (Prescription and Control of Supply) Regulations 1996, the Medicinal Products (Prescription and Control of Supply) (Amendment) Regulations 1996, the Medicinal Products (Prescription and Control of Supply) (Amendment) Regulations 1999, the Medicinal Products (Prescription and Control of Supply) (Amendment) Regulations 2000, the Medicinal Products (Control of Paracetamol) Regulations 2001 and the Medicinal Products (Prescription and Control of Supply) (Amendment) Regulations 2002.

Information Law and the Ombudsman

ESTELLE FELDMAN, Research Associate, Trinity College, Dublin

INFORMATION COMMISSIONER

All statutory references in this section are to the Freedom of Information Act 1997 (hereafter "the Act"), unless otherwise stated. The Act has been previously considered in *Annual Review of Irish Law 1997*, p.2 *et seq.*; *Annual Review of Irish Law 1999*, p.1 *et seq.*, p.350 *et seq.*; *Annual Review of Irish Law 2000*, p.273 *et seq.*; *Annual Review of Irish Law 2001*, p.391 *et seq.*; *Annual Review of Irish Law 2002*, p.306 *et seq.; Annual Review of Irish Law 2003*, p.373 *et seq.* In addition to hard copy, documents referred to may be found at the Information Commissioner's website: www.oic.ie.

FREEDOM OF INFORMATION (AMENDMENT) ACT 2003

Significant decline in FOI requests   In her Introduction to the *2003 Report*, the Information Commissioner noted that the most striking finding to emerge from her Office's *Review of the Operation of the Freedom of Information (Amendment) Act 2003* was the significant decline in Freedom of Information ("FOI") requests for non-personal information. In her *2004 Report* the Commissioner indicates that there has been a 50 per cent decline in requests:

> "I do not believe that the Oireachtas could have anticipated so great a decline in usage of the Act when amending the Act and approving the scale of fees to be charged. I believe that so great has the decline in usage been that a review of the scale and structure of the charges, particularly in relation to my Office should be undertaken. I should point out that Ireland is very much in the minority in charging fees for internal review and for an appeal to the Information Commissioner. In eight comparable jurisdictions looked at as part of the investigation, Ireland proved to be the only country which charges for internal review and is one of just two jurisdictions that charges for an appeal to the Information Commissioner." *Annual Report of the Information Commissioner 2004*, p.35.

SUPREME AND HIGH COURT APPEALS

Section 42 of the Act governs the right to take an appeal from a decision of the Information Commissioner on a point of law to the High Court. Such decisions issue consequents on a s.34 review: *Annual Review of Irish Law 1999*, p.351 *et seq.* The statutory barrier preventing appeals from the High Court to the Supreme Court was withdrawn by the Freedom of Information (Amendment) Act 2003: *Annual Review of Irish Law 2003*, p.391. Of the five High Court judgments delivered in 2004, four have been appealed to the Supreme Court; one of these appeals was subsequently withdrawn. The Supreme Court delivered its first substantive freedom of information judgment in May 2005, and a second appeal is scheduled for hearing in November 2005.

School league tables Section 53 of the Education Act 1998 and its relationship to the release of school information under the provisions of the Freedom of Information Act 1997 was first considered in *Minister for Education and Science v Information Commissioner* [2001] I.E.H.C. 116, *Annual Review of Irish Law 2001*, pp.396–391. Section 53 provides that in relation to examinations, the Minister for Education and Science has discretion to refuse access to any data that would enable the compilation of information (not otherwise available to the general public) with regard to the comparative performance of schools in respect of academic achievement, notwithstanding any other enactment. *Sheedy v Information Commissioner* [2004] I.E.H.C. 192; [2004] 2 I.R. 533; [2005] I.E.S.C. 35 considered a request for the release of five Inspector's Reports (Tuairiscí Scoile) on primary schools. The appellant, the Principal of Scoil Choilm, one of the five schools involved, appealed the decision of the Information Commissioner to release the reports, *inter alia* citing the requirements of s.53. In the High Court Gilligan J. affirmed the Information Commissioner's decision (Case No. 000238), but the Supreme Court—in its first judgment on an appeal under the Act—overruled that decision in relation to s.53 of the Education Act 1998 and its relationship with s.32(1) of the Act.

Trumping Freedom of Information Act Kearns J. (Denham J. concurring; Fennelly J. dissenting) stated: "In my view s.53 of the Act of 1998 overrides or 'trumps' any provision of the Act of 1997, unless of course, it can be shown that the school reports in question do not come within the protection offered by s.53."

Commissioner's understanding of exemption sections affirmed The Supreme Court unanimously affirmed the decision of Gilligan J. in the High Court and upheld the Commissioner's decision and the inherent interpretation of s.21(1) (a) of the Act, *i.e.* exemption from disclosure where access might prejudice future reports, and of s.26(1), *i.e.* exemption where information is given in confidence.

A detailed analysis of the Supreme Court's decision will be given in the *Annual Review of Irish Law 2005.*

Court representation

Third party rights The Commissioner, respondent to the appeal in *Sheedy*, challenged whether Mr Sheedy had sufficient *locus standi* to proceed with the case. The main parties in his decision on the request for the Tuairiscí Scoile were *The Irish Times*, requester, and the Department of Education and Science. Granting *locus standi*, Gilligan J. took the view that the applicant, as Principal of one of the schools reported, was a person affected by the Commissioner's decision [2004] I.E.H.C. 192 at para.8. The Supreme Court noted this decision and the fact that it was not appealed to the Supreme Court.

Procedure: Information Commissioner is a necessary respondent In *Re an Application by C.W. Shipping Co.* [2004] I.E.H.C. 49; [2004] 2 I.R. 321, the third-party appellant objected to the presence of the Information Commissioner as a notice party at a High Court appeal against the Commissioner's decision to grant access to a report held in records of the Department of Communications, Marine and Natural Resources notwithstanding, in the appellants' submission, that the information contained in the report was commercially sensitive: s.27 of the 1997 Act, Case No. 030036. The Rules of the Superior Courts (No.3) (Freedom of Information Act 1997) 1998 (S.I. No. 325 of 1998), as amended, apply. Murphy J. held that the Information Commissioner was entitled to be a party to the proceedings and was a necessary party to the proceedings.

Information Commissioner's costs The appeal to the Supreme Court initiated in this preliminary point of law was subsequently withdrawn, as was the earlier substantive appeal to the High Court. The appellant in *C.W.* was required to make a payment towards the Commissioner's costs.

Separated parent's right of access to records of minor *N. McK. v Information Commissioner* [2004] I.E.H.C. 49; [2004] 2 I.R. 12, granted the appeal brought by a separated parent against the decision of the Information Commissioner to affirm a hospital's refusal to grant access to medical records relating to his minor daughter (Case No. 000128). The hospital in question was the Adelaide & Meath Hospital, Dublin, incorporating the National Children's Hospital. The judgment is the subject of an appeal by the Information Commissioner to the Supreme Court.

Access to minor's records shall be granted This case involved consideration of the Freedom of Information Act 1997 (s.28 (6)) Regulations 1999, S.I. No. 47 of 1999, in particular, Art.3(1), which states that a request for access to a record that involves the disclosure of personal information shall be granted, *inter alia*, where:

"(a) the requester is a parent or guardian of the individual to whom the record concerned relates and that individual belongs to one of the following classes of individuals:

    (i)   Individuals who, on the date of the request, have not attained full age (within the meaning of the Age of Majority Act, 1985 ...) access to whose records would, in the opinion of the head having regard to all the circumstances and to any guidelines drawn up and published by the Minister, be in their best interests."

Quirke J. held that these terms are prima facie "imperative and positive requiring that access to appropriate records *shall* be granted where the requester is a parent or guardian and where the record relates to a minor (as in this case)." The only relevant qualification upon this requirement is that such access:

> " '... *would, in the opinion of the head, having regard to all the circumstances and to any guidelines drawn up and published by the Minister, be in [the minor's] best interests ...*'
>
> It has been acknowledged that no guidelines of the kind contemplated in the Regulations have been drawn up or published so it follows that the regulation imposes an obligation upon the [Information Commissioner] to form an opinion as to whether access to the records would, having regard to all the circumstances, be in the minor's best interests". [2004] I.E.H.C. 49 at paras 17–18.

It was held that the Information Commissioner had misconstrued these provisions by placing an onus on the applicant to prove that granting of access would be a tangible benefit to the child:

> "The respondent is not of the opinion that access by the appellant to the records will accrue to *the detriment* of the minor. The respondent construes the section as requiring that access must invariably be *denied* unless and until *'tangible'* evidence has been furnished demonstrating that the access will result in a benefit to the minor.
>
> I do not believe that this construction is the correct one. It imposes upon an applicant such as the appellant in this case, the obligation to discharge an onus which is not apparent from the terms of the legislation. The Act and the Regulations, when read together, provide that access *'shall'* be granted where, in the opinion of the deciding officers it is in the best interests of the minor *'having regard to all the circumstances'* ". [2004] I.E.H.C. 49 at paras 24–25.

Strained family relationship irrelevant The background to *N. McK.* is that during separation proceedings between the applicant and his wife, an allegation was made that the applicant had sexually abused his daughter. He vigorously denied, and still denies, this allegation. A Garda investigation into the allegations concluded that there was "no evidence to warrant a prosecution". The applicant was granted supervised access to his children. Subsequently, the wife died and, by agreement, the two children of the marriage went to live with the late Mrs McK.'s brother and his wife, with whom Mr McK. had a strained relationship. It was agreed, *inter alia*, that they and the applicant would be appointed as joint guardians of the two children. In January 2000 the daughter, then aged 12, was admitted to hospital.

With regard to the applicant's history, Quirke J. stated:

> "Although a complaint has in the past been made about the appellant, it remains unsubstantiated and the appellant comes before this Court enjoying the presumption of innocence which is enjoyed by every citizen of the State. The evidence indicates that he is concerned with the welfare of both of his children and avails of his rights of access to them in a conscientious fashion". [2004] I.E.H.C. 49 at para.29.

The judgment is rooted in Hardiman J.'s judgment in the Supreme Court in *North Western Health Board v H.W.* [2001] 3 I.R 622, which declared that any legislation vindicating and defending the rights of children must be interpreted in light of the Constitution, particularly Art.41 (The Family) and Art.42 (Education).

Parental primacy Quirke J. quoted extensively from this judgment:

> "… a presumption exists that the welfare of the child is to be found in the family exercising its authority as such. … The presumption … is not, of course, a presumption that the parents are always correct in their decisions according to some objective criterion. It is a presumption that where the constitutional family exists and is discharging its functions as such and the parents have not for physical or moral reasons failed in their duty towards their children, their decisions should not be overridden by the State or in particular by the Courts in the absence of a jurisdiction conferred by statute". [2004] I.E.H.C. 49 at para.27.

Having noted that there had been no suggestion of such a failure of duty on the part of the appellant, Quirke J. continued:

> "Accordingly the appellant, as a parent, joint guardian and joint custodian of the child concerned enjoys the parental primacy identified by Hardiman J. in *North Western Health Board v. H. W.* [2001] 3 I.R 622 and the presumption that he has the welfare of his child at heart, in the absence of evidence to the contrary.

The presumption is, of course, rebuttable, but there is no suggestion of rebuttal in this case.

Reluctance by another family member to agree to access does not, in the absence of any supporting evidence, amount to rebuttal sufficient to displace the said presumption". [2004] I.E.H.C. 49 at paras 31–33.

Regulations limiting prescription of public body misconstrued   In *Radio Telefís Éireann v Information Commissioner* [2004] I.E.H.C. 113 (June 11, 2004) the appeal centred on the interpretation of the provisions of the Freedom of Information Act 1997 (Prescribed Bodies) (No.2) Regulations 2000, S.I. No. 115 of 2000, (hereafter "the Regulations"). In accordance with s.3(5) of the 1997 Act, the Regulations applied the Act exclusively to non-programme-related functions of Radio Telefís Éireann (RTÉ) and certain specified subsidiaries: *Annual Review of Irish Law 2000*, p.278.

The appeal was brought by RTÉ against a decision of the Information Commissioner (Case No. 020336), to grant a requester access to data collected regarding the amount of radio and television broadcast time allocated daily to each political party during the general election campaign of 2002. The Commissioner gave a narrow interpretation to the exclusions under Sch.3 of the Regulations. Consequently, he found that the records at issue were created and held by RTÉ in the context of performing its management function of ensuring impartiality in broadcasting of news and current affairs under s.18 of the Broadcasting Authority Act 1960. On the other hand, RTÉ contended that the collection of the data—the subject of the request—was not a management function but an editorial function, and therefore fell within the exemptions of the Regulations. Ó Caoimh J. held that the exclusions to those functions of RTÉ covered by the 1997 Act must be interpreted widely. He concluded that the former Commissioner had erred in law in his construction of the Regulations and accordingly set aside the Commissioner's decision.

Onus in course of s.34 review Ó Caoimh J. queried whether a request for information from a body that is not a prescribed body under the 1997 Act, or is a public body only in limited respects—as in the case of RTÉ—and where the information so requested may not pertain to that body insofar as it may be a public body in those limited respects, whether such request can constitute an application under s.7 of the 1997 Act. This arose in the context of the Commissioner's reliance on s.34(12) of the Act, which, in relation to a request made to a public body, places the onus on the public body to justify its decision to the satisfaction of the Information Commissioner. While the substance of the case made by RTÉ was that it was not a public body for the purposes of the application in question, RTÉ did not seek to argue that the onus of proof did not lie on it. Ó Caoimh J. declared himself satisfied that the onus on an appeal on a point of law lies on the appellant and for the purposes of the instant appeal, irrespective of s.34(12), the onus of proof lay on RTÉ.

Inability of public body to find requested record   This issue was addressed in the *Annual Review of Irish Law 2003*, pp.386–388, in the analysis of *Ryan v Information Commissioner*, unreported, High Court, May 20, 2003. *Ryan* was affirmed in an *ex tempore* judgment of Smyth J. in *Holland v Information Commissioner* [2004] I.E.H.C. 176 (April 23, 2004). Here, the appellant was serving a sentence in Portlaoise prison on drug charges. Under freedom of information provisions, he had sought a copy of the report of Assistant Garda Commissioner Carty into the conduct of certain gardaí during the trial of Paul Ward in the Special Criminal Court. The Department of Justice, Equality and Law Reform refused the request under the provisions of s.10(1)(a) of the 1997 Act. This section provides for refusal of a request if the record concerned does not exist, or cannot be found after reasonable steps to ascertain its whereabouts have been taken. The Commissioner upheld the Department's refusal and this decision was appealed to the High Court.

Whyte J. noted that it is not the Commissioner's function to search for records, but rather to review the decision of the public body having regard to the evidence available to the decision-maker and the reasoning employed by the decision-maker in arriving at the decision. The Commissioner must decide whether the decision-maker had regard to all relevant evidence and whether he was justified in arriving at his decision. In addition to citing *Ryan*, Whyte J. affirmed the principles for the correct interpretation of the 1997 Act and the principles to be applied when considering only a point of law, as laid down by McKechnie J. in *Deely v Information Commissioner* [2001] I.E.H.C. 91; [2001] 3 I.R. 439, *Annual Review of Irish Law 2001*, pp.405–407, noting that in *Ryan* Quirke J. had similarly cited *Deely*. In addition, *Mara v Hummingbird* [1982] 2 I.L.R.M., at pp.426–427, was cited as authority that any findings of facts by the respondent cannot be set aside unless there is no evidence to support such findings, or they are—as was contended by the appellant in *Mara*— unsustainable and incontrovertible.

Procedural appeal to Supreme Court   The appellant had taken a preliminary appeal to the High Court, where he was refused leave to cross-examine the Information Commissioner's investigator on an affidavit filed as part of the proceedings in the substantive appeal. The appellant appealed to the Supreme Court from this refusal. The Supreme Court delivered judgment on December 15, 2003 and upheld the decision of the High Court to refuse cross-examination on the affidavit. (See also in Constitutional Law chapter, p.163.)

Personal liberty demands careful scrutiny   The court was conscious of its responsibility *vis-à-vis* personal liberty:

> "It is true, and in this Mr. Holland is correct, that where the liberty of the person is involved the Court must scrutinize very carefully the actions of the Respondent to be satisfied, as I am in this case, that the Respondent

acted within his powers and that he made all such enquiries and proper enquiries as were appropriate. It would not satisfy his functions if he were to do to so on a superficial basis or an inadequate basis and I am satisfied there was no superficiality or inadequacy in the enquiries made by the Respondent in this case."

Painstaking review by Information Commissioner The careful scrutiny applied by the Commissioner to such cases is also evident in her report concerning the adequacy of a records search conducted by Naas Town Council, see elsewhere in this chapter.

Certificate of exemption Under s.25(1) a Government Minister may exempt a record from the application of the Freedom of Information Act: *Annual Review of Irish Law 2000*, p.275; *Annual Review of Irish Law 2001*, p.409; *Annual Review of Irish Law 2002*, p.308; *Annual Review of Irish Law 2003*, pp.391– 392. In 2004 no new certificates were issued, but the Minister for Justice, Equality and Law Reform did renew for a further two years two previously issued certificates. A copy of the report in respect of these certificates is included in Appendix I of the *Annual Report of the Information Commissioner 2004*.

Notices of non-compliance
Section 37 Notice Under s.37 the Act provides for the issue of a notification to the head of the public body requiring the production of information and/or records.

Section 35 Notice Section 35 of the Act provides that, where a statement of reasons for refusing a request is deemed inadequate, the Commissioner may require the head concerned to furnish a further statement: *Annual Review of Irish Law 2002*, p.275.

　　In 2004 the Information Commissioner issued six s.37 notices—two of which were as a consequence of extraordinary obstruction—and one s.35 notice.

EXTRAORDINARY AND OBSTRUCTIVE
BEHAVIOUR OF TWO PUBLIC BODIES

Unreasonable attitude to Information Commissioner In the 2004 Report the Commissioner highlights a decision pertaining to records held by the National Maternity Hospital and relating to the Post Mortem Inquiry (the Dunne Inquiry). The substantive issue in this decision (Case No. 030830) is on appeal to the High Court. The Commissioner's purpose in the Report is to draw attention not to the findings of the review but to the behaviour of the Hospital in relation to the provision of the records to her Office, and to the approach adopted by the Hospital as to how she should conduct the review.

"On both counts, I regard the attitude of the Hospital as falling well short of the standard of reasonableness one is entitled to expect from a publicly funded body engaging in a process with a statutory office such as that of the Information Commissioner. I would go so far as to say that the behaviour of the Hospital in this case amounted to obstruction of my Office in the performance of its functions. This obstruction manifested itself in the following ways: in an unwarranted delay in the provision to my Office of the records at issue in the review; in an attempt to set pre-conditions before the Hospital would agree to co-operate with my review; in the adoption of an adversarial and confrontational approach in its dealings with my Office in relation to the review". *Annual Report of the Information Commissioner 2004*, p.17.

Right of entry to premises In light of the National Maternity Hospital's refusal to provide the requested records, the Commissioner invoked her powers under s.37(2) of the FOI Act, which provide for a right of entry to premises occupied by a public body. This is the first occasion since the establishment of the Office of Information Commissioner that the Commissioner has felt the need to invoke these powers.

Unnecessary reliance on legal advisers In its dealings with the Information Commissioner the Hospital engaged counsel in addition to solicitors. Expressing surprise that a public body should need to involve legal advisers in the routine issue of providing her Office with records requested in the course of a review, the Commissioner commented: "I am also concerned that, in conducting its business with my Office in this manner, the Hospital is likely to have incurred substantial and mostly unnecessary legal costs which ultimately must be at the expense of the taxpayer". *Annual Report of the Information Commissioner 2004*, pp.17–19, quote at p.17.

Admonition to hospital The Commissioner concluded her detailed account of her Office's interaction with the Hospital and its solicitors as follows:

"I find it difficult to accept that a public body should involve its solicitors in the quite routine matter of making records available to enable the review get underway. Indeed, even when minor routine queries arose in the course of the review, in relation to matters such as the numbering of certain records, these matters were dealt with by the solicitors rather than by the Hospital's FOI Officer as is usual. The practice of my Office is that reviews are conducted on an inquisitorial rather than on an adversarial basis. Unfortunately, the Hospital and its solicitors seemed not to appreciate this fact and adopted what I believe was an adversarial approach not only in relation to the original requester but, surprisingly, in relation to the adjudicating authority (my Office). **For the future, I**

believe the Hospital would do well to reflect on the nature of the instructions it gives its solicitors. It would do well, also, to reflect on whether it is justified in incurring what must be substantial legal costs in engaging solicitors to represent it in a way which hinders rather than helps the overall FOI review process". *Annual Report of the Information Commissioner 2004*, p.19 (emphasis added).

Inadequate search for records   In a case relating to Naas Town Council (Case No. 030520), referred to elsewhere in this chapter, the Commissioner notes that in its efforts to secure information necessary to carry out the review, her Office was forced to go beyond what would normally be expected in such circumstances. The adequacy of the search for any additional records was the central issue in her review.

Section 2(5) means all records under public body's control During the course of the review it transpired that the council had not checked with its solicitors as to whether relevant records were held:

> "In this regard, Section 2(5) of the Act makes it clear that a reference to records held by a public body includes a reference to records under its control. It was explained to the Council that, whether or not the records fell to be released under the FOI Act or, indeed, whether all of them were properly within the scope of the request, was a matter for my Office and that the information requested was necessary to enable the review to be conducted. In the event, the Council's solicitors did hold relevant records and these were eventually released. ...
>
> An inordinate amount of time had to be spent in pursuing what were perceived as possible 'gaps' in the records held and statutory notices were served on the Town Clerk and on the Council's solicitors before we were satisfied that all of the records had been provided". *Annual Report of the Information Commissioner 2004*, p.19.

Continuing failure of Oireachtas to review non-disclosure enactments
Section 32 of the FOI Act refers to non-disclosure enactments not included under any other section of the Act. Access shall be refused to any record whose disclosure is prohibited, or whose non-disclosure is authorised, in certain circumstances, by statute (including statutory instrument). In circumstances where such a statute is listed in the Third Schedule to the Act, the disclosure of records is assessed solely by reference to the other provisions of the FOI Act. Further, s.32 provides for a review of the operation of these provisions by a Joint Committee of both Houses of the Oireachtas. In the course of this review ministers must report to the Committee all secrecy provisions contained in the enactments falling within their respective areas of authority; each minister must state his or her view on whether these secrecy provisions should be

amended, repealed, or allowed to continue in force and, in addition, whether a reference to any of those provisions should be included in the Third Schedule to the Act. Each minister must lay a copy of his or her report before each House of the Oireachtas and also forward a copy to the Information Commissioner.

Since April 1999, the date of the first report, these reports fall due every five years, therefore one fell due in May 2004. The previous Commissioner appeared before the Oireachtas Joint Committee in November 1999, when he gave his opinion and conclusions relating to the reports the ministers provided. The Director General of the Office attended a subsequent meeting of a sub-committee of the Joint Committee in July 2000. It is the Commissioner's understanding that no report in respect of the 1999 review was presented by the Joint Committee to each House of the Oireachtas, as stipulated.

Neglect of ministerial obligation   In respect of the 2004 review, the Commissioner received copies of the reports of a number of ministers in satisfaction of their obligation under s.32(3) of the FOI Act. The reports of other ministers remained outstanding at the end of the year. The Commissioner concludes her report on the neglect of s.32 as follows:

> "I consider section 32 to be a vitally important provision of the FOI Act. It is the provision which maintains coherence throughout the FOI Act, ensuring that the widest and most informed perspective is taken on all provisions of all enactments which prohibit the disclosure, or authorise the non-disclosure, of certain records by holding these records up to scrutiny against the central purpose of the FOI Act which is 'to obtain access, to the greatest extent possible consistent with the public interest and the right to privacy, to information in the possession of public bodies ...'". *Annual Report of the Information Commissioner 2004*, pp.22–23, quote at p.23.

Trojan Horse effect   Section 53 of the Education Act 1998 is an example of a provision that has not been included in the Third Schedule. As noted elsewhere in this chapter, in its first consideration of the Freedom of Information Act, the Supreme Court ruled that s.53 trumped the provisions of the Act. In the absence of Oireachtas scrutiny of secrecy provisions, as required by statute, it remains to be seen what other non-disclosure provisions of legislation lie in wait to render the openness of freedom of information of null effect. This issue was previously discussed in *Annual Review of Irish Law 1999*, p.354 *et seq.* and *Annual Review of Irish Law 2003*, p.394.

OMBUDSMAN

In addition to hard copy, documents referred to may be found at the Ombudsman's website, http://ombudsman.gov.ie, unless otherwise stated. The Ombudsman is governed by the Ombudsman Act 1980.

Information Commissioner and Ombudsman compared   While both the Information Commissioner and the Ombudsman deal with matters of administrative accountability, as has been noted previously there are significant differences in the statutory role and responsibility of each Office: *Annual Review of Irish Law 2000*, p.276 *et seq.*; *Annual Review of Irish Law 2001*, p.409 *et seq.*; *Annual Review of Irish Law 2002*, p.310; *Annual Review of Irish Law 2003*, p.395.

Statutory Notices of Non-Compliance with Ombudsman Requests   A s.7 notice is a statutory demand for the provision of information required by the Ombudsman's Office in examining a complaint and is normally issued only as a last resort, when there has been an unacceptable delay on the part of the public body in providing the information requested: *Annual Review of Irish Law 2002*, p.314. Six such notices were issued in 2004. The Ombudsman welcomed this as by far the lowest number recorded since her Office began publishing the relevant figures: *Annual Report of the Ombudsman 2004*, p.28.

NURSING HOME CHARGES

The Ombudsman's Special Report on *Nursing Home Subventions*, published in January 2001, features prominently in the debate on nursing home charges. In brief, this report dealt with the payment by health boards of subsidies, or subventions, to patients in private nursing homes. It also dealt with the role of the Department of Health and Children in making regulations and overseeing the introduction and operation of the scheme nationally. In addition, the report considered the nature of the relationship between the Department and the Oireachtas, on the one hand, and between the Department and the health boards, on the other. The report identified a failure to allow a pocket-money provision in the calculation of the elderly person's means, and the erroneous calculation of family circumstances in the calculation of those means. As a result of the investigation, fundamental changes—which mirrored the Ombudsman's concerns—were made to the regulations and appropriate arrears were paid in affected cases: *Annual Review of Irish Law 2001*, pp.416–417.

Improper practices highlighted since 1988   In the 2004 Report the Ombudsman comments:

"The potential devastating impact—at a national level—of certain acts of maladministration has of course been brought home to all of us most forcibly through the ongoing nursing homes debacle. In that case a decades long failure to acknowledge the illegality of regulations put in place to charge public patients for nursing home care has now led to a potentially enormous cost on the Exchequer and by definition, on the taxpayer." *Annual Report of the Ombudsman 2004*, p.5.

She notes that over the years her predecessors had made the Department of Health and Children and the health boards aware of their opinion that long-stay care amounts to in-patient services and that medical card holders should not be charged for such services. This view was communicated regularly by her Office during meetings with officials of the health boards and of the Department: *Annual Report of the Ombudsman 2004*, p.28. Indeed, as far back as 1988, and repeatedly in the intervening years, the Annual Report records a complaint about nursing home charges: *Annual Report of the Ombudsman 1988*, pp.84–85. See also Feldman, "The Ombudsman: Redressing the Balance for the Older Person", in O'Dell (ed.) *Older People in Modern Ireland: Essays on Law and Policy* (Firstlaw, Dublin, 2005) (forthcoming).

Following the decision of the Supreme Court in *Re Article 26 of the Constitution and the Health (Amendment) (No.2) Bill 2004*, [2005] I.E.S.C. 7, the Ombudsman received a number of additional complaints in relation to repayment of the nursing home charges which the court had found unconstitutional. At the time of writing the 2004 Annual Report, the Ombudsman had already entered into preliminary discussions with the Health Services Executive (HSE) concerning the manner in which such complaints will be processed: *Annual Report of the Ombudsman 2004*, p.28.

Ombudsman's concerns regarding private nursing homes In view of the history and severity of the problems confronting the relevant authorities in resolving the difficulties surrounding the issue of nursing home charges, it is appropriate to quote the balance of the Ombudsman's remarks *in extenso*:

"It is my intention to examine these complaints under the terms of the Ombudsman Act, 1980, as amended. In doing so, I will take into account the individual circumstances of the complaint, the individual and general administrative actions of the health boards and the Department in the matter and any submissions they may make in relation to any complaint, relevant legislation and any determination of relevant issues by the courts. In any particular case where I find that maladministration has adversely affected a complainant, I will make recommendations for redress to the relevant health agencies or to the Department, as appropriate. As in the past, my focus will be on the administrative actions of the Department and the health agencies.

The current controversy has focused solely on the question of patients in public institutions. It does not deal with the issue of those patients, both medical card holders and non medical card holders, who had been directed by the health boards towards private care, without in any way acknowledging their own responsibilities in the area. I remain of a similar view to my predecessors in relation to the legal situation in this regard *viz.*, everybody resident in the State is eligible to be provided with in-patient services, where necessary, by the HSE. The services can be provided directly by the HSE in one of its own hospitals, in another publicly funded hospital, or by way of a contracting out arrangement between the HSE and a private institution.

It seems to me that those patients who were directed towards private nursing home care, and who subsequently made their own private arrangements, have an arguable case that they were acting out of practical compulsion or necessity in so doing. Equally, they might argue that they made their own arrangements in a mistaken belief (similar to patients in public nursing homes) as to their liability to pay for in-patient services. If those patients who were directed towards private nursing home care made their own arrangements out of practical compulsion or necessity or mistake, and consequently discharged an obligation which was, in fact, owed by the State, they may well have an arguable case for compensation equal to the amount of the State's obligation. In practical terms, the State's obligation could be regarded as (i) the actual amounts paid out in the private care, or (ii) the economic costs of providing the State service, or perhaps, more realistically, (iii) 80 per cent of the rate of non-contributory old age pension applicable at the material time". *Annual Report of the Ombudsman 2004*, pp.28–29.

STATUTORY INSTRUMENTS

There are no statutory instruments to record for 2004; source: Government Stationery Office.

Land Law, Landlord and Tenant Law and Conveyancing

**RUTH CANNON, Barrister-at-Law, Lecturer in Law,
Trinity College, Dublin**

CONVEYANCING

Time Clauses—Conditional Contracts

O'Connor v Coady [2004] 3 I.R. 271   A contract of sale between the appellant vendor and the respondent purchaser in respect of sale lands at Ashbourne, County Meath, was expressly made subject to the obtaining of planning permission within four months of the date of conclusion of same. When planning permission failed to issue within this specified period, the appellant wrote to the respondent stating that he was treating the contract as at an end. The respondent opposed this on the basis that no completion notice had been issued and subsequently commenced proceedings for specific performance. Carroll J. in the High Court found in favour of the respondent. She relied on the decision of Costello J. in *Sepia Limited v O'Hanlon* [1979] I.L.R.M. 11 to hold that the condition relating to planning permission was a condition precedent; that time was not automatically of the essence as regards such conditions; and that the appellant was not entitled to withdraw from the contract on expiry of the four-month period without serving a valid completion notice and waiting for the time period in same to expire without completion.

The Supreme Court allowed the appellant's appeal, rejecting the interpretation of *Sepia v O'Hanlon*. Two separate judgments were delivered, by Geoghegan and McCracken JJ. The third member of the Court, McGuinness J., concurred with both judgments. Geoghegan J. approved the ruling of the Privy Council in *Aberfoyle Plantations v Cheng* [1960] A.C. 115 to the effect that where a conditional contract of sale fixes a date for completion of the sale, then the condition must be fulfilled by that date, or, where no date is specified, within a reasonable time. Such time limits were not to be extended by reference to equitable principles. Although, *per* Geoghegan J., the expiry of the four-month period without a grant of planning permission did not automatically void the contract of sale, either party became entitled to rescind it, as and from this date, by communication to the other of the intention to rescind. Such communication could take place, as in this case, by letter; the service of a formal completion notice requiring completion within a specified period was not necessary. McCracken J. also regarded the service of a formal completion notice as superfluous in the circumstances. His judgment differed from that of Geoghegan J., however, insofar as he appeared to regard the contract of sale as automatically coming to an end if planning permission were not obtained within the period specified in the condition, stating that:

> "In my view there is certainly an argument to be made that where there is a fixed date by which there must be completion of a condition, the contract automatically becomes void on failure to comply with the time limit."

Much of the discussion before the court had been devoted to the question of whether the condition relating to planning permission was a condition subsequent, or a condition precedent. The court did not see it as necessary that the condition be so classified, however, since in its view the same rules should apply to both categories of conditions.

The issue of non-compliance with time clauses in planning permission conditions is one that occurs regularly in practice. The requirement imposed by Carroll J. in the High Court that a completion notice be served in the case of non-compliance with same appears to be out of line with UK and Australian authority and, in an era of rapidly rising house prices, to be unduly beneficial to the dilatory purchaser. In this regard the Supreme Court judgment is to be welcomed. However, given the expense of High Court litigation in conveyancing cases and the need for clarity in this area, it is regrettable that the question of whether such non-compliance renders a contract void, or voidable, remains unclear.

Hand v Greaney, unreported, High Court, Clarke J., December 15, 2004   A contract whereby the defendant agreed to sell and the plaintiff agreed to buy lands in County Offaly contained the following Special Conditions:

> *"Special Condition 7*
> This sale is strictly subject and conditional, to the vendor obtaining a Grant of full Planning Permission for 93 detached two storey dwelling houses, from Offaly County Council on foot of planning permission planning register reference number PL2/02/470, which said application for such planning permission has been applied for to date via a joint application between Golden Vale Marts Limited and Bridie Lee. Upon the said grant of planning permission issuing from Offaly County Council pertaining to the lands the subject matter of this sale, this sale shall be completed 14 days thereafter and/or 14 days subsequent to the issue of the original grant of probate of the estate of the late Annie Kearney deceased whichever is the latest. Once the said grant of planning permission has issued it is then the responsibility of the

purchaser to comply with any/all conditions attached thereto, insofar as it relates to that portion of the lands the subject matter of this sale, and duly comprised in part of Folio 8649 of the Register of County Kings AND also in conjunction with the owners of the neighbouring lands duly owned by Golden Vale Marts Limited in relation to (a) the common entrance, (b) the roundabout and (c) the common services pertaining to this entire development on foot on the entire grant of planning permission planning register reference number PL2/02/470. In that respect the vendor herein must enter into an agreement with the owner/developer of the adjoining neighbouring lands duly owned at present by Golden Vale Mart Limited in relation to the main access road (i.e. the common entrance) roundabout and common/work services affecting the boundaries of each of the respective properties."

"Special Condition 19
The purchaser shall not be obliged to close until:
  (a) the final grant of permission has issued from the local authority and An Bord Pleanála satisfactorily in all respects to the purchaser in his absolute discretion and particularly as regards compliance with the section schedule to planning permission reference PL2/02/470 being requirements of the local authority and approval required to be lodged before any development can commence and any other matter.
  (b) the vendor shall make all necessary arrangements as per the amendments to condition 7 herein to agree with Golden Vale Marts Limited arrangements satisfactory to the purchaser in his absolute discretion in relation to the services to be constructed for the joint benefit of Golden Vale Marts Limited and the vendor. The purchaser shall be advised of these arrangements as they progress and shall be notified of the arrangements prior to any final agreement being concluded between the vendor and Golden Vale Marts Limited regarding the provision of the services necessary to the development of the lands in sale and adjoining lands of Golden Vale Marts Limited."

"Special Condition 21
In the event that conditions 19(a) or 19(b) above are not met to the satisfaction of the purchaser then and in that case the deposit will be returned immediately with interest accruing to the purchaser. If the purchaser confirms that conditions 19(a) and 19(b) are met to his satisfaction then the sale will close not later than 21 days following on the grant of satisfactory permission and conclusion of an agreement with Golden Vale Marts Limited and the issuing of a grant of probate to the estate of Annie Kearney, deceased, whichever event is the later."

The defendant purchaser obtained a grant of planning permission from Offaly County Council, but same was overturned by An Bord Pleanála on appeal. The plaintiff vendor returned the deposit and commenced court proceedings, seeking a declaration that it was entitled to withdraw from the contract. This was opposed by the defendant, who argued that Special Condition 19 had been waived validly by him.

Clarke J. refused to hold that Special Condition 19 had been waived by the defendant. Waiver by a purchaser of a Special Condition that had been inserted for his benefit could only take place within the time limits specified in the Condition itself. Once fulfilment of the Condition was no longer possible according to its terms, the plaintiff was no longer entitled to waive it. In this case, compliance with the Special Condition became impossible when An Bord Pleanála allowed the appeal against the decision to grant permission; any waiver by the defendant had occurred after this point and was consequently ineffective. *Per* Clarke J., since compliance with the Special Condition was no longer possible according to its terms, either the contract ended automatically (*per* McCracken J. in *O'Connor v Coady* [2004] 3 I.R. 271, see above, p.333), or either party was entitled to rescind it by serving notice of the intention to rescind on the other party (*per* Geoghegan J. in the same case). In the instant case, as notice of intention to rescind had clearly been given by the plaintiffs, the contract was at an end from that date, if not before, and it was not necessary to choose between the two approaches.

Completion Notices
Birmingham v Coughlan, unreported, High Court, Smyth J., June 9, 2004   The plaintiffs, the vendors of lands in Folio 14915F of the Register of Freeholders, County Westmeath, brought an action against the defendant purchasers for a delay in completing the contract of sale. The contract in question incorporated General Condition 40 of the Law Society standard form Conditions of Sale (1993 ed.). On the twelfth day of July 2001, following the expiration of this closing date as specified in the contract, the vendors served a completion notice on the purchasers pursuant to General Condition 40. The defendants failed to comply with same within the specified period, whereupon the plaintiffs brought an action for specific performance together with interest in respect of the period between expiration of the notice period given in the completion notice and the date of actual completion. Such completion occurred prior to the hearing of the case, whereupon the specific performance claim was dropped, but the plaintiffs elected to proceed with the claim for interest. The defendants opposed this claim on the ground that the completion notice of the twelfth day of July 2001 was invalid because the plaintiffs were not, in fact, ready, willing and able to complete at the time it was served. Smyth J. accepted this argument and rejected the plaintiffs' claim. He identified four problems as to title, which existed in relation to the property, the subject of the sale. Three of these problems had ceased to exist at the date of service of the completion notice,

but the defendants had not been made aware of same by the plaintiffs. The remaining problem, namely the issue of wayleaves held by Westmeath County Council over the property, the subject of the sale, remained unresolved at the date of service of the notice.

Citing the decision of the Supreme Court in *Tyndarius v O'Mahony*, unreported, March 3, 2003, Smyth J. referred to the penal and draconian nature of a completion notice and stated that it was vital that the party serving same be ready, willing and able to complete. In this case:

> "The problem of the Purchasers was that they purchased a parcel of land and when documentation was received the conditions on site varied from those shown on such map or maps as were furnished to them. They could not be expected to buy into a lawsuit or close a sale when the Vendors were not in a position to give good marketable title and clearly explain whatever discrepancies had been highlighted in the correspondence. Appreciating the argument that was made in the course of the hearing that any developer would be anxious to have as clean a site as possible so as to maximise such development as might be possible on the site, I am nonetheless satisfied that notwithstanding that the number of linear metres by which the pipeline might be said to be out of "alignment" per the maps furnished with the way leave, does not mean that the Purchasers were obliged to conclude a sale which had certainly, to adopt the Plaintiffs/Vendors' euphemism, "<u>paper difficulties</u>". In my judgment, this was not a case of mere paper difficulties—the difficulties were real and not imaginary."

At the date of service of the completion notice:

> "[T]he Plaintiffs/Vendors, through their solicitors, had been advised by their own engineers that certain steps still required to be taken to resolve the mapping, measurement and boundaries of the wayleaves."

In the circumstances, the plaintiffs could not be said to have been ready, willing and able to complete at the time of service of the completion notice, which consequently rendered it invalid. The plaintiffs' claim was dismissed pursuant to the inherent jurisdiction of the court to stay frivolous and vexatious proceedings.

EASEMENTS

Express and implied grants and reservations
Conneran v Corbett, unreported, High Court, Laffoy J., December 15, 2004 The plaintiffs, tenants of retail property in a shopping mall, claimed

that their leases of October 21, 1991 and September 30, 1991, received from the first-named defendant, had the effect of giving them express, or alternatively implied, easements over adjoining land originally retained by the first-named defendant and subsequently sold by him to the second-named defendant. Each of the leases gave the plaintiffs the express right to use "car park delivery doors" for the purpose of receiving deliveries of stock and materials. Although it was not expressly stated that the car park delivery doors could be accessed by going through the land retained by the first-named defendant, this was clearly implicit from the location of the doors and was also the common intention of the parties at the date of execution of the lease. In the circumstances, Laffoy J. held that a right on the part of the plaintiffs to cross over the land in question, by foot or by lorry, for the purpose of accepting deliveries of stock and material for their retail units should be implied in the leases in order to give effect to that common intention.

The defendants argued that any such grant was limited by reservations 3 and 6 of the lease, which conferred on the lessor and his successors in title the right to redevelop, or build on any other part of the shopping mall and/or control, regulate, or limit the traffic passing through it and the delivery, or storage of stocks and goods. *Per* Laffoy J., the principle that "a man must not derogate from his grant" required that any conflict between the rights granted to the plaintiffs and the rights reserved to the defendants be resolved in favour of the former:

> "[W]hen a man transfers his land to another person, knowing that it is going to be used for a particular purpose, he may not do anything which is doing to defeat that purpose and thereby frustrate the intention of both parties when the transfer is made."

Per Laffoy J., the principle of non-derogation from grant required that the above reservations be construed narrowly, so as not to deprive the plaintiffs of the reasonable enjoyment of the easements and rights granted them by the Leases.

Bennett Construction Limited v Greene, unreported, Supreme Court, February 25, 2004   The plaintiff in this case had purchased land from the defendants. Prior to the sale the defendants had already obtained outline planning permission for a housing development on the land, and the plan accompanying the application for outline planning permission clearly showed a sewage drain running from the proposed development across adjoining land, retained by the defendants, to a foul water sewer on a road adjoining the site. The plaintiff was aware of this outline planning permission at the date of entering into the contract of sale with the defendants. However, the subsequent transfer to the plaintiff made no reference to an easement of drainage across the retained lands. Following completion, the defendants informed the plaintiff that they were not prepared to grant such an easement. The plaintiff argued that same was implied in the transfer pursuant to the principle of non-derogation from grant, s.6 of the Conveyancing Act 1881, or the doctrine of promissory estoppel. O'Higgins J. in the High Court rejected the plaintiff's claim and it was appealed to the Supreme Court. In a judgment delivered by Keane C.J. (Murray and Geoghegan JJ. concurring), the Supreme Court affirmed the conclusion of O'Higgins C.J. that no easements should be implied into the transfer. Since the right of drainage over the retained land had never actually been exercised prior to the sale, it was not a situation in which either the principle of non-derogation from grant or s.6 of the Conveyancing Act 1881 applied. Nor was there a clear and unambiguous promise by the defendants such as to ground a claim in promissory (or, presumably, proprietary) estoppel.

Prescription
Orwell Park Management v Henihan, unreported, High Court, Herbert J., May 14, 2004   The plaintiff, being the Management Company for a residential complex off Orwell Park Road, claimed to have acquired a right of way over a neighbouring lane, owned by the defendant, by prescription. The plaintiff relied on long user by its predecessors in title throughout the period 1937–1972 and based its claim alternatively on the Prescription Act 1832 (as applied to Ireland by the Prescription (Ireland) Act 1858) and the doctrine of lost modern grant. Herbert J. rejected the claim under the Prescription Act on the basis that the plaintiff and its predecessors in title had not enjoyed the right-of-way for the necessary period of 40 or 20 years immediately prior to the commencement of proceedings, as required by same. However, he held that the requirement that the user continue up to the date of commencement of proceedings did not apply to a claim based on the doctrine of lost modern grant. In the circumstances, the plaintiff had shown to be a continuous user of a sufficient duration to entitle it to succeed under this doctrine.

Herbert J. rejected the defendant's argument that any easement acquired by lost modern grant had been extinguished by abandonment since 1978. *Per* Herbert J., before abandonment of an easement acquired by lost modern grant (as opposed to an easement acquired under the Prescription Act) could take place, a fixed intention on the part of the owner of the dominant tenement never again to assert the easement or attempt to transmit same to anyone else would have to be proved. In the circumstances of the particular case, such intention was not shown to be present.

LICENCES

Deignan v Emmett, High Court, Carroll J., October 15, 2004   The Constitution of Erin's Isle GAA Club provided for the formation of a separate sub-committee dedicated to the promotion of pitch and putt, the section so formed being known by the name of Erin's Isle Pitch and Putt Club. As licensee of the GAA Club, the Pitch and Putt Club was allowed to occupy an area of the GAA Club. A dispute subsequently arose between the GAA Club and the Pitch and Putt Club, and the GAA Club sought to suspend its committee. The Pitch and Putt Club responded by claiming that, as a licensee of the Club, it had acquired rights under s.2 of the Landlord and Tenant (Amendment) Act 1971, which entitled certain sports clubs in occupation of property under a licence or tenancy to apply for a sporting lease in respect of that property.

While recognising that a licensee, as well as a tenant, could claim a sporting lease if they satisfied the conditions in s.2, Carroll J. emphasised that the wording of that section specifically restricted its application to "sports clubs". It was a necessary corollary of this that the claimant should qualify as a distinct and separate sports club from the individual or body against whom they were asserting rights. The Pitch and Putt Club did not satisfy this condition as it was merely a section, or sub-committee, of the GAA Club and not a separate sports club from same. In addition, the Pitch and Putt Club failed to satisfy other requirements of s.2, in particular that money have been spent on developing, or improving, or adapting the land so as to render it more suitable for the sport in question.

LANDLORD AND TENANT

Covenant by landlord regarding user of adjoining property
Kennedy, Bismilla v Mahon, High Court, Peart J., August 20, 2004   The plaintiff tenants sought an interlocutory injunction against the defendant landlords prohibiting them from consenting to, or permitting any of the other retail units in the development being used as a convenience store or off-licence. The plaintiffs relied on a written undertaking given by the defendants at the time of entering into the lease not to sell, or lease any other retail units in the development with the permitted use of convenience or off-licence. Although the defendants had arguably breached this clause insofar as they had sold an adjoining unit without imposing a covenant restricting its user, Peart J. refused to grant the interlocutory relief sought on the grounds that there was nothing to be restrained by injunction at this stage as deals regarding all adjoining units had been completed at the date of the court proceedings.

New Residential Tenancies Scheme
The Residential Tenancies Act 2004   The Residential Tenancies Act applies to all tenancies of dwellings, except those specified in s.3(2) of the Act. Within the terms of the Act, "tenancy" is defined so widely as to include most, if not all, situations where there is a landlord–tenant relationship. The definition of the term in the Act includes both periodic and fixed-term landlord–tenant relationships, whether oral or in writing, and also includes a sub-tenancy.

Individuals who occupy property under a licence from the property owner do not come within the scope of the Act. If the occupier of property has been granted exclusive possession of that property by the owner, he/she will more than likely be regarded as a tenant. An individual is regarded as having exclusive possession of property if he/she has the right to exclude anyone he/she wishes from the property, including the owner. The fact that the owner has the right to come onto the property for certain, limited purposes does not prevent the occupier having exclusive possession.

The initial reaction of landlords to the Act might be to try to avoid it by creating licences over their property, rather than tenancies. The Irish courts are very reluctant to treat an agreement as a licence however, and tend to construe occupation agreements as giving rise to tenancies wherever possible, particularly where the courts consider that the owner of the property is attempting to avoid statutory rights. Although licensees of the owner are excluded from the operation of the Act, it is worth noting that licensees of tenants are granted some statutory rights. A person who is in occupation of property as a licensee of the tenant during the subsistence of a Pt 4 tenancy may request the landlord to allow him/her to also become a tenant of the dwelling; the landlord may not unreasonably refuse such a request.

The definition of the term "dwelling" is also crucial in determining the scope of the Act. "Dwelling" is defined, in s.4, as including any building or part of building let as a self-contained residential unit and "any out office, yard, garden or other land appurtenant to it or usually enjoyed with it".

Certain tenancies are specifically excluded from the operation of the Act by s.3(2). These are as follows:

1. Where the dwelling is used wholly or partly for purpose of carrying on a business. The business must be of a type sufficient to give rise to a business equity under Pt II of the 1980 Act. It is worth noting that the definition of "business" in Pt II is very broad and includes charitable and non-profit activities. It also includes part-time business users. The business must, however, be bona fide; if carried on in breach of a term in the tenancy agreement, it will not be bona fide.

2. Where the dwelling is a dwelling to which Pt II of the Housing (Private Rented Dwellings) Act applies.

3. Where the landlord or tenant is a public authority or a body approved under s.6 of the Housing (Miscellaneous Provisions) Act 1992. The term "public authority" includes a government minister, a local authority, a health board, a voluntary body approved by Minister for Health or health board, or a recognised educational institution. State authoritites, local authorities and health board landlords are therefore not bound by the provisions of this Act.

4. Where the occupier of the dwelling is entitled to buy out the fee simple.

5. Where the dwelling is occupied under a shared ownership lease within the meaning of s.2 of the Housing (Miscellaneous Provisions) Act 1992.

6. Where the tenant's entitlement to occupation is solely for the purpose of a holiday.

7. Where the landlord also resides in the dwelling.

8. Where the spouse, parent, or child of the landlord also resides in the dwelling and no written tenancy agreement has been entered into by any person resident in the dwelling.

9. Where the dwelling is the subject of a tenancy granted under Pts II and III of the 1980 Act, or under Pt III of the 1931 Act, or in relation to which an application for a new tenancy under the Act is pending.

Part 2 of the Act imposes important obligations on landlords and tenants of residential property. These are implied in every residential tenancy agreement and, significantly, cannot be contracted out of by the parties. Chapter 1 of Pt 2 deals with the landlord's implied obligations. Not only does it replicate, in statutory form, the existing common law warranty of quiet possession but it goes on to specifically impose an ongoing duty of repair on the landlord in relation to both the structure and the interior of the dwelling (the terms "structure" and "interior" to be defined more precisely by the Residential Tenancies Board). This new obligation is much more extensive than the existing common law implied repair obligation on landlords: it applies not just to furnished lettings but to all lettings of dwellings, and it does not apply only at the beginning of the lease but rather is an ongoing duty that continues throughout the lease period. Part 2 also provides that if the landlord refuses to carry out repairs and it is unreasonable to postpone the repairs, the tenant is entitled to carry them out himself/herself and the landlord is obliged to reimburse the full cost. This imposes an extensive decorative duty on the landlord. The tenant has no responsibility for wear and tear under the Act. Although the tenant cannot do any act that would cause deterioration in the condition of the buildings, he/she is not liable for ordinary wear and tear; it is the responsibility of the landlord.

    Other new implied duties imposed on the landlord are: the duty to insure against destruction and liability; the obligation to repay any deposit paid by the tenant unless there has been failure to pay rent or damage caused to the dwelling; the obligation to notify the tenant of the name of the person authorised to act on his/her behalf in relation to the tenancy; and the duty to detail to the tenant how he/she or his/her authorised agent can be contacted. The landlord also has a duty not to penalise the tenant for enforcing his/her rights under the Act, and a duty to third parties to enforce the obligations of the tenant. Further, the landlord has an obligation to return any deposit paid by the tenant, unless there has been default in the payment of rent or an act causing deterioration in the value of the dwelling.

The obligations of the tenant are set out in Chapter 2 of Pt 2, which states that these obligations are "in addition to the obligations arising by or under any other enactment". The tenant is under a duty to pay the rent and also to pay any charges or taxes required by the tenancy agreement. The tenant is also under a duty not to act/fail to act in such a way as to prevent the landlord's statutory obligations in relation to the dwelling from being complied with. The tenant is under a duty to allow the landlord access to the premises at reasonable intervals for the purpose of inspecting the dwelling, to notify the landlord of any defect in the dwelling that requires repair and to provide the landlord with reasonable access for the purpose of carrying out such works.

Other duties of the tenant are as follows:

1. Not to do any act that would cause a deterioration in the condition the dwelling was in at the commencement of the tenancy (but normal wear and tear is excepted from this).

2. Not to behave or allow others in the dwelling to behave in an anti-social manner, or to act in a way that might invalidate insurance policy or cause an increase in the landlord's insurance premium.

3. Not to assign or sublet without prior written consent of landlord; however, it is worth noting that the Act states that a tenant can terminate the tenancy immediately if the landlord's consent to an assignment or subletting is withheld.

4. Not to alter or improve the dwelling without the prior written consent of the landlord.

5. Not to use the dwelling for any purpose other than a dwelling without the prior written consent of the landlord.

6. To notify the landlord of the identity of each person residing in the dwelling.

The Act specifically states that the above obligations cannot be contracted out of. Additional obligations can be imposed on the tenant "only if those obligations are consistent with every other part of the act". Part 2 also provides that a landlord of a dwelling shall not penalise a tenant for referring any dispute to the Residential Tenancies Board, giving evidence in any proceedings under the Residential Tenancies Board, or giving notice of his/her intention to do same.

Part 3 of the Act deals with rent. The initial rent under a tenancy shall not be greater than the market rent at the time of commencement of the tenancy and any subsequent rent imposed on foot of a rent review shall not be greater than the market rent at the time of that rent review. Market rent is defined as the rent a willing tenant, not already in occupation, would give and a willing landlord would take for the dwelling on the basis of vacant possession. The Act also implies a term in every lease or tenancy in which either party may require a review of the rent, even if the lease or tenancy does not contain a rent review clause. However, a rent review—whether expressly provided for under the lease/tenancy or implied under the Act—may not occur more frequently than once every 12 months, nor can there be a rent review within the first 12 months of the tenancy unless there is a substantial change in the nature of the dwelling.

Part 4 of the Act creates a new right to a statutory tenancy. If a tenant is in occupation of a dwelling for a continuous period of six months after the coming into effect of the Act and no notice of termination is served during that period, he/she will get the right to continue in occupation for a period of up to four years from the date of initial commencement of occupation under the tenancy. This right is known as a "Part 4 tenancy". Subject to contrary agreement between the parties, the same terms are to apply to the Part 4 tenancy as to the original tenancy and obviously it is subject to rent review according to the conditions set out in Pt 3 of the Act.

The Act further provides that the landlord can prevent a second, or subsequent, "Part 4 tenancy" arising by serving a notice of termination before the expiry of the earlier Part 4 tenancy, or six months after the commencement of the subsequent Part 4 tenancy. Once notice has been served, the tenant will have the right to stay on until either the end of the earlier Part 4 tenancy or until the expiry of the notice period, whichever is the later. Therefore, if the landlord follows the correct procedure, he/she can avoid a second, or subsequent, Part 4 tenancy being granted, without having to give any reason for same.

The tenant can at any time use the termination procedure in Pt 5 of the Bill to bring to an end a Part 4 tenancy. The landlord, on the other hand, can only terminate a Part 4 tenancy in certain, specified situations as detailed in s.34 of the Act, namely where:

- the tenant fails to comply with any of his/her obligations in relation to the tenancy and fails to remedy that failure on request;

- the dwelling is no longer suitable to the accommodation needs of the tenant;

- the landlord intends to enter into an enforceable agreement for the transfer to another for full consideration of the transfer of his/her interest;

- the landlord requires the dwelling or the property containing the dwelling for his/her own occupation, or for occupation by a member of his/her family;

- the landlord intends to substantially refurbish or renovate the dwelling or the property containing the dwelling in a way that requires the dwelling to be vacated for that purpose and for which renovations planning permission has been obtained, if necessary;

• the landlord intends to change the use of the dwelling and any necessary planning permission has been obtained.

The Act also sets out a number of situations in which the tenant is deemed to have terminated a Part 4 tenancy and the landlord may recover possession, namely, if the tenant vacates the dwelling while owing rent and having served a termination notice that does not give the required period of notice, or if he/she falls more than 28 days behind with the rent payments, provided that the tenancy in either case has not been sublet or assigned.

The Act provides that a residential tenant can renounce his/her entitlement to a statutory tenancy under Pt II of the Landlord and Tenant (Amendment) Act 1980 by executing a renunciation in writing. In addition, it provides that the rights of residential tenants as per Pt II will come to an end five years after the coming into force of the Act.

Chapter 6 of Pt 4 applies to multiple tenants. A "multiple tenant" is defined as a person(s) who co-owns the leasehold interest in the dwelling with one or more other persons. The fact that the continuous period of occupation by one or more of the multiple tenants is less than six months does not prevent a Part 4 tenancy coming into being in respect of the dwelling if another of the multiple tenants has been in continuous occupation of the dwelling for six months. Once a Part 4 tenancy comes into being, each of the multiple tenants benefits from the protection afforded by that tenancy and if, after the creation of the Part 4 tenancy, the landlord accepts another person as a co-tenant of the dwelling, then that person will also benefit automatically from the Part 4 tenancy.

No act done by any one or more of the multiple tenants, which would lead to the termination of the Part 4 tenancy, shall have such result if the other tenant can provide an explanation to the landlord from which a landlord would reasonably conclude that that act was done without consent of that other tenant. However, the tenant who carried out the act and any other multiple tenants who consent to it lose the protection of the Part 4 tenancy and the landlord can obtain a determination requiring them to vacate possession of the dwelling. Neither the vacating of possession of the dwelling concerned by the multiple tenant whose occupation gave rise to the Part 4 tenancy nor the death of that tenant shall deprive the other multiple tenants of the benefit of that tenancy protection.

Although licensees of the owner are excluded from the operation of the Bill, it is worth noting that licensees of tenants are given some statutory rights. A person who is in occupation of property as a licensee of the tenant during the subsistence of a Part 4 tenancy may request the landlord to allow him/her to also become a tenant of the dwelling; the landlord may not unreasonably refuse such a request.

The issue of the rights of sub-tenants under sub-tenancies created by Part 4 tenants is dealt with in the Schedule to the Act rather than in Pt 4. Clause 2 of the Schedule states that if a sub-tenancy is created out of a Part 4 tenancy with the written consent of the landlord, then the sub-tenancy shall continue in being for so long as the Part 4 tenancy continues in being. Any notice of termination served by the landlord in respect of the Part 4 tenancy must also include a requirement to terminate the sub-tenancy. If the landlord terminates the Part 4 tenancy, the sub-tenant may make an application to the Board to the effect that he/she has been unjustly deprived of possession of the dwelling. The above provisions apply only if the landlord gives written consent to the sub-tenancy and landlords should therefore be aware of the implications of giving such written consent.

Part 5 of the Act abolishes old termination procedures, such as forfeiture and notice to quit, and replaces them with a new "notice of termination" procedure for all residential tenancies. The notice of termination must be in writing and must be signed by the landlord or his/her authorised agent. It must specify its date of service and the termination date. If the duration of the tenancy is more than six months, the notice must specify the reason for the termination. It must further state that any dispute about the validity of the notice be referred to the Residential Tenancy Board.

Once the notice of termination is served, the notice period must expire before the tenancy ends. The notice periods vary depending on the duration of the occupation from the date of coming into effect of the Act and also on the reason for the termination. In assessing the appropriate notice periods, it is necessary to look at the duration of the occupation from the date of coming into effect of the Act rather than the type of landlord–tenant relationship involved. The notice period may also vary if there has been a breach of obligations. The parties may agree between themselves to reduce the notice periods, but only after the landlord has communicated to the tenant his/her intention to terminate the tenancy.

The notice of termination procedure may be initiated either by the tenant or by the landlord. However, a landlord cannot serve a notice of termination if the tenancy is one to which Pt 4 applies, except in accordance with the provisions of that Part. In addition, the notice of termination procedure cannot be used by the tenant or by the landlord to shorten a fixed-term lease, unless there has been a failure by the other party to comply with their obligations. It is unclear whether the landlord must serve a notice when a fixed-term lease comes to an end, a point that should have been clarified in the Act.

Additional requirements are necessary where a tenancy has been sublet. A notice of termination in respect of the head tenancy must state whether or not the landlord requires the head tenant, under the head tenancy, to terminate the sub-tenancy. If this is the case a copy of the notice of termination must also be served on the tenant of the sub-tenancy. Within 28 days of receipt of the notice the head tenant must serve a notice of termination in respect of the sub-tenancy on the sub-tenant, unless the head tenant is disputing the validity of the notice and referring a complaint to the Board. Where the notice does not require the head tenant to terminate the sub-tenancy, it must nonetheless be forwarded to the sub-tenant. If the notice does not require the head tenant to terminate the sub-tenancy and a dispute in relation to the validity of the notice is referred to the Board, the head tenant must notify the sub-tenant of this.

Part 6 applies to any issue between the parties regarding compliance by either party with their obligations as landlord and tenant, or regarding the legal relations between the parties. From the date of coming into effect of this Part:

> "proceedings may not be instituted in any court in respect of a dispute that may be referred to the Board for resolution under that Part unless one of the following reliefs is being claimed in the proceedings
>   (a) damages of an amount of more than 20,000 Euros
>   (b) recovery of arrears of rent of an amount of more than 20,000 Euros
>   (c) recovery of other charges of an amount of more than 20,000 Euros."

Once an issue comes within Pt 6, the Residential Tenancies Board has exclusive jurisdiction. Either party may refer the issue to the Board for resolution, with or without the consent of the other side. There are strict time limits regarding referral of disputes and relating to the validity of a notice of termination; such disputes cannot be referred to the Board more than 28 days after the receipt of the notice by the other side. However, the Board has jurisdiction to extend this time limit. Otherwise the normal time limits laid down in the Statute of Limitations 1957 apply.

The party who refers the matter to the Board can withdraw the matter at any time. The existence of an arbitration clause in the lease or tenancy agreement cannot be used to preclude referral to the Board. The Board can invite parties to submit to mediation; if both sides consent, this can be done. Where no agreement to refer to mediation is reached, the Board will appoint an adjudicator. It is possible to appeal the determination of the adjudicator to the Tenancy Tribunal, which is a three-person body appointed by the Board. From the determination of the Tenancy Tribunal an appeal on a point of law can be made only to the High Court. However, it is possible to make an application to the Circuit Court to enforce determination orders made by the mediator, the adjudicator, or the Tenancy Tribunal that have not been obeyed.

Under Pt 7 of the Act the landlord of a dwelling is obliged to apply to the Board to register a tenancy of that dwelling. This obligation arises within one month of the commencement of the tenancy. In the case of tenancies created before the coming into effect of the Act, the landlord has three months from the coming into effect of the Act to register the tenancy. It is not a criminal offence to fail to register a tenancy, however. It is only a criminal offence to furnish false or misleading particulars to the Board. If it comes to the attention of the Board that a tenancy has not been registered, the Board shall serve a notice on the landlord of that tenancy. This action can be followed by a further notice being served on the landlord. If the landlord fails to register on foot of the further notice, he/she is guilty of a criminal offence.

MORTGAGES

Judgment Mortgages

Irwin v Deasy, unreported, High Court, Finlay Geoghegan J., March 1, 2004   The defendant had obtained three judgments against the plaintiff that it converted into judgment mortgages over registered land that she held as joint tenant with her husband. These judgment mortgages were subsequently registered on the appropriate Land Registry folio. The plaintiff mortgagee brought proceedings seeking an order of sale in lieu of partition.

Finlay Geoghegan J. stated that the judgment mortgages had the effect of severing the joint tenancy of the property and that they applied to the moiety in favour of the plaintiff, which arose as a result of the severance. She considered the nature of the right to sale in lieu of partition under the Partition Act 1868 and drew attention, in particular, to the wording of s.3 and s.4 thereof, which provided that such right arose only where the court had jurisdiction to make an order for partition under the Partition Act 1542. She rejected the suggestion made by Murphy J. in *O'D v O'D,* unreported, High Court, November 18, 1983, that the Statute Law Revision (Pre-Union Irish Statutes) Act 1962 might have had the effect of removing the jurisdiction to grant partition under that Act, preferring the view of Barr J. in *FF v CF* [1987] I.L.R.M. 1 that such jurisdiction was preserved by s.2(1) of the 1962 Act.

Although ultimately concluding that, as the property, the subject of the judgment mortgage, was registered land, no right to sale in lieu of partition arose in favour of the Plaintiff under the 1868 Act (due to the fact that a judgment mortgagee of registered land does not have ownership rights over the premises, the subject of the mortgage, but merely a charge over same), Finlay Geoghegan J. took the view that s.71 of the Registration of Title Act 1964, which expressly provided that a judgment mortgagee of registered land should have "such rights and remedies as may be conferred on him by order of the Court", provided her with an alternative jurisdiction to grant a partition order in this case.

Holohan v Aughey, unreported, High Court, Finlay Geoghegan J., June 28, 2004   In 1993 an initial judgment mortgage was registered over the defendant's property by one John Browne. Subsequently, Browne assigned his judgment debt to the plaintiff under s.28(6) of the Judgment Mortgages Act 1877. The plaintiff registered a subsequent judgment mortgage in respect of the same debt in 2000 and sought a well-charging order in respect of same. The defendant argued that the 2000 judgment mortgage in favour of the plaintiff was invalid and of no effect because at the time it was created there was an existing judgment mortgage on the property in respect of the same debt. The plaintiff submitted that the 2000 judgment mortgage was valid because the 1993 mortgage had been extinguished by that date, due to failure to re-register same within five years of its creation and because the assignment of the judgment debt by the original judgment mortgagee justified the registration of a second judgment mortgage by the assignee. Finlay Geoghegan J. expressed reservations regarding the plaintiff's argument that the 1993 mortgage had been extinguished by s.4 of the 1877 Act, taking the view that this section applied only to judgment mortgages obtained prior to the coming into effect of that Act. In her view, s.6 of the 1877 Act would have been a more appropriate section to raise in this regard. However, she did accept the plaintiff's second argument to the effect that the assignment of the debt by the 1993 judgment mortgagee had the effect of terminating that judgment mortgage so as to permit the registration of a fresh judgment mortgage by the assignee.

Negative Pledge Clauses
Re Salthill Properties Limited, unreported, High Court, Laffoy J., July 30, 2004   The receiver of the above-mentioned company brought an application under s.316 of the Companies Act 1963 seeking directions, *inter alia*, on whether certain leases entered into by the company in 1999 breached a negative pledge clause in a prior mortgage agreement binding the property. The clause in question precluded the company from selling, transferring, lending, leasing, or otherwise disposing of the property without the consent of the mortgagee. Laffoy J. extended the rules developed in relation to the effect of negative pledge clauses in floating charges to cover the situation before the court: in order to avoid taking subject to the mortgage, the lessee must show that he/she had no actual notice of same. On the facts of the particular case, the lessee had failed to discharge this burden and consequently took subject to the mortgages.

PROPRIETARY ESTOPPEL

JC v WC [2004] 2 I.R. 312   The plaintiff in this case commenced legal action in the Circuit Court seeking to exclude the defendant, his son, from his lands. The defendant counter-claimed, claiming an interest under a constructive trust, or alternatively the right to specific performance of a partly performed agreement for transfer of the lands to him. The plaintiff succeeded in the Circuit Court and the defendant's counter-claim was dismissed. The defendant appealed to the High Court against the finding on the specific performance issue, arguing that his father had promised him that he would inherit the lands in return for working on them and that he had relied on same to his detriment. Murphy J. rejected the defendant's appeal. There had been no definite terms of offer and acceptance sufficient to constitute an agreement between the parties regarding the transfer of the land. Nor had any consideration been requested from the defendant by the plaintiff. As there was no contract, the question of part-performance did not arise. However, Murphy J. indicated that even if there had been a contract to transfer the land to the defendant, the defendant's work on the land could not be said to constitute part-performance of same since he had been paid for this work and had also been provided with a house and other land by the plaintiff. In the circumstances, the alleged acts of part-performance were not unequivocally referable to the type of contract alleged.

Although the defendant's grounds of appeal appear to have been based on breach of contract rather than on proprietary estoppel, Murphy J. specifically distinguished the case before him from those situations in which a court would be prepared to grant a remedy on the basis of an estoppel, pointing out that whereas the vast majority, if not all, of the Irish proprietary estoppel cases involved claims against the estates of deceased persons, in this case the defendant was asserting a present entitlement to land rather than an expectation of inheriting it under a will. In addition, the defendant did not appear, in fact, to have suffered any detriment by reason of his expectation that the land would be transferred to him.

Owens v Duggan, unreported, High Court, Hardiman J., April 2, 2004   This case also involved the issues of part-performance and proprietary estoppel. The plaintiff was the owner of Enniskerry Lodge, County Wicklow. In addition to owning an acre behind this property, known as "the Arena", the defendant had a right-of-way along the drive of Enniskerry Lodge and owned a small area of land ("the Sliver") adjacent to same. The defendant decided to build a house on "the Arena" and reached an oral agreement with the plaintiff to the effect that, if the plaintiff did not object to the defendant's application for planning permission in respect of same, the defendant would execute a deed releasing this right-of-way and transferring ownership of "the Sliver" to the plaintiff. No note or memorandum of this oral agreement was ever signed by the defendant, however in reliance on same, the plaintiff refrained from objecting to the planning application. After obtaining planning permission, the defendant refused to relinquish his rights over the driveway and "the Sliver", arguing that the agreement was only an oral agreement and not binding. The plaintiff succeeded in Circuit Court proceedings for breach of contract/ proprietary estoppel, whereupon the defendant appealed to the High Court. Hardiman J. rejected the defendant's appeal, stating that the situation was a classic case of proprietary estoppel. In the circumstances, the plaintiff had incurred detriment in reliance on the defendant's undertaking by giving up his right to object to the defendant's proposed development. The detriment suffered by the plaintiff made it unconscionable for the defendant to go back on the assurance given by him. In the circumstances, the defendant was obliged to release the right-of-way and transfer "the Sliver" to the plaintiff.

Licensing

INTOXICATING LIQUOR

The primary purpose of the Intoxicating Liquor Act 2004 was to amend the Intoxicating Liquor Act 1988 in order to provide a clear statutory basis for the holding of alcohol-free events and activities for young persons under the age of 18 years in licensed premises, such as a nightclub, or in part of a premises, such as a function room in a hotel or the main hall of a registered club, at a time when intoxicating liquor is not being sold, supplied or consumed and physical access to it is securely prevented. Prior to the 2004 Act, s.34 of the Intoxicating Liquor Act 1988, as substituted by s.14 of the Intoxicating Liquor Act 2003, generally prohibited persons under the age of 18 years from the bar of licensed premises after 9.00 p.m. The restriction in the 2003 Act constitutes part of the Government's response to concerns about alcohol-related harm among young people (see *Annual Review of Irish Law 2003*, pp.448–451). A further provision was added during the debate concerning the "watershed" for children to be on licensed premises during the summer tourist season.

During the Oireachtas debate on the 2004 Act it was stated that it had not been the intention of the Oireachtas, when enacting the 2003 Act, to restrict in any way alcohol-free events for young people. However, shortly after the entry into force of s.14 of the 2003 Act concerns were expressed that the restrictions provided for in s.14 could have this effect. The Minister for Justice, Equality and Law Reform stated that legal opinion had been sought from a leading expert in licensing law, which advice received held that where licensed premises, or a part of such premises, are not being used for the sale or supply of intoxicating liquor and the bar counter is closed, such premises do not constitute a bar for the purposes of the 1988 Act. But the Minister also noted that the Director of Public Prosecutions had directed that prosecutions be taken in certain cases where alcohol-free events have been held on licensed premises in just such circumstances. It was noted that, at the time of the Oireachtas debate, no prosecution of this nature had resulted in a conviction. The Minister for Justice, Equality and Law Reform considered that it would not be appropriate, in light of the differing views as to the effect of the 2003 Act, to place organisers of events "in the position of being guinea pigs in a legal experiment where one person may or may not be proven to be correct." In those circumstances it was concluded that it was more appropriate to remove any doubt on the matter.

Section 1(1) of the 2004 Act therefore provides that, for the purposes of s.34 of the Intoxicating Liquor Act 1988, it shall not be unlawful for a licensee to allow a person under the age of 18 years to be on a licensed premises, or part of a licensed premises, at a time when intoxicating liquor is not being sold, supplied or consumed there and physical access to intoxicating liquor on those premises, or part thereof, is securely prevented. The original text of the 2004 Act had referred to the bar counter being closed, but this was replaced with a reference to access to intoxicating liquor being securely prohibited.

Section 1(2) provides that, for the purposes of s.34A of the 1988 Act—which requires persons aged at least 18 years, but under the age of 21 years, to have an age document with them in order to be in the bar of a licensed premises after 9.00 p.m.—it shall not be unlawful for the licensee to allow such a person who has not produced an age document to be on licensed premises in similar circumstances. It would be manifestly absurd to say, for example, that the trainer of the judo class should have in his possession a card showing his age just because there was a bar at the end of the function room of the local sports club.

Section 1(3) provides that, for the purposes of ss.33 and 34 of the 1988 Act, it shall not be unlawful for a person under the age of 18 years to be on licensed premises in the circumstances mentioned in subsection (1). Section 1(4) provides that, for the purposes of s.34A of the 1988 Act, it shall not be unlawful for a person aged at least 18 years, but under the age of 21, who does not have an age document with him or her to be on the licensed premises in the circumstances mentioned in subsection (1).

Section 1(5) provides a defence in line with the legal advice received by the Minister for Justice for a person charged with an offence under the relevant sections of the 1988 Act, where bar shutters are closed. Section 1(6) provides that nothing in the 2004 Act prevents a person raising any point of law, or other plea, or objection that would be open to a person to raise in proceedings under the relevant provisions of the 1988 Act.

Section 1(7) of the 2004 Act was inserted by way of a Committee Stage amendment in the Dáil to deal with another issue that received a great deal of public airing in late 2003 and early 2004. It takes account of concerns expressed about the impact of the 9.00 p.m. rule for children on family holidays. The 2003 Act had altered this watershed for young people in pubs from 8.00 p.m. to 9.00 p.m. Section 1(7) of the 2004 Act moves this back further to 10.00 p.m. between the months of May and September. This was intended to deal with arguments raised about the need for further flexibility during the tourist season, in particular.

Limitation of Actions

CONSTITUTIONALITY OF SHORT, UNQUALIFIED LIMITATION PERIOD

In the *Annual Review of Irish Law 2002*, pp.105–109, we discussed Ó Caoimh J.'s decision in *White v Dublin City Council*, striking down as unconstitutional s.82(3B)(a)(i) of the Local Government (Planning and Development) Act 1963, as inserted by s.19(3) of the Local Government (Planning and Development) Act 1992. This provision prescribed a two-month period for those challenging by way of judicial review the validity of a decision of a planning authority on an application for a permission or approval under Pt IV of the Act. The court had no power to extend this period even in cases of injustice or hardship. Ó Caoimh J. considered that the absence of any saver rendered the provision unconstitutional by unduly restricting the right of access to the courts.

The Supreme Court affirmed Ó Caoimh J.'s judgment on June 10, 2004. Denham J. delivered the judgment of the court, whose other members were Murray, McGuinness, Fennelly and McCracken JJ. In determining the correct approach to take, Denham J. was guided by *Tuohy v Courtney* [1994] 3 I.R. 1, where Finlay J., delivering the judgment of the court had stated:

> "It has been agreed by counsel, and in the opinion of the Court, quite correctly agreed, that the Oireachtas in legislating for time limits on the bringing of actions is essentially engaged in a balancing of constitutional rights and duties. What has to be balanced is the constitutional right of the plaintiff to litigate against two other contesting rights or duties, firstly, the constitutional right of the defendant in his property to be protected against unjust or burdensome claims and, secondly, the interest of the public constituting an interest or requirement of the common good which is involved in the avoidance of stale or delayed claims.
>
> The Court is satisfied that in a challenge to the constitutional validity of any statute in the enactment of which the Oireachtas has been engaged in such a balancing function, the role of the courts is not to impose their view of the correct or desirable balance in substitution for the view of the legislature as displayed in their legislation but rather to determine from an objective stance whether the balance contained in the impugned legislation is so contrary to reason and fairness as to constitute an unjust attack on some individual's constitutional rights."

That passage, observed Denham J., set a high standard to be met by any person impugning the constitutionality of a period of limitation.

Denham J. went on to analyse other decisions, including *Re Article 26 of the Constitution and Re sections 5 and 10 of the Illegal Immigrants (Trafficking) Bill 1999* [2000] 2 I.R. 360, where the Supreme Court upheld the validity of a 14-day limitation period for taking judicial review, subject to the power of the extension of time for "good and sufficient reason".

Denham J. considered that "a number of helpful principles" could be deduced from *Tuohy v Courtney* and the *Illegal Immigrants Bill* case:

> "More lengthy limitation periods are laid down for civil actions between private persons or bodies. Their length is an important consideration when judging whether they are fair and just. It is not necessarily unconstitutional to omit a stipulation for extension of time for cases where the wrong was not reasonably discoverable within the longer time allowed. Anxiety, worry and cost for the defendant are important elements in those cases.
>
> It is inherent in the principle of respect for the rule of law that citizens should have the right to challenge the legality of decisions, made under public law, by administrative bodies. Judicial review is the appropriate procedural vehicle for such challenges. There is a strong public interest in the certainty and finality of administrative decisions. Any attack on their validity should be made at the earliest reasonable date."

There were obvious distinctions between common-law actions and applications for judicial review. The reasoning of the court in *Tuohy v Courtney* was, in some important respects, particular to that case and, to that extent, distinguishable. The court had clearly been very much influenced by the substantial period of six years involved in that case. The protection of defendants from stale claims and the need for a court to have before it oral evidence based on the accuracy of recent recollection and complete documentary evidence were less compelling justifications for the absence of a power of extension, where the limitation period was a mere two months. In that type of case, it was very much less likely that recollection would have faded or that relevant documents would not be available.

Denham J. went on to note that, where planning decisions were in question, members of the public were involved. A development might affect the environment generally, but was most likely to affect the amenities of those living or working closest to the proposed site. It followed that persons, such as the respondent, had a right to reasonable notice of what was proposed. In the circumstances of the instant case, the respondents had been deprived of any reasonable opportunity to challenge the validity of the planning permission by an unlawful act of the planning authority within the two-month limit; the effect of s.82(3B)(a)(i) was to deny them access to the court to extend the time.

Counsel for the Attorney General had claimed that the Oireachtas had made the deliberate choice to re-enact the absolute time limit in 1992 after an earlier absolute time limit had (albeit ineffectively in the event) been struck down by Costello J. in *Brady v Donegal County Council* [1989] I.L.R.M. 282 (analysed in the *Annual Review of Irish Law 1987*, pp.243–246). The Attorney General urged the court to accept that this demonstrated that the choice was not irrational. Denham J. did not agree. She stated:

> "While it is legitimate for the Attorney General to rely on the re-enactment of the provision, it must, therefore, be equally relevant to note that section 50 of the Planning and Development Act, 2000 permits an extension of the eight-week time limit there enacted where 'there is good and sufficient reason for doing so.' While counsel is right to say that the latter provision does not necessarily imply that section 82(3B)(a)(i) is unconstitutional, it is a useful and relevant indicator of what may be considered fair and just in such an enactment. Moreover, the Oireachtas may indeed, having regard to the considerations addressed above, be entitled to fix an absolute time limit of a short duration, such as two months, where the persons to which it applies have in fact had a full opportunity to bring proceedings within that limited period but that is not the situation here for the reasons already explained.
>
> The Court considers that section 82(3B)(a)(i) constitutes an injustice to such an extent that in exercising its discretion to exclude any power to extend time for cases such as the present, the legislature undermined or compromised a substantive right guaranteed by the Constitution, namely the right of access to the courts. The applicants, through no fault of their own, but through the unlawful act of the decision-maker, were deprived of any genuine opportunity to challenge the legality of the decision within the permitted time. For these reasons, the Court concludes that the High Court was correct in holding that the provision in question is repugnant to Article 40 section 3 of the Constitution."

Accordingly the Supreme Court dismissed the appeal.

The court did not attempt to sketch in detail the contours of a legislative measure that would survive constitutional scrutiny. Clearly it was the absoluteness of the short cut-off period which raised the greatest constitutional concern; some qualification is clearly called for. This can range from the narrowest power of extension only in cases where the applicant was deprived of an opportunity to challenge the legality of the decision to the broadest and open-ended judicial discretion based on the requirements of justice. Perhaps such a completely open-ended discretion could raise constitutional issues relating to the public interest in orderly development and the constitutional rights of developers.

ACCRUAL OF CAUSE OF ACTION

When does accrual occur?   In *Manning v Benson and Hedges Ltd* [2005] 1
I.L.R.M. 190, where claims were taken by smokers against cigarette
manufacturers based on alleged negligence in exposing them to the risk of
injury and addiction and in failing to warn them of the dangers, Finlay
Geoghegan J. approached the issue of dismissal for want of prosecution and
inordinate delay on the basis that the claims were not statute-barred, this defence
not having been raised against the plaintiffs. The claims had been made within
three years of the date of diagnosis of emphysema or lung cancer. Finlay
Geoghegan J. was of the view that the court should consider each application
for dismissal in the way most favourable to the plaintiff. This required the
assumption that the date of diagnosis was either the date of the completion of
the tort or the date of knowledge for the purposes of the 1991 Act. In her
opinion, the former was probably the position more favourable to the plaintiffs
and accordingly she adopted it.

It must be acknowledged that this approach is certainly generous to
plaintiffs. It is hard to reconcile with the rationale for the enactment of the
1991 legislation, which was that a cause of action can indeed accrue without
the victim of the tort being in a position to know that fact.

Severance of claims   In *Butler v Regan*, High Court, July 1, 2004, the plaintiff,
who had received serious injuries in a car crash in 1980, compromised his
claim against the other driver in 1984 for around £85,000. In 1987, he initiated
litigation against the defendant surgeon, arguing that the defendant had
negligently failed to report all of his injuries and their likely *sequelae* to his
legal advisers. This failure, he claimed, had resulted in an inappropriately low
settlement to his original claim and had resulted in his suffering depression
when being belatedly informed in 1986 of the prospect of future arthritis. Abbot
J. rejected the element in the claim relating to depression. Abbott J. held,
however, that the claim for economic loss relating to the inadequate settlement
was not defeated by the Statute of Limitation period. He stated:

> "As the claim is sustained only in relation to economic loss and not
> personal injuries, the six year period of limitation applies from date of
> accrual of action. As the right of return accrued (at the earliest) on the
> date of the last medical report in 1982, the proceedings were commenced
> within the six year period thereafter and hence the claim as accepted by
> this Court is not statute barred."

Abbott J. made no express finding that the plaintiff's claim for personal injuries
was statute-barred. If it was, then s.11(2)(b) of the Statute of Limitations 1957
(as amended) would have the effect of killing off the element of the negligence
claim based on negligently caused pure economic loss, since that provision

states that an action for negligence, *inter alia*, "where the damages claimed by the plaintiff for the negligence ... consist of *or include* damages in respect of personal injuries to any person, *shall not be brought* after the expiration of three years ..." (emphasis added). The court is not given the entitlement to sever the claims in respect of personal injuries and economic loss and to apply the Statute to the former but not the latter. It is up to the plaintiff to address the strategic question of whether to limit the claim to one for economic loss.

Could it be argued that the claim for economic loss made in the instant case was actually one seeking damages "in respect of personal injuries", in that the plaintiff's alleged economic loss was sustained in the context of an action for personal injuries sustained by the plaintiff? We suggest that such an argument is misconceived. The actual subject matter of that litigation was not central to the plaintiff's claim.

One is reminded of the process whereby negligence claims arising from a single incident can be broken into different categories, each with its own cause of action. We discuss this phenomenon, most recently manifested by *Hayes v Callinan*, High Court, March 25, 1999 and *Kerwick v Minister for Defence*, High Court, March 19, 1999, in the *Annual Review of Irish Law 2003*, pp.613–614.

DISCOVERABILITY OF INJURY

Unnecessary medical intervention In the *Annual Review of Irish Law 2003*, at pp.455–462, we analysed the important Supreme Court decision of *Gough v Neary* [2003] 3 I.R. 92. The members of the court could not agree on how to characterise a case where a doctor misrepresents to a patient that a medical intervention was therapeutically required: the patient is of course aware that the intervention has taken place and fully appreciative of the fact that an incursion upon his or her bodily integrity has occurred, but the patient will naturally regard it as beneficial rather than injurious. The Statute of Limitations (Amendment) Act 1991 stops the limitations clock in personal injuries litigation until the plaintiff could reasonably become aware that he or she has sustained an injury, that this injury is significant and that it is attributable to the allegedly negligent conduct of the defendant (even though it is not necessary that the plaintiff should reasonably have been aware that this conduct constituted negligence as a matter of law). In *Gough v Neary,* Hardiman J. thought that the misled plaintiff in this scenario ought reasonably to appreciate that he or she has sustained an injury: the suspension of the operation of the Statute for fraud provided by s.71 of the 1957 Act was in his view significant protection for victims of breaches of trust by the medical profession. Geoghegan J. disagreed: in his view the patient in such a situation could not reasonably have known that an injury had been sustained. Even if this was not so, the patient ought to be aware that an injury has been sustained but should not be considered

reasonably capable of attributing that injury to the conduct of the doctor.
McCracken J. agreed with the latter proposition.

In *Cunningham v Neary* [2004] 2 I.L.R.M. 498, a somewhat differently
constituted court of McGuinness, Hardiman and Fennelly JJ. returned to the
theme. The facts involved the same defendant and an essentially similar
complaint: that he had engaged in an unnecessary surgical intervention which
he had misrepresented to the patient as being necessary to save her life. There
were, however, some differences between the two cases which led ultimately
to the dismissal of the claim on the basis that it was barred under the Statute as
amended.

In the instant case, the plaintiff had been admitted to the hospital where the
defendant worked in 1991. He operated on her for a ruptured ectopic pregnancy,
removing a fallopian tube but also removing one of her ovaries. In her affidavit
in the subsequent litigation, the plaintiff asserted that the defendant, in extremely
rude terms, had justified the removal of the ovary on the basis that this had
been necessary to save her life. Her own general practitioner had endorsed
that explanation. The plaintiff trusted her general practitioner and accepted
what he said.

In October 1998, the plaintiff was admitted to another hospital for a
hysterectomy. While there, she told a nurse about her experience with the
defendant. The nurse encouraged her to complain about him to the Medical
Council. The plaintiff did this in December 1998. It appears that towards the
end of 1998, after her hysterectomy, she had become aware of rumours about
the defendant's practice which included rumours of how some expectant
mothers had had experiences "far worse" than hers and that some of them
were contemplating suing the defendant.

The plaintiff did not go to a solicitor until May 2000. In April 2001, an
independent expert obstetrician provided a report in which he advised that the
removal of the plaintiff's ovary had been unnecessary and represented
incompetent medical practice. A plenary summons was issued in March 2002.

In the High Court, Ó Caoimh J. held that the plaintiff's claim was not
barred. Basing his findings on *Gough v Neary* he held that the relevant
knowledge for the purposes of s.2(1) of the 1991 Act was "that the operation
had been unnecessarily performed". He held that the plaintiff had neither actual
nor constructive knowledge of this fact until the expert obstetrician submitted
his report in 2001.

On appeal, the Supreme Court unanimously reversed this decision,
essentially on the basis that the plaintiff had acquired the relevant knowledge
in late 1998. Two judgments—by Fennelly and McGuinness JJ.—were
delivered. Hardiman J. preferred on this occasion to limit himself to a simple
concurrence with both judgments.

Fennelly J. observed that "[t]he important point of principle" decided in
Gough v Neary had been that knowledge that the injury was attributable in
whole or in part to the act or omission alleged to constitute negligence for the

purpose of s.2(1)(c) of the 1991 Act included knowledge that the operation was unnecessary. Fennelly J. went on to observe that in *Gough v Neary:*

> "Geoghegan J drew a distinction between that knowledge and knowledge that the act in question was, as a matter of law, a negligent act, which is, of course, rendered irrelevant by the proviso to sub-section 1. On that particular matter, Hardiman J dissented and the matter may be open to debate in a future case. However, it seems clear to me that the Court may not, in this case, reopen that issue … it has not been invited to do so. In fact, however, this case can be decided by reference to sub-section 2."

It is not in fact clear that Hardiman J.'s dissent was on this particular point. Hardiman J. could scarcely have contested the proposition that is contained in this proviso. Hardiman J.'s dissent was on the prior question of what should be characterised as an "injury".

Fennelly J. was prepared to accept that the plaintiff had been entitled reasonably to rely on the advice of her general practitioner in 1991 but he considered that the position had changed significantly in late 1998. When the plaintiff had the conversation with the nurse in the hospital:

> "[t]he nurse encouraged her to complain about the defendant to the Medical Council, a very serious step. The letter of 19th December 1998 makes a number of grave allegations against the defendant. Among them is an account of two separate complaints about the absence of an explanation for the removal of an ovary. In addition, the plaintiff learned from media reports that a number of women had made serious complaints about the defendant. This is confirmed by the statement in her letter that, if she had complained earlier, 'she might have saved many other women from going through the same kind of treatment'. It was suggested at the hearing that this sentence did not necessarily mean any more than that she had been badly treated herself. However, given the other evidence of the plaintiff's knowledge, from media reports, that 'some expecting mothers had experiences with him that were far worse than mine', I think it highly likely that the plaintiff was referring in her letter to these cases.
>
> Thus, at the stage when the plaintiff wrote to the Medical Council, she had knowledge of the fact that the defendant had removed her ovary in 1991, that she had twice asked him why he had done so, that she had received no explanation at all and that other women had made serious complaints about the defendant. This knowledge was such that it was then 'reasonable' for her to seek medical or other expert advice."

After the plaintiff had gone to her solicitor in May 2000, it had taken a further

11 months to obtain the report of the expert witness. This could be explained by the time needed to obtain the plaintiff's medical records from the hospital. It showed, however, that, if the plaintiff had gone to a solicitor in December 1998, she would have obtained the sort of advice which would have made out a case in negligence against the defendant. Therefore, the key fact that the removal of the ovary had been unnecessary had been "ascertainable" and, for the purposes of the section, the plaintiff was deemed to have had knowledge of it as of that date. Consequently, the three-year period began to run against the plaintiff's claim not later than December 19, 1998 and her claim was out of time.

McGuinness J. in her judgment placed emphasis on a passage in Geoghegan J.'s judgment in *Gough v Neary* in which he stated:

> "While it may not be necessary for the purposes of starting the statute to run to know enough detail to draft a statement of claim, a plaintiff in my opinion must know enough facts as would be capable at least upon further elaboration of establishing a cause of action even if the plaintiff has no idea that those facts of which he has knowledge do in fact constitute a cause of action as that particular knowledge is irrelevant under the Act."

McGuinness J. noted that, although the plaintiff in evidence had sought to explain her failure to initiate proceedings in December 1998 on the basis that she "had nothing to go on", and while it was indeed true that she had at that time no definitive medical report indicating that the removal of her ovary had not been necessary, the plaintiff had if anything rather more information available to her than had Mrs Gough. She had, in the words of Geoghegan J., "enough facts as would be capable at least upon further elaboration of establishing a cause of action."'

McGuinness J. went on to observe:

> "It was argued on behalf of the plaintiff that she as an ordinary lay person did not have the required medical knowledge to take immediate action in December 1998. It is perhaps understandable in the circumstances that she may have been hesitant about taking the step of consulting her solicitor. However, once she had done so she not only had the information already available to her but also had the benefit of legal advice. It must be presumed that this legal advice included knowledge of the operation of the Statute. In May 2000 proceedings initiated by the plaintiff would have been within the statutory limit.
>
> It was submitted on behalf of the plaintiff in this court that it would be unwise for a solicitor to embark upon a medical negligence action without convincing, or at least persuasive, independent medical evidence to establish the claim. Such a practice, it was argued, would have

unnecessary and harmful effects on the medical profession. In general terms this is true but, as was pointed out by senior counsel for the defendant, in a case where there is a danger of the Statute running against the plaintiff it is perfectly possible and legitimate to issue a plenary summons and to delay serving it on the proposed defendant while investigating the available medical evidence.

Even apart from this argument, the plaintiff's medical expert, Dr. Porter, presented his report to her solicitor in April 2001. If one accepts, as I do, that the plaintiff did not acquire the requisite knowledge that the removal of her ovary was unnecessary until December 1998 her claim would not be statute barred until December 2001. Had her proceedings been initiated promptly after the receipt of Dr. Porter's report the present problem would not have arisen. In these circumstances it is difficult to understand why the plaintiff's plenary summons was not issued until 22nd March 2002."

One issue of detail on which there was a nuanced difference of judicial opinion was whether the rumours in the newspapers had put the plaintiff on notice for the purposes of the Statute. A passage from McGuinness J.'s judgment suggests that it may have; Fennelly J. was more doubtful:

"Media reports of complaints that the defendant had performed unnecessary operations on other women may certainly have put the plaintiff on inquiry, but it can scarcely be said that, from such reports alone, she knew rather than suspected that her own operation had been unnecessary."

Some may be reminded of what Keane C.J. had to say in *Fletcher v Commissioners of Public Works* [2003] 1 I.R. 465:

"A person who prefers to rely on the ill informed comments of friends or acquaintances or inaccurate and sensational media reports rather than the considered view of an experienced physician should not be awarded damages by the law of tort."

In the instant case, of course, the subject matter of the reports concentrated on the issue of the bona fides of a particular person rather than a broader issue of the aetiology of a disease, yet the need for caution and due process in responding to media allegations is a common denominator in both cases.

One has to express a note of caution about the holding in *Cunningham v Neary*. The plaintiff could perhaps be criticised for her delay in going to a solicitor but the 1991 Act was not intended to operate as a guillotine on the claims of injured people who lack legal sophistication. The very notion of limitation of actions is completely foreign to many victims of torts. The gradual process of realising that a person in whom one placed trust may possibly have betrayed that trust can invoke complex and confusing emotions and factual hypotheses, with faith and disbelief jockeying for dominance. In the instant case, the plaintiff displayed early evidence of a sense of outrage at the betrayal of trust; clearly she was not concerned at that time about suing the defendant. To attribute to her the requisite knowledge to activate the limitations clock under s.2 of the 1991 Act when three Supreme Court judges cannot agree as to when and why the clock starts to tick in cases of such betrayal may be considered harsh.

There is a further difficulty with *Cunningham v Neary*, which has implications for future litigants. This concerns the reliance placed on what Geoghegan J. had to say in *Gough v Neary* to the effect that:

> "[w]hile it may not be necessary for the purposes of starting the statute to run to know enough detail to draft a statement of claim, a plaintiff ... must know enough facts as would be capable at least upon further elaboration of establishing a cause of action even if the plaintiff has no idea that those facts of which he has knowledge do in fact constitute a cause of action as that particular knowledge is irrelevant under the act."

Geoghegan J. made this remark as a side comment during his analysis of English case law. In England, s.11(2) of the Limitation Act 1980 provides that an injury is significant "if the person whose date of knowledge is in question would reasonably have considered it sufficiently serious to justify his instituting proceedings for damages against a defendant who did not dispute liability and was able to satisfy judgment". There is nothing like this in the Irish Act. See *Bolger v O'Brien* [1999] 2 I.R. 431, analysed in the *Annual Review of Irish Law 1999*, pp.285–288. The reference in the English position to the justification for instituting proceedings is merely to provide a measure for determining what constitutes a significant injury: it has nothing to do with the actual litigation with which the court is concerned. Knowledge of the facts sufficient to render the plaintiff capable of establishing a cause of action is simply irrelevant to the Irish definition of the knowledge that triggers the Statute. If a particular plaintiff was fully aware that he or she had sustained a significant injury and fully aware that as a matter of fact it was caused by the defendant, the clock will start to tick even in cases where the plaintiff simply could not have known that the defendant's conduct constituted an actionable tort. Knowledge of the legal aspects or implications of the requisite facts is simply irrelevant. The language of s.2 allows no other construction.

Even if it were the case that knowledge of enough facts "as would be capable at least upon further elaboration of establishing a cause of action" had the effect of starting the clock to tick, this formula would not be a satisfactory one since it leaves unclear how much foundation or substance the facts without such elaboration must have. What Geoghegan J. appears to be addressing is the point at which the facts, as established, are sufficiently full to constitute the requisite knowledge. Some situations will arise where the facts may not of themselves be sufficient to give a victim anything like actual knowledge of the three elements of the injury, yet they would put a reasonable person on enquiry, placing that person under an obligation to become a detective. Geoghegan J.'s position is that, once that point has been reached, the clock starts to tick even though much detective work may be necessary before the position is clarified. One may question whether the clock should start quite so early. It is the hallmark of good detectives that they keep an open mind rather than rush to judgment. There is also the difficulty that Hercule Poirot may need less evidence on which to elaborate than Constable Plod. Geoghegan J.'s formula is unclear on the *quantum* of evidence that is necessary: its capacity for elaboration is too elastic a test.

In *Fortune v McLoughlin*, Supreme Court, June 9, 2004, a court composed of McCracken J. (who had been part of the court in *Gough v Neary*), Keane C.J. and Murray J. had already revisited the issue. Here the plaintiff in 1993 had engaged the defendant, a registered midwife, to provide midwifery services during her pregnancy, with the intention of giving birth at home. One night the plaintiff had convulsions and lost consciousness. It was alleged by the plaintiff that her partner telephoned the defendant and asked whether he should call an ambulance and that the defendant had told him not to, but that nonetheless he had called an ambulance; the plaintiff was taken to a maternity hospital where she gave birth by caesarian section. She had further seizures after the birth. She alleged that she sustained serious brain injuries during this period which left her with significant permanent brain damage with intellectual impairment. In proceedings launched in 2000, the plaintiff alleged that the defendant had been negligent in failing to monitor her condition adequately and in failing to have regard to her own clinical findings which should have indicated to a reasonable competent midwife the onset of pre-eclampsia and the need for increased monitoring and early delivery of the child.

Kearns J. held that, in spite of the long delay, the proceedings were not statute-barred. Kearns J. came to this conclusion on two grounds. The first was that the plaintiff had not the requisite knowledge for the purposes of s.2 of the 1991 Act until she had received advice from a general practitioner in September 1999 and the relevant records obtained and expert medical advice based on those records had been given thereafter to her solicitor. The plaintiff had for many years regarded what had happened to her as being "one of those things" which could befall a woman of her age with a first-time pregnancy. So far as she thought of attributing any blame, she had been disposed to direct it towards the maternity hospital.

On the appeal to the Supreme Court, the defendant argued that the word "attributable" in s.2(1)(c) of the 1991 Act was "satisfied by the plaintiff's knowledge of the factual situation". By this it appears that counsel was contending that knowledge of the sequence of facts that occurred without any attribution of *factual* (or, *a fortiori*, legal) causation was sufficient to start the limitation clock ticking.

The Supreme Court did not agree. McCracken J. (Keane C.J. and Murray J. concurring) stated:

> "The knowledge referred to in [section 2(1)(c)] is knowledge of attribution, in other words knowledge that there was a connection between the injury and the matters now alleged to have caused the injury. This is a connection which the plaintiff did not make in this case. If a plaintiff is to have knowledge within the meaning of the sub-clause, she must have knowledge at least of a connection between the injury and the matters now complained of sufficient to put her on some inquiry as to whether the injury had been caused by the matters complained of. At what stage she is put on inquiry must be a matter to be determined in each case, but in the present case the plaintiff quite clearly did not make the connection at all, as even when she was alerted to the fact that there might have been negligence, her reaction was to attribute her injuries to the actions of [the] hospital rather than of the defendant. It should be emphasised that the plaintiff's knowledge of these matters is largely a question of fact."

The Supreme Court was undoubtedly correct to require actual or constructive knowledge of causal attribution rather than of a mere sequence of facts. Section 2(1)(c) clearly refers to knowledge "that the injury was *attributable* in whole or in part to the act or omission which is alleged to constitute negligence..." (emphasis added). It is worth noting that in the instant case the claim made against the defendant was in essence one of alleged culpable failure to act. Negligence by omission can present distinctive problems in the context of s.2(1)(c). In such claims the plaintiffs will often be perfectly aware that the defendant has not acted; they may in some cases be aware that, if the defendant had acted, the injury, loss or damage would not have occurred. Yet they may not ascribe any factual causal connection between the omission and the injury, loss or damage simply because they are not aware that the law imposed an actionable affirmative duty on the defendant. Their completely understandable ignorance of the law will blind them to the factual connection.

The truth of the matter is that to speak in this context of a factual connection involves a high level of artificiality. Factual causal attribution for omissions is not a process that can meaningfully take place independently of legal causal ascription. Assume for a moment that you are ignorant of the law on affirmative obligations in negligence. You are shown a video that was taken of me in which I continually passed by a starving young beggar outside my door for a week; you witness the decline and ultimate death of the beggar on my doorstep. The question whether I factually caused the death of the beggar cannot easily be answered in isolation from the legal context. If I was under a legally enforceable affirmative duty towards him, then the factual question seems easy to answer; if not, then you might hesitate before making a factual ascription of causal responsibility. If it turns out that the beggar was my child whom I had disowned, the causal ascription appears to clarify appreciably.

All of this is relevant to s.2 of the 1991 Act since s.2(1) states that "knowledge that any acts or omissions did or did not, as a matter of law, involve negligence... is irrelevant". What is intended here, of course, is that, for the clock to start ticking, it is not necessary that the plaintiff ought to have been aware that he or she could sue the defendant for negligence. In that sense factual ascription is all that need reasonably be capable of being made. Yet, where claims for allegedly negligent omissions are involved, the clock will in many cases be started only where the plaintiff becomes aware of the legal duty to act resting on the defendant.

In the instant case the alleged omission bore no relationship to the types of example mentioned above, which concern situations where arguably no legal duty to act arose at all. Clearly omissions occurring in the context of an ongoing duty to provide a particular service or, more generally, to act in a particular way, present neither legal nor factual problems of ascription. The surgeon who is engaged to remove your appendix but negligently fails to do so cannot argue convincingly that he or she is neither factually nor causally implicated because he or she did nothing. Similarly, the bus driver who fails to apply the brakes. As Fleming observed in *The Law of Torts* (9th ed., LBC Information Services, Sydney, 1998), p.163:

> "What superficially looks like non-feasance is often, upon correct analysis, a case of misfeasance. A motorist's failure to brake in time to prevent a collision is not an example of supine inaction: an omission is involved, but it is merely the element that makes his *active* conduct – driving – negligent."

In *Fortune v McLoughlin*, there was a second, quite separate, reason for Kearns J.'s holding, affirmed on appeal, that the limitation clock had not started to tick. Section 2(3)(b) of the 1991 Act makes it clear that a person is not fixed with knowledge of a fact relevant to the injury which that person has failed to acquire as a result of that injury. In the instant case, the injury received by the plaintiff prevented her from having, or being reasonably capable of having, knowledge of the facts mentioned in s.2(1).

Knowledge that the injury is "significant"   In *Keogh v Minister for Defence*, High Court, January 20, 2004, the plaintiff had been a member of the FCA for 46 years, retiring in 2003 at the rank of battalion sergeant major. He sought compensation for a condition of deafness allegedly caused by negligent exposure to noise during his time with the FCA. Pursuant to defence force regulations and circulars, his hearing had been tested in 1998 and he received documentation showing that he fell within the H2 category, which was "early warning of hearing loss. No NIHL" (noise-induced hearing loss). This permitted him to engage in all training activity while wearing double protection. In 1999 he had a further annual hearing test. He was not informed of the result because the printer on which the result would have been printed for him was not working properly. Although the authorities fully intended to let him have his test result as soon as the printer came back into service, this was not actually done and the plaintiff thereafter remained in ignorance of the fact that, between the 1998 test and the 1999 test, his hearing had deteriorated to the point where by the end of 1999 he was in the H4 category. This category involved hearing loss described as "moderate NIHL or age induced HL". Members of the defence forces with H4 hearing loss were not permitted to engage in certain activities relating to particular weapons. The plaintiff attempted to have his hearing test done, on the normal annual basis, both in 2000 and in 2001, but because of pressure of work on those persons carrying out the tests, he was unable to get an appointment to have his audiogram carried out. This meant that it was not until October 2002 that he had a hearing test carried out. When he received his print-out of that test, he saw that in fact in 1999 he had been in the H4 category. The defendants sought to argue that the plaintiff's claim, initiated in December 2002 was defeated by the Statute of Limitations. Perhaps not too surprisingly, Peart J. rejected this argument. Peart J. devoted part of this judgment to focusing on the defendants' negligence in failing to notify the plaintiff of the result of the 1999 test:

> "I have no doubt that, if the defendants had, in accordance with their normal practice, given the plaintiff the result of his test on 16th November 1999 showing that he was now in the category of H4, ... the defendants would have taken it upon themselves to comply with the requirements of Training Circular TC 10/96, and the plaintiff himself would have taken appropriate steps in relation to the fact that he was now in a worse category than previously. The defendants were in my view obliged to notify the plaintiff of the result of his test in November 1999, as it contained information which he was entitled to be aware of in his own interests, but, even if they failed to notify him of the result of that test, they themselves must be deemed to have known the result of the test, and accordingly they must be regarded as negligent in not taking the necessary steps with regard to the plaintiff's well-being, as required by their own regulations.
>
> It also follows in my view that the defendants cannot rely upon the delay between 15th December 1998 and 15th October 2002 in order to successfully plead the Statute of Limitations against the plaintiff. To do so would enable the defendants to benefit from the consequence of their own negligence and that could not be just. ...
>
> There can be no question but that the plaintiff, as an experienced

member of the FCA, would have been aware of the fact that a person's hearing can be damaged by exposure to arms fire, especially over a prolonged period of time. He would also have been fully aware from 1998 onwards that many members of the defence forces were taking proceedings to recover damages in respect of hearing loss, but it is also quite clear that the plaintiff had been tested in 1998 and was shown to be in the category of H2, which is not a category indicating a significant level of hearing loss. In my view the plaintiff was entitled to assume, since he had been tested again in 1999, that there was nothing adverse arising as a result of that test, even though it would have been prudent of him to have chased up a copy of the test result. However his failure to do so cannot absolve the defendants from their responsibilities to the plaintiff. Even if they did not give him a copy of his test result, they must be fixed with knowledge of that result, and they cannot benefit from what must be regarded as their own negligence in failing to either notify him of the result, or take precautions with regard to his participation in fire arms activity which would have been appropriate for a person in the category of H4. The plaintiff in his own evidence has stated that he had not noticed any deterioration in fact in his hearing between the time he was H2 and becoming H4, but Mr Dermot Dougan, when giving evidence on behalf of the plaintiff, stated that there can be an incremental progression in loss of hearing to which a person can become habituated. ... In other words the deterioration is so gradual that the person concerned does not notice its deterioration, unlike a situation where the deterioration might be sudden. ...

I am satisfied that the plaintiff first obtained knowledge that his injury was 'significant' when he was informed on 15th October 2002, for the first-time, that he was in the H4 category of hearing loss. That is the date therefore from which time began to run against the plaintiff for the purposes of section 2 of the Statute of Limitations (Amendment) Act, 1991.

As far as section 2, subsection (2)(a) of that Act is concerned, the plaintiff cannot have been expected to know of the deterioration in his hearing from facts observable or ascertainable by him. He has stated in evidence that he did not notice any deterioration, and Mr Dougan has said that that is reasonable, since any such deterioration would have been gradual and the plaintiff could have habituated to it.

In relation to subsection 2 (b) of section 2, I am not satisfied that it is reasonable that the plaintiff should have sought medical advice or other appropriate expert advice in the circumstances where he did not notice any deterioration in his hearing, and in circumstances where the defendants failed to discharge their obligation to the plaintiff to notify him of the actual deterioration which had occurred in his hearing.

I am satisfied that the claim herein is not statute-barred."

The conclusion that the claim was not statute-barred seems eminently sensible and fair. There is something unattractive about an argument by a defendant that a plaintiff should have been aware of a fact that the defendant had culpably not communicated to the plaintiff. Nevertheless, the issue in this case was when the plaintiff first could reasonably have become aware that he had received a significant injury; the defendants' possible neglect in failing to communicate information to the plaintiff was relevant only in so far as it threw light on this issue. Even if the defendants had not been unreasonable in failing to communicate the information to the plaintiff, the plaintiff could well have been regarded as not having reached the point where he ought reasonably have known of the relevant facts. If, for example, a postal worker had stolen the 1999 Report after it had been put in the post by the defendants, no blame could conceivably attach to the defendants but the plaintiff's action would still be held to fall within the limitation period.

Of course, the question of whether the defendants had been careless in failing to communicate the relevant information to the plaintiff would be highly relevant to a negligence claim taken by the plaintiff in respect of damage following from that carelessness. If, for example, the plaintiff's action had been held to have been defeated by the Statute of Limitations, the possibility of the defendant being sued by the plaintiff for negligence causing that defeat could not be discounted. (Whether such an action would succeed is another matter. The loss in such a case would be economic and *Glencar* does not look with favour on allowing awards of damages for negligently caused pure economic loss. As against this, if the defendant's default were to be framed in constitutional language, it might be less easy for a court to reject on policy grounds the sustainability of a claim for compensation for infringement of the plaintiff's constitutionally based entitlement of access to the courts to seek to vindicate a claim arising from the violation of his right to bodily integrity. Perhaps it is unduly alarmist to raise concerns about the possible applications of *Glencar* in this context: see *Butler v Regan*, High Court, July 1, 2004.)

FORFEITURE

The Proceeds of Crime Act 1996 is a muscular statutory initiative clothed in the finery of constitutional proprieties. It needed the most sophisticated drafting strategies to meet the challenge of complying with the requirements of due process and fair trial. In *McK v D* [2004] 2 I.L.R.M. 419, the issue relating to limitation of actions was a narrow one: whether s.3 of the 1996 Act involved a "forfeiture" for the purposes of s.11(7)(b) of the Statute of Limitations 1957 which provides that:

> "[a]n action to recover any penalty or forfeiture, or sum by way of penalty or forfeiture, recoverable by virtue of any enactment shall not

be brought after the expiration of two years from the date on which the cause of action occurred."

Section 3 of the 1996 Act provides for the making of what it describes as "an interlocutory order". It requires the court, on the basis of certain evidence that specified property constitutes proceeds of crime, to make an "interlocutory order" prohibiting the respondent from disposing of it or otherwise dealing with it, unless the respondent shows that it does not constitute proceeds of crime. Section 4 provides for the disposal of the property seven years later.

In *McK v D*, the appellant contended that an application under s.3, in spite of its own characterisation, amounted to an action for civil forfeiture to which s.11(7)(b) of the Statute of Limitations applied. He relied on a statement of Keane C.J. delivering the judgment of the court in *Murphy v G.M.* [2001] 4 I.R. at 137, to the effect that "[t]he orders which the court is empowered to make accordingly, under the Act, may equate to the forfeiture of the property in question..."

The Supreme Court in *McK v D* did not agree with this interpretation of Keane C.J.'s remarks. Fennelly J. (Keane C.J., Denham, Murray and McCracken JJ. concurring on this issue) considered that the Chief Justice's statement was referable to the Act as a whole and not specifically to s.3. In the passages leading up to it, Keane C.J. had explained the place of a s.3 order in the statutory scheme. He described the making of the "interim order" (s.2) and the "interlocutory order" (s.3) and then pointed out:

> "However, in the interval between the making of the interlocutory order and the expiration of that seven year period, the court may discharge the order on the application either of the garda officer or the person to whom it was directed or who claims an interest in the property. In the latter case, the order is to be made by the court where it is satisfied that the property was not, directly or indirectly, the proceeds of crime or that it would cause 'any other injustice'."

He had gone on to state:

> "The effect of the statutory scheme, accordingly, is to 'freeze' property which senior members of the gardaí suspect of representing the proceeds of crime for an indefinite period, subject to the limitations indicated."

Keane C.J. had further described the status and effect of the interlocutory order as follows:

> "Unless an order is made under s.4 at the expiration of the seven year period for the disposal of the property, the owner of the property does not cease to be its owner by virtue of anything done in exercise of the

powers conferred by the Act. He or she is, however, in effect deprived
of the beneficial enjoyment of the property even before such a disposal
order is made. ..."

The dictum cited by the appellant appeared in the same paragraph and had to
be understood as referring to the potential effect of the order under s.4. It was
clear that the court in *Murphy* had not said that a s.3 order effected a forfeiture.
Fennelly J., while deeming it unnecessary in the instant case to decide whether
an order under s.4 of the 1996 Act amounted to a forfeiture for the purposes of
s.11(7)(b) of the Statute of Limitations, considered it:

> "sufficient to say that the effect of section 3 is, as stated in *Murphy*, to
> freeze the interest of the property owner but not to deprive him of it. It
> allows the Court to make an order restraining the owner 'from disposing
> of or otherwise dealing with the whole or, if appropriate, a specified
> part of the property or diminishing its value...' Such an order is not, in
> any normal sense, an order of forfeiture. It would do violence to the
> language of s.3 to hold that it effects a forfeiture."

ESTOPPEL

In *Yardley v Boyd*, High Court, December 14, 2004, a plea of estoppel failed.
A fatal accident had taken place in Ireland involving English parties. There
was some uncertainty as to whether the litigation should proceed in Ireland or
England. The defendant's insurers wrote a letter to the plaintiff's English
solicitors stating that: "based upon information that we have seen so far liability
for the accident would not appear to be an issue". In a later letter, the defendant's
insurers wrote:

> "We are not saying that there is any other information to see, simply
> that what we have seen so far suggests that liability is not a relevant
> issue. In the interests of all concerned can we not now make some
> headway with these claims? As previously requested and (*sic*) we await
> full details with some indications as to the parameters of the intended
> claims including documentary evidence."

Having heard the evidence and considered the correspondence, Herbert J. found
that the defendant's insurers had not made a clear and unambiguous promise,
assurance or representation to either the English or Irish solicitors that liability
would not be an issue. Both the English and Irish solicitors were convinced
that negligence or contributory negligence would never be real issues in the
proceedings. It was clear from their evidence that neither considered that he
had received a promise or assurance that the insurers, if the claims were not

compromised, would not raise an issue of negligence, breach of duty or contributory negligence. Both accepted that the issue of the claims becoming statute-barred was never adverted to: the issue did not arise under English law because of the length of time involved and the person dealing with the claim in the Irish solicitors' firm did not appear to have adverted to the two-year, as distinct from the (then) normal three-year, period of limitation in personal injury claims, provided for by s.9(2) of the Civil Liability Act 1961, in respect of causes of action surviving against the estate of a deceased person.

Even if the letters from the defendant's insurers meant that liability was conceded except in the most unlikely event of some new and very material facts concerning the accident coming to light, this was far short of the sort of clear and unambiguous promise, assurance or representation that liability would not be an issue necessary to enable the doctrine of promissory estoppel to be invoked by the plaintiff. In Herbert J.'s judgment, the principles of the law of promissory estoppel as expounded and applied in *Doran v Thomas Thompson and Sons Ltd* [1978] I.R. 223 applied to the facts to the instant case. Kenny J. had stated:

> "There was no representation of any kind by the insurers… that they were admitting liability, or that the only issue in the case was the amount of damages or that they would not rely on the Statute of Limitations. Therefore, there is no foundation for the application of the doctrine of promissory estoppel."

Herbert J. commented:

> "Even if these letters could—and I do not accept that they could—be construed in the context as amounting to an unambiguous promise or assurance intended to affect the legal relations between the parties, that liability—that is, negligence, breach of statutory duty or contributory negligence—would not be an issue in any proceedings, this would not necessarily of itself make it reasonable for the solicitors for the plaintiff to assume that the institution of proceedings—even if by way of assessment of damages only—could be deferred beyond the limitation period."

PROCEDURE

Amendment of statement of claim and delivery of replies   In *Croke v Waterford Crystal Ltd* [2005] 1 I.L.R.M. 321, the Supreme Court, reversing Smyth J., permitted the plaintiff to amend his statement of claim against the first defendant and gave him liberty to deliver replies to the defences of the first and second defendants, both of which had pleaded the Statute of

Limitations. The statement of claim in its original formulation contained allegations of deceit and fraudulent concealment; Geoghegan J. (Murray C.J., Denham, McGuinness and Fennelly JJ. concurring) observed that, whilst the latter allegation "might not in itself be a cause of action ... presumably [it] would be directed towards a potential plea of the Statute of Limitations". One of the proposed amendments was to claim that the plaintiff discovered the alleged untruth of the representations in 1999 whereas no date had been provided in the original formulation of the statement of claim. Geoghegan J. considered that, while making this change constituted "a helpful piece of clarification", it was not necessary for the purpose of meeting a plea of the Statute of Limitations. It was in the reply that the date of knowledge had to be inserted. It would not be right for a court on an interlocutory application such as was now before the Supreme Court to speculate in any way as to whether a date of knowledge proposed to be inserted was in some way bogus or not.

Geoghegan J. did not see how the amendment would give rise to legal prejudice:

> "If by reason of the [plaintiff]'s date of knowledge the action which might otherwise have been statute barred is not in fact statute barred it cannot be said that prejudice has arisen."

While it was true that time limits applied to the delivery of a reply, there would have to be extraordinary circumstances, in Geoghegan J.'s view, for a court "to deprive a plaintiff of the right to adduce a perfectly good answer to a plea of the Statute of Limitations effectively on a time point".

Withdrawal of notice of discontinuance   If a plaintiff who has issued notice of discontinuance against a defendant seeks many years later to withdraw the notice, in circumstances where the claim is now statute-barred, what should the attitude of the court be? In England over a century ago the answer was plain. The Court of Appeal, in an unreserved judgment by Lord Esher M.R. in *Weldon v Neal* (1887) 19 Q.B.D. 394, held that withdrawal should not be permitted. Lord Esher stated:

> "If an amendment were allowed setting up a cause of action which, if the writ were issued in respect thereof at the date of the amendment, would be barred by the Statute of Limitations, it would be allowing the plaintiff to take advantage of her former writ to defeat the statute and taking away an existing right from the defendant, a proceeding which, as a general rule would be, in my opinion, improper and unjust."

A later amendment in the Rules led to a change of heart so as to enable courts to permit withdrawal of notice of discontinuance wherever it would be just to do so. In Ireland, in *Krops v Irish Forestry Board Ltd* [1995] 2 I.R. 113, Keane

J. endorsed this general approach.

In *Smyth v Tunney* [2004] 1 I.L.R.M. 464, the plaintiff sought to withdraw notice of discontinuance against the third defendant, Crofter Properties Ltd. The plaintiff was a retired Garda Chief Superintendent. He and his brother were directors of a company which was the parent company of Genport Ltd, which was a lessee of the third-named defendant. The plaintiff's brother was the majority and controlling shareholder of Genport and the first defendant was the major shareholder of the third defendant. The second defendant was a director and officer of the third defendant. There had been protracted litigation between Genport and the defendants. Much of this litigation has been analysed in several previous Annual Reviews. An important part of the litigation concerned a serious defamation of the plaintiff's brother made by the second defendant who alleged falsely that he had been involved in money laundering on behalf of the IRA through Genport's parent company. The second defendant claimed that a co-director of this company was a Garda Chief Superintendent who had actively inhibited enquiries about his brother's alleged associates by misuse of authority whilst head of personnel in An Garda Síochána. There was an investigation by An Garda Síochána and the plaintiff was cleared. The plaintiff had sued for defamation in 1996. He had discontinued proceedings against the third defendant in 1998, on the basis that it seemed unnecessary to involve the third defendant in order to vindicate his reputation and because of the difficulty in establishing that the second defendant, when engaging in the defamatory communication, had been acting on behalf of the third defendant. The Supreme Court in 2002, in defamation proceedings taken by Genport, held that the third defendant was indeed vicariously liable for the second defendant's tortious conduct.

In a detailed judgment, O'Sullivan J. held that the plaintiff should be entitled to withdraw notice of discontinuance. He was willing to follow the approach of the British Columbia Court of Appeal in *Adam v Insurance Corporation of British Columbia* (1985) 66 B.C.L.R. 146, where Esson J.A. had expressed the view that, where the limitation period had elapsed, "the circumstances must be very special" to permit such withdrawal. In the instant case, the claim of tortious wrongdoing contained allegations of deception and fraudulent wrongdoing which might override a defence based on the Statute of Limitations. O'Sullivan J. considered it preferable that this complex issue should be determined on the basis of full evidence rather than on affidavit evidence at an interlocutory stage.

O'Sullivan J. went on to observe:

> "It may be argued that the plaintiff should not be permitted to blow hot
> and cold and in particular should not be permitted to secure for himself
> a perceived tactical advantage by serving a notice of discontinuance in
> August, 1998 and then, following a Supreme Court ruling four years
> later, bring an application (seven months later again) to reverse that

tactical decision. However, to deprive the plaintiff on the grounds that he made a tactical decision of the perceived benefit of reversing that decision solely on the grounds that he cannot blow hot and cold or that the third defendant is entitled to treat the plaintiff's claim against it as finally concluded (save for the matter of costs) seems to me to be closer to punishing or disciplining the plaintiff for a decision taken when the notice of discontinuance was served (to use the concept endorsed by Murphy J in *Aer Rianta International CPT v Walsh Western International Ltd.* [1997] 2 ILRM 45 at p 51) rather than ensuring that the real issues between these parties be dealt with at the trial. I would think that the plaintiff's sense of grievance that his issue was on the narrow ground foreclosed would be greater than any sense of relevant or legitimate prejudice that might be suffered by the third defendant if the present application is permitted. The third defendant has pointed to no prejudice arising from the serving of the notice of discontinuance which I should legitimately take into account in exercising my discretion on this matter. The plaintiff's application may, perhaps, be described merely as a 'change of heart' – but insofar as that reference might suggest an element of whimsicality, it is not applicable. The decision of the Supreme Court on his brother's counterclaim is clearly highly relevant and something which not only he but this court, I believe, should take into account."

Joinder of a new defendant   If an application is made to add a new party to litigation and that party resists being joined on the basis that the claim against him or her is statute-barred, what is the solution? The Supreme Court might be considered to have given the definitive answer in *Allied Irish Coal Supplies v Powell Duffryn International Fuels Ltd* [1998] 2 I.L.R.M. 61, where Murphy J. noted that:

> "[i]t is a well established rule of practice that a Court will not permit a person to be made a defendant in an existing action at a time when he could rely on the Statute of Limitations as barring the plaintiff from bringing a fresh action against him."

Whether this answer may easily be reconciled with the court's earlier decision in *O'Reilly v Granville* [1971] I.R. 90 troubled Shanley J. in *Southern Mineral Oil Ltd v Cooney* [1998] 2 I.L.R.M. 377 and Geoghegan J. in *B.V. Kennermerland Groep v Montgomery* [2000] I.L.R.M. 370. Geoghegan J. concluded that the answer depended on whether the action was "quite clearly barred". If so, the application to join the party should be rejected *in limine*; if, however, there was a doubt on the question, the party should be joined, leaving the matter to be resolved in the substantive litigation.

In *Purcell v Taylor*, High Court, May 26, 2004, Peart J. followed Geoghegan

J.'s approach. The plaintiff alleged that he had slipped and fallen from a balcony when he was a customer at the first and second defendants' licensed premises in 2000. His claim was based on occupiers' liability principles. In December 2003, the plaintiff sought to add the architect who designed the premises as another defendant. His solicitor stated in an affidavit that at no time prior to the delivery of the defence in 2003 had he been aware of earlier correspondence between the first and second defendants and the architect's solicitor in which they had sought an indemnity from the architect and indicated that they intended to default on his agreement to join him as a third party.

The plaintiff's solicitor contended that this point was the earliest date on which the plaintiff had the requisite knowledge for the purposes of s.2 of the 1991 Act. He also averred that this knowledge as to the possible involvement of the architect was not knowledge which the plaintiff might reasonably be expected to have acquired from facts observable by him or ascertainable by him even with the assistance of expert help.

Peart J., upholding the order of the Master, held that the joinder of the architect as a party to the litigation was the proper course. The averment of the plaintiff's solicitor gave an appropriate foundation based on s.2 of the 1991 Act. The court could not reasonably conclude, contrary to this averment, that the information about the architect's possible liability had earlier been reasonably ascertainable by the plaintiff. When the case proceeded further, and all the issues had been clarified, there could be a hearing of the limitations dispute as a preliminary issue. The architect would be entitled to seek discovery as to whether there had been any previous correspondence between the plaintiff or his solicitor and the first and second defendants or their solicitors regarding the possible involvement of the architect in the liability for the plaintiff's injury.

One can perhaps wonder why the issue of the architect's possible liability should have been regarded as beyond the range of knowledge of the plaintiff from the earliest stages. The nature of the occupiers' liability alleged against the first and second defendants was that they had failed to take reasonable care for the plaintiff's safety, exposed him to a risk which could have been avoided, maintained a hidden trap and/or danger for him and other members of the public, failed to warn of the danger, failed to adequately light the stairs serving the differing levels in the premises, and failed to provide adequate hand-rails. In essence, this was a claim about the structure of the balcony and about decisions made as to its safety. The notion that the proprietors of licensed premises might engage an architect to assist them is scarcely an outlandish one.

Planning Law

GARRETT SIMONS, B.L.

JUDICIAL REVIEW

Time limits An eight-week time limit is prescribed under s.50 of the Planning and Development Act 2000 (hereafter "PDA 2000") for proceedings challenging certain decisions taken by a planning authority, or by An Bord Pleanála. The High Court has the discretion to extend this time limit where there are "good and sufficient" reasons for so doing. The judgment in *Marshall v Arklow Town Council (No.1)*, unreported, High Court, Peart J., June 30, 2004 deals with a number of practical issues arising in the context of an application to extend the time limit. In this case the applicants were local residents. The principal issue raised in the judicial review proceedings was an allegation that a site notice had not been erected and maintained in accordance with the requirements of the regulations. The applicants claimed they had not been aware of the making of the application for planning permission, learning of the application only after a decision to grant planning permission had been made. The fact of the decision came to the applicants' attention within the eight-week period specified for bringing judicial review proceedings. However, the judicial review proceedings were not issued until some 14 days after the eight-week deadline had expired. The notice of motion issued did not seek an order extending the time for the making of the application for judicial review. The High Court dealt with this omission by allowing the applicants to amend the notice of motion.

Peart J. decided that it was necessary to rule on the application to extend the deadline as a preliminary issue, in advance of hearing the actual application for leave to apply for judicial review:

> "It follows that this Court must determine first of all whether an extension is required and, if so, whether it should be granted for good and sufficient reason. A refusal of such an extension has the effect of finally determining the application from the applicants' viewpoint, in the sense that without it they cannot proceed further. To deal with the merits of the application at the same time as determining the time point would result in the Court dealing unnecessarily with the substantive merits in a case where an extension of time is found not to be merited. That consideration must outweigh any countervailing consideration such

as having the entire matter aired at one sitting, rather than dealing with each aspect separately. I have therefore decided to proceed with my decision in relation to time and delay, and if finding in favour of the applicants on that issue, I will then proceed to fix as early a date as possible for the hearing of the substantive application for leave."

With respect, while this approach has much to recommend it, it is questionable if it will be appropriate in every instance. In certain cases, for example, the question of an extension of time will be inextricably linked to the substantive merits of the case. Indeed, it is arguable that this was the position on the facts of *Marshall*, where the principal ground put forward for challenging the validity of the planning permission (namely, that a site notice was not erected and maintained in compliance with the regulations) was also the point relied upon in seeking an extension of time. In the circumstances there must be something to be said for dealing with all matters together rather than, in effect, giving the applicants the benefit of the doubt. As it happens, the applicants in *Marshall* were ultimately successful in the substantive application for judicial review, but one can readily envisage cases where an extension of time might be granted—with all the attendant uncertainty and delay for the developer—only for the applicants to fail to obtain leave to apply for judicial review.

In assessing whether there was good and sufficient reason to extend time, Peart J. attached particular significance to the conduct of the applicants from the date on which they first alleged they had learned of the existence of the decision to grant planning permission. Peart J. found that the applicants had moved with as much haste as was reasonably possible in the circumstances. In this regard, Peart J. also attached significance to the fact that a letter had been sent to the notice party developer, within the statutory eight-week period, intimating possible judicial review proceedings. The delay in the case was relatively short (14 days) and Peart J. held that, in his view, it was accounted for solely by the intervening of the Easter holiday period.

Constitutionality of previous time limit   In *White v Dublin City Council* [2004] 1 I.R. 545; [2004] 2 I.L.R.M. 509 the Supreme Court had to consider the constitutionality of the limitation period governing applications for judicial review proceedings under the previous legislation. Under s.82(3A) of the Local Government (Planning and Development) Act 1963 a time limit of two months was prescribed. There was no provision made whereby this time limit could be extended in any circumstances.

The facts of *White* were that an application for planning permission had been made in respect of certain residential development. In the course of processing this application the planning authority had exercised its powers under the regulations to invite the applicant to submit revised plans. The effect of these revised plans was to radically alter the nature of the proposed development. The Supreme Court held that the planning authority had erred in law by not requesting further public notice in the circumstances. As a result of its finding on this issue, the Supreme Court had then to consider the constitutionality of the two-month time limit applicable under the Local Government (Planning and Development) Act 1963 (as amended).

The Supreme Court held that the absolute nature of the time limit constituted an injustice because by excluding any power to extend time, the legislature had undermined, or compromised, a substantive right guaranteed by the Constitution, namely the right of access to the courts. The applicants, through no fault of their own but rather through the unlawful act of the planning authority, were thereby deprived of any genuine opportunity to challenge the legality of the decision to grant planning permission within the permitted time.

It should be noted that under s.50 of the PDA 2000 the High Court has an express power to extend the eight-week time limit prescribed under that legislation.

Substantial interest and prior participation   Under s.50 of the PDA 2000 a person seeking leave to apply for judicial review is required to demonstrate a "substantial interest" and prior participation in the decision-making process. Prior to the 2000 Act an applicant was simply required to demonstrate a "sufficient interest". In *Lancefort Ltd v An Bord Pleanála* [1999] 2 I.R. 270, the Supreme Court had interpreted the requirement as obliging an applicant to raise before the decision-maker any legal objection that would subsequently be relied upon in judicial review proceedings. The effect of the statutory requirement for prior participation was considered by the High Court in *Ryanair Ltd v An Bord Pleanála* [2004] 2 I.R. 334. It was held that the failure of the applicant to raise an objection to a particular aspect of the proposed development precluded it from making complaints in judicial review proceedings as to how that aspect had been dealt with in the decision taken by An Bord Pleanála.

> "In the instant case it is clear that the applicant could have raised at the appeal stage certain of its concerns relating to the new pier itself which it did not raise until the bringing of this application. In this regard I refer to its failure to address the proposal for bridges on the southern side of the new pier. Insofar as that is the situation I am satisfied that to that extent also it lacks the necessary *locus standi* and cannot show that it has a 'substantial interest'."

Rolled-up application   A special judicial review procedure is prescribed under s.50 of the PDA 2000 for challenges made against certain types of planning decision. The special procedure differs in a number of respects from that governing conventional, or non-statutory, judicial review. In particular, the application for leave to apply for judicial review must be made on notice and a higher threshold ("substantial grounds") applies. Occasionally, an applicant will seek a combination of reliefs, some of which are within s.50.

For example, an applicant may wish to challenge the legality of an objective of the statutory development plan (conventional judicial review) and also to challenge a subsequent decision to grant planning permission based on that objective (statutory judicial review). In such circumstances the question arises as to the standard that should be applied at the leave stage, for example, should the High Court simply apply the lower threshold of an arguable or stateable case to those reliefs which do not involve a direct challenge to a decision of the type protected by s.50?

This question arose on the facts of *Kinsella v Dundalk Town Council,* unreported, High Court, Kelly J., December 3, 2004. The applicant alleged that the respondent planning authority had acted unlawfully in processing an application for planning permission. In particular, it was alleged that the planning authority should have required further public notice on receipt of a response to a request for further information. It was alleged that the response contained "significant additional data" such as to trigger the statutory requirement for further public notice. The applicant sought to quash the "decision" of the planning authority not to require further public notice, and also to quash the subsequent decision to grant planning permission. On the precedent of *Huntstown Air Park Ltd v An Bord Pleanála* [1999] 1 I.L.R.M. 281, it would seem that only the latter decision was subject to the special judicial review procedure available under s.50. In the circumstances, the applicant sought to argue that he was only required to meet the lower threshold of an arguable or stateable case in respect of the challenge to the earlier "decision" of the planning authority not to require further public notice. Kelly J. rejected this submission, holding that it would serve no useful purpose to set aside this earlier decision without going on to quash the decision to grant planning permission:

> "It was suggested on the part of the applicant that whilst the application for leave to apply for *certiorari* against the decision to grant permission undoubtedly fell within the ambit of s. 50, the application for leave to apply for *certiorari* in respect of the decision of 25th June, 2004, did not. It was said that it fell to be decided by reference to ordinary judicial review principles and that the threshold of arguable case identified by the Supreme Court in *G. v D.P.P.* [1994] 1 I.R. 374 was all that had to be achieved.
>
> I rejected that submission at an early stage in the hearing for reasons which I enunciated then. I took the view that it was quite clear that the whole thrust and ambition of these proceedings was to quash the decision of 3rd August, 2004. As the applicant was quite plainly questioning the validity of the decision to grant planning permission he could not avoid or evade meeting the necessary threshold of proof required under s. 50 of the PDA 2000. Indeed as I pointed out in giving my ruling on this topic, if the applicant were correct in his submission in this regard an

absurd result could be achieved which would be entirely contrary to the letter and intent of s. 50.

Accordingly, as I ruled at the outset it is necessary for the applicant to demonstrate substantial grounds for contending that the decisions which he impugns in these proceedings are invalid or ought to be quashed."

Alternative remedies A person seeking to challenge at first instance the decision of a planning authority to grant planning permission has, in theory at least, a choice of remedies. He may either appeal to An Bord Pleanála or bring judicial review proceedings before the High Court. Judicial review is a discretionary remedy, however, and the courts may refuse relief to a person otherwise entitled to relief on the basis that an appeal would have been the more appropriate remedy in the circumstances. The prior case law in relation to this issue is confusing and it is often difficult to ascertain which of the two alternative remedies is the more appropriate in any particular set of circumstances. One test seems to be whether the challenge simply raises legal issues (in which case judicial review seems more appropriate), or whether it touches on the planning merits of the planning authority's decision.

The question as to alternative remedies was considered by the High Court in *Kinsella v Dundalk Town Council*, unreported, High Court, Kelly J., December 3, 2004. There, the applicant for judicial review had also brought an appeal to An Bord Pleanála. The *gravamen* of the applicant's case in the judicial review proceedings was that the planning authority had acted unlawfully in failing to direct further public notice in circumstances where a response to a request for further information contained what the applicant alleged to be "significant additional data". The High Court ultimately refused leave to apply for judicial review on the basis that the applicant had failed to make out "substantial grounds" of challenge. Kelly J. stated that it was not necessary for him to decide the case on the basis of the existence of an alternative and adequate remedy to judicial review, but he did comment as follows:

> "In my view the applicant has in his right of appeal to An Bord Pleanála not merely an adequate but a preferable remedy to that which is sought here. I do not perceive that these proceedings display any of the exceptional characteristics which would justify the court in intervening in the self-contained planning process. Thus were it necessary I would be inclined to refuse this application on the basis of the existence of an adequate alternative remedy. Given that the applicant has availed himself of that right my inclination to refuse would be all the stronger."

Statement of main reasons and considerations Under s.34(10) of the PDA 2000, the planning authorities and An Bord Pleanála have a statutory duty to state reasons for their decisions. First, the planning authorities and An Bord

Pleanála are required to state the main reasons and considerations on which any decision is based. Secondly, where the decision to grant or to refuse planning permission is different from the recommendation in the inspector's report, the planning authorities and An Bord Pleanála must indicate the main reasons for not accepting the recommendation put forward in the report.

It would appear from the judgment in *Ryanair Ltd v An Bord Pleanála* [2004] 2 I.R. 334, that the change introduced under the PDA 2000, whereby planning authorities and An Bord Pleanála must now state the "main reasons and considerations" for their decisions, will in practice add little to the previous statutory requirement to state "reasons". The High Court rejected a challenge based on an allegation that a decision of An Bord Pleanála failed to comply with the new statutory requirements.

Leave to appeal to Supreme Court   It is necessary to first obtain the leave of the High Court before an appeal may be brought to the Supreme Court against a decision on an application under s.50 of the PDA 2000. Leave to appeal may only be granted by the High Court: there is no procedure whereby an application for leave can be renewed before the Supreme Court. This mechanism gives rise to potential difficulties in the context of applications for preliminary rulings from the European Court of Justice (ECJ). Under Art.234 a more exacting standard applies in the case of a court against whose decision there is no remedy under national law—the court must bring the matter before the ECJ, where a decision on the question is necessary for it to give judgment. The difficulty presented by the provisions of s.50 is that it will not be known whether the High Court will be the final court until such time as a ruling is made on any application for leave to appeal to the Supreme Court; this will not normally occur until such time as the High Court has made its decision on the judicial review application, by which time it is, presumably, too late to make a reference as judgment will have already been given: *McNamara v An Bord Pleanála* [1998] 3 I.R. 453. One practical solution might be for counsel to indicate to the court during the course of the hearing that a reference to the ECJ is being sought. The court should then consider whether or not to make such a reference before moving on to make its substantive decision on the application for judicial review.

A practical example of the difficulties which can arise in this regard is to be found in the judgment of the High Court in *Arklow Holidays Ltd v Wicklow County Council* unreported, High Court, Murphy J., February 4, 2004.

APPLICATION FOR PLANNING PERMISSION

Site notice   The judgment in *Marshall v Arklow Town Council (No.2)*, unreported, High Court, Peart J., August 19, 2004 concerned an allegation that the site notice requirement under Art.19 of the Planning and Development

Regulations 2001 had not been complied with and, allegedly, no site notice had been erected at all. The applicants complained that as a result of this breach they did not become aware of the application for planning permission until after the decision to grant had been made by the planning authority.

In his judgment Peart J. decided that the conflict of evidence arising between the parties regarding the existence, or non-existence, of the site notice was impossible to reconcile and he could not, therefore, determine that factual issue with absolute certainty. To decide either way would be to say either that the notice party's professional did not comply with planning requirements and was deliberately untruthful, or that the site notice, not seen by the many passers-by resident on that street, did not fulfil the requirement that it "be easily visible and legible" by persons using the road, as mandated by Art.19(1)(c) of the regulations.

Instead, Peart J. preferred to decide the case by reference to the failure of the planning authority to inspect the site notice within five weeks, beginning on the date of the receipt of the application for planning permission. An applicant for planning permission is required to maintain the site notice *in situ* for a period of five weeks. Peart J. ruled that there was an obligation on the planning authority to inspect the land to which the application related within the five-week period. There is no such express duty under the Planning and Development Regulations 2001. However, Peart J. was prepared to infer an implied duty from the provisions of Art.26(4) of the Planning and Development Regulations 2001.

It is submitted that this proposition puts the planning authority under an enormous burden to visit each and every proposed site and creates an obligation that was not intended by the Planning and Development Regulations 2001. Under the terms of the Regulations there is no express requirement to carry out such an inspection, instead the planning authority is empowered to inspect the lands under Art.26. The decision in *Marshall* thus has implications for all planning authorities.

Request for further information   The validity of a request for further information was considered in *Illium Properties Ltd v Dublin City Council*, unreported, High Court, O'Leary J., October 15, 2004. Towards the end of the statutory period allowed for the determination of an application for planning permission (two months under the previous legislation), the planning authority approached the applicant company with a view to obtaining consent to an extension of time for the determination of the application. This was refused. Thereafter, the planning authority purported to serve a request for further information, which was divided into five categories. The court ruled that four out of five of these categories were beyond the scope of a proper request for further information. Insofar as the remaining category was concerned, the court held that, whereas it might have been legitimate in other circumstances, the surrounding facts rendered it likely that it was included as part of a document with a hidden and illegal purpose of gaining more time for the planning authority to do its work. The court also held that at the time of the serving of the request for further information the planning authority already had enough information to refuse planning permission (and probably enough information to approve same with conditions). Accordingly, a declaration was made as to a default planning permission.

Revised plans   In *White v Dublin City Council* [2004] 1 I.R. 545; [2004] 2 I.L.R.M. 509, an application for planning permission had been made in respect of certain residential development; a similar application had previously been refused by the planning authority. In the course of processing the subsequent application, the planning authority exercised its powers under the regulations to invite the applicant to submit revised plans. The effect of the revised plans was to radically alter the nature of the proposed development. The planning authority did not, however, exercise its discretion to require further public notice.

The Supreme Court held that the planning authority had erred in law. In particular, it was held that the relevant official of the planning authority had, in effect, asked himself the wrong question in deciding whether to require further public notice. The proper test was whether, in the circumstances of the application before the planning authority, some members of the public might reasonably wish to object to the plans as modified. Instead, the relevant official had acted as if he was deciding whether or not planning permission should be granted. The Supreme Court held that not to require further public notice was unreasonable and irrational in the circumstances.

As a result of its finding on this issue, the Supreme Court then had to consider the constitutionality of the two-month time limit applying under the Local Government (Planning and Development) Act 1963 (as amended). The Supreme Court held that the absolute time limit constituted an injustice because by excluding any power to extend time, the legislature had undermined, or compromised, a substantive right guaranteed by the Constitution, namely the right of access to the courts. The applicants, through no fault of their own but rather through the unlawful act of the planning authority, were thereby deprived of any genuine opportunity to challenge the legality of the decision within the permitted time.

To a certain extent, the facts in the subsequent case of *Dietacaron Ltd v An Bord Pleanála*, unreported, High Court, Quirke J., October 13, 2004 represented the obverse of those in *White*. An Bord Pleanála exercised its power under the regulations to invite an applicant for planning permission to submit revised plans. An Bord Pleanála indicated that the revised plans would be circulated to the parties to the appeal and that those parties would be given a further opportunity to make submissions and observations in relation thereto. One of the parties to the appeal argued that the nature and extent of the revisions sought by An Bord Pleanála went beyond mere modifications and, in fact, so radically altered the development as to comprise a new development, requiring a fresh application for planning permission.

One of the preliminary issues to be determined by the High Court was as to the standard of review to apply. Quirke J. held that the decision fell to be reviewed against the standard of administrative unreasonableness. On the facts, Quirke J. held that the decision of An Bord Pleanála to invite revisions of the type sought was not unreasonable.

A subsidiary issue arose as to the aspirational 18-week time limit applying to decisions of An Bord Pleanála. It had been argued that An Bord Pleanála was not entitled to seek revisions of the type sought in circumstances where this would put any decision by An Bord Pleanála well beyond the 18-week time limit. This argument was also rejected by the High Court.

Response to request for further information   The requirements for public notice were also considered in *Kinsella v Dundalk Town Council*, unreported, High Court, Kelly J., December 3, 2004. The facts were slightly different from those of *Dietacaron* in that what was at issue was not revised plans but rather the response to a request for further information. It was alleged that the planning authority should have required further public notice on receipt of a response to a request for further information. It was alleged that the response contained "significant additional data" such as to trigger the statutory requirement for further public notice. Kelly J. upheld the actions of the planning authority. The decision in *White* was distinguished on the basis that the planning authority had, in fact, addressed its mind to the correct question:

> "In this case (unlike *White's* case) there can be no doubt but that the question posed to Mr. Ewbanks was the correct one. Ms. McDonnell's memorandum of 25th June, 2004, could not have been clearer. She asked him to decide if the further information submitted the previous day in relation to the application contained significant additional data. Not merely that, but she went on to point out that if that were so then the planning authority must require Coverfield to publish notice of the new information and invite submissions or observations on it. She referred specifically to article 35 of the regulations."

Given that the planning authority had addressed its mind to the correct question, the High Court held that the only remaining basis for challenging the decision could be that the decision was unreasonable or irrational. Kelly J. held that this ground was not made out on the facts.

DEVELOPMENT

Declaratory relief   The principal issue for determination by the Supreme

Court in *Grianán An Aileach Interpretative Centre Company Ltd v Donegal County Council* [2004] 2 I.R. 625 was as to whether the High Court retained jurisdiction to grant declaratory relief in circumstances where a procedure was prescribed under the legislation for the reference of disputes involving the question as to whether or not planning permission was required. The Supreme Court held that the existence of the s.5 reference procedure precluded the High Court from determining such issues. In this regard, it was suggested that for the High Court to retain a jurisdiction to give declaratory relief would create a danger of overlapping and unworkable jurisdictions.

It is submitted that this aspect of the judgment is incorrect and should not be followed. First, the determination as to whether or not planning permission is required is pre-eminently a question of law and one that the High Court should have jurisdiction to determine. Secondly, in any event both the High Court and the Circuit Court are called upon regularly to address these issues in the context of planning injunctions under s.160 of the PDA 2000. It has long since been established that, in the exercise of their jurisdiction in respect of the planning injunction (both under the present and previous legislation), the courts are not inhibited by the fact that there is a parallel procedure available to determine such matters. Given the ongoing existence of this overlapping jurisdiction it seems somewhat anomalous to suggest that the High Court's inherent jurisdiction to give declaratory relief is extinguished. This is especially so where there is no express suggestion to that effect under the PDA 2000.

Standard of review   An interesting question arises as to the weight, if any, a court should assign to the views of a planning authority as to whether or not a particular matter requires planning permission. A planning authority will regularly have to take a view (to use a neutral term) as to whether a particular activity requires planning permission, for example, in deciding whether or not to take enforcement action. A planning authority also has a more formal role under s.5 of the PDA 2000, whereby questions can be referred to it for determination as to whether development/exempted development is involved. If the matter proceeds to litigation, the question arises as to what weight should be assigned to the views of the planning authority in this regard. Approaching the matter from first principles, one would have presumed that there was no need for a court to show any deference to the planning authority's view in that it is a question of law (not a question of fact and degree) as to whether development or exempted development is involved.

The position is complicated, however, by the fact that under the newly structured s.5 reference procedure the statutory right of appeal to the High Court has been removed. Instead, a reference is made, in the first instance, to a planning authority, with a subsequent appeal to An Bord Pleanála. The jurisdiction of the High Court can only be invoked by way of an application for judicial review. The fact that the planning authorities and An Bord Pleanála have now been entrusted with an express statutory function in this regard might suggest that the courts should show deference and interfere only if the decision is shown to be unreasonable or irrational. Such an approach would seem to be consistent with the tenor of the Supreme Court's judgment in *Grianán An Aileach Interpretative Centre Company Ltd v Donegal County Council* [2004] 2 I.R. 625. As against this, it was certainly the position under the previous s.5 reference procedure that a statutory appeal to the High Court should take the form of a re-examination, from the beginning, on the merits of the decision appealed from, with a view, if appropriate, to the substitution by the High Court of its adjudication for that of An Bord Pleanála: see *Glancré Teoranta v Cafferkey*, unreported, High Court, Finnegan P., March 22, 2004. The fact that the statutory right of appeal has now been removed, leaving only jurisdiction by way of judicial review, should not necessarily alter this approach.

Waste disposal It can be a difficult question as to whether a fresh planning permission is required in the case of a change of use to one involving waste disposal/recovery. The Court of Appeal in England and Wales has indicated that the use of land for waste disposal/recovery can, in principle, represent a substantive use of lands in its own right, even where it occurs as part of some other process (typically, manufacturing): see *R. v Durham County Council Ex p. Lowther* [2002] 1 P. & C.R. 22. It is therefore a question of fact and degree as to whether the land is subject to a single use (waste disposal/recovery), or to a dual use (waste disposal/recovery and some other use), or whether the waste disposal/recovery is simply ancillary or incidental to the principal use of the lands.

In *Glancré Teoranta v Cafferkey*, unreported, High Court, Laffoy J., April 26, 2004 the High Court found that a change in use from use for the purpose of drying peat and the manufacture of fuel to use for the purpose of waste disposal/recovery represented a material change in use. In reaching this conclusion the High Court placed particular emphasis, first, on the fundamental difference in the purpose to which the two activities were directed: the proposed activity was primarily directed to waste disposal, albeit that a by-product in the form of a granulated fertiliser would arise, whereas the use permitted under planning permission was directed to the manufacture of a fuel product, one of the components of which was dried peat; and, secondly, on the differences in process (in terms of quarantining, odour treatment, treatment of waste water, specialised storage of sludge and emissions) arising from the differences in the raw materials.

Advertisements The application of planning control to advertisements has given rise to much confusion in the case law. In particular, the courts seem unsure whether to regard advertisements as development by way of works or by way of material change in use. The better view seems to be that advertisements should be treated as giving rise to a use of land: this follows from s.3 of the PDA 2000, which expressly declares there to be a material change in use where any structure or other land, or any tree or other object on land becomes used for the exhibition of advertisements. Under s.2 of the PDA 2000 "advertisement" means any word, letter, model, balloon, inflatable structure, kite, poster, notice, device, or representation employed for the purpose of advertisement, announcement, or direction.

In *Dublin Corporation v Lowe*, unreported, Supreme Court, December 17, 2004, the Supreme Court treated advertisements as giving rise to development works. The gable-end of premises was used, under agreement, for the display of advertisement hoardings. The trial judge had found as a fact that on the appointed day, namely October 1, 1964, an advertisement hoarding had been in existence on the gable wall of the premises. The trial judge had also found that hoardings had been renewed or replaced from time to time, with the time periods between the removal and replacement being no more than a few days on any occasion. In or about the end of December 1995, the owner of the premises had entered into a new agreement with a different advertising company, which resulted in the removal of one advertising hoarding and its replacement by another a number of days later. The new hoarding was identical in its dimensions to that which immediately preceded it.

Notwithstanding the provisions of s.3 of the PDA 2000, the Supreme Court addressed the case as one involving development works. Thus, even though the use of the lands had clearly not changed since October 1964, the Supreme Court nevertheless considered whether planning permission might have been required. The Supreme Court ultimately held that the works involved were exempted development under the equivalent provision to what is now s.4(1)(h) of the PDA 2000. The relevant parts of this subsection provide for an exemption in favour of alterations that do not materially alter the external appearance of the structure so as to render its appearance inconsistent with the character of the structure itself, or that of neighbouring structures. The Supreme Court held that the term "alteration" was not confined to a mere visual alteration. For the purposes of assessing the impact of the alteration the relevant structure was that which had been in place prior to October 1964, namely, the building, or gable wall of the building, with an advertisement hoarding attached to it. It would be unrealistic to look at a hoarding of this nature as a structure in isolation from the rest of the building:

> "The Appellant also submits that in any event the advertisement hoarding did materially affect the external appearance of the premises so as to render its appearance inconsistent with the character of the premises itself or that of neighbouring structures. It is, of course, true that the building itself is an old Georgian building, and no doubt advertising hoardings such as the present one would not have been present or in contemplation of the owners of the original building in Georgian times. However, what this Court is concerned with is the alteration of the hoarding by the substitution of a new hoarding, and

that in itself in my view cannot possibly be said to have materially affected the external appearance of the premises."

Exempted development: waste disposal   The fact that a particular activity may be subject to both the planning legislation and the waste management legislation can present practical difficulties. For example, the requirements of a waste licence in respect of works or structures might be different from those of the relevant planning permission. This issue is, to some extent, addressed under the Waste Management Act 1996. Specifically, s.54(4) and (5) provides that works which are necessary to give effect to any conditions to be attached to a waste licence are to be classed as exempted development. There is a procedural requirement for the Environmental Protection Agency to consult with the relevant planning authority in this regard.

The wording of s.54(4) is somewhat unusual and refers to circumstances not only where planning permission has previously been granted for development comprising, or for the purposes of, a waste disposal activity, but also where "an application has been made for such permission". The possibility of exempted development occurs where the necessary works are "not the subject of a permission or an application" for planning permission. The meaning and effect of this exemption was considered in *Yellow Bins (Waste Disposal) Ltd v Environmental Protection Agency*, unreported, High Court, Ó Caoimh J., July 9, 2004. On the facts of the case, an application for planning permission had been refused by An Bord Pleanála in respect of works considered necessary by the Environmental Protection Agency. The sequence of events left it open to the developer to make the ingenious argument that the provisions of s.54(4) arose notwithstanding the fact that an application for planning permission had actually been refused for the necessary works.

The High Court rejected this argument, holding that the provisions of s.54(4) were triggered only where there was either an existing planning permission or a *pending* application for planning permission. The High Court also accepted the submission made on behalf of the Environmental Protection Agency to the effect that s.54(4) applied only in the limited circumstances where a developer had been granted, or was seeking land use permission for the *general* works required in connection with the activity requiring the waste licence, but had not been granted nor had sought permission for the *particular* works necessary to give effect to the conditions which the Agency believed were appropriate.

In *Mason v KTK Sand and Gravel Ltd*, unreported, High Court, Smyth J., May 7, 2004, a further limitation on the exemption under s.54(4)(a) was highlighted. The High Court held that the exemption applied only to development works and did not extend to a material change in the use of lands. Thus, a change from use as a sand and gravel quarry to use as a landfill would not be covered by the exemption. (On the facts, s.54(4)(a) would appear not to have been applicable in any event in that it seems that the developer held only a waste permit and not a waste licence.)

TRAVELLERS

Traveller Accommodation Programme The development of a travellers' halting site is subject to the provisions of both the statutory Development Plan and the statutory Traveller Accommodation Programme. In addition, where the development involves expenditure beyond a certain threshold, it is subject to a form of public consultation (previously under Pt X of the Local Government (Planning & Development) Regulations 1994, now under Pt 8 of the Planning and Development Regulations 2001). The precise relationship between these various overlapping controls fell for consideration by the High Court in *Jeffers v Louth County Council*, unreported, High Court, Gilligan J., December 19, 2003. In summary, the High Court found that the carrying out of the site-specific statutory public consultation procedure under Pt X of the 1994 regulations did not absolve the local authority from engaging in a more general form of public consultation—in advance of any particular site having been selected—where this had been provided for under the terms of its Traveller Accommodation Programme.

The respondent local authority's Traveller Accommodation Programme had included a provision that in implementing the programme the local authority would endeavour to ensure that "all traveller families secure accommodation of a type, standard and location acceptable to them" and, furthermore, that "there is full and meaningful consultation with travellers themselves, traveller representative groups, statutory and voluntary agencies, the appropriate local traveller accommodation consultative committee, elected members, the public generally and any other interested persons or bodies". The applicant argued that the local authority had failed to comply with its (self-imposed) obligation to consult under the Traveller Accommodation Programme. In response, the local authority argued that the fact that it had undertaken the public consultation procedure under Pt X of the 1994 Regulations was sufficient to meet its obligations under the Traveller Accommodation Programme. Gilligan J. rejected this line of defence, holding that the Pt X procedure is site-specific and therefore should only come into play when a preferred location for a halting site has been identified and has thus achieved the status of a proposed development. Gilligan J. further held that what was required under the terms of the Traveller Accommodation Programme was that a full and meaningful consultation with various parties would take place *prior* to the identification of the preferred location for a halting site to examine all available options for traveller accommodation.

The local authority thus found itself hamstrung by the terms of its own Programme. By including generous provisions in the Traveller Accommodation Programme in respect of public consultation, the local authority had, in effect, submitted to a more exacting regime than that provided for under statute. There does not appear to be any statutory obligation under the Housing (Traveller Accommodation) Act 1998 to engage in the level of public consultation envisaged by the Traveller Accommodation Programme. The provisions in respect of a local traveller accommodation consultative committee under s.21 are somewhat vague and do not appear to entail an obligation to consult in relation to the development of particular sites. Nonetheless, the High Court decided to hold the local authority to its (volunteered) commitment under the Programme. This outcome is somewhat surprising as there is nothing in the 1998 Act that suggests development in breach of the Traveller Accommodation Programme is unlawful; this can be contrasted with the express provisions under the planning legislation in respect of a material contravention of the Development Plan. It is difficult to reconcile this aspect of the judgment with the statutory obligation imposed on the local authority *qua* housing authority to provide accommodation.

The judgment in *Jeffers v Louth County Council* is also of interest insofar as it addresses the effect of the exception provided under s.27(2) of the Housing (Traveller Accommodation) Act 1998. Section 26 of the 1998 Act introduced, for the first time, an *express* requirement that a local authority include objectives in its Development Plan for the provision of accommodation for travellers and the use of particular areas for that purpose (see now s.10 of the PDA 2000). Subsection 27(2) went on to provide that any thing done or any act carried out by a housing authority for the purpose of implementing an accommodation programme shall be deemed not to contravene a Development Plan in the period between the coming into operation of this new requirement and the inclusion of such objectives in the Plan. This transitional provision seems intended to cover the *interregnum* between the amendment or variation of a Plan (so as to comply with the statutory requirement to include objectives for the provision of accommodation for travellers) and the use of particular areas for that purpose.

On the facts of *Jeffers*, the Development Plan had not yet been amended to include such objectives. The High Court went on to hold that the transitional provision applied only where the material contravention arose as a result of a failure to include in the Plan objectives in relation to travellers. In other words, it was not every type of material contravention that was absolved by the subsection. The High Court also held that the transitional provision was available only where the material contravention of the Development Plan arose where same was done for the purpose of implementing the Traveller Accommodation Programme: if an act does not comply with any requirements imposed under the Traveller Accommodation Programme, it is not an act for the purpose of "implementing" the Programme and, therefore, cannot avail of the protection afforded under s.27(2) of the 1998 Act. The local authority in *Jeffers* was not, therefore, entitled to rely on the exception in circumstances where the material contravention involved a breach of junction design standards (the proposed sight distances and gradients were not in compliance with the standards prescribed under the Development Plan), and where the High Court had already found that there had been a failure to comply with the consultation requirements under the Traveller Accommodation Programme.

PLANNING PERMISSION

Extension of duration of planning permission Provision is made under the PDA 2000 for the extension of the duration or "life" of a planning permission in certain circumstances. Section 42 sets out the requirements in this regard. The principal requirements are: (i) the development to which the planning permission relates must have commenced before the expiration of the period sought to be extended; (ii) substantial works must have been carried out pursuant to the planning permission during that period; and (iii) the development will be completed within a reasonable time. The equivalent provisions in the previous legislation (Local Government (Planning & Development Act 1982) had been considered in a number of judgments. These judgments established that on an application for an extension the planning authority's function is very narrow. In particular, it would seem that once the relevant statutory conditions have been fulfilled, the planning authority has no choice but to grant the extension: *State (McCoy) v Dun Laoghaire Corporation* [1985] I.L.R.M. 533. See also *John A. Woods Ltd v Kerry County Council*, unreported, High Court, Smyth J., October 31, 1997, and *Littondale Ltd v Wicklow County Council* [1996] 2 I.L.R.M. 519. Thus, for example, it would seem improper for a planning authority to purport to take into account factors such as the desirability or otherwise of the development being completed. The previous case law also emphasised that substantial works must have been carried out "pursuant to" the planning permission sought to be extended. For example, in *Garden Village Construction Ltd v Wicklow County Council* [1994] 3 I.R. 413; [1994] 2 I.L.R.M. 527, the Supreme Court held that, in the context of a major housing scheme covered by several planning permissions, works under other planning permissions "designed to benefit" the particular development covered by the expiring planning permission could not be taken into account.

This latter requirement, that substantial works have been carried out "pursuant to" the planning permission sought to be extended, fell for further consideration in *McDowell v Roscommon County Council*, unreported, High Court, Finnegan P., December 21, 2004. The planning authority had, seemingly, taken the view that the development as actually carried out was not in compliance with the planning permission and was, therefore, unauthorised. An extension of time was refused. The allegation was that the house was being built some two metres or more lower than permitted.

The High Court held that the planning authority had acted unlawfully in purporting to have regard to the alleged unauthorised nature of the development. Two principal reasons were put forward for this conclusion. First, it was suggested that on an application to extend time the function of the planning authority was a narrow one, that the planning authority was confined to a consideration of the statutory criteria set out under s.42 and did not enjoy some form of residual discretion to take into account whether or not the development was authorised.

> "The Respondent further contends that as it has concluded that the development does not comply with the planning permission it cannot be said that the planning permission relates to the development in fact being undertaken. In any particular set of circumstances the position may be that the development is fully in compliance with the planning permission or the development relates to the planning permission but is not fully in compliance with it. In the latter case it will be clear that the development although not in compliance therewith relates to a particular planning permission rather than to some other planning permission or to no planning permission at all. The reasons stated for the refusal recognise a relationship between the development and this particular planning permission. I am satisfied from a perusal of the plans that the development is that contemplated by the planning permission. I am further satisfied that the true effect of section 42 is that the Planning Authority must therefore consider the application in that light having regard to the matters enumerated in the section and those matters only. This it has failed to do by taking into account a matter not specified in the section that is compliance with the planning permission."

Secondly, in circumstances where the planning authority had available to it a range of enforcement mechanisms under Pt VIII of the PDA 2000, it was improper to use the occasion of an application for an extension to prevent the completion of what the planning authority regarded as an unauthorised development.

> "In this case I am satisfied that the primary object of section 42 of the Act of 2000 is to enable a development already commenced to which a planning permission relates to be completed: it is not permissible to use the section to prevent the completion of a development to which the planning permission relates which the Planning Authority has concluded does not comply fully with that permission. What the Planning Authority must consider is whether the development relates to the permission and not whether it is in full compliance with the same. It is not permissible to use a statutory power conferred for a particular purpose for some other purpose."

It is respectfully submitted that the reasoning on both counts is unconvincing. Insofar as the discretion of the planning authority is concerned, it is submitted that the requirement that the planning authority address its mind to the question as to whether substantial works have been carried out "pursuant to" the planning permission will, in some cases, require the planning authority to consider the issue of compliance. It is further submitted that it is incorrect for the court to suggest that it is sufficient that the development carried out to date "relates" to the planning permission: s.42 expressly requires that the works have been carried out "pursuant to" the planning permission. The two phrases are not synonymous. It is a question of fact and degree as to whether works can fairly be said to be pursuant to the planning permission. Whereas it may well be that in the present case any deviation from the terms of the planning permission was immaterial, and thus the works could properly be said to have been carried on pursuant to the planning permission, it is submitted that it is incorrect to suggest that the planning authority is not entitled to address its mind to this question.

The position obtaining in this jurisdiction as a result of the judgment in *McDowell v Roscommon County Council* is to be contrasted with that applying in England and Wales. There, provision is made for the expiry of planning permissions not implemented within a certain time. Development must begin within a certain period and is taken to begin on the earliest possible date on which any material operation comprised in the development begins to be carried out. It is well established that in order for operations to amount to the commencement of development under a planning permission, those operations must be authorised by the permission in question, read together with its conditions: *Henry Boot Homes Ltd v Bassetlaw DC* [2002] EWCA Civ 983, [37]; [2003] 1 P. & C.R. 23, citing *Whitley and Sons v Secretary of State for Wales* (1992) 64 P. & C.R. 296. In general, operations carried out in breach of a condition cannot be relied upon. If the operations do not comply with the planning permission, they constitute a breach of planning control and for planning purposes will be deemed unauthorised and thus unlawful.

Turning now to the second ground put forward in the judgment, namely that the refusal of an extension was for an improper purpose, *i.e.* to prevent the completion of an unauthorised development, it is submitted that this analysis simply begs the question at issue. Either the planning authority is entitled to take into account the fact that development may be in breach of the terms of the planning permission—and, for the reasons set out above, it is submitted that the planning authority is so entitled—or it is not. This turns on the meaning to be attached to the phrase "pursuant to" the planning permission. If the planning authority is entitled to take into account the fact that development may be in breach of the terms of the planning permission, then there is no improper purpose.

In any event, it is artificial to characterise the refusal of an extension as the action that prevents the completion of the development: if the development truly is unauthorised, then it has been unauthorised since the beginning and the refusal of an extension does not change that status.

The concepts of "development" and "unauthorised development" are central to the planning legislation and a planning authority will often have to address its mind to whether a development is unauthorised in contexts other than enforcement proceedings. For example, in adjudicating on an application for planning permission, a planning authority is entitled to consider whether the development in respect of which planning permission is being sought is in aid of other unauthorised development. Moreover, the planning authority has an express power, under s.5, to make a determination on the question of whether an act is or is not development (this is subject to an appeal to An Bord Pleanála). The Supreme Court decision in *Grianán An Aileach Interpretative Centre Company Ltd v Donegal County Council* [2004] 2 I.R. 625 suggests that the planning authorities are particularly well qualified to assess this. It is submitted that there is nothing inconsistent in allowing the planning authority to address its mind to this question in the context of an application to extend the life of a planning permission.

Abandonment of planning permission   The concept of abandonment is an important one in planning law, with relevance both in the context of a pre-1964 use and in the context of the seven-year limitation period on enforcement proceedings. It is well established that a manifest interruption in the use of lands or in the carrying out of works will represent an abandonment, with the result that the resumption of the activity will represent a fresh act of development. Most of the previous case law in this regard relates to claims for an established pre-1964 use, *i.e.* there being no formal grant of planning permission in existence.

In *Molloy v Minister for Justice Equality and Law Reform*, unreported, High Court, Gilligan J., April 30, 2004, the High Court had to consider whether a grant of planning permission can be "abandoned". Planning permission had been granted for the erection of a three-storey residential hostel block. Initially the premises was used for the permitted use, but after a period of six years the use changed to use for religious purposes—an unauthorised use. The unauthorised use of the premises continued for a period in excess of 20 years. The position in England and Wales seems to be that a planning permission (works) capable of implementation cannot be abandoned, but that once a planning permission has been implemented, it is spent, with the result that if the permitted use is displaced by another use, then the resumption of the permitted use itself represents a *fresh* act of development, which requires planning permission. Thus on the facts of the present case, the resumption of the hostel use would appear to require a further grant of planning permission.

The High Court, seemingly, took a different view. It has to be said that the reasoning of the High Court in this regard is somewhat unclear. The key issue seems to have been the question of what is meant by a planning permission "capable of implementation". In the case of development involving mining or quarrying, the planning permission may be implemented in various stages. Conversely, in the case of a material change in use, the planning permission is, arguably, implemented once the permitted use is first commenced: the development is the *change*, not the use *per se*. The High Court seems to have taken the view that reversion to the permitted use is always available, even where the lands have been put to a different use for a lengthy period of time (on the facts, in excess of 20 years). Gilligan J. stated that what he meant by "capable of implementation" was that there has been no material or structural alteration of the land or property that would render the original planning permission incapable of being implemented. The inconsistency between the position of the courts of England and Wales and our own High Court might be explicable by reference to the provisions of s.28(6) of the Local Government (Planning and Development) Act 1963, which allows a planning permission to specify the purposes for which a structure may or may not be used: this might be thought to be broader than simply permitting a once-off change in use.

Planning permission as derogation from grant An important point of conveyancing law fell for consideration by the Supreme Court in *William Bennett Construction Ltd v Greene* [2004] 2 I.L.R.M. 96. Outline planning permission had been obtained for certain residential development. On the site layout plan accompanying the application for planning permission, a drain for the disposal of sewage was shown running in a south-easterly direction to connect with a foul water sewer under the road adjoining the site. Part of the land was sold on, conditional on the purchaser obtaining an approval pursuant to the outline planning permission. The part of the land sold excluded the land on which the drain for the disposal of sewage was to run. The purchaser brought proceedings, claiming that it had a wayleave in this regard and arguing that where land had been sold for a specific purpose known to both parties, *i.e.* the development of the land as shown on the site layout plan on the basis of which the outline permission had been granted, and the uncontradicted evidence established that it would be prohibitively expensive for the purchaser to develop the land in any other way insofar as the disposal of the sewage was concerned, then the conduct of the vendor in refusing to allow the development proceed in that manner constituted a derogation from the grant of the land. The Supreme Court rejected this argument, holding that at the time of the sale there was not in existence an easement in the nature of a wayleave that, when part of the land was sold, remained in existence as a quasi-easement for the benefit of the lands sold:

> "The defendants in this case had never at any stage used any part of their land for the disposal of sewage by means of a pipe connecting with the main sewers of the local authority. They did no more than indicate in the site layout plan lodged with the application for permission that that was how they would propose to dispose of the sewage, in the event of permission being granted for the development and the

development proceeding. There was, accordingly, no easement in existence being used at the time of the grant by the grantor for the benefit of the property granted over the property retained and hence no room for the application of the doctrine that the grantor cannot derogate from his grant."

The Supreme Court also made the point that a purchaser of the land becomes entitled to the benefit of a planning permission, not by virtue of the conveyance but because of the general principle that a grant of permission to develop land inures for the benefit of the land and of all persons for the time being interested therein.

PLANNING CONDITIONS

Points of detail Provision is made under s.34(5) of the PDA 2000 whereby a condition attached to a planning permission may provide that points of detail relating to a grant of permission be agreed between the planning authority and the person to whom the permission is granted and that in default of agreement the matter is to be referred to An Bord Pleanála for determination. It seems that a similar power was implicit in the previous legislation. The judgment of the Supreme Court in *Boland v An Bord Pleanála* [1996] 3 I.R. 435 set down the requirements for such conditions. The overall objective to be achieved by the matters left for agreement, and the purpose of such details, should be clearly stated in the condition. The condition should also have laid down criteria by which the developer and the planning authority can reach agreement. Thus, when a compliance submission is made, it is simply a matter for the planning authority to implement what has already been decided in essence. The planning authority enjoys a very limited discretion and must ascertain what is the true or correct meaning of the conditions attached to the planning permission and confine itself and the developer to such proposals as are in compliance with those conditions. See, generally, *O'Connor v Dublin Corporation (No.2)*, unreported, High Court, O'Neill J., October 3, 2000.

The judgment in *Kenny v Dublin City Council*, unreported, High Court, Murphy J., September 8, 2004 involved the application of these established principles to a particular set of facts. The High Court rejected a challenge that the decision of the planning authority to agree a compliance submission went beyond the scope of the conditions or represented a material alteration to the development.

"The faithful implementation of the decision of An Bord Pleanála in relation to its conditions depends in the first instance on the degree of specificity of those conditions. The more specific, the less discretion there is regarding their implementation. The more general they are the

> more scope there is between the planning authority and the developer.
> There is clear evidence that there are several ways whereby a general
> condition such as that relating to the western arm of building number 3
> could be reduced in height in the interest of visual amenity by the
> omission of the first floor."

The applicant in the judicial review proceedings had previously challenged
the decision of An Bord Pleanála to grant planning permission, arguing, *inter
alia*, that the conditions imposed by An Bord Pleanála amounted to the board's
unlawful delegation of its decision-making power to the planning authority
and was thus *ultra vires*. It had been argued that the developer and the planning
authority were at large as to the appearance, nature and scale of the ultimate
development, all of which matters, or so it was alleged, could subsequently be
agreed in private without any input from, or access by, members of the public.
In rejecting this earlier challenge, the High Court in *Kenny v An Bord Pleanála*
[2001] 1 I.R. 565 emphasised that the subsequent conduct of the planning
authority in agreeing submissions under the impugned conditions could itself
be subject to judicial review proceedings, if necessary. The High Court also
stated that it should not be assumed that the planning authority would seek to
exceed the limited discretion allowed to it in agreeing points of detail under
the conditions:

> "In addition I do not believe that it would be correct of me to assume
> that the Planning Authority, which as a matter of law ought to be aware
> of its functions and responsibilities including its limitations, when
> dealing with conditions of this nature, would exceed its role which is to
> further the faithful, true and core implementation of the permission. It
> would be wrong in my view to ascribe to it any ultra vires intention
> when none has or could be so identified."

The provisions of s.34(5) fell for direct consideration in *Ryanair Ltd v An
Bord Pleanála* [2004] 2 I.R. 334. The applicant for judicial review sought to
make the argument that the express power to attach conditions, leaving points
of detail over for agreement, was confined to the planning authority and was
not available to An Bord Pleanála on appeal. The argument in this regard
appeared to be to the effect that because there is no express reference under
s.37 to s.34(5), this power is available only in respect of a decision by the
planning authority. The powers of An Bord Pleanála in relation to an appeal
are set out under s.37 of the PDA 2000. It is expressly provided that subss.(1),
(2), (3) and (4) of s.34 shall apply, subject to any necessary modifications, in
relation to the determination of an application by the board on an appeal under
s.37 as the subsections apply in relation to the determination under that section
of an application by a planning authority. The High Court rejected this
argument:

"While it has been submitted on behalf of the applicant that the power of a planning authority to impose such a condition derives from s. 34 (5) alone, it has to be recalled that this Court has previously decided in the case of *Kenny v. An Bord Pleanála (No. 1)* [2001] 1 I.R. 565 that the power enjoyed by the Board to impose a condition that matters should be agreed between a planning authority and the recipient of a permission is one arising under s. 26 of the Act of 1963. In this regard, the court was following the earlier decision in *Boland v. An Bord Pleanála* [1996] 3 I.R. 435. It has not been suggested that the principles outlined in Bennion *Statutory Interpretation,* referred to by counsel for the Board on this application, do not represent a correct statement of the law such that any intended removal of the power previously enjoyed by the Board should be removed by measured and considered provisions and that the least alteration of the law should be presumed, all matters being equal. I am also inclined to the reasoning of counsel for the Board as to the purpose of s. 34 (5). I am further inclined to accept the submissions of counsel for the notice party that subs. (5) does not in fact confer the power in question but rather identifies the existing power."

Restoration conditions   A planning permission will sometimes contain conditions requiring the restoration of the land after permitted development, such as quarrying, is completed. Although a planning permission will generally have a "life" of five years, certain conditions survive the expiration of the planning permission. In particular, the obligation of any person to comply with any condition, whereby something is required either to be done or not to be done, survives. In *Mason v KTK Sand and Gravel Ltd*, unreported, High Court, Smyth J., May 7, 2004, the somewhat ingenious argument was put forward that certain conditions under a long-since expired planning permission allowed a disused sand and gravel quarry to be filled with inert waste. A waste permit had been granted under the Waste Management Acts, but no fresh grant of planning permission had been obtained. The developer argued that the backfilling of the excavated quarry with inert waste was authorised by a restoration condition under the planning permission. The relevant condition was in the following terms:

"The whole of the surface area, including slopes and sections containing deposits accruing from the working of the pit shall be reinstated as closely as possible to the contours of the original ground. The date of commencement of restoration works, the phasing of such works, the sections to be reinstated and the final contours and levels to which the restoration shall be carried out shall be agreed with the Planning Authority."

Smyth J. appeared to accept that, in principle, a condition requiring restoration works to be carried out could implicitly include permission for those works. The scope of the planning permission, however, was a matter for construction, subject to the principle that the planning permission could not go beyond the scope of the initial application. Smyth J. held that the test to be applied was as to whether or not the operation of a landfill site was a different development from that which was originally intended in the way of restoration works under the planning permission. In applying this test, Smyth J. emphasised that in determining the nature and extent of development permitted under a planning permission, regard had to be had to the description of the development in the application for planning permission. The purpose of the requirement to state the nature and extent of the proposed development was to ensure that both the planning authority and members of the public could evaluate, or come to an appreciation of, what development was intended. On the facts, Smyth J. held that the proposed and existing use of the land (as a landfill site) was not the subject of the original planning permission and was not reasonably incidental either to the primary purpose of such use, for which permission was obtained, or incidental to the conditions attached thereto. The fact that one or more conditions in a planning permission left outstanding obligations did not *per se* permit the carrying out of development of a radically different character (both as to its nature and extent) in purported discharge of such obligations. The operations, works, use and effects of the intended landfill site were a radically different development both in nature and extent than that which could be reasonably foreseen or envisaged from that to "extend existing sandpit into adjoining field", as stated in the original planning permission.

In reaching his conclusions, Smyth J. rejected a submission that particular weight should be attached to the (favourable) interpretation by the planning authority of the planning permission, holding that the interpretation of a planning permission was ultimately a matter for the courts.

DEVELOPMENT PLAN

Variation of development plan   The procedural steps to be followed by a planning authority in varying its development plan are set out in detail in s.13 of the PDA 2000. To a large extent, these procedural steps are similar to those prescribed in relation to other actions on the part of a planning authority, for example, there is a requirement to give public notice and the manager is required to prepare a report summarising the issues raised in submissions or observations made. In *Sandyford Environmental Planning and Road Safety Group Ltd v Dun Laoghaire Rathdown County Council*, unreported, High Court, McKechnie J., June 30, 2004, a variation of a development plan was challenged on the basis that there had not been proper compliance with the requirements of s.13.

The first ground of challenge was that the public notice failed to state

properly the reason, or reasons, for the proposed variation, as required under
s.13. The stated reason was in the following terms: "The draft of the proposed
variations proposes the rezoning of four acres in the county from open space
to residential use to provide for future residential development and the deletion
of a long term roads proposal." It was argued, on behalf of the applicant
company, that the true justification for the proposed rezoning was to implement
the planning authority's own housing strategy and to ensure compliance with
the regional planning guidelines. The applicant company based this argument
on the fact that the manager's report made express reference both to the housing
strategy and to the regional planning guidelines. McKechnie J. rejected this
argument, holding that the manager's reference to the housing strategy and
the regional planning guidelines was merely for the purposes of establishing
the context of the proposed variation. McKechnie J. stated that given the
complementary and interactive workings of a local authority, it would be quite
proper that in reporting to his council the manager would establish the context
and give the relevant background to any proposal contained within that report.

The High Court held that the stated reason for the variation was adequate:

> "The objective is to put the public on notice of matters likely to interest
> those concerned and to do so in such a way that any member, who
> informatively considers the notice, will recognise the essentials of the
> proposal, and depending on detail or complexity, will be alerted
> sufficiently to further evaluate the underlying reasons for that proposal.
> For any proposal there may be reasons, some of which are proximate,
> some of which are less so, and indeed, some of which are so remote
> that any connection with the subject matter is highly tenuous. What is
> required, in my view, in order to comply with the duty of the provision
> in question, is to meaningfully impart information, sufficiently
> intelligible to a reasonable person, who could, from such information,
> understand the said proposal."

[...]

> "What would a reasonable person take from the suggested future
> residential development of the land in question? In my view, this type
> of phrase would immediately convey an intention behind the proposal,
> to provide for those lands, if the variation was adopted, a scheme which
> resulted in the construction of a residential development with such
> associated and ancillary services which follow from such a development.
> What in broad terms that would have involved, not only for the existing
> use but also for its future direction, was or, with ease, could have been
> ascertained. In addition, having specified the exact location of the subject
> lands, one would have been able to immediately identify the adjacent
> location of Fitzsimons Wood. Again, an enquiring person would readily
> have been able to envisage, at least some consequences for that

designated conservation area. As a result, I am quite satisfied that the notice served its intended statutory purpose and that it was far more meaningful than if there was simply a reference to a Housing Strategy or to the Strategic Planning Guidelines, even if either or both of these were the true reasons for the said proposal, a suggestion which, in fact, I reject."

Interestingly, in reaching his conclusion on this issue, McKechnie J. attached significance to the nature of the decision being challenged, stating that the decision was simply a proposal emanating from a local authority and not one that could have profound and immediate consequences for those affected. Nor was the court dealing with a statutory report from an inspector or other designated person, whether under the Planning Acts, the Housing Acts, or otherwise. McKechnie J. also gave some weight to the fact that the public notice was to be given by way of newspaper notice and that, by its very nature, it was not practical or feasible to give extensive reasons through the medium of a newspaper notice.

McKechnie J. did, however, sound the following note of caution:

"In saying this, however, I wish to emphasise that, in my view, a local authority should not have or adopt a minimalist standard to the contents of such a notice and, if anything, should err on the side of an expansive approach. If for example the true reasons for this proposal were the Council's Housing Strategy and or the Strategic Guidelines, then, whilst these would have to be referred to, I doubt strongly if a mere reference to such documents, and no more, would have conveyed in recognisable language the meaningful information which, in my opinion, the public are entitled to expect from such a notice. So, whilst I believe that the notice in this case did contain reasons which were 'proper, intelligible and adequate', I would caution strongly against any practice or policy, used or designed, directly or indirectly to limit, whether by omission, phraseology, or otherwise, information which should be supplied to the public."

As a separate ground of challenge, it was alleged by the applicant company that the manager's report had been defective in a number of respects, as follows. First, it was claimed that the entire submissions and observations made in response to the public notice should have been circulated to each of the elected members prior to the first of the relevant meetings. Secondly, it was suggested that the manner of summarising the content of those submissions was inadequate and, when taken against the manager's response, conveyed an incomplete and unfair representation of those observations and submissions. Thirdly, it was claimed that the objectors' names should have been assigned against their particular objection.

Again, the High Court rejected the applicant company's arguments. McKechnie J. held that the duty upon the manager was but to summarise the submissions and observations received; this duty could not be interpreted as obliging the manager to circulate, in full, all the submissions and observations received. In any event, copies of the submissions and observations were made available for inspection. In complying with his obligation to summarise the submissions and observations, the manager was not bound to use any formula nor to follow any specific method. On the facts, McKechnie J. found that, although dealt with quite briefly, the issues raised, both in substance and in materiality, were adequately outlined in the manager's report.

Finally, McKechnie J. observed that although he was not deciding the case on the point, he had great reservations as to whether it could be said that this application for judicial review was brought promptly as required under Ord.84, r.21. McKechnie J. went on to state that even in the absence of express prejudice, and appreciating the difficulties of an association like the applicant in mounting High Court proceedings, he nevertheless believed that would-be litigants were running a serious risk by deferring proceedings for lengthy periods of time.

APPEALS TO AN BORD PLEANÁLA

Statutory notices An Bord Pleanála has a power, under s.131 of the PDA 2000, to request submissions or observations in relation to any matter arising in relation to an appeal. The notice must specify a period within which such submissions or observations are to be made. This period is not to be less than two weeks or more than four weeks, beginning on the date of service of the notice. The consequences of a failure to comply strictly with the requirements of a similar provision under the previous legislation (s.9 of the Local Government (Planning and Development) Act 1992) were considered in *Hickey v An Bord Pleanála*, unreported, High Court, Smyth J., June 10, 2004. On the facts, it was admitted that the applicant for judicial review had only been given 13 days, rather than 14 days, within which to make her submissions or observations. Smyth J. refused to quash the decision of An Bord Pleanála, ruling that there was no evidence that the applicant had sustained any prejudice as a result of the shortened time limit: a response had actually been made by the applicant and there was no evidence that one further day would have made any difference to that response. Smyth J. relied in this regard on the judgment in *Ryanair Ltd v An Bord Pleanála* [2004] 2 I.R. 334. In *Ryanair Ltd* the High Court had held that once the submission had been made within the statutory period, the letter inviting same could not act in a manner to defeat the legal rights of the applicant.

In order to avoid the strictures of the judgment of the Supreme Court in *Monaghan UDC v Alf-a-bet Promotions Ltd* [1980] I.L.R.M. 64, Smyth J. held that there had been "substantial compliance" with the statutory requirements. This approach can be contrasted with that usually taken in relation to time limits, to the effect that a time limit is either met or it is not met: there can be no halfway house or partial compliance. See, for example, *McCann v An Bord Pleanála* [1997] 1 I.R. 264; [1997] 1 I.L.R.M. 314. See also *Graves v An Bord Pleanála* [1997] 2 I.R. 205.

ENFORCEMENT

Section 160 injunction: discretion   In *Mason v KTK Sand and Gravel Ltd*, unreported, High Court, Smyth J., May 7, 2004, the High Court granted relief notwithstanding an objection on the part of the respondent developer that the applicants had delayed. Smyth J. found that the applicants' solicitors had written to the respondent before the use complained of was first undertaken, and that the applicants had not waited until expenditure was incurred by the respondent before making known their concerns.

ENVIRONMENTAL IMPACT ASSESSMENT

Division of function   The long running debate as to whether the environmental impact assessment directive had been properly implemented into national law prior to the PDA 2000 may, at last, be drawing to a conclusion with the decision of the High Court in *Martin v An Bord Pleanála (No.2)*, unreported, High Court, Smyth J., November 30, 2004. The gist of the objection to the form of implementation of the directive might be summarised as follows: it was argued that the division of function as between An Bord Pleanála and the Environmental Protection Agency—demarked by the concept of "environmental pollution"—produced the unsatisfactory result that no one body was entitled to carry out an integrated assessment of the proposed development.

The principal argument of the applicant in *Martin (No.2)* represented a variation on this theme. It was argued that planning permission constituted the only "development consent" for the purposes of the directive, and in circumstances where An Bord Pleanála was precluded from assessing "environmental pollution" (save in respect of the actual construction works), there had been a clear breach of the directive. It was suggested that the Environmental Protection Agency had no formal function as "competent authority" insofar as the directive was concerned.

Smyth J. rejected these arguments, holding that the complementary decisions of An Bord Pleanála and the Environmental Protection Agency represented the "development consent" for the purposes of the directive. Smyth J. distinguished the earlier judgment of the Supreme Court in *O'Connell v Environmental Protection Agency* [2003] 1 I.R. 530 on the basis that that judgment was principally concerned with a different issue, namely the procedure for deciding whether an environmental impact statement should be required in respect of a sub-threshold project. Smyth J. did, however, grant leave to appeal to the Supreme Court. This appeal was heard in April 2005.

It should be emphasised that this debate regarding the division of function as between An Bord Pleanála and the Environmental Protection Agency is now largely of historical interest. This is because the PDA 2000 introduced a more flexible system, which allows for An Bord Pleanála to consider matters of environmental pollution. Thus the argument is really only relevant to applications for planning permission made prior to the commencement of the new statutory regime.

Integrated pollution control Under the previous legislation the division of function as between An Bord Pleanála and the Environmental Protection Agency only arose where the activity, the subject-matter of an application for planning permission, also required a waste licence or an integrated pollution control licence. In *Hickey v An Bord Pleanála*, unreported, High Court, Smyth J., June 10, 2004, a decision to grant planning permission was challenged, *inter alia*, on the basis that An Bord Pleanála should have treated the development as one which required an integrated pollution control licence and should, accordingly, have limited its consideration to issues other than environmental pollution. This argument was rejected by the High Court. Smyth J. attached significance to the fact that the Environmental Protection Agency had confirmed, in writing, to the planning authority that in its opinion an integrated pollution control licence was not required in respect of the activity. Smyth J. held that the legislative entitlement to determine when and where a licence is necessary and upon what terms it should issue had been conferred on the Environmental Protection Agency by Pt IV of the Environmental Protection Agency Act 1992. With respect, this aspect of the judgment may go too far. Although as a matter of practicality the Agency will often have to address its mind to the question as to whether a particular activity comes within the list of activities prescribed for the purposes of integrated pollution control, it is submitted that in the event of dispute the interpretation of the schedules must be a matter of law for the courts. In this regard, reference is made, by analogy, to the approach adopted in relation to the interpretation of environmental impact assessment projects: see, for example, *Shannon Regional Fisheries Board v An Bord Pleanála* [1994] 3 I.R. 449 and *Maher v An Bord Pleanála* [1999] 2 I.L.R.M. 198.

Development consent The ECJ has indicated, in *R. (On the application of Wells) v Secretary of State for Transport, Local Government and the Regions* (Case C–201/02, January 7, 2004), that in cases where the initial development consent was not subject to environmental impact assessment, or where that initial assessment was inadequate, then a requirement for environmental impact assessment might be triggered by an application for a further development consent. On the facts of *Wells*, the further development consent was the decision on an application for registration and determination of planning conditions on an old mining planning permission.

The question as to whether an environmental impact assessment might be required on the occasion of some further consent or approval in respect of a project already authorised arose for consideration in *Dunne v Minister for the Environment, Heritage & Local Government*, unreported, High Court, Laffoy J., September 7, 2004. The proceedings concerned the construction of part of the M50 motorway at Carrickmines. The motorway scheme had been approved by the Minister for the Environment in October 1998. On the same date, the Minister for the Environment had also given an approval for the purposes of the environmental impact assessment directive. As part of the mitigation measures the environmental impact statement required that archaeological excavation be carried out during the course of construction. It was accepted by all parties that the excavations subsequently carried out had actually uncovered a whole range of features that were not known of at the time of the environmental impact assessment in 1998.

It was argued in the High Court that the giving of ministerial directions under the amended national monuments legislation constituted, in all the circumstances, the giving of a "development consent" such as to trigger a requirement for a further environmental impact assessment. Laffoy J. rejected this analysis, holding that, as a matter of fact, the ministerial directions neither replaced nor altered the approved road development. Laffoy J. accepted a submission on behalf of the Minister that the constraints imposed by the national monuments legislation, including the requirement to obtain ministerial consent, represented an extra layer of regulation that was separate and distinct from the regulatory regime to which the earlier decisions, in 1998, had given effect. Accordingly, the ministerial directions, did not constitute a development consent.

This judgment is under appeal to the Supreme Court.

Remedies In *Cosgrave v An Bord Pleanála* [2004] 2 I.R. 435 the High Court ruled that an alleged breach of the environmental impact assessment directive could not be raised in judicial review proceedings challenging a decision to grant planning permission; rather, it seems that any challenge should have been brought as against the State alone. With respect, this ruling would appear to be at odds with the approach adopted by both the House of Lords in *Berkley v Secretary of State for the Environment, Transport and the Regions* [2001] 2 A.C. 603 and the European Court of Justice in *R. (On the application of Wells) v Secretary of State for Transport, Local Government and the Regions* (Case C-201/02, January 7, 2004). The ECJ rejected an argument that the directive could not be invoked against a particular "development consent" as this would otherwise involve inverse direct effect:

"In the main proceedings, the obligation of the Member State concerned to ensure that the competent authorities carry out an assessment of the environmental effects of the working of the quarry is not directly linked to the performance of any obligation which would fall, pursuant to Directive 85/337, on the quarry owners. The fact that the mining operations must be halted to await the assessment is admittedly the consequence of the belated performance of the State's obligations. Such a consequence cannot, however, as the United Kingdom claims, be described an inverse direct effect of the provisions of that directive in relation to quarry owners."

It is to be noted that a similar procedural objection was not pursued by the State respondents in *Martin v An Bord Pleanála (No.2)*, unreported, High Court, Smyth J., November 30, 2004.

DEVELOPMENT CONTRIBUTIONS

Development contribution scheme   The extent of information that a planning authority is required to include in a development contribution scheme was considered by the High Court in *Construction Industry Federation v Dublin City Council*, unreported, High Court, Gilligan J., March 2, 2004. The applicant company, which claimed to represent the interests of a number of builders, sought to challenge the validity of Dublin City Council's development contribution scheme. A number of grounds of challenge were put forward. The principal ground raised was that a draft scheme or a scheme should specify the individual projects the planning authority intends to fund wholly or partly from money raised under that scheme, and that a scheme is required to set out the level of detail as to cost or timing. Objection was also made that insofar as any detailed information was provided, it was contained in an extraneous document, namely a report prepared for the planning authority. It was argued that this information should have been included in the draft scheme. Complaint was also made that the draft scheme was amended before adoption, without any further public consultation.

The High Court rejected the challenge. Gilligan J. held that the legislation did not require that individual projects and facilities be specifically referred to and costed in a scheme or draft scheme. Nor was there any legal infirmity in not including the information in the consultants' report in the scheme or draft scheme.

"In my view it was permissible for the respondent to have referred to the consultants' report and to have incorporated it into the scheme. The consultants' report was clearly an integral part of the consultation process and was freely available to all concerned persons including the applicant and it constituent members. The respondent did not in my view have to set out the basis for the scheme but did have to set out the basis for determining the contribution. In my view the consultants' report, in fact, is supplementary to the scheme itself. The real criticism in this aspect is to the extent of the information contained in the consultants' report. It is accepted by the respondent that all the information available is not set out in the consultants' report for a number of reasons. The reality however is that, in my view, the scheme itself complies with s.48 and if the legislature had intended that every piece of information as considered by the respondent must be set out in the scheme it could clearly have said so in the provisions of section 48. The scheme does no more or less than it is obliged to do and the consultants' report provides significant background detail."

On appeal, the Supreme Court rejected the challenge on the basis that the applicant company did not have "sufficient interest" to sustain a challenge to the development contribution scheme: unreported, March 18, 2005.

Practice and Procedure

RAYMOND BYRNE *and* HILARY DELANY

ABUSE OF PROCESS

Order 19, rules 27 and 28 of the Rules of the Superior Courts 1986 provide a mechanism for bringing a motion to strike out "any matter in any indorsement or pleading" or "any pleading" respectively on stated grounds. Rule 27 provides that the court may at any stage in proceedings order any matter in the pleadings to be struck out on the grounds that it may be "unnecessary or scandalous" or may "tend to prejudice, embarrass, or delay the fair trial of the action". An example of matters characterised as scandalous, prejudicial or embarrassing in this context is provided in the judgment of Smyth J. in *Hanly v Newsgroup Newspapers Ltd* [2004] 1 I.R. 471 in which Smyth J. ordered that certain paragraphs in a statement of claim should be struck out pursuant to Ord.19, r.27. In his view the issues referred to were in the nature of evidence referable to unrelated proceedings and were scandalous in that they sought to introduce immaterial matters which would lead to the introduction of irrelevant evidence at the trial of the action.

The Supreme Court has reiterated that the jurisdiction to strike out under Ord.19, r.28 is one which a court will be slow to exercise. As was stated by Denham J. in *Aer Rianta cpt v Ryanair Ltd* [2004] 1 I.R. 506, "a court will exercise caution in utilizing its jurisdiction" in this regard, although she added that if a court is convinced that a claim will fail, pleadings will be struck out. Denham J. also made it clear that Ord.19, r.28 refers to an entire pleading and not to parts of a pleading, in contrast to the provisions of r.27. Denham J. stated that she was satisfied on the plain words of the rule that this was the correct construction and that under Ord.19, r.28 the court has jurisdiction to strike out an entire document, for example a statement of claim, but not a portion of it.

CIVIL LIABILITY AND COURTS ACT 2004

The Civil Liability and Courts Act 2004 is, as its title suggests, a wide-ranging legislative enactment. Part 2 of the 2004 Act (ss.6 to 32) deals with civil liability in personal injuries actions and largely implements recommendations of the 2002 *Report of the Motor Insurance Advisory Board* (MIAB). The MIAB

Report had also led to the enactment of the Personal Injuries Assessment Board Act 2003 (see *Annual Review of Irish Law 2003*, p.608 *et seq.*). Part 3 of the 2004 Act (ss.33 to 56) contains a number of miscellaneous items, including provisions on funds of suitors, the jurisdiction of the courts, significant changes to the *in camera* rule, provisions on court officers and provisions for an increase in the number of judges.

Limitation period in personal injuries actions Sections 6 and 7 of the 2004 Act amend the general limitation period for personal injuries actions. When published as a Bill, it was proposed to reduce the general limitation period in personal injuries actions from three years to one year, in line with the MIAB Report. After the Committee Stage debate in the Seanad, the Minister for Justice, Equality and Law Reform accepted that, particularly in medical negligence claims, a reduction to one year was too dramatic and so the eventual reduction is from three to two years for all personal injuries claims.

Letter of claim Section 8 of the 2004 Act requires that, within two months of the incident giving rise to the claim, the plaintiff must notify the proposed defendant in writing, giving details of the nature of the claim and the intention to institute legal proceedings; this is referred to as a letter of claim. Failure to serve such a notice will not, of course, preclude an action from proceeding, but it may be dealt with in terms of costs orders.

Nature of pleadings Section 13 of the 2004 Act provides that all pleadings in personal injuries actions must be descriptive and not set out in general terms. Section 10 of the 2004 Act states that a personal injuries summons in the High Court, Circuit Court or District Court must specify the plaintiff's name and address, PPS number, defendant's name and address (if known), the injuries suffered by the defendant's alleged wrong (which has the same meaning as in the Civil Liability Act 1961, being a "tort, breach of contract or breach of trust"), full particulars of special damage, full particulars of the defendant's acts constituting the wrong and of each instance of negligence. In effect, this requires the plaintiff to set out his or her understanding of the factual basis of the claim and the basis on which the defendant is liable. Section 11 provides that the plaintiff must, if requested by the defendant, give particulars of any personal injuries actions previously brought (whether leading to a court award or withdrawn and settled), his or her medical history, and earnings. Section 12 states that defendants must, in their defence or if they are counterclaiming, specify which allegations they admit and which they dispute and state the basis on which liability is denied, and if the defendant is suggesting a different version of events, the defendant must specify that version.

Affidavits supporting factual assertions Section 14 of the 2004 Act provides that both claimants and defendants will be required to swear affidavits verifying that any factual assertions they have set out in the pleadings submitted to the court are accurate. If subsequently the court decides they were fraudulent or exaggerated, the plaintiff or defendant swearing the false affidavit could be, if it was done knowingly, liable on conviction on indictment to a fine of €100,000 and/or imprisonment of up to 10 years (see ss.25, 26 and 29). They also stand to lose the right to recover any damages, even if the exaggeration was partial. They may also be liable to pay the other party's costs. The final version of the 2004 Act does not require all pleadings to be filed immediately (current practice that they are filed at the setting down stage is therefore continued) but these affidavits will have to be filed in the relevant court office immediately so that there is a "trail" that can be later taken up if criminal proceedings become relevant.

Woolf-like case management in personal injuries claims The 2004 Act also includes important new case management reforms along the lines of the "Woolf" reforms which came into force in the UK in 1999, albeit the 2004 Act is confined to personal injuries actions. Thus, s.9 of the 2004 Act provides that the courts are required to ensure that parties to personal injuries actions comply with relevant rules of court so that hearings occur "within a reasonable period of their having been commenced". Similarly, the 2004 Act encourages the parties to make all possible efforts to settle proceedings. Either party will have the power to convene a mediation conference to settle claims (ss.15 and 16) and courts will have the power to arrange pre-trial hearings and conferences, with a view to shortening the trial (s.18). Before a case goes to trial, the parties must exchange formal written offers of settlement. But if the case goes to trial, the trial judge will not be made aware of the final offers until after judgment has been delivered. However, the judge will be entitled to take the final offer into account when deciding on costs (s.17). Evidence may be given on affidavit if the court directs (s.19). Courts are also empowered to appoint suitably qualified assessors to assist them on any matter relating to expert evidence (s.20) and the Supreme Court may invite such parties as it thinks fit to address it on issues of liability or damages that it considers to be of "exceptional public importance" (s.21).

Book of Quantum Section 22 of the 2004 Act requires courts in assessing damages to "have regard to" the Book of Quantum published by the PIAB under the PIAB Act 2003 (the first edition of which was published in June 2004), while ss.23 and 24 provide that Regulations may be made setting out actuarial tables for future loss of income and the "discount rate" for assessing future financial loss.

Collateral benefits Section 27 deals with the deductibility of collateral benefits and implements in large measure the Law Reform Commission's 2002 *Report on the Deductibility of Collateral Benefits* (see the *Annual Review of Irish*

Law 2002, p.517. Section 27 amends s.50 of the Civil Liability Act 1961 and s.2 of the Civil Liability (Amendment) Act 1964 to provide that in assessing damages in a personal injuries action (including a fatal injuries action), account is not to be taken of any charitable gift (whether in the form of money or property) made to the plaintiff in respect of the injuries suffered by the plaintiff, unless the defendant is the donor of the gift and, at the time the gift was made, the plaintiff was informed that a deduction would be made from any award subsequently made or, where the plaintiff is employed by the defendant, the gift resembled pay or other remuneration.

Undeclared income Section 28 of the 2004 Act provides that undeclared income will usually be disregarded in assessing damages, unless the court considers it would be unjust to do so.

Register of personal injuries actions Section 30 provides for the establishment by the Courts Service of a register of personal injuries actions. It had originally been proposed that this would be published on the Internet, but this was altered during the Oireachtas debate on the basis that it might subject litigants to unwanted public attention. Instead, the final version of s.30 states that the Courts Service will make the register available to such persons who can establish a sufficient interest in seeking access to it (this would include solicitors and counsel and probably also insurance companies).

Personal Injuries Assessment Board Act 2003 Sections 31 and 32 amend the PIAB Act 2003 (see *Annual Review of Irish Law 2003*, p.608 *et seq.*), including inserting a new s.54A into the 2003 Act empowering the Board to require persons (including solicitors) to provide it with such records, documents or information as it may reasonably require to carry out one of its functions under the 2003 Act, which includes assessing the cost-benefit of the current personal injuries regime. There was a good deal of debate in the Oireachtas about whether this would infringe, for example, solicitor-client confidentiality, but the Minister for Justice, Equality and Law Reform expressed the view that it could not, particularly bearing in mind the presumption of constitutionality and of compatibility with the European Convention on Human Rights.

Funds of suitors Sections 33 to 38 of the 2004 Act involve considerable reform of the funds of suitor account (in effect, money lodged in court which has never been claimed, somewhat similar to dormant funds in banks).

In camera rule Section 40 of the 2004 Act considerably modifies the *in camera* rule, in particular in family cases, in line with recommendations of the Working Group on the Courts Commission (which had been chaired by Denham J.) and further recommendations from the Courts Service. It allows solicitors, barristers and "a person falling within any other class of persons" to be specified in

Regulations concerning access to court (subject to the final directions of the judge) to report on *in camera* proceedings. No reporting can identify the litigants and there are other restrictions. Section 40 does not open up these cases to general media reporting, but the intention is to allow general trends to be monitored. Section 40 also allows for orders made and evidence given in *in camera* proceedings to be used in other hearings. Indeed orders made may also be used for the purposes of obtaining mortgages and loans; this is the only element of s.40 which is retrospective.

Interest on costs and orders Section 41 amends the Court and Court Officers Act 2002 on interest on costs and orders.

Registrars of Central Criminal Court Sections 42 and 44 of the 2004 Act allow a High Court registrar to act as registrar in the Central Criminal Court (until now, only Circuit Court registrars were so assigned).

Taxing Master Section 43 deals with temporary vacancies and illnesses of Taxing Masters.

Valuation as basis for jurisdiction of courts Sections 45 to 48, and 50 to 53, amend various Courts Acts to ensure that the new "market value" approach to land valuation, introduced by the Valuation Act 2001 (rather than rateable valuation) is the basis for the jurisdiction of the courts.

Electronic service of summonses Section 49 amends the Courts (No.3) Act 1986 to facilitate electronic service of summons, which is especially connected with the penalty points system.

Excluding witnesses from personal injuries actions Section 54 empowers a court to exclude from the courtroom witnesses from a personal injuries action (excluding the parties and expert witnesses).

Register of reserved judgments Section 55 amends the provisions of the Court and Court Officers Act 2002 on the register of reserved judgments.

Increase in number of judges Section 56 provides for an increase of judges: three more judges of the High Court (bringing the maximum to 32); three more in the Circuit Court (bringing the maximum to 34); and two more in the District Court (bringing the maximum to 55).

Fennelly Working Group recommendations It had been suggested that the 2004 Act would include the proposals from the 2003 *Report of the Working Group on the Jurisdiction of the Courts* (the Fennelly Group Report, on which see the *Annual Review of Irish law 2003*, pp.497–498) on the redistribution of criminal trials. This did not happen ultimately.

COSTS

Solicitor instructing fee: tribunal of inquiry In *Minister for Finance v Flynn*, High Court, July 31, 2003, the applicant Minister applied for a review of an order of taxation made by the taxing master in respect of the costs of two politicians incurred in the course of the Tribunal of Inquiry into the Beef Processing Industry, which had been established in 1991 and had reported in 1994. The taxing master allowed an instruction fee to the solicitor retained by the two politicians of £580,500. The applicant contended that the amount allowed was excessive and sought to have it reduced. Herbert J. agreed. He held that the taxing master had incorrectly concluded that no guidance could be obtained as to the correct level of the instruction fee from instruction fees agreed between parties or allowed on taxation in a number of other cases to which he was referred. In allowing an instruction fee of £580,500 to the solicitor, the taxing master had erred in failing to apply the correct principles in the calculation of the sum. Herbert J. concluded that the fee was so in excess of fees allowed in comparable cases that it must be considered unjust. Had the taxing master applied the correct principles of comparison in assessing the appropriate instruction fee he could not reasonably have allowed more than £450,000.

DELAY—DISMISSAL FOR WANT OF PROSECUTION

The well established principles set out by the Supreme Court in *Primor v Stokes Kennedy Crowley* [1996] 2 I.R. 459, were applied again by the High Court in *O'Connor v John Player and Sons Ltd* [2004] 2 I.L.R.M. 321. The plaintiff appealed against an order made pursuant to Ord.63, r.1(8) whereby the Master dismissed the plaintiff's claims against the defendants for want of prosecution. There had been a delay of four years and 11 months between the issue of the plenary summons (December 1997) and the delivery of the statement of claim (November 2002). Notices of motion seeking dismissal were issued on behalf of the second and third named defendants in September 2002 and on behalf of the first named defendant in August 2003. Quirke J. stated that although the onus of establishing that the delay complained of had been inexcusable clearly rested on the person so alleging, the onus might be discharged by way of evidence and argument demonstrating that no reasonable or credible explanation had been offered or could reasonably be said to exist which would account for or excuse the delay. Quirke J. concluded that the plaintiff's delay had been inordinate and inexcusable and that having so found he would consider whether, on the facts, the balance of justice was in favour of or against the plaintiff's case proceedings. The determination of this issue required the consideration of the following factors: (1) the conduct of the defendants; (2) whether the delay was likely to cause or had caused serious prejudice to the defendants; and (3) whether, having regard to the implied constitutional principle of basic fairness of procedures, the plaintiff's claim against the defendant should be allowed to proceed or should be dismissed. He concluded that there had been no conduct on the part of the defendants which induced the plaintiff to embark on any particular task thereby causing delay nor had there been any delay on the defendants' part in delivering any particular pleadings or taking any particular step. In relation to prejudice, Quirke J. stated that there was no concrete evidence of specific prejudice but he quoted from the judgment of O'Flaherty J. in *Primor* to the effect that once there is inordinate and inexcusable delay, establishing prejudice seems to follow almost inexorably. He concluded that the interests of justice required that the plaintiff's claim should be dismissed for want of prosecution.

The principles relating to an application to dismiss for want of prosecution were also considered by Finlay Geoghegan J. in *Manning v Benson and Hedges Ltd* [2004] 3 I.R. 556 who reaffirmed that the applicable law is as set out by the Supreme Court in *Primor plc v Stokes Kennedy Crowley* [1996] I.R. 459. The first two plaintiffs had been diagnosed with emphysema and the third with lung cancer and they claimed that their injuries had been caused by the negligence and breach of duty of the defendants in the manufacture and distribution of cigarettes. In each of the actions the defendant sought an order pursuant to the inherent jurisdiction of the court dismissing the plaintiffs' claims for want of prosecution and two specific issues were in dispute between the parties in relation to this claim. First, should the court consider any delay by the plaintiff in the period between the date of the alleged wrongful acts or accrual of the cause of action and the date of commencement of the proceedings; and secondly, in considering the balance of justice issues, what period of delay is relevant to the issue of prejudice to the defendant or risk that it is not possible to have a fair trial.

On the first question, Finlay Geoghegan J. stated that it appeared that "in considering an application to dismiss for want of prosecution, the court should, in general, consider the period starting with the accrual of the cause of action for the purpose of determining whether there has been a delay by the plaintiff". She pointed out that she was saying "in general" because earlier decisions to which she had referred including *Primor* did not concern a personal injuries claim with a date of knowledge within the meaning of s.3 of the Statute of Limitations (Amendment) Act 2000 which was later than the date of accrual of the cause of action. In relation to the second issue, Finlay Geoghegan J. made it clear that in considering an application to dismiss for want of prosecution the court should not take into account prejudice caused to the defendant or the risk that it would not be possible to have a fair trial by reason of the lapse of time between the alleged wrongful acts and the accrual of the cause of action. However, she added that the fact that there was such a lapse of time may be an issue when considering the factors relevant to the question of the balance of justice and that the court should not ignore the fact that the alleged wrongful acts took place a long time ago. She concluded that the balance of the delays between the accruals of the causes of action and the point in each proceedings reached by the date of the issue of the motions before the court was both inordinate and inexcusable. Considering the impact of the delay since the accrual of the causes of action, and having referred to the nature of the claims and the lack of any real progress made in relation to them since the commencement of proceedings, Finlay Geoghegan J. concluded that the balance of justice was against permitting the plaintiffs to proceed with their claims.

The defendants also sought an order dismissing the plaintiffs' claims as being in breach of their rights under the Constitution, including the right to a fair trial and to fair procedures. Referring to the decisions of the Supreme Court in *Toal v Duignan (No.1)* [1991] I.L.R.M. 135, *Toal v Duignan (No.2)* [1991] I.L.R.M. 140 and *Ó Domhnaill v Merrick* [1984] I.R. 151, Finlay Geoghegan J. accepted that the courts have recognised the existence of a jurisdiction to dismiss a claim by reason of a lapse of time without there being any culpable delay by the plaintiff where the interests of justice or the constitutional principles of fair procedures so require. She concluded that by reason of the lapse of time between the alleged wrongful acts and the probable hearing date of the plaintiffs' claims there was a real and serious risk of an unfair trial if the claims were to be permitted to continue and that there would be a clear and patent unfairness in asking the defendants to defend the actions brought against them. Finlay Geoghegan J. therefore made an order dismissing the plaintiffs' claims in each case.

An interesting question which has been canvassed on a number of occasions is whether the slightly broader test put forward by Finlay C.J. in *Toal v Duignan (No.1)* [1991] I.L.R.M. 135, is more appropriate than that set out in *Primor* when the delay complained of takes place principally between the events complained of and the commencement of proceedings. This suggestion was made by counsel for the defendant in *Kelly v O'Leary* [2001] 2 I.R. 526, although in the circumstances Kelly J. applied the *Primor* test which he acknowledged was more demanding from the defendant's point of view in concluding that the plaintiff's claim must be dismissed. This argument was raised again before Kelly J. in *Ryan v Doyle* High Court, Kelly J., April 23, 2004, where again most of the delay had occurred prior to the commencement of proceedings. It was contended on behalf of the second named defendant that the court ought not to apply the *Primor* test as it applied only to post-commencement delays and that it should instead approach the matter on the basis of the principles set out in *Ó Domhnaill v Merrick* [1984] I.R. 151 and *Toal*. It was contended that the *Primor* test involved a consideration of blameworthiness for delay which was not a feature of the approach adopted in *Toal* and that the only matter with which the court should be concerned is the existence of a clear and patent unfairness in asking a defendant to defend a case after a very long lapse of time. Kelly J. commented that "the defendant may very well be correct in this assertion" but concluded that it did not make much difference on the facts of the case before him. Given that he had already made a finding of inordinate and inexcusable delay in relation to the first named defendant's application to strike out, Kelly J. stated that regardless of which test he applied, he had simply to consider whether there was a real and serious risk of an unfair trial due to prejudice caused to the second named defendant by delay. Given the circumstances, particularly the death of a crucial witness in the interim, Kelly J. concluded that there was not a real risk of an unfair trial in so far as this defendant was concerned and he made orders striking out the plaintiff's claim against the first and second named defendants.

Although Kelly J. did not go so far as to state that the *Toal* test, which is less stringent from the point of view of the defendant than that in *Primor,* is the more suitable one where most of the delay has occurred prior to the commencement of proceedings, he was clearly sympathetic to this approach. However, where there has been inordinate delay prior to the commencement of proceedings, it is almost inevitable that some blame for this will attach to the plaintiff and in practice which test is applied would rarely make any difference to the plaintiff's ability to resist an order dismissing his claim. In both cases, as Kelly J. pointed out in *Ryan v Doyle*, the issue will be whether there is a real and serious risk of an unfair trial because of the prejudice caused to the defendant as a result of the delay.

Often where a plaintiff brings a motion seeking an extension of time to serve a statement of claim, the defendant may seek an order striking out the proceedings for want of prosecution. This was the case in *Rainsford v Limerick Corporation* [1995] 2 I.L.R.M. 561, where Finlay P. made it clear that the onus of establishing that the delay had been inordinate and inexcusable lay on the party seeking to have the proceedings dismissed. Having concluded that the delay had been inordinate and inexcusable in the case before the court, but that the balance of justice lay in favour of allowing the case to continue, Finlay P. granted the plaintiff's motion seeking an extension of time to serve a statement of claim.

However, it is clear from the decision of the Supreme Court in *Irish Family Planning Association v Youth Defence* [2004] 1 I.R. 374, that different principles may apply where the application before the court is simply a motion seeking an extension of time. In this case the plaintiff's application for an extension had been granted by the High Court on appeal from the Deputy Master and the defendants appealed to the Supreme Court. Counsel for the defendants contended that the High Court judge had erred in effectively placing the onus on them in considering the application to extend time and submitted that where a party makes an application of this nature to the court the onus must lie on him. McCracken J. stated that in cases such as *Primor* where what is sought is an order striking out proceedings for want of prosecution, the defendant is actively seeking the termination of the proceedings and in so far as there may be an onus of proof, it is logical that it should lie on the defendant.

On the other hand, in the case before the court, the defendants were not seeking any relief from the court but were simply opposing an application by the plaintiff for a discretionary remedy. However, McCracken J. pointed to the fact that the application was to extend time to serve a statement of claim which on its face did not disclose any cause of action against the defendants and concluded that the court in its discretion should not extend time in such a case. Denham J. also stated that there was no statement alleging a wrongful act on the defendants' part in the statement of claim which was before the court. While she was satisfied that on an application to extend time for the service of a statement of claim the court has an inherent jurisdiction to control the procedure and to dismiss an application where the justice of the case required, she also made it clear that there was an onus on an applicant to present a statement of claim in an appropriate form. Denham J. added that if the statement of claim discloses no cause of action against the defendants then the court should exercise its inherent jurisdiction to control proceedings and that it may not order an extension of time for the service of a document which is defective on its face. She concluded, in refusing the application to extend time, that the issues raised by counsel in relation to cases such as *Rainsford* and *Primor*, while of interest, did not arise for decision in the case before the court.

One further point to note in the judgment of McCracken J. in *Irish Family Planning Association v Youth Defence* is his statement that while the dictum of Finlay P. in *Rainsford* to the effect that "where a delay has not been both inordinate and inexcusable it would appear that there are no real grounds for dismissing the proceedings" is relevant in the context of an application to dismiss proceedings, it has no application to a motion seeking to extend time for service of a statement of claim. It would appear then that where the application before the court is simply one to extend time, the onus of proof—described by McCracken J. as an unfortunate phrase in the context of a discretionary remedy—lies on the plaintiff and that the authorities relating to applications to dismiss for want of prosecution should be treated with a degree of caution.

In *Nevin (decd) v Nevin*, Supreme Court, March 5, 2004, the court (Murray, Hardiman and McCracken JJ.) also applied these principles in an *ex tempore* judgment. In this case, the applicant sought an order dismissing the respondent's appeal against an order of the High Court concerning the estate of her deceased husband. The applicant sought to have the appeal dismissed. It was argued for the respondent that the delay in the bringing of the appeal was excusable in light of her murder conviction and subsequent appeal to the Court of Criminal Appeal: see *People (DPP) v Nevin* [2003] 3 I.R. 321 (*Annual Review of Irish Law 2003*, pp.224 and 325). The court did not accept this submission, noting that no steps had been taken by the respondent in relation to her late husband's estate since the decision of the Court of Criminal Appeal. In the affidavit filed on behalf of the respondent, there was no indication that any steps would be taken by her to advance the appeal other than to await the outcome of the proceedings lodged with the European Court of Human Rights (ECtHR) in Strasbourg, but the proceedings before the ECtHR had no bearing on the parties to the present appeal. In balancing justice between the parties, the court held that it must have regard to the rights of all the parties and that the applicant was entitled to have questions concerning the estate of the deceased decided upon within a reasonable time. The court concluded that the delay by the respondent since the decision of the Court of Criminal Appeal was not in the circumstances excusable.

Order 27, rr.1 and 8 of the Rules of the Superior Courts 1986, as originally formulated, set out provisions dealing with the consequences of a failure to deliver a statement of claim and a defence respectively in a timely manner but neither rule went further than saying that the court might in such circumstances dismiss an action or grant a motion for judgment. The revised Ord.27, r.1, introduced by the Rules of the Superior Courts (Order 27 (Amendment) Rules) 2004 (S.I. No.63 of 2004), now reads as follows:

> "1. If the plaintiff, being bound to deliver a statement of claim, does not deliver the same within the time allowed for that purpose, the defendant may, subject to the provisions of rule 1A, at the expiration of that time, apply to the Court to dismiss the action, with costs, for want of prosecution; and on the hearing of the first such application, the Court may order the action to be dismissed accordingly, or may make such other order on such terms as the Court shall think just; and on the hearing of any subsequent application, the Court shall order the action to be dismissed as aforesaid, unless the Court is satisfied that special circumstances (to be recited in the order) exist which explain and justify the failure and, where it is so satisfied, the Court shall make an order
>   (a) extending the time for delivery of a statement of claim,
>   (b) adjourning the motion for such period as is necessary to enable a statement of claim to be delivered within the extended time, and on such adjourned hearing
>   (i) if a statement of claim has been delivered within the extended time, the Court shall allow the defendant the costs of and in relation to the motion at such sum as it may measure in respect thereof;
>   (ii) if a statement of claim has not been delivered within the extended time, the Court shall order the action to be dismissed, with costs, for want of prosecution."

Rule 8, as amended, makes similar provision in relation to circumstances in which a defendant fails to deliver a defence within the time allowed for that purpose. Therefore, both rules now provide that where a second application has to be brought, the court *shall* order the action to be dismissed or the plaintiff to be granted judgment unless it is satisfied that special circumstances, which must be recited in the order, exist to explain and justify the failure to act. Commenting on the amendments introduced to the provisions of Ord.27 in 2004 in *Gilroy v Flynn* [2005] 1 I.L.R.M. 290, Hardiman J. stated that: "[T]hese changes, and others, mean that comfortable assumptions on the part of a minority of litigants of almost endless indulgence must end". He also stated that the courts have become increasingly conscious of the unfairness and increased possibility of injustice which may ensue when an action which depends on witness testimony is allowed to proceed a considerable time after the accrual of the cause of action. In his view, following such cases as *McMullen v Ireland* European Court of Human Rights, July 29, 2004 and the enactment of the European Convention on Human Rights Act 2003, "the courts, quite independently of the action or inaction of the parties, have an obligation to ensure that rights and liabilities, civil or criminal, are determined within a reasonable time".

Hardiman J. added that in particular the assumption that even grave delay will not lead to the dismissal of an action if it does not occur as a result of the fault of the plaintiff, but of a professional adviser, may now prove to be unreliable. In the case before him, having referred to the fact that the matter was set to proceed on an assessment only basis, Hardiman J. decided to allow the plaintiff's appeal against the order of the High Court striking out the claim for want of prosecution and he substituted an order giving one week to file a statement of claim. However, the tenor of his judgment generally and the significant amendments made to the provisions of Ord.27 make it clear that the courts will not tolerate excessive delays by either side when it comes to the delivery of pleadings and previous authorities in this area such as *Rainsford v Limerick Corporation* [1995] 2 I.L.R.M. 561, must now be read in the light of these developments.

COSTS

Security for Costs—striking out for failure to comply   The issue of the circumstances in which a claim may be struck out for failure to comply with an order for security for costs received detailed consideration by both O'Sullivan J. in the High Court and by the Supreme Court in *Lough Neagh Exploration Ltd v Morrice (No.2)* [1999] 4 I.R. 515, and these principles were subsequently approved of and applied in *Superwood Holdings plc v Sun Alliance and London Insurance plc (No.3)* [2004] 2 I.R. 407. Keane C.J. stated that it was beyond argument that the decision recognised that the court possessed an inherent jurisdiction to dismiss proceedings by a company which has been ordered to provide security for costs under s.390 of the Companies Act 1963 where security has not been provided. He added that it would be remarkable if the court did not enjoy such jurisdiction as otherwise proceedings might remain indefinitely in being, contrary to the general principle of public policy that litigation must terminate sooner or later. This jurisdiction was in his view necessary for the proper administration of justice and not in any way inconsistent with the constitutional right of persons to have access to the courts or to appeal to the Supreme Court where such appeal was not excluded by law. Keane C.J. concluded that he was satisfied that the history of the proceedings since the plaintiffs had been required to furnish security made it clear beyond doubt that there was no reasonable prospect that they would provide the sum required and held that there was no alternative to striking out the plaintiffs' appeal.

DISCOVERY

Garda files In *Livingstone v Minister for Justice, Equality and Law Reform*, High Court, April 2, 2004, the plaintiffs sought an order for discovery of documents relevant to the arrest of the first-named plaintiff in 1993. In 1992, the first-named plaintiff found his wife lying bound, gagged and fatally injured, having received a gunshot wound to the head. The first-named plaintiff was arrested in 1993 and detained overnight for questioning. The first-named plaintiff claimed damages for false imprisonment, abuses of legal process, abuse of power, conspiracy, conversion and detinue, slander and breach of his rights under Art.13 of the European Convention on Human Rights. All of the plaintiffs claimed damages for intentional and/or negligent infliction of emotional suffering, negligence, breach of duty, breach of statutory duty and breach of their constitutional rights. In its defence, the defendant claimed that the Gardaí regarded the first-named plaintiff as a suspect in their murder investigation and that such belief was held on reasonable grounds. In relation to the discovery application, the defendant claimed that the discovery sought constituted a trawling exercise and that it was not necessary for fairly disposing of the proceedings. Murphy J. accepted that a distinction can be made between civil and criminal proceedings, and that the desirability of protecting the confidentiality of documents may be of vastly greater significance in matters of a criminal nature. But he also concluded that Garda communications are not, as a class, privileged, and that there does not appear to be a blanket ban against making an order for discovery where a litigant seeks his or her Garda file or documents relating to a criminal investigation. He accordingly made an order for discovery in respect of some of the categories of documents sought.

Time of discovery in judicial review applications It was clear from the judgment of Finlay Geoghegan J. in *KA v Minister for Justice, Equality and Law Reform* [2003] 2 I.R. 93, that discovery might be granted in judicial review proceedings before the grant of leave but only in very limited cases. A more flexible view of the circumstances in which discovery may be granted in such a case was taken by Peart J. in *Syziu v Minister for Justice, Equality and Law*

Reform High Court, March 19, 2004. Peart J. stated that he was satisfied that the applicant was not simply engaged in a fishing expedition and said that the only question was whether the documents sought were such that they should be discovered before the grant of leave or whether they would more properly be relevant and necessary at a later stage if leave were granted. He concluded that on balance it seemed that the applicant must be in a position to make the best possible case at the leave stage and the documents sought were those that a person to whom leave had been granted would have been entitled to on discovery. Peart J. added that not to order discovery at the pre-leave stage had the potential to place the applicant in a less advantageous position in making his application for leave than if discovery were granted and he ordered discovery in respect of some of the documents sought.

Underlying purpose of discovery   Some differences of opinion have recently emerged about the underlying purpose of the discovery process. In *Taylor v Clonmel Healthcare Ltd*, High Court, July 7, 2003, Murphy J. suggested that discovery must provide added value to a case and narrow the issues between the parties so enabling them to settle the matter. However, in the Supreme Court ([2004] 1 I.R. 169; [2004] 2 I.L.R.M. 133) Geoghegan J. said that he found that statement difficult to reconcile with the normal understanding of what discovery is all about. In his view it was a novel idea to suggest that discovery was to enable settlement of a case and said that, on the contrary, "discovery is with a view to fighting the case". Whichever view is preferred it is fair to say that the discovery process is designed to narrow the issues which must be resolved between the parties and to facilitate the resolution of the case in as speedy and cost efficient a manner as possible.

Changes effected by new discovery rules   It has been suggested (see *Abrahamson* (2002) 7 BR 360, 362) that Morris P. in *Swords v Western Proteins Ltd* [2001] 1 I.R. 324, may have overstated the effect of the requirement in the amended discovery rules relating to the contents of the letter seeking voluntary discovery and certainly a more flexible approach was taken towards this requirement by the Supreme Court in *Taylor v Clonmel Healthcare Ltd* [2004] 1 I.R. 169 in which the Supreme Court allowed the plaintiff's appeal against a refusal of discovery by the Master and by the High Court. Geoghegan J. was satisfied on the facts before him that there had not been non-compliance with the rules but went on to state that even if he were wrong on this point, it would not be fatal in this case. He added that he did not think that the Master is confined in exercising his jurisdiction to making orders based on strict compliance with the rules and said that the latter has power to waive any technical breach of the rules if the object of the provision has in reality been achieved.

A further change effected by the amendment to the rules is that the notice of motion is required to specify the precise categories of documents in respect of which discovery is sought. Some guidance in relation to this requirement is provided by Geoghegan J. in *Taylor v Clonmel Healthcare Ltd* where he stated that in interpreting the nature of the particular category of documents being sought by reference to its description, the court must look at the context and that surrounding correspondence which is exhibited may be relevant. Geoghegan J. concluded that in the circumstances the categories of documents sought had been set out with sufficient precision to comply with the rules.

The third change to previous practice is that motions for discovery must now be grounded on an affidavit which shall verify that the discovery sought is necessary for disposing fairly of the matter or for saving costs and shall furnish the reasons why each category of documents is required to be discovered. In *Ryanair plc v Aer Rianta cpt* [2003] 4 I.R. 264 Fennelly J. held that the plaintiff had sufficiently verified that discovery of the categories of documents sought was necessary for the fair disposal of the action and had complied with its obligation to provide reasons why each category was required. A similar conclusion was reached by Geoghegan J. in *Taylor v Clonmel Healthcare Ltd* where he stated that in his view it was sufficient compliance with the rules if the letters seeking voluntary discovery which contained the reasons why discovery was sought were exhibited in the affidavit and that it was not necessary to set out the reasons seriatim. Geoghegan J. added that even if he were wrong in this conclusion, he felt that it was clear that the object of the rule had been achieved in the circumstances.

The relationship between the requirements of "relevance" and "necessity" in the discovery process was also examined by Geoghegan J. in *Taylor v Clonmel Healthcare Ltd*. Geoghegan J. stated that over the years the "necessity" aspect of the rule had been rather overlooked until it was resurrected in the case of *Brooks Thomas Ltd v Impac Ltd* [1999] 1 I.L.R.M. 171. He expressed the view that the strengthening of the requirements in the amending rule was so that the legal advisors of the moving party would apply their minds not only to whether the documents were relevant but also to whether they were necessary. He added that "in most instances if they are relevant they will be necessary" but acknowledged that there will be situations in which this is not the case. In his view it would defeat the whole purpose of discovery if detailed reasons as to necessity had to be given in the grounding affidavit and he was satisfied that there had been a sufficient verification of necessity in the case before the court.

In the opinion of the Master in *Linsley v Cadbury Schweppes International Beverages Ltd*, February 19, 2004 the decision in *Taylor* clearly suggests that the court and the Master may waive non-compliance with the specific requirements of S.I. No.233 of 1999 where necessity is self-evident. However, the Master stressed that necessity does not arise simply because there is an issue between the parties or because counsel advises that such is the case; rather it arises "when the plaintiff has an evidential deficit in respect of a material fact". He also stated that non-material facts, even if in issue, will never be the basis of a successful discovery application. In his view disputes concerning "surplus" facts are of no interest to the court, so, *e.g.* a safety statement, if it is not probative of any disputed material fact, is neither "genuinely necessary" *(Ryanair plc v Aer Rianta cpt* [2003] 4 I.R. 264 at 277 *per* Fennelly J.) nor "really needed" (*Taylor v Clonmel Healthcare Ltd* [2004] 2 I.L.R.M. 133 at 145).

Security for the Costs of Discovery The circumstances in which security for the costs of discovery will be granted has been considered in some detail by Herbert J. and by the Supreme Court in *Framus Ltd v CRH plc* [2003] 1 I.L.R.M. 462; [2004] 2 I.R. 20. The plaintiff companies were engaged in the business of manufacturing and selling cement products and concrete blocks and when they ceased trading, the second-, third- and fifth-named defendants acquired the assets and goodwill of these companies. The plaintiffs issued proceedings against the defendants alleging that they had engaged in anti-competitive practices and abused a dominant position and that they had sought to exclude the plaintiffs from the markets in which they operated. The plaintiffs sought discovery from the defendants and the High Court made an order of discovery against a number of these defendants. The latter then sought an order requiring the plaintiffs to provide security for the costs of certain aspects of discovery which was granted by the High Court.

On appeal the plaintiffs submitted that the order for security for costs should not have been made or alternatively should have been made for a lesser amount. While Murray J. said that he would have no difficulty agreeing generally with the factors set out by Herbert J. (see *Annual Review of Irish Law 2002*, p.420) which may be taken into account when considering an application for security for costs, he disagreed in relation to the amount of security which should ordinarily be provided in such cases. Murray J. stated that in his view the scope of the discretion to be exercised by the court in an application for security for costs pursuant to Ord.31, r.12, being an exercise of its inherent jurisdiction pursuant to the Rules, is the same as that outlined by Kingsmill Moore J. in *Thalle v Soares* [1957] I.R. 182, where the latter had spoken about it being customary to require an amount of not more than about one third of the costs which would probably be incurred by the defendants as security. However, Murray J. stressed that the discretion to be exercised is a very broad one and said that the plaintiffs had been incorrect in submitting that security fixed pursuant to the inherent jurisdiction of the court should be confined to a maximum of one third of the estimated costs. In his view the practice of the court in cases like *Thalle* reflects the fact that it strives to achieve a balance of justice between the parties with a view to ensuring that the security is not a mere token and at the same time not an obstacle to a full and fair disposal of the issues between the parties. Murray J. found that on the facts of the case before the court, there were no special circumstances which would indicate that the court should depart from the practice of awarding "an amount of not more than about a third of the costs which would probably be incurred".

Murray J. concluded that Herbert J. had given insufficient weight to two factors, namely, that the plaintiffs would be seriously handicapped in making their claim if the amount of security was fixed at such a level that there was a real likelihood that they would be unable to proceed with discovery; and that the estimated costs of discovery were likely to be a relatively small proportion of the overall costs of the proceedings. He therefore set aside the order of the High Court fixing the amount of security at €77,000 and substituted an order requiring the plaintiffs to pay the sum of €27,000, which was approximately 30 per cent of the estimated costs of discovery.

It is clear from the judgment of the Supreme Court in *Framus Ltd v CRH plc* that the principles applied by the courts in relation to applications for security for costs pursuant to Ord.29 of the Rules of the Superior Courts are equally applicable to an application for security brought under Ord.31, r.12 and that it is appropriate to take the same approach as regards the amount of security. It should also be noted that Murray J. did not fully subscribe to the attitude adopted by Herbert J. that there is a clear distinction between the effect that an order for security might have in amounting to an obstacle to a party having access to the courts at all, and simply being an obstacle to obtaining discovery. As Murray J. pointed out, where discovery is essential to a party's ability to make a claim or defend an action this is a "distinction without a difference". So in many respects the principles which should be applied to an application for security for the costs of discovery are those already well established in relation to applications brought pursuant to Ord.29.

PLEADINGS

Unnecessary or scandalous claim   In *Hanly v Newsgroup Newspapers Ltd* [2004] 1 I.R. 471, the defendant sought an order under Ord.19, r.27 of the Rules of the Superior Courts 1986, as amended, striking out certain elements of the plaintiff's statement of claim on the basis that they were unnecessary or scandalous, or tending to prejudice, embarrass or delay the fair trial of the plaintiff's libel action. In the Statement of Claim, the plaintiff specified that, in 2002, the *Irish Sunday People* had published a photograph of the plaintiff with a series of articles and headlines and that as a consequence of the publication the plaintiff's character and reputation was injured and he was exposed to ridicule and contempt. The publication contained reports of the behaviour of certain members of the Roscommon football team after a night in a Derry hotel following a GAA match against Donegal in May 2002. The plaintiff subsequently sought and obtained an apology from the *Irish Sunday People* which was published in May 2002. The Statement of Claim went on to state that a subsequent publication by the *Irish Sun* of the same defamatory material a short time after the publication in the *Irish Sunday People* neutralised the effect of this apology and further aggravated the damage to the plaintiff's character and reputation and exposed him to further ridicule and contempt and as a consequence he was entitled to aggravated damages. The defendant argued that the first article and apology was inadmissible in the context of the libel complained of in these proceedings as each publication even by the same newspaper gives rise to a separate cause of action.

Smyth J. agreed and accepted that the relevant material in the statement of claim was scandalous, prejudicial and embarrassing in the legal sense of the words. He held that it was not permissible for the plaintiff in a statement of claim to seek to set forth in the pleadings in a narrative form intended factual evidence in anticipation of or pre-emptive of possible evidence in mitigation of damages that may be tendered at trial arising based on matters in a defence that had not yet been formulated. He noted that the function of pleadings was to ascertain with precision the matters on which the parties differ and the points on which they agree, and thus to arrive at certain clear issues on which both parties require a judicial decision. Only the material facts—and not the evidence on which they are to be proved—should be pleaded. The matters referred to in paras 6, 7 and 8 of the Statement of Claim were in the nature of evidence, were referable to unrelated proceedings with a different party, and were scandalous in that they sought to introduce immaterial matters which would lead to the introduction of irrelevant evidence at the trial of the action. He concluded that the plaintiff's entitlement to aggravated damages must be related to or connected to the original subject of the cause or matter of the publication of July 19, 2002. The instant case was referable to a publication in the *Irish Sun* and not the *Irish Sunday People*.

REMITTAL FROM HIGH COURT TO CIRCUIT COURT

Family law In *D v D* Supreme Court, December 5, 2003, the Supreme Court affirmed the decision of the High Court to remit a judicial separation case to the Circuit Court. The respondent had argued that the issues in the case were not particularly complex and that the matter could be dealt with at less cost in the Circuit Court. The appellant argued that there could be complex evidence in relation to the valuation of an asset belonging to the parties and that it was not appropriate to remit. The Supreme Court (McGuinness, Fennelly and McCracken JJ.) first outlined the principles applicable where the Supreme Court hears an appeal in such a case. It held that, although the court may interfere with the discretion of a High Court judge if it feels it has been wrongly exercised, great weight will nevertheless be given to the discretion of the trial judge and the court would be reluctant to interfere with that discretion without strong reasons. As to the specific issues in this case, the court noted that it was the policy of the law that family law matters should in the main be dealt with in the Circuit Court: this was evidenced by the provisions of the Judicial Separation and Family Law Reform Act 1989 and subsequent legislation such as the Family Law Act 1995. The court also noted that the matters involved in the present case were not of such complexity that they required a hearing in the High Court. The Supreme Court noted that the Circuit Court was accustomed to dealing with complex issues in relation to valuation evidence arising in the exercise of its landlord and tenant jurisdiction (though it may be noted that much of this jurisdiction has now been transferred from the Circuit Court to the Residential Tenancies Redress Board under the Residential Tenancies Act 2004: see the Land Law Chapter above, p.333). In any event, the Supreme Court concluded that, in all probability, the matter would be dealt with more rapidly and with less cost in the Circuit Court. On that basis, the court affirmed the remittal order.

RULES OF COURT

The following Rules of Court were made in 2004.

Rules of the Superior Courts

- The Rules of the Superior Courts (Commercial Proceedings) 2004 (S.I. No.2 of 2004) inserted a new Ord.63A into the Rules of the Superior Courts 1986 in order to facilitate the operation of the Commercial List in the High Court. These Rules gave effect to recommendations in the 28th Interim Report of the Committee on Court Practice and Procedure (see the *Annual Review of Irish Law 2003*, p.482), in particular by providing for case management and electronic facilities for commercial proceedings involving claims in excess of €1 million.

- The Rules of the Superior Courts (Order 27 (Amendment) Rules) 2004 (S.I. No.63 of 2004) are discussed above, p.419.

- The Rules of the Superior Courts (Shorthand Reporting) 2004 (S.I. No.137 of 2004) inserted a new Ord.123, r.7 into the Rules of the Superior Courts 1986 in order to specify that a shorthand writer will no longer be provided at the public's expense at the trial or hearing of chancery and family law proceedings begun after April 30, 2004.

- The Rules of the Superior Courts (Right of Attorney General and Human Rights Commission to notice of Proceedings involving Declaration of Incompatibility Issue) Rules 2004 (S.I. No.211 of 2004) inserted a new Ord.60A into the Rules of the Superior Courts 1986. They provide that, if any issue as to the making of a declaration of incompatibility under s.1(1) of the European Convention on Human Rights Act 2003 arises in any proceedings, the party having carriage of the proceedings shall serve notice on the Attorney General and the Irish Human Rights Commission.

- The Rules of the Superior Courts (Amendment to Order 118) Rules 2004 (S.I. No.253 of 2004) amended Ord.118 of the Rules of the Superior Courts 1986, and have the effect of extending opening hours of the public offices of the High Court and Supreme Court to a uniform time of 4.30 p.m. throughout the year.

- The Rules of the Superior Courts (Order 130 (Amendment)) Rules 2004 (S.I. No.471 of 2004) amended Ord.130 of the Rules of the Superior Courts 1986 in light of the Freedom of Information (Amendment) Act 2003.

- The Rules of the Superior Courts (Personal Injuries Assessment Board Act 2003) Rules 2004 (S.I. No.517 of 2004) prescribe the procedures in the High Court in applications under the Personal Injuries Assessment Board Act 2003. In particular, they provide for details of authorisations to be included in indorsements of claim, for the ruling by the court by way of approval of assessments in the case of persons with incapacities, and for the enforcement of assessments made by the Personal Injuries Assessment Board where these have been accepted by the parties.

- The Rules of the Superior Courts (Solicitors Acts 1954 to 2002) 2004 (S.I. No.701 of 2004) inserted an amended Ord.53 into the Rules of the Superior Courts 1986), which concerns the admission of solicitors and related matters.

- The Rules of the Superior Courts (Order 85) 2004 (S.I. No.767 of 2004) amended Ord.85 of the Rules of the Superior Courts 1986, which concerns procedures in the Central Criminal Court.

Circuit Court Rules

- The Circuit Court Rules (No.2) (Section 39 Criminal Justice Act 1994) 2004 (S.I. No.448 of 2004) prescribe the procedures in the Circuit Court in applications under s.39 of the Criminal Justice Act 1994.

- The Circuit Court Rules (Personal Injuries Assessment Board Act 2003) 2004 (S.I. No.542 of 2004) prescribe the procedures in the Circuit Court under the Personal Injuries Assessment Board Act 2003. In particular, they provide for details of authorisations to be included in indorsements of claim in Civil Bills, for the ruling by the court by way of approval of assessments in the case of persons with incapacities, and for the enforcement of assessments made by the Personal Injuries Assessment Board where these have been accepted by the parties.

- The Circuit Court Rules (Protection of Employees (Part-Time Work) Act 2001) 2004 (S.I. No.721 of 2004) prescribe the procedures in the Circuit Court in applications under the Protection of Employees (Part-Time Work) Act 2001.

- The Circuit Court Rules (Equal Status Act 2000) 2004 (S.I. No.879 of 2004) prescribe the procedures in respect of applications brought in the Circuit Court under the Equal Status Act 2000.

- Circuit Court Rules (Employment Equality Act 1998) 2004 (S.I. No.880 of 2004) prescribe the procedures in respect of applications brought in the Circuit Court under the Employment Equality Act 1998.

- The Circuit Court Rules (Jurisdiction and Recognition and Enforcement of Judgments in Matrimonial Matters) 2004 (S.I. No.881 of 2004) prescribe the procedures in the Circuit Court for Regulation 1347/2000/EC, the Brussels II Convention on jurisdiction and the recognition and enforcement of judgments in matrimonial matters.

- The Circuit Court Rules (Jurisdiction and Recognition and Enforcement of Judgments in Civil or Commercial Matters) 2004 (S.I. No.882 of 2004) prescribe the procedures in the Circuit Court for Regulation 44/2001/EC on jurisdiction and the recognition and enforcement of judgments in civil or commercial matters. They also provide for the provision of documentation under Art.54 of Regulation (EC) No.44/2001 and Art.33 of Regulation 1347/2000/EC, the Brussels II Convention on jurisdiction and the recognition and enforcement of judgments in matrimonial matters.

- The Circuit Court Rules (Service in Member States of Judicial and Extra-Judicial Documents in Civil or Commercial Matters) 2004 (S.I. No.883 of 2004) prescribe the procedures in the Circuit Court for Regulation 1348/2000/EC on the service in Member States (other than Denmark) of judicial and extra-judicial documents in civil or commercial matters and any amendments thereto.

District Court Rules

- The District Court (Intellectual Property) Rules 2004 (S.I. No.411 of 2004) inserted a new Ord.31B into the District Court Rules 1997 and prescribe the procedures in the District Court in certain applications under the Trade Marks Act 1996, the Copyright and Related Rights Act 2000 and the Industrial Designs Act 2001.

- The District Court (Personal Injuries Assessment Board Act 2003) Rules 2004 (S.I. No.526 of 2004) prescribe the procedures in the District Court under the Personal Injuries Assessment Board Act 2003.

- The District Court (Railway Infrastructure) Rules 2004 (S.I. No.534 of 2004) prescribe the procedures in the District Court in applications under the Transport (Railway Infrastructure) Act 2001.

- The District Court (Estreatment of Recognisances) Rules 2004 (S.I. No.535 of 2004) provide for amended forms concerning the estreatment of recognisances and repealed and replaced the District Court (Estreatment of Recognisances) Rules 2003.

• The District Court (Children) Rules 2004 (S.I. No.539 of 2004) and the District Court (Children) (No.2) Rules 2004 (S.I. No.666 of 2004) prescribe the procedures in the District Court in applications under the Children Act 2001.

• The District Court (Taxes Consolidation Act 1997) (Amendment) Rules 2004 (S.I. No.586 of 2004) amended Ord.38 of the District Court Rules 1997 and prescribe procedures under s.908A of the Taxes Consolidation Act 1997, as amended most recently by the Finance Act 2004, under which an authorised officer of the Revenue Commissioners may apply to the District Court to inspect and take copies of books or records held in financial institutions where he or she suspects that there are reasonable grounds to suspect that an offence in serious prejudice to the proper assessment and collection of tax is being, or has been or is or was about to be committed, and where such information is likely to be of substantial value to the investigation.

• The District Court (Food Safety) Rules 2004 (S.I. No.700 of 2004) prescribe the procedures in the District Court where the Food Safety Authority of Ireland require information under the Food Safety Authority of Ireland Act 1998 and in relation to non-compliance with improvement notices issued under the 1998 Act.

SEPARATE OR JOINT HEARINGS

In *Doherty v North Western Health Board*, Supreme Court, January 15, 2004, the court declined to interfere with an order for separate hearing of actions which initially had been listed together. The defendant health board appealed against an order of the High Court directing separate trials for the plaintiff's case against the defendant and the case between the defendant and the third party. The plaintiff's claim arose out of the alleged negligence of the defendants at the time of her birth. The plaintiff applied to the High Court to have her case against the defendant heard separately from the case between the defendant and the third party. The High Court directed that the third party's medical reports should be served on the plaintiff to allow her to decide whether it would be prejudicial to her to have both cases heard together. Following perusal of the reports, the plaintiff renewed her application and an order was made directing separate trials. In an *ex tempore* judgment for the Court, McGuinness J. noted that the Court, on appeal, would have to feel very strongly that the trial judge had erred in his discretion before it would interfere with the manner in which a trial was to be run by him. In the present case, the High Court judge had exercised his discretion to order separate trials in a perfectly reasonable way and the setting aside of the listing of the two cases together was within the ambit of his discretion.

Prisons

ACCESS OF PRISONER TO MEDIA

In *Holland v Governor of Portlaoise Prison*, High Court, June 11, 2004, the applicant brought proceedings by way of judicial review seeking to challenge the refusal of the respondent to allow him access by way of correspondence and prison visits to members of the media while in custody. The applicant was serving a sentence of 12 years' imprisonment, but claimed that his conviction amounted to a miscarriage of justice. In particular he claimed that a prosecution witness had committed perjury, that admissions allegedly made by him in custody had been forged, and that documents which would have demonstrated his innocence had been wrongly withheld from him. The applicant hoped that media interest in his case might result in further evidence being gathered which in turn could entitle him to have his conviction reviewed. The respondent unconditionally refused his request. This was in line with a policy of the Irish Prison Service not to allow prisoners conduct campaigns for their release through the media, in the interests of, *inter alia*, maintaining good order and security in the prison. The Rules for the Government of Prisons 1947 allowed the prisoner visits from "respectable friends". McKechnie J. granted the relief sought. He held that the court had to consider whether the policy of the prison service was proportionate to its objectives of maintaining security and good order. He acknowledged that the respondent had a considerable discretion under the 1947 Prison Rules, but he noted that there was no exclusion of the media under those rules. Nor was there anything in the 1947 rules which entitled the respondent to adopt the position of the Irish Prison Service or indeed any independent policy which would entitle him to refuse every prisoner, in all circumstances, every request, no matter what the purpose of the intended communication was. He therefore concluded that the policy of the respondent was contrary to the applicant's right to have his request properly considered and evaluated. Since the policy fettered the decision-maker's discretion, the respondent was not entitled to apply the policy in the manner in which he had. He was obliged to give individual consideration to each request made.

Safety and Health

CHEMICAL SAFETY

Classification, packaging and labelling of single chemicals The European Communities (Classification, Packaging Labelling and Notification of Dangerous Substances) Regulations 2003 (S.I. No.116 of 2003), referred to as the CPL Regulations, gave effect in consolidated form to Directive 67/548/EEC on the classification, packaging and labelling of dangerous substances, that is, single chemicals, as most recently amended in 2001 by Directives 2001/58/EC and 2001/59/EC. They revoked and replaced the European Communities (Classification, Packaging, Labelling and Notification of Dangerous Substances) Regulations 2000 (see *Annual Review of Irish Law 2000*, p.391) and came into effect on March 27, 2003. The CPL Regulations 2003 require manufacturers of chemicals to notify the Health and Safety Authority when new chemicals are placed on the market and to submit detailed technical dossiers on the chemicals (this requirement has been in place in preceding Regulations since 1981). They also require manufacturers of all chemicals to classify chemicals according to the criteria (explosive, flammable, etc.) in the 1967 Directive, as amended, to package and label them in accordance with the requirements of the 1967 Directive and to ensure that appropriate Material Safety Data Sheets (MSDSs) are provided to users.

Classification, packaging and labelling of chemical mixtures The European Communities (Classification, Packaging and Labelling of Dangerous Preparations) Regulations 2004 (S.I. No.62 of 2004) implemented Directive 1999/45/EC, which replaced Directive 88/379/EEC. The 2004 Regulations also implemented the first adaptation to technical progress (ATP) of the 1999 Directive, Directive 2001/60/EC. The Regulations apply to all dangerous preparations, that is, mixtures of single chemicals, with exceptions for certain categories of preparations such as medicines and cosmetics, which are covered by other EU Directives. The 2004 Regulations require persons placing a dangerous preparation on the market, to classify and label it according to the inherent hazards including, for the first time, danger to the environment. Certain preparations that would not be classified as dangerous by the Directive and these Regulations are nevertheless subject to specific labelling requirements if the particular preparations are listed in Annex 5 to Directive 1999/45/EC, as amended by Directive 2001/60/EC. The classification, labelling and packaging requirements of the 2004 Regulations have also been extended to include plant protection products from July 30, 2004. The requirements for classification and provision of Material Safety Data Sheets (MSDSs) have been extended to explosive and pyrotechnic preparations for the first time. The 2004 Regulations also implemented Directive 2001/58/EC, which amended Directive 91/155/EC concerning the provision of specific information relating to dangerous preparations in the form of MSDSs, requiring the provision of MSDSs on request to professional users of certain preparations not classified as dangerous. The Regulations revoke and replace the European Communities (Classification, Packaging and Labelling of Dangerous Preparations) Regulations 1995 and 1998.

Chemicals: restrictions on manufacture The European Communities (Dangerous Substances and Preparations (Marketing and Use) Regulations 2003 (S.I. No.220 of 2003) gave effect in consolidated form to Council Directive 76/769/EEC on the marketing and use of chemicals and preparations, that is single chemicals and chemical compounds, as most recently amended by Directives 2001/41/EC, 2001/62/EC, 2001/90/EC, 2001/91/EC, 2002/45/EC and 2002/61/EC. They revoked and replaced the European Communities (Dangerous Substances and Preparations (Marketing and Use) Regulations 2000 (see *Annual Review of Irish Law 2000*, p.391) and came into effect on June 4, 2003. By contrast with the CPL Regulations, above, the Marketing and Use Regulations are primarily confined to imposing complete bans on certain chemicals, such as PCBs and PCTs, or imposing severe restrictions on their use, such as excluding the use of certain chemicals in toys. The European Communities (Dangerous Substances and Preparations) (Marketing and Use) (Amendment) Regulations 2004 (S.I. No.852 of 2004) amended Schedules 1 and 3 to the European Communities (Dangerous Substances and Preparations) (Marketing and Use) Regulations 2003, above. The 2004 Regulations implemented Directive 2003/53/EC which places restrictions on the marketing and use of nonylphenol, nonylphenol ethoxylate and cement. The Regulations also implemented Directive 2004/21/EC, relating to restrictions on the marketing and use of "azo colourants". The Regulations also implemented Directive 2004/96/EC, which deals with restrictions on the marketing and use of nickel for piercing post assemblies. Finally, the 2004 Regulations implemented Directive 2004/98/EC as regards restrictions on the marketing and use of pentabromodiphenyl ether in aircraft emergency evacuation systems.

Cosmetics The European Communities (Cosmetic Products) (Amendment) (No.5) Regulations 2003 (S.I. No.553 of 2003) amended the European Communities (Cosmetic Products) Regulations 1997 to implement Directives 2002/34/EC, 2003/1/EC and 2003/16/EC relating to cosmetic products.

DANGEROUS SUBSTANCES

Petrol stations and stores   The Dangerous Substances (Retail and Private Petroleum Stores) (Amendment) Regulations 2004 (S.I. No.860 of 2004) amended the Dangerous Substances (Retail and Private Petroleum Stores) Regulations 1979 to 2002. Under the 2004 Regulations, as adapted by s.29 of the Safety, Health and Welfare at Work Act 1989, a retail and private petroleum store requires to be licensed by the local or harbour authority or, where the store is owned by such authority, by the Health and Safety Authority, the regulatory body under the 1989 Act. The 2004 Regulations provide, *inter alia*, for safety requirements in certain circumstances for petrol filling stations, constructed before the 1979 Regulations commenced, to enable them to be licensed to operate until December 31, 2006.

MANUFACTURING STANDARDS

General product safety   The European Communities (General Product Safety) Regulations 2004 (S.I. No.199 of 2004) gave effect to Directive 2001/ 95/EC on general product safety. The 2004 Regulations revoked and replaced the European Communities (General Product Safety) Regulations 1997 (*Annual Review of Irish Law 1997*, pp.672–677). The 2004 Regulations require that consumer products placed on the market are safe and obliges producers to place only safe products on the market. The 2004 Regulations specify the duties of producers and distributors and make it an offence to place dangerous products on the market. The Director of Consumer Affairs is given authority to ensure that products placed on the market are safe and that producers and distributors of such products comply with their obligations under these Regulations and the Directive. The General Product Safety Directive and the 2004 Regulations apply in the absence of specific technical standards Directives and their implementing national legislation, such as the specific Directives and implementing Regulations listed below. The relevance of the 1997 Regulations in the context of product liability was discussed by Carroll J. in *Rodgers v Adams Childrens Wear Ltd*, High Court, February 11, 2003.

Cableway installations   The European Communities (Cableway Installations Designed to Carry Persons) Regulations 2003 (S.I. No.470 of 2003) gave effect to Directive 2000/9/EC relating to cableway installations designed to carry persons by introducing a regulatory framework for cableway installations and their subsystems and safety components. They came into force on October 3, 2003.

Medical devices: breast implants   The European Communities (Medical Devices) (Amendment) Regulations 2003 (S.I. No.358 of 2003) gave effect to

Directive 2003/12/EC as regards the reclassification of breast implants to the higher classification of class III medical devices within the meaning of Directive 93/42/EEC. In this respect, they amended the European Communities (Medical Devices) Regulations 1994 (*Annual Review of Irish Law 1994*, p.403) and came into force on September 1, 2003.

Medical devices: tissues of animal origin The European Communities (Medical Devices) (Tissues of Animal Origin) Regulations 2003 (S.I. No.554 of 2003) amended the European Communities (Active Implantable Medical Devices) Regulations 1994 (*Annual Review of Irish Law 1994*, p.403) to give effect to Directive 2003/32/EC, which also amended Directive 93/42/EEC, introducing detailed specifications with respect to medical devices manufactured utilising tissues of animal origin. They came into effect on November 13, 2003.

Transportable pressure equipment The European Communities (Transportable Pressure Equipment) Regulations 2004 (S.I. No.374 of 2004) implemented Directive 1999/36/EC on Transportable Pressure Equipment, as adapted to technical progress by Directive 2001/2/EC and Directive 2002/50/EC. The 2004 Regulations apply to any new transportable pressure equipment placed on the market and manufactured on or after July 1, 2001, which may be subject to assessment of conformity. The 2004 Regulations also apply to existing equipment, which may be subject to reassessment of conformity. Transportable pressure equipment is defined as a receptacle or tank which is used or intended to be used for the carriage by road or rail of Class 2 goods (gases) and certain other dangerous goods, including any valve or other accessory fitted to the equipment and used for carriage. The Regulations provide that transportable pressure equipment must be safe and suitable for its intended purpose and comply with the international agreements concerning transport of dangerous goods by road and rail. Where appropriate, the transportable pressure equipment must be assessed by a notified body or an approved body and bear the conformity marking. The Regulations provide for offences, which are subject to summary prosecution and provide for penalties of up to €3,000 per offence.

MATERNITY PROTECTION

Maternity Protection (Amendment) Act 2004 The Maternity Protection (Amendment) Act 2004 amended the Maternity Protection Act 1994, which had implemented Directive 92/85/EEC on the protection of pregnant workers. The 2004 Act implemented the recommendations made in the 2001 *Report of the working group on the review and improvement of the maternity protection legislation*, which had been established under the social partnership agreement, the *Programme for Prosperity and Fairness*. In presenting the legislation to the Oireachtas, the then Minister of State at the Department of Justice, Equality and Law Reform stated that the 2004 Act constituted an element of work-life balance initiatives. It was also noted that the enactment of the 2004 Act coincided with the highest ever participation of women in the Irish workforce. In 2002, this stood at over 678,000, which was more than twice that recorded in the 1981 census. Of the women in employment, over 67.8 per cent were aged between 25 and 54, which indicates that a significant proportion of women in the workforce were of childbearing age. In 2002, 60,521 children were born and 30,211 maternity benefit payments were awarded to employed or self-employed women, representing a 4 per cent increase over 2001. For commencement of the 2004 Act, see the Maternity Protection (Amendment) Act 2004 (Commencement) Order 2004 (S.I. No.652 of 2004) and the Maternity Protection (Amendment) Act 2004 (Commencement) Order 2005 (S.I. No.131 of 2005).

Maternity leave Sections 2 and 5 of the 2004 Act amended ss.8 and 14 of the 1994 Act to give effect to the recommendation of the working group to increase the period of maternity leave attracting maternity benefit payment from 14 weeks to 18 weeks and the period of unpaid maternity leave from four weeks to eight weeks. In fact, this recommendation had already been implemented by the Maternity Protection Act 1994 (Extension of Periods of Leave) Order 2001 (S.I. No.29 of 2001): the 2001 Order was consequently revoked by s.26 of the 2004 Act. Section 6 inserted a new s.14A into the 1994 Act to provide that, in the event of the sickness of the employee, she may, with the agreement of the employer, terminate her period of additional maternity leave. Once terminated, the employee will not be entitled to take the remainder of the additional maternity leave at a later date. Any absence from work due to illness following the termination of the period of additional maternity leave shall be treated in the same manner as any absence from work due to sickness. Section 7 of the 2004 Act inserted a new s.14B into the 1994 Act and provides that, in the event of the hospitalisation of the child, an employee may, with the employer's agreement, request to postpone her maternity leave and/or additional maternity leave and return to work on an agreed date. It will be possible to postpone maternity leave only where the employee has taken at least 14 weeks' maternity leave, four of which are after the end of the week of the birth. Where the employer agrees to a postponement and where the employee has adhered to certain notification requirements, the employee will be entitled to take her postponed leave in one continuous block known as resumed leave. This resumed leave must commence not later than seven days after the discharge of the child from hospital. If the employee is absent from work due to sickness during the period of the postponement, the employee is deemed to have commenced her resumed leave, unless she opts to forfeit the right to resumed leave. The absence from work due to sickness shall be treated in the same manner as any absence from work due to sickness. The details are set out in the Maternity Protection (Postponement of Leave) Regulations 2004 (S.I. No.655 of 2004).

Compulsory pre-confinement period Section 3 of the 2004 Act amended s.10(1) of the 1994 Act to provide for the reduction of the compulsory period of pre-confinement maternity leave from four weeks to two weeks. Section 4 safeguards an employee's entitlement to the extended minimum period of 18 weeks' maternity leave where premature births are concerned. The Minister of State stated during the Oireachtas debate that it had been argued that a reduction in the compulsory pre-confinement period might be interpreted as a reduction in the level of protection for pregnant employees, and that this might have contravened Art.1.3 of the 1992 EU Directive on Pregnant Workers, which prohibits any new restrictions on protection. But the advice received from the Office of the Attorney General was that the reduction was not prohibited by the 1992 Directive, provided that employees can avail of non-compulsory pre-confinement leave in excess of the two-week period.

Ante-natal classes The Maternity Protection Act 1994 provided for time off without loss of pay for ante-natal and post-natal care, in accordance with Regulations, but the definition of ante-natal care did not include ante-natal classes. Implementing another recommendation of the working group, s.8 of the 2004 Act inserted a new s.15A into the 1994 Act and provides a new entitlement for mothers to paid time off from work for the purposes of attending ante-natal classes. The details are included in the Maternity Protection (Time Off for Ante-Natal Classes) Regulations 2004 (S.I. No.653 of 2004). Section 15A also provides that expectant fathers are now also entitled to time off work without loss of remuneration to attend the last two ante-natal classes in a set. A limited exclusion is provided in the case of members of the Defence Forces, the Garda Síochána serving overseas or in other exceptional circumstances.

Breastfeeding Section 9 of the 2004 Act inserted a new s.15B into the 1994 Act and provides that an employee who is breastfeeding and has informed her employer that she is doing so shall be entitled until the child is six months old to breastfeeding breaks, where facilities for breastfeeding are provided in the workplace, or to a reduction of working hours, without loss of pay in either case. This provision reflects the 2003 national breastfeeding policy, which encourages exclusive breastfeeding up to six months, in line with World Health Organisation recommendations. Section 15B(2) provides that employers will not be required to provide facilities for breastfeeding breaks in the workplace where the provision of such facilities "would give rise to a cost, other than a nominal cost, to the employer". Where breastfeeding breaks are not provided, the employer is required to agree a reduction of working hours with the employee without reducing pay. The detailed arrangements relating to breastfeeding breaks or a reduction of working hours with respect to the amount of time off and the number and frequency of breastfeeding breaks to be allowed, the reduction of working hours to be allowed, the terms and conditions relating to breastfeeding breaks and/or reduction of working hours, the notification procedures and the evidence to be furnished to the employer concerning the date of confinement, are set out in the Maternity Protection (Protection of Mothers who are Breastfeeding) Regulations 2004 (S.I. No.654 of 2004).

Leave entitlement for fathers Section 10 of the 2004 Act amended s.16 of the 1994 Act and incorporates the increased periods of leave entitlement for fathers where the mother dies during the period of her maternity leave, which had already been provided for in the Maternity Protection Act 1994 (Extension of Periods of Leave) Order 2001 (S.I. No.29 of 2001). Section 11 inserted a new s.16A into the 1994 Act and applies similar provisions as apply to termination of leave along the lines of s.6 of the 2004 Act, to fathers who are entitled to such leave under the 1994 Act, in the event of the death of the mother during the course of her leave. Similarly, s.12 inserted a new s.16B into the 1994 Act and applies to fathers similar provisions as those in s.7 of the 2004 Act to termination of leave in the event of hospitalisation of the child.

Protective leave Section 13 amended the definition of "protective leave" in s.21 of the 1994 Act and provides that the period of leave taken prior to postponement and the period of resumed leave after postponement shall be treated as separate periods of protective leave.

Effect of absences on employment rights Section 14 amended s.22 of the 1994 Act to provide that employees absent from work on additional maternity leave will be treated for the purposes of all employment rights, other than remuneration and superannuation benefits, as if they remained at work. It also adds new rights to attend ante-natal classes or to breastfeed to the list of absences in s.22 of the 1994 Act, for which the employee shall be treated as if she were not absent from work. Sections 15 and 16 of the 2004 Act amended ss.23 and 24 of the 1994 Act to provide that employees who avail of the new entitlements to ante-natal classes and breastfeeding are afforded protection under the 1994 Act as to the termination or suspension of their employment. Section 17 amended s.25 of the 1994 Act to ensure that periods of probation, training and apprenticeship, apply to both female and male employees who are absent from work on protective leave. Section 18 of the 2004 Act amended s.26 of the 1994 Act and strengthens the provisions relating to the return to work of an employee who was on protective leave to give effect to the 2002 EU Directive on Gender Equal Treatment. An employee returning to work from protective leave will have a statutory entitlement to any improvement in the terms or conditions of the employment to which she would have been entitled if she had not been absent on protective leave. Section 19 amended s.27 of the 1994 Act and applies to employees returning to work on the expiry of protective leave who are offered suitable alternative work because the resumption of the work which they carried out before their protective leave is not practicable. In such a case, the terms or conditions of the alternative work shall not be less favourable to the employee than those of her contract of employment immediately before protective leave. An employee in this position will also be entitled to any improvement in the terms or conditions of the employment to which she would have been entitled if she had not been absent on protective leave. This also gives effect to the 2002 EU Directive on Gender Equal Treatment.

OCCUPATIONAL SAFETY AND HEALTH

General duties of employers The Safety, Health and Welfare at Work (General Application) (Amendment No.2) Regulations 2003 (S.I. No.53 of 2003) involve four important changes to the general duties of employers to employees. They state that it is not a defence in any criminal prosecution to state that the failure to comply with a relevant statutory duty under the Safety, Health and Welfare at Work Act 1989 (or any Regulations made under the 1989 Act) arose from an act or omission of an employee or a competent person; they introduce for the first time a statutory definition of "competent person" (the person or persons who must be designated to implement safety and health policies for the employer); they require all employers to have fire-fighting arrangements in place, including designated fire-fighters; and they require employers to designate first-aiders. The changes involve further implementation of the 1989 "Framework" Directive on safety and health at work, 89/391/EEC, whose main provisions were implemented in the Safety, Health and Welfare at Work (General Application) Regulations 1993 (*Annual Review of Irish Law 1993*, pp.483–505). The 2003 Regulations are the State's response to European Commission queries as to whether the 1993 Regulations had fully implemented the text of the 1989 Directive. The 2003 Regulations came into effect on January 30, 2003, the date they were signed by the Tánaiste and Minister for Enterprise, Trade and Employment. The fire safety aspect of the 2003 Regulations has also been affected by the provisions of the Licensing of Indoor Events Act 2003, discussed below. The 2003 Regulations will be replaced by the consolidating and amending provisions of the Safety, Health and Welfare at Work Act 2005, which replaced the 1989 Act, and to which we will return in the *Annual Review of Irish Law 2005*.

Construction sites: qualifications The Safety, Health and Welfare at Work (Construction) (Amendment) Regulations 2003 (S.I. No.277 of 2003) amended the Safety, Health and Welfare at Work (Construction) Regulations 2001 (*Annual Review of Irish Law 2001*, pp.514–518) to allow "new starters" who need to obtain the relevant qualification under the Construction Skills Certification Scheme (CSCS) to begin work in the specified areas (*e.g.*

scaffolding, tower crane operation) without the qualification, but only if they are "under the direct supervision" of a person who does possess the relevant CSCS qualification.

Explosive atmospheres   The Safety, Health and Welfare at Work (Explosive Atmospheres) Regulations 2003 (S.I. No.258 of 2003) implemented the 1999 Explosive Atmospheres Directive 1999/92/EC, from June 30, 2003, subject to some transitional provisions which allow some places of work to phase in some requirements up to June 30, 2006. The 2003 Regulations set out a comprehensive approach to the protection of workers where there is a risk of explosion from dust and other fumes in the workplace. It does not deal with the risk of fire or risk from the use of explosives. The Regulations define a potentially explosive atmosphere as a situation where flammable substances, whether gases, vapours, mists or dusts, might under atmospheric conditions ignite with air and result in combustion. The Regulations apply to all places of work within the meaning of the Safety, Health and Welfare at Work Act 1989 and also replace and revoke existing provisions on dust explosions and flammable atmospheres, especially those contained in the Safety in Industry Acts 1955 and 1980: see the Safety, Health and Welfare at Work (Revocation of Sections 37 and 38 of the Factories Act 1955) Order 2003 (S.I. No.257 of 2003).

Major accident hazards   The European Communities (Control of Major Accident Hazards Involving Dangerous Substances) (Amendment) Regulations 2003 (S.I. No.402 of 2003) amended the European Communities (Control of Major Accident Hazards Involving Dangerous Substances) Regulations 2000 (*Annual Review of Irish Law 2000*, p.395) in order to ensure that the public is consulted on external emergency plans as required by Directive 96/82/EC on the control of major accident hazards involving dangerous substances, which had been implemented by the 2000 Regulations. They came into force on September 8, 2003.

Maternity protection   The Maternity Protection (Amendment) Act 2004 is discussed separately, above.

Smoking ban   The effect of the Public Health Tobacco (Amendment) Act 2004 is discussed separately below.

PUBLIC SAFETY

The Licensing of Indoor Events Act 2003 has two main purposes: first, to provide for the licensing of certain indoor events; secondly, and notably, to make substantial amendments to the Fire Services Act 1981 by bringing all "workplaces" within the scope of the 1981 Act. As to the licensing of indoor events, Pt 2 of the 2003 Act makes provision for the licensing by fire authorities (that is, larger local authorities) of certain indoor events, such as concerts. In that respect, the 2003 Act implements the main "indoor" elements of the 1990 Hamilton Committee Report, the *Report of the Committee on Public Safety and Crowd Control* (*Annual Review of Irish Law 1990*, p.476). The main recommendations of the Hamilton Committee on "outdoor" events were, in effect, implemented by Pt 16 of the Planning and Development Act 2000, which introduced a special licensing system for open air public performances and funfairs. As to fire safety in places of work, Pt 3 of the 2003 Act brought all "workplaces" under the Fire Services Act 1981. Pt 3 was brought into force on July 14, 2003 by the *Licensing of Indoor Events Act 2003 (Commencement) Order 2003* (S.I. No.291 of 2003). Notably, s.29 of the 2003 Act, which inserted a new s.18 into the 1981 Act, is the key provision. The new s.18 of the 1981 Act includes all "workplaces" under the 1981 Act, as well as other places already covered by the 1981 Act, notably premises to which the public have access. The new s.18 has no exclusions, such as those for premises to which the Dangerous Substances Acts 1972 and 1979 apply, explosives premises and oil jetties. While these premises will also be covered by more specific fire safety requirements, the 1981 Act, as amended by the 2003 Act, now also applies to them. Sections 25 and 26 of the 2003 Act also provide a new power for fire authorities to opt to prosecute offences under the 1981 Act or Regulations made under s.37 of the 1981 Act either as summary offences or indictable offences and also updates the penalty provisions in the 1981 Act. Section 30 of the 2003 Act provides that if an authorised officer is of the opinion that a very grave and immediate risk is posed to the safety of people in or on a premises, he or she may serve a closure notice "on the spot" on the person who owns, occupies or is in control of the premises.

SEA POLLUTION

Civil liability for oil pollution   The Oil Pollution of the Sea (Civil Liability and Compensation) (Amendment) Act 2003 amended the Oil Pollution of the Sea (Civil Liability and Compensation) Acts 1988 and 1998 (*Annual Review of Irish Law 1988*, pp.437–439, and *Annual Review of Irish Law 1998*, p.580) in order to give effect to the 2003 Protocol amending the 1992 International Convention on the Establishment of an International Fund for Compensation for Oil Pollution Damage. The 1992 Fund Convention, as amended, provides for the establishment of an international fund from which to supplement the amount of compensation for oil pollution where shipowners' liability is exceeded. The fund is financed each year by levies charged to receivers of oil carried by sea, on amounts over 150,000 tonnes received in the previous calendar year.

Dumping at sea   The Dumping at Sea (Amendment) Act 2004 amended the Dumping at Sea Act 1996 to reflect in statutory form certain non-statutory arrangements. Thus, s.3 of the 2004 Act, which inserted a new s.5A into the 1996 Act, imposes a statutory obligation on applicants for dumping at sea permits to advertise their applications in a local newspaper. Interested parties will have 21 days after publication of the newspaper advertisement in which to comment to the Minister for Communications, Marine and Natural Resources on the proposals in the applications, except in urgent cases involving navigational safety, where public advertisement only is being provided for. The new s.5A of the 1996 Act also requires the Minister for Communications, Marine and Natural Resources to publish by electronic means all applications for dumping at sea permits received on or after January 1, 2001 and all submissions or observations from the public in relation to such applications. The 2001 date was inserted during the *Seanad Debates* on the 2004 Act, which occurred in 2000.

Sea pollution prevention   The Sea Pollution (Prevention of Oil Pollution) (Amendment) Regulations 2003 (S.I. No.191 of 2003), made under the Sea Pollution Act 1991 (*Annual Review of Irish Law 1991*, pp.366–369), amended the 1994 Regulations of the same title (*Annual Review of Irish Law 1994*, p.398) to provide for additional measures relating to the prevention of oil pollution from tankers in the event of collision or stranding. The 2003 Regulations gave effect to further amendments of the International Convention for the Prevention of Pollution from Ships (the MARPOL Convention) and came into effect on April 30, 2003. The European Communities (Port Reception of Facilities for Ship-Generated Waste and Cargo Residues) Regulations 2003 (S.I. No.117 of 2003) gave effect to Directive 2000/59/EC and aim to reduce discharges of ship-generated waste and cargo residues in the sea. They came into force on September 27, 2003.

TOBACCO CONTROL AND WORKPLACE SMOKING BAN

The Public Health Tobacco (Amendment) Act 2004 amended in important respects the Public Health (Tobacco) Act 2002, primarily in relation to prohibiting tobacco advertising and introducing a prohibition on smoking in virtually all indoor places of work, including bars and other licensed premises. As explained during its passage through the Oireachtas, the principal genesis of the 2004 Act was the institution in June 2002 of three sets of High Court proceedings by representatives of the tobacco industry and other related trades which challenged various elements of the 2002 Act.

The technical standards "transparency" Directives   The essence of these cases was that there had been a failure to notify the European Commission in advance of the enactment of the 2002 Act in accordance with the requirements of the technical standards "transparency" Directives, 98/34/EC and 98/48/EC. The transparency Directives require EU Member States to notify draft national technical standards to the European Commission and to other Member States in advance of their adoption. This is intended to provide transparency and control concerning technical regulations which impose binding legal rules, regulating the characteristics required of a product such as levels of quality, performance, safety or dimensions, including the requirements applicable to the product as regards the name under which the product is sold, terminology, symbols, testing and test methods, packaging, marking or labelling and conformity assessment procedures. As national measures of this nature could create unjustified barriers to trade between Member States, their notification in draft form and the subsequent evaluation of their content in the course of the procedure help to diminish this risk. The principal elements of the 2002 Act affected by these notification requirements, which comprised 14 of the 53 sections of the 2002 Act, related mainly to the sale and marketing of tobacco products.

It is worth noting that the Minister of State for Health provided a significant insight into the discussions which had occurred between the State and the European Commission in connection with compliance with the transparency Directives. He noted that, as the 2002 Act was a public health measure, it was originally considered that it was not notifiable to the Commission as a technical Regulation. It was also considered that the requirement to introduce Commencement Orders to bring the relevant provisions of the 2002 Act into force would allow for notification of the standards in draft form, thereby meeting the requirements of the transparency Directives. But, the Minister stated, following correspondence and discussions with European Commission officials on this matter and having obtained legal advice from the Office of the Attorney General, that it became clear that any attempt to commence the affected sections would result in considerable uncertainty as to their enforceability. In the context of the three sets of High Court proceedings, therefore, the court was advised of the attempts made through the Commission to resolve the issue and each set of proceedings was discontinued, with the State in effect conceding the issues raised.

Advertising and sale of tobacco products   Accordingly, from a legislative perspective, it was decided that the most appropriate way of resolving the issue was to repeal the affected sections of the 2002 Act and to reintroduce them by way of new sections to be inserted into the 2002 Act which would then be notified under the transparency procedure and, on completion of this procedure, would be re-enacted. The Government was, the Minister stated, also advised by the Office of the Attorney General that with a view to assisting in the defence of any challenge brought to the re-enacted legislation, the 2004

Act should be used as an opportunity to strengthen the 2002 Act in a number of areas. This was done by, among other things, changing the Long Title of the 2002 Act to indicate that the 2002 Act is designed to give effect to those EU and international measures that have been adopted at that date. The re-enacted provisions of the 2002 Act thus include those EU measures relating to tobacco products to be transposed into national law. The EU measures include Directive 2001/37/EC on the approximation of the laws, regulations and administrative provisions of Member States concerning the manufacture, presentation and sale of tobacco products, and Directive 2003/33/EC on the approximation of those laws, regulations and administrative provisions of Member States which prohibit tobacco advertising and related sponsorship. In addition, the World Health Organisation Framework Convention on Tobacco Control was adopted at Geneva in May 2003 and the State became a signatory in September 2003. The provisions in the 2002 Act dealing with indirect advertising were removed as the EU Directive on the advertising and sponsorship of tobacco products does not cover indirect advertising. Indirect advertising is often referred to as "brand stretching". The removal of this provision was advised on the basis that it would also serve to insulate the 2002 Act from further legal challenge. The provision on the prohibition of smoking of tobacco products in specified places was amended to include the principles and policies which will inform the making of Regulations under the relevant section.

Workplace smoking ban   A general ban on smoking in places of work and public places, including bars and restaurants, had been due to come into effect in January 2004, under the *Tobacco Smoking (Prohibition) Regulations 2003* (S.I. No.481 of 2003), which had been made under the Public Health (Tobacco) Act 2002. These Regulations were, in fact, revoked before they came into effect by the *Tobacco Smoking (Prohibition) (Revocation) Regulations 2004* (S.I. No.31 of 2004). It was also proposed that amendments would have been made to the Safety, Health and Welfare at Work (Carcinogens) Regulations 2001 which would have defined "Environmental Tobacco Smoke" as a carcinogen for the purposes of the 2001 Regulations. Due to concerns arising from the three claims initiated in 2002, referred to above, the Government was advised by the Office of the Attorney General that the provisions for smoke-free workplaces should be introduced by means of primary legislation, rather than by means of secondary legislation, as had been anticipated under the original s.47 of the 2002 Act. As a result, the general ban on smoking was included in s.47 of the Public Health (Tobacco) Act 2002, as inserted by s.16 of the Public Health (Tobacco) (Amendment) Act 2004. This came into effect on March 29, 2004.

General ban, subject to exceptions Section 47(1) of the 2002 Act states that, subject to a number of important exceptions, "the smoking of a tobacco product in a specified place is prohibited". Section 47(2) states that a person who contravenes the prohibition is guilty of an offence. Section 5(2A) of the 2002 Act, as amended by the 2004 Act, states that a person guilty of an offence under s.47 can be prosecuted in the District Court and that, on conviction, the maximum fine is €3,000. Section 47(3) states that where s.47(1) is breached, "the occupier, manager and any other person for the time being in charge of the specified place concerned shall each be guilty of an offence". Section 47(4) provides for an important defence, namely, that it is a defence for a person prosecuted "to show that he or she made all reasonable efforts to ensure compliance with" s.47. The Office of Tobacco Control has published *Guidance for Employers and Managers* on the "reasonable efforts" defence, available at www.otc.ie.

Specified places where smoking is prohibited Section 47 of the 2002 Act, as inserted by the 2004 Act, lists the following "specified places" where smoking is prohibited:

(*a*) a place of work,

(*b*) an aircraft, train, ship or other vessel, public service vehicle, or a vehicle used for the carriage of members of the public for reward other than a public service vehicle, insofar as it is a place of work,

(*c*) a health premises, insofar as it is a place of work,

(*d*) a hospital that is not a health premises, insofar as it is a place of work,

(*e*) a school or college, insofar as it is a place of work,

(*f*) a building to which the public has access, either as of right or with the permission of the owner or occupier of the building, and which belongs to, or is in the occupation of—
   (i)   the State,
   (ii) a Minister of the Government,
   (iii) the Commissioners of Public Works in Ireland,
         or
   (iv) a body established by or under an Act of the Oireachtas,
   insofar as it is a place of work,

(*g*) a cinema, theatre, concert hall or other place normally used for indoor public entertainment, insofar as it is a place of work,

(*h*) a licensed premises, insofar as it is a place of work, or

(*i*) a registered club, insofar as it is a place of work.

Exempted places A number of places of work are exempted from the general ban in s.47 of the 2002 Act, as inserted by the 2004 Act. These are as follows:

(*a*) a dwelling,

(*b*) a prison,

(*c*) subject to paragraph (*d*), a place or premises, or a part of a place or premises, that is wholly uncovered by any roof, whether fixed or movable,

(*d*) an outdoor part of a place or premises covered by a fixed or movable roof, provided that not more than 50 per cent of the perimeter of that part is surrounded by one or more walls or similar structures (inclusive of windows, doors, gates or other means of access to or egress from that part),

(*e*) a bedroom in—
   (i)   a premises registered under Pt III of the Tourist Traffic Act 1939 in a register established and maintained under that Part,
   (ii) a premises for the time being specified in a list published, or caused to be published, under s.9 of the Tourist Traffic Act 1957, or
   (iii) any other premises in which a person carries on business, being a business that consists of or includes the provision, in those premises, of sleeping accommodation to members of the public,

(*f*) a room that, in furtherance of charitable objects, is used solely for the provision of living accommodation,

(*g*) in premises owned or occupied by a person whose main objects are the provision of education, a room that, in furtherance of those objects (other than objects relating to the provision of primary or secondary education), is used solely for the provision of living accommodation,

(*h*) a nursing home,

(*i*) a hospice,

(*j*) a psychiatric hospital, or

(*k*) the Central Mental Hospital.

In summary, these exemptions cover: outdoor locations such as beer gardens and smoking shelters, provided they comply with the 50 per cent rule in s.47 of the 2002 Act; prisons and places of detention; places that are similar to a private dwelling such as bedrooms in hotels, guesthouses, hostels and B&Bs; some care institutions such as nursing homes, hospices, psychiatric hospitals and certain charitable institutions; and third level education residential facilities.

Signage Section 46 of the 2002 Act, as amended by s.15 of the 2004 Act, states that places to which the smoking ban applies must display a sign indicating that smoking is prohibited, the name of the owner or person in charge, and the name of the person to whom a complaint can be made, if necessary.

TRANSPORT

Carriage of dangerous goods by road   The Carriage of Dangerous Goods by Road Regulations 2004 (S.I. No.29 of 2004) (the CDGR Regulations), which were made under the Carriage of Dangerous Goods by Road Act 1998, replace the Carriage of Dangerous Goods by Road Regulations 2001 (*Annual Review of Irish Law 2001*, p.523). They set down detailed requirements for the vehicles, tanks, tank containers, receptacles and packages containing dangerous goods, including petrol products, as defined in the UN's ADR Agreement on the Carriage of Dangerous Goods. The 1998 Act implemented the general principles of the ADR Agreement, while the 2004 Regulations implement its detailed requirements. The 2004 Regulations require, for example, that the drivers and others, such as the consignor, involved in the carriage of the dangerous goods by road (including their packing, loading, filling, transport and unloading) be adequately trained and, in the case of drivers, hold certificates of such training. The 2004 Regulations also contain provisions on an EC harmonised approach to the road checks aspect of their enforcement. The 2004 Regulations came into force on January 21, 2004. The 2004 Regulations implemented Directive 94/55/EC on the Transport of Dangerous Goods by Road, as amended by Directive 95/50/EC on uniform procedures for checks on the transport of dangerous goods by road, Directive 2000/61/EC, Directive 2001/26/EC and Directive 2003/28/EC.

Transport of dangerous goods by rail   The European Communities (Transport of Dangerous Goods by Rail) Regulations 2003 (S.I. No.701 of 2003) give effect to Directives 2001/6/EC and 2003/29/EC adapting for the third and fourth time Directive 96/49/EC on the approximation of the laws of the Member States with regard to the transport of dangerous goods by rail. The 1996 Directive had been implemented by the European Communities (Transport of Dangerous Goods by Rail) Regulations 2001 (*Annual Review of Irish Law 2001*, p.524). The 2003 Regulations came into effect on December 18, 2003.

Social Welfare Law

GERRY WHYTE

During 2004, two Social Welfare Acts were passed, 29 social welfare regulations were promulgated, and one case concerning the social welfare code was decided in the Superior Courts.

PRIMARY LEGISLATION

Part II of the Social Welfare (Miscellaneous Provisions) Act 2004 provides for a number of amendments to the social welfare code. (Part III provides for miscellaneous amendments to other enactments, including the implementation of the Race and Framework Directives—Directives 2000/43 and 2000/78 respectively—in relation to occupational pensions. Sections 22 and 23 in this Part were commenced by Social Welfare (Miscellaneous Provisions) Act 2004 (Sections 22 & 23) (Commencement) Order 2004 (S.I. No.141 of 2004). Part I provides for the short title, construction and commencement of the 2004 Act).

Section 2 defines certain terms used in the Act, while ss.3 and 4 provide for increases in the rates of Child Benefit and Respite Care Grant respectively. Section 5 extends the Payments After Death scheme (whereby the surviving spouse or partner of a social welfare claimant continues to receive the social welfare payment paid to that claimant for a period of six weeks following his/ her death) to all social welfare claimants. Section 6 provides for an additional increase in the rate of Death Benefit Pension to claimants aged 80 years or more while s.7 provides for an increase in the minimum rate of Unemployment Assistance payable to a claimant whose means derive from parental income. Section 8 amends the Maternity Benefit scheme by reducing from four weeks to two weeks the minimum period of such benefit that must be taken before the expected date of birth, and by empowering the Minister to make regulations providing for the splitting of the period of Maternity Benefit where the infant is hospitalised. This section was commenced by S.I. No.658 of 2004. Section 9 provides for an increase in the maximum duration of Adoptive Benefit from 14 to 16 weeks. This section was commenced by S.I. No.756 of 2004. Section 10 continues the transitional arrangements put in place in 2001 dealing with entitlement to short-term social insurance benefits following on from the alignment of the income tax and calendar years in 2002. Section 11 provides for the inclusion of four additional agencies in the list of public bodies authorised to use the Personal Public Service (PPS) Number as a public service identifier. Section 12 authorises social welfare inspectors carrying out an enquiry in relation to PRSI to determine also whether the employer is enabling those of his/her employees for whom a pension scheme is not provided to access a Personal Retirement Savings Account. Section 13 provides for certain technical amendments, consequent on the decision in 2003 to charge PRSI and levies on certain benefits-in-kind, to the definitions in the Social Welfare (Consolidation) Act 1993, while s.16 provides for a further technical amendment to s.14(5) of the 1993 Act arising out of these changes. These two sections were commenced by S.I. No.406 of 2004. Sections 14 and 15 provide for the charging of PRSI in circumstances where an employer reaches an agreed settlement with the Revenue Commissioners in relation to irregular and minor benefits-in-kind, while ss.20 and 21 make similar provision in respect of health contributions and the training fund levy. Section 17, read together with the First Schedule to the Act, introduces a requirement of "habitual residence in the State" for the purposes of determining eligibility for social assistance schemes and Child Benefit. This new requirement was introduced in response to the enlargement of the European Union from 15 to 25 States in 2004. By virtue of s.208A(1) (inserted by s.17), there is a presumption, until the contrary is shown, that a person is not habitually resident in the State for this purpose unless s/he has been present in the State or in the United Kingdom for a continuous period of two years. Section 17 was commenced by S.I. No.184 of 2004. Finally, ss.18 and 19 provide that a "qualified adult" for the purpose of nine administrative schemes, including the Free Travel Scheme, the National Fuel Scheme and the Back to Education Allowance, is the spouse or cohabiting partner of the beneficiary of the relevant scheme.

The Social Welfare Act 2004 provides for the annual increases in the rates of social welfare payments, together with a number of other changes to the social welfare code. Section 1 provide for the definition of certain terms used in the Act, while ss.2 and 3 provide for the increases in the rates of social welfare payments. Section 4 provides for increases in the weekly net income thresholds used to determine eligibility for Family Income Supplement. Sections 5 and 6 provide for increases in the annual earnings ceiling up to which social insurance contributions are payable by employees and optional contributors respectively. Section 7 provides for an increase from 70 per cent to 75 per cent in the percentage of reckonable weekly earnings referred to in calculating the rate of Maternity Benefit, while s.8 provides for increases in the Health Levy thresholds. Finally, s.9 provides for the short title and construction of the Act.

SECONDARY LEGISLATION

During 2004, the following regulations were promulgated by the Minister for Social and Family Affairs:

Social Welfare (Miscellaneous Provisions) Act 2002 (Section 16) (Commencement) Order 2004 (S.I. No.8 of 2004) This Order provides for the commencement of certain items of the Schedule to the Social Welfare (Miscellaneous Provisions) Act 2002 in order to permit the electronic registration of births and deaths in the Civil Registration Office in Limerick from January 19, 2004 and in Nenagh, East Clare and Limerick West from January 26, 2004 and to allow for the capture of additional information at the time of registration.

Social Welfare (Consolidated Payments Provisions) (Amendment) (No.1) (Qualified Child Increase) Regulations 2004 (S.I. No.9 of 2004) The Social Welfare Act 2003 provided that, with effect from January 19, 2004, any increase for a qualified child applicable to Unemployment Benefit, Disability Benefit, Injury Benefit and Health and Safety Benefit will only be payable where the weekly income of the spouse or partner of the claimant does not exceed a prescribed amount. These Regulations provide that the prescribed amount shall be €300 per week.

Social Welfare (Consolidated Payments Provisions) (Amendment) (Overlapping Payments) Regulations 2004 (S.I. No.17 of 2004) These Regulations provide for the removal of the entitlement to half-rate Disability Benefit, Injury Benefit, Unemployment Benefit, Unemployability Supplement, Maternity Benefit, Adoptive Benefit and Health and Safety Benefit where the recipient is already in receipt of a widow's or widower's pension or one-parent family payment. They also provide that where a person is in receipt of a reduced rate widow's or widower's pension or one-parent family payment and has an entitlement to Disability Benefit, Injury Benefit, Unemployment Benefit, Unemployability Supplement, Maternity Benefit, Adoptive Benefit, or Health and Safety Benefit at a higher rate of payment, they may continue to receive the widow's or widower's pension or one-parent family payment and be paid a "top-up" by way of the benefit payment. This top-up payment is the difference between the maximum rate of benefit the person is entitled to and the reduced rate of widow's or widower's pension or one-parent family payment they are in receipt of, as the case may be. The Regulations also provide a saver whereby anyone in receipt of half-rate benefit and a widow's or widower's pension or one-parent family payment prior to the commencement of these Regulations will continue to receive such overlapping payments for the duration of their claims.

Social Welfare (Miscellaneous Provisions) Act 2002 (Section 16) (No.1) (Commencement) Order 2004 (S.I. No.75 of 2004) This Order provides for the commencement of certain items of the Schedule to the Social Welfare (Miscellaneous Provisions) Act 2002 in order to permit the electronic registration of births and deaths in the Civil Registration Office in Kilmallock from February 9, 2004; in Thurles from February 11, 2004; and in Roscrea from February 13, 2004, and to allow for the capture of additional information at the time of registration.

Social Welfare (Miscellaneous Provisions) Act 2002 (Section 16) (No.2) (Commencement) Order 2004 (S.I. No.77 of 2004) This Order provides for the commencement of certain items of the Schedule to the Social Welfare (Miscellaneous Provisions) Act 2002 in order to permit the electronic registration of births and deaths in the Civil Registration Office in Kilrush from February 23, 2004, and in Ennistymon from February 25, 2004 and to allow for the capture of additional information at the time of registration.

Social Welfare (Miscellaneous Provisions) Act 2002 (Section 16) (No.3) (Commencement) Order 2004 (S.I. No.97 of 2004) This Order provides for the commencement of certain items of the Schedule to the Social Welfare (Miscellaneous Provisions) Act 2002 in order to permit the electronic registration of births and deaths in the Civil Registration Office in Letterkenny, Leitrim, and Stranorlar from March 16, 2004 and to allow for the capture of additional information at the time of registration.

Social Welfare (Consolidated Payments Provisions) (Amendment) (No.1) Regulations 2004 (S.I. No.125 of 2004) These Regulations provide for increases in the income disregarded for the purposes of Carer's Allowance to €250 per week in the case of a single person and €500 per week in the case of a married person. The Regulations also provide for the abolition, with effect from April 7, 2004, of the assessment of Benefit and Privilege for the purposes of unemployment assistance and pre-retirement allowance in the case of those claimants aged 27 years and over living in the parental home.

Social Welfare (Miscellaneous Provisions) Act 2004 (Sections 22 & 23) (Commencement) Order 2004 (S.I. No.141 of 2004) This Order provides for the commencement of ss.22 and 23 of the Social Welfare (Miscellaneous Provisions) Act 2004.

Social Welfare (Consolidated Payments Provisions) (Amendment) (No.3) (Overlapping Payments) Regulations 2004 (S.I. No.145 of 2004) These Regulations provide for the restoration of the entitlement to half-rate Disability Benefit, Injury Benefit, Unemployment Benefit, Unemployability Supplement, Maternity Benefit, Adoptive Benefit, or Health and Safety Benefit which was payable to recipients of widow's or widower's pension or one-parent family payment prior to January 19, 2004.

Social Welfare (Miscellaneous Provisions) Act 2002 (Section 16) (No.4) (Commencement) Order 2004 (S.I. No.158 of 2004) This Order provides for the commencement of certain items of the Schedule to the Social Welfare (Miscellaneous Provisions) Act 2002 in order to permit the electronic registration of births and deaths in the Civil Registration Office in Kenmare and Castletownbere from April 13, 2004, and in Dingle from April 20, 2004 and to allow for the capture of additional information at the time of registration.

Social Welfare (Transitional Arrangements) (Alignment of Income Tax Year with Calendar Year) Regulations 2004 (S.I. No.159 of 2004) These Regulations provide for the continuation of the transitional arrangements necessary to preserve entitlement to social insurance-based benefits, consequent on the alignment of the income tax and calendar years with effect from January 1, 2001.

Social Welfare (Miscellaneous Provisions) Act 2004 (Section 17) (Commencement) Order 2004 (S.I. No.184 of 2004) This Order provides for the commencement of s.17 of the Social Welfare (Miscellaneous Provisions) Act 2004 with effect from May 1, 2004.

Social Welfare (Miscellaneous Provisions) Act 2002 (Section 16) (No.6) (Commencement) Order 2004 (S.I. No.250 of 2004) This Order provides for the commencement of certain items of the Schedule to the Social Welfare (Miscellaneous Provisions) Act 2002 in order to permit the electronic registration of births and deaths in the Civil Registration Office in Navan and Galway from May 12, 2004 and to allow for the capture of additional information at the time of registration.

Social Welfare (Miscellaneous) Act 2004 (Section 13 & 16) (Commencement) Order 2004 (S.I. No.406 of 2004) Sections 13 and 16 provide for technical amendments to the PRSI definitions contained in the Social Welfare (Consolidation) Act 1993 consequential on the decision in Budget 2003 to charge PRSI and levies on certain benefits-in-kind. These amendments will come into effect from January 1, 2004.

Social Welfare (Consolidated Contributions and Insurability) (Amendment) Regulations 2004 (S.I. No.428 of 2004) These Regulations amend the Social Welfare (Consolidated Contributions and Insurability) Regulations so as to provide for an exemption on the return on certain foreign funds and life policies from PRSI.

Social Welfare (Consolidated Contributions and Insurability) (Amendment) (No.1) Regulations 2004 (S.I. No.429 of 2004) These Regulations amend the Social Welfare (Consolidated Contributions and Insurability) Regulations so as to provide for the payment of PRSI in relation to benefits-in-kind which are irregular in nature and minor.

Social Welfare (Miscellaneous Provisions) Act 2002 (Section 16) (No.8) (Commencement) Order 2004 (S.I. No.450 of 2004) This Order provides for the commencement of certain items of the Schedule to the Social Welfare (Miscellaneous Provisions) Act 2002 in order to permit the electronic registration of births and deaths in the Civil Registration Office in Dublin from August 3, 2004; in Dublin South City 4 from August 5, 2004; in Naas from August 9, 2004; and in Wicklow from August 11, and to allow for the capture of additional information at the time of registration.

Social Welfare (Miscellaneous Provisions) Act 2002 (Section 16) (No.9) (Commencement) Order 2004 (S.I. No.657 of 2004) This Order provides for the commencement of certain items of the Schedule to the Social Welfare (Miscellaneous Provisions) Act 2002 in order to permit the electronic registration of births and deaths in the Civil Registration Office in Waterford from October 11, 2004, and to allow for the capture of additional information at the time of registration.

Social Welfare (Miscellaneous Provisions) Act 2004 (Section 8) (Commencement) Order 2004 (S.I. No.658 of 2004) This Order provides for the commencement of s.8 of the Social Welfare (Miscellaneous Provisions) Act 2004.

Social Welfare (Consolidated Payments Provisions) (Amendment) (No.4) (Maternity Benefit) Regulations 2004 (S.I. No.660 of 2004) These Regulations provide, for the purposes of the Maternity Benefit scheme, that the minimum payment period prior to the expected date of birth will be two weeks and, where Maternity Benefit has been in payment for a minimum period of 14 weeks, that payment may be postponed in the event of the hospitalisation of the child. The Regulations further provide that an application to postpone payment must be made in writing; that the maximum duration of the postponement of benefit will be six months; and that payment will resume within seven days following written notification of the discharge of the child from hospital. Payment will then continue until completion of the period of entitlement to benefit.

Social Welfare (Miscellaneous Provisions) Act 2002 (Section 16) (No.10) (Commencement) Order 2004 (S.I. No.735 of 2004) This Order provides for the commencement of certain items of the Schedule to the Social Welfare

(Miscellaneous Provisions) Act 2002 in order to permit the electronic registration of births and deaths in the Civil Registration Office in Wexford from November 29, 2004, and to allow for the capture of additional information at the time of registration.

Social Welfare (Miscellaneous Provisions) Act 2004 (Section 9) (Commencement) Order 2004 (S.I. No.756 of 2004) This Order provides for the commencement of s.9 of the Social Welfare (Miscellaneous Provisions) Act 2004.

Social Welfare (Miscellaneous Provisions) Act 2002 (Section 16) (No.11) (Commencement) Order 2004 (S.I. No.802 of 2004) This order provides for the commencement of certain items of the Schedule to the Social Welfare (Miscellaneous Provisions) Act 2002 in order to permit the electronic registration of births and deaths in the Civil Registration Office in the District of Portlaoise from December 13, 2004; in the District of Mullingar from December 14, 2004; in the District of Dundalk from December 17, 2004; and in the District of Cavan from December 20, 2004, and to allow for the capture of additional information at the time of registration.

Social Welfare (Occupational Injuries) (Amendment) Regulations 2004 (S.I. No.845 of 2004) These Regulations provide for increases in the reduced rates of certain Occupational Injuries Benefits.

Social Welfare (Consolidated Payments Provisions) (Amendment) No.6 (Miscellaneous Provisions) Regulations 2004 (S.I. No.846 of 2004) These Regulations provide, where a recipient of one parent family payment exceeds the weekly income threshold of €293, for the circumstances in which the recipient may receive, for a further six months, a transitional one parent family payment payable at half rate.

Social Welfare (Consolidated Payments Provisions) (Amendment) (No.7) (Qualified Child Increase) Regulations 2004 (S.I. No.847 of 2004) These Regulations provide that, with effect from January 19, 2004, any increase for a qualified child applicable to Unemployment Benefit, Disability Benefit, Injury Benefit, and Health and Safety Benefit will only be payable where the weekly income of the spouse or partner of the claimant does not exceed €350 a week.

Social Welfare (Transitional Arrangements) (Alignment of Income Tax Year With Calendar Year (No.1) Regulations 2004 (S.I. No.848 of 2004) These Regulations provide for the continuation of the transitional arrangements necessary to preserve entitlement to social insurance based benefits, consequent on the alignment of the income tax and calendar years with effect from January 1, 2001.

Social Welfare (Rent Allowance) (Amendment) Regulations 2004 (S.I. No.849 of 2004) These Regulations provide for increases in the amount of means disregarded for people affected by the decontrol of rents and the minimum rent for the purposes of the Rent Allowance scheme with effect from January 1, 2005.

Social Welfare (Consolidated Payments Provisions) (Amendment) (No.5) (Increase in Rates) Regulations 2004 (S.I. No.850 of 2004) These Regulations provide for increases in the reduced rates of Disability Benefit, Unemployment Benefit, Health and Safety Benefit, Old Age (Contributory) Pension, Retirement Pension, Widow's and Widower's (Contributory) Pension, Deserted Wife's Benefit, and also provide for increases in the rates of tapered increases in respect of qualified adults. The Regulations also provide for increases in the minimum weekly rate of Maternity Benefit and Adoptive Benefit with effect from January 3, 2005.

Finally, S.I. Nos 768 of 2004, 864 of 2004 and 865 of 2004 provide for the payment of certain maintenance allowances administered by the Department of Health and Children.

CASE LAW

Readers of the *Annual Review of Irish Law 2003* may recall that in *Castleisland Cattle Breeding Society v Minister for Social and Family Affairs* (High Court, November 7, 2003), O'Donovan J. had held that the Chief Appeals Officer had failed to conduct a proper review of a decision of an appeals officer that an individual engaged in the artificial insemination of cattle was an insurable employee of the plaintiff society. (The Chief Appeals Officer had held that there was no mistake of law or fact in the appeals officer's decision and consequently refused to revise this decision.) In the course of his judgment, O'Donovan J. took the view that his function pursuant to s.271 of the Social Welfare (Consolidation) Act 1993 was confined to deciding whether the Chief Appeals Officer was correct in refusing to revise the appeals officer's decision on grounds of mistake of fact or law and that he could not address the substantive decision of the appeals officer.

This decision was, in turn, appealed to the Supreme Court—*Castleisland Cattle Breeding Society v Minister for Social and Family Affairs* (Supreme Court, July 15, 2004, [2004] I.E.S.C. 40). In a unanimous decision, the court (*per* Geoghegan J.) dismissed the appeal, in the process taking a very different view of the role of the courts in appeals taken pursuant to s.271 of the 1993 Act to that adopted by O'Donovan J.

The court began by reviewing some of the procedures under the Social Welfare Acts for resolving contested issues. Section 263 of the Social Welfare (Consolidation) Act 1993 empowers the Chief Appeals Officer to revise any decision of an appeals officer, if it appears to him that the decision was erroneous by reason of some mistake having been made in relation to the law or the facts. According to the court, this section provided for a revising, rather than an appellate, procedure:

> "[T]he Chief Appeals Officer may go through the materials which were before the appeals officer and check whether there was any error in law or on the facts. If he were to find that the appeals officer did not have enough facts or the facts which were before him or her were ambiguous there may be circumstances in which the Chief Appeals Officer would require additional evidence … (p.1)".

The court then turned to s.271, which provides:

> "Any person who is dissatisfied with (a) the decision of an appeals officer, or (b) the revised decision of the Chief Appeals Officer, on any question, other than a question to which section 265 applies, may appeal that decision or revised decision, as the case may be, to the High Court on any question of law".

The court took the view that this entitled the respondent to bring two appeals, one against the decision of the appeals officer that a particular individual was an insurable employee of the respondent and the other against the decision of the Chief Appeals Officer that there was no mistake of law or fact in the appeals officer's decision such as to warrant a revision of that decision. The distinction between these two appeals had, however, become blurred in the High Court where O'Donovan J. treated the entire appeal as an appeal against the refusal of the Chief Appeals Officer to revise the decision of the appeals officer. This had the further consequence that a concession made by the respondent in the context of the appeal against the Chief Appeals Officer's decision that the High Court need not concern itself with the substantive issue of the legal status of the worker at the centre of this case was incorrectly treated by the High Court judge as also being a concession for the purposes of the appeal against the appeals officer's decision. Moreover, the High Court had dealt with the appeal against the Chief Appeals Officer ahead of the appeal against the appeals officer, a sequence that was considered inappropriate because if the appeals officer had been wrong in law, it did not matter whether the Chief Appeals Officer had carried out his revising procedure correctly or not. This point was reinforced by the Supreme Court's view that, properly construed, s.271 did not provide for a right of appeal from the *refusal* of the Chief Appeals Officer to review a decision of an appeals officer, the situation in the instant case. Accordingly, the Supreme Court decided to address the substantive issue in the case before considering whether the Chief Appeals Officer had correctly discharged his function under s.263. In that context, the court held, in contrast to O'Donovan J. in the High Court, that it was entitled to consider whether it was open to the appeals officer to come to the decision which she did arrive at and, if not, whether the evidence conclusively established that the worker in question was an independent contractor. The court further noted that a statutory appeal on a question of law includes the question of whether the evidence supports only one conclusion.

With regard to the legal status of the artificial inseminator, the Supreme Court, applying the principles set out in *Henry Denny & Sons Ltd v Minister for Social Welfare* [1998] 1 I.R. 34, concluded that the individual in question was an independent contractor rather than an employee. Two factors were fundamental in coming to this conclusion. First, the artificial inseminator, who had formerly done this work as an employee of the company, was aware that he and others had been made redundant in order to facilitate the establishment of new arrangements between the company and independent contractors for carrying out this work. As a result of this change, the worker was now self-employed for tax purposes, had to carry his own insurance, and lost his pension entitlements. The second factor was that this type of work was regulated by legislation which removed any significance from the inclusion in the new contract of terms requiring the company's approval for the use of any substitute inseminator. Other elements of the relationship between inseminator and company supported the conclusion that it entailed a contract for services rather than a contract of service. Thus, repeat inseminations had to be carried out without payment and payment was made on foot of monthly invoices. The new contract required the worker to provide his own transport, communication system, protective clothing, equipment, and insurance. The inseminator also indemnified the company against any claim arising out of his gross negligence in the performance of, or deliberate refusal to perform, his functions. As the inseminator controlled his own timetable, this meant that he could increase his profits with his own efficiency. In the light of these and other factors, the Supreme Court held that it was not open to the appeals officer to conclude that the worker was an insurable employee of the company. It followed that the appeal from the decision of the Chief Appeals Officer had to be struck out.

Sports Law

NEVILLE COX, Law School, Trinity College, Dublin

INTRODUCTION

The level of interaction between sport and the law in Ireland continued to increase in 2004. Thus major developments occurred in the area of criminal law, administrative law, and the law governing doping in sport.

THE SPORTS COUNCIL AND ANTI-DOPING RULES

In 2004, the Irish Sports Council continued to develop its pivotal role in the fight against doping in sport. In particular it continued to take responsibility for the bulk of drug testing in Irish sport. In 2004, 918 tests were carried out, including 153 user-pays tests. Sixty per cent of such tests were conducted on an "out-of-competition" basis. The tests focused on 37 different sports with 75 tests taking place overseas. There were seven positive tests, of which one was justified by a retrospectively granted therapeutic use exemption, four received sanction, and two remained to be considered.

More significantly, however, in January 2004, the Irish Sports Council published the Irish Anti-Doping Rules, which, it is hoped, will govern the conditions under which all drug testing in Irish sport will henceforth take place. All Irish governing bodies in receipt of government grants are required to sign up to these rules. The essential function of the rules is to incorporate the terms of the World Anti-Doping Agency (WADA) code signed by sports federations and governments in March 2003 (and the international standards and models of best practice adopted by WADA in support of the code). Such rules essentially represent one of the contractual terms by which competitors in sporting events agree to be bound as a result of their contractual relationship with the relevant governing body. A possible exception to this (and one that would prove significant in 2005) concerns equestrian sport, in that it is entirely arguable that the WADA code (and hence the Irish Rules) only applies to *human athletes* (including jockeys) whereas Equestrian Federation rules continue to govern the application of anti-doping policy where horses are concerned.

The 2004 rules deal with many of the vexed questions that have traditionally beset the operation of anti-doping policies. First and foremost, a clear definition of what constitutes doping is provided. Thus a doping offence is committed whenever any of the following can be demonstrated:

• Presence of a prohibited substance, its metabolites or markers in an athlete's bodily specimen (and the code insists that it is the athlete's personal duty to ensure that no prohibited substance enters his or her body).

• Use or attempted use of a prohibited substance.

• Refusal or failure to submit to, or evasion of a sample collection.

• Violation of applicable requirements regarding out-of-competition testing including failure to provide reliable information as to the athlete's whereabouts.

• Tampering or attempting to tamper with any part of doping control

• Possession of prohibited substances or methods, save where it can be established that the substances in question were permitted for therapeutic reasons.

• Trafficking in any prohibited substance or method.

• Administration or attempted administration of a prohibited substance or method to any athlete.

• Assisting, encouraging, aiding, abetting, concealing, covering up, or any other type of complicity ... involving a breach [or attempted breach] of the rules.

The rules further deal with questions of burden and standard of proof. Thus, it is stressed that the anti-doping organisation has the burden of establishing that a violation of an anti-doping rule has occurred, and it must prove that allegation "to the comfortable satisfaction of the court"—a standard between the traditional criminal and civil standards of proof. There is a presumption that WADA-accredited laboratories have conducted sample analyses and custodial procedures in accordance with international standards of best practice. Moreover, whereas departures from international standards that do not cause an adverse analytical finding do not invalidate test results, equally if the athlete proves that such departure *has* occurred, then the burden shifts back to the anti-doping organisation to establish that the departure does not cast doubt on the analytical finding. Finally, if an athlete who has tested positive for a banned substance wishes to assert moral innocence with a view to having his sanction reduced, then the burden of proof in this regard rests with him.

The Irish Rules also adopt the WADA international standard for Therapeutic Use Exemptions (TUE). Thus, athletes with a documented condition who require to use a prohibited substance must obtain a TUE either from the Sports

Council or from the relevant international federation *prior to* competing in any sporting event—although provision is made for retrospective approval of a TUE in exceptional or emergency circumstances. If the athlete is granted a TUE by the international federation, then he/she must inform the Sports Council of this fact. Finally, if the athlete is competing in an international event, then he/she must obtain a TUE from the international federation irrespective of whether or not he/she has previously obtained one from the Sports Council. A TUE shall only be granted where:

- the athlete would suffer a significant impairment to health if he/she was unable to avail of the prohibited substance or method;

- the therapeutic use thereof would not provide performance-enhancing benefits over and above those that would derive from a return to a state of normal health. Thus, the use of a prohibited substance or method to boost below normal levels of endogenous hormones is not regarded as an acceptable therapeutic intervention;

- there is no reasonable therapeutic alternative to the use of the prohibited substance or method;

- the need to use the prohibited substance or method is not the consequence of prior non-therapeutic use of the same.

In order to avail of a TUE, the athlete must comply with strict rules regarding the submission of supporting medical evidence to the sports council.

The rules also adopt the WADA provisions in respect of testing, providing for a rigorous programme of testing both in and out of competition. The Irish Sports Council is obliged under the rules to identify a registered testing pool (subject to revision from time to time) of athletes to be tested. Athletes who have been informed that they are in this pool are obliged to fill out quarterly reports specifying their location for the next period (and such information may be altered as the need arises). Failure to provide such a report after receipt of two formal warnings from the sports council in the previous 18 months constitutes a doping offence. Should an athlete prove unavailable for testing on three occasions in an 18 month period, he/she will be considered to have committed a violation of the anti-doping rules. Testing of minors may only take place with the consent of a person with legal responsibility for such minors, but such consent is a condition precedent to the participation of the minor in sport. Finally, the rules provide that no liability for inconvenience or loss resulting from the testing process shall arise, and no cause of action shall accrue.

The Irish Rules outline the manner in which the rights of athletes accused of doping offences are to be protected. The Irish Sports Council is required to appoint an Irish sport anti-doping disciplinary panel consisting of a chair, two vice chairs (lawyers of not less than ten years' standing), three medical experts with relevant experience, and three sports administrators, who will preside over disciplinary hearings and determine all issues arising from any matters referred to it pursuant to the rules, including the consequences of violation thereof. Decisions of the panel may be appealed to the Court of Arbitration for Sport. The rules provide for:

- A timely hearing (it is envisaged that the hearing process should be completed within three months of the completion of the results management process). Moreover there is an absolute time limit of eight years from the date of a violation in which to bring an action.

- A fair and impartial panel.

- The right to be represented by counsel and where appropriate to have an interpreter.

- The right to be informed of the alleged violation and the resulting consequences.

- The right to present evidence and to summon witnesses.

- The right where necessary to an interpreter.

- A timely, written, and reasoned decision.

Equally the obligations on the Disciplinary Panel are not as onerous as those that would apply in a court room. Thus for example the hearing panel may receive evidence (including hearsay evidence) as it thinks fit. Decisions of the hearing panel shall be in the form of one brief, reasoned opinion with no dissenting decisions produced. Finally, the rules make provision for circumstances where, by reason of an agreement with the Sports Council (which may be rescinded), determination of a doping matter is transferred to the disciplinary panel of a National Governing Body.

In line with the WADA code, the Irish Rules provide that in the event of a positive test, all the athlete's results in an event in which the violation occurs will be disqualified, as shall all results obtained from the date of the production of the positive sample through the commencement of any period of suspension. Beyond this, the athlete will also receive a two-year ban for a first offence, and a lifetime ban for a second offence, subject to the possibility of his or her being able to present mitigating evidence which can lead to a reduction in sanction. The period of ineligibility starts on the date of the hearing decision, and any period of provisional suspension shall be credited against the total period of ineligibility. Importantly, this means that an athlete is suspended from *all* sporting competitions organised by any governing body that has signed up to the code. The athlete must submit to reinstatement testing as a condition to regaining eligibility.

Equally, in the context of most doping offences (excluding manipulation of a sample and trafficking in drugs), if the athlete can demonstrate that he/she bears no fault or negligence in respect of a doping offence then the otherwise applicable period of ineligibility shall be eliminated, and if he/she can demonstrate that he/she bears no significant fault or negligence then the period of suspension can be reduced, yet must not be less than half of the minimum period of ineligibility otherwise applicable. It is also specifically provided that where the offence involves the presence of a banned substance in an athlete's system, then the athlete must demonstrate how the substance entered his system. Finally the rules provide for the reduction of a suspension where the athlete has provided assistance to an anti-doping organisation which assists the latter in discovering or establishing an anti-doping violation by another party.

The rules also provide for the creation of an Anti-Doping Appeal Panel, comprising two legal practitioners of not less than ten years' standing, two medical practitioners of not less than ten years' standing and two members each of whom is either a sports administrator or an athlete. This body has power to hear and determine all appeals arising out of the above process. The required procedures before the appeal body are similar to those before the original disciplinary panel, and seek to provide a high level of protection for the athlete and to ensure that, as far as possible, issues of this nature are kept out of the civil courts.

The rules give the Sports Council a greatly increased power not just to organise the testing procedure of governing bodies, but now effectively to ensure that anti-doping policy in Irish sport is brought into line with the approach of WADA. There will no doubt, be pitfalls ahead, not least the fact that the WADA rules are undoubtedly designed for professional or near professional sport, where it is reasonable to demand that athletes should be able to provide detailed "whereabouts" information, and to take responsibility for everything that goes into their systems. The GAA has long argued that such standards cannot reasonably be expected of amateur athletes. Nonetheless, from the lawyer's point of view, the rules are admirable in their clarity and in the thorough manner in which they reconcile the competing claims of the individual athlete and the anti-doping movement.

EUROPEAN UNION FREEDOMS AND SPORT

The decision of the European Court of Justice in *Union Royale Belge des Societes de Football Association ASBL v Jean Marc Bosman,* Case C–415/93, [1995] E.C.R. I–4921; [1996] 1 C.M.L.R. 645; [1996] All E.R. (EC) 97, continues to have an enormous impact on professional sport in Europe, by reason of its conclusion that in as much as professional sport is a business, the European Community freedoms—and especially the freedom to provide services, the free movement of workers, and the freedom to establish one's business—apply to it. Equally, it is clear from the EC treaty that such freedoms are not absolute, and indeed it also seems clear that the interests of sport weigh heavily in any evaluation of the legitimacy of any restriction on such freedoms. The question of acceptable restrictions on the freedoms has arisen recently in the context of a challenge to a law that restricted advertising of alcoholic drinks at sporting events. (Generally see Cox & Schuster, *Sport and the Law* (First Law, 2004) at Chap.8.)

At issue in *Bacardi-Martini SAS, Cellier des Dauphins v Newcastle United Football Company Ltd*, Case C–318/00 (January 21, 2003), was a French law (Loi No. 91/32). This law effectively prohibited the advertising of alcohol on French television. Moreover, under a (non-binding) code of conduct created by the Conseil Superior de l'Audiovisuel (CSA), broadcasters are instructed to take a non-indulgent approach to alcohol advertising at sporting events, whether those events take place in France or abroad. Thus, where the law of a host country allows the advertising of alcoholic drinks at sporting venues but the transmission is aimed at a French audience, it is the responsibility of all parties negotiating contracts with the holders of transmission rights to use all available means to prevent brand names relating to alcoholic drinks from appearing on the screen. (No such prohibition on alcohol advertising is to be found in the British Code of Advertising.) The well known Premiership soccer club Newcastle United had agreed a contract with an advertising company DORNA whereby the latter was appointed to sell and display advertisements on the hoardings around the touchline at Newcastle home games. Under the terms of this contract, DORNA had agreed to provide the claimants with advertising time on an electronic revolving display system during a UEFA cup third-round game between Newcastle and the French side Metz in December 1996. Shortly before the game, however, Newcastle became aware of these arrangements, and, feeling that they violated the French legislation (because the French station, Canal Plus, had bought the rights to show the game live on French television), they instructed DORNA to remove the claimant's advertisements from the system. This was impossible, because of the imminence of the game, but the display system was instead programmed so that the claimant's advertisements appeared for only two seconds at a time rather than for the 30 seconds arranged. The claimants sued the defendants under the tort of inducing a breach of contract, but the defendants claimed that this inducement was justified in order to ensure that there was not a breach of French law, to which the claimants counter-argued that this was not an acceptable justification, in that the French law was in violation of Art.49 of the treaty. On this basis, the English High Court referred the case to the European Court of Justice (ECJ) asking whether, indeed, the French rule violated Art.49 of the Treaty.

The French Government (and the Commission) had argued that the questions referred to the court were inadmissible, in that there was no extra-territorial application of French law affecting Newcastle United. Rather it was the French channel (Canal Plus) that would have had to answer for any breach of French law, and the appropriate jurisdiction in which such litigation would occur would of course be France. Ultimately the court agreed with this position, pointing out that whereas generally the question of whether a case should be referred to the ECJ was one for the national court, equally the court was entitled to refuse jurisdiction over a case where it is asked to give an interpretation of a piece of community law that does not directly impinge on the facts of the case, especially where, in reality, the court was being asked to assess the validity of a piece of law of another Member State. Here, there was nothing in the High Court's analysis of the matter to suggest whether or why Newcastle was obliged to comply with the relevant French legislation (as a matter of contract or otherwise), and hence the court did not feel that it had any evidence before it to show that it was necessary to rule on the compatibility with the Treaty of the relevant French legislation.

A more substantive analysis of the compatibility of this French Law with Art.49 was provided in 2004 in the opinion of Advocate General Tizzano in the joined cases *Commission v France, Bacardi France SAS v Television Française TF1, Groupe Jean-Clàude Darmon SA Girosport Sarl* (Cases C–262/02 and C–429/02, Reference CJE/04/15 (March 12, 2004)). Again, the question was asked whether these rules violated Art.49, but this time in the context both of a Commission claim, and also in the context of claims by Bacardi that the French television channel, TF1, had obliged the Groupe Jean-Clàude Darmon and Girosport companies (both of whom negotiated television broadcasting rights for football matches) to ensure that the brand names of alcoholic drinks did not appear on television screens where matches aimed at the French public were concerned. This practice had meant that a number of foreign football clubs had refused to supply Bacardi with advertising space around their grounds. A case was taken to the French Cour de Cassation, which referred to the ECJ the question whether the French rules were in violation both of Art.49 of the Treaty and of the provisions of the Television Without Frontiers Directive.

Advocate General Tizzano agreed that the rule was prima facie in breach of the Treaty, but also accepted that there was a Treaty-based justification for it—namely to secure the protection of public health. The important question, therefore, was whether the rules in question were a proportionate response to this justification. The Advocate General noted that excessive consumption of alcohol could generate health risks and that the ban on alcohol advertising could potentially reduce the level of consumption thereof. He further noted that French law did not seek to ban the sale or consumption of alcohol (in other words, the restriction at stake was a comparatively minimalist one), and, because of the expensive nature of image-masking techniques, it would have been exceptionally difficult for television broadcasts to secure this objective through other means (for example by obscuring hoardings advertising alcoholic beverages). In other words, in all the circumstances the French measure represented a proportionate response to the problem as perceived. At the end of 2004, the case was under consideration by the ECJ.

A further major area of involvement of the EU institutions in sport has been in the area of transfer rules in sport. Typically this has arisen in the context of challenges (such as in *Bosman*) based on the "free movement" provisions of the Treaty, although there is plainly a competition law component to the issue. Since *Bosman* (a challenge to FIFA transfer rules), the European Commission has continued to have difficulties with aspects of the FIFA transfer rules that did not come under the impact of the decision in *Bosman*. Following a protracted period of discussion involving FIFA and the Commission (with significant intervention from national governments), an agreement was reached in 2001 providing for various matters including the creation of a scheme for the purposes of compensating clubs which have trained players when those players are transferred and re-transferred, in order to encourage small clubs to assist in the training of such young players. Thus for example, if a young League of Ireland soccer player signs terms with a Premiership club and is then sold to another club, the League of Ireland club is entitled to be compensated for its training of that young player, depending on the number of years that it has trained that player and the category of club involved

In 2004, such rules appeared likely to come under scrutiny in Irish courts. The relevant case involved Alan Cawley, a 23-year-old former Leeds United and Sheffield Wednesday player. Having returned from England, Mr Cawley played for two seasons at UCD, and when his contract expired (and UCD were relegated from the Eircom Premier League), Cawley was approached by Shelbourne FC—one of the top League of Ireland clubs—and offered €500 per week to play for them. Cawley wished to play for Shelbourne but, because he was 23, under FAI rules (which derived from the FIFA rules) UCD were entitled to compensation for training him. They demanded €50,000, which was later reduced by an FAI tribunal to €20,000. Shelbourne refused to pay this figure and repudiated its agreement with Cawley. As a result, Cawley issued High Court proceedings against the refusal of the National League to register him as a player, claiming that the imposition of the €20,000 fee which now effectively accompanied him wherever he sought work constituted a severe restraint on trade and a breach of EU law. In late April 2004, an interim deal was reached with the FAI, allowing Cawley to register with Shelbourne pending a full hearing of the action which was due to take place in the autumn of 2004 and which has the capacity to throw the validity of the new transfer system into jeopardy.

EQUALITY LAW AND SPORT

In the *Annual Review of Irish Law 2003*, p.522, we referred to the circumstances in which the Equality Authority sought to take action against Portmarnock Golf Club for its policy of not admitting women members. (Generally see Costello, "Equality Law" at Chap.10 in Cox & Schuster, *Sport and the Law*

(First Law, 2004)). Proceedings in this regard were brought before the District Court in which the club captain argued strongly that the refusal to admit women members was an expression of diversity and should be just as acceptable as "... ladies' boutiques, hairdressers and even ladies' rugby teams" on the basis that equality and sameness could be separated. For the purposes of s.9 of the Equal Status Act (which provides that a club is not a "discriminating club" if its principal purpose is to cater only for the needs of, *inter alia*, a person of a particular gender), the club argued that its principal purpose was to cater for the playing of *men's* golf. Judge Collins in the District Court rejected this logic, however, concluding that in fact the principal purpose of the club was to facilitate the playing of golf generally (as distinct from men's golf specifically). She pointed out that whereas women were not allowed to become full members, they were permitted to play on the course—an illogical state of affairs if the principal purpose of the club was that claimed by the Portmarnock Committee. As a result, the club had its drink licence suspended for seven days. However, enforcement of this sanction was itself suspended pending the hearing of a constitutional action taken by the club.

CRIMINAL LAW AND SPORT

In 2004 there was a surprisingly large number of incidents in which sport interacted with the criminal law in Ireland.

In March 2004, a hurling club selector, John Burke, was sentenced to four months in prison at Athenry District Court for assaulting a player on an opposing team with a hurley during a Galway City League final match in February 2003. The injured player sustained a gash to the top of his head requiring nine stitches after the defendant knocked his protective helmet off by repeatedly hitting him with a hurley. Following an appeal to the Circuit Court (during the course of which Judge Kenny was highly critical of what he perceived as a failure on the part of the GAA to discipline players and officials who bring the game into disrepute), the defendant's sentence was reduced to 200 hours of community service.

On the other hand, in December 2004 Judge Mary Devins in the Castlebar District Court dismissed charges of assault against a university student arising out an incident in the Mayo under-21 Championship final in 2003. During the game, one player, Michael Colleran, suffered a fractured jaw and broken teeth and alleged that this was the result of having been "intentionally clocked" by the defendant Jason Coy. Judge Devins, however, was unable to conclude that there was the relevant *mens rea* on the part of the defendant, and referred to the fact that the only relevant evidence was a video of the match, which was simply incapable of proving the guilt of the accused. Indeed it should be noted that one of the reasons why there are in general so few convictions for on-field violence is because of evidentiary issues of this kind.

The most notable incident in which the relationship between the criminal law and sport came to public attention in 2004 (and, given the high profile nature of the players involved, arguably the most significant such case ever under Irish law) was the case of the All-Ireland medal winner and Down footballer James McCartan. In October 2004, Mr McCartan was accused of assaulting an opponent, Kenneth Larkin, during a "friendly" match between Westmeath and Down, causing a broken jaw, which led to Mr Larkin having three steel plates inserted in his jaw. The victim and the accused naturally had different views of the incident which led to the criminal proceedings; Mr Larkin said that he was marking Mr McCartan during the game, and at one point, when the ball was not in the vicinity of the two players, the latter had simply turned and punched him in the jaw with his clenched fist. McCartan on the other hand denied that he had turned around to hit Larkin but instead said that Larkin had been holding onto him during the game while he (McCartan) had the ball, and that any contact between the two was the accidental result of his swinging his arms in an attempt to break free from the challenge. Evidence was also given by the Westmeath manager and goalkeeper and the Down physiotherapist, and was split on team lines.

In the Dublin District Court, Judge Early, convicting the defendant, rejected as "a lie" Mr McCartan's explanation of the incident. Significantly, the judge said that whereas Gaelic football was a combative sport and accidental injury would inevitably occur, nevertheless, "to strike someone without legal justification is a crime, whether it takes place in the street, in the family home or the football pitch". Eventually, and following payment of €10,000 by Mr McCartan to charity, as well as €1,243 in legal costs, Judge Early decided to apply the probation act to Mr McCartan.

Such incidents highlight the fact that it is notoriously difficult to discern from an analysis of relevant case law, and indeed from an analysis of police activity in this area, any firm rules for determining whether particular incidents of foul play will lead to criminal prosecution. This is for a number of reasons (See Cox & Schuster, *Sport and the Law* (First Law, 2004) at Chap.4), but the result is a good deal of uncertainty. A decision of the English Court of Appeal in December 2004 may, however, have provided a good deal of much needed clarity in this area. In *R. v Barnes* [2005] 2 All E.R. 113, Lord Woolf, upholding an appeal against a conviction for assault of an amateur soccer player who had injured another as a result of a "late tackle", held that in the sporting context, criminal prosecution should be reserved for those cases where the impugned conduct was sufficiently grave that it could genuinely be characterised as criminal. The primary response to foul play should come from internal disciplinary mechanisms within sport, and beyond that it was possible for an injured party to institute civil proceedings. It was only where the conduct in question went well beyond what a player could reasonably be regarded as having taken part in the sport that it would not be covered by the consent of the injured party.

Moreover, the question of whether the conduct was serious enough to justify criminal prosecution was one of fact to be determined on a case-by-case basis. If the conduct was within the rules of the game, then this clearly indicated that it did not reach the threshold. Beyond this, however, and because foul play does occur in the heat of the moment in sport, it might well be that even that type of foul play for which the protagonist might be sent off would not reach the threshold. This would fall to be determined having regard to factors such as the type of sport, the level at which it was played, the nature of the act, the degree of force used, the extent of the risk of injury, and the state of mind of the defendant. In a case such as this, the jury should ask itself whether the conduct was so obviously late or violent that it could not be regarded as an instinctive reaction or an error or a misjudgment in the heat of the game.

CIVIL LIABILITY FOR ON-FIELD VIOLENCE

In June 2004, an action taken by a GAA footballer against the trustees of the GAA in respect of injuries suffered while playing an organised Gaelic football match was settled without admission of liability. The plaintiff, Michael Miller, had claimed that while playing for Enniscorthy Starlights against Duffry Rovers he was violently struck in the lower abdomen by a member of the opposing team leading to a major tear in part of the small bowel which required emergency surgery and which led to him being hospitalised for two weeks.

FAIR PROCEDURES AND INTERLOCUTORY RELIEF

In previous editions of the *Annual Review of Irish Law*, we referred to the increasing propensity of sportspeople who had been suspended from playing for a period in which a major sporting event was to take place to challenge the imposition of such suspension in the courts, claiming that the relevant disciplinary proceedings were somehow procedurally deficient, and to seek an interlocutory injunction staying such suspension until the trial of the action—relief which, if granted, would have had the effect of meaning that they could take part in the major event in question. Because of the relatively low threshold for obtaining such interlocutory relief at Irish law, this tactic had a high success rate, with "suspended" athletes taking part in the relevant event and then discontinuing the substantive proceedings in respect of which the interlocutory relief was sought and granted.

This trend continued in 2004, to the extent that the GAA (the body against whom such interlocutory relief was inevitably sought) intimated that it would be seeking to amend its rules in 2005 by the insertion of an arbitration clause which would mean that all such claims would now have to be brought before a newly created Disputes Resolution Authority that could expeditiously resolve the matter in its entirety.

In May 2004, a Longford county footballer, Dave Barden, secured an interlocutory injunction from the High Court restraining the GAA from enforcing an eight-week suspension imposed on him following an incident during a club match on April 9 when he was sent off. Mr Barden had claimed that the club match in question was not a properly constituted competition under GAA rules because the competing clubs had not sought clearance from their county boards and provincial councils, and, not being a properly constituted GAA competition, a sending off in such a match could not generate a suspension that would apply to GAA competitions generally.

On the other hand, in October 2004, Andrew Gallagher the player-manager of St Naul's Mountcharles Gaelic football team was unsuccessful in his attempt to obtain an interlocutory injunction that would have had the effect of lifting a 12-week suspension that had been imposed on him and which would have permitted him to play in an intermediate championship final. In this case, Mr Gallagher had been suspended following a melee during a Donegal All-County League Match—a match in which he was not actually playing. According to the referee's report of the melee, he (the referee) had asked one particularly vociferous participant in the melee whether he was the St Naul's manager and the individual in question had replied in the affirmative. At all stages, including at a disciplinary meeting organised by the Donegal County Board, Mr Gallagher denied both taking part in a melee and also ever having been spoken to by the referee, or having said to the referee that he was the manager of St Naul's. He also alleged that the disciplinary hearing was unfair in that two clubs, Glenswilly and Glencolumcille had representatives on the committee which was adjudicating on his case, and St Naul's was due to play both teams in vital matches in (respectively) the intermediate championship and the All-County League. In other words, both representatives would have an interest in his being suspended. In the High Court, however, Carroll J. rejected his application for interlocutory relief, implicitly accepting the conclusion of the County Board that the relevant committee had acted in a fair and impartial manner in reaching its decision.

This case appears to manifest a further trend in the dealings of the courts with sports-related cases, namely that whatever about upholding challenges to decisions made by governing bodies or games committees, there is a marked reluctance to make any decision that would have the effect of undermining a decision of a referee. This is arguably why the decision of the High Court granting an interlocutory injunction to Westmeath GAA footballer Rory O'Connell which had the effect of lifting a three-month suspension for stamping on an opponent, thereby rendering him available to take part in the Leinster senior football final in July 2004, was one with particularly far-reaching implications. O'Connell had been sent off during an inter-county match in May 2004. It was common cause that he had been involved in what was described as "an entanglement after a tussle for the ball" and it seems clear that such entanglement was with an opposing player, Paschal Kellaghan. The referee's report, however, stated that Mr O'Connell had been guilty of stamping on Mr Kellaghan—a suggestion that Mr O'Connell emphatically denied. Following a conversation with Mr O'Connell some time after the issuing of the referee's report, Mr Kellaghan wrote a letter in which he said that whereas he had received a blow to the face, equally he was unable to confirm that Mr O'Connell was the offender. When his case came before the Games Administration Committee and the management committee, however, this letter was deemed inadmissible on the basis that because it did not have Mr Kellaghan's address on it, nor had it come through the Offaly County Board (Mr Kellaghan being an Offaly player), it could have been written by anyone and hence should not be considered.

In the High Court, O'Leary J. held that there was a stateable case that fair procedures had not been followed in this instance, in that there was nothing in GAA rules requiring that for a letter to be considered by the Games Administration Committee it would have to come through official channels. This in itself was not particularly concerning. What *was* significant, however, was the fact that if the contents of the letter *had* been accepted, they would have had the effect of undermining the conclusions in the referee's report. Director General of the GAA, Liam Mulvihill, had pointed out in an affidavit that the disciplinary structures and committees of the GAA were premised on treating the referee's report as conclusive with regard to matters contained in the report. Thus, the impact of the court's conclusion in this case—that fair procedures required the consideration of a document aimed at undermining the referee's report—is arguably enormous.

Finally, in September 2004, Irish international handball player, Tom Sheridan, obtained an interlocutory injunction lifting a six-month suspension imposed on him, and thereby freeing him to play in the All-Ireland Handball Final. Mr Sheridan had been suspended in August 2004 for six months in respect of an incident that had arisen in a match in August 2003. During the match he alleged that he had spoken to the referee and told him that one of his opponents had threatened to break his jaw. On the other hand, the referee's report—which Mr Sheridan said was only delivered to him in January 2004 but which the relevant sub-committee of the Irish Handball Council said was received by Sheridan in October 2003—cited *him* for a pushing incident. Mr Sheridan alleged that whichever version of the timeframe was accepted, the GAA had failed to comply with its own rules which required that the referee submit his report within 14 days after a game. He further argued that because of procedural flaws he was denied an appeal against the relevant decision of the sub-committee that suspended him. On the other hand, the Irish Handball Council and the GAA argued that he should be refused the equitable relief, *inter alia*, for lack of candour in that he had not disclosed to the court the fact that the referee had stopped the 2003 match temporarily to issue a warning to

Mr Sheridan in respect of the pushing incident. It further argued that Mr Sheridan had failed to co-operate with the internal disciplinary investigation into the alleged incident in November 2003. In granting the interlocutory relief sought, White J. pointed out that there were procedural flaws in the manner in which the rules of the association were applied in this case. He further noted that had the rules been complied with at a prompt disciplinary hearing in November 2003, then any six-month suspension would now have run its course and the matter need not have troubled the court.

Succession Law

ALBERT KEATING, B.C.L., LL.B., LL.M., B.L.
Senior Lecturer in Law
Law Department, Waterford Institute of Technology

UNDUE INFLUENCE—DURESS—DELAY— INORDINATE AND INEXCUSABLE DELAY

Things were unusually quiet on the probate and succession law front in the year 2004. Even s.117 of the Succession Act 1965, which can normally be relied upon to produce at least one annual variation on the theme, has also been unusually quiet. This is in marked contrast to the three rather interesting s.117 applications which came before the courts in 2003—*In the Estate of ABC, XC, YC and ZC v RT, KU and JL*, unreported, High Court, Kearns J., April 2, 2003; *DS v KM and D*, unreported, High Court, Carroll J., December 19, 2003; *K.C. v C.F.*, unreported, High Court, Carroll J. December 16, 2003— and one case involving the duties of a personal representative, *Sarah Gunning v Eileen Gunning Hameed*, unreported, High Court, Smyth J., July 31, 2003 (see *Annual Review of Irish Law 2003*, p.434.) In fact, there would have been nothing to report for the year 2004 but for one gem of a case involving an application to strike out proceedings for duress and undue influence on the grounds of inordinate and inexcusable delay.

An application to have proceedings struck out may be made to the courts because of a delay on the part of plaintiffs in circumstances where such delay would result in prejudice being suffered by defendants to the extent that it poses a real and serious risk of an unfair trial. The test to be applied in this regard may depend on whether there is a pre-commencement or a post-commencement delay in proceedings. The test for a pre-commencement delay is that taken from the decisions of the Supreme Court in *O'Domhnaill v Merrick* [1984] I.R. 151 and in *Toal v Duignan (No.1)* [1991] I.L.R.M. 135. (See also *Kelly v O'Leary* [2001] 2 I.R. 526.) The test in those cases is a wider one, based on general principles of fairness regardless of whether or not the delay was excusable. The test for post-commencement delay is more stringent. The Supreme Court decision in *Primor v Stokes Kennedy Crowley* [1996] 2 I.R. 459, provides the principles on which the inherent jurisdiction of the courts ought to be exercised in cases involving such delay. (See also *Anglo Irish Beef Processors Limited v Montgomery* [2002] 3 I.R. 510 and *Ewins v Independent Newspapers (Ireland) Ltd* [2003] 1 I.R. 583.) It would appear, however, as a result of *Ryan v Doyle*, unreported, High Court, Kelly J., April 23, 2004, that a defendant may accept the more stringent test in *Primor* to be applied to his case, even though the bulk of the delay is pre-commencement of proceedings. Regardless of the test to be applied, the court has to consider whether there is a real and serious risk of an unfair trial as a result of the prejudice engendered by the delay.

In *Ryan v Doyle*, unreported, High Court, Kelly J., April 23, 2004, the first defendant sought an order striking out the plaintiff's claim, pursuant to the inherent jurisdiction of the court, on the grounds of prejudice resulting from inordinate and inexcusable delay in the institution and/or prosecution of the proceedings by the plaintiffs. The second defendant sought a similar order.

The proceedings were initiated by the issue of a plenary summons on October 25, 2001. The plaintiffs were the sisters of John Doyle Junior, deceased (hereafter "Junior"). The plaintiffs and Junior were the children of John Doyle Senior, deceased (hereafter "Senior"). The first defendant was the widow and sole executrix of Junior, who was being sued in her capacity as executrix of Junior's estate. Senior died on December 15, 1985; he had made his will on October 19 of that year. At the time of Senior's death he owned a substantial number of shares in a company called John Doyle and Co. (Horticultural Specialists) Limited (hereafter "the company"). Senior bequeathed his estate, including shareholding in the company, equally to all his children. On October 14, 1986 the plaintiffs entered into a deed of arrangement whereby they disclaimed their interest under the will of Senior together with their interest in the residue of the estate and any share of the estate to which they might have been entitled on intestacy, in consideration of the payment of the sum of £12,260 to each of them. By a further deed of April 28, 1987 the plaintiffs appointed and confirmed to Junior the lands that formed part of the estate of Senior, together with 1,831 shares in the company. The effect of these arrangements was to confer on Junior almost the entire legal and beneficial interest in the company and the residue of Senior's estate.

The first part of the plaintiffs' claim sought a declaration that the arrangements of October 1986 and April 1987 were void because they had allegedly been procured under duress and undue influence, or in the alternative constituted an improvident transaction or unconscionable bargain. The plaintiffs alleged that Junior was domineering, bullying and intimidating and by those means procured the execution of the deeds in question. An order was sought setting aside these transactions. The second part of the plaintiffs' claim was that there existed a collateral agreement, drawn up at or about the time that the transactions were made between Junior and the plaintiffs, the terms of which were that in consideration of the plaintiffs executing the relevant documents, the plaintiffs would remain entitled to receive an equal division of the proceeds of sale and/or rezoning and/or redevelopment and revaluation of the lands that formed part of Senior's estate.

The defendants requested the court to exercise its inherent jurisdiction and strike out the proceedings. They argued that that the plaintiffs were seeking to litigate arrangements and agreements entered into by them in 1986 and 1987 and were therefore guilty of inordinate and inexcusable delay, which gave rise to actual prejudice suffered by them in attempting to defend the case, most particularly by reference to the fact that Junior, who was pivotal to the arrangements, was deceased. Given these factors, the defendants argued that there was a real and serious risk of an unfair trial.

Kelly J., having referred to the Supreme Court decision in *Primor plc v Stokes Kennedy Crowley* [1996] 2 I.R. 459, remarked that although *Primor* dealt with post-commencement delay in proceedings and the case before him dealt largely with pre-commencement proceedings, the decision was still applicable. He went on to say that in *Primor* the Supreme Court had set down the principles upon which the inherent jurisdiction of the court ought to be exercised. A party seeking a dismissal of proceedings by reason of delay must demonstrate that such delay was both inordinate and inexcusable. Even when a delay can be so categorised, the court must also exercise a judgment on whether, in its discretion and on the facts, the balance of justice was in favour of, or against the case proceeding to trial. In considering this obligation:

> "the court is entitled to take into consideration and have regard to the following—(1) the implied constitutional principles of basic fairness of procedures, (2) whether the delay and consequent prejudice in the special facts of the case are such as to make it unfair to the defendant to allow the action to proceed and to make it just to strike out the plaintiff's action, (3) any delay on the part of the defendant—because litigation is a two party operation, the conduct of both parties should be looked at, (4) whether any delay or conduct of the defendant amounts to acquiescence on the part of the defendant in the plaintiff's delay, (5) the fact that conduct by the defendant which induces the plaintiff to incur further expense in pursuing the action does not, in law, constitute an absolute bar preventing the defendant from obtaining a striking out order but it is a relevant factor to be taken into account by the judge in exercising his discretion whether or not to strike out the claim, the weight to be attached to such conduct depending upon all the circumstances of the particular case, (6) whether the delay gives rise to a substantial risk that it is not possible to have a fair trial or is likely to cause have cause serious prejudice to the defendant, (7) the fact that the prejudice of the defendant referred to in (6) may arise in many ways and be other than that merely caused by the delay, including damage to a defendant's reputation and business. Those principles were subsequently reiterated by the Supreme Court in *Anglo Irish Beef Processors Limited v Montgomery* [2002] 3 I.R. 510."

The proceedings were commenced in October 2001, 15 years after the execution of the deeds of October 1986 and 14.5 years after the execution of the subsequent agreement of April 1987. Throughout that time it was open to the plaintiffs to bring proceedings, but they did not do so. Kelly J. was of the opinion that the delay in commencing these proceedings was inordinate, from any point of view.

In one of the grounding affidavits lodged by the plaintiffs an attempt was made to excuse the delay on the basis that it was not until Junior's death that the plaintiffs' case of complaint arose, as it was only then that they realised that he had not honoured the terms of the collateral agreement. They claimed that at the time they executed the documents, and for the remainder of his life, Junior was a very domineering, bullying and intimidating man. They also alleged that he was evasive, and the combination of these traits meant they did never had access to the information that became available to them after he died. However, in reply to these allegations Kelly J. asked: "Why would one hold off instituting proceedings seeking to set aside the deeds by reference to a belief that a man of such character would honour his obligation?" He was not satisfied that any of the excuses proffered by way of explanation for the commencement of proceeding as late as 2001 were valid, and concluded that the delay in instituting the proceedings were both inordinate and inexcusable.

Kelly J. referred to the Supreme Court decision in *Anglo Irish Beef Processors Ltd v Montgomery* and stated that it appeared to him that he had to ask himself whether Junior's absence gave rise to a substantial risk of an unfair trial. In his view that question had to be answered in the affirmative. He went on to say:

> "... because of the inordinate and inexcusable delay in commencing these proceedings very substantial prejudice has been suffered by the first defendant in attempting to defend them. To allow the action to proceed to trial would be to put justice to the hazard and accordingly I propose to exercise my discretion by striking out the plaintiffs' claims against the first defendant."

The essence of the case that was made against the second defendant was that he had failed to advise the plaintiffs in respect of the agreement they had entered into with Junior. It was claimed that he was obliged to advise them to obtain independent legal advice and because he had failed to do so they had entered into an improvident transaction, one foisted upon them by their brother's bullying behaviour. This defendant stated that the court ought not to apply the *Primor* against him as it was applicable only to post-commencement delays. The only matter with which the court was concerned was the existence of a "clear and patent unfairness" in asking a defendant to defend a case after a lengthy time had elapsed. Kelly J. was satisfied that, given the lapse of time between the events complained of and the prejudice to this defendant arising principally from Junior's inability to give evidence, it had been established that there did exist a substantial risk to the possibility of conducting a fair trial. The plaintiffs' claims were also struck out against the second defendant.

Torts

DUTY OF CARE

In *Sharkey v Dunnes Stores (Ireland) Ltd*, High Court, January 28, 2004, the defendant company terminated the plaintiff's contract after nearly 30 years of employment with the company in circumstances that greatly upset the plaintiff. At a meeting to which he was summoned, the head of personnel, after social introductions, said to the plaintiff: "The Company has reviewed its future plans and you are no longer part of their future plans." In spite of repeated requests by the plaintiff, he was never told what the plans were or why he did not figure in them.

The plaintiff's action for damages for breach of contract failed as the cessation package offered by the defendant was, in Smyth J.'s view, sufficient to discharge its contractual obligations, provided (as Smyth J. clarified) this offer was considered still open for acceptance by the plaintiff. The plaintiff's claim for damages for the negligent infliction of emotional suffering also failed, both on the evidence and on legal grounds, apparently on the basis of lack of foreseeability and the absence of a duty of care resting on the defendant in the circumstances of the case.

In the *Annual Review of Irish Law 2003*, pp.526–532, we critically analysed the Supreme Court decision of *Fletcher v Commissioner of Public Works in Ireland* [2003] 1 I.R. 465, dismissing on policy grounds the claim for negligence of an employee who had developed a foreseeable psychiatric illness rendering him afraid of developing mesothelioma, as a result of having been negligently exposed by his employer to asbestos for a long period. The court left open the question whether, in order to have a sustainable claim, it was necessary to develop the disease or whether the onset of pleural plaques would suffice.

In *Packenham v Irish Ferries Ltd*, Supreme Court, January 3, 2005 (*ex tempore*), reversing High Court, February 26, 2004, a defendant employer sought dismissal of claims for negligent exposure of employees to the risk of injury from asbestos. The plaintiffs had not averred that they had sustained, or were likely to sustain, lesions to their lungs or that they suffered from any psychiatric illness.

Finnegan P. made an order staying the action. The Supreme Court reversed this. Geoghegan J. (Fennelly and McCracken JJ. concurring) described Finnegan P.'s order as "unorthodox", though "well meaning". The proper course was to strike out the action. In view of the controversy surrounding *Fletcher* it is useful to quote from Geoghegan J.'s judgment in some detail to see whether it gives us any clues as to the court's present thinking on the issue:

> "Neither the statement of claim nor any evidence that was before the
> court disclosed a cause of action having regard to the judgment of this
> court in *Fletcher*. As Mr. Hayden has rightly pointed out *Fletcher* is
> not the last word on this question of risk of asbestos diseases. Obviously,
> if someone develops asbestosis or an asbestos related disease there will
> be an action. Quite apart from that in my judgment and to a certain
> extent in the former Chief Justice's judgment in *Fletcher* also, questions
> were left open. They were not decided because they did not arise. They
> certainly were not in the proceedings. What would the position be if it
> was found that there were pleural plaques or even possibly microscopic
> fibres and so on? It would depend on what the evidence was and what
> the consequences of that as a matter of probability were likely to be.
> Possibly, there may be an action in a suitable case where either of these
> events can be proved but that is a question for a separate case."

Striking out the action did not preclude the plaintiffs from bringing a "fresh
action on fresh information which they could not have been expected to have
known at the time". Counsel for the defendant had "rightly conceded that no
question would arise of statute bar". Nor did it appear that any question of *res
judicata* could possibly arise.

It is interesting to note Finnegan P.'s willingness to adopt a new approach
to the traditional rule that a tort action must be disposed of once and for all in
one hearing. A similar disposition is apparent in Finnegan's decision in *Smyth
v Ward*, High Court, December 11, 2004, which we discuss below, p.551.

EMPLOYERS' LIABILITY

Who is an "employer"? The question of whether employers' liability should
depend on a formal definition of what constitutes an employer has largely
been answered in the negative by the courts. In contrast to the contexts of
vicarious liability and health and safety legislation, where formalism can feature,
the common law action for negligence is not so fussy. Negligence liability,
after all, depends on the notion of proximity of relationship and it is clearly
possible for parties to be proximate to one another in ways that fall outside a
strict employment relationship. The case law on this issue is discussed by
McMahon & Binchy, *Law of Torts* (3rd ed., 2000), para.18.23.

In *Marsella v J & P Construction Ltd*, High Court, November 30, 2004,
the plaintiff, a plasterer who worked in close conjunction with the third party,
another plasterer, was injured when he fell from scaffolding erected negligently
by the defendant, a main contractor with whom the plaintiff and the third party
were working. The defendant sought to establish that the third party was the

plaintiff's employer or, alternatively, his partner; in either case, the defendant claimed that the third party had owed the plaintiff a duty of care in respect of the security of the scaffolding.

The two men had known each other since they were teenagers and had worked together for many years as a plastering team. They were not partners in the strict legal meaning of that term. There was no partnership agreement, either verbal or written, but they worked as a team on jobs and they had an agreed basis upon which the price for any job done would be split between them after allowing for the overheads and deductions. While this relationship defied any strict legal categorisation, it enjoyed a form of acceptance or recognition by the Revenue Commissioners. It was based on a Form C45 used by registered subcontractors. It also contained a certain informal fluidity. If a particular job was obtained through a contact of the third party, a business name of his would be named on the C45 form as the subcontractor to whom the main contractor would make his payment for the job sub-contracted, and the profit after overheads and disbursements would be equally shared among what was known as "the group", which would comprise the plaintiff and any other plasterers on that job. The plaintiff therefore would be named on the C45 as the recipient of a certain sum, and would himself thereafter make his own return to the Revenue in respect of his tax liability.

Conversely, if a particular job was obtained through a contact of the plaintiff's, the payment would be made to him by the main contractor, and the third party would be named on the C45 as part of the group, and would be shown on the C45 as having received a certain sum, and would make his own return to the Revenue Commissioners. This type of working relationship was well known in the trade, and apparently applied not only to plasterers but also to other trades working regularly as subcontractors.

On the basis of the evidence in the case, Peart J. was satisfied that the relationship between the two men was not one which imposed any duty of care on the third party to the plaintiff in respect of the injuries that the plaintiff received in the accident.

Peart J. considered it :

> "virtually impossible to categorise the relationship by the use of any term normally used to describe the relationship between two men working together. But I am satisfied that although there is some loose form of profit-sharing within the relationship, both are in reality self-employed persons who come together from time to time and work as a team, but without either being subsumed into any relationship with the other as an employee or into a partnership as such. One could perhaps describe it as a *sui generis* relationship enjoyed between sub-contractors in the plastering trade. I am satisfied on the evidence that the plaintiff was never employed by the third party in the normal sense of the term 'employed'."

Whatever the relationship between the plaintiff and the third party, it was not that of employer/employee in the normal sense of that term such as would create obligations on the third party as employer. Obviously the third party would owe the duty of care not to do a negligent act during the course of working with him on the scaffolding but that was "another matter altogether" and not relevant to the case.

Peart J. went on to hold that the defendant had owed, and breached, a duty of care to the plaintiff. In his view, the question of liability could be decided "by the ordinary principles regarding the duty of care owed in certain situations by one person to another". There was no need to decide whether the plaintiff was contractor in any sense relevant to the health and safety regulations. It had been clearly foreseeable that someone such as the plaintiff, a plasterer, would be using the scaffolding and the element of proximity was also clearly present since the senior member of the defendant company had engaged what he believed to be a plastering subcontractor to do the work. It was "of no relevance really" whether he believed he was engaging just the third party rather than the "team" comprising the third party and the plaintiff. What was beyond any doubt was that the duty of care had been owed to whatever person was in fact plastering with the aid of the scaffolding.

Work stress   If an employee is placed under severe stress in his or employment to such a degree that he or she suffers from a psychological or psychiatric injury, in what circumstances is the employer liable, under common law or statutory principles? Laffoy J answer this question in the *McGrath v Trintech Technologies Ltd*, High Court, October 29, 2004.

The plaintiff claimed that his employer had been guilty of negligence and breach of statutory duty for causing him psychiatric damage as a result of work-related stress and for failing to respond adequately to his condition as it unfolded. The plaintiff had been employed in the information technology sector, working in a number of countries, including Korea, South Africa and Uruguay.

Laffoy J gave a comprehensive analysis of the common law developments in other jurisdictions. It may be useful to quote a statement of the 16 "practical propositions" set out by the English Court of Appeal in *Hatton v Sutherland* [2002] 2 All E.R. 1 as determinants of liability for stress-induced psychiatric injury in an employment context:

> "(1) There are no special control mechanisms applying to claims for psychiatric (or physical) illness or injury arising from the stress of doing the work the employee is required to do. What this means is that 'policy' considerations of the type referred to by Geoghegan J. in his judgment in ... *Fletcher v Commissioner for Public Works* [2003] 1 I.R. 465 do not arise. Distinctions which are made in determining liability for psychiatric harm in other circumstances, for example, distinguishing between "primary" and "secondary"

victims, have no application in the case of psychiatric injury arising from stress in the workplace.

(2) The threshold question is whether this kind of harm to this particular employee was reasonably foreseeable. This has two components:

    (a) an injury to health (as distinct from occupational stress), which

    (b) is attributable to stress at work (as distinct from other factors). In the earlier analysis of the issue of foreseeability, it was stated … that the question is not whether psychiatric injury is foreseeable in a person of "ordinary fortitude". The employer's duty is owed to each individual employee.

(3) Foreseeability depends upon what the employer knows, or ought reasonably to know, about the individual employee. Because of the nature of mental disorder, it is harder to foresee than physical injury, but it may be easier to foresee in a known individual than in the population at large. An employer is usually entitled to assume that the employee can withstand the normal pressures of the job unless he knows of some particular problem or vulnerability.

(4) The test is the same whatever the employment: there are no occupations which should be regarded as intrinsically dangerous to mental health.

(5) Factors likely to be relevant in answering the threshold question included the following:

    (a) The nature and extent of the work done by the employee. Is the workload much more than is normal for the particular job? Is the work particularly intellectually or emotionally demanding for this employee? Are demands being made of this employee unreasonable when compared with the demands made of others in the same or comparable job? Or are there signs that others doing the job are suffering from harmful levels of stress? Is there an abnormal level of sickness or absenteeism in the same job or the same department?

    (b) Signs from the employee of impending harm to health. Has he a particular problem or vulnerability? Has he already suffered from illness attributable to stress at work? Have there recently been frequent or prolonged absences which are uncharacteristic of him? Is there reason to think that these are attributable to stress at work, for example, because of complaints or warnings from him or others?

(6) The employer is generally entitled to take what he is told by his employee at face value, unless he has good reason to think to the contrary. He does not generally have to make searching enquiries of the employee or seek permission to make further enquiries of his medical advisers.

(7) To trigger a duty to take steps, the indications of impending harm
     to health arising from stress at work must be plain enough for any
     reasonable employer to realise that he should do something about
     it.

(8) The employer is only in breach of duty if he has failed to take the
     steps which are reasonable in the circumstances, bearing in mind
     the magnitude of the risk of harm occurring, the gravity of the
     harm which may occur, the costs and practicability of preventing
     it, and the justifications for running the risk.

(9) The size and scope of the employer's operation, its resources and
     the demands it faces are relevant in deciding what is reasonable;
     these include the interests of other employees and the need to treat
     them fairly, for example, in any redistribution of duties.

(10) An employer can only reasonably be expected to take steps which
     are likely to do some good and the court is likely to need expert
     evidence on this.

(11) An employer who offers a confidential advice service, with referral
     to appropriate counselling or treatment services, is unlikely to be
     found in breach of duty.

(12) If the only reasonable and effective step would have been to dismiss
     or demote the employee, the employer will not be in breach of
     duty in allowing a willing employee to continue in the job.

(13) In all cases, therefore, it is necessary to identify the steps which
     the employer both should and could have taken before finding
     him in breach of his duty of care.

(14) The plaintiff must show that the breach of duty has caused or
     materially contributed to the harm suffered. It is not enough to
     show that occupational stress has caused the harm. Earlier, in its
     analysis of the issue of causation, the Court ... illustrated the
     distinction inherent in this proposition. Where there are several
     different causes, as will often be the case with stress related illness
     of any kind, the plaintiff may have difficulty proving the employer's
     fault was one of them. This will be a particular problem if the
     main cause was a vulnerable personality which the employer knew
     nothing about.

(15) Where the harm suffered has more than one cause, the employer
     should only pay for that proportion of the harm suffered which is
     attributable to his wrongdoing, unless the harm is truly indivisible.
     It is for the defendant to raise the question of apportionment.

(16) The assessment of damages will take account of any pre-existing
     disorder or vulnerability and of the chance that the claimant would

have succumbed to a stress-related disorder in any event. Earlier, in dealing with the issue of quantification, the Court ...stated that where the tortfeasor's breach of duty has exacerbated a pre-existing disorder or accelerated the effect of pre-existing vulnerability, the award of general damages for pain, suffering and loss of amenity will reflect only the exacerbation or acceleration. Further, the quantification of damages for financial losses may take some account of contingency for example, the chance that the plaintiff would have succumbed to a stress-related disorder in any event and this may be reflected in the multiplier to be applied in quantifying future loss of earnings."

Laffoy J went on to discuss the decision of *Barber v Somerset County Council* [2004] 2 All E.R. 385, in which one of the plaintiffs in the *Hatton* group of cases had appealed to the House of Lords.

Laffoy J. observed that:

"[t]he effect of the decisions of the Court of Appeal and the House of Lords in the Hatton/Barber case is to assimilate the principles governing an employer's liability at common law for physical injury and for psychiatric injury where an employee claims that the psychiatric injury has resulted from the stress and pressures of his or her working conditions and workload. In my view, there is no reason in law or in principle why a similar approach should not be adopted in this jurisdiction. I consider that the practical propositions summarised in the judgment of the Court of Appeal in the Hatton case are helpful in the application of legal principle in an area which is characterised by difficulty and complexity, subject, however, to the caveat of Lord Walker in the *Barber* case – that one must be mindful that every case will depend on its own facts."

If in the instant case, Laffoy J held on the evidence that the defendant had not been guilty of negligence. It had not been aware of the plaintiffs vulnerability to psychological harm. The plaintiff's workload had not been unduly demanding and there are no warning signs of existing or impending injury.

As regards alleged breaches of the Safety Health and Welfare at Work Act 1989 and the Safety, Health and Welfare at Work (General Applications) Regulations 1993 (S.I. No.44 of 1993), Laffoy J considered that, even if the defendant's safety statement had addressed the issue of stress, and structures had been in place for monitoring stress in the workplace and, even if the defendant had an employee assistance programme in place in its Irish operations, these measures would not have made a difference to the outcome.

Laffoy J rejected the plaintiff's argument that, where a prima facie case had been made out, the onus shifted onto the defendant to advance an alternative cause for his injuries:

> "The issue is not whether the stress the plaintiff suffered was caused by work, but whether the stress-induced injury was a consequence of a breach by the defendant of its statutory duties. Where an employee is injured because of the malfunction of a faulty piece of equipment given to him by his employer, the causative link is obvious. The injury would not have been inflicted if the faulty piece of equipment had not been given to the employee. The question which arises here is whether it can be said, as a matter of probability, that if the defendant took all of the steps which the plaintiff contends it was statutorily obliged to take (dealing with workplace stress in the safety statement, having in place a system for monitoring stress and an employee assistance programme and providing further training for the plaintiff) the plaintiff would not have suffered psychological injury. In my view it cannot."

Contributory negligence In *Marsella v J & P Construction Ltd*, High Court, November 30, 2004, which we have just discussed, the plaintiff, who had many years' experience, fell through a gap in the floor of scaffolding erected negligently by the defendant. Peart J. reduced the award by 20 per cent to take account of the plaintiff's contributory negligence. Peart J. was:

> "satisfied that the plaintiff was at the time a very experienced plasterer. That experience will have told him that care is required to ensure that an item such as a scaffold is a potentially dangerous position to work from. That potential danger is reflected in the need for regulations in the manner in which scaffolding over a certain height is concerned. Even if the height of this platform was not over that limit, the plaintiff himself cannot work on an assumption that the platform is safe. However, clearly the main contractor bears a larger portion of the responsibility to ensure that the scaffolding is safely constructed."

Peart J. was prepared to accept that on a casual observation of the structure from the floor the plaintiff might not have noticed the fact that the planks were short at one end, thereby causing a gap to exist which was dangerous. Moreover, while working on the platform in the act of putting plaster on the ceiling, he would be looking upwards and not towards the planks in the direction in which he was working. But this latter fact, in Peart J.'s view, placed on the plaintiff, before he commenced his work, the obligation to check that the area where his feet would travel while he was looking upwards at the ceiling was safe.

Reducing the plaintiff's award by 20 per cent, Peart J. observed that:

> "[i]f he was less experienced, that would be reflected in a lesser finding of contributory negligence perhaps, but it defies commonsense, if

> nothing else, to mount a structure such as this one and for the purpose in this case, not to adequately check its safety before commencing work upon it."

An interesting question arises in regard to the relationship between the parties in this case because Peart J. held that it was not one of employer/employee. Where an employer/employee relationship exists, the courts have traditionally been indulgent to carelessness on the part of employees when deciding whether to condemn their carelessness as involving contributory negligence. The reason for this indulgence was of course that, prior to 1961, contributory negligence afforded a complete defence to an action for negligence. The idea that an employer, guilty of negligence of an egregious kind, should be relieved of any liability to a somewhat careless employee was unpalatable to courts even in the most *laissez faire* times.

In claims for breach of statutory duty taken by employees against employers, the courts were, if anything, even more resolute not to let the social policy underlying the legislative provisions imposing such a duty be frustrated by dismissal of a claim on account of relatively minor carelessness on the part of the employee. The enactment of the Civil Liability Act 1961 might perhaps have been considered to have encouraged a change from the traditional judicial indulgence towards careless employees since the courts would be free to make a modest reduction in the amount awarded rather than have to confront the crude option of a complete dismissal of the claim. There has not, however, been any discernible hardening of judicial attributes towards moderately careless employees over the past four decades. The courts have also retained the distinction between claims against employers for common law negligence and claims for breach of statutory duty. Contributory negligence falling within the latter category is still treated more leniently than in the former. (Whether this can be justified under the 1961 Act is a real issue.)

At all events, courts have yet to address specifically the question whether the lenient policy towards employees in negligence claims against employers should be carried over to claims against defendants who are not employers but whose relationship with the plaintiff bears some close similarity to that of employer. We suggest that the answer should depend on the particular nature of that relationship. If it involves long-term, ongoing control of an enterprise by the defendant, the court may well find resonances that encourage it to adopt a paternalistic approach. If, however, the relationship between the parties is one at arm's length, with no obvious imbalance of power, the argument for application of paternalistic norms seems misplaced. In the instant case, the plaintiff was, in essence, an independent contractor, a skilled plasterer engaging with the defendant on equal terms. This may perhaps explain why Peart J. showed him no leniency in reducing his compensation by 20 per cent to take account of his contributory negligence.

In *Keogh v Minister for Defence*, High Court, January 20, 2004, an "army deafness" claim, Peart J. held that the failure of a member of the FCA with many years' experience to wear appropriate ear protection did not constitute contributory negligence. As far as the plaintiff was concerned at the relevant time, on the basis of information provided to him by the defendants, he did not suffer from such hearing loss as would warrant him wearing such protection. He was not aware that his condition was a good deal more serious, requiring resort to such protection, as the defendants had failed negligently to pass on to him the relevant result of a hearing test, in circumstances that induced in him the reasonable belief that all was well.

OCCUPIERS' LIABILITY

Recklessness Under s.4(1) of the Act, an occupier, in respect of a danger existing on premises, owes towards a recreational user of the premises or a trespasser a duty not to injure him or her (or his or her property) intentionally nor "to act with reckless disregard for the person or the property of the person". What does recklessness involve?

In *McGowan v Dun Laoghaire/Rathdown County Council and Sandycove Bathers' Association*, High Court, May 7, 2004, de Valera J. ruled that the defendants had been guilty of acting with reckless disregard for the safety of the plaintiff who had been paralysed when he struck a rock outcrop when diving at the Forty Foot in Sandycove. The outcrop was invisible. There was no warning of the danger. Had there been, de Valera J. indicated that the defendants would have discharged their duty to the plaintiff. De Valera J.'s analysis of s.4 of the 1995 Act suggests that he interpreted the several factors listed therein as prescribing, in substantial effect, a test somewhere between negligence and gross negligence.

This was not the interpretation favoured by the Supreme Court in *Weir Rodgers v The S.F. Trust Ltd*, on January 21, 2005. There the court, while not taking a final position on the question, canvassed interpretations of recklessness as involving negligence even more egregious than gross negligence or a subjective test; we shall analyse this alarming decision in the *Annual Review of Irish Law 2005*. It is also worth noting the recent decisions of the High Court of Australia in *Mulligan v Coffs Harbour City Council* and *Vairy v Wyong Shire Council*, on October 21, 2005, in favour of the councils on facts quite similar to those in *McGowan*.

"Activity" duty An intriguing and important question relates to the scope of operation of the Occupiers' Liability Act 1995. Section 3(1) imposes on an occupier of premises a "common duty of care" towards a visitor. Section 3(2) provides that this duty is to take such care as is reasonable in all circumstances to ensure that the visitor of the premises does not suffer injury or damage "by reason of any danger existing thereon". "Danger" in relation to any premises is, in turn, defined by s.1 as meaning "a danger due to the state of the premises". Does this imply that a danger due to some other cause—such as the active conduct of the occupier—falls outside the scope of the 1995 Act, and continues to be determined by common law principles?

In *Hackett v Calla Associates Ltd*, High Court, October 21, 2004, an affirmative answer was given to the question. The plaintiff had lost the sight in one eye when struck by a weapon carried by a bouncer at a nightclub. Peart J. held that the defendants could not be sued as occupiers under s.3 of the 1995 Act as the danger had not related to the state of the premises. Having quoted the definition of "danger" in s.1, Peart J noted:

> "It must follow from this that the plaintiff's claim is not one coming within the duty of care imposed by Section 3 as the allegations of negligence are not related in any way to the state of the premises but rather the behaviour of the bouncers on the night in question. It is necessary to consider this claim by reference to the more usual non-statutory criteria in relation to the possible breach of the common law duty of care owed to the plaintiff by the owners/occupier of the premises, diluted possibly by the contribution which the plaintiff's own behaviour made to what befell him at the hands of their employees, servants or agents."

In the instant case, the difference between common law liability and liability under s.3 was not significant. In the years before the enactment of the 1995 Act, the courts had increasingly treated the duties owed to invitees as in essence one of negligence: the refinements and limitations as to "unusual dangers" prescribed by *Indermaur v Dames* (1866) L.R. 1 C.P. 274 had lost much of their force. The plaintiff in the instant case would probably even have been categorised as a contractual entrant, to whom (in the absence of express terms) an implied duty of due care would have been owed. The real area of controversy relates to trespassers and the new category of recreational users created by the 1995 Act. Under s.4 of the Act, the only obligation that the occupier has relative to them is not to injure them intentionally and not to act in reckless disregard of them. Section 4, of course, reversed the developments at common law in *Purtill v Athlone UDC* [1968] I.R. 205 and *McNamara v ESB* [1975] I.R. 1, which permitted trespassers with sufficient proximity of relationship to occupiers to sue the occupiers for negligence. If the definition of "danger" in s.1 has the effect of replacing common law claims by the 1995 Act only where the danger is due to the state of the premises, then it may be argued that a trespasser who was injured as a result of the occupier's conduct rather than the state of the premises will still be able to invoke *Purtill* and *McNamara*. If this is so, farmers who lobbied for the legislation will receive an unpleasant surprise.

We should note here that Herbert J. took a somewhat different view of the issue in *Meagher v Shamrock Public Houses Ltd t/a the Ambassador Hotel*,

High Court, February 16, 2005. We shall examine this case in detail in the *Annual Review of Irsih Law 2005*.

Who is the occupier?   In *Hackett v Calla Associates Ltd*, High Court, October 21, 2004 the question of who was occupier of the premises on which the plaintiff was attacked by a bouncer fell for consideration. We have already discussed the facts of this case. The bouncer received his payment from an employer of the owner (Calla). There was a lease between Calla and the second defendant (Mr O'Reilly), who was also the transferee of the licence. Although the bouncer was not paid by Mr O'Reilly, Peart J. held on the evidence that both Calla and Mr O'Reilly were occupiers of the premises. After a detailed review of the terms of the agreement under which Calla let the premises to Mr O'Reilly, Peart J. stated:

> "It is clearly recognised in this Agreement that Mr. O'Reilly's interest as occupier is to be noted on the insurance policies which the Lessor Calla has covenanted to put in place. It is also clearly stated as one would expect that Calla will indemnify Mr. O'Reilly against all Public Liability Claims arising from incidents at the premises. That implies that Mr. O'Reilly is intended to be the first target of any such claim, and that Calla will simply indemnify him in respect of same. I do not believe that the fact that the bouncers are stated to have been paid in cash at the end of the night by an employee of Calla can render nugatory the terms of a legally binding agreement which has formed the basis of a licence transfer in the District Court and under which Mr. O'Reilly holds the licence to run the premises. I am not privy to what precise arrangements have or have not been made outside the terms of that agreement, and they ought not to interfere with what appears to be the legal position arising from the document itself.
>
> It is also relevant that under the Agreement, as set forth above, Mr. O'Reilly has responsibility for Employee Liability insurance claims, as well as ensuring that the premises are run properly.
>
> In my view there is such a mingling of functions between both Calla and Mr. O'Reilly, according to the evidence, and such a relationship created by the Agreement, that it can reasonably and properly be said that both the defendants are occupiers of the premises and that each owe a duty to the visiting public, including the plaintiff. Since the Agreement actually refers to Mr. O'Reilly as an occupier for the purposes of insurance, he cannot now say that he is not an occupier, particularly as he is the holder of the licence by virtue of the Transfer of the licence to him by virtue of this agreement. Equally, Calla has accepted that as a matter of fact the bouncers were their employees. I am satisfied therefore that the liability to the plaintiff is one which is joint and several. The plaintiff ought to be entitled to recover from

either defendant, and the paying defendant will be entitled on the basis
of joint and several liability to recover appropriately from the non-paying
defendant."

Visitors *Hall v Meehan*, High Court, December 17, 2004 is of interest even
though it was decided on the basis of common law occupiers' liability
principles. It concerns a six-year-old pupil who was injured when he collided
with another pupil when running in the playground of the defendant's school.
He fell backwards onto a kerb and suffered an internal injury to his left kidney
when he came in contact with a breeze block. The accident occurred in 1992.
In the late 1980s the school in question had been in need of repair but the
school authorities were not in a position to obtain any funds from the
Department of Education.

As a result various parents had come together and brought in sand and soil
in order to make a playing area. They had surrounded this area with concrete
breeze blocks which were laid on their side to separate the path area immediately
outside the school from the playing field area. The Department of Education
was probably not aware that this voluntary work had been carried out.

Gilligan J. imposed liability on the school. He characterised the plaintiff
as an invitee under common law. Although he quoted the somewhat restrictive
test in regard to invitees which Willes J. had laid down in *Indermaur v Dames*
(1866) LR CP 274, Gilligan J. noted that, in *Foley v Musgrave Cash & Carry*,
Supreme Court, December 20, 1985, McCarthy J. had taken the view that the
court should no longer be talking about "unusual dangers" in the type of case
before the court and that the general negligence approach was to be preferred.
Griffin J., while admitting that the plaintiff was an invitee, took the view that
the duty of the occupier was to take reasonable care in all the circumstances to
see that the premises were reasonably safe for the invitee.

Gilligan J. concluded on the evidence that the kerbing that was in place
"was of a makeshift variety consisting of rough concrete breeze blocks with a
sharp edge and broken in places". This kerbing was inappropriate for installation
on a school premises where six-year-old boys would be running and, as would
be normal, falling. The sharp rough edge of the kerbing presented an unusual
danger to school children, particularly of a tender age, and a danger of which
the defendant knew or ought reasonably to have known. It appeared self-evident
from photographs put in evidence that, if a child were to fall against the sharp
rough edge of the kerb stone, an injury was likely to follow and the significance
of that injury would be determined by the velocity involved in impact against
the sharp edge. Gilligan J. rejected a causal challenge on the evidence and
also noted that "[q]uite correctly no allegation to contributory negligence [had
been] made out against the plaintiff having regard to his tender years at the
time of the accident". (This latter holding can best be understood as meaning
that the plaintiff could not reasonably have appreciated the particular danger
of the breeze block kerb in view of his lack of age and experience rather than
that six-year-olds are incapable of contributory negligence.)

Hall v Meehan is of interest because it applies, in essence, a negligence test, following *Foley*. It is therefore easily adaptable to claims by school pupils under s.3 of the Occupiers' Liability Act 1995.

An interesting feature of the case was that relating to resources. The school in question was a two-teacher premises in need of repair. Gilligan J. noted that:

> "unfortunately the school authorities were not in a position to obtain any funds from the Department of Education as a result of which various parents came together and brought in sand and soil in order to make a playing area and surrounded this area with concrete breeze blocks which were laid on their side to separate the path area immediately outside the school from the playing field area. This was voluntary work on behalf of the parents and [the person] who was the school principal at the time of this accident has given evidence that the breeze blocks would have been in position for approximately 4–5 years prior to the accident the subject matter of these proceedings."

The former school principal accepted in evidence that the Department of Education were probably not even aware that this voluntary work had been carried out by the children's parents in order to better the school facilities in the absence of any funds being available.

Gilligan J., in his holding regarding liability, did not return to this aspect of the case. No doubt questions may arise in the future as to whether the State should be exposed to liability, exclusively or in conjunction with a school, where inadequate funding has been provided and the premises are clearly dangerous as a result. Another issue may relate to work done by parents without the knowledge of the Department of Education. In the unlikely case where work is completed surreptitiously, without the knowledge or approval of the school principal, then it is possible that the school authorities will not be liable, provided of course that in the ordinary course of events, the school management, as reasonable occupier, would not have discovered the work. Where, as will surely be the position in the overwhelming majority of cases, the school management is or ought to be aware of the work, then its duty of care cannot be shuffled off onto the parents.

Contributory negligence The defence of contributory negligence applies in relation to claims under the Occupiers' Liability Act 1995. Of course, the issue of the entrant's carelessness will already have arisen when determining the prior question as to whether the occupier was in breach of his or her statutory duty. Thus, for example, s.3(2) provides that "the common duty of care" means "a duty to take such care as is reasonable in all the circumstances (*having regard to the care which a visitor may reasonably be expected to take for his or her own safety ...*) to ensure that a visitor to the premises does not suffer injury or damage by reasons of any danger existing thereon" (emphasis added). So, also, s.5(5) provides that:

> "[w]here injury or damage is caused to a visitor or property of a visitor by a danger of which the visitor had been warned by the occupier or another person, the warning is not, without more, to be treated as absolving the occupier from liability unless in all the circumstances, *it was enough to enable the visitor, by having regard to the warning, to avoid the injury or damage, so caused*" (emphasis added).

To take a clear example, if an occupier were to explain to a visitor that a particular light fitting in the ceiling will give an electric shock and to request the visitor not to touch it, the foolish visitor who touches the fitting will lose his claim not on the ground of contributory negligence but on the prior ground of the absence of any liability on the part of the occupier in the first place.

In two cases, the issue of an entrant's contributory negligence was addressed. In *Hall v Meehan*, High Court, December 17, 2004, which we have just discussed, a six-year-old plaintiff was injured when he fell backwards on sharp-edged breezeblocks in the defendant's school playground. Gilligan J. simply observed that "[q]uite correctly no allegation of contributory negligence is made out against the plaintiff having regard to his tender years at the time of the accident". Gilligan J. was here scarcely reviving the old judicial tendency—mercifully in abeyance—to try to identify the minimum age at which children are capable of contributory negligence. To such an unwise question there simply can be no definitive answer since the development of such capacity depends on the particular circumstances of each individual child. What Gilligan J. surely meant was that a six-year-old child could not be regarded as acting carelessly in playing in a school yard with the sharp breeze blocks *in situ*. The child may well have been already aware of the bricks' sharp edges but what was he to do in the light of such knowledge?

In *Hackett v Calla Associates Ltd*, High Court, October 21, 2004, where a nightclub patron was injured by a bouncer, Peart J. reduced his compensation by 50 per cent, stating that, although a member of the security staff had used unreasonable force:

> "the plaintiff has to share in the responsibility for what happened to him that night. His involvement ... amounts to contributory negligence. The question as always is to what degree. One is more accustomed to assessing contributory negligence in the context of a car accident or an accident at work. In such cases it would be unusual to make a large deduction on account of contributory negligence, because in most cases the element of contributory negligence arises due to perhaps not wearing a seat-belt, exceeding a speed limit, failing to observe an on-coming car and so forth. What I am trying to convey is that in such cases the

plaintiff is guilty of relatively minor negligence not worthy of being severely marked by a large reduction in damages. In the present case the plaintiff's behaviour is of a different character. It was criminal behaviour such as should not be implicitly condoned by a sympathetic approach to contributory negligence. It cannot be equated to the type of contributory negligence more commonly found in road accidents or workplace accidents. It is culpable behaviour for which the plaintiff must retain responsibility. In my view, even though the defendants are liable to him for an unreasonable use of force, and even though the Court feels great sympathy for the fact that the plaintiff has now only the use of one eye, he has himself to blame to a significant extent, and to an extent far in excess of the more normal type of case to which I have referred."

PRODUCT LIABILITY

The question of the need for an inflammability warning on children's clothes and the manner in which such a warning should be conveyed has arisen in several Irish cases over the past decade and a half. They include *O'Byrne v Gloucester*, Supreme Court, November 3, 1988, analysed in the *Annual Review of Irish Law 1988*, pp.433–434; *Duffy v Rooney and Dunnes Stores (Dundalk) Ltd*, High Court, June 23, 1997, affirmed by Supreme Court, April 23, 1998, analysed in the *Annual Review of Irish Law 1997*, pp.745–752; and *Cassells v Marks and Spencers plc* [2002] 1 I.R. 179, analysed in the *Annual Review of Irish Law 2001*, p.595.

In *Rodgers v Adams Children's Wear Ltd*, High Court, February 11, 2003, the six-year-old plaintiff received severe burns when the summer dress she was wearing went on fire when it came in contact with an open turf fire in her kitchen. She sued the defendant, as manufacturer and retailer of her dress, for negligence and breach of statutory duty.

The dress when bought had a label sewn into the side seam about 9cm above the hem with a button sewn on beside it and with information as to the type of material (100 per cent viscose) and a warning in red to "keep away from fire". On the reverse side there were care instructions and the defendant's address.

The plaintiff's mother said she had checked to see if there was a fire warning on the dress. There was none at the neck or on the hanging label. She said that she would not have bought it if there was a fire warning. She did not check inside the dress for a label and she did not know it was there until after the accident. If she had found the warning after she got home, she would have brought it back to the shop. She said she would not have to read the label for care instructions as she would know how to treat the garment. She claimed she could identify viscose by the feel as it was silky whereas cotton would be dry to feel.

The essence of the plaintiff's claim was that the defendant should be stigmatised for having failed to test for flammability; for having produced a garment which it ought to have known had low flame resistance and was highly inflammable; for having failed to give an adequate fire warning; for having failed to treat the garment with chemical fire retardant; for having failed to comply with its own policy document by failing to put the fire warning at the neck or beside the label which stated the size of the garment; and, finally, under the European Communities (General Product Safety) Regulations 1997 (S.I. No.197 of 1997), (a) as a producer, for having put a product on the market that was not a safe product (in breach of reg.4), for having failed to provide all relevant information (in breach of reg.5) and for having failed to carry out sample testing (in breach of reg.6), and (b) as a distributor, for having failed to act with due care to ensure that the dress was safe (in breach of reg.7(1)) and for having supplied what it knew or should have known was a dangerous product (in breach of reg.7(2)).

Carroll J. dismissed the action. Carroll J. dealt first with the argument based on failure to have tested for flammability. Her analysis of this (and a number of the plaintiff's other arguments) involved an integration of the requirements of the 1997 Regulations with those of common law negligence. She regarded these Regulations as setting the standard of care, even though the Regulations do not prescribe civil liability. She noted that, under reg.6(b), testing was required only "if appropriate". The need to test fabrics was dealt with in IS 138/1998. Under that standard, only fabric used in children's nightdresses and dressing gowns had to be tested. The Director of Consumer Affairs had given no direction in relation to sample testing of the product. The fact that another manufacturer—Marks and Spencers—had introduced internal testing did not mean that the defendant was also obliged to do so. Accordingly it was not "appropriate" to have carried out sample testing under reg.6.

Carroll J. turned next to the plaintiff's argument that the defendant had been negligent in producing a garment it knew or ought to have known had low flame resistance and was highly flammable without giving adequate warning to the plaintiff. She noted that all fabric was flammable. The dress in the instant case had not been made of the most flammable material. Carroll J. found it:

> "impossible to say what is 'highly' flammable when there is no scientific definition. A fabric can become more flammable by a person standing near a fire and heating the fabric by radiation. If it catches fire it will burn more quickly than the same fabric if it is cold.
>
> It was held in *Cassell*'s case that the wording taken from IS 148/ 1988 was an adequate warning in a dress which was described as 'highly flammable'. It was not argued that the wording in this case should be different.
>
> A dress is not dangerous per se. It does not self ignite. It can go on

fire if a child is permitted to be so close to a fire that the flames reach the fabric. That is what happened in this case. It has been held that the duty of care of the manufacturer is fulfilled if a fire warning is given. The words contained in IS 148/1998 'keep away from fire' have been held to be adequate."

Carroll J. noted that there were no statutory requirements as to where the label should be placed. Requirements relating to the placement of labels in children's nightwear other than nightdresses and dressing gowns under IS 148/1998 did not apply to daywear.

Carroll J. regarded as "incredible" the argument of the plaintiff's mother that, when she did not see a fire warning at the neck or on a hanging tag, she presumed the dress was safe:

"She knew of the existence of fire warning tags. She ignored them in the case of cotton, whether t-shirts, shorts or summer dresses. How could she assume a viscose dress was 'safe' if there were no tags?"

Even if the plaintiff's mother had not seen the warning tag, the test was whether a reasonable person would be expected to notice the tag in the seam. An expert witness had given evidence that he was not aware of any manufacturer who put the label other than in the seam. In Carroll J.'s opinion a fire warning on the tag in the side seam was an adequate warning, regardless of whether it also showed the size.

Carroll J. did not consider that the failure to treat the fabric with fire retardant constituted negligence. She noted that it had been held in *Duffy* and in *Cassells* that it was not necessary to have fire retardant treatment. In the instant case, there had been evidence that it was not feasible. There were no statutory requirements to treat the fabric in children's clothes with fire retardant (other than nightdresses and dressing gowns). The Regulatory Authority had not considered it necessary to treat children's clothes with fire retardant other than nightdresses and dressing gowns.

Neither did the failure by the defendant to comply with its own policies by failing to put a fire warning at the neck or in or beside the size label constitute negligence. The manuals produced by the defendant were directed to its suppliers and did not create any legal obligation as between the defendant and the plaintiff. The defendant was free to alter its policies as it saw fit and it had done so by putting the fire warning on the label sewn into the side seam because that was the quickest way to implement the principal policy of having a fire warning on all children's clothing. The positioning of the warning was secondary. The duty of care required that a fire warning be given and that had been fulfilled by the label in the side seam.

Turning to the General Product Safety Regulations of 1997, Carroll J. first addressed the question of whether the dress was a safe product within the meaning of the definition. It had to be one which under normal and reasonably foreseeable conditions of use did not present any risk or only minimum risk compatible with the product's use, considered as acceptable and consistent with the high level of protection for the safety and health of persons. In determining safety, labelling was to be taken into consideration as well as the categories of consumer at risk, in particular children. Where appropriate, a producer should carry out testing. Where there were no specific rules, no voluntary national standard or community technical specifications, the conformity of a product to the general safety requirements had to be assessed taking into account standards drawn up in the State, codes of good practice in respect of health and safety in the product sector concerned and the state of the art and technology, the safety of which consumers reasonably expect.

Carroll J. dealt with these requirements as follows:

> "The standards which have been laid down are those defined by the High Court and Supreme Court having taken into account the duty of care owed by both a producer and distributor to the person injured. All the case law confirms that if a fire warning is given, the duty of care owed by the manufacturer/retailer is discharged. The Supreme Court has therefore considered it acceptable, that children's daywear with a fire warning may be sold. In doing so they were concerned with the health and safety of the child wearing the product. The labeling was adequate and testing was not appropriate. Also, … 'normal reasonably intended use' did not involve exposure to fire. There are no regulations in any EU Member State for nightwear other than the U.K. and Ireland. There are no regulations in any EU State for daywear. There is no credible evidence to support putting the label at the neck.
>
> In my opinion the dress was a safe product and the Defendant, whether looked at as producer or distributor incurred no liability under the 1997 Regulations."

The dismissal of the plaintiff's claim comes as little surprise. Once the location of the warning on the seam of the dress was considered to be acceptable, there was little prospect of success.

Carroll J.'s interpretation of the General Product Safety Regulations and negligence principles when determining the question of civil liability is interesting. The General Product Safety Directive, either in its original form (which was considered by Carroll J.) or in its revised form (which we discuss below at p.498), does not prescribe civil liability. The Product Liability Directive of 1985, of course, prescribes such liability. The relationship between the two Directives is complex since, in their definitions of key concepts, they do not coincide, though there is a significant overlap. If civil liability is to attach to breaches of the General Product Safety Directive, then anomalies will inevitably arise.

A wider question arises as to the theory of statutory interpretation. In "domestic" tort litigation, where a plaintiff argues that breach of a particular statutory provision enacted by the Oireachtas warrants the imposition of civil liability, the court must engage in the process of trying to establish whether the Oireachtas *intended* there to be such a remedy at civil law. Usually the statutory provision is silent on the question, as are the Oireachtas Debates. The process is not truly one of genuine statutory interpretation but in fact involves policy-based analysis of the merits of imposing civil liability in the particular context.

In regard to the General Product Safety Directive, it would be very difficult to discern a genuine legislative intent to establish civil liability. Whether a European Directive should involve the imposition of civil liability at the national level is not a question that should be answered without some considerable analysis. It is true that the Product Liability Directive operates without prejudice to national rules of tortious liability "existing at the moment when this Directive is notified" (Art.13). Arguably the action for breach of statutory duty—and of course the action for negligence—could be so described; but does that mean that they can extend to the imposition of liability for breach of a European Directive which contains no provisions prescribing civil liability?

The whole question of the relationship between the Product Liability Directive and the General Product Safety Directive is comprehensively analysed by Fabrizio Cafaggi in "A Coordinated Approach to Regulation and Civil Liability in European Law: Rethinking Institutional Complementarities" (EUI Working Paper LAW No. 2005/13).

One simple, though perhaps ultimately less than satisfying, solution would be for a court to "marry" the two Directives by holding that breach of the General Product Safety Directive rendered the product in question defective. Lovell's *Product Safety in the European Union: A Practical Guide to the General Product Safety Directive*, para.9.2, considers that such a development is "conceivable", at least to the extent that proof of such breach would constitute prima facie evidence of defectiveness. It also raises the possibility that it could constitute evidence of negligence under traditional common law principles. It may be, therefore, that *Rodgers* represents a pioneering decision, rather than involving the inappropriate reference to the General Product Safety Directive.

PROFESSIONAL NEGLIGENCE

Doctors   In *Griffin v Patton*, Supreme Court, July 27, 2004, the Supreme Court affirmed a finding by O'Donovan J. of liability in negligence against a consultant obstetrician and gynaecologist who, when removing the remains of a deceased unborn baby of 17 weeks' gestational age from its mother's uterus, had failed to retrieve a piece of bone over 5cm in length. Geoghegan J. (Murray C.J., McGuinness, Hardiman and Fennelly JJ. concurring) disagreed with

O'Donovan J.'s view that, under the principles set out in *Dunne v National Maternity Hospital* [1989] I.R. 91, where two medical experts disagreed as to whether a doctor had fallen below an acceptable standard of care, the judge was not entitled to prefer one view rather than the other and make a finding of negligence. Geoghegan J. considered that the reference in *Dunne* to an "honest difference of opinion between doctors" related to differences regarding diagnosis and ways of treating a patient. Nothing in *Dunne* supported the view that, if two medical experts expressed opposing honestly-held opinions on the negligence issue, the judge was precluded from making a finding of negligence in relation to the way a particular treatment was carried out. O'Donovan J. had been entitled, if the evidence supported it, to form a view that the respondent had not carried out the evacuation process properly, there being no disagreement between the experts as to how that process should be done.

Geoghegan J. went on to hold that, so far as O"Donovan J. had based his finding of negligence on the failure of the respondent to have carried out an ultrasound scan, it could not be supported. Such an allegation would have to depend on the third principle enunciated in *Dunne*, which stigmatised a customary practice only where it had "inherent defects which ought to be obvious to any person giving the matter due consideration". In the instant case, such a line of argument should have been made from the start and pursued in the course of trial. This had not occurred. Accordingly, liability had to be based on the manner in which the respondent had checked whether she had removed all relevant material from the plaintiff's uterus. There was ample evidence to support O'Donovan J.'s finding on this question.

Geoghegan J. finally addressed the issue of the limits of statistical evidence. In *Daniels v Heskin* [1954] I.R. 73, where a needle had broken in the course of a home delivery, Laverty J. in the Supreme Court had expressed the opinion that it was:

> "certainly not open to a jury, ... to hold that the breaking was caused by imperfection of technique on the ground that say in 60 per cent of cases of broken needles it is so caused, and the same is true of any other statistical record of such happenings until the point is reached where the preponderance is such as to make it a case of *res ipsa loquitur* shifting the burden of proof to the defendant to give an explanation and to establish that the mishap was not due to his negligence."

In the instant case, using the same percentage sample, Geoghegan J. accepted that, if the evidence before O'Donovan J. had established that in 60 per cent of all instances where a limb of a foetus was mistakenly left behind in the uterus there would have been fault on the part of the operating surgeon, there could not on that evidence alone be a finding that as a matter of probability there was negligence. Geoghegan J. ventured the opinion that percentages of that kind "would probably have to be disregarded altogether". But that did not mean that in a case where the evidence established that it would be rare in the extreme for a piece of isolated bone to be left behind, that fact would not be relevant, combined with all the other evidence in the case, in a judge arriving at a finding of negligence.

Loss of chance If I negligently cause you injury, I will have to compensate you. But what is the position where my negligence reduces your prospects of survival, let us say, from 45 per cent to 10 per cent? Should I have to compensate you for the 35 per cent reduction or may I avoid liability on the basis that you were more likely to die than to survive even if I had not acted at all? This issue has been widely discussed in the academic literature for several decades. See King, "Causation, Valuation and Chance in Personal Injury Torts involving Preexisting Conditions and Future Consequences" (1981) 90 Yale L.J. 1353. It divided the House of Lords in *Gregg v Scott*, H.L., January 27, 2005, analysed by Stapleton, "Loss of the Chance of a Cure for Cancer", 68 Modern L. Rev. 996 (2005).

In Ireland, the matter was addressed in *Philp v Ryan*, Supreme Court, December 17, 2004. There, the negligent failure by the first-named defendant to diagnose that the plaintiff was suffering from prostate cancer led to an eight-month delay in the provision of treatment appropriate to that condition. Peart J. awarded the plaintiff damages. The basis on which he did so was not absolutely clear. In summary, he held that the plaintiff's belief that his life had been shortened was a reasonable one, though not actually a finding made by the court. Doctors were divided as to whether an early resort to hormonal treatment (of the possibility of which the plaintiff had been deprived by the negligent diagnosis) was the preferable course. That division reflected disagreement on its efficacy in extending life expectancy and also disagreement as to how it compared to other treatment in other respects (such as its effect on sexual potency). Peart J. did not attempt to resolve this divergence of medical opinion. He did, however, consider that the plaintiff had been deprived of the entitlement to make an informed choice as to how he would be treated.

On appeal by the defendants to the Supreme Court, Fennelly J. (Murray C.J. and McCracken JJ. concurring) presented an analysis of the question whether the loss by the plaintiff of the chance of successful treatment should have been compensated. He observed that it seemed to him:

> "to be contrary to instinct and logic that a plaintiff should not be entitled to be compensated for the fact that, due to the negligent diagnosis of his medical condition, he has been deprived of appropriate medical advice and the consequent opportunity to avail of treatment which might improve his condition. I can identify no contrary principle of law or justice. It is commonplace that allowance is made in awards and in settlements for the risk that an injured plaintiff may in the future develop arthritis in an injured joint. The risk may be high or low—a 15 per cent

risk is often mentioned—but damages are paid. I cannot agree that this is any different from what is sought in the present case. It does not matter that the damage suffered by the plaintiff consists of the loss of an opportunity to avail of treatment. It might, with equal logic, be described as an increased risk of shorter life expectancy. It seems to me as illogical to award damages for a probable future injury as if it were a certainty, as to withhold them where the risk is low on the basis that it will not happen at all."

Fennelly J. went on to observe:

"The assessment of future losses is, on occasion, a matter of mathematical calculation. In certain cases, the courts are accustomed to resorting to the evidence of actuaries, who are expert in calculating the present capitalised value of a combination of future events of greater or lesser likelihood. They can build in allowance for the occurrence of a variety of possibilities including likely age of death or retirement. Nobody suggests that their calculations must be posited on the probable as distinct from the possible happening of each event. Their reports would be deeply flawed if they were.

In my view, the plaintiff should receive an award for the loss of the opportunity to be advised correctly and treated accordingly."

We shall return to the theme of loss of chance in the *Annual Review of Irish Law 2005*. Here we limit ourself to a couple of observations.

First, the issue is a large one, extending well beyond the context of medical negligence. It would require serious and extended consideration of the question before the court should commit itself to accepting the idea that a reduction in the percentage of the chance of a more happy outcome should inevitably warrant compensation. The court would have to consider whether to adopt a general principle or to fashion particular rules to deal with particular types of loss (economic or physical injury, for example) or particular contexts in which the defendant acted (as a professional or as a person in whom the plaintiff reposed trust, for example). In the instant case, regardless of how the court might answer the question of the actual efficacy of the alternative treatment, the plaintiff had surely suffered some loss in having been denied the opportunity to make an informed choice as to how he would be treated.

Secondly, it is worth contrasting *Vavasour v O'Reilly*, High Court, January 28, 2005, in which Fennelly J.'s approach was applied in the economic context, with *Quinn v Mid Western Health Board*, Supreme Court, April 8, 2005, where a separately constituted Bench (Denham, Geoghegan and Kearns JJ.) endorsed the approach favoured in *Gregg v Scott*, without reference to the Supreme Court judgment in *Philp v Ryan*.

RES IPSA LOQUITUR

In *Doherty v Reynolds and St James's Hospital*, Supreme Court, July 14, 2004 the plaintiff, who went to hospital for an operation to deal with acid reflux and heartburn, emerged with a "frozen shoulder", which caused him intense pain. The hospital records failed to record adequately this fact but, in a conflict of evidence on the matter between the plaintiff, his wife and a priest, on the one hand, and certain witnesses on behalf of the defence on the other, O'Donovan J. held in favour of the plaintiff and, on appeal, Keane C.J. (Murray and Fennelly JJ. concurring) had not "the slightest doubt" that O'Donovan J. had been entitled to do so. The Chief Justice commented that the absence of any records of the plaintiff's complaints of severe pain in his shoulder area by any of the hospital staff was "certainly remarkable and reflect[ed] at best from their point of view, a singularly inadequate system of record keeping."

As to the cause of shoulder pain, there was a dispute. The plaintiff's expert witnesses maintained that it was a traction injury. The defendant's expert witness argued that it was the result of brachial neuritis. He said that surgery or anaesthesia could precipitate the condition in one in 10,000 cases. Early recovery would occur in 90 per cent to 95 per cent of cases; this case must have been one of 5 per cent to 10 per cent where it had not. The essence of this evidence, therefore, was that the plaintiff had suffered an injury such as would occur only once in 100,000 to 200,000 cases.

O'Donovan J. preferred the plaintiff's expert evidence and held that the pain was attributable to traction injury. Accordingly the *res ipsa loquitur* principle applied. He was not greatly impressed by the failure of all relevant employees on behalf of the defence to give evidence or by the fact that the thrust of the evidence actually adduced was that, while the witnesses could not recall the day on which the operation had occurred, the treatment given to patients was of a high standard. O'Donovan J. observed:

> "In this case, the defendants have not established precisely how and when the plaintiff sustained the injury of which he complains and, accordingly, have not demonstrated that it cannot be attributed to any blame on their part and, although they have purported to lead evidence to establish that, from the beginning to the end of the procedure to which the plaintiff was subjected on 13th December, 1996, there was no negligence on their part, the fact of the matter ... is because the persons responsible for caring for the plaintiff during that period have no actual recollection of what occurred, all that has been proved is what should have happened in an ideal hospital situation; not what actually occurred. Accordingly, ... I am not persuaded that the defendants have excluded the likelihood on the balance of probability that the injury suffered by [the plaintiff] was occasioned by sub-standard care on their part. Accordingly, it is my judgment that the plaintiff is

entitled to succeed in his claim here against the second named
defendant."

The Supreme Court reversed this decision and ordered a retrial, for two reasons.
First, O'Donovan J., when determining whether the plaintiff's "frozen shoulder"
was attributable to a traction injury or brachial neuritis, should have weighed
in his assessment the evidence by members of the hospital staff of their general
practice of good treatment of patients. Secondly, O'Donovan J. when addressing
the *res ipsa loquitur* issue, had not given sufficient weight to that evidence.
Keane C.J. stated:

> "The trial judge held that because, as he put it, no-one was in a position
> to state positively that their admittedly safe system had been
> implemented in the case of the plaintiff, he could not exclude the
> possibility that an incident did occur as a result of which the plaintiff
> sustained the traction injury Such an incident, he held, could not have
> happened without negligence on the part of the hospital.
>
> That approach seems to me difficult to reconcile with the law as
> stated in *Lindsay v Mid-Western Health Board* [1993] 2 I.R. 147. The
> fact that, for the most part, the anaesthetist, surgeon and nursing staff
> were unable to recall, at that remove of time, the specific details of
> what transpired during the operation itself or the peri-operative period
> generally did not have, as its necessary consequence, as the trial judge
> appeared to assume, that they could not discharge the burden of proof
> resting on them of establishing that there was no negligence on their
> part. In my view, that would be to impose a burden of proof on
> defendants in a case such as this which is unfair and unreasonable. The
> fact that the staff of the hospital cannot, at a particular remove of time,
> give honest evidence that they recall how a particular patient was dealt
> with is, of course, a fact to which the court must have regard. But it
> must also give the appropriate weight to evidence, such as was adduced
> in this case, as to the procedures which would normally be applied, the
> inferences that can properly be drawn from the hospital records and the
> evidence, if it exists, as it did in this case, of those concerned that,
> while they did not recall the specific operation, they had no recollection
> in any operation of the procedures being departed from with the
> consequences alleged to have resulted in this case."

It has to be said that this analysis seems indulgent to the defendants. The
effect of *res ipsa loquitur* is to place the burden on a defendant of proving, on
the balance of probabilities, that he or she has not been guilty of negligence
(or has not caused the injury). Evidence that one recollects nothing specific
about the occasion in question but one's day-to-day practice is of a high standard
scarcely discharges that onus. O'Donovan J. did not impose liability because
the defendants could not remember the occasion: he found that this

forgetfulness, in combination with evidence as to day-to-day practice, did not suffice to discharge that burden.

CONTRIBUTORY NEGLIGENCE

Occupiers' liability   Earlier in the chapter, in the section on occupiers' liability, we discussed two decisions in which the issue of contributory negligence was considered. In *Hall v Meehan*, High Court, December 17, 2004 (above, p.491) no reduction was made in relation to a six-year-old plaintiff. In *Hackett v Calla Associates Ltd*, High Court, October 21, 2004, (above, p.493), a 50 per cent reduction was made where the plaintiff was held significantly to blame for the circumstances in which he was subjected to unreasonable force, resulting in the loss of sight in one of his eyes.

Professional negligence   In *Philp v Ryan*, High Court, March 11, 2004 (affirmed, with modifications as to damages, by the Supreme Court, December 17, 2004) there was a negligent failure to diagnose the plaintiff's prostate cancer, resulting in delay in his treatment: see above, p.500. Peart J. acquitted the plaintiff of any contributory negligence. The plaintiff could not:

> "be presumed to have any prior knowledge regarding the nature of his ailment, what possible diagnoses might be open, what tests might be appropriate, the significance of any such tests, or any possible or appropriate treatment. This feature distinguishes the relationship of doctor and patient from that which exists in some other relationships such as that of master and servant, where a finding of contributory negligence can be made against an employee who has acted in a way which perhaps lacked ordinary common-sense, or was contrary to some training which he had received. In the doctor/ patient relationship there is a total reliance placed by the patient upon the doctor."

In the instant case, although the plaintiff ought to have made contact with the specialist, he had not been guilty of contributory negligence in failing to do so since he had not been informed of what a PSA test was and what consequences hung on the results. (This finding was not challenged on the later appeal to the Supreme Court.)

In *Butler v Regan*, High Court, July 1, 2004, discussed above, p.356, the plaintiff, who had been injured in an accident, settled his claim at an undervalue because his surgeon had failed to diagnose his condition fully and had thus not reported fully on his condition to his legal representatives. Abbott J. held that the plea of contributory negligence was "not sustainable by reason of the fact that the defendant did not bring the hip injury into sufficient focus to place an onus on the plaintiff or his advisors to receive clarification". Moreover, the action had been settled on the basis that it was for full value on the advice of two eminent and experienced senior counsel who had been "best positioned to judge whether [it] should be moved forward by setting it down for trial..."

Employers' liability Earlier in the chapter, in the section on employers' liability, we referred to a number of decisions in which the issue of contributory negligence was addressed.

In *Marsella v J & P Construction Ltd*, High Court, November 30, 2004, the plaintiff plasterer, not an employee, but in a somewhat analogous relationship which generated a duty of care, had his damages reduced for his failure to examine the floor area of the scaffolding on which he was to work. We enlarge upon the court's analysis of this issue above at p.480.

In *Keogh v Minister for Defence*, High Court, January 20, 2004 (above, p.487), in a deafness claim, Peart J. acquitted a member of the FCA of any contributory negligence in relation to wearing ear protection.

Schools' liability In *Murphy v County Wexford VEC*, Supreme Court, July 29, 2004, a 16-year-old pupil succeeded in an action for negligence when he was struck in the eye by a chocolate bar thrown by a fellow pupil during the lunchtime break. In the absence of supervision, there was a great deal of horseplay taking place. The plaintiff's counsel, in opening the case, had said that the plaintiff would "freely concede" that he might have thrown one or two chocolate bars and that he did not think that the plaintiff would dispute the allegation of contributory negligence alleging that he had indulged in excessive horseplay. The trial judge, de Valera J., did not, however, find the plaintiff guilty of contributory negligence and the Supreme Court affirmed his holding. McCracken J. (McGuinness J. concurring) commented: "[t]he learned trial judge must decide the case on the evidence before him, and not on the concessions possibly made by the respondent's counsel in opening the case."

Seat-belt defence

a. Conceptual basis for reducing damages If I fail to wear a seat-belt and, as a result, receive an injury to my shoulder in a traffic accident caused by the defendant's negligence, what should be my legal fate? The traditional approach in Ireland, since the Supreme Court decision in *Hamill v Oliver* [1977] I.R. 73, has been to reduce the total award of compensation by a modest proportion, usually 10 per cent to 20 per cent. A more sophisticated, but controversial, approach would be to let the contributory negligence regime operate only on such of my injuries as is (or are) attributable to my failure to wear the seat-belt: so, if I sustain €20,000 damage to my nose as result of that failure and €30,000 to my foot which would have been sustained even had I been wearing the seat-belt, the contributory negligence regime will apply only to the €20,000 and I will be entitled in any event to the €30,000.

But how much should such be deducted from the sum of €20,000, and why? Section 34(2)(b) of the Civil Liability Act 1961 makes a distinction between contributory negligence prior to the injury and a careless failure to mitigate damage. The latter is deemed contributory negligence "in respect of the amount by which such damage exceeds the damage that would otherwise have occurred".

The failure to wear a seat-belt is foolhardy in exposing oneself to the risk of injury; but that injury will never occur unless some other act (usually, but by no means invariably, one of negligence) intervenes. Only then may my foolhardiness result in injury to me. On one view, my carelessness in not wearing the seat-belt should be regarded as a form of anticipatory failure to mitigate foreseeable future damage. If this approach is taken, then it can have real practical consequences, since the case will fall under s.34(2)(b) rather than s.34(1). This means that any injuries I sustain in an accident which are not attributable to my failure to use the seat-belt simply cannot be touched when reducing my damages for my deemed contributory negligence.

In *Rogan v Walsh*, High Court, April 22, 2004, the plaintiff sustained a relatively minor injury to his shoulder as a result of his failure to wear a seat-belt. He sustained far more serious injuries to his elbow and knee, which had nothing to do with that failure. Peart J. reduced his compensation for the shoulder injury by 50 per cent (from €6,000 to €3,000), leaving the award for the injuries to his elbow and knee unaffected (at €50,000). On these mathematics the total reduction of the plaintiff's compensation was in the region of 3 per cent but it is clear that, had the relative injuries been reversed, it would have been in the region of 50 per cent.

Peart J.'s reduction of 50 per cent is far higher than that adopted by the small number of judges who have adopted the sophisticated strategy of focusing on the particular injuries which are attributable to the failure to use the seat-belt. In *Cassidy v Clarke* (High Court, 1999), Doyle's Personal Injuries Judgments: Trinity and Michaelmas 1999, p.183 for example, Finnegan J. made a reduction of only 15 per cent in respect of the particular injury that was attributable to such a failure. We suggest that the best way of interpreting Peart J.'s judgment is that the large reduction was made precisely because the quantum of injury attributable to the failure to wear the seat-belt was very small relative to the injuries the plaintiff sustained as a whole. Support for this interpretation may perhaps be found in *Hussey v Twomey*, High Court, January 18, 2005 where the plaintiff passenger was injured in a traffic accident where the driver was intoxicated. Reducing her compensation by 40 per cent, Peart J. observed:

> "If the courts see fit to substantially reduce damages for not wearing a seat-belt, it should do so all the more in respect of a person who voluntarily, or carelessly, or even recklessly places herself in danger at the hands of someone such as the [driver] in this case."

One can perhaps question whether an elastic approach towards the reduction of damages, dependent on the proportion of the total injury that the element of injury attributable to the non-use of the seat-belt represents, necessarily advances the law much beyond the simply global percentage reduction that has been applied in most cases in Ireland since *Hamill v Oliver*. If the judicial concern is not to reduce overall damages by more than (say) 20 per cent, maybe it is simply more straightforward to adopt the traditional approach rather than engage in sophisticated calculations, only to manipulate them thereafter so as to ensure that a plaintiff is not punished too severely for the failure to wear the seat-belt?

b. Rear seat passenger The issue of seat-belts for rear seat passengers is beginning to be addressed by our courts. Studies have indicated that wearing such seat-belts reduces mortality by 20 per cent, as well as protecting front seat passengers: see Cummings & Rivara, "Car Occupant Death According to the Restraint Use of Other Occupants: A Matched Cohert Study", 291 J.A.M.A. 343 (2004); Mayrose, Jehle, Hayes, Tinnesz, Piazza & Wilding, "Inference of the Unbelted Rear-Seat Passenger Mortality: 'The Backseat Bullet'", 12 Acad. Emergency Med. 130 (2005).

How great a reduction should the courts make for failure by a rear seat passenger to wear a seat-belt? No definitive answer was given in 2004. In *Higgins v Smith*, High Court, November 15, 2005, however, it was agreed by the parties that there should be a deduction of 5 per cent for the plaintiff's contributory negligence in failing to wear a seat-belt. In the *Annual Review of Irish Law 2005* we shall discuss *Kelly v Hackett* High Court, July 5, 2005, where O'Donovan J. acquitted a mother, a rear seat passenger, of any contributory negligence in removing her seat-belt to enable her to bottle-feed her four-month-old infant son.

Battery It is noteworthy that the plaintiff's claim appears to have been framed in negligence rather than being based on vicarious liability for battery. In some other common law jurisdictions, courts hesitated for a considerable time before permitting the defence of contributory negligence to apply to claims for battery, and some doubts remain even today: see Lord Rodger of Earlsferry's observations in *Standard Chartered Bank v Pakistan National Shipping Corporation* [2003] 1 A.C. 959. Of course other, more radical defences, notable *ex turpi causa*, may be available.

In *Hackett v Calla Associates Ltd*, High Court, October 21, 2004, the plaintiff was struck in the eye by a weapon carried by a bouncer when the plaintiff was attending the defendants' nightclub. He lost the sight in the eye. The plaintiff had orchestrated a disturbance in the nightclub which had warranted his removal from the premises. He had then started kicking the doors and shouting abuse. This had led to a wider disturbance. The bouncer was held to have used unreasonable force. Peart J. observed that, even if the bouncer had not intended to cause an injury of the magnitude of that sustained by the plaintiff, it mattered not, since it was "a reckless, negligent and dangerous act..." Peart J. went on, however, to reduce the award against the proprietors by 50 per cent to take account of the plaintiff's contributory negligence. He stated that:

> "The question as always is to what degree. One is more accustomed to assessing contributory negligence in the context of a car accident or an accident at work. In such cases it would be unusual to make a large deduction on account of contributory negligence, because in most cases the element of contributory negligence arises due to perhaps not wearing a seat-belt, exceeding a speed limit, failing to observe an on-coming car and so forth. What I am trying to convey is that in such cases the plaintiff is guilty of relatively minor negligence not worthy of being severely marked by a large reduction in damages. In the present case the plaintiff's behaviour is of a different character. It was criminal behaviour such as should not be implicitly condoned by a sympathetic approach to contributory negligence. It cannot be equated to the type of contributory negligence more commonly found in road accidents or workplace accidents. It is culpable behaviour for which the plaintiff must retain responsibility. In my view, even though the defendants are liable to him for an unreasonable use of force, and even though the Court feels great sympathy for the fact that the plaintiff has now only the use of one eye, he has himself to blame to a significant extent, and to an extent far in excess of the more normal type of case to which I have referred."

CONSTITUTIONAL TORT

In *O'Donoghue v Legal Aid Board*, High Court, December 21, 2004, Kelly J. awarded damages to a woman whose desire to take legal proceedings for a divorce and for maintenance for her disabled son had been thwarted by her failure for more than two years to receive appropriate legal services from the Legal Aid Board. The Legal Aid Board had been starved of sufficient resources, especially for the period after the introduction of divorce. Kelly J. held that the Legal Aid Board was liable neither for negligence nor for breach of statutory duty, since it had done the best that it could with the shamefully inadequate resources provided by the State. He held that the State had infringed the plaintiff's constitutionally-based entitlements of access to the courts and fair procedures. It was not enough for the State to set up a scheme for the provision of legal aid to necessitous persons and then to render it effectively meaningless for a long period of time. The State, in the words of Gannon J. in *M.C. v Legal*

Aid Board, had to ensure that the scheme was "implemented fairly to all persons and in a manner which fulfils its declared purpose". The purpose of the 1995 Act was that persons who met the necessary criteria should receive legal aid. That carried the implication that the entitlement to legal aid would be "effective and of meaning". Kelly J. commented: "How can it be if a delay of 25 months is encountered? Equally, how can the scheme be fair if a qualified person cannot get to see a solicitor for such a lengthy period?"

The Civil Legal Aid Act of 1995 gave substance, in many ways, to the constitutional entitlement to legal aid for appropriate persons. The legislature was entitled to define reasonable limits to that right; but the right could not be effectively set at nought for years in the manner that had occurred in the instant case.

Counsel for the State had argued that the court was powerless to intervene in the case regardless of the nature of the right being asserted by the plaintiff, whether it be statutory, constitutional, or a right under the European Convention on Human Rights. To do so would involve trespassing into an area outside its competence under the Constitution. (Counsel cited *Sinnott v Minister for Education* [2001] 2 I.R. 545 and *T.D. v Minister for Education* [2001] 4 I.R. 259 in support.) Kelly J. rejected this argument. The case was not concerned with a claim for any form of mandatory relief against the State. The court was doing no more than what the courts had been doing since at least *Ryan v Attorney General* [1965] I.R. 294, namely, ensuring that a right under the Constitution was protected and given effect. In *Sinnott v Minister for Education* Keane C.J. had stated:

> "That is not to say that where a plaintiff successfully claims that his constitutional rights have been violated by the State in the past and will continue to be so violated in the future (which is not the case here) unless the court intervenes, the courts are impotent when it comes to the protection of those rights."

Keane C.J. had also said that, while in principle there was nothing to preclude the granting of mandatory relief against a Minister to meet a constitutional obligation, the courts should "presume that where this court grants a declaration that he or she had failed to meet his or her constitutional obligations the Minister will take the appropriate steps to comply with the law as laid down by the courts".

In the instant case, there was no question of a future breach and Kelly J. saw no reason why the court should not be entitled to deal with a past breach by means of an appropriate declaration and an award of damages if necessary.

In *Cronin v the Minister for Education and Science*, High Court, July 6, 2004, Laffoy J. granted an interlocutory mandatory injunction directing the Minister, during the pre-school phase of the education of the plaintiff, who suffered from attention deficit hyperactivity disorder, autistic features and hearing deficit and speech delay, to provide for the cost of 29 hours per week one-to-one Applied Behaviour Analysis tuition from appropriately qualified personnel throughout the calendar year in his home and the cost of supervision of his education programme, measured at €300 per week.

The plaintiff invoked in support of his claim both his constitutional right to free primary education appropriate to his needs as recognised by the Supreme Court in *Sinnott v The Minister for Education* [2001] 2 I.R. 545 and his statutory rights under the Education Act 1998, especially under s.6, para.(g) which provides that everyone concerned in the implementation of the Act should have regard to the objects set out, including:

> "(g) To promote effective liaison and consultation between schools and centres for education, patrons, teachers, parents, the communities served by schools, local authorities, health boards, persons or groups of persons who have a special interest in or experience of the education of students with special educational needs and the Minister."

Counsel for the plaintiff laid particular emphasis on the observations of Hardiman J. in *Sinnott v Minister for Education*, pointing to the possibility of enforcement of statutory duties in relation to the provision of education for autistic children through court intervention.

While the Minister was committed to continuing to fulfil his obligations to the plaintiff and to ensuring that suitable and appropriate education was made available for him having regard to his needs, counsel for the Minister referred to s.5(4) of the Act which mandated the Minister in carrying out his functions under the Act to have regard, *inter alia*, to the resources available. Moreover, his duty under s.6, para.(b) of the Act was "to provide that as far as is practicable and having regard to the resources available, there is made available to people resident in the State a level and quality of education appropriate to meeting the needs and abilities of those people."

Counsel for the first defendant emphasised in particular the reference in para.(b) to "the resources available" and to "quality of education appropriate to meeting the needs and abilities of those people". Counsel submitted that what was required of the Minister was to adopt a reasonable approach and this could not mean that he might be enjoined to give effect to a programme, just because it was proposed by a psychologist.

Counsel for the Minister submitted that, as the plaintiff was seeking mandatory relief at an interlocutory stage, the criterion which the court should apply was whether the plaintiff was likely to succeed at the trial, there being currently the clearest indication that the Minister was not in breach of his constitutional or statutory duties to the plaintiff.

Laffoy J. did not agree. The suggested test involved making a judgment as to the strength of the respective cases of the plaintiff and the Minister, which the court was not entitled to do at the interlocutory stage, as had been made clear by the Supreme Court in *Westman Holdings v McCormack* [1992] 1 I.R. 15. In the instant case, given the divergence of professional opinion, it would be impossible to make such a judgment in any event. The plaintiff clearly fulfilled the first element of the *Campus Oil* test: there was "undoubtedly" a bona fide issue to be tried as to the appropriate pre-school provision of education for the plaintiff.

Laffoy J. considered that the balance of convenience lay in favour of the grant of an injunction. The plaintiff's parents could not, without incurring serious hardship, fund the programme of education from their own resources. The provision sought was specific to the plaintiff, was limited both in *quantum* and duration and could have no significant resource or budgetary implications for the first defendant. Damages would not be an adequate remedy if the injunction were refused and the plaintiff was ultimately successful. Inherent in the circumstances of the plaintiff's family was the real possibility that, without the benefit of the provision which was sought, his educational progress would be hindered.

Explaining the basis of her order, Laffoy J. stated:

> "In reaching this conclusion, I have had particular regard to the decision of the Supreme Court in *T. D. -v- The Minister of Education* [2001] 4 IR 259, and, in particular, to the observations of Keane, C. J. at page 287. I am satisfied that granting a mandatory injunction does not fall foul of that decision. The relief granted is limited to the particular needs of the plaintiff and merely extends a programme which the first defendant has already sanctioned."

BATTERY

In *McCormack v Olsthoorn*, High Court, December 21, 2004, Hardiman J. awarded €3,500 damages for battery (described colloquially as assault) and false imprisonment where a retired garda superintendent was apprehended briefly by a horticulturalist who mistakenly believed that he had stolen a plant from his stall at a market. The incident occurred in public but was of brief duration.

Hardiman J. stated that:

> "I accept that the plaintiff was, albeit very briefly, technically assaulted and falsely imprisoned. The latter simply means that he was (briefly) deprived of his liberty to go where he wanted. I am satisfied that there was no real violence in the assault which I believe consisted of grabbing the plaintiff by the arm. I believe that the episode lasted, if only by five or ten seconds, longer than the defendant now recalls and that there was some element of propulsion towards the shop. Any level of force

whatever was quite unnecessary in respect of a man who, even if his
utter respectability was unknown to the defendant, cannot have presented
as being a risk of violence or of escape. No physical harm was done but
the plaintiff was technically assaulted, briefly deprived of his liberty
and as a result of this was very understandably upset, distressed and
shocked. This is a most unfortunate thing to happen to anyone, and
particularly to a man of advancing years. But it was by no means a very
grave episode. I am satisfied that the defendant resiled from his position
within a very short time and I am happy to note the very ample apology
his solicitor made in correspondence. I must also consider that the
defendant contradicted the plaintiff in certain respects where I am
satisfied the plaintiff is both truthful and accurate and this must have
added to his distress."

ANIMALS

There is very little reported litigation under s.21 of the Control of Dogs Act
1986, perhaps because the general rule of strict liability which it prescribes
admits of no legal argument. In *Quinlisk v Kearney*, High Court, June 10,
2004, Murphy J. addressed a specific question arising under s.21: whether a
dog which attacked the plaintiff was in the care, or under the management or
control, of the defendants. Section 9 of the 1986 Act provides that:

> " 'Owner' in relation to a dog includes the occupier of any premises
> where the dog is kept or permitted to live or remain at any particular
> time unless such occupier proves to the contrary; . . ."

Most of Murphy J.'s judgment addresses the evidential question of the degree
of connectedness between the offending dog and the defendants. There was
evidence that, while the defendants did not own dogs, dogs were around their
house.
    Murphy J. imposed liability. He stated:

> "The court has to be satisfied on the balance of probabilities, from the
> evidence of the second and third named defendants, that none of the
> three defendants kept a dog or permitted a dog to live or remain for any
> particular time in their premises."

Reading the judgment, it is not entirely clear why the onus of proof of this
kind should have been placed on the defendants. The essential issue in the
case related to the identity of the dog and of those who might be its owners or
exercised control over it. If the offending dog in this case could thus be linked
to the defendants, then, by reason of the definition of "owner" in s.1 of the

Act, liability would follow automatically unless the occupiers of the premises where the dog was kept or permitted to live proved that in fact they were not its owner. If, however, this evidential link could not be established, nothing in s.1, or in any other provision of the Act, would assist the plaintiff in one task of proving her case on the balance of probabilities. It may perhaps be the position that Murphy J. considered that there was sufficient evidence in the case to show that the defendants had kept or permitted the dog to remain at their home and that they simply had not adduced sufficient evidence to contradict the evidence adduced by the plaintiff.

DEFAMATION

Whether the words were capable of carrying a defamatory meaning   In *McGarth v Independent Newspapers (Ireland) Ltd*, High Court, April 21, 2004, the defendants published in one of their newspapers a photograph of the plaintiff, a fitter with Irish Rail who was a worker director on its board. The photograph appeared above an article entitled "Eircom investors still hold out for better bid". The photograph contained a caption which stated: "Losses; businessman Pat McGarth stands to lose thousands after investing £50,000 in Eircom". The plaintiff regarded this false assertion as defamatory in suggesting that he had been hypocritical with his co-workers in hiding wealth and representing himself as a committed trade union representative. He sought an apology and correction. The defendant later published a correction in the paper which consisted of a photograph of "CIE tradesman Pat McGarth who was described as a business man in Friday's Your Money borrowed to invest £9,600 in Eircom shares not £50,000 as reported." The photograph and correction statement were published under the heading "Big business linked to family of terrorist". The heading related to an article concerning various well-known international comparisons doing business with the Bin Laden empire. Reference was made to Osama Bin Laden's having over 50 brothers and sisters and to the family's company Saudi Bin Laden Group's having a turnover of $5 billion a year. The plaintiff sued the defendants for defamation. He alleged that no attempt had been made by the defendants to distance or distinguish the photograph of himself from the contents of the article.

The plaintiff alleges that by virtue of the placing of the photograph and the correction statement in conjunction with the article, the contents of the latter in their natural and ordinary meaning meant or were understood to mean that the plaintiff:

1. was a terrorist;

2. was a criminal;

3. had ties with known and/or reputed terrorist organisations;

4. would conduct himself in such a manner as to invite a criminal prosecution for involvement in terrorist activities;

5. was involved in big business for the purpose of raising money to fund terrorist activities;

6. was part of a family of terrorists;

7. would see no reason to sever ties with terrorist organisations;

8. would condone the commission of terrorist activity in any manner;

9. was one of a family of terrorists.

As an aspect of the damage to his reputation, part of the plaintiff's claim was that the publication contributed to defeat of his re-election campaign to the position of worker director.

Gilligan J., on a motion by the defendants, held that the published matter was not capable of a defamatory interpretation. He observed:

> "In determining whether the words are capable of a defamatory meaning the court is obliged to construe the words according to the fair and natural meaning which would be given to them by reasonable persons of ordinary intelligence and will not consider what a person setting themselves to work to deduce some unusual meaning might extract from them. The court should avoid an over elaborate analysis of the article because the ordinary reader would not analyse the article as a lawyer or accountant would analyse documents or accounts. In deciding the issue I am satisfied that I am entitled to consider the impression that the article has conveyed to me personally in considering what impact it would make on the hypothetical reasonable reader and lastly the court should not take a too literal approach to its task.
>
> Accordingly taking the article … as a complete entity including the headline, the content of the article, the placing of the photograph of the plaintiff and the caption underneath the photograph and placing myself in the shoes of the ordinary reasonable fair minded reader I take the view that the article complained of in paragraph 7 of the statement of claim is not capable of meaning that the plaintiff was a terrorist or a criminal or was involved with persons who had terrorist or criminal involvement nor is the article capable of bearing any of the defamatory meanings pleaded [elsewhere] in the statement of claim."

This conclusion seems reasonably easy to understand. Any possible confusion of a tentative character induced in a reader by the headline would be immediately resolved by the most brief perusal of the text of the article. But what about a casual and lazy reader who did not take the trouble to read the text of the article? It seems hard to see how even such a reader could conclude that the headline related to the plaintiff. The text relating to the plaintiff made it clear that no such suggestion was being made about him. It must be admitted that the words used to correct the previous error were less than gracious but that aspect of the publication was not relevant to the large complaint made by the plaintiff in respect of the proximity of the headline to the picture of him. Of course it is possible that the positioning of headlines of different stories and of pictures with captions could be such as foreseeably to mislead the casual reader into a conclusion that the headline related to the "wrong" text. In such circumstances a defendant would not escape liability by pointing to the truth of the text which, as it were, had wandered away from its own headline. This does not appear to have been the position in the instant case.

Qualified privilege   If I am a shopkeeper and I wrongly believe that you have stolen an item from my shop, am I guilty of defamation if I accuse you of theft in the presence of others? The old High Court case of *Coleman v Kearns Ltd* [1946] Ir. Jur. Rep. 5 said yes, in any event where there were no reasonable grounds or evidence for so acting. Hardiman J., in *McCormack v Olsthoorn*, High Court, December 21, 2004, says no. The plaintiff was a retired garda superintendent in his mid-70s at the time of the incident. He was mistakenly accused, in the presence of others, of theft of a plant by the defendant, a horticulturalist selling horticultural produce.

Hardiman J. stated:

> "I believe that the occasion at … [a] market was one of qualified privilege. The plaintiff had a legal right to protect his property and in doing so to 'tax' an individual whom he suspected of a theft. Situations such as that which arose between these parties in … [a] market arise quickly and without notice. For this reason I think it would be utterly unreasonable to require of the defendant any fine judgement or considered selection of the words which he used. Accordingly I do not consider that the direct statement which he made deprived him of privilege. Furthermore I do not consider that the presence of bystanders in itself had that effect, because, as Gatley observes: 'The law has been fairly liberal in allowing charges to be made in the presence of others.' I have no doubt that this, too, is because of the hurried circumstances in which such accusations tend to be made. In one of the classic cases, *Toogood v. Spyring* (1834) 1 Cr M & R 181, the allegation was made in the presence of a third party two days after the event, and that did not displace the privilege. I do not need to consider whether that decision should now be followed."

Hardiman J. noted that, in *Coleman v Kearns Ltd* a butcher's accusation that a woman had stolen some bacon from a shop had been held not to be privileged because it was made with the desire to recover the property, instead of a desire to bring a thief to justice. Hardiman J. observed:

> "I cannot regard that decision as correct. There is no doubt that something said with a view to bringing a thief to justice is privileged, but it is not the only heading of privilege that arises in such circumstances. Privilege exists where a legally recognised duty or interest in speaking exists: in my view the legitimate desire to recover one's property is just as much a legitimate interest as the desire to bring a thief to justice. Very often these desires will co-exist. Realistically, where there is a sudden theft or suspected theft, the owner or his agent will not pause to analyse his own motives in detail but will act immediately out of an instinctive and proper desire to stop a theft. I agree with what is said on this topic in McDonald, *'Irish Law of Defamation'* at page 149.
>
> Equally, I have to disagree with the dictum in the judgment in *Coleman v. Kearns* to the effect that a person seeking to avail of the privilege 'must have reasonable grounds or evidence before so acting. He must not immediately jump to a rash conclusion.' I do not believe that the requirement of 'reasonable grounds' is a correct statement of the law. Privilege is lost by malice, excessively wide publication or one of the other established causes. It is not lost merely because the belief turns out to be erroneous, or because the defendant was hasty. The presence or absence of reasonable grounds for the defendant's belief may be very relevant in a case where malice (that is, some improper motive) is pleaded but there is no such plea here, and on the facts, there could not have been. Having seen and heard the parties I am in any event quite satisfied of Mr. Olsthoorn's *bona fides* and I believe that he acted as he did on the spur of the moment (delay would obviously have been fatal to his chances of recovering the plant he believed stolen) and after a most unfortunately coincidental sighting of what he believed to be a theft."

While dismissing the claim, Hardiman J. described that:

> "there must of necessity be an element of hardship where one honest man due to an unfortunate coincidence of circumstances *bona fide* accuses another honest man of theft. It is a nice question as to whether the reputation of the latter should not predominate over the privilege of the former, but I do not think that it does. The law must make realistic allowances for the absolutely unheralded manner in which these circumstances arise, the lack of time to formulate a polite form of words to use and the need for haste generally."

The possible effects of this decision are worth considering. May security staff in large supermarkets now accuse shoppers of theft, in the hearing of others, where there is no reasonable ground for the belief that they stole? What may seem a defensible calibration of hardship in the case of a corner shop may not seem quite so palatable in the case of the larger commercial emporium.

Loss of reputation   In *Cooper-Flynn v Radio Telefís Éireann*, Supreme Court, April 28, 2004, the Supreme Court made it clear that, in circumstances where a particular defendant has not sought the protection of s.22 of the Defamation Act 1961 but the evidence that emerges during the trial makes it clear that the plaintiff's reputation has been severely compromised, it is not open to the plaintiff to obtain damages for that reputation. Very briefly, the facts were as follows. The plaintiff, a Dáil Deputy, had formerly been a member of the investment staff of a bank. A reporter of RTÉ alleged that she had advised the third defendant, a retired farmer, not to avail himself of an available tax amnesty but to invest the money in a scheme in the Isle of Man which would conceal its existence from the Irish revenue authorities. In a later broadcast, the RTÉ reporter alleged that a number of other customers of the bank had been told by the plaintiff that the revenue authorities would never find out about their money in the Isle of Man.

In libel proceedings, RTÉ and its reporter pleaded, among its defences, s.22, which provides as follows:

> "In an action for libel or slander in respect of words containing two or more distinct charges against the plaintiff, a defence of justification shall not fail by reason only that the truth of every charge is not proved, if the words not proved to be true do not materially injure the plaintiff's reputation having regard to the truth of the remaining charges."

The third defendant did not plead s.22, however, although he pleaded justification.

The third trial lasted 28 days. The jury found that the plaintiff had not induced the third defendant to evade his tax obligations but that she had advised or encouraged a number of others to evade their tax obligations. It went on to address the third question, which asked them whether, in view of their answer that the plaintiff had encouraged others to evade tax, the plaintiff's reputation had suffered material injury by reason of the matters published relating to the third defendant. They answered this question in the negative. They went on to answer further questions, making it clear that no damages should be awarded to the plaintiff. They also awarded costs against the plaintiff.

One of the grounds of appeal was that the trial judge had erred in allowing the third defendant to rely on the jury's answers to the second and third questions. He had not, after all, invoked s.22. Moreover, under the rule in *Scott v Sampson* (1882) 2 Q.B.D. 491, a defendant seeking to rely on matters in mitigation of damages was bound to rely on evidence of general reputation rather than specific acts of misconduct.

The Supreme Court did not agree. Keane C.J. referred to the rule in *Scott v Sampson* and noted that it was said to be based on the difficulty that any other rule would create for the plaintiff in showing "a uniform propriety of conduct during his whole life" and would give rise to interminable issues having only a remote bearing on the real issue in the case. Although it had been regarded as correctly stating the law in *Kavanagh v The Leader* [2001] I.R. 538 (a decision of the former Supreme Court as long ago as 1955), there was at least one older Irish authority to a different effect, *i.e. Bolton v O'Brien* (1885) 16 L.R. (Ir.) 97. Moreover, as had been pointed out in *Browne v Tribune Newspapers plc* [2001] 1 I.R. 521, the Law Reform Commission in their *Report on the Civil Law of Defamation* (1991) had recommended that the defendant should be permitted to introduce in mitigation of damages any matters, general or particular, relevant at the date of the trial to that aspect of the plaintiff's reputation with which the defamation was concerned.

It had also been held by the English Court of Appeal in *Pamplin v Express Newspapers* [1988] 1 W.L.R. 116 that, despite the rule in *Scott v Sampson*, the defendant was entitled to rely in mitigation of damages on any evidence properly before the jury, including evidence of specific acts of misconduct or other evidence adduced in support of an unsuccessful plea of justification.

Keane C.J. was:

> "satisfied that where, as here, evidence is before the jury of specific acts of misconduct which were relevant to that aspect of the plaintiff's reputation with which the defamation was concerned, there is no reason in principle why a defendant should not be allowed to rely on such evidence by way of mitigation of damages. Since the purpose of the law of defamation is to compensate a plaintiff for damage to his or her reputation, it would be singularly unsatisfactory if a jury were obliged to award anything other than nominal or contemptuous damages to a plaintiff whom they had found in effect not to be entitled to any reputation in the relevant area. While the procedure actually adopted of, in effect, allowing [the third defendant] to rely on an answer to question 3 which was unfavourable to the plaintiff may not have been, in procedural terms, the best way of eliciting the verdict of the jury, it is clear that they could not have come to a significantly different conclusion had the questions been framed in such a way as to draw the suggested distinctions between the position of RTÉ and [its reporter] on the one hand and [the third defendant] on the other hand. If they had, such a verdict would have to be set aside as perverse or replaced with an award of nominal damages."

The same course had been taken by the majority of the House of Lords in

Grobbelaar v Newsgroup Newspapers Ltd [2002] 4 All E.R. 732. Lord Bingham of Cornhill had said:

"The tort of defamation protects those whose reputations have been unlawfully injured. It affords little or no protection to those who have, or deserve to have, no reputation deserving of legal protection."

Denham J. put the matter succinctly:

"The plaintiff chose to sue the defendants in one action and cannot now argue that the jury could find that she had two contradictory reputations, which would be a consequence of her submission. In a single case, as here, with multiple defendants and a wider frame of issues, a verdict cannot be that she has multiple (contradictory) reputations."

Defamation of the dead In *Murray v Commission to Inquire into Child Abuse*, High Court, January 27, 2004, where members of the congregation of the Christian Brothers challenged the entitlement of the Commission to make findings of facts against deceased persons, Abbott J. gave short shrift to the argument that deceased persons enjoyed constitutional rights. He observed that:

"[t]he plaintiff's own submissions recognise the validity of there being a legislative prohibition against the estates of deceased persons maintaining actions for defamation in respect of publication regarding the deceased. This is justified by reference to good policy reasons, presumably relating to the difficulties which will be caused to the writing and recording of a recent history. This policy was less significant than the ascertainment of facts surrounding matters of legitimate public concern as are in issue before the Commission. The case of *Hilliard v. Penfield Enterprises Ltd* [1990] 1 I.R. 138 supports the view that because the deceased are neither alive nor citizens they have no personal rights."

Perhaps the point could have been given greater consideration. Both the Law Reform Commission and the Legal Advisory Group on Defamation have recommended that the reputation rights of deceased persons receive some protection and the German Constitutional Court has recognised that respect for human dignity may require such protection. There are complex arguments on both sides of the question. See Böttner, "Protection of the Honour of Deceased Persons: A Comparison between the German and Australian Legal Situations" [2001] Bond L. Rev. 109.

Procedure In *Hanly v Newsgroup Newspapers Ltd*, High Court, March 10,

2004, the plaintiff, a member of a football team, sued one newspaper for defamation in allegedly communicating to its readers that he had engaged in drunken, seriously offensive behaviour in a hotel on the night after a match, whereas he had not been at the hotel at all. In his statement of claim, he included details of a similar allegation made earlier in another newspaper regarding the night in question which had resulted in an apology and the payment of compensation. The defendant in the instant proceedings successfully applied for an order pursuant to Ord.19, r.27 of the Rules of the Superior Courts 1986, as amended, striking out the paragraphs containing these details. The plaintiff resisted on the basis that their inclusion was designed to establish that the defendant's article had negated and neutralised the effect of the earlier apology of the other newspaper and that as a consequence the plaintiff was entitled to aggravated damages.

Smyth J. stated:

> "In my judgment it is not permissible for a plaintiff in a Statement of Claim in an action such as this to seek to set forth in the pleadings in a narrative form intended factual evidence in anticipation of or pre-emptive of possible evidence in mitigation of damages that may be tendered at trial arising from matters in a defence yet to be formulated. The material in the paragraphs of the Statement of Claim is scandalous, prejudicial and embarrassing in the legal sense of those terms ..."

TRESPASS TO LAND

Injunction In *Dublin City Council v McGrath*, High Court, March 12, 2004, Carroll J. granted an interlocutory injunction restraining trespass by a tenant in Eamonn Ceannt Tower in Ballymun, which was due to be demolished as part of the Ballymun Regeneration Programme. The Council had offered the tenant alternative accommodation and had given her notice to quit. The tenant resisted, not because she wanted to remain in the Tower, where the conditions were designed as "horrific", but rather because she wished to be rehoused in Finglas, for family reasons, in particular because this would offer the best environment for her disabled son. The Council averred that it had no suitable accommodation in Finglas and that in any event the defendant would have to take her place in the queue.

Carroll J. was satisfied that the *Campus Oil* test had been met as regards the requirement to establish that there was a fair question to be tried. The defendant had invoked *Dublin Corporation v Burke*, Supreme Court, October 9, 2001, where the Supreme Court had reversed what was basically an order for possession of a shopping centre, made against a defendant who was in possession when the Corporation bought the property and who claimed title to a tenancy. Geoghegan J. had said that he was:

"extremely doubtful that there would even be a *prima facie* case for an injunction where a defendant with some back-up evidence (if ultimately accepted) is alleging an actual tenancy in the premises and the plaintiff is for all practical purposes merely sceptical of the truth of the allegation."

In Carroll J.'s view there was:

"no comparison between the defendant in that case claiming a commercial tenancy in a shopping centre and the present defendant claiming she is entitled not to be disturbed in a flat where the conditions are sub-human and where the safety and health of herself and her young son are in danger. She does not want to remain and says so. What she wants is a tenancy in the area of her choice.

While generally the court will preserve the *status quo*, in my opinion, in the extraordinary circumstances of this case, the court is not constrained *ab initio* from considering whether an injunction might be granted."

Nor did the Supreme Court decision in the landmark decision of *McDonald v Feeley*, July 23, 1980 avail the defendant. While this case was authority for the proposition that a local authority which failed to consider the housing needs of a person within their jurisdiction was not acting in accordance with its duty and could not eject a trespasser, it was also authority for the corollary that, if there had been a reasonable discharge of this duty by considering the housing needs, an authority would not be restrained from ejecting a trespasser.

Carroll J. was satisfied that damages would not be an adequate remedy for the plaintiff. The balance of convenience also tilted in its favour. The defendant wanted to go to the area of her choice; she was not defending a home in which she wanted to stay.

Defence of property   At common law occupiers of property are perfectly entitled to use reasonable force in the protection of that property. This ancient entitlement has been expressly preserved by s.8 of the Occupiers' Liability Act 1995. What constitutes reasonable force will depend on the circumstances; these include the nature of the threat to the property, the likelihood (or actuality) of its occurrence and the possibility of resorting to other, non-violent, ways of protecting the property. Thus, in *McKnight v Xtravision*, Circuit Court, July 15, 1991, Carroll J. held that, in a commercial dispute between landlord and tenant about a lease, the tenant had acted unreasonably in using force to protect its position rather than taking the somewhat slower, but effective and more pacific, strategy of seeking an injunction.

In *Hackett v Calla Associates Ltd*, High Court, October 21, 2004, Peart J. provided an interesting analysis of the issue of reasonable force. He was approaching it from the standpoint of negligence rather than trespass to the person. The plaintiff, who had attended a disco at the defendants' nightclub, had orchestrated a disturbance in the nightclub which had warranted his removal from the premises and had then started kicking the doors and shouting abuse. This led to a wider disturbance which involved others hurling missiles at the premises, resulting in some damage to windows. Thereafter bouncers working on behalf of the defendants emerged from the side door. One of them struck the plaintiff with a weapon, blinding him in one eye. It was not management policy that weapons should be available for use.

Peart J. analysed the issue as follows: the security staff members were not entitled to use more force than was reasonably necessary in any particular circumstances which might present during the evening. It was clearly reasonably foreseeable that an excessive use of force by staff had the potential to cause injury. The next hurdle to be overcome under the test for liability as pronounced by Keane C.J. in *Glencar Exploration Ltd v Mayo County Council* [2002] 1 I.L.R.M. 481 was to exclude any public policy consideration which ought to exclude liability arising. In Peart J.'s opinion there could be no public policy consideration which should result in no duty of care being owed by employers of security staff to members of the public in the circumstances of facts such as had occurred:

> "In fact the opposite would be the case, since a situation would then exist in which security could go about their tasks with complete impunity regarding the level of force they might use, and in effect a situation would exist where it was permissible for the owners of licensed premises and other such premises to hire their own private army in order to enforce their version of law and order. That could never be acceptable."

The final hurdle to be overcome by a plaintiff under the *Glencar* principles was that the court had to be satisfied that it would be fair, just and reasonable that the law should impose a duty of care on the defendants for the benefit of the plaintiff. In the instant case, this consideration was quite closely linked to the public policy consideration, and there was also some blurring between consideration of the concept of fairness and reasonableness and the concept of any contributory negligence on the part of the plaintiff. One could consider the concept of fairness, justice and reasonableness also from the point of view of the *ex turpi causa* principle. On this approach, the actions of the plaintiff might be regarded as so egregious that he ought not to be allowed to recover any damages for an injury resulting from that behaviour.

Peart J. did not consider that that the facts of the case would warrant such a stark response:

> "The latter methodology must in my view be reserved for the very worst type of behaviour in order to serve the punitive purpose of denying an

injured plaintiff any remedy for otherwise culpable behaviour on the part of a defendant. I believe that in the present case it is fair, just and reasonable that the defendants remain under the duty of care towards the plaintiff and other patrons even in the unpleasant and potentially dangerous circumstances which arose outside the premises on this night. The whole purpose of the job of being a security staff member is to deal with situations which arise in premises of this kind and which cannot be reasonably dealt with by what I might conveniently describe as 'ordinary staff'. It is part of the normal working life of such security men to encounter patrons in various states of intoxication, and who even when not intoxicated, are nevertheless aggressive and sometimes violent. Such staff ought to be, and in most cases, are trained to deal efficiently with such situations. It is perfectly fair, just and reasonable that such persons should carry out their duties in a way which is consistent with a reasonable use of force and restraint, and I can see no reason why any special dispensation should be extended to them in the manner in which they carry out their tasks."

Peart J. was therefore satisfied that the defendants had owed a duty of care to the plaintiff which extended to avoiding causing injury to him through an unreasonable or unnecessary use of force or violence in dealing with the situation. A decision had been taken to allow the bouncers to run out of the side door and get in amongst the crowd outside and disperse them. In Peart J.'s view the appropriate course of action would have been to contact the Gardaí and to wait for them to arrive in order to deal with the situation. In the instant case that had been done, but the management had not waited for the Gardaí to arrive. Peart J. observed:

"This was not a disturbance within the premises themselves. It was a disturbance outside. The staff of the premises were inside the premises, and even though there may have been some shouting and kicking of the doors, and even a couple of windows broken, it does not seem to me that it was appropriate for the management to send out their own troops, so to speak, in order to break up the disturbance. That action led to direct confrontation between the troublemakers outside and the security staff and it was inevitable that somebody would be injured..."

The fact that the plaintiff might have been the instigator of much of the disturbance did not mean that the security staff could single him out in any way or treat him with more than reasonable force. Peart J. had no doubt that it was an unreasonable use of force to hit him so severely in the face with some sort of heavy blunt instrument that he had effectively been rendered blind in his right eye. Even if a security man had not intended to cause an injury of that magnitude, it mattered not. It was a reckless, negligent and dangerous act committed after the security staff had taken the inappropriate step of going out to themselves deal with the trouble outside, rather than allowing the members of An Garda Síochána to arrive and intervene. What happened amounted to negligent behaviour.

The imposition of liability in this case seems well justified. It is, however, slightly odd that the analysis had to proceed in terms of the duty of care in negligence rather than of defence of property against a trespasser. Peart J. was surely justified in holding that the bouncers were not relieved of any duty of care under *Glencar*; to grant bouncers a complete immunity from legal repercussions for their actions would be a recipe for anarchy.

PRIVACY

In *Rooney v Minister for Agriculture, Food and Forestry*, High Court, July 13, 2004, the plaintiff wrote a letter addressed to the President, the Taoiseach, the Ceann Comhairle and the Chief Justice complaining that he had been "denied judicial determination of issues raised (as a lay litigant) in proceedings before the Superior Courts". He outlined specific complaints against several former and serving judges of the Superior Courts. In relation to one judge he alleged that he had "conferred an unfair advantage on the defendants". He alleged that each of the others had "exercised his judicial functions improperly". The defendant in the instant case had been the primary defendant in the proceedings to which the allegations related. The private secretary to the Taoiseach acknowledged receipt of the letter on behalf of the Taoiseach and passed it on to the defendant for appropriate attention. The plaintiff claimed that in thus receiving his letter, the defendant had infringed his right to privacy.

Laffoy J. dismissed this claim summarily. She stated:

> "In my view, no right of privacy could enure to the author thereof in relation to a letter to a constitutional officer of the State alleging improper conduct against members of the judiciary in the conduct of legal proceedings in which the author is the plaintiff and the State is effectively the defendant. The plaintiff's claim for damages for alleged breach of his constitutional right to privacy is wholly unstatable and devoid of merit. It is undeserving of any further serious consideration..."

COMPANY

In *Heaphy v Heaphy*, High Court, January 15, 2004, Peart J. applied the rule in *Foss v Harbottle* (1843) 2 Hare 461 and struck out the part of the plaintiff's claim against his brother that asserted rights on behalf of a company in which the plaintiff was the shareholder. The plaintiff had left Ireland in 1986, having placed the running of two hotels owned by his company in the hands of the defendant. The plaintiff claimed that there was an oral agreement between him and his brother which involved the ultimate return of the hotels into the plaintiff's control after a period of 14 years. The hotels had been sold in 2000. The plaintiff sued the defendant for damages for fraud, breach of contract, misrepresentation and breach of judiciary duty.

Peart J. naturally did not attempt to resolve the factual matters at issue between the parties. He focused on the rule in *Foss v Harbottle*, to the effect that only the company can take proceedings in respect of damage done to it and that an individual shareholder has generally no such right (subject to four exceptions, which clearly had no application in the instant case).

Peart J. referred to the explanations for the rule which had been given in *Prudential Assurance Co. v Newman Industries Ltd* [1982] Ch. 209 and endorsed by Blayney J. in the Supreme Court decision of *O'Neill v Ryan* [1990] I.L.R.M. 140:

> "A personal action would subvert the rule in *Foss v Harbottle* and that rule is not merely a tiresome procedural obstacle placed in the path of a shareholder by a legalistic judiciary. The rule is the consequence of the fact that a corporation is a separate legal entity. Other consequences are limited liability and limited rights. The company is liable for its contracts and torts; the shareholder has no such liability The company acquires causes of action for breaches of contract and for torts which damage the company. No cause of action vests in the shareholder. When the shareholder acquires a share he accepts the fact that the value of his investment follows the fortunes of the company, and that he can only exercise his influence over the fortunes of the company by the exercise of his voting rights in general meeting. The law confers on him the right to ensure that the company observes the limitations of its memorandum of association and the right to ensure that other shareholders observe the rule, imposed upon them by the articles of association."

In the instant case, the company was by now in liquidation. Peart J. noted that the plaintiff could make enquiries to find out whether the liquidator was still *in situ*. If he was, the plaintiff's allegations that the assets of the company had been fraudulently disposed of would have to be investigated. Peart J. referred to the plaintiff's allegation that his signature to the contracts for sale of the hotels had been forged. He commented:

> "That, if true, would be a criminal offence, which the Fraud Investigation Branch of An Garda Síochána ought to have an interest in investigating. I am told that solicitors represented the vendor company. That firm presumably was under the impression that it was receiving instructions

from a person entitled to speak on behalf of the company and to execute any necessary documents. It is easy enough to appreciate that the firm in question would have assumed that the person who gave instructions to that firm was the person he said he was, and that he was entitled to bind the company in the sale of the hotels. But one's experience of life tells one that such strange things do happen where things are not necessarily as they might appear to be."

DAMAGES

1. The Civil Liability and Courts Act 2004 This important legislation is mainly directed towards restricting the latitude afforded under the law previously to plaintiffs in personal injuries litigation. It reduces the limitations period from three to two years. It requires plaintiffs to issue a letter of claim, within two months as a general rule, notifying the alleged wrongdoer of the alleged wrong. It transforms the process of initiating litigation, and of pleadings generally, by requiring greater specificity, earlier than under the previous dispensation. It requires the plaintiff to swear a verifying affidavit and creates criminal sanctions for knowingly false or misleading statements therein, as well as for the giving or adducing of evidence known to be false or misleading.

The Act also includes new machinery for a mediation conference, designed to encourage settlement, and for the making of formal offers. It empowers the court to appoint an independent expert and changes several aspects of the law relating to damages, most notably by requiring the court to have regard to the *Book of Quantum* published by PIAB. As a further discouragement to fraudulent claimants it establishes a register of personal injuries actions, which will reveal the number of times plaintiffs have previously participated in litigation.

These are the main features of the legislation. It has been followed by amendments to the Rules of the Superior Courts (S.I. No. 248 of 2005) and the District Court Rules (S.I. No. 257 of 2005). We still await the appropriate amendments to the Circuit Court Rules. For analysis of the Act see Craven & Binchy (eds), *Civil Liability and Courts Act 2004: Implications for Personal Injuries Litigation* (2005); Nolan, "The Civil Liability and Courts Act 2004", 9 Bar Rev. 181 (2004), 10 Bar Rev. 38 (2005). The new rules for "personal injuries summonses", requests for further information, defences, counterclaims, replies and defences to counterclaims and verifying affidavits are analysed comprehensively by Ciarán Craven & Binchy, *op. cit.*, pp.10–39.

Let us now look in more detail at provisions of the Act that are likely to impact on the substance of tort litigation, directly or indirectly.

Limitation of actions Personal injury litigation, prior to the enactment of the 2004 Act, had to be initiated within three years of the date of accrual of the right of action or the "date of knowledge" (whichever occurred later), as a result of the passage of the Statute of Limitations (Amendment) Act 1991, which introduced the "discoverability" principle for personal injury litigation. In essence, the clock does not start to tick under the 1991 Act until one could reasonably be aware that one has been injured, that the injury is significant and that it is attributable to the defendant's conduct.

Section 7 of the 2004 Act reduces the relevant period from three years to two years, from both the date of accrual of the cause of action and the "date of knowledge". The limitation provision in the Bill as initiated provided for only a one-year limitation period. This was roundly condemned by Senators and the Minister, at the close of the Second Reading in the Seanad, indicated that he would reflect on the matter. By Committee Stage, the Minister had capitulated. Responding to an amendment proposed by Senator Terry, Mr McDowell explained his change of mind on the basis that the States Claims Agency had communicated with him its belief that one year was too short a period for medical negligence claims:

> "Although this Bill has gone through a drafting and scrutiny process in the Attorney General's office, it strikes me, when I think about the effect on medical negligence cases, there could be a question mark over its proportionality in constitutional terms, for example, where somebody in the rehabilitation hospital in Dun Laoghaire has one year in which to decide on these weighty matters...
>
> The Law Society has also made the point to me that cases of medical negligence are complex and require time to establish the facts. I know from my experience as a barrister that even an enthusiastic solicitor seeking to marshall all the facts and get all the relevant reports will be hard pressed to get much of the material lined up so that the barristers can advise the client, if it is a case that requires advice, on who the appropriate defendant should be and on whether it was the anaesthetist, the surgeon or the hospital who was responsible for the medical catastrophe. Also, obtaining medical reports here frequently requires going outside the country and the laying out of considerable amounts of money.
>
> I pay tribute to members of the legal profession who carry much of the slack in terms of undertaking to pay fees for consultants in cases where there is a considerable risk to themselves that nothing will come of it. Often one must arrange for one's client to be examined by somebody outside the country, arrange trips abroad and join a queue if the client requires examination by a busy specialist in the United Kingdom or wherever. One cannot just click one's fingers and get an instant report from such a person, even in an ideal world."

The Minister proved impervious, however, to the suggestion—forcibly made by several senators and deputies—that medical negligence claims might need a longer limitation period than two years and might be deserving of a special period. In favour of a special, longer, period, several arguments were canvassed: the difficulty of getting expert witnesses, the trust that many patients repose in their doctors which may cause them to hesitate before initiating a claim against them, as well as the fact that, under the Personal Injuries Assessment Board Act 2003, the Statute of Limitations is suspended for a personal injury claim while it is being assessed by the PIAB, whereas medical negligence claims fall outside the scope of the 2003 Act and thus lose this period of grace. Moreover, forcing lawyers to initiate claims before the case has been properly prepared compromises the plaintiff, the defendant and the administration of justice.

The Minister's arguments against an extension for medical negligence claims are not fully convincing:

> "I reflected carefully on this and it is not as easy as members might think. Frequently a single incident has several consequences. For example, where a person is knocked down and breaks a limb, he or she is brought to hospital and treated, either correctly or not. It may happen some months after the injuries have settled that he or she should have been warned that the bone had settled in the wrong position, that there should have been an X-ray follow-up and, had he or she been properly advised, a new treatment to mitigate the effects of the accident should have been given. There is a series of single incidents that lead to a multiplicity of claims.
>
> I am concerned that, if the two year limit were to be imposed but it would be extended to three years where an additional claim for medical negligence would be made, a claimant would be tempted to allege that he was badly treated. In turn, he would launch a joint action against the original motorist and the doctor, claiming that between them his injuries resulted in a limp. Mixed claims would be difficult to disentangle.
>
> Defensive medicine is also damaging to the national interest. Claiming that the boat must be put out for victims of medical negligence because they are a special category ignores that we want doctors to treat people in an effective and efficient way. It is not a public policy aim to encourage medical negligence claims and put them into a wholly different category from ordinary negligence claims. It is never pleasant to be on the receiving end of a professional negligence claim. A doctor, in working out what went wrong, will have to recreate the situation from the patient's treatment notes to determine if care was adequate. On public policy grounds, I am not as sympathetic as most Deputies are to free range for medical negligence plaintiffs. I tend to believe that the pendulum may have swung too far in favour of liability. If one has a case in medical negligence, then bearing in mind the new law and the new time period which starts at the point of knowledge, which is quite

generous in its own way, two years should be sufficient for people with claims against doctors to have those claims articulated, put in writing and commenced."

This defence of the two-year period for medical negligence claims does not address the concerns that were advanced in favour of a longer period. The instance cited by the Minister of a claim against both a motorist and a doctor is clearly an exceptional one.

The reduction of the limitation period throws up significant anomalies in relation to PIAB applications, plaintiffs under a disability and fatal accident claims. These are insightfully analysed by Ciarán Craven, "Civil Liability and Courts Act 2004: Procedural Aspects" in Craven & Binchy (eds), *Civil Liability and Courts Act 2004: Implications for Personal Injuries Litigation* (2005), pp.7–10.

Letter of claim Section 8 contains a new requirement, that plaintiffs in personal injury litigation serve notice on the alleged wrongdoer, stating the nature of the wrong alleged to have been committed. It provides as follows:

"(1) Where a plaintiff in a personal injuries action fails, without reasonable cause, to serve a notice in writing, before the expiration of 2 months from the date of the cause of action, or as soon as practicable thereafter, on the wrongdoer or alleged wrongdoer stating the nature of the wrong alleged to have been committed by him or her, the court hearing the action may—
    (a) draw such inferences from the failure as appear proper, and
    (b) where the interests of justice so require—
        (i) make no order as to the payment of costs to the plaintiff, or
        (ii) deduct such amount from the costs that would, but for this section, be payable to the plaintiff as it considers appropriate.

(2) In this section "date of the cause of action" means—
    (a) the date of accrual of the cause of action, or
    (b) the date of knowledge, as respects the cause of action concerned, of the person against whom the wrong was committed or alleged to have been committed, whichever occurs later."

The Minister was confident that the section would not involve oppression on the plaintiffs. He observed in the *Seanad Debates*, June 3, 2004, Col.1588, that:

"anybody who knows the general disposition of the court knows that section will not be interpreted in a draconian or unreasonable way. It will only be invoked where the interests of justice require that something be done in regard to the costs because the plaintiff, without reasonable cause, failed to put the defendant on notice that a case was being taken. It is not simply that there was a failure without reasonable cause. It is also that the interests of justice require that the defendant be assisted by the penalisation as to cost issues.

In practice, it will not have a dramatic effect on genuine cases or people who did not get their act together. I do not think the courts would so interpret it. There is every reason to believe the courts will interpret it in a reasonable way. They will say that if a solicitor had a clear indication of the crash or an industrial accident, he or she should have written a letter to the other side stating, for example, that a person dropped a hammer on his foot at work last week and was not wearing protective boots. There is no reason that they should not be alerted within two months of being made aware of it. That is not draconian."

One can see the merit of encouraging solicitors not to sit on claims: it is unfair to defendants that they should learn of a claim perhaps a month short of the expiry of the limitation period, when they have little or no recollection of the day of the alleged accident. Of course the courts have the power to dismiss litigation taken within the limitation period on the basis of inordinate and inexcusable delay, but this will help only a small number of defendants facing such difficulties.

Nevertheless, two months is a very short period. In a matter of less than nine weeks, many victims of a tort will simply be recovering from their injuries; they will not yet have consulted a lawyer. Other victims may not yet be aware that they have a right of action against the wrongdoer. The "discoverability" principle introduced by the Statute of Limitations (Amendment) Act 1991 and incorporated into s.8 of the 2004 Act will often not avail them as they will be perfectly aware that they have received a significant injury as a result of the wrongdoer's conduct but may lack the legal sophistication to be aware that they have a right to sue the wrongdoer.

It will be hard to know how s.8 will harmonise with the policy of the Personal Injuries Assessment Board Act 2003. Section 8 requires very early intervention by victims of tortious wrongdoing. Prudence would dictate that this intervention be made only after legal advice has been obtained: a badly framed statement of the nature of the alleged wrong could damage the prospects of success in litigation. Yet the 2003 Act is designed to encourage victims (mistakenly, it may be suggested) *not* to see the need for lawyers to vindicate their claim. It may be questioned whether the need to serve a notice under s.8 is yet widely known in the community especially the community of employees, pedestrians and adventurous young boys who comprise a sizeable proportion of personal injury claimants. The best advice that can be given to the victims of a tort is that they should *immediately* contact a lawyer. How this is going to reduce the incidence of litigation is not easy to discern. For further consideration of the provisions relating to the letter of claim, see Craven, *op. cit.*, pp.10–15.

Mediation conferences   Let us now examine the effect of ss.15 and 16 of the Act which provide for the holding of a mediation conference, with a chairperson, under the direction of the court. For detailed analysis of these provisions, see Val Corbett, "Mediation in Actions for Personal Injury: Is It Good to Talk?" in Craven & Binchy (eds), *Civil Liability and Courts Act 2004: Implications for Personal Injuries Litigation* (2005), p.103.

Section 15 empowers the court, on the request of any party, at any time before trial, if it considers that the holding of a meeting would assist in reaching a settlement, to direct the parties "to meet and discuss and attempt to settle the action". The parties are obliged to "comply with that direction". This meeting, referred to as a "mediation conference", is to take place "at a time and place agreed by the parties" or, where they do not agree, at a time and place specified by the court.

The mediation conference has a chairperson appointed by agreement of all the parties or, in default of agreement, by the court. In the latter (but not the former) case, the chairperson must be a practising barrister or solicitor of five years standing or a person nominated by a body prescribed by order of the Minister. These bodies, prescribed by S.I. No.168 of 2005, are Friary Law; Mediation Forum-Ireland; Mediators' Institute Ireland; the Bar Council; the Chartered Institute of Arbitrators Irish Branch; and the Law Society.

The notes of the chairperson and all communications during the mediation conference and any records or other evidence of the conference are confidential and may not be used in evidence in any proceedings, civil or criminal. Val Corbett, *op. cit.*, p.130 warns practitioners to be on their guard when making revelations during a mediation conference: "[e]xamination of the wording of section 15(5) and case law from other jurisdictions indicates that it may only be the substance of the mediation that will be privileged". The costs incurred in the holding of the mediation conference are to be paid "by such party to the personal injuries action concerned as the court hearing the action shall direct".

The chairperson submits a report to the court under s.16(1). If the mediation conference did not take place, the report must state the reasons why it did not. Where it did take place, the report must state whether or not a settlement has been reached and, if so, its terms; the agreement must be signed by the parties. Each party is given a copy of this report. At the conclusion of the action the court hears submissions from the parties. If satisfied that "a party to the action failed to comply with a direction under s.15(1)", the court may direct that party to pay all or some of the costs of the action incurred after the giving of the direction under ss.15(1) and 16(3). For discussion of whether this complies with Art.6 of the European Convention on Human Rights, see Corbett, *op. cit.*, pp.132–134.

This section provokes a number of comments. First, it is to be noted that the initiative for the holding of a mediation conference rests with any of the parties to the litigation; the court cannot direct that such a conference take place of its own motion. Even where a party makes a request for a mediation conference, the court will make a direction for it to be held only if it considers that this would assist in reaching a settlement in the action. Whether the court must have specific grounds for that view or can make a direction, acting on the *a priori* principle that settlement should always be attempted, is not clear. the language of s.15(1)(b) suggests that the former interpretation is preferable. For consideration of this aspect see Corbett, *op. cit.*, pp.122–124.

Next, the section envisages that only one mediation conference will take place: it refers to "a time" rather than "a time or times". Common sense would suggest that this could hardly mean that a conference, once initiated, could not be adjourned by the chairperson, with the consent of the parties, with the intention of concluding it at some later stage; but if, at the end of a conference, there is no agreement that the conference be reconvened, that would appear to be that. It may even be the case that common sense must yield to the actual language of s.15 and that a consensual adjournment is not permitted under the section—that what is provided for is one shot at a settlement rather than a settlement process. See further Corbett, *op. cit.*, pp.125–126.

The next issue concerns the parties' obligations under s.15. What are they actually required to do? The crucial provision is s.15(1), under which the court directs that the parties "meet to discuss and attempt to settle the action". Failure to comply with this direction renders a party liable to an order relating to costs. Clearly a point-blank refusal, or a wilful omission, to meet the other party at all will constitute such a failure; but what is the position where a party turns up but indicates no desire whatsoever to settle the case? Do the words "attempt to settle the action" import some genuine substantive attempt? There are serious difficulties with such an interpretation. Let us take a case where a defendant sincerely believes that a claim is fraudulent. The only terms on which he or she will "settle" the action are that the plaintiff withdraw the claim. Clearly there can be no obligation on the defendant to offer a penny. If a defendant takes the stance of complete opposition to the claim, is the chairperson to involve himself or herself in an assessment of whether that stance is bona fide or reasonable? How could the chairperson come to any sound conclusion on the basis of one meeting? Section 15 does not require the chairperson to brief himself or herself on the merits of the claim: that would be an adjudicatory function well beyond what the mediation (or settlement) process envisages. Moreover, the terms of the report prescribed by s.16 give no support for this interpretation of the chairperson's role.

It may well be, therefore, that failure to comply with a direction under s.15(1) will, in practice, be limited to cases where the party simply does not participate in the conference rather than adopts what, in the view of the chairperson, is an entirely unreasonable stance. It could, however, be the case that the refusal by a party to take part in any meaningful way could be cited by the mediator as one of the reasons why the mediation conference failed: see

Corbett, *op. cit.*, p.131.

Section 15 is lacking in any detail of the chairperson's role, other than to chair a process the purpose of which is to seek to reach a settlement of the action. Whether the chairperson is strongly interventionist or entirely passive seems to be a matter for him or her to determine.

It is worth noting that anyone can be a chairperson if the parties agree: no qualifications are required. It is only where the court makes the appointment, in default of such agreement, that the qualifications mentioned in s.15(4)(b)(ii) are relevant.

Formal offers   A new procedure, requiring the parties to make formal offers of terms of settlement to each other, is prescribed by s.17. It is important because it is backed by a sanction: the court, when addressing the costs issue, must have regard to the terms of the respective formal offers and the reasonableness of the conduct of the parties in making them.

The section provides as follows:

> "(1) The plaintiff in a personal injuries action shall, after the prescribed date, serve a notice in writing of an offer of terms of settlement on the defendant.
>
> (2) The defendant in a personal injuries action shall, after the prescribed date, serve a notice in writing on the plaintiff—
>
> (a) of an offer of terms of settlement, or
>
> (b) stating that he or she is not prepared to pay any sum of money to the plaintiff in settlement of the action.
>
> (3) A copy of a formal offer shall, after the expiration of the prescribed period be lodged in court by, or on behalf of, the plaintiff or defendant, as the case may be.
>
> (4) The terms of a formal offer shall not be communicated to the judge in the trial of a personal injuries action until after he or she has delivered judgment in the action.
>
> (5) The court shall, when considering the making of an order as to the payment of the costs in a personal injuries action have regard to—
>
> (a) the terms of a formal offer, and
>
> (b) the reasonableness of the conduct of the parties in making their formal offers.
>
> (6) This section is in addition to and not in substitution for any rule of court providing for the payment into court of a sum of money in satisfaction of a cause of action or the making of an offer of tender of payment to the other party or parties to an action.
>
> (7) In this section—
>
> 'formal offer' means an offer under subsection (1) or (2)(a), or a statement under subsection (2)(b);
>
> 'prescribed date' means such date before the date of the commencement

of the trial of the personal injuries action concerned as is prescribed by order of the Minister;

'prescribed period' means such period commencing on the prescribed date as is prescribed by order of the Minister."

The Civil Liability and Courts Act 2004 (Section 17) Order 2005 (S.I. No.169 of 2005) provides that the prescribed date is the date upon which the personal injuries summons is served on the defendant. The prescribed period, in the case of proceedings in the High Court or Circuit Court, is the period commencing on the prescribed date and ending on the expiration of 14 days after the service of the notice of trial in the proceedings; in the District Court, it is the period commencing on the prescribed date and ending on the expiration of four days after the delivery of the defence in the proceedings.

Section 17 does not make matters easy for a plaintiff. While clearly a plaintiff who asks for "a million euro for a broken finger and not a halfpenny less" will be acting totally unreasonably and perhaps deserving of some sanction in costs, the position becomes more troublesome where the plaintiff places a very high value on his or her claim. Why should the plaintiff not do so? Is the underlying thrust of s.17 that the plaintiff should be intimidated by the fear of a costs sanction into formally offering less than he or she estimates the claim at its best? Is s.17 really about forcing plaintiffs to compromise on the fullest worth of the claim?

Note that the defendant is under similar, but not identical, pressures. The defendant may be contesting liability. If the defendant reasonably believes that there is a 60 per cent chance of successfully defending a claim worth €100,000, offers €40,000 and ultimately loses the case, is the court to investigate, not merely the *quantum* issue, but the propriety of the defendant's assessment of the strength or weaknesses of the claim? A judge who has just found in favour of a plaintiff on the issue of liability is hardly likely to sympathise with a defendant's assessment that the claim was unmeritorious.

Expert evidence Let us now consider s.20, which enables the court to appoint an expert witness, in addition to any other expert witness called by the parties. The section provides as follows:

"(1) In a personal injuries action, the court may appoint such approved persons as it considers appropriate to carry out investigations into, and give expert evidence in relation to, such matters as the court directs.

(2) A party in a personal injuries action shall cooperate with a person appointed under this section and shall, in particular, provide the person with—

(a) (i) any report or other document prepared by the party, or

(ii) any report or other document prepared on behalf of the party concerned, for the purposes of or in contemplation of the personal injuries action,

and

(b) any document or information used or referred to for the purpose of preparing the report.

(3) The costs incurred in the appointment of, and carrying out of an investigation by, a person appointed under this section shall be paid by such party to the personal injuries action concerned as the court hearing the action shall direct.

(4) A party in a personal injuries action shall be entitled to cross-examine a person appointed under this section in relation to any matter that he or she was appointed to investigate and give expert evidence on.

(5) The President of the High Court in consultation with the President of the Circuit Court and the President of the District Court shall approve such persons as he or she considers appropriate for the purposes of this section, and a person so approved is in this section referred to as an 'approved person'."

The Minister sought to justify this innovation as follows:

"In many personal injuries actions, conflicting evidence from experts must be decided by the court. Section 19 allows a court to appoint approved persons to investigate and give expert evidence on any issue the court may direct. The section also provides that any party to a personal injuries action shall co-operate with an approved person. An 'approved person' is a person approved by the President of the High Court, in consultation with the Presidents of the Circuit and District Courts, for the purposes of the section. The intention behind this provision is that an expert, independent of any expert witness retained by the parties, could be appointed to assist the court. To take a medical example, a court might decide to appoint its own medical assessor, who will testify and be liable to cross examination, but will give an objective view to the court having listened to the medical experts on either side."

Although it is true that the parties may cross-examine the court-appointed expert and may call expert witnesses themselves, one may wonder about the justification for this change. Let us consider some of the difficulties it involves.

First, it appears to call into question the truthfulness and objectivity of expert witnesses called by the parties. The court-appointed witness is presented by the Minister as giving an "objective view": the implication is that the court is not otherwise in receipt of such evidence. Undoubtedly some expert witnesses may tend towards partisanship and it would be sensible to acknowledge this fact clearly, but such a weakness is not limited to expert witnesses; judges are well used to responding to it when it presents itself. Moreover, it is the function of cross-examination to expose it to the gaze of the court.

Secondly, there is a danger that a court-appointed witness might be regarded by the court as offering more reliable evidence than the parties' experts. That will clearly not necessarily be the case where these experts give objective evidence.

Thirdly, the use of a court-appointed expert witness may have an effect detrimental to plaintiffs who are seeking to advance a theory that contradicts orthodox practice. In the case of medicine, for example, the test for professional negligence set out in *Dunne v National Maternity Hospital* [1989] I.R. 91 imposes liability where a particular customary practice is one with inherent defects that ought to be obvious to anyone giving the matter consideration. This involves a challenge to the accepted wisdom of the profession. A person chosen by the court from a panel of experts may tend towards the centre of conventional thought within the profession. This means that, in such a case, the plaintiff may have the handicap of having to pitch his or her expert witness, arguing in favour of a new approach, against two expert witnesses. Conversely, a defendant doctor who has conscientiously deviated from customary practice may well find that his or her expert has to do battle with two expert witnesses.

Next we may ask: What will be the position where a scientific controversy is at the heart of the litigation? One can discern two difficulties with the role of the court-appointed expert here. First, the selection by the court of a particular expert may have an influence on the outcome of the case. Let us take a practical example. A plaintiff claims that her condition of multiple sclerosis is attributable to an accident caused by the defendant's negligence. The crucial scientific issue in the case is whether multiple sclerosis can be caused by trauma. If the panel of experts contains experts taking opposing views of this issue, what is the court to do? Is it to apprise itself of the respective views of the experts before making a selection of one of them or should it simply take pot luck? What is it to do where it is aware of the view of some of the experts on the panel but not of others?

The second difficulty arises where an expert is chosen from the panel and gives evidence (let us say) that multiple sclerosis cannot be caused by traumatic injury. The court is theoretically free to reject that view and to favour the evidence given by the plaintiff's expert witness. To do so, however, would be to stigmatise the quality of the evidence of the expert witness on a straightforward scientific issue and, indirectly, the wisdom of the President of the High Court in having put that witness on the panel. A new pressure has been placed on judges which is unfair to them and even more unfair to litigants.

At a philosophical level, there are problems with compromising the values underlying the adversarial system. These may seem remote from daily practice but that is not in fact the case. No enterprise can thrive if based on inconsistent values as to what it should seek to achieve.

At the core of the adversarial system, surely, is the notion that the parties to the litigation have the function of defining the issues, adducing evidence and challenging each other's case through cross-examination and the adducing of opposing evidence. The trial judge has the function of adjudicating on the issues on the evidence presented to the court. It is not the judge's function, generally speaking, to assume the mantle of Hercule Poirot, prescribing the scope of the evidence that should be adduced and engaging in an enquiry into the true situation. The inquisitorial process, favoured in continental European legal systems, serves that goal. The judge takes control and the parties play a secondary, subservient, role.

This is not to suggest that the adversarial system is an inadequate vehicle for the emergence of the truth. On the contrary, with the central role it gives to cross-examination—in Wigmore's famous description, "beyond doubt the greatest legal enquiry ever invented for the discovery of the truth"—the adversarial system can claim to advance the interests of truth, generally, in a rigorous manner.

Now it may be possible to argue that we should replace the adversarial system with the inquisitorial system. This would be a truly radical change for our legal culture and should be contemplated only after a most thorough comparative analysis of the competing systems and an assessment of the probable outcome from the standpoint of justice. No such enquiry has even been proposed, let alone begun, in Ireland. Yet this Act introduces into the very heart of the adversarial system an essentially inquisitorial element, based on the thinnest of rationales, with no clear guidance to the court as to how to accommodate and nurture the cuckoo that has been placed in the nest.

One should keep a sense of proportion; the change is not seismic, in view of the fact that the trial judge retains a discretion as to whether to appoint an expert witness and the parties retain the right of cross-examination. As against this, it would be wise to keep in mind that the PIAB procedure is deeply inquisitorial. The PIAB computation of assessment of damages has been linked to the courts by s.22 of the 2004 Act; there may be here an inexorable underlying shift away from the adversarial process of compensation for personal injury in Ireland.

The Act does not explain the scope of the court-appointed expert witness power to carry out investigations into "such matters as the court directs"(s.20(1)). How extensive can these investigations be? Is the expert to take on the role of investigator of the truth of the plaintiff's assertions or of the evidence of other witnesses? Does the duty of cooperation resting on parties to the action (but not, expressly at all events, on witnesses other than the parties) include the obligation to answer fully and truthfully all questions that the expert chooses to ask?

Neither does the Act clarify the status of the expert evidence given by the expert witness to the court after he or she has carried out these investigations. The easy answer would be that this expert evidence should be treated in the same way as the evidence given by experts chosen by the parties; but it is of a somewhat different character, being based on a power of investigation backed by compulsion. Section 20 expresses no specific sanction for breach of the obligation to cooperate prescribed in s.20(2). It would seem, at a minimum, that such a breach would constitute civil contempt; it could well be criminal contempt and perhaps constitute the offence of interfering with the administration of justice.

Damages awards   Let us now turn to consider some of the changes in relation to damages awards which the Act makes.

1. Actuarial tables Section 23 provides as follows:

> "(1) The Minister may, by regulations, prescribe actuarial tables for the purpose of their being referred to by the courts when assessing damages in personal injuries actions in respect of future financial loss.
> (2) A court in a personal injuries action shall, in assessing damages in respect of future financial loss, refer to such actuarial tables (if any) as are prescribed under subsection (1).
> (3) In this section 'actuarial tables' means actuarial tables prepared by a person designated for that purpose by a body prescribed by regulations made by the Minister."

The Minister explained the purpose of the provision as follows:

> "This is a new innovation, but it is not unprecedented internationally, whereby the Minister can prescribe actuarial tables by regulations for the purpose of their being referred to by the courts when assessing damages in respect of future financial loss.
>   If one loses an income stream for the rest of one's life, at the moment in Ireland if it is a serious case an actuary comes to court and gives evidence by reference to actuarial tables as to what the appropriate multiplier for a capital sum should be. I am not in the slightest anti the actuarial profession whose members are skilled and wonderful people, but it is a waste of their time to have them hanging around courts to give fundamentally statistical advice by way of evidence when, as in certain other common law countries comparable to ours, it is possible to do so by a standard form table which can be varied from time to time to reflect realities. Somebody once asked: 'What is the definition of an extrovert actuary?' to which the reply was 'An extrovert actuary is one who looks at your shoes when he is talking to you.'"

2. Discount rate Section 24 gives the Minister power to prescribe the discount rate for determining the current value of future financial loss for the purposes of assessing damages. The section provides as follows:

"(1) The Minister may, by regulations, prescribe the discount rate that shall apply for the purposes of the assessment of damages in respect of future financial loss.

(2) Regulations under subsection (1) may prescribe different rates in respect of different classes of financial loss or different periods of time.

(3) The court may apply a discount rate other than the rate prescribed under subsection (1) if it considers that the application of the rate prescribed would result in injustice being done.

(4) In this section 'discount rate' means, in relation to the assessment of damages by a court, the rate commonly referred to by that name that is applied by the court for the purpose of determining the current value of any future financial loss."

A few points may be noted. First, the court has the power, under s.24(3), to depart from the ministerial preference, but only where not to do so "would result in injustice being done". That is a fairly stiff test. Secondly, although the section is not expressly limited to personal injuries actions, s.6 would seem to limit it in this way, since it provides that (subject to certain identified sections other than s.24) a provision of Pt 2—of which s.24 is one—"applies only to personal injuries actions brought after the date of the commencement of that provision".

As to how matters had been operating up to the passage of the 2004 Act, see *McEneaney v Monaghan County Council*, High Court, July 26, 2001 noted in the *Annual Review of Irish Law 2001*, pp.649–651.

3. The Book of Quantum The legislation contains an important provision relating to the *Book of Quantum* created under the Personal Injuries Assessment Board Act 2003.

Section 22 of the 2004 Act provides as follows:

"(1) The court shall, in assessing damages in a personal injuries action, have regard to the Book of Quantum.

(2) Subsection (1) shall not operate to prohibit a court from having regard to matters other than the Book of Quantum when assessing damages in a personal injuries action.

(3) In this section 'Book of Quantum' means the Book of Quantum required to be prepared and published by the Personal Injuries Assessment Board under the Act of 2003."

The Minister explained his understanding of the provision as follows:

"There is a precedent in that there was a guideline for the Army deafness claims. It is not mandatory, a court is free to disregard it if it wishes but it asks courts to have regard to the Book of Quantum.

If one is a judge in a Circuit Court in Tipperary town, with counsel from both sides addressing a case, and one is trying to decide how much a broken leg or hand is worth, it is useful at least to have a document which addresses that issue. It may be that the judge in his or her independent judicial function regards it as low or high in the circumstances of the particular case but it is in the interests of uniformity in the administration of justice that there should be some general document available to which the judiciary can have regard, even if it is not strictly legally bound. Subsection (2) makes it clear that this is not an exhaustive procedure or that the court cannot have regard to matters not covered by the Book of Quantum. It is a serious advance in an effort to bring consistency in uniformity to the question of damages...

I want to make it clear to judges that they are expected to have regard to the contents of this Book of Quantum, that it is their legal duty to have regard to it and to consult it. I do not want a price list that is invariable in every case which counsel could consult and say a case is worth a given amount and that is it. Injuries vary from case to case, for example, a broken ankle can be very serious or less so.

It is beyond the wit of man and woman to devise an exact scale of damages in these matters...

This is a major new step. It would be unlawful for a court to decide damages without having regard to the Book of Quantum, but it would not be unlawful to deviate from it. The High Court, on appeal from the Circuit Court, would be in a position to ask why was there a departure from the Book of Quantum and if there were grounds to justify it. It is an effort to bring consistency but not uniformity into the application of the law."

It may be recalled, in the context of the army deafness litigation, that the Government enacted the Civil Liability (Assessment of Hearing Injury) Act 1998, s.4 of which provides as follows:

"(1) In all proceedings claiming damages for personal injury arising from hearing loss, the courts shall, in determining the extent of the injuries suffered, have regard to Chapter 7 (Irish Hearing Disability Assessment System) of the Report and, in particular, to the matters set out in paragraph 1 (Summary) and Table 4 (Disability Percentage Age Correction Factor) to paragraph 7 (Age Related Hearing Loss Correction) of that Chapter, and the said paragraph 1 and Table 4 are, for convenience of reference, set out in Part I and Part II, respectively, of the Schedule to this Act.

(2) In all proceedings claiming damages for personal injury arising from tinnitus, the courts shall, in determining the extent of the injuries

suffered, have regard to the classification method contained in paragraph 9 (Tinnitus) of Chapter 7 (Irish Hearing Disability Assessment System) of the Report."

Commenting on this provision, in *Hanley v Minister for Defence* [1999] 4 I.R. 393. Keane J. observed:

> "The policy underlying the Act is obvious. Although it is not confined in its terms to the many cases brought against the present defendants, it was, of course, the legislative response to what may fairly be described as a 'litigation crisis' confronting the State. The objective was clearly to ensure that, while those who had suffered hearing loss as a result of negligence were fairly compensated, the amount of that compensation should, so far as possible, be assessed by courts in a manner which reflects the basic principle that like cases should be treated alike. It was also no doubt envisaged that such an approach would facilitate the early compromise of claims of this nature with a consequent significant reduction in the huge burden of legal costs involved.
>
> While it is the duty of the courts to give effect to the legislative policy enshrined in the Act, every case which comes before them for assessment must be considered in the light of its particular facts. The Act indeed implicitly acknowledges that this should be the appropriate approach by doing no more than requiring the court to 'have regard' to the relevant sections of the Green Book."

Keane J. approved of what Lavan J. had said in *Green v Minister for Defence* [1998] 4 I.R. 464:

> "The requirement to 'have regard to' the Green Book does not... impose a duty upon the Court to adhere strictly to its terms. Therefore, while the Court must consider the approach adopted in the Green Book, it reserves the right to consider alternative approaches. The Court may then determine which is the most appropriate solution in each individual case. In the absence of a more appropriate alternative solution... established to the satisfaction of the Court, the statutory formula should be applied. The circumstances in which the statutory formula is not applied may in fact transpire to be as limited as the defendants' submissions suggest. However, this will be a matter for the determination of the Court in the circumstances of each individual case."

It seems clear that s.22 of the 2004 Act would not be declared unconstitutional on the basis of interference by the Oireachtas in the exercise of the judicial power. It is nothing like the offending provision in *Maher v Attorney General* [1973] I.R. 140 which purported to give to a certificate regarding the alcohol in a blood specimen the status of conclusive evidence. Section 22 merely requires the court to "have regard" to certain evidence, while leaving the court perfectly free to have regard to other evidence. A purist court might complain about being *required* to have regard to evidence to which it otherwise might attach absolutely no weight; it seems far more likely that a court would consider this obligation as going no further than to take account of the *Book of Quantum*, for what it is worth evidentially, which may be very little or not at all in some cases. Thus, for example, in a case involving post-traumatic stress disorder, which is not covered by the *Book of Quantum*, the trial judge would merely state in his or her judgment that he or she had "had regard" to the *Book of Quantum* and found that it had thrown no light on the issue requiring resolution. (Herbert J. adopted this strategy in *Power v Governor of Cork Prison*, High Court, July 20, 2005.)

Nonetheless, s.22 represents a coded message from the Oireachtas to the courts that the former would greatly prefer if the latter went a considerable distance towards adopting the ranges of awards prescribed by the *Book of Quantum*. This appears to be what Herbert J. did in *Meagher v Shamrock Public Houses Ltd t/a the Ambassador Hotel*, High Court, February 16, 2005. Indeed, in the decision of the Supreme Court in *Nolan v Murphy* on March 18, 2005, the *Book of Quantum* was referred to without any sign of hesitation or attempt to establish some judicial distance from it.

Fraud or exaggeration   Before considering s.26 of the 2004 Act, one should refer briefly to the previous case law: *Vesey v Bus Éireann* [2001] 4 I.R. 192, analysed in the *Annual Review of Irish Law 2001*, pp.657–658; *Shelly-Morris v Bus Átha Cliath/Dublin Bus* [2003] 2 I.L.R.M. 12, analysed in the *Annual Review of Irish Law 2002*, pp.527–529 and *O'Connor v Bus Átha Cliath/Dublin Bus* [2003] 4 I.R. 459, analysed in the *Annual Review of Irish Law 2003*, pp.604–607. It would be fair to say that there is some evidence of a difference in approach among the court: Hardiman J. seems disposed to take a strong position against exaggerated claims; Murray C.J. prefers a somewhat gentler approach.

Section 26 *requires* the court to dismiss a personal injuries action where the plaintiff gives or adduces, or dishonestly causes to be given or adduced, evidence that is false or misleading, in any material respect, and that he or she knows to be false or misleading, *unless*, for reasons that the court must state in its decision, the dismissal would result in injustice being done. An act is done "dishonestly" by a person if he or she does it with the intention of misleading the court. It should be noted that s.26 applies even in cases where liability is not contested.

The introduction of s.26 represents a clear attempt by the Oireachtas to weaken the position of plaintiffs whose claim is tainted by untruthfulness in some respect. Its proviso probably preserves the common law position, so far as it can be gleaned from *Vesey*, *Shelly-Morris* and *O'Connor*. It leaves for another day resolution of the exact circumstances in which an exaggerating plaintiff should be denied any remedy. Clearly s.26 would not apply to someone such as the plaintiff in the *O'Connor* case, who was not dishonest, having no intent to mislead the court.

The Minister was apparently content with the principle that untruthfulness should be met by an outright dismissal. He stated that:

> "People must understand that if they take personal injuries actions, they will lose out if they come other than with clean hands as genuine claimants. If they come with dishonest intent either to exaggerate or tell lies about their case, they will get nothing.
>
> If, for example, a plaintiff states that as a result of fracturing his or her leg he or she can no longer play golf and subsequently a video is shown to the court of the person playing golf, the person will not only lose the extra damages he or she would have got as a result of not being able to play golf but will also lose the full damages and the case will be thrown out of court emphatically."

It remains to be seen whether the courts will take a more nuanced view. What is not clear is whether the court is free to take, and articulate, a position, *a priori*, that a general rule denying compensation to a plaintiff who is untruthful in any material respect is one that would result in injustice being done. In other words, does the "out clause" given by the section on the issue of justice permit the court to articulate a value that is inconsistent with the value adopted by section? Of course the issue is unlikely to surface because the court is always free to conclude, in *the particular circumstances*, that to deny compensation to the particular plaintiff would result in injustice being done.

Mulkern v Flesk, High Court, February 25, 2005 is the first decision in which s.26 of the Act is analysed. The plaintiff had been involved in a traffic accident. Liability was not contested. The defendant obtained through discovery the records of a job application made by the plaintiff subsequent to the accident in which she had not mentioned the accident and asserted that she was in good health and specifically that she had never suffered from back injury. When the inconsistency between her claim and what she had stated in these documents was put to her in correspondence by the defendant's solicitor, she acknowledged the disparity but explained it was on the basis that she had been working as a shop assistant, that her back pain was so intense that she needed to avoid constantly standing and that the new job offered this possibility.

Kelly J. declined to dismiss the claim. Having heard the plaintiff's evidence as well as the evidence of doctors who had treated her, he concluded:

> "Before the court could apply the provisions of s.26(1) of the Act it would have to be satisfied as a matter of probability that the evidence given by the plaintiff was false or misleading in a material respect and

that the plaintiff knew her evidence to be false and misleading.

I do not accept that the plaintiff gave false or misleading evidence. It is not to her credit that she told untruths to her prospective employer. I am satisfied that she very much wanted and indeed needed to obtain employment with Boston Scientific. That may explain why she was untruthful in her dealings with that employer although it does not excuse such behaviour. But I do not accept that she gave false or misleading evidence to the court…

I am of opinion that once the plaintiff realised that the defendants had found her out in her untruths she decided to make a clean breast of it and admit to the court her wrongdoing in that regard. That wrongdoing was admitted at the outset. It was admitted in pre-trial correspondence, by her counsel in opening the case and in her own evidence in chief. She may well have given false and misleading information to her employer but I do not believe that she did so on oath before the court and consequently I am satisfied that the provisions of the section do not apply."

One has to wonder whether the interests of justice are truly being served by s.26. *Mulkern v Flesk* captures the dilemma that many people who are not well off may confront. They may be driven by economic necessity to suppress certain facts in order to avoid financial disaster. If in this case the documents had not been discovered but instead a surprise witness from the new employer had given evidence, there is a real prospect that the claim would have been dismissed. Would that really have been a fair result?

Undeclared income Section 28 of the Act requires the court to disregard any income, profit or gain in respect of which the plaintiff is making a claim which has not been returned or notified to the Revenue Commissioners unless in all the circumstances it would be unjust to disregard it. For consideration of this provision, see Neville Cox, "The New Rules Relating to Collateral Benefits and Undeclared Income", in Craven & Binchy (eds), *Civil Liability and Courts Act 2004: Implications for Personal Injuries Litigation* (2005), pp.94–102.

Invited submissions to Supreme Court Let us now consider a very curious innovation. Section 21 provides as follows:

"(1) The Supreme Court may, upon an appeal to it in a personal injuries action, invite such persons as it considers appropriate to make submissions to the court-
  (a) in relation to any matter concerning either liability or damages that it considers to be of exceptional public importance, and
  (b) if the action belongs to a class of causes of action in which the same or a similar matter arises.

(2) The Supreme Court may perform functions under subsection (1), either—

    (a) upon receiving a request in that behalf from a party to the personal injuries action concerned, or from a person who is not such a party, or

    (b) where no such request is made.

(3) Where a person declines an invitation to make submissions under this section he or she shall inform the court in writing stating his or her reason for so declining."

What is this section seeking to achieve? First, it is clear that the Supreme Court's power of invitation can be activated either on the request of a party to the personal injuries action or of anyone else or by the court itself, without any request to it. Secondly, it appears that the Supreme Court is free, but not obliged, to adhere to such a request by inviting "such persons as it considers appropriate" to make submissions to it. The section gives no guidance as to the qualifications or other qualities that might render persons "appropriate" to the task, nor does it throw light on their number or on whether they need represent both sides of the issue that requires determination on appeal. It would appear that they need not.

As to the kind of case in which the power may be exercised, it must be one involving "any matter concerning either liability or damages" that the Supreme Court considers to be of exceptional public importance and the action "belongs to a class of causes of action in which the same or a similar matter arises." The word "liability" is highly elastic. It obviously includes issues relating to the duty or standard of care. Less obviously, it may extend to issues relating to contributory negligence, voluntary assumption of risk or the *ex turpi causa* defence, all of which, in part or in whole, arguably relate to the *non-ascription* of liability. A matter concerning "damages" clearly includes such issues as the categories for assessment of damages. Arguably it includes issues relating to remoteness of damage, which is concerned with the limits of liability. This was the Minister's interpretation of the provision: *Seanad Debates*, March 4, Col.1809. See further McMahon & Binchy, *op. cit.*, Chap.3. It may well be that the notion of liability could be regarded by the court as being sufficiently broad to encompass any case raising the question of whether a defendant should be found liable to compensate the plaintiff *in the particular circumstances of that case*.

The provisos, as we have seen, are twofold. The first is that the court must consider that the matter is one of "exceptional public importance". We are familiar with this concept in the context of limitations on the entitlement to appeal against certain judgments, generally in a public law context. The second is that the action must "belon[g] to a class of causes of action in which the same or a similar matter arises". What exactly does a "class of causes of action" comprise? Must there be a series of related claims before the courts? If so, what degree of connectedness must there be as regards defendant or defendants or as regards plaintiffs? If the concept of class does not carry with it a connotation of several actual claims but rather an abstract category of claims that could be taken, what are the parameters of this concept? It is easy to regard the tort of negligence as being capable of being broken into categories of duty: one recalls Lord Macmillan's observation that "[t]he categories of negligence are never closed". But how sharply should the notion of class of causes of actions be defined in this context?

One suspects that the court will not attempt to lay down any clear guidelines on this question but will instead proceed more by way of broad intuition that a particular claim has the potential for significant downstream effects in the incidence of litigation. An example may help. In *Barclay v An Post* [1998] 2 I.L.R.M. 385, McGuinness J. rejected a claim by a postal worker that An Post (and its predecessor, the Department of Posts and Telegraphs) had been negligent in exposing him and other workers to the risk of back pain from having to bend to deliver mail to letterboxes placed at the bottom of front doors in private residences. The plaintiff's argument was that the defendant either ought to have secured from the Department of the Environment a bye-law locating letterboxes higher up on doors or ought not to have required its workers to deliver letters to doors with dangerously low letterboxes. McGuinness J. held on the evidence that the defendant, an employer, had just about done enough to discharge its duty of care to its postal workers. Had she come to the opposite conclusion, An Post would no doubt have potentially faced thousands of claims. Yet there was nothing novel about the relevant legal principles in this litigation. The issue was one merely of applying traditional, well established principles to the facts and making a value-judgment as to whether the defendant had complied with the standard of care required of employers generally. No extension of the frontiers of liability or of the duty of care was in issue: all that was involved was the prospect that a defendant could be exposed to claims from a great many plaintiffs. The same, incidentally, could be said of the Army deafness litigation, though the subjective character of the injury in that context was an exacerbating factor so far as estimating the potential range of claims was concerned.

Why should the prospect of the imposition of widespread liability on an admittedly negligent defendant whose negligence is well established by traditional principles be a reason for the Supreme Court to invite submissions from outsiders? It may be unpleasant for defendants to have to face a large bill but it is hard to articulate a principled reason for the Supreme Court to go to their aid by inviting submissions from people or groups who are not involved in the litigation, the intended effect of which will be to make it more likely for the court to find in favour of the defendant? Yet this is what the framers of the section appear intent on encouraging.

The Minister stated:

"Section 20 is an important provision dealing with intervention in personal injuries action. It provides that where an appeal is taken to the Supreme Court, the court may, where it considers that any matter in the case is of exceptional public importance and the action is one of a class of claims in which the same or similar matters arise, invite appropriate persons to make submissions to it. Such an intervention may come about at the initiative of the court, at the request of any party or of any person who is not a party. An issue may arise in a series of cases which is of exceptional public importance and goes beyond the interests of the parties before the court.

This could, for example occur within the ambit of nervous shock. If, for example, when walking down a street I witness a collision between two people causing fatal injury to one of them and I suffer shock and injury on account of what I have witnessed, the ambit of that right to claim damages has serious implications. Recently, for example, we had a case where somebody working in a hospital accident and emergency unit or a morgue claimed damages after suffering nervous shock arising from a traffic accident.

This gives rise to the question of reasonable foreseeability and proximity. This is not just a matter of a good or bad barrister spending an afternoon in court arguing the toss between a plaintiff or a defendant and coming to a conclusion on this issue. The Attorney General or others may want to tell the Supreme Court that such a High Court decision extends the concept of reasonable foreseeability or proximity too far and will have general repercussions if it becomes a general application."

What seems to be envisaged here is that, where there is a prospect that one defendant, or a range of defendants, may face wide-ranging liability, the Supreme Court should seek to ensure that the strongest arguments against that prospect are advanced. This does not seem a very even-handed approach. If we take the case of the wrongful sustained exposure by an employer of its employees to the risk of injury, would it be fairer for the court to side with the negligent employer or the injured employees? The best answer perhaps is that it should not be in the business of siding with either party; the next best answer, it may be suggested, is that the court should strive to advance the vindication of the rights of the injured victims of a serious tort rather than protect the interests of the wrongdoer.

It may well be the case that the Minister's apparent interpretation of the sections is mistaken and that the Supreme Court will exercise its jurisdiction under the section even-handedly, extending to non-parties the entitlement to make submissions advocating the enlargement of the duty of care on the same basis as those making opposite submissions. The s.26 procedure is an obvious precedent of such an even-handed approach.

It is not clear why this controversial power of recruitment of outside submissions should be exercised only by the Supreme Court. If it is a good power, why should it not also be available to the High Court trial judge? And are there not dangers to the separation of the powers if the Government is able to convey to the Supreme Court its desire, in particular cases, that liability should be trimmed back, out of concern for the public interest? For a thoughtful analysis of s.21, see Ray Ryan, "The Impact of the Act on the 'Compensation Culture': Big or Small?" in Craven & Binchy (eds), *Civil Liability and Courts Act 2004: Implications for Personal Injuries Litigation* (2005), pp.155–157.

2. Constitutional infringements In *Redmond v Minister for the Environment*, High Court, February 1, 2004, Herbert J. gave a robust refutation to the argument advanced on behalf of the defendants that the doctrine of the separation of powers rendered it inappropriate, save in the most extreme circumstances, to make an award of damages against the legislative arm of the State for the infringement in an Act of the Oireachtas of a right guaranteed by the Constitution. In the instant case Herbert J. had earlier struck down legislative provisions requiring the payment of deposits by candidates for elections to the Dáil and the European Parliament: see [2001] 4 I.R. 61, analysed in the *Annual Review of Irish Law 2001*, pp.103–107. Herbert J. observed:

> "It was held by the Supreme Court in the case of *T.D. & Ors. v. Minister for Education & Ors.* [2001] 4 IR 259, that the doctrine of separation of powers required that none of the three institutions of government be paramount. In my judgment, it is essential in a constitutional democracy such as this State, where a rule or convention of parliamentary sovereignty has no place, that the courts should have the power and be prepared wherever necessary to, vindicate by, 'all permitted and necessary redress,' (to borrow the phrase of Henchy, J., in the case of *Murphy v. Attorney General* [1982] I.R. 241 at 313), including where justice so requires by an award of damages, the constitutional rights of anyone, even where the transgression on those rights is in an Act of the National Parliament passed into law by the votes of the elected representatives of the People and signed by the President. This does not, I believe, amount to unwarranted judicial activism trespassing on the legislative function of the Oireachtas. No evidence was advanced at the hearing of this Issue and I am not prepared to assume that this particular power and, indeed, duty of the courts, would in any way inhibit or interfere with the proper functioning of the legislative arm of the State within its own unique sphere of activity under the Constitution.
>
> From the decision of the Supreme Court in the cases of *The State (Quinn) v. Ryan* [1965] I.R. 70; *Byrne v. Ireland and the Attorney General* [1972] I.R. 241, and *Murphy v. Attorney General* [1982] I.R. 241, and decisions in other cases to which I was referred during the

hearing of this Issue but which I consider it unnecessary to cite here, I am satisfied that this Court does have full power to award damages ordinary compensatory damages or aggravated or increased compensatory damages and even punitive or exemplary damages, (see *Conway v. Irish National Teachers Organisation & Ors.* [1991] 2 I.R. 305), against the legislative arm of the State for breach of a constitutional right by an Act of the Oireachtas or by a provision of such an Act. However, I do not think that it is reasonably possible or even desirable to attempt to formulate any principles of general application as to the circumstances in which the Court might so award damages or as to the type or amount of those damages. In this respect I adopt what was held by Henchy, J., in the case of *Murphy v. Attorney General* [1982] I.R. 241 at 315, where he stated, when speaking of such redress and of the sometimes 'transcendent considerations' which may render any or some particular forms of redress unavailable i.e., damages or restitution — 'in any event, I think experience has shown that such constitutional problems are best brought to solution, step by step, precedent after precedent, and when set against the concrete facts of a specific case.'"

Herbert J. awarded the plaintiff only nominal damages because he concluded on the evidence that the plaintiff had not established that he had been deprived of the chance of being elected. Although the case was one of injury without loss, the infringement of the plaintiff's constitutional right was actionable without proof of actual loss. In awarding nominal damages of €130, Herbert J. stressed that these damages "should not be considered to be in any sense derisory or contemptuous. He referred in this context to *Kearney v Minister for Justice* [1986] I.R. 116 where Costello J. had awarded £25 for an infringement of a prisoner's constitutional right to communicate.

3. The Reddy v Bates principle In *O'Connor v O'Driscoll*, High Court, February 23, 2004, Ryan J. applied the *Reddy v Bates* principle expansively so as to reduce an award for loss of earning capacity from €535,000 to €380,000— a reduction of about 29 per cent. The plaintiff was a very high-ranking bank official who sustained injuries when he was 46 years old. Ryan J. noted that a consultant psychiatrist who had given evidence on behalf of the defence had made the observations "that the plaintiff's personality was such that there was a risk of burn out as a person gets older". He said there was some risk of this happening before retirement, assuming that no accident had occurred. He "did not of course say that this was a likelihood but merely identified the possibility".

On the question of whether the *Reddy v Bates* principle had any application, counsel for the defendant submitted that some account should be taken of the possibility that the plaintiff might have suffered burn-out or some similar psychological crisis, even if there had been no accident. Counsel for the plaintiff argued that, before such a reduction could be considered to be appropriate, there would have to be specific evidence relating to the plaintiff to suggest in some particular way that he was vulnerable to some such illness or crisis. Ryan J. stated:

"My view is that if there is evidence to show that the plaintiff would have been at risk in the absence of an accident, that is a feature that is particular to that case and must be reflected in the assessment of damages in proportion to the scale of the risk. The Supreme Court did not intend in *Reddy v Bates* and other cases to give an exhaustive list of the matters that are to be taken into account in considering future loss of earnings. The principle is that life's uncertainties and exigencies have to be taken into account in general terms so as to modify the certainties implied by actuarial calculations, which are based on the assumption that events will progress to a particular date without any disruption or interruption. If there are particular circumstances in a case, then they obviously must be taken into account.

In this case, the principle in *Reddy v Bates* has application. Apart from the basic and general principle, one has particular features in the nature of [the plaintiff's] personality, the high stress levels to which he was exposed and the different kinds of job in the Bank of Ireland network which he was asked to do. As he progressed upwards in the bank's management structure, I think it likely that the stresses and strains would have increased. These factors make very real the possibility expressed by [the psychiatrist] of burnout, which I understand to be a psychological crisis which would have rendered [the plaintiff] either incapable of continuing to work or much less capable of doing so...

Having regard to the evidence of the psychiatrists and particularly [the psychiatrist already mentioned] as to the risk of burn-out in a person in the plaintiff's position, the evidence of the severe stresses to which his work exposed the plaintiff, the evidence of his own personality with its high demands made on himself, his perfectionist tendencies and intolerance of failure, a substantial reduction has to be made by reason of *Reddy v. Bates*. I make a reduction of a sum that is between one-quarter and one–third in order to take account of these risks and uncertainties, which brings the €535,000 down to €380,000."

There can be no difficulty with the principle that an appropriate reduction should be made in the *quantum* of damages for loss of earning capacity to take account of an identifiable risk, established in evidence, specifically relating to the plaintiff. So, if a particular plaintiff was at risk of burn-out before the accident, a reduction to take account of that risk would be required. The broader question of whether people working in a particular kind of work face the risk of burn-out as an occupational hazard fits more conventionally into the type of situation envisaged by *Reddy v Bates*. In the instant case, it is not entirely clear whether the psychiatrist's evidence fell into the first or second category of risk: in truth, it may well have fallen into both.

4. The *"once and for all"* rule The traditional structure of an action for personal injuries in torts has been that the decision-maker—the jury or, since 1988, the judge—must make a once and for all assessment of the damages that the plaintiff had already suffered and would suffer in the future. The difficulty with this approach is obvious: there are many situations in which the prognosis is uncertain; the plaintiff may have a 30 per cent chance of premature death or of developing arthritis, for example. Is the court in these circumstances to give 30 per cent of the projected possibility, 100 per cent of the possible outcome, or nothing at all? If the court awards 30 per cent to take account of that possibility and that possibility actually occurs, the plaintiff will receive 70 per cent less than the damages sustained. A "once-off" award risks either over-compensation or under-compensation. See the Law Reform Commission's *Report on Personal Injuries: Periodic Payments and Structured Settlements* (LRC 54–1996) paras 16.2–16.5.

This raises the question as to whether, at least in particular circumstances, it might be possible for the court to postpone its final award in order to take into account the uncertain projections into the future. One solution would be an award of periodic payments, conditional on the actual medical progress of the plaintiff and the risks to which he or she may be exposed by the tortfeasor. Another would be for the court to make a substantive once-off award on the basis of the injuries and loss sustained by the plaintiff to date and in the future, so far as these may be measured accurately, and to defer to some future time the possibility of awarding future damages, if some foreseeable damage befalls the plaintiff.

In *Smyth v Ward*, High Court, December 11, 2004, the plaintiff, aged 11, had suffered a hearing loss as a result of the defendants' admitted negligence in an accident in 1999. There was a possibility that she would sustain a complication in her right ear which would require major surgical repair to the ear and result in further reduction in her hearing capacity. The medical reports disclosed that there was "a significant chance" of this occurring but that it was very difficult to form an opinion as to how significant that chance was. If it did occur, Finnegan P. considered that it would be "disastrous" for the plaintiff.

The plaintiff sought to have the hearing of the action deferred until she was 18. At that time, if there had been no deterioration in her right ear, a prognosis could be given with greater certainty. The third-named defendant, the Motor Insurers Bureau of Ireland, opposed the deferral.

Finnegan P. considered that his task, in the light of the circumstances and the interests of justice, was to balance the defendant's interest in a prompt hearing of the action with the plaintiff's interest in having established with as much certainty as possible what the future might hold for her. He had regard to the medical reports indicating that greater certainty could attach to the prognosis regarding the plaintiff if some years were allowed to go by before the hearing. He did not believe that any special or particular injustice would be caused to the third defendant by this deferral of the assessment of damages as in the intervening period the third-named defendant would have the use of the amount of the ultimate award.

Finnegan P. acknowledged that he had to have regard to Art.6(1) of the European Convention on Human Rights which guaranteed a trial within a reasonable time and which placed on the court the responsibility actively to ensure that there was no delay. He considered, however, that this did not present a barrier to deferring the hearing as reasonableness was assessed in the light of all the circumstances of the case, having regard in particular to the complexity of issues in the case. Moreover, the court had to take into account what was at stake for the plaintiff in the litigation. He cited *Mikulic v Croatia* (2002) II B.H.R.C. 689 in support of this latter element.

Finnegan P. was satisfied that justice demanded that there should be some further delay to enable the prognosis in respect of the plaintiff to be rendered more certain. The date of the plaintiff's 18th birthday was admittedly arbitrary but, having regard to the time which had passed since the accident, a further period of just over two years was acceptable.

It has to be said that the principle underlying the postponement is eminently sensible—that the plaintiff should be entitled to have established with as much certainty as possible what the future might hold for her. Finnegan P. would not have been entitled on the evidence to award her 100 per cent compensation for a contingency of such uncertain predictability. Yet, if the principle is sound, does this not commit the court to a more radical acknowledgement of a move away from the idea that a once-and-for-all award should be made at the end of a trial in the normal time period for litigation to run its course?

Perhaps this is reading too much into the judgment. Two years is not a tremendously long period. It may be better to treat the judgment as dependent very much on its particular facts rather than presaging a fundamental shift in the policy relating to awards for damages in personal injury litigation.

It is interesting, nonetheless, to bear in mind that Finnegan P. displayed a similar "wait and see" attitude in the decisions of *Rafter v Attorney General*, High Court, February 26, 2004 and *Packenham v Irish Ferries Ltd (formerly B & I Ltd)*, High Court, February 26, 2004, when he stayed rather than dismissed proceedings in order to see whether the plaintiffs, who had allegedly been negligently exposed to asbestos, would develop physical injuries. The Supreme Court reversed Finnegan P. in an *ex tempore* judgment in *Packenham* on January 31, 2005. That reversal might be regarded as one of formal propriety but there surely is some evidence in Finnegan P.'s approach in the two separate contexts of an underlying disposition to increase the rationality of the compensation system for personal injuries.

5. Loss of earning capacity In *O'Sullivan v Kiernan and Bon Secours Health*

Systems Ltd, High Court, April 2, 2004, O'Neill J. addressed the question of whether damages should be awarded to a plaintiff the range of whose prospective modes of employment has been restricted by the injury that had been sustained. The plaintiff was the victim of negligence in her delivery. She sustained an Erbs palsy on the right side which left her with a very significant deformity of her right shoulder and arm and right scapula. She was unable to get her right hand behind her head actively or behind her back. She also had difficulty in reaching outwards and upwards. The dexterity of her right hand was reduced, so that she lacked normal writing capacity and speed in this hand.

At the time of the trial the plaintiff was eight years old. She was a very bright child, doing very well academically, at the top of her class. O'Neill J stated:

> "I take it as a probability that with the support of her parents and good schooling she will continue to enjoy academic success and it is a probability that she will attain the appropriate standard for a third level education and her career will progress on that basis. It is impossible at this stage to say what choice of career she would make in that context, but what is significant from the damages point of view is that there are a number of careers that she would be excluded from because of her disability. These include membership of An Garda Síochána or of the defence forces, an airline pilot, those branches of the medical or paramedical professions which require some degree of balanced physical strength and manual dexterity, the veterinary profession, and architecture because she would not be able to climb ladders or scaffolding.
>
> At this stage it cannot be said as a matter of probability that the plaintiff will suffer any loss of earning capacity as a result of her disability but what can be said as a matter of certainty is that the range of choice of career available to her will be significantly reduced and that is a fact which must redound in general damages."

O'Neill J. considered that there was a likelihood that the plaintiff would suffer "considerable stress" because of the disability and the appearance of her shoulder and scapula. In awarding high general damages—€75,000 to the time of judgment and €175,000 for the future—O'Neill J. bore in mind the fact that the plaintiff had been largely dominated by the injury which had caused her a great deal of pain and distress.

The total sum of €250,000 is approaching the maximum prescribed by the *Book of Quantum*. O'Neill J. did not clarify the amount he was awarding for the constriction of the plaintiff's career choice although the plaintiff had not suffered any actual loss of earning capacity. It would have been interesting to know the exact principles on which O'Neill J. calculated this amount. One plaintiff who sustained a certain injury might be deprived of the opportunity to take up any of several careers involving a particular physical capacity and this may be psychologically devastating for him or her; another plaintiff, with precisely the same injury and inhibition of prospects in respect of these careers, may be completely serene because he or she intends, and is still able, to pursue a cerebral career which requires no physical dexterity. If the court were to introduce a sharply defined causal analysis in this context, it might conclude that the second of these plaintiffs should be awarded nothing (or virtually nothing). Whether such close scrutiny of a plaintiff's career intentions would be appropriate may, however, be debated.

6. Property damage In *Murnaghan v Markland Holdings Ltd*, High Court, December 1, 2004, Laffoy J. applied the principles set out by the Supreme Court in *Munnelly v Calcon Ltd* [1978] I.R. 387 on the measurement of damages where a building has been negligently damaged or destroyed. There the Supreme Court had held that reinstatement damages should not be awarded as a prima facie right; even if they were, the plaintiff's intentions as to reinstatement should be the determining factor. The crucial principles were to put the plaintiff in the same position as he would have been if the tort had not been committed and to award damages that were reasonable as between the parties. Henchy J. had observed that it was:

> "in the application of those principles that difficulty may arise, for the court, in endeavouring to award a sum which will be both compensatory and reasonable, will be called on to give consideration, with emphasis varying from case to case, to matters such as the nature of the property, the plaintiff's relation to it, the nature of the wrongful act causing the damage, the conduct of the parties subsequent to the wrongful act, and the pecuniary, economic or other relevant implications or consequences of reinstatement damages as compared with diminished-value damages."

In the instant case, the defendant's construction work on its own property had damaged the plaintiff's home. The plaintiff and his wife had rented another property as they had received advice that the damage rendered their home dangerous to their health. The plaintiff had also sold the home.

Laffoy J. held that there could be no question of the plaintiff's being awarded damages commensurate with the cost of demolishing and rebuilding his property since he had ceased to own it and was not in a position to effect reinstatement. The only basis on which the diminution in value of the property could be established was "by reference to what a prospective purchaser would consider to be the impact on the value of the damage, having regard to its nature and extent and the cost of remedying it". The purchase price obtained for the sale of the home was not a good indicator as the home had not been properly marketed. The plaintiff was entitled to compensation for the fact that he had rented accommodation. While Laffoy J. was not satisfied that the home was actually a health hazard, there was significant water damage and disrepair caused by the defendant's activities to such a degree that the plaintiff and his family could not reasonably be expected to continue to live there.

7. Exemplary damages In *Sharkey v Dunnes Stores (Ireland) Ltd*, High Court, January 28, 2004, where the plaintiff's contract was terminated in a somewhat hurtful manner (see above, p.479), Smyth J. declined to award exemplary damages or aggravated damages, stating:

> "This is not a case for exemplary, punitive or aggravated damages—a want of tact at the meeting [when the termination was communicated to the plaintiff] is not equivalent to the outrageous conduct considered by Griffin J in *Conway v INTO* [1991] 2 IR 305 at 323."

A couple of observations may be appropriate. The passage might seem to distinguish between exemplary and punitive damages but it would seem unwise to read too much into this. Smyth J. was *rejecting* an award outside the traditional compensatory framework on the facts of the case. He was scarcely seeking to take a considered position on the question of whether any conceptual distinction can be made between exemplary and punitive damages. Secondly, it is not entirely clear from the judgment whether it involves a holding that the defendant had committed any actionable wrong, in respect of which damages of any category might be awarded. It appears that Smyth J. found that no breach of contract had in fact occurred and he rejected all claims in tort made by the plaintiff.

8. Aggravated damages It will be recalled that, in *Conway v Irish National Teachers Organisation* [1991] 2 I.R. 305 Finlay C.J. addressed the question of aggravated damages, stating that they were:

> "compensatory damages increased by reason of:
> (a)   the manner in which the wrong was committed, involving such elements as oppressiveness, arrogance or outrage, or
> (b)   the conduct of the wrongdoer after the commission of the wrong, such as a refusal to apologise or to ameliorate the harm done or the making of threats to repeat the wrong, or
> (c)   conduct of the wrongdoer and/or his representatives in the defence of the claim of the wronged plaintiff, up to and including the trial of the action."

He went on to observe:

> "Such a list of the circumstances which may aggravate compensatory damages until they can properly be classified as aggravated damages is not intended to be in any way finite or complete. Furthermore, the

circumstances which may properly form an aggravating feature in the measurement of compensatory damages must, in many instances, be in part a recognition of the added hurt or insult to a plaintiff who is being wronged, and in part also a recognition of the cavalier or outrageous conduct of the defendant."

The question whether aggravated damages may be awarded in negligence litigation has troubled the Supreme Court over the years since *Conway* was decided. In *Cooper v O'Connell*, Supreme Court, June 5, 1997, aggravated damages were awarded in a case which, although sounding in negligence, involved a course of action by the defendant dentist which had intentionally subjected the plaintiff to unnecessary treatment. In *Swaine v Commissioners of Public Works* [2003] 1 I.R. 521, the defendants had been guilty of "the grossest negligence" towards their employee in negligently exposing him to the risk of mesothelioma but the Supreme Court overruled an award of aggravated damages. Keane C.J. referred to what Finlay C.J. had said in *Conway* and observed that, although Finlay C.J. had emphasised that his list of circumstances in which aggravated damages might be awarded was not intended to be exhaustive, "those circumstances which he has identified do not typically arise in cases of negligence and, if they do, are not a ground for increasing the amount of compensatory damages."

In *Philp v Ryan and Bon Secours Hospital*, Supreme Court, December 17, 2004, the plaintiff sued the defendants for professional negligence in failing to diagnose that he was suffering from prostate cancer. The first defendant was found by the trial judge, Peart J., to have deliberately and knowingly altered his clinical notes, which he must have been aware would be used in court proceedings, with the intention of assisting his case. On appeal, McCracken J. interpreted this holding as meaning that the first defendant had had "the intention of deceiving the court and of attempting to deprive the plaintiff of damages to which he [was] subsequently …found to be lawfully entitled". The plaintiff had also prepared a case summary for his expert witness in which he maintained, as he had in the altered clinical notes, that he had told the plaintiff to arrange to have a particular test carried out six weeks after his consultation.

The first defendant had also misled his own legal advisers who, in ignorance of the true position, had conducted an active defence based on his false assertion contained in the clinical notes. He did, however, tell them the truth between one and two weeks before the commencement of the action. McCracken J. regarded this as "[t]he truly appalling feature" in the case. He found it:

"almost incomprehensible that in those circumstances they did not inform the plaintiff's solicitors of the true facts. While a great deal of blame attaches to the first defendant for having altered the document in the first place, he did at least disclose the facts to his own legal advisors, and in my view at least equal if not greater blame must be attributable to them. It is instructive that they did not seek to use the clinical notes in cross-examination of the plaintiff or his advisors, although they did suggest in such cross-examination that he had been instructed to have a further test taken in six weeks' time. They did not seek to have their own client prove the notes until they were called for by the learned trial Judge, although they knew they were being put on proof of the notes. There must be at least a suspicion that there was a deliberate attempt to keep the true facts from the Court notwithstanding that the altered document had been furnished to the plaintiff's solicitors as being genuine, and that the facts stated in the alteration had formed part of the instructions to [the expert witness]."

McCracken J. had no doubt that the instant case was "a classic example" of one where aggravated damages should be awarded in a negligence claim. The plaintiff had not given evidence of the effect which the misinformation which he had received had on him; this was not something about which the defendants could complain as it was attributable entirely to what McCracken J. could "only describe as the misconduct of the defendants' advisors in not disclosing the alteration". The court could only imagine the additional stress and anxiety which the plaintiff must have suffered in the belief that, in documents shown to him, there was a strong defence to his action. McCracken J. accordingly concluded that an award of €50,000 for aggravated damages was appropriate. The other members of the court (Murray C.J. and Fennelly J.) concurred.

9. Pain and suffering In *O'Connor v O'Driscoll*, High Court, February 23, 2004, the plaintiff suffered physical injuries in a traffic accident and developed a very serious post-traumatic stress disorder and a major depressive illness, complicated by generalised anxiety disorder. Ryan J. awarded €100,000 for pain and suffering up to the time of judgment and €50,000 for future pain and suffering.

In *Hackett v Calla Associates Ltd*, High Court, October 21, 2004, Peart J. awarded €100,000 damages for the loss by the plaintiff of sight in one eye and the scarring due to the blow that caused the injury. The plaintiff was 26 years old at the time of the incident. Peart J. observed that he took into account the fact that the plaintiff was a young man who "could have to live with this disadvantage for about fifty years".

In *Higgins v Smith*, High Court, November 15, 2004, Peart J. awarded €130,000 for pain and suffering to the time of judgment and €25,000 for future pain and suffering where the plaintiff, aged 18 at the time of the accident, suffered serious injuries. She had to be cut out of the car, which had struck a telephone pole. She sustained injuries to her arm and leg as well as scars on several parts of the body.

In *Curley v Dublin City Council*, Supreme Court, November 26, 2004,

Denham J. adverted to the forensic challenge presented by soft tissue injuries. Upholding the award made by Galligan J., Denham J. (Geoghegan and Fennelly JJ. concurring) observed:

> "This was an injury of which there were little or no objective findings, but that is often the case with soft tissue injuries. This is a case where the doctors and courts heard evidence of subjective symptoms. That is often the only evidence in soft tissue injuries. The nature of the injuries may make objective findings virtually impossible. That does not mean there can be no evidence. It means that the nature of the evidence is different to that of an injury, such as a broken bone, where there can be objective findings. In this case there were no findings by the trial judge of lying or malingering by the plaintiff."

In *O'Sullivan v Kiernan and Bon Secours Health Systems Ltd*, High Court, April 2, 2004, the plaintiff sustained an Erbs palsy on the right side and a fractured clavicle when she was the victim of negligence in her delivery. The extent of those injuries are described above at p.553. O'Neill J. awarded general damages of €75,000 to the time of judgment and €175,000 for the future. (A complicating factor was that the plaintiff's restriction in the range of her career choices also featured in this award of general damages, though it seems reasonable to infer that this did not constitute a significant element in the award.)

It is interesting to note that O'Neill J. was willing to award such a high sum for injuries which, while serious and involving pain and stress over very many years, were not approaching paraplegia in their seriousness.

PUBLIC AUTHORITY

In *Flynn v Waterford County Council*, High Court, October 20, 2004, the absence of a stop sign was at the heart of the litigation. Section 95(5)(a) of the Roads Traffic Act 1961 (as amended) provides that: "A road authority shall provide for public roads in their charge such regulatory signs (other than special category signs) as may be requested by the Commissioner."

Finnegan P. referred to the difference between s.95(5)(a), which used the word "shall" and s.95(3)(a), which used the word "may". He stated:

> "On this basis I find that section 95(3)(a) confers a discretionary power on a Road Authority and not an obligation. Applying the principles enunciated by the Supreme Court in *Glencar v Mayo County Council and Another* [2002] (1 I.R. 112) to section 95(3)(a) I am satisfied that it was not the intention of the Legislature in enacting that provision to confer on an individual an entitlement to claim for damages."

Finnegan P. observed that, where a statutory provision did not give a private right to sue it would be most unusual that it should nevertheless give rise to a duty of care at common law. He cited Lord Hoffmann's remarks in *Gorringe v Calderdale Metropolitan Borough Council* [2004] 2 All E.R. 326 at 336:

> "In the absence of a right to sue for breach of the statutory duty itself it would in my opinion have been absurd to hold that the Council was nevertheless under a common law duty to take reasonable care to provide accommodation for homeless persons whom we could reasonably foresee would otherwise be reduced to sleeping rough. And the argument would in my opinion have been even weaker if the Council, instead of being under a duty to provide accommodation merely had a power to do so."

In the instant case the defendant merely had a power to erect signs. Finnegan P. was satisfied that that power did not give rise to a cause of action in a person who suffered injury as a result of the local authority's failure to erect signs. Neither could that failure give rise to an action for negligence at common law:

> "The Roads Act 1993 I am satisfied, does not alter the common law save and except that it includes within the duty to maintain a road a duty to provide and maintain public lighting. The failure of a Road Authority to maintain a public road does not confer upon an individual a right to civil redress for damages: *Brady v Cavan County Council* [2000] 1 ILRM 81 and *Harbinson v Armagh County Council* [1902] 2 IR 538".

Accordingly, if the plaintiff was to sustain his claim, he had to do so at common law. Assuming that the sign was in disrepair and that it was largely obscured by vegetation and that the result of this was that the sign was not visible to a motorist going along the road until he was almost upon the sign, could this give rise to a claim in negligence? The plaintiff relied on the proposition in Pratt and McKenzie, *Law of Highways* (20th ed.,1962) to the effect that:

> "Where a highway authority places something in the highway under statutory powers and not for the purposes of maintaining the highway ... they are bound to keep and repair the statutory work so placed and are liable to an action for injury arising out of their failure to do so."

Finnegan P. was satisfied that if no sign had been erected this could not have given rise to a claim by an individual for damages for breach of statutory duty; *Glencar v Mayo County Council* [2002] 1 I.R. 112 supported this conclusion. If the failure to erect a sign could not give rise to liability, the question arose as to whether he could be liable if, having erected a sign, it failed to maintain it by ensuring that it remain visible. In *Gorringe v Calderdale MBC* [2004] 2 All E.R. at 334 Lord Hoffmann had said:

> "If the highway authority at common law had no duty other than to keep the road in repair and even that duty was not actionable in private law, it is impossible to contend that it owes a common law duty to erect warning signs on the road. It is not sufficient that it might reasonably have foreseen that in the absence of such warnings, some road users might injure themselves or others. Reasonable foreseeability of physical injury is the standard criterion for determining the duty of care owed by people who undertake an activity which carries a risk of injury to others. But it is insufficient to justify the imposition of liability upon someone who simply does nothing: who neither creates the risk nor undertakes to do anything to avert it."

In the instant case had the defendant done nothing it would not have attracted a common law duty of care. Finnegan P. observed:

> "Having given a warning the circumstances which prevailed on the day of the accident were such that the warning was less than that which was desirable but even then the Defendant had done more than it was at common law obliged to do. In these circumstances it seems to me that no liability at common law arises."

The plaintiff also relied on *Bird v Pearse* [1979] R.T.R. 369. In that case the highway authority had carried out resurfacing which obliterated white lining on the road which had established a system of priorities at a junction. It was held foreseeable that there was a risk of drivers misunderstanding their priorities at the junction in that the highway authority had created a pattern of traffic flow which did not exist before they placed the white lines on the road, a pattern which drivers could be expected to rely upon. In these circumstances there was a duty of care to the plaintiff to prevent accidents occurring as a result of the removal of the white lines. Finnegan P. distinguished *Bird v Pearse* on the basis that, in *Bird v Pearse*, the decision had been based on the highway authority encouraging a pattern of behaviour among road users and altering the same without warning. No such conduct on the part of the defendant arose in the instant case.

Finnegan P. dismissed the plaintiff's claim. The plaintiff had not established to his satisfaction that the defendant was in breach of a statutory duty or, if it was, that such a breach conferred on the plaintiff a right of action. Further he had failed to establish the existence of a duty on the defendant at common law to maintain the sign which it had erected so that it would be clearly visible.

It must be said that the full force of *Glencar* is apparent in Finnegan P.'s holding. The broader implications of negligence claims against public authorities are stark.

A decision in stark contrast to *Flynn* is *Carey v Mould*, High Court, April 20, 2004. In *Carey*, Peart J. held that the second defendant, Donegal County Council, was liable to the extent of 85 per cent of the plaintiff's damages and the first defendant, the driver of the vehicle that had collided with him, was liable for 15 per cent where an accident occurred at a road junction between a major and a minor road where the first defendant emerged without stopping from the minor road. The County Council had erected a stop sign on the minor road, but this had been interfered with and turned completely around (rendering it useless) some time before the accident. About 100m back from the junction there was a yellow sign with words in black informing drivers on the minor road that there was a stop sign ahead at 100m. There was also a white stop line at the junction though this was partially faded. The first defendant, who lived in Northern Ireland, was unfamiliar with the area.

Peart J. held the first defendant liable in travelling at an excessive speed and in failing to see the yellow sign. He also held the County Council liable on the following basis:

> "It has the statutory obligation to maintain a safe road system. While it cannot be expected to be aware automatically of every occasion on which a sign is turned around the wrong way, perhaps by mischief, it retains an overall responsibility to ensure that roads are safe and that all traffic users are aware of potential dangers, including persons such as the first defendant, a tourist, who would not be familiar with a potentially dangerous junction, such as that involved in this accident. I am satisfied that this junction is, and was on this date, even ignoring the fact that the Stop sign was facing the wrong way, an inherently hazardous junction, and one requiring that very clear warnings be apparent to any road-user, particularly one such as the first defendant who was a visitor to the area. It is an unfortunate fact of everyday life that signs such as this Stop sign can become turned in the wrong direction for whatever reason. No doubt this is why the Council felt it was desirable to give road users an early warning of the junction by placing the yellow sign 100 metres back from the junction. However it is also clear to me that the Council would not have regarded that yellow sign alone as an adequate warning to a road-user such as the first defendant, to stop at the junction, hence the fact that it placed the Stop sign, and also the white Stop line at the junction itself. That white line marking was partially faded on this date, according to the evidence of Garda Wallace, which I accept in that regard....
>
> I am satisfied that while the Council had fulfilled the letter of their statutory obligation by erecting the Stop sign at this junction, that is not the full extent of its obligations to the public. Firstly, this is an inherently dangerous junction requiring special steps to be taken in

order to ensure as far as possible that an accident such as the present one did not happen. In recognition of this it went further than its statutory obligation by providing a white Stop line at the junction, and a yellow warning 100 metres back from the junction. However the white line was partially faded, and the yellow sign, it has to be said, from the photographs, is not a large, unmissable type of sign. Nevertheless, I believe that the first defendant ought to have seen it, and if he had, he might possibly have realised that he was at a junction at which he was required to stop and give way to the plaintiff."

A few points about this decision may be in order. First, it was handed down only 19 days after the House of Lord's decision in *Gorringe*. Secondly, the scope of duty that Peart J. used was broad: it did not depend on how long the sign had been turned in the wrong direction and Peart J. imposed liability in spite of the existence of the yellow warning. The contrast between *Flynn* and *Carey* could scarcely be greater. One may apprehend that, of the two, *Flynn* will emerge victorious at appellate level.

Transport

AIR TRANSPORT

Warsaw and Montreal Conventions on international carriage by air   The Air Navigation and Transport (International Conventions) Act 2004 implemented the 1999 Montreal Convention for the Unification of Certain Rules for International Carriage by Air. The 1999 Convention was intended to update and, ultimately, to replace the previous international regime, the Warsaw regime, which stretches back to the 1929 Warsaw Convention for the Unification of Certain Rules Relating to International Carriage by Air, as amended a number of times since by various instruments, including the 1944 Chicago Convention, which created the International Civil Aviation Organisation (ICAO). The Warsaw regime was implemented in this State by the Air Navigation and Transport Act 1936, as amended. As the Montreal Convention will ultimately replace the Warsaw regime, the opportunity was taken to restate the law relating to the existing Warsaw Convention and its amendments in the 2004 Act, so that the entire subject is now covered in a single Act. The 2004 Act therefore, and of necessity, repealed Pt III of, and the First Schedule to, the Air Navigation and Transport Act 1936, which had implemented the original Warsaw Convention.

Essential elements of 1999 Montreal Convention   In the course of the Oireachtas debate on the 2004 Act, it was pointed out that the 1999 Montreal Convention represents a major improvement over the liability regime established under the Warsaw Convention and its related instruments relative to passenger rights in the event of an accident. Among other benefits, the 1999 Convention holds carriers strictly liable for damages up to 100,000 Special Drawing Rights (SDRs), or approximately €118,000 of proven damages for each passenger. This is a big increase from the approximate 16,600 SDRs, approximately €20,000, applicable under the Warsaw system. The 1999 Convention also removes the upper limit on damages for accident victims that had existed in the Warsaw system; extends the range of jurisdictions in which claims for damages may be brought; clarifies the duties and obligations of carriers engaged in code-share operations; and, with respect to cargo, provides for modernised documentation. Significantly for passengers, the 1999 Convention makes it easier for them to bring legal action. In addition to those jurisdictions in which legal action for damages may be taken under the Warsaw system, the 1999 Convention further allows legal action to be taken in the State where the passenger lives, if the carrier operates services to or from that State. In almost all cases this provision will allow the passenger to take legal action in the courts with which he or she is most familiar.

The 1999 Montreal Convention will supersede the Warsaw system in every State that implements it. However, as was pointed out in the Oireachtas debate, the Warsaw system will continue to apply to international air travel where either or both of the States has not yet ratified the Montreal Convention. The 2004 Act deals with this by providing that the most recent Convention common to both Ireland and another State will apply to air travel to or from that State. The rules of the 1999 Montreal Convention are already included in European law for all European airlines and their passengers through Council Regulation (EC) No. 2027/97 on air carrier liability in the event of accidents. Ratification of the Montreal Convention will extend the higher liability limits worldwide, thereby providing very significant benefits for passengers travelling with non-EU airlines. It was also pointed out that ratification of the Montreal Convention by all EU Member States and the European Community before May 1, 2004—which occurred—would ensure that the Montreal Convention would be extended automatically to the 10 new accession countries when they became EU members on May 1, 2004.

Key elements of 2004 Act Section 4 of the 2004 Act provides for the two main versions of the Warsaw Convention (the 1929 Convention, as amended by the 1944 Convention) and the 1999 Montreal Convention to have the force of law in Ireland. The first two had already been implemented under the Air Navigation and Transport Act 1936, as amended. The texts of the three Conventions are set out in the three Schedules to the 2004 Act. Section 11 of the 2004 Act repealed Pt III of, and Schedule 1 to, the 1936 Act. Section 5 of the 2004 Act provides for the French language version of the two Warsaw Conventions to prevail where there is a dispute regarding differences between the English texts and the original French texts. Those Conventions were originally drafted in French only, and these original texts are deposited with the Ministry of Foreign Affairs in Poland.

Section 6 empowers the Government to certify which States are contracting parties to this Convention. Section 7, which is based on s.18 of the Air Navigation and Transport Act 1936, sets out the liabilities of a carrier in the event of the death of a passenger, specifying who is entitled to claim compensation. Section 8 empowers the Minister for Transport to make a notification, as provided for in Art.57 of the Montreal Convention, to the effect that the Convention will not apply to international flights carried out by the State for non-commercial purposes, nor to military flights. While it was stated in the Oireachtas that there were "no immediate plans to make such notifications", it was also pointed out that in international aviation it is customary to treat "state aircraft" separately from civilian aircraft. Section 9 empowers the Minister to extend the Convention to apply to internal, non-international flights. In practice, internal flights are already subject to equivalent provisions through the Council Regulation (EC) No. 2027/97 on air carrier liability in the event of accidents.

Detailed elements of Montreal Convention The Montreal Convention has been described as the successful culmination of work by the ICAO to modernise the patchwork of liability regimes around the world. Its success is apparent in the fact that 52 countries immediately signed it in 2000, including many EU Member States, such as Ireland. In November 2003 the United States became the thirtieth country to ratify the Convention, thereby causing it to enter into force among the States that have ratified it.

Chapter 1 of the Convention covers the general provisions contained therein and deals mainly with who and what is covered under its terms. Chapter 2 deals with both the documentation and the duties of the parties relating to the carriage of passengers, baggage and cargo. Articles 3–11 of the Convention deal with the documentation requirements for international air carriage of passengers, baggage and cargo. Most significantly, these Articles benefit the cargo industry by providing for modernised electronic documentation, including the elimination of the need for consignors of cargo to complete detailed air waybills prior to consigning goods to a carrier. Consignors may instead use simplified electronic records to facilitate shipments, thereby expediting the movement of goods.

Chapter 3 of the Convention deals with the liability of the carrier and the extent of compensation for damage. Article 21 provides for compensation in the case of death of, or injury to passengers. First, the carrier will be strictly liable for the first 100,000 SDRs, or approximately €118,000, of proven damages for each passenger. This is a significant increase from the approximate 16,600 SDRs, approximately €20,000, available under the Warsaw system. A carrier cannot avoid liability for this amount, even if it can prove that the harm was not caused by its negligence. This means that even if an accident was caused by weather or by a third party, such as a terrorist, the carrier is still liable for damages up to 100,000 SDRs. The only way a carrier can exonerate itself from this liability is if it can prove that the passenger for whom the damages are sought either caused or contributed to the accident. In addition to the liable sum of 100,000 SDRs, carriers are further subject to unlimited liability if the plaintiff can show that the carrier was negligent. This is another significant change from the Warsaw system, which placed a low upper limit of 16,600 SDRs on the amount of damages, except in very unlikely cases where it could be proved that the carrier or its staff intentionally or recklessly caused the accident. As these limits were already in force in Ireland under Council Regulation (EC) No. 2027/97 on air carrier liability in the event of accidents, the implementation of the 2004 Act held no cost implications for Irish air carriers. In addition, under the 1997 EU Regulation all European air carriers must insure themselves sufficiently to meet these liability limits. Consequently, ratification of the 1999 Convention will not increase costs for carriers in Europe, nor will it lead to increased fares for passengers. Article 28 provides for advance payments, which acknowledges the right of States to have national laws that require their own carriers to make such payments in the event of passenger death or injury, and addresses certain procedural issues related to such payments. In addition, a resolution adopted by the diplomatic conference as part of the final Act encourages all States to adopt such laws. The 1997 EU Regulation had already provided for advance payments of the type referred to in Art.28. Amounts of at least 16,000 SDRs, approximately €19,000, are to be made without delay to meet immediate financial needs of persons entitled to make claims. These advance payments do not involve an admission of liability and may be offset against the total amount of damages deemed payable. Articles 29–35 provide for rules relating to the basis for making claims and include a new provision allowing persons to bring actions in the State where the passenger lives, if the carrier operates services to or from that State. Disputes may also be settled by arbitration.

Chapter 4 of the Convention deals with combined carriage. This is where a person or cargo makes a journey partly by air and partly by surface transport. In that case the Convention applies only to carriage by air. Chapter 5 deals with carriage by air performed by a person other than the contracting carrier. This is primarily to cover what is known as "code-sharing" among airlines. Code-sharing is where airline "A" agrees to carry passengers on behalf of airline "B", but the tickets issued by airline "B" carry its flight number and not the flight number of the craft on which the passenger is travelling. This has become a very common arrangement among airlines because it allows much wider international marketing by, for example, linking internal flights in America by US airlines with Aer Lingus' transatlantic flights. When a claim arises under the Convention under these circumstances a claimant may take an action against the carrier from which the carriage was purchased, or against the code-sharing carrier that was operating the aircraft at the time of the accident.

Chapter 6 of the Convention deals with other provisions, such as nullifying clauses in contracts that do not comply with the Convention and which require insurance. Chapter 7 contains the final clauses, covering such matters as signature, ratification and entry into force. Article 53 includes provision to allow regional economic integration organisations, such as the European Union, to ratify the Convention.

Rules of the air   The Irish Aviation Authority (Rules of the Air) Order 2004 (S.I. No.72 of 2004) consolidates, with amendments, the Irish Aviation Authority (Rules of the Air) Orders 2001 to 2002, which it also revoked. It gives effect to the Standards in Annex 2 and certain Standards in Annex 11 to the Chicago Convention, discussed above in the context of the Air Navigation and Transport (International Conventions) Act 2004.

RAIL TRANSPORT

Access to railway infrastructure   The European Communities (Access to Railway Infrastructure) Regulations 2003 (S.I. No.536 of 2003) gave effect to Directive 2001/12/EC, amending Directive 91/440/EC on the development of the European Community's railways. The 2003 Regulations also revoked the European Communities (Access to Railway Infrastructure) Regulations 1996.

Licensing of railway undertakings   The European Communities (Licensing of Railway Undertakings) Regulations 2003 (S.I. No.537 of 2003) gave effect to Directive 2001/13/EC, amending Directive 95/18/EC on the licensing of railway undertakings. They also revoked the European Communities (Licensing of Railway Undertakings) Regulations 1999 (S.I. No.238 of 1999).

ROAD TRAFFIC

Road Traffic Act 2004   A key element of the Road Traffic Act 2004 was to provide for the metrication of road traffic speed limits. Following its initial publication as a Bill in 2004, the Comptroller and Auditor General published a report on the operation of the fixed charge and penalty points systems. The final elements of the 2004 Act reflect the legislative response to this Report and subsequent debate in the Oireachtas Committee of Public Accounts. The 2004 Act also contains provisions on the use of hand-held speed detection guns in the detection of road traffic speeding offences, as well as introducing the possible capping of cover for vehicle insurance.

Metrication of speed limits   Part 2 of the 2004 Act provides for the introduction of metric speed limits: these came into effect in January 2005. It was stated during the Oireachtas debate that the changeover to the metric system would involve the provision of over 58,000 metric speed limit signs to serve the 96,000km of public road network. Section 4 empowers the Minister for Transport to determine the maximum speed limits that should be applied to vehicle classes through Regulations. The 2004 Act provides four "default" speed limits. Section 5 provides that the speed limit in built-up areas will be 50km/h, replacing the 30mph limit in these areas. Section 6 introduces a new speed limit of 80km/h for all regional and local roads outside of built-up areas. It was stated during the Oireachtas debate on the 2004 Act that this limit, which is a reduction of approximately 16km/h (or just over 10mph) in the speed limit previously applying on these roads, is applicable to over 90 per cent of the rural road network. Section 7 provides for a new speed limit of 100km/h for to all national roads outside of built-up areas. This replaced the general speed limit of 60mph on national roads outside urban areas. It is worth noting that the 2004 Act authorises local authorities to apply the higher speed limit of 100km/h on specified stretches of regional and local road where such action is deemed by the local authority to be appropriate. Section 8 provides that the speed limit for motorways will be 120km/h, which replaced the previous motorway speed limit of 70mph.

The speed limits, provided for under ss.5–8 will apply unless special speed limit by-laws are enacted by County and City Councils under s.9 of the 2004 Act, which replicates a power first introduced in the Road Traffic Act 1994. Such decisions are reserved to elected members. Section 9(4) of the 2004 Act introduces a new public consultation process through which members of the public can submit objections to a Council's proposals. The prior consent of the National Roads Authority to all proposals relating to national roads continues to be required under the 2004 Act, and the prior arrangements relating to consultation with the Gardaí and urban local authorities also remain in place. The range of speed limits that may be deployed as special speed limits include 120km/h, 100km/h, 80km/h, 60km/h and 50km/h. Local authorities can apply special speed limits of 30km/h and 60km/h. The availability of the use of the 30km/h speed limit will allow Councils to impose a legal requirement on traffic to adopt very low speeds at locations that are sensitive from a road safety perspective. The use of the 30km/h speed limit must be in accordance with guidelines set down for local authorities, which will be issued by the Minister for Transport under the 2004 Act. Section 9 of the Act also empowers local authorities, for the first time, to make provision in by-laws to apply different speed limits on separate carriageways of a road and to apply special, lower speed limits for specified periods of the day, for example, in the vicinity of schools during the times children are entering and leaving school. Section 11 provides for the substitution of s.47 of the Road Traffic Act 1961, which establishes that it is an offence to breach a speed limit.

Hand-held speed detectors Section 15 of the 2004 Act is the legislative response to an issue raised in some prosecutions under the Road Traffic Acts by providing clarity on the evidence from the operation of all forms of equipment used by the Gardaí in the enforcement of speed limits.

Fixed penalty charges Part 3 of the 2004 Act introduced a number of amendments to the administration of the fixed charge and penalty points systems previously introduced under the Road Traffic Act 2002. Section 18 of the 2004 Act empowers the Minister for Justice, Equality and Law Reform to engage third parties in functions relating to the system. These are of an administrative nature only and do not involve the detection work of the Gardaí and traffic wardens.

As already indicated, after the publication of the 2004 Act as a Bill in June 2004, the Comptroller and Auditor General published a Report on the operation of the fixed charge system, which Report was then considered by the Oireachtas

Committee of Public Accounts. One of the issues on which the report focused was corporate registered owners of vehicles. The Road Traffic Act 2002, which introduced fixed charge and penalty points systems, established requirements with which a registered owner must comply. Sections 19 and 20 of the 2004 Act respond to the Report of the Comptroller and Auditor General by providing more stringent requirements on corporate owners to ensure they do not escape their responsibilities. Section 22 provides for a number of amendments to the operation of the penalty points system, notably the addition to the list of scheduled offences under the 2002 Act of the offence of driving without reasonable consideration. This offence will attract four penalty points on conviction in court, and two penalty points on payment of a fixed charge.

Emergency service drivers Section 27 of the 2004 Act was enacted in response to concerns expressed by representatives of the emergency services regarding the need for greater clarity as to the circumstances where emergency vehicles can be exempted from requirements, restrictions and prohibitions imposed under the Road Traffic Acts, such as exceeding speed limits, or driving through red traffic lights. The exemption now contained in s.27 is subject to the overriding requirement that the safety of road users must not be endangered where such an exemption is permitted.

Supply of vehicle to minors Section 30 introduces a new offence relating to the supply of mechanically propelled vehicles to minors. The new offence will generally apply to the supply of all mechanically propelled vehicles to persons aged under 16 years of age.

Production of driving licence Section 33 provides for a new power to enable Gardaí to demand production of a driving licence or provisional licence subsequent to the commission of a road traffic offence. This issue was also raised in the Comptroller and Auditor General's Report referred to above.

Cap on motor insurance cover Section 34 of the 2004 Act enables the Minister for Transport to replace the existing requirement on insurance companies in the Road Traffic Acts to provide unlimited motor cover with provision for a specified level or cap. Any such change will be subject to positive approval of both Houses of the Oireachtas.

Subject Index